MÎZÂN

Studien zur Literatur in der islamischen Welt

Herausgegeben von
Stephan Guth, Roxane Haag-Higuchi
und Mark Kirchner

Band 17

Essays in Arabic Literary Biography

General Editor: Roger Allen

Teil 3

2010
Harrassowitz Verlag · Wiesbaden

Essays
in Arabic Literary Biography
1850–1950

Edited by
Roger Allen

2010
Harrassowitz Verlag · Wiesbaden

The signet on the cover was designed by Anwārī al Ḥusaynī and symbolizes a scale.

Collage *Fajr al-adab al-ʿarabî al-muʿâṣir*, assembled by Stephan Guth.

Bibliografische Information der Deutschen Nationalbibliothek
Die Deutsche Nationalbibliothek verzeichnet diese Publikation in der Deutschen
Nationalbibliografie; detaillierte bibliografische Daten sind im Internet
über http://dnb.d-nb.de abrufbar.

Bibliographic information published by the Deutsche Nationalbibliothek
The Deutsche Nationalbibliothek lists this publication in the Deutsche
Nationalbibliografie; detailed bibliographic data are available in the internet
at http://dnb.d-nb.de.

For further information about our publishing program consult our
website http://www.harrassowitz-verlag.de
© Otto Harrassowitz GmbH & Co. KG, Wiesbaden 2010
This work, including all of its parts, is protected by copyright.
Any use beyond the limits of copyright law without the permission
of the publisher is forbidden and subject to penalty. This applies
particularly to reproductions, translations, microfilms and storage
and processing in electronic systems.
Printed on permanent/durable paper.
Printing and binding: Hubert & Co., Göttingen
Printed in Germany
ISSN 0938-9024
ISBN 978-3-447-06141-4

Contents

Contents

Introduction

ROGER ALLEN

University of Pennsylvania

This is the third (and last) volume in a series devoted to the biographies of renowned Arab littérateurs. The three volumes have been organized into the following periods[1]:

> Volume 1: 950-1350
> Volume 2: 1350-1850
> Volume 3: 1850-1950.

While it will be noted that these "periods" are indeed the product of a process of periodization, a favorite activity of historically-based scholarship, it is important for readers of the series to be aware that, as Series-Editor for the volumes, I have selected these chronological subdivisions on the basis of criteria that pay less attention to the more political and dynastic phenomena that have often dictated the organization and subdivision of historical studies devoted to the Arabic-speaking regions, literary-historical studies having been in most cases no different from other foci of historical accounts. By contrast, the principles applied in establishing these timeframes for the four volumes have endeavored to be more reflective of changes in intellectual and cultural milieus and, almost deliberately, to transcend the more traditional historical boundaries of many previous studies of the Arabic literary heritage.

In brief, such previous and more traditional approaches to periodization have identified: (a) a pre-Islamic era (up to 622 CE); (b) an era of Muhammad and the four "Rightly-Guided" caliphs (622-660); the Umayyad dynasty of caliphs (660-750); the Abbasid dynasty (750-1258), often subdivided into two or three sub-periods, and ending with the Mongol sack of Baghdad; a "period of decadence" (1258-1798), sometimes also subdivided into "Mamluk" and "Ottoman" periods, the preferred dividing line being 1516, the Ottoman capture of Cairo; and a "modern period," from 1798 (Napoleon's invasion of Egypt) until whatever the present may be at the time of writing the work in question. Without going into unnecessary detail (at least, in this context), this process of historical periodization has the obvious virtue of linking cultural trends with often cataclysmic processes of political transformation (although it manages to ignore both the fall of Constantinople in 1453 and of Granada in 1492). But the negative aspect of such an approach lies in the fact that the continuities of the literary tradition and the emergence and transformation of literary genres tend to be subordinated to a logic dictated by non-literary criteria. Thus, while it has to be admitted that the "divides" reflected in the subdivisions of the four volumes of this series are, in a sense as "artificial" as any others in their designation of "breaks" rather than "continuities," I would suggest that they do nevertheless serve as more effective boundaries to the development of literary trends than the more traditional ones briefly described above that rely mostly on other principles.

With regard to the time-period of this fourth volumes in the series, it will immediately be observed that its period of coverage stops at the year 1950, thus focusing in the main on the earlier phases in the development of what is generally known as a "modern" tradition of

---

[1] It should be noted that a previous volume devoted to the earlier period, 500–950, was published under different circumstances: see *Arabic Literary Culture 500–950*, ed. Shawkat Toorawa and Michael Cooperson, Dictionary of Literary Biography series no. 311 (Detroit: Thompson Gale, 2005).

Arabic literature and, in more political terms, on the pre-independence and/or colonial period in most of the Arabic-speaking regions. This is a deliberate decision on my part, in that the last half-century (I am writing these words in the summer of 2007) has witnessed both creative writing and literary scholarship developing in ways that suggest that not only would the identification of 40 authors for a post-1950 volumes be an extremely difficult, indeed controversial, task, but also the very generic and geographical diversity of the Arabic-speaking region would render modes of organization other than the chronological one adopted in these four volumes more appropriate. I should also stress that the selection of authors for inclusion in this volume—a difficult task in any case—is based on the "floruit" period of the authors concerned. Just to provide one example, and one that I realize from my own scholarly interests will be controversial enough, the name of Najīb Mahfūz—the Egyptian Nobel Laureate in Literature of 1988 is not included among those discussed in this volume, because, even though he was born in 1911, I would submit that his "floruit" period belongs in the post-independence phase of Egyptian and Arabic literature. It is obviously an aspiration of the present writer and his colleagues to see the volumes of this current project continued into a further set of volumes devoted to the immensely rich tradition of Arabic literary creativity during and following the eventful decade of the 1950s and particularly the many important developments that have followed the so-called "al-naksah" (the setback), the June War of 1967, an event that had the most profound impact on the community of intellectuals throughout the Arabic-speaking world.

These volumes then present to their readers biographical and critical essays on some 120 authors who number among the major figures in the tradition of Arabic literature. As will always be the case when a selection has to be made, other major figures have had to be omitted, not least because these volumes have strived, to the extent possible, to represent the geographical breadth of the region within which Arabic literature has been created and disseminated.

Precedents and Problems

In view of the alternative modes of periodization that have just been discussed, it is already obvious that the use of 1850 as a beginning date for the current volume marks a different approach to the chronology and sequence of Arabic literary production in the 19th and 20th centuries. 1850 is the mid-point in a century that witnessed great changes within many regions of the Arabic-speaking world, but, as recent scholarship has tended to suggest (that of Edward Said being the most prominent), great changes also in the ways in which the Western world regarded the region and its peoples. As Thomas Bauer has clearly demonstrated in a recent article devoted to the problems of traditional literary historical approaches and, in particular, the relationship between the modern and its precedents (*Mamluk Studies Review*, 9.2 [2005]: 105-32), European interest moved from a fascination with the exotic and different, a trend forwarded, if not triggered, by the image of the culture fostered by the widespread availability of translations of *A Thousand and One Nights*, to more specifically focused colonial initiatives aimed at the protection of commercial interests (the British in India, for example) and the importation of what were considered "superior" cultural values to regions and cultures that were viewed as "backward" and thus in need of "reform" (and, in many regions, of evangelism as well). Bauer goes on to suggest that the identification of a "decadent" period of Arab and Islamic culture preceding the 19th century is not the result of any indigenous scholarly process that set out to analyze elements of continuity and rupture within the intellectual milieus involved, but rather was imposed from the outside; indeed the very notion of such a break in the Arabic literary tradition was to become a very important means whereby to justify this kind of European colonialist logic. What serves to confuse the picture even further is that several Arab cultural historians who were among the most prominent intellectuals, especially in Egypt, during the formative years of the process of modernization—Ahmad Amīn (d. 1954) and Tāhā **Husayn** (d. 1973), for example—traveled to France to study their own culture within a very different academic milieu and returned to their homeland to reproduce the above European attitudes to their pre-modern cultural history in their own works.

The highly questionable validity of these literary-historical premises has been explored in some detail within the articles of Volume 2 of the present series, devoted to the "pre-modern" period in question (albeit with chronological boundaries different from those usually applied). However, as we move towards a discussion of the mid-19th century as the starting-point of this volume and the relationship of its trends to what went before, it seems useful to identify, as Bauer does in his article cited above, some of the literary trends that cast doubt on the ascription of "decadence" to the period in question, not least because many of those same trends are prominent features of the initial phases of the post-1850 period.

To begin with, there is a delight in all literary genres in exploring, and indeed playing with, the lexical and rhetorical dimensions of the Arabic language: cryptograms in poetic form that use the numerical value of the graphemes of the Arabic alphabet to produce lines of poetry that add up to the year of its composition (or, more appropriately, the birthdate of the ruler of the time, panegyric still occupying the position that it has held for many centuries as the most widespread and profitable poetic genre), and elaborate exercises in rhyming, cadenced prose (the Arabic term is saj') whereby the prestige narrative form of the maqāmah, originally developed in the 10th century CE, is used for variety of purposes—depictions of the life of the populace, veiled criticism of political and religious figures, moral and homiletic wisdom, and sheer entertainment. There is, particularly among the increasingly important secretarial class within the chancelleries of the court, a continuing interest in compilation of information and anecdote of astonishing variety and of manuals prepared by members of this class for their peers and successors devoted to every aspect of the scribal profession and its adjuncts. There is also evidence of a wide variety of performance-media that may be termed "dramatic." These range from scripts of actual plays, to the enactment of religious rituals (particularly among the Shiʿa popula-

tions), to puppet performances and shadow-plays; it is only within a context in which one demands the existence of a building called a "theater" and the acceptance of a particular dramatic work as being part of a literary canon that it is possible to claim that the pre-modern Arabic-speaking regions had no tradition of drama. Finally, among these general features we can point to the existence of a number of works that indicate a narrowing of the large chasm that traditionalist scholarship had established between "elite" and "popular" literature, the dividing line being mostly based on assessments of the "probity" of different levels of the Arabic language, between al-lughah al-fushā (the more correct language), the level with the Qurʾān itself as its inimitable model, that is characteristic of (required for) any ascription of cultural value on the one hand, and al-lughah al-dārijah (or ʿāmmiyyah), the language of the plebs on the other. Robert Irwin (in his introductory survey, The Arabian Nights: a companion [London: Penguin Books, 1995] has done an excellent job in making scholars aware of the large amount of literature (including the types and themes mentioned above) composed or compiled during this pre-modern era that uses one of a large variety of medial levels of language between these two poles.

It is clear, I trust, that the trends just mentioned are merely a small part of a period in Arabic literary history (c. 1150-1850), the first centuries of which Bauer is prepared to term "one of the apogees of Arabic literature" (p. 129). It is equally clear that, from a critical and esthetic stand-point, the values implicit in the continued publication and popularity of these types of literary expression reflect modes of appreciation and assessment that are widely at variance with those that have been applied to Western literary works over several centuries. While acknowledging (and regretting) the failure of much Western scholarship to engage with such critical differences and their implications for literary-historical evaluation, I have chosen here merely to identify these particular aspects of that "pre-modern" era since they are precisely those that are encountered by the earliest representatives of the century that is our concern in this third volume in the series. They thus serve both to counter many traditional (and mostly Western-inspired) attitudes to the periodization of Arabic literary history and to indicate those elements of continuity that link the post-1850 period to its antecedents.

"Al-Nahdah"

The Arabic term *al-nahdah* implies a process of moving in an upwards direction; it is the preferred term to describe the process of cultural change—albeit within widely variant chronological frameworks—that took place within the Arabic-speaking regions during the 19th century and well into the 20th. It is often linked to the European notion of "renaissance," but I hope that by now it is clear that the linkage between the European and Arabic concepts of that term cannot in any way be considered analogous. The European renaissance, at least as a broadly-based literary-historical concept, is part of an assessment of the development of European culture that succeeds in tracing continuities; even the so-called "Middle Ages" (or even, "Dark Ages") become interesting objects of study as being sites of alternative cultural priorities and critical values that lead into other eras to which a higher cultural value has been ascribed. As noted above, such is not the case with the example of Arabic literary history, in that the pre-modern period (at least, the 16th-18th centuries, and often more than that) is considered so lacking in value (and thus so under-studied) that few, if any, elements of continuity have been identified or agreed upon (to be fair, there are a few examples, as in Peter Gran's significant contribution to this debate, *The Islamic Roots of Capitalism*, 1979). Some significant Arab intellectuals living through this very process had occasion to question the parameters that seemed to be implied and applied in the coinage of the term. One such is the Lebanese poet, short-story writer, and critic, Mīkhā'īl **Nu'aymah**[2], who spent the

early part of his career until the 1930s in the United States:

I've often wondered what we mean by the word nahdah. Do we mean that we were not paying attention, but now we've woken up? Were we flat on our backs, but now we've stood up? Or that we were walking at the back of the procession of life, whereas now we're in the middle or even close to the front? As we move one step at a time, how can we know whether we're moving forwards or backwards, or just staying where we are? (Nu'aymah, *Fatāwā*, cited in *Akhbār al-Adab* 217 [7 Sept. 1997]: 15)

In response to questions such as these, the above-mentioned Tāhā Husayn, who might be dubbed "Egypt's school-teacher" on such matters, suggests to his contemporaries that they perform a huge chronological leap-frog over seven centuries of Arabic literary production and search for the values needed for the development of their sense of national and cultural identity in the glorious classical heritage of the 11th century CE and earlier.

This 19th century movement of cultural change in the Arabic-speaking world, widely known as "*al-nahdah*," thus needs to be seen on its own terms rather than in any kind of comparative framework. It can be conveniently viewed as a combination of two separate trends: one that involves a search into the past, and a second that seeks to examine and imitate those values that are being imported from Europe, particularly in the wake of the series of colonial incursions that begin with France's annexation of Algeria in 1830. As will already be obvious, however, the analysis of this twin process of research and assimilation is already heavily tilted in one direction, in that the search into the indigenous past is heavily colored by the posture of the critical communities of the region towards their own immediate past and its cultural achievements (or lack thereof).

In what follows I will discuss these two cultural movements, that in their initial manifestations appear to be entirely separate and discrete but that gradually come to participate as contrasting poles in a joint enterprise of modernization.

---

2   Authors whose names are indicated in bold print are the subjects of biographical articles in this volume.

The Revival of the Past

The second volume in this series has clearly shown, I believe, the extent to which the period immediately prior to the 19th century was not the unmitigated literary "slough of despond" that it has traditionally been portrayed as being. To be sure, the esthetic principles and the tastes of listeners or readers were, as we have already noted, quite different from those that have been used to assess the value of the products of other literate cultures, but research currently in progress on the pre-modern history of many sub-regions in the Arabic-speaking world clearly illustrates the existence of thriving literary and critical communities.

In the realm of poetry, and in both its elite and popular forms and contexts, the practitioners of the poetic art were continuing to make use of the forms and principles that had been handed down to them over the centuries. In Syria Manjak Pāshā al-Yūsufī (d. 1669) continues the tradition of the court poet, seeking remuneration for the panegyrics that he addresses to the rulers of the age, while the renowned figure of Shaykh ʿAbd al-Ghanī al-Nābulusī (d. 1731) is one of the era's greatest polygraphs, penning not merely poems of a wide variety (including cryptograms), but also works devoted to travel, jurisprudence, and mysticism. Another poetic figure discussed in the previous volume is the Egyptian popular poet Yūsuf al-Shirbīnī (fl. 1665-87), who composed a famous poem on the subject of Egypt's peasantry; like the plays of the dramatist-oculist, Ibn Dāniyāl (d. 1310) that have survived from earlier times, these texts afford us insight in what was clearly a lively tradition of popular literature and performance.

It is also in Egypt that another renowned scholar of Indian origin, Murtadā al-Zabīdī (d. 1791), not only completed the compilation of the enormous dictionary of the Arabic language, *Tāj al-ʿArūs*, begun centuries earlier by al-Fayrūzābādī (d. 1414), but also convened a literary salon in which students and colleagues discussed the treasures of the literary heritage. Thus it was that Shaykh Hasan al-ʿAttār (d. 1834), one of those students, learned to appreciate the erudition and stylistic virtuosity to be found in the prose narratives, called *maqāmāt*, that had been

perfected by al-Harīrī (d. 1122) and replicated centuries later by Jalāl al-Dīn al-Suyūtī (d. 1505), another of Arabic literature's great polygraphs. Al-ʿAttār in turn produced his own set of *maqāmāt*, thus providing not only a link to the narratives of the past, but also pointing forward to further use of the genre and style during the 19th and 20th centuries—one of those "continuities" that revised approaches towards the premodern can engender. Also in the realms of prose-narratives, a remarkable Syrian figure, Ilyās al-Mawsilī (d. 168?), continued the earlier tradition of travel accounts in Arabic, exemplified most notably by those of Ibn Battūtah (d. 1377), in undertaking a lengthy voyage to South America.

Another student in al-Zabīdī's literary salon was ʿAbd al-Rahmān al-Jabartī (d. 1822) whose history of Egypt, *ʿAjāʾib al-āthār fī ʾl-tarājim waʾl-akhbār* (Wondrous Relics Concerning Biographies and Events), can be regarded as a continuation of the account begun in the work of his predecessor, Ibn Iyās (d. 1523), *Badāʾiʿ al-zuhūr fī ʾl-waqāʾiʿ waʾl-duhūr* (The Choicest Blooms Concerning Events and Dooms); while the latter includes within its pages an account of the capture of Cairo by the Ottomans in 1516; the former provides invaluable details of that event which is widely regarded as marking the divide between the pre-modern and modern, namely Napoleon's invasion of Egypt in 1798.

Contacts with Europe

The examples that have been provided thus far of cultural activities in the Arabic-speaking world in the centuries preceding the 19th have primarily focused, it will be observed, on what may be termed the "central" part—Egypt and Syria. In fact, the French invasion of Egypt is, within the context of our current discussion of inter-cultural contact, something of an exception, and it is, no doubt, the very abruptness of that contact and the fact of Egypt's centrality in the region (both geographically and culturally) that have made it a favorite model for discussions of the processes of modernity and change. However, it needs to be pointed out that patterns of contact existed in other regions as well, and indeed that some of those patterns had existed for several centuries. Histories of the Maghrib (North-West Africa), for example, make it clear that the linkages that had for centuries tied the region to Spain to its North and also to Italy had not been completely severed as a result of the events of 1492; indeed there continued to be a flourishing commercial exchange been ports such as Sale in Morocco, Bājiyah (Bougie) in Algeria, and Amalfi and Genoa in Italy. Nor were such links merely commercial; cultural linkages across the Straits of Gibraltar were maintained, and to this day Algeria remains the primary center for the study of what is still termed "Andalusian" music. Further to the East, the region of Mount Lebanon, then part of the Ottoman province of Syria, housed, as it continues to house, a vigorous community of Maronite Christians, one that maintained continuous contacts with the Catholic church, not least through the establishment of a Maronite College in Rome complete with its own Arabic printing press.

Such differing patterns of contact between the various sub-regions of the Arabic-speaking world and Europe during the pre-19th century era help to explain not only the variations in that series of developments that is termed "modernization" in each region, but also the widely different chronologies involved. Henceforth we will continue to make use of the "central" region as a model for those developments, not merely because of the relatively "early" period in which the signs of change begin to occur in chronological terms, but also because an intercommunal civil war in Syria during the mid-19th century and the subsequent departure of large numbers of Christians from the region (many of them to Egypt) served to bring together within a single region many aspects of the lengthy process of change.

Importation, Translation, Imitation

The impact of Napoleon's invasion of Egypt was not merely military, in that the expedition included in its numbers a large contingent of scholars in a variety of disciplines. The latter group spread out across the country and gathered data that became part of the *Description de l'Egypte*, a series of folio-sized volumes that remain prized items to this very day and contain exquisite illustrations of life in the Egyptian countryside that are as valid today as they were when they were originally crafted, even though many other aspects of the record have, of course, been radically transformed over the course of the two subsequent centuries. Many French scholars engaged in discussions with the local intellectual community, one among whom was the already mentioned historian, 'Abd al-Rahmān al-Jabartī, who left us an invaluable record of these exchanges, particularly those involving the *'ulamā'* (religious scholars) of al-Azhar, the great seat of Islamic learning in Cairo. Theater troupes and other modes of entertainment were brought to the Egyptian capital in order to entertain the French occupying forces, all of which were dutifully observed and recorded by al-Jabartī.

While the importance of these contacts was clearly considerable, it may appear at first that the military aspect was essentially a failure, in that, following the defeat of the French fleet at the hands of the British admiral, Lord Nelson, at what is generally known as the Battle of the Nile in July 1798, French forces withdrew. However, as a result of the French invasion, the Ottoman government in Istanbul had dispatched an armed force to bolster the local Egyptian forces. The commander of that force was an officer of Albanian origins named Muhammad 'Alī. The combined Egyptian and Ottoman forces had been roundly defeated at the Battle of the Pyramids just a few days before the fateful naval battle mentioned above, and Muhammad 'Alī had made due note of the enormous differences in weaponry with which the two sides were equipped. With the withdrawal of French forces and the creation thereby of what was essentially a power-vacuum, Muhammad 'Alī stepped into the breech, consolidated his own authority, orchestrated the massacre of his Mamluk rivals (in 1811), and thereafter established what was to become an Egyptian dynasty that lasted until the revolution of 1952 during which Muhammad 'Alī's last successor, King Fārūq (Farouk), was sent into exile. Having established his power in this way, Muhammad 'Alī was determined to create an entirely new kind of armed force whose weapons and military competence could rival that of the French. For that purpose, he dispatched missions of young Egyptians (the Arabic term is "*ba'thāt*"), initially to Italy but eventually and predominantly to France, in order to study military tactics and the science of weaponry. While the initial goals of these missions were obviously specific in their focus on military and technical subjects, a crucially important pattern had now been created whereby young Egyptians would be sent to Europe for training. Over the course of subsequent decades, the purposes of such missions, both publicly and privately financed, were considerably expanded.

With the mission of 1824, Muhammad 'Alī dispatched an *imām* whose primary task was to supervise the maintenance of Islamic worship among the members of the mission. His name was Rifā'ah Rāfi' al-**Tahtāwī** (d. 1873), the earliest of the writers to be included in this volume; since he was a pupil of Shaykh Hasan al-'Attār—himself a pupil of al-Zabīdī (both mentioned above), we thus have a direct linkage to the immediate past, but, in the context of our current discussion of the processes involved in the 19th century "*al-nahdah*," al-Tahtāwī serves as an excellent and early illustration of the Janus-like process (he being the Roman house-god whose image on the lintel of houses points in two opposite directions) of looking forwards as well as backwards. Al-Tahtāwī spent his time in France not only fulfilling his religious obligations, but also in learning the French language and recording his impressions of as many aspects of French society, government, and culture as he could. Upon his return to Egypt in 1831, he recorded these impressions in a classic work, *Takhlīs al-Ibrīz fī talkhīs Bārīz* (the title of which reflects the patterns of pre-modern Arabic works that almost always expected a rhyming phrase, an effect that might be replicated in translation as something like: The Purest Gold Refined, A Summary of Paris Defined). The work was published through the newly established printing-press that Muhammad 'Alī had established in 1822 at Būlāq, a district of Cairo close to the River Nile, and its author was subsequently charged with the organization of a

school of translation (in order to translate the French military manuals with which the missions returned to Egypt) and the editorship of a new official "gazette," *al-Waqā'i' al-Misriyyah* (Egyptian Events). It almost goes without saying that each of these separate endeavors constituted a major step in Egypt's ability to advance Muhammad 'Alī's goals of replicating European advances in a number of fields. To be sure, the cultural sector was not one of his major priorities. At the turn of the 19th/20th century, Muhammad al-**Muwaylihī** (another of the figures represented in this volume) could declare, in a frequently censored chapter of his famous work, *Hadīth 'Īsā ibn Hishām* ('Īsā ibn Hishām's Tale), that Muhammad 'Alī knew no Arabic; in fact, the only words in that language that he is alleged to have used on a regular basis were "*kurbāsh*" (whip) and "*bakhshīsh*" (bribe, tip). While that may be a somewhat embellished description (like many other segments of al-Muwaylihī's work), it does suggest the way many Egyptians viewed the language preferences of their new rulers. In any case, what Muhammad 'Alī regarded as a somewhat subordinate priority was to be taken up with gusto by his later successor, Ismā'īl (who ruled from 1863 until he was deposed and exiled in 1879), He was responsible for the building of a modern section of Cairo known then as "Ismā'īliyyah," with broad boulevards modeled on Haussmann's Paris; for the inauguration of a National Library (Dār al-Kutub al-Misriyyah) and the construction of both the Suez Canal and the Cairo Opera House (along with the commissioning of Verdi opera, *Aida*, to open it; unfortunately the opera was not completed in time, and *Rigoletto* was performed in its place). These measures had two primary effects: firstly they managed to bankrupt the Egyptian state, leading initially to European "supervision" of the finances of the country and subsequently (1882) to British occupation of the country; secondly to Egypt's being viewed throughout the Arabic-speaking world as a model of change, modernity, and freedom of thought, the last being a category that was being varying monitored and suppressed in Arabic-speaking regions under more direct Ottoman control (Syria and Iraq, for example) with the rigorous system of censorship that was imposed from the central administration in Istanbul.

It was within that particular environment that the Christian communities of Mount Lebanon continued and expanded their own contacts of long-standing with Europe.

In 1847, for example, Mārūn al-**Naqqāsh** (d. 1855), a member of a prominent family, returned from a visit to Italy where he had become devoted to the theatre and obtained permission from the Ottoman authorities to mount a production of *al-Bakhīl*, an adaptation of Molière's well known play *L'avare*. In view of what we have noted above about the nature and existence of drama in the pre-modern era, it is important to stress that this performance in Naqqāsh's house was an important initial gesture in the process of establishing the idea of "theatre" as involving a particular place and a publicly available text (and, in these early days, a frequent recourse to a source-tale in *A Thousand and One Nights*). It was precisely the social issues aroused by this public dimension and the availability of a text for examination that brought so much trouble to Naqqāsh and even more so to his contemporary, Abū Khalīl al-**Qabbānī** (d. 1902), who, after much harassment from religious and secular authorities in Damascus, emulated many of his colleagues and moved his troupe to the more liberal environment of Egypt, as just described.

Another prominent Lebanese family that was heavily involved in these movements of revival and change was that of al-**Yāzijī**. Nāsīf al-Yāzijī (d. 1871) was a devotee of the Arabic language and its pre-modern literary heritage, those being topics of particular interest within the Christian communities of Lebanon that can be traced back to a number of eminent precursors, and most especially to Germanus Farhāt (d. 1732), Maronite Bishop of Aleppo and a major figure in lexicography and grammar studies. Al-Yāzijī set himself to replicate the virtuosity of past masters (and particularly al-Harīrī) by composing a set of *maqāmāt* under the title, *Majma' al-bahrayn* (The Meeting-place of the two seas, a Qur'ānic reference). This set of *maqāmāt* is a genuine work of neo-Classicism, a language-lover's gesture of appreciation to the masterworks of his forebears and a clear illustration of the revivalist

aspects of the 19th century "*al-nahdah*." Nāsīf al-Yāzijī instilled his love of Arabic and its history in his son, Ibrāhīm (d. 1906), who not only contributed studies of Arabic lexicography but also participated in a project that was to have significant ramifications for Arabic and its texts in their process of adaptation to new cultural realities, namely the Protestant translation of the Bible into Arabic. Here, of course, the element of Western evangelism, noted briefly above, enters the picture, especially through the initiatives of the American Presbyterian Church that not only established its own college, the Syrian Protestant College (1866)—now known as the American University in Beirut but also embarked upon a large-scaled project to translate the Protestant Bible into Arabic. In so doing, they employed the most prominent scholars of Arabic from the Christian community. We have already mentioned the Yāzijī family, but prominent roles were also played by the Bustānī and Shidyāq families.

The Bustānī family was to play an extremely important role in the earlier stages of the development of a tradition of modern Arabic literature. Butrus al-Bustānī (d. 1883), educated within the Maronite tradition, converted to Protestant Christianity and assisted American missionaries, prominent among whom was Dr. Cornelius van Dyke, in the translation of the Bible. He produced a major dictionary of the language, *Muhīt al-muhīt*, and started work on an encyclopedia, *Dā'irat al-ma'ārif*, work on which was carried on by his successors. He also edited the newspaper, *al-Jinān*, and translated certain works of Western literature into Arabic, including Defoe's *Robinson Crusoe* and John Bunyan's *Pilgrim's Progress*. *Al-Jinān* in fact became a major outlet for the publication of initial attempts at fiction writing. One of the major contributors to that initiative was Butrus's own son, Salīm (d. 1884), who penned a number of novels modelled on Western prototypes that explored love and marriage within the framework of a rigidly determined set of moral values. *Al-Huyām fī jinān al-Shām* (Passion in Syrian Gardens, 1870), set during the Arab invasions of Syria during the earliest days of Islam (7th century), is one of the earliest attempts at the writing of the historical romance in Arabic. Another member of the Bustānī family, Butrus's cousin, Sulaymān (d. 1925) travelled widely in the Middle East and Europe and published a translation into Arabic of Homer's *Iliad*.

Ahmad Fāris al-**Shidyāq** (d. 1887) was born into the same Maronite community, but his brother, As'ad, ran up against the rigid system of the clergy and died in prison. With that Fāris converted first to Protestantism and later to Islam (adopting the name Ahmad); opinions differ as to whether he reconverted upon his death-bed (in Istanbul, where he had served for many years as editor of the newspaper, *al-Jawā'ib*).

With his monumental work *al-Sāq 'alā 'l-sāq fī-mā huwa al-Fāryāq* (1855), yet another playful title that uses two parts of al-Shidyāq's own name (Fār- and -yāq) in the second part, while the first is a semantic maze that can either mean "One Leg over Another" or "The Pigeon on the Tree-Branch," al-Shidyāq provides yet another major Janus-like gesture, pointing to both past and future. As language-amateur, lexicographer, journalist, translator, and traveller, he invokes the traditions of the past. Indeed the work contains four examples of the *maqāmah* genre, each of them amazingly complex examples of word-play and linguistic virtuosity that reflect the values and entertainments of previous centuries. The travel-theme is, of course, also a highly developed genre in the pre-modern era, but in this case it is applied to a visit to Europe, thus relating it to a certain extent to al-Tahtāwī's account mentioned above. Now however, al-Shidyāq introduces not only a pseudo-fictional narrator, *Fāryāq*, but also his wife, *Fāryāqah*, who accompanies him on his visits to Paris and London. Quite apart from the way in which Arab readers are given yet another (and even broader) picture of the West and its cultural traditions, al-Shidyāq's resort to the fictionalization of autobiographical narrative in this work serves as a major precedent for the emergence of experiments in the composition of Western fictional genres and their incorporation into the literary life of the different regions of the Arabic-speaking world.

As we have already noted, the policies of the Egyptian Khedive, Ismā'īl, in particular, advocated the most rapid importation of Western institutions and values into the fabric of Egyptian society during the mid-19th century. It is thus not a source of surprise that, when civil war broke out between Muslims and Christians in Syria during the 1850s, many of the Christian families whom we have already mentioned moved to Egypt (while others emigrated to the Americas and to Europe). Acting troupes, newspapers and their owners, littérateurs, and language scholars were all involved in this exodus, one that was to have a profound impact both on the history of Syrian literature and that of Egypt. As has been the case in a number of literary traditions, the development of the press tradition was to play a central role in the debates over the twin issues that we raised above: the indigenous and the imported, the traditional and the modern (and the criteria upon which those terms were to be defined), the Western colonial presence and the Arab quest for national and/or local identity.

We have already drawn attention to the role of the Bustānī newspaper, *al-Jinān*, in publishing early attempts at fiction-writing. During the course of the latter half of the 19th century, as Syrian intellectuals and writers joined their Egyptian counterparts in Cairo and Alexandria, there was an enormous increase in the establishment of newspapers; Phillipe de Tarrāzī, the author of the authoritative account of this development, records that by the year 1900 there were 152 newspapers in Cairo and 60 in Alexandria (as cited in J. Brugman, *An Introduction to the History of Modern Arabic Literature in Egypt*, Leiden: E. J. Brill, 1984, 63). Following on the precedent created by Muhammad 'Alī in the establishment of an official gazette, *al-Waqā'i' al-Misriyyah*, in 1828, Syrians and Egyptians cooperated in the founding of newspapers that adopted particular points-of-view regarding tradition and change and the varying postures towards the occupying British forces and the more distant suzerainty of the Ottoman government, with its claims to serve as a focus of pan-Islamic beliefs. *Al-Ahrām*, still Cairo's major newspaper, was founded in 1876 by the Lebanese Taqlā brothers (and was the publication venue for *Dhāt al-Khidr* (Lady of the Boudoir,

1884), one of the above mentioned Salīm al-Bustānī's novels). In 1885, Ya'qūb Sarrūf (d. 1927), who had been working at the Syrian Protestant College in Beirut, came to Cairo, bringing his journal, *al-Muqtataf*, with him. In 1889 he and his Lebanese colleague, Fāris Nimr, established the newspaper, *al-Muqattam*, which came to serve as a mouthpiece for pro-British sentiment. Sarrūf himself contributed to developments in fiction in his newly adopted land, publishing novels in his own magazine, *al-Muqtataf*; they include *Fatāt Miṣr* (Girl of Egypt, 1905) and *Amīr Lubnān* (Prince of Lebanon, 1907).

However, one name stands out from all the other composers of these early attempts at novels of historical romance, Jūrjī **Zaydān** (d. 1914), yet another Lebanese littérateur and journal editor; in his case the journal was and still is *al-Hilāl*, which continues to play a major role in the publication of literature within Egypt and beyond.

Zaydān aimed to give his Arab readers a collection of works that would educate them concerning their cultural history. He wrote a history of Islamic civilization and a history of Arabic literature, but what is most significant in our current context is that, modeling himself very much on Sir Walter Scott, he decided to foster the emerging sense of identity (in the context of foreign occupation) by penning a series of historical novels.

Each of them took a particular period of Arab and Islamic history and used the major events of the period as a backdrop for what we might term a "local interest" story, one that involved one or more members of a family in the ramifications of the larger story.

These novels began with *al-Mamlūk al-sharīd* (The Fugitive Mamluk, 1891)—about the famous massacre of the Mamluks by Muhammad 'Alī that we alluded to earlier, and continued on their course through history, from earliest 7th century times to Spain, to Khurasan, to the Crusades, and the Ottoman conquests; it is a tribute to their continuing popular appeal that they remain in print today.

Thanks to the increasing availability of magazines and newspapers (including some, like *al-Riwāyāt al-shahriyyah* [Monthly Novels]), the early works of these writers garnered a wide readership for fiction, but, as literary historians have pointed out, the works in question raise issues concerning the type of fiction being published and the broader purposes as fiction in general. These early novels were certainly demanding the development of a new kind of Arabic writing-style and were also serving to develop a much enhanced sense of heritage and identity. But, as the title and summaries we have essayed above show reasonably clearly, they were not concerned with present realities and the advocacy of social change. It is in this latter realm that the work of the already mentioned Muhammad al-**Muwaylihī** and his renowned narrative, *Hadīth 'Īsā ibn Hishām*, serves an important function in the history of modern Arabic fiction. With al-Shidyāq's *al-Sāq 'alā 'l-sāq fī-mā huwa al-Fāryāq* as a clear precedent, al-Muwaylihī chooses to invoke the past and its stylistic modes in order to pass trenchant comment on the present. His work has often been described as a "bridge," and the image seems appropriate. The picture of fin de siècle Cairo, published in his own family newspaper, *Miṣbāḥ al-Sharq*, and later converted into book form, displays a close observation of social reality and a bitingly sarcastic wit that are lacking in any of the other works that we have discussed thus far; furthermore such social criticism as one finds in *Hadīth 'Īsā ibn Hishām* is not replicated in Egyptian fiction until the 1930s.

Al-Muwaylihī's work of social criticism is couched in the language of the pre-modern narrative genre, the *maqāmah*, both through its use of the rhymed prose style of *saj'* and its episodic structure (although a developing sense of plot-sequences in certain episodes is a new feature in this context). Those features link *Hadīth 'Īsā ibn Hishām* with the earlier tradition of Arabic prose narrative, via al-Shidyāq, al-Yāzijī, al-'Attār, al-Suyūtī, and others, but within that particular framework we need to introduce another author, one who belongs to a category of littérateurs that now demands inclusion in the history of the 19th and 20th century, albeit under publication circumstances that differ from those we have encountered thus far. I am referring to women writers, and in this particular case to 'Ā'ishah al-**Taymūriyyah** (d. 1902). The daughter of a prominent family of Turco-Circassian origins, she grew up in a home surrounded by literature and its practitioners, but she spent much of her life countering the prejudices of her family and later her husband against women publishing literature. However, following the death of her husband in 1875, she proceeded to place her works into the public domain. In the context of the continuity of the *maqāmah* tradition in the 19th century and into the 20th, it is her work, *Natā'ij al-ahwāl fī 'l-aqwāl wa'l-af'āl* (the play on rhymes evident yet again, translatable perhaps as "The results of conditions concerning both statements and commissions," 1887-8). Invoking her own persona as narrator of this *maqāmah*-revival, she uses a variety of story-types to provide a kind of modern example of the "mirrors for princes" genre, but her adherence to a more coherent notion of plot points to future developments in narrative rather than past. 'Ā'ishah al-Taymūriyyah's achievements are recorded in the work of another female pioneer whose role has recently come to be appreciated, Zaynab **Fawwāz** (d. 1914). Yet another immigrant to Egypt from Lebanon, she moved from a relatively poor Shi'ite family background to become an important advocate of women's rights. The author of works of both fiction and drama, she also published a compilation of the biographies of famous women, under the title *al-Durr al-manthūr fī tabaqāt rabbāt al-khudūr* (Scattered Pearls, concerning the Categories of Ladies Secluded, 1894). 'Ā'ishah al-Taymūriyyah was one of the subjects included in the compilation.

Of all the literary genres whose initial phases occurred within this bifurcated process known as "*al-nahdah*," it is almost certainly drama and its public manifestation as theater that present the literary historian with some of the most complex and interesting trans-cultural issues. Since it is, of course, the most public of literary genres, it presents the best vehicle whereby to illustrate the social dimensions of the debates that were taking place around this process and period of change. As was the case with Mārūn al-Naqqāsh within the Syrian

context, an Egyptian Jew named Ya'qūb **Sannū'** (d. 1912) had travelled to Europe and witnessed the potential impact and social significance of theatrical performances. Upon his return to Egypt he gathered together some local actors and, more controversially Christian and Jewish actresses, and produced performances of his own plays on a stage in the Ezbekiyyah Gardens in central Cairo. They were comedies of social satire and became extremely popular. The troupe was invited to perform for the Khedive Ismā'īl in person, and the ruler is alleged to have dubbed Sannū' the "Molière of Egypt." Unfortunately one of his plays was interpreted as being an attack on the Khedive's uxorious tendencies; the theatre was closed in 1872 and Sannū' was later sent into exile from where he published a number of newspaper in Arabic, many of them variants on his nickname, "Abū Nazzārah zarqā'" (the man with blue glasses). However, the tradition of popular drama that he had fostered was continued by Najīb al-Rīhānī (d. 1949), another Egyptian actor and director, who earned an enormous reputation for his portrayal of a typical Egyptian figure, the rural *'umdah* (head of the village), whose venal instincts are only matched by his naiveté in the face of the modern city. Alongside this kind of popular drama in the colloquial dialect, other writers and performers tried to continue along the path set by earlier figures such as al-Naqqāsh and al-Qabbānī, the latter of whom, as noted above, had himself moved his troupe to Cairo. The process of introducing more serious themes into the dramatic medium and presenting them to an audience was to prove considerably more challenging. Contemporary accounts of performances (including a memorable one in al-Muwaylihī's *Hadīth 'Īsā ibn Hishām*) make it clear that the audience tended to regard such presentations as a participatory event and expected interludes of singing and music along with the segments of monologue and dialogue. As a result of these problems, the development of a tradition of drama as literature in Arabic and its introduction into the public arena was to demand a longer period of cultural adaptation. In the meanwhile, drama acquired a somewhat risqué reputation, somewhat akin to that of vaudeville and burlesque; to go to watch such a performance, with women appearing in public on stage, was to risk one's reputation. These early problems concerning the goals and methods of drama was to become the topic of an experimental play written in the 1970s by the Syrian playwright, Saʿdallāh Wannūs (d. 1997), *Sahrah maʿa Abī Khalīl al-Qabbānī* (A Soirée with Abū Khalīl al-Qabbānī), in which the frustrations of presenting a "serious" play in such conditions, one based on a tale from *A Thousand and One Nights*, are explored.

In the preceding paragraphs I have tried to show the various ways in which the factors of the indigenous and traditional on the one hand and the imported and "modern" on the other operated both separately and together in the general process of cultural change that is generally known as *al-nahdah*. Among other things it has emerged clearly that, while the general parameters governing the process occurred in the same sequence, the actual chronology differed widely among the various sub-regions of the Arabic-speaking world. I have concentrated on that region, mostly Egypt and Syria, within which the trends are visible at a relatively early stage and where, as we have seen, they were considerably strengthened by the combination of the efforts of littérateurs from both regions.

Looking back on the early stages in the development of a sense of modernity and national identity, many indigenous scholars have come to regard *al-nahdah* as a continuing project, even a multi-phased one. One such is the Moroccan critic (and novelist), ʿAbdallāh al-ʿArwī (Laroui), who, in the wake of one of the Arab world's major modern watersheds, the June War of 1967, examines the relationship between present and past and suggests that modernity is a constantly changing posture of the present to the past and that thus the cultural movement known as *al-nahdah* needs to be viewed in such a light.

Having now examined the parameters of the process and its manifestation in different regions and genres, I will now shift the focus of the remainder of this introduction in order to focus on the three genres of poetry, narrative fiction, and drama, in turn.

Developments in Genres

Poetry

Apart from a very few prominent figures such as the Syrian poet, critic, and religious scholar, ʿAbd al-Ghanī al-Nābulusī already mentioned, the poets who composed in Arabic during the centuries immediately preceding the year 1850 remain mostly unknown and unstudied. A recent study of the subject and period by Muhammad Lutfī al-Yūsufī (*The Post-Classical Period* [Cambridge History of Arabic Literature], 2005) reveals that there was, not unexpectedly, a large number of poets composing odes that conformed with the models established many centuries earlier; along with the most favored and best rewarded genre of panegyric, there was wine and love poetry and, to accompany the continuing and widespread prevalence and influence of Sufi orders within the region, a large amount of mystical verse (with al-Būsīrī's [d. 1296] famous "*Burdah*" poem maintaining its position at the head of the list).

In terms of form Arabic poetry was to maintain its reliance on traditional structures and their prosodic expectations for several decades into the 20th century. In that regard, Mahmūd Sāmī al-**Bārūdī** (d. 1904) adheres to the pattern, but he is widely regarded as the first genuine neo-classical poet in the modern Arabic tradition. Thus he chose to replicate Tāhā Husayn's counsels and sought his major inspiration in the great poets of Arabic literature's "classical" period; indeed in 1909 he published an anthology of the greatest poets of the period beginning with Bashshār ibn Burd (d. 784). His own poetry was very much modeled on the genres and styles of this earlier tradition, a trait that was duly recognized by his contemporary, Husayn al-Marsafī (d. 1890), who compiled a work on principles of literary analysis under the title, *al-Wasīlah al-adabiyyah* (The literary method, 1872-5) and praised the ways in which al-Bārūdī was replicating the great models of the past. However, alongside these more traditional features, the "neo" part of neo-classical is represented by al-Bārūdī's vigorous involvement in the politics of his day, particularly his opposition to the ruling family and the British occupiers, a posture that led to his exile to Sri Lanka for several years and thus to a poetry of nostalgia and complaint not a little redolent of Ovid's poems from "ultima Thule." Another way in which al-Bārūdī expressed his desire to incorporate aspects of his own era into his poems was through the inclusion of modern terms—photographs, telephones, and electricity, for example—into his otherwise thoroughly traditional compositions, the effect of which was often somewhat jarring.

Like many other early pioneers to whom we have already drawn attention, al-Bārūdī served a bridging function, drawing his inspiration from the past but also providing through his participation in the political and cultural life of his times a foundation upon which his successors could not only build but also use to embark upon new directions and experiments. Such was the continuing cultural power of the poetic tradition in Arabic, in terms of both its forms and elevated levels of language, that the choice of priorities exemplified by al-Bārūdī's poetry was to be replicated in the compositions of neo-classical poets across the Arabic-speaking world, poets who found themselves confronting new political realities and utilizing new publication outlets as they sought to integrate elements of the modern into their revivals of the poetic heritage of the past. Of those many poets we have selected three for inclusion in this volume. The first and undoubtedly the most renowned is the Egyptian, Ahmad **Shawqī** (d. 1932). Born into a high-class family and a favorite at the Egyptian court from an early age, he came to be known as "the Prince of Poets." In his ringing odes, both occasional poetry and more personalized expressions, he managed to capture the imaginations of his listeners with beautifully cadenced verses, many of which became (as was the case with his most eminent classical forebears) proverbial quotations. His reputation was also enhanced by the series of verse plays that he composed, many of them based on themes from the pre-modern history of the region; set to music and performed on stage by some of Egypt's most popular singer-actors and actresses, they were to become immensely popular. Shawqī's Egyptian colleague and friend, Ḥāfiz **Ibrāhīm** (d. 1932), came from more popular origins. A career in the

Egyptian army took him to the Sudan, an experience that led him to compose a good deal of public poetry in which he was both a staunch advocate for nationalist causes and critic of the British occupation of his homeland. This and his popular origins led him to be differentiated from his colleague, Shawqī, by the title "Poet of the Nile." The third of these neo-classical poets to be included here is the Iraqi, Maʿrūf al-**Rusāfī** (d. 1945). A teacher of Arabic who had received a thoroughly traditional training in Arabic and Turkish, al-Rusāfī used his poetic gifts to both inspire and educate. While adhering, like his fellow neo-classical poets, to the forms and genres of his predecessors, he was anxious to rid his poetry of embellishment for its own sake and to use a less complex language-level in order to introduce his listeners and readers to contemporary concerns and concepts, both political and social (including, for example, the emancipation of women.

The Lebanese poet Khalīl **Mutrān** (d. 1949), who emigrated, like so many of his fellow countrymen, to Egypt and thus became known as "the poet of the two regions" [Lebanon and Egypt], displays many of these same traits in his poetry, not least in his adherence to expectations regarding form. That said however, Mutrān is often described with the epithet "pre-romantic," a phrase that certainly applies to his writings about poetry where he clearly advocates the primacy of the imagination and the need for poetic unity, but that can also be seen in several of his own poems, of which "al-Masāʾ" (Evening) and "al-Asad al-bākī" (The Weeping Lion) are the most often cited in this context.

Before we turn to the advent of romanticism in its fullest form to modern Arabic poetry, it needs to be pointed out that the great tradition of occasional poetry in Arabic, extending back to the beginnings of poetry in the pre-Islamic era and manifested in the prevalence of panegyric throughout the intervening centuries, has been maintained by a number of poets throughout the Arabic-speaking world alongside the many radical transformations to which Arabic poetry has been exposed. In this context, al-Akhtal al-Saghīr (penname of the Lebanese poet Bishārah al-Khūrī, d. 1968) and Badawī al-Jabal (penname of the Syrian poet Muhammad al-Ahmad, d. 1981) deserve to be mentioned, but the poet whom we have selected to exemplify the continuing presence of the traditional poem and its social functions throughout the 20ᵗʰ century is the Iraqi poet Muhammad al-**Jawāhirī** (d. 1997) who, like so many other Arab neo-classical poets, reflected the political situation in the first half of the 20ᵗʰ century by composing vigorous occasional poems on nationalist and anti-colonialist themes. Like his fellow countryman and poet, ʿAbd al-Wahhāb al-Bayātī (d. 1999), he had an ambivalent relationship with the succession of governments in his homeland; both poets served as cultural ambassadors for their country in Europe (in al-Jawāhirī's case, in Prague, in al-Bayātī's in Madrid). Both of these great Iraqi poets, similar in their aspirations for Iraq, yet so different in their modes of expressing them in poetic form, lived the latter part of their lives in exile.

The encounter between a firmly entrenched tradition of Arabic poetry and the various elements of change during the latter half of the 19ᵗʰ century and the early decades of the 20ᵗʰ produced, as we have noticed above, a widespread and vigorous school of neo-classical writing. Changes in the purpose and context of poetry and in the perceived role of the poet within the Arabic-speaking world were to be part of a lengthier and more gradual process. That may well serve to explain why the first full flowering of romanticism, as a reaction to the tenets of classicism and its neo-classical forms, emerged in distant lands; specifically among the emigré communities of Lebanese Christians who had traveled to the Americas, both North and South. For that reason they are generally known as the *mahjar* (emigré) school of poets. In the South they became known as *al-ʿUsbah al-andalusiyyah* (the Andalusian group), and one of its most prominent members was Ilyās **Farhāt** (d. 1976) who left Lebanon for Sao Paolo in Brazil in 1910 and composed several volumes of poetry that were published in both Brazil and Lebanon. It is the Northern group however that has been the subject of the most attention, not least because of the fame of its leading figure, Jubrān Khalīl **Jubrān** (d. 1932, usually spelled

"Gibran" in English), who served as president of the group known as *al-Rābitah al-qalamiyyah* (The Bond of the Pen), while his close friend, Mīkhāʾīl **Nuʿaymah** (d. 1989, who wrote his name in English as "Naimy") was the group's secretary. Jubrān is, of course, well known for his writings in English, but both these writers were to have a profound influence within the Arabic literary context, and in both poetic and prose genres. For readers of English Jubrān's *The Prophet*, with its mellifluous blend of moral philosophy and aphoristic discourse, has maintained a widespread popularity. In his Arabic poetry, of which the lengthy strophic poem, *"al-Mawākib"* (Processions, 1918), is probably the most famous, he adopts a poetic persona that projects to his listeners eternal verities about existence and nature. Nuʿaymah remained in the United States until the death of his close friend, after which he returned to his native Lebanon. Under the inspiration of Jubrān and their North American *mahjar* colleagues in the "Bond of the Pen," including Īliyyā **Abū Mādī** (d. 1957), Rashīd Ayyūb (d. 1941), and Nasīb ʿArīdah (d. 1946), Nuʿaymah wrote a good deal of poetry, the most famous example of which is his bitter poem, *"Akhī"* (My Brother), in which he reflects on the wanton waste of human life in the First World War that he himself had witnessed as a soldier in the American armed forces. However, while Nuʿaymah was an important contributor to the development of the romantic spirit that was so characteristic of the poetry of this group, his major role in what may be considered this secondary phase in the development of modern Arabic literary genres lies more in the realms of both narrative prose and criticism.

As the *mahjar* poets encountered the poetry of English and American writers and encouraged each other to embark on their new experiments with voice, imagery, and language, they were their own audience. However, they also made efforts to publish their works more widely, firstly in a journal, *al-Funūn* (The Arts), and, when that closed for financial reasons, in special issues of the journal, *al-Sāʾih* (The Traveler). Copies of these collected poems made their way back to the Arabic-speaking regions where they were received with an anticipated combination of excitement and opposition. Their more radical experiments with voice and imagery were to be matched in a more gradualist fashion by groups of Arab poets who were operating within the more fractious critical environment of the ongoing process of "al-nahdah."

In 1912, the Egyptian poet 'Abd al-Rahmān Shukrī (d. 1958) returned to his homeland after spending three years studying in Sheffield, England. In his two Egyptian contemporaries, Ibrāhīm al-Māzinī (d. 1949) and 'Abbās Mahmūd al-'Aqqād (d. 1964) he found kindred spirits in their joint admiration for the English romantic school of poets, and particularly those poets and poems that were included in the famous anthology, Palgrave's *Golden Treasury*. Critics agree that, of the three, Shukrī was the most gifted poet, and he was also the least involved in the more public aspects of cultural life. During the seven or so years after Shukrī's return to Egypt, this group of poets worked closely together and provided each other with the same kind of inspiration as the "Bond of the Pen" had done in the United States. However, a dispute broke out (over accusations that al-Māzinī had plagiarized some English poetry in his own verses), and in 1921 al-Māzinī responded with a vicious attack on Shukrī's poetry in a periodical called *al-Dīwān*, jointly edited by al-'Aqqād and al-Māzinī. As is reasonably obvious, it is thus less than useful to call this group of three poets "the *Dīwān* group," but the name has stuck. Within the Arabic-speaking region itself, this publication (along with *al-Ghurbāl*, a collection of critical essays by Mīkhā'īl Nu'aymah, with an introduction by al-'Aqqād) was to have a significant impact on critical opinion and the direction of Arabic poetry, not least because al-'Aqqād also launched a fierce attack, this time on the poetry of Ahmad Shawqī, the most famous neoclassical poet of his time. Both al-Māzinī and al-'Aqqād later involved themselves in other aspects of the Egyptian cultural milieu, the former in fiction (to be discussed below), while the latter became, along with the above-mentioned Tāhā Husayn, a much respected arbiter of literary taste and a vigorous participant in the political life of the country.

The decades of the 1930s and '40s were to be the heyday of romantic poetry in Arabic. In a quest for an archetypal figure to represent the movement, we can do no better than point to the Tunisian poet Abū 'l-Qāsim al-Shābbī (d. 1934). A naturally gifted poet from an early age who had imbibed not only the heritage of Arabic poetry but also the newly imported poems of the Mahjar school in the Americas, he managed to shock his contemporaries at the age of twenty by delivering a lecture on the role of the imagination, in which he advocated a changing role for the poet and more critical view of both the role of the past and of the status of women in society. In his own poetry he followed the model of Jubrān in seeing the poet in an almost prophetic function, and wrote stirring odes on the themes of love and love of homeland; his nationalist odes are still part of the consciousness of every Tunisian. And, when he discovered that he was stricken with an incurable heart condition, his thoughts turned to death and a defiance of its irreversible dictates. Like many other poets of this era, al-Shābbī turned to Egypt in order to have his poetry published. In 1932 the Egyptian poet Ahmad Zakī Abū Shādī (d. 1955)—who had traveled to study in England in 1912, the very year when the above-mentioned 'Abd al-rahmān Shukrī had returned—founded his renowned poetry magazine, *Apollo*, named after the society that he established to foster the development of romantic poetry. It was there that al-Shābbī, along with many other poets, published their poems. Abū Shādī was himself a prolific poet (besides having a specialty in medicine and an avocation as a bee-keeper); he produced no fewer than nineteen collections of poetry, one of which, *al-Shafaq al-bākī* (Weeping Twilight, 1926), runs to well over 1,300 pages. While not all his poems were of equal value, his particular forte was in the realms of love poetry and nature poetry. Above all, the magazine *Apollo* served as a rallying-ground for romantic poetry and poets, although personality conflicts did not prevent some of the founding figures (such as al-'Aqqād) from roundly criticizing some of its publications.

Many prominent exponents of romantic poetry could be mentioned at this point—the Egyptian Ibrāhīm Nājī (d. 1953), the Lebanese Ilyās Abū Shabakah (d. 1947), and the Sudanese Yūsuf Tījānī al-Bashīr (d. 1937) are three examples taken from different regions of the broader Arabic-speaking world, but from among them we have chosen to include ʿAlī Maḥmūd **Ṭāhā** (d. 1949) in this volume. He too published poems in *Apollo* and was an able translator of European poetry into Arabic. He was thus well acquainted with the romantic tradition and, through his seven collections, went on to achieve a very wide readership. He too is very concerned with the poet's self-image and his almost other-worldly status, but he manages to include within his poems of love and suffering the more alienated and rebellious aspects of the poetic inspiration.

The latter half of the 1940s decade witnesses the end of the Second World War, the foundation of the Arab League (1945), and the United Nations' decision to create an Israeli State (1947). These political events of enormous moment are accompanied by an era of deep discontent within the Arab world, with roots in a continuing pattern of colonial occupation, a whole series of corrupt and complacent regimes, and, in the broader social and cultural spheres, a continuing confrontation between tradition and change. On the political level this atmosphere provided the primary motivation for those forces that were to turn the 1950s into a decade of revolution and change throughout much of the Arabic-speaking region.

In addition to these broader political and social trends, 1947 was to witness a major event in the history of modern Arabic poetry. Two Iraqi poets (and argument rages as to which of the two was the first), Nāzik al-Malāʾikah (b. 1923) and Badr Shākir al-Sayyāb (d. 1964), decided to break away from the formal expectations regarding the prosody and structure of the traditional poem (*qaṣīdah*) that poets had for the most part adhered to for many centuries. One might suggest that, with the walls of tradition now breached, the way was open for a whole series of innovations that mark the 1950s and beyond. The changing role of the poet and commitment to the national cause, the relationship between form and content, the prose poem and the rela-

tionship of poetry with other literary genres, all these were to become issues to which Arab poets addressed themselves in the post-independence era.

Narrative

The narrative genre that Arab visitors to Europe first encountered was that of the novel, which, by the first half of the 19th century, had not only become recognized as a major conduit for ideas about social change but also had gained a wide popularity through serialization in the press. As we noted above, it was examples of the novel that were first translated into Arabic and then imitated by the earliest pioneers in fiction-writing. Alongside them, other Arab authors chose to continue the traditions of prose narrative inherited from previous centuries.

The other characteristic fictional genre, the short story, did not initially attract much attention in the Arabic-speaking world, but, if we bear in mind that it was by comparison a young and still developing genre in Europe during the period in question, that should not come as much of a surprise. That said however, those Arab authors who aspired to compose in the novel genre required a significant amount of experiment with themes and techniques (and not least, that of style) before it was finally integrated into what one might term the modern Arabic literary canon—a process in which the Nobel Laureate of 1988, the Egyptian novelist Najīb Maḥfūẓ, was to play an important role in the 20th century.

The pre-modern tradition of Arabic narrative includes a large number of story-types that are short, including anecdotes, fables, and maxims. As writers in the second half of the 19th century participated in debates over the traditional and the imported and exploited the new press medium as a means of expressing their views on social and political topics, the resort to the comical and morally uplifting emerges as a natural consequence of the intellectual atmosphere of the time. Of the former category, ʿAbdallāh Nadīm (d. 1896) was a pioneer, both as editor of a series of sarcastic reviews (one of them bearing the characteristic title, *al-Tankīt wa'l-Tabkīt* "Ridicule and Reproach") and as author of his own brand of humorous vignette, particularly those involving a clash of cultural values. Of the morally uplifting category Mustafā Lutfī al-**Manfalūtī** (d. 1924) has long been acknowledged as the master, as well as being an important figure in the early development of a modern narrative style. Using the newspaper, *al-Mu'ayyad*, as his vehicle, he published a whole series of highly sentimental stories that painted moral and social issues in colors of black and white; they were published in two separate volumes, *al-Nazarāt* (Essays, 1910, 1912) and later *al-'Abarāt* (Tears, 1915). Among the more curious, yet significant aspects of the interaction of different cultural forces that were at work during this period is that al-Manfalūtī, who apparently knew no foreign languages, also published versions of several classics of French literature that became enormously popular: Rostand's *Cyrano de Bergerac* (1921) and de Saint Pierre's *Paul et Virginie* (1923).

Alongside these early developments in Egypt other writers concerned themselves with shorter narrative forms, including two that we noted above in connection with the Mahjar School in North American and developments in romantic poetry: Jubrān Khalīl Jubrān and Mīkhā'īl Nu'aymah. Early in his career Jubrān published a whole series of stories full of nostalgia for his Lebanese homeland and commenting (as had Ahmad Fāris al-Shidyāq at an earlier stage) on the status of women in marriage and the hypocritical postures of the Maronite clergy. To this day they retain a certain popularity in both their original Arabic and English versions: *'Arā'is al-murūj* (1905; *Nymphs of the Valley*, 1948); *al-Arwāh al-mutamarridah* (1908; *Spirits Rebellious*, 1947); and *al-Ajnihah al-mutakassirah* (1912; *Broken Wings*, 1957). In the case of Mīkhā'īl Nu'aymah (who was educated in Russian schools in turn-of-the-century Syria and later in a Ukranian seminary) the contact with the rapidly developing short-story genre in Europe was more direct, in that he read with great admiration the works of the Russian masters of the genre, Gogol, Chekov, Turgenev, and others. His own developing awareness of the structural and stylistic features of this new and dynamic literary medium is evident in the suc-

cession of short story collections that he published following his return to Lebanon from the United States, such as *Kān mā kān* (Once upon a time, 1937), *Akābir* (VIPs, 1956), and *Abū battah* (The Big-calfed Man, 1959). Belonging to this same early period is another writer who received training in Russian schools, the Palestininan, Khalīl **Baydas** (d. 1949), whose short story collection, *Masārih al-adhhān* (Mind Stages, 1924) reflects the anticipated struggles of a generation of writers coming to terms with the structural and stylistic demands of a new narrative genre.

Throughout this prolonged period of development that we investigate in this volume, it has been noticeable that genuine change has tended to occur when a group of like-minded writers have got together to inspire and criticize each other's efforts. Following on the efforts of these pioneers in short fiction, it is with an Egyptian group, one that consciously dubbed itself "*Jamā'at al-madrasah al-hadīthah*" (The Modern School Group), that the short story comes to be fully integrated into the literary life of the region and to fulfill its generic purposes. The leader of the group was Muhammad Taymūr (d. 1921), but his promising career as a short-story writer was cut short by his early death. The mantle then passed to a number of colleagues, including his own brother, Mahmūd **Taymūr** (d. 1973), Mahmūd Tāhir **Lāshīn** (d. 1954), and Yahyā **Haqqī** (d.1993), all of whom were to become major contributors to the genre. Taymūr was a prolific writer, with over twenty volumes of stories to his credit, many of them reworkings of earlier publications, and he was also the earliest to gain a wide reputation, with his collections *al-Shaykh Jum'ah wa-qisas ukhrā* (Shaykh Jum'ah and other stories, 1925) and *'Amm Mitwallī* (1925). Dubbed "Egypt's de Maupassant" by his contemporaries, his stories reflected the modes of his French model and other European writers in their attention to local detail and their portraits of unusual characters. At the beginning of his career Taymūr contributed greatly to the forwarding of the case for the use of the colloquial dialect in fiction, but he gradually withdrew from this posture and, in many of his rewrites of earlier stories, he began to use the standard written version of the language, a decision that seems to have been of some moment in his election to the Arabic Language Academy in Cairo. Lāshīn's career was many ways the opposite of Taymūr's, in that he spent much of his life as a post-office employee and eventually stopped writing when his works failed to achieve the recognition that he thought they deserved. Subsequent critical opinion has tended to share his views and has come to regard him as one of the finest exponents of the short-story genre during this relatively early stage in its development; indeed some of the stories in both *Sukhriyyat al-nāy* (Flute's irony, 1926) and *Yuhkā anna* (It's related that…, 1930) now seem far ahead of their time in their skillful use of economy of structure and language to portray aspects of Egyptian society. Of this trio of writers, Yahyā Haqqī is the one whose influence on subsequent generations of would-be writers of short-stories was the most profound and long-lasting. His creative output was not large, and each story is a carefully crafted stylistic and structural jewel. He is best remembered for his novella *Qindīl Umm Hāshim* (The Lamp of Umm Hāshim, 1944; *The Saint's Lamp*, 1973), a wonderful evocation of a popular district of Cairo and its traditions that is used to illustrate the clash of religion and science as part of the confrontation between East and West to which we have alluded above. However, each of his short stories is an excellent demonstration of the most economical use of language to portray character and situation in a manner that is totally authentic and constantly fascinating.

During the 1930s and '40s the Arabic short story, based on the foundations set down by these pioneers, began to fulfill its generic purpose across the Arabic-speaking world. In that process it was, of course, much helped by the expansion of the press in various regions, although at the same time the unwelcome attentions of censorship authorities governed what might be published and what subterfuges might be needed to circumvent such attentions. From a potentially large number of contributors to this genre, we have selected a cross-section for inclusion here. Within the Lebanese context Tawfīq Yūsuf **'Awwād** (d. 1989) was among the

first, and in both short-story and novel form, to depict in realistic terms the suffering of his homeland during the first World War and of the people in the countryside in their ongoing struggles against the forces of nature. In Iraq, Dhū 'l-Nūn **Ayyūb** (d. 1988), a translator of both English and Russian literature into Arabic, undertook a similar project to depict the realities of his own society; a prolific writer he published no fewer than 11 anthologies of short-stories, but, like so many of his fellow-countrymen during the 20th century (and into the 21st), he fell victim to the political turmoil in his homeland and spent various segments of his life in Vienna. One of the above-mentioned Khalīl Baydas's successors in depicting the realities of the Palestinian tragedy in short-story form was Samīrah 'Azzām (d. 1967), who, beginning in the 1940s, published a number of collections in which she depicts the miseries of daily existence but focuses in some of her stories specifically on the plight of women within a society in which men establish and maintain social norms.

Tunisia provides one of the most interesting illustrations of the different forces that were at work during this lengthy and variegated period of development in the fictional genres. Mahmūd al-**Mas'adī** (d. 2004) attended the most renowned, French-based secondary school in his native Tunis, obtained a doctorate from the Sorbonne in Paris, and returned to become one of the major upholders of the classical norms of style and discourse and critics of modernizing tendencies in language. His fictional works, all of them interesting explorations of broader philosophical issues couched in a variety of trans-generic combinations, are written in a peerless level of the literary language that has made them models of the high style that tends to tilt against the more populist instincts of many contemporary authors. Al-Mas'adī's fellow-countryman, 'Alī al-**Du'ājī** (d. 1949), represents exactly the opposite trend: educated in traditional Islamic schools, he lived a somewhat dissolute existence in the Tunisian capital, in particular frequenting a well-known café, "Taht al-Sūr" (Under the Wall) in the old city of Tunis, where he and his colleagues would discuss the course of Tunisian literature. Al-Du'ājī took a very sardonic look at the life of his fellow-countrymen; like many of his literary forebears, he too traveled, but the results, published as *Jawlah bayna hānāt al-bahr al-mutawassit* (A Trip Around the Bars of the Mediterranean, 1935), are an apt reflection of his attitudes to life and its vicissitudes. Much of al-Duʿājī's output remains unpublished, but his short-story collection, *Sahirtu minhu al-layālī* (1969; *Sleepless Nights*, 1991) gives ample demonstration of his developing mastery of the genre.

We have already noted that the novel genre was among the first types of narrative to be translated into Arabic in the mid-19th century but that its development and incorporation into the fabric of literary and intellectual life in the Arabic-speaking region was a longer process. Many of the writers of short stories that have been mentioned above also contributed works to this gradual developmental process, thereby participating in a project which had begun not only with the early works of Fransīs Marrāsh, Salīm al-Bustānī, and Jūrjī Zaydān, and others but also with the often more "realistic," yet traditional narrative offerings of al-Shidyāq and al-Muwaylihī. In such a context it seems less than accurate or useful to characterize the famous novel of Muhammad Husayn **Haykal** (d. 1956), *Zaynab*, as the first Arabic novel (or even the first "real" Arabic novel), as so many commentators have tended to do. Unless we are to redefine the structural and stylistic parameters of the novel genre, *Zaynab* has many precedents, including in Egypt itself Mahmūd Tāhir Haqqī's *'Adhrā' Dinshawāy* (1905; *The Maiden of Dinshway*, 1986) based on an actual incident in which several Egyptian villagers were hanged for firing on a British hunting party. That said, *Zaynab* clearly does represent an important stage in the development of the Arabic novel. Haykal, living in France at the time (1911), pens a thoroughly nostalgic picture of life in the Egyptian countryside and of the plight of its peasant population. Much influenced by the advocate of women's rights, Qāsim Amīn (d. 1908), he also criticizes the status and treatment of women in Egyptian society. It is an interesting insight into the process of social reception of new genres such as fiction and drama that Haykal, an aspiring lawyer and thereafter politician and journalist, felt it necessary to publish his novel in 1913 under a pseudonym, *misrī fallāh* (peasant Egyptian) and only later acknowledged his authorship.

A further step in this socialization process whereby the novel genre was adopted, adapted and internalized occurred in 1926 when the already mentioned Tāhā Husayn began to publish an account of his provincial childhood under the title, *al-Ayyām* (The Days; *An Egyptian Childhood*, [1932] 1981). While this narrative certainly falls into the general category of autobiography, the author manages to place a distance between himself and his child-protagonist by couching the narrative in the third person, something that not only enhances the more fictional aspect of the account but also allows for a ironic approach to portrayal of the vast chasm that separates the blind child growing up amid the poverty of rural Egypt from the towering figure who was to become Egypt's most important intellectual in the 20th century. The instant popularity of *al-Ayyām*, coupled with the publication of a second edition of Haykal's *Zaynab* in 1929, ushered in a decade in which experimentation with the novel genre began in earnest. Following the lead of European novel traditions (and that of Haykal, for that matter), several writers used women's names in the titles of their variegated experiments in novel-composition. The most accomplished was Mahmūd Tāhir Lāshīn with *Hawwā' bi-lā Ādam* (*Eve without Adam*, 1934), not least because it appears to be the least autobiographical, but there was also al-ʿAqqād's *Sārah* (Sarah, 1938) and later Mahmūd Taymūr's *Salwā fī mahabb al-rīh* (Salwa Blown by the Wind, 1944). Ibrāhīm al-Māzinī insisted, somewhat unconvincingly, that he was not to be identified with the hero of *Ibrāhīm al-Katib* (Ibrāhīm the Author, 1931), the winner of a prize for the best novel offered at the beginning of the decade, in which the hero recounts his love-affairs with three women. Tāhā Husayn also participated in this "novel-writing decade," penning the semi-autobiographical *Adīb* (1935), the story of the confrontation of cultures to which an Egyptian student is exposed during his time studying in Paris) and later two important novels, *Duʿā' al-karawān* (1941; *The Call of the Curlew*,

1980) and *Shajarat al-bu's* (1944; *Tree of Misery*, 1997). But perhaps the major contributor to the advancement of the novel as a literary genre during this decade was Tawfīq al-**Hakīm** (d. 1987). In three novels, *'Awdat al-rūh* (1933; *Return of the Spirit*, 1990), *Yawmiyyāt nā'ib fī 'l-aryāf* (1937; *The Maze of Justice*, [1947] 1989), and *'Usfūr min al-Sharq* (1938; *Bird of the East*, 1966) he not only addresses himself to some of the major social and political issues of the time—the confrontation of East and West and the process of change and its effects on people in both city and countryside—but also makes major contributions to the development of novelistic technique in Arabic, not least through the use of the colloquial dialect in dialogue.

This pattern of experimentation is to be replicated in many other regions of the Arabic-speaking world during this decade. Both Tawfīq Yūsuf 'Awwād and Dhū 'l-Nūn Ayyūb begin their novelistic careers during this decade, and in Syria **Shakīb al-Jābirī** (b. 1912) follows a familiar path by devoting his first novel, *Qadar yalhū* (Fate at Play, 1939), to the theme of the life of an Arab student living in Germany.

During this same decade (1930s), a young Egyptian student, Najīb Mahfūz (b. 1911), began writing a series of newspaper articles and short stories. As part of the prevailing interest in ancient Egypt (the so-called Pharaonism movement) that had been much stimulated by the discoveries in Tutankhamun's tomb in 1922, he also became interested in ancient Egyptian history and translated an English work on the subject, Baikie's *Ancient Egypt*, into Arabic. Becoming more and more interested in the emerging genre of the novel as being experimented with by the members of the older generation, he set himself (in a fashion that is to remain typical of his methodical approach to writing throughout his career) to studying the "new" genre. Having studied John Drinkwater's *Outline of Literature*, he proceeded to read as many examples of the recommended novels as possible and from several European traditions. On these bases he then planned a series of novels set in ancient Egypt and wrote three of them before deciding, under the impetus of the Second World War and its effects on Egyptian society, to turn his attention to the present day.

The consequence of that momentous decision was a series of novels set in quarters of old Cairo that take Arabic fiction to new levels of sophistication, culminating in the enormous trilogy of novels, *Bayn al-qasrayn* (1956; *Palace Walk*, 1990), *Qasr al-Shawq* (1957; *Palace of Desire*, 1991), and *al-Sukkariyyah* (1957; *Sugar Street*, 1992). This last project was actually finished in 1952 before the Egyptian revolution of that year, but it appeared in 1956-7. That was, of course, a new era, one that followed the withdrawal of British occupying forces, the Czech Arms Deal, the Bandung Conference, the Suez Canal debacle of 1956, and the rise to power of President 'Abd al-Nāsir (Nasser). The trilogy of novels was almost instantly recognized for what it was and is, a lovingly accurate record of a particular phase in the development of 20th century Arab societies and their prolonged confrontation with change from within and without. The entire world was to learn to acknowledge that feat and to accord Mahfūz a world-wide status in the award of the Nobel Prize for literature in 1988.

That there is no chapter on Mahfūz in this volume may come as a surprise to some, not least because I myself have devoted much of my career to studies (and translations) of his works. He is without doubt the Arab writer who has brought the novel genre in particular to a level of maturity that has allowed it to participate fully in the cultural life of the region as a whole and indeed brought it to the attention of a much broader world audience. Even so, I would suggest that such recognition and indeed a retrospective realization of the developing importance of his works penned before the 1952 revolution only occurred after the publication of his trilogy in 1956. One might say perhaps that he too is one of those bridges that I have mentioned above, someone who carried the novel genre across a major intellectual and cultural divide—the late 1940s—into the latter half of the 20th century.

Drama

Earlier in this introduction, I mentioned some of the great pioneers in the lengthy and problematic process whereby the notion of drama as a contribution to literature was introduced to the

Arabic-speaking world, to be placed alongside more traditional modes of public performance. A survey of the means whereby this performance medium made its way to the various regions make it abundantly clear that the acting troupes that flourished in Egypt played an enormous role in this process, paying visits to Easy and West, to Iraq and Morocco.

The project to link performance on stage to literary text was to be one that required a lengthy period of trial and error, and not a little social contumely. In that process one figure stands out above all others, the already mentioned Tawfīq al-Hakīm.

Following the earlier patterns of Tāhā Husayn and Muhammad Husayn Haykal, al-Hakīm was sent to France for further studies (like Haykal, in law). However, al-Hakīm had already shown an extreme interest in drama (much to his parents' alarm) and had published some plays under a pseudonym (yet another symptom of the status of drama at this time). Al-Hakīm returned to Egypt from Paris in 1928 with a certain amount of knowledge in law (later reflected in his novel *Yawmiyyāt nā'ib fī 'l-aryāf*, noted above), but with a far greater exposure to and interest in drama as a literary medium. Beginning with his play *Ahl al-kahf* (People of the Cave, 1933), based on the legend of the seven sleepers of Ephesus that is cited in the text of the Qur'ān itself (Sūrah 18), and proceeding with *Shahrazād* (1934), *Pygmalion* ((1942), and *al-Malik Ūdīb* (King Oedipus, 1949), al-Hakim showed not only that drama written in Arabic could take on the kind of philosophical issues that characterized the major monuments of Western drama but also that the resulting texts could be subsumed under the all-important cultural term of "*adab*" (literature). Tāhā Husayn himself, the self-appointed guardian of the gates to this elite category, welcomed *Shahrazād*, noting that it "represented a new art form in our modern literature ..., a carefully wrought work of art, enjoyable, subtly crafted, and certainly worthy of a long life." He went on to point out the major issue that was to confront al-Hakim for much of his career, namely the process of transferring these works to the stage in a way that would appeal to an Egyptian audience

more accustomed to action (often comic) and music. Al-Hakīm was to struggle with this and other issues throughout his career; initially he developed the notion of his dramas as being "*masrah dhihnī*" (theater of the mind), but the decades of the 1940s and thereafter see him experimenting in a number of interesting ways with both format and language.

As is the case in other genres noted above, the period that followed the various processes of revolution and the achievement of independence throughout the Arabic-speaking world ushered in a new era in Arabic drama, most especially in Egypt which retained its particularly central position for several decades. As with Mahfūz in the novel genre, so al-Hakīm was without question the writer who succeeded in laying the groundwork upon which subsequent generations of dramatists could build.

Conclusion

The three volumes in this series devoted to the Arabic literary tradition are arranged in such a way as provide space for studies of some forty authors within each time-frame. Since each of those studies is a discrete entity, it has been the aim of this introduction to show some of the continuities that link this particular period, 1850-1950, to what is both before and after it, and to illustrate some of the developments within each of the three genres of poetry, fiction, and drama and their debts to their more recent and distant forebears.

As we have suggested above, the period immediately before this one remains an era on which an enormous amount of research still needs to be undertaken in order for anything resembling a responsible literary history of a period of at least three centuries to be attempted. At the other end of our period, the post-1950 era is one in which the genres that have been studied in this volume have expanded and diversified across the Arabic-speaking world and all its sub-regions in spectacular ways; not only that, but so has the indigenous critical tradition that comments on such trends. These trends have also been the object of the attention of a small but increasing group of Western literary specialists who have undertaken to immerse themselves in the cultural tradition not merely by reading the texts involved but by spending significant amounts of time within the region itself, perfecting a knowledge of the various levels of the language and making valuable contacts with littérateurs and critics. It is to a cross-section of those colleagues that I here express my thanks for their contributions.

FURTHER READING IN ENGLISH

General

Roger Allen, *The Arabic Literary Heritage* (Cambridge: Cambridge University Press, 1998; abbreviated version: *Introduction to Arabic Literature*, Cambridge; Cambridge University Press, 2000);

—— and D. S. Richards (eds.), *The Post-Classical Period*, The Cambridge History of Arabic Literature series (Cambridge: Cambridge University Press, 2006);

M. M. Badawi (ed.), *Modern Arabic Literature*, The Cambridge History of Arabic Literature series (Cambridge: Cambridge University Press, 1992);

Issa J. Boullata, *Trends and Issues in Contemporary Arab Thought* (Albany: SUNY Press, 1990);

Albert Hourani, *Arabic Thought in the Liberal Age* (London: Oxford University Press, 1962; reprinted Cambridge: Cambridge University Press, 1983).

Bibliographies

Salih J. Altoma, *Modern Arabic Literature in translation: a companion* (London: Saqi Books, 2005);

——, *Modern Arabic poetry in English translation* (Tangier, Morocco: The King Fahd School of Translation, 1993).

Translation Anthologies

Salma Khadra Jayyusi (ed.), *Modern Arabic Poetry: An Anthology* (New York: Columbia University Press, 1987);

—— (ed.), *Modern Arabic Fiction: An Anthology*, (New York: Columbia University Press, 2005);

—— and Roger Allen (eds.), *Modern Arabic Drama: An Anthology* (Bloomington, Indiana: Indiana University Press, 1995).

Poetry

M. M. Badawi, *A Critical Introduction to Modern Arabic Poetry* (Cambridge: Cambridge University Press, 1975);

Salma Khadra Jayyusi, *Trends and Movements in Modern Arabic Poetry*, 2 vols. (Leiden: E. J. Brill, 1977);

S. Moreh, *Modern Arabic Poetry, 1800–1970* (Leiden: E. J. Brill, 1976).

Narrative

Roger Allen, *The Arabic Novel: an historical and critical introduction* (Syracuse: Syracuse University Press, 1982; 2nd ed., 1995);

Sabry Hafez, *The Genesis of Arabic Narrative Discourse: a study in the sociology of modern Arabic literature* (London: Saqi Books, 1993);

Matti Moosa, *The Origins of Modern Arabic Fiction* (Washington D.C.: Three Continents Press, 1983);

Joseph Zeidan, *Arab Women Novelists: the formative years and beyond* (Albany: SUNY Press, 1995).

Drama

M. M. Badawi, *Early Arabic Drama* (Cambridge: Cambridge University Press, 1988);

——, *Modern Arabic Drama in Egypt* (Cambridge; Cambridge University Press, 1987);

Philip Sadgrove, *The Egyptian Theatre in the Nineteenth Century: 1799–1882* (Reading: Ithaca Press, 1996);

Criticism

Roger Allen (ed.), *Modern Arabic literature*, Library of Literary Criticism series (New York: Ungar Publishing Co., 1987).

EDITORIAL COMMENTS

Bibliographies

It will be noted that the Bibliographies which are an important part of the essays that follow show considerable variation in both size and detail.

That is partially a consequence of the repute of the author concerned, the region of the Arabic-speaking world (or elsewhere) in which the author lived and worked, and, needless to say, of the scholarly interest devoted to the author in question—at least, up till now. It is hoped that this volume will served as a spur to younger scholars to investigate those authors who come from regions and time-periods that have tended to be neglected by previous generations of specialist.

Transliteration
The transliteration system that has been adopted for this volume represents a compromise. The elongated vowels in Arabic names and terms have been indicated by macron-signs placed

over the vowel in question (ā, ī, and ū), but other diacritical marks have been omitted (the dots normally placed beneath transliterations of the Arabic emphatic (velarized) consonants, for example. Thus, *dāl* and *ḍād* are both transliterated as "d".

Acknowledgments
I would like to take this opportunity to acknowledge with gratitude the contribution that my esteemed colleague, Dr. Stephan Guth of the University of Oslo, Norway, has played by accepting these three volumes for publication in the series of which he is co-editor, and also to Dr. Barbara Krauss of the Harrassowitz publishing house in Wiesbaden for her willingness to undertake this substantial project.

Īliyyā Abū Mādī
(circa 1889 – 1957)

CHRISTOPHER STONE
Hunter College of the City University of New York

WORKS
Tadhkār al-mādī ("Memory of the Past", Alexandria: al-Matbaʿah al-Misriyyah, 1911);
al-Juzʾ al-thānī min dīwān Īliyyā Abū Mādī ("Part Two of Īliyyā Abū Mādī's poetry", New York: Matbaʿat *Mirʾāt al-Gharb* al-Yawmiyyah, 1919); includes introduction by Khalīl Jibrān;
al-Jadāwil ("Brooks", New York: Matbaʿat Mirʾāt al-Gharb al-Yawmiyyah, 1927); includes introduction by Mikhāʾīl Nuʿaymah;
al-Khamāʾil ("Thickets", New York: Matbaʿat Jarīdat *al-Samīr* al-Yawmiyyah, 1940);
Tibr wa-turāb ("Gold and Dust", Beirut: Dār al-ʿIlm liʾl-Malāyīn, 1960).

Works in Translation
A. J. Arberry, *Modern Arabic Poetry: An Anthology with English verse translations* (New York: Cambridge University Press, 1975), 60-63;

Salma Khadra Jayyusi, *Modern Arabic Poetry: An Anthology* (New York: Columbia University Press, 1987), 45-48.
Mounah A. Khouri and Hamid Algar, *An Anthology of Modern Arabic Poetry* (Berkeley: University of California Press, 1974), 35-37.

Īliyyā Zāhir Abū Mādī is considered by many to be the most important poet of the group of Arab literary figures known as the writers of the *mahjar* (place of migration). These writers, primarily from the Levant, settled in North and South America beginning in the second half of the 19th century and in the early decades of the 20th. Abū Mādī enjoys this reputation despite the fact that he is neither as well-known nor as copiously translated as some his *mahjar* colleagues such as Khalīl **Jubrān** and Mikhāʾīl **Nuʿaymah** [Naimy]. Abū Mādī is known for his adherence to some aspects of the classical Arabic poetic form, a fact that might well explain the paucity of samples of his poems in translation. Less well-remembered today, perhaps because these writings have not yet been collected even in Arabic, Abū Mādī was a prolific journalist, journal editor and newspaper owner throughout most of his years in the US. Born in today's Lebanon, Abū Mādī, like many of his contemporaries, was forced to migrate due to the unstable economic and political conditions in the Levant in the latter half of the 19ᵗʰ century. After spending several years in Egypt, Abū Mādī moved to the US where he remained until his death almost fifty years later. Abū Mādī did not consider his life worthy of biography, or at least that is what he wrote to one of his friends: "As for my life story there is nothing in it that deserves publication or at least this is what I think. There is nothing in it that would pique anyone's curiosity." This may explain why we know somewhat less about him than some of his *mahjar* colleagues. The Egyptian poet and critic, Salāh ʿAbd al-Sabūr (d. 1981) also notes the lack of details about Abū Mādī's life, but contends that much can be learned about the man though his poetry. In any case, there can be no question that Abū Mādī's literary achievements make him a major figure of 20th century Arabic letters.

Īliyyā Zāhir Abū Mādī was born around 1889 in the village of al-Muhaydithah in the mountains to the East of Beirut. We do not have many details about his childhood, and particularly about his early education, though we do know that he was a pupil in the local village school and that his formal education did not go beyond that. His father worked with silk worms, a trade which made it difficult for him to provide for his family of eight (five sons and one daughter). The result was the migration of a number of Abū Mādī's siblings to Egypt and the US. What we know of the family situation in Lebanon early in Abū Mādī's life confirms that, while the period of self-rule *(al-mutasarrifiyyah)* on Mt. Lebanon granted by the Ottoman Empire may have provided a measure of stability for the area, it did not bring prosperity for all. The immigration waves of 1860 and then again during World War One may have been well documented, but the fact that Abū Mādī himself and so many of his

siblings left the Levant in between these periods demonstrates that this outward flow was an ongoing phenomenon.

Abū Mādī left Mt. Lebanon in 1902 for Alexandria where he lived with an uncle. It was around this time that he is said to have penned his first poem. During his ten or so year stay in Egypt he wrote enough poetry to publish a small collection in 1911 entitled *Tadhkār al-mādī* (Souvenir of the Past [although there is no indication that he intended a pun on his name by using such a title]). He did not make a living from his poetry (and in fact never would) but rather worked as a tobacconist. The story goes that he would often write his poetry while at work, and that this is how he was discovered by Antawān Jumayyil, who published his poems in his magazine *al-Zuhūr*. Abū Mādī would go on to publish his poetry from this period in other Egyptian and Arab journals. It is also said that he was aware of the literary currents of the day in Egypt, but that he remained on the margins, his modest background no doubt limiting the amount of time he could spend on intellectual activities.

Scholars also note that Abū Mādī returned to Lebanon several times during his stay in Egypt, though it is said that he never found it economically feasible to stay. It is also known that even from this early period his writing demonstrated a keen nostalgia for his homeland, a trait that would only become more pronounced in his writing and which he shared with other *mahjar* writers. The great Egyptian "Dean" of Arab letters, Tāhā **Husayn** (d. 1973) once complained that "The Syrian and Lebanese do not forget for a moment that they are sons of Lebanon or Syria and that they have a mother, father and siblings at home…who remember him whenever the sun rises and whom he likewise remembers…". At the same time, it is clear that this period in Egypt left its mark on him. The country appears not only in his first volume but in subsequent volumes as well, as evidenced by poems such as "ʿĪd al-nuhā" (Holiday of Reason) from his third collection *al-Jadāwil*. The poem was composed for the 50ᵗʰ anniversary of the Beirut journal *al-Muqtataf*, mentioning, in addition to the unforgettable sweets he ate there, the important role

Egyptians and its many non-Egyptian residents were playing in a very exciting period of Arabic literary activity. It did not require the passage of years for Abū Mādī to develop strong feelings for Egypt; his first volume of poems is dedicated to the country. He writes that, while custom demands that he dedicate the volume to an individual, he deems it more appropriate in this case to thank Egypt as a whole.

Tadhkār al-Mādī, his first collection of poems, contains 55 poems. It received very little critical attention when it came out and only mixed reviews from later critics. Robin Ostle contends that its main interest lies in the contrast it provides to his later works. Some who have written about the volume are particularly negative about his portrayal of women in his love poems. Īliyyā Hāwī wrote that the women in these poems are like dolls with no flesh and blood. In general, the poems in this volume tend to be traditional in form and somewhat romantic in content, not so different from those written by contemporaries in Egypt such as Khalīl **Mutrān** and Hāfiz **Ibrāhīm**. If one were looking for a general theme to the volume, one could say that it is about injustice: the injustice of the Ottomans (e.g. "Tahayyat al-dustūr al-ʿUthmānī (Long Live the Ottoman Constitution), of the British (e.g. "1910"), of men against women (e.g. "Shakwā fatāt" (A Girl's Complaint)). The volume also contains occasional poems, a consistent feature of Abū Mādī's collections to come, including elegies for such well-known figures as the renowned nationalist leader, Mustafā Kāmil (d. 1908), and Shaykh Muhammad ʿAbduh (d.1905), one of the foremost religious reformers of the era. He also wrote one for his brother Tānyūs who died in Egypt in 1909. Aside from these pieces, there are no poems in praise of individuals. It is in these elegies, according to al-Maʿūsh, that his work most evokes the poets of the classical period, such as Ibn al-Rūmī (d. 896) and al-Mutanabbī (d. 965). Even though Abū Mādī appears here to be relatively traditional in terms of form, in contrast to his *mahjar* colleagues, he would eventually experiment with the mixing of meters. This volume, however, sticks mostly to the mono-rhyme, mono-meter format followed by centuries of predecessors. If there is any formal innovation it comes in his attempt at narrative verse. But even these samples, such as "Masraʿ Habībayn" (The Two Lovers' Downfall) were not an advance on similar and slightly earlier attempts by Khalīl Mutrān.

Soon after submitting these poems for publication, Abū Mādī emigrated to Cincinnati, Ohio, where he joined his brother Murād for four years before moving on to New York. Scholars disagree on the details of his migration. Najdat Safwat says he left from Alexandria for the US, while others suggest that he first returned to Lebanon (e.g. al-Kattānī). One scholar—Jūrj Salīm—claims that Abū Mādī was wanted by the Ottoman authorities and for that reason he left Lebanon for the US. Not a great deal about his time in Cincinnati is known either, except that he was not able to find a satisfactory balance between work and writing. It was here that he began reading American literature and translated some American poetry and song into Arabic. This included an African American song which he translated as "ʿAbd" (Slave), a poem that fit in with his ever-present concern with oppression. The reasons behind his move to New York in 1916 are unclear, but it is known that his brother Dimītrī committed suicide in Cincinnati a few months before he departed for the East Coast. Having already contributed poems to New York journals, Abū Mādī was also well aware of what any other Arab American at that time knew; namely that New York was the center of a robust Arab American cultural and economic scene and home to the largest Arab community in North America. It was there that Abū Mādī first came into contact with Khalīl Jubrān, Mīkhāʾīl Nuʿaymah, Nasīb ʿArīdah, Rashīd Ayyūb, ʿAbd al-Masīh, Amīn al-Rīhānī and others. It was also in the New York area that Abū Mādī would live for the remainder and majority of his life, and where he found his life's work in journalism as a writer, editor and finally owner.

Though he is known today primarily as a poet, his fame during his life was at least partly due to his work in journalism. Toward the end of his life Abū Mādī had planned to collect some of his prose writings but never finished that project.

Jurjī Saydah, who assembled Abū Mādī's post-humous poetry collection to be discussed below, also attempted to collect Abū Mādī's daily writings from his paper *al-Samīr*, but said that he could not find enough material to make it worthwhile. Nuʿaymah, who did not always see eye to eye with Abū Mādī, once said that of all the *mahjar* writers the prose of only two were worthy of publication: Khalīl Jubrān and Abū Mādī. This is quite a statement when one keeps in mind the large number of Arabic-language publications during this period. The first US periodical in Arabic, *Kawkab Amrīkā* (Star of America) had been published by Najīb Diyāb in 1888. By the beginning of the 20th century there were already approximately 100 such publica-tions. Abū Mādī's first such job in New York was as editor in chief of the youth and Palestine oriented *al-Majallah al-ʿArabiyyah*. While exact dates are not known, he next moved on to work at the magazine called *al-Fatāh*, owned by Shukrī al-Bakhkhāsh. In 1918 he was hired to edit the magazine *Mirʾāt al-gharb*, which was owned by the wealthy businessman Najīb Diyāb. Abū Mādī married his daughter Dorothy in 1920, and they would have three sons: Richard, Edward and Robert.

Abū Mādī's second volume of poetry, *al-Juzʾ al-thānī min dīwān Īliyyā Abū Mādī* (Part Two of Abū Mādī's Collected Poetry), was published in New York in 1919 and is his largest non-posthumous collection: it contains 79 poems, most of which are dated. The introduction to this volume was written by Khalīl Jubrān who, in a two-page introduction, summarizes his view of the poet as one who sees things that non-poets cannot see. He ends the introduction by saying that according to this definition Abū Mādī is indeed a poet and that the volume provides links between the seen and the unseen, the apparent and the unapparent. Elsewhere, in his famous collection of critical essays, *al-Ghirbāl* (The Sieve), Mikhāʾīl Nuʿaymah wrote that this was a transitional volume between two periods of Abū Mādī's poetic output, that of imitation and that of creation. Formally, the volume is a minor departure from his first in that Abū Mādī begins to mix his meters, though the meter *tawīl* (long) remains the prominent one. Also, in this volume,

Abū Mādī sometimes varies the mono-rhyme mono-narrator format of his first collection.

Like the first collection, this volume is a mix-ture of elegies, and political, nationalistic, love, and occasional poems. It also resembles his first volume in that he demonstrates a nostalgia not just for the Levant, but for Egypt as well. What is new in this volume is a greater self-reflexivity, a recurring tendency to write about the role of the poet as a kind of prophet, as in the poem "al-Shāʿir" (The Poet). According to this poem, it is the poet's role to teach people what they do not know, to discover what they cannot discover. There are additional poems in this collection that ponder philosophical issues, such as "al-Khulūd" (Immortality). Other poems in the collection are placed in settings from the Umay-yad (660-750) and Abbasid (750-1258) periods. This technique extends to questions of form as well, such as his use of the structures of Andalu-sian strophic poem, the *muwashshah* (e.g. "Fiʾl-layl", At Night). But this is not to say that this volume is mired in the past. Since all the poems were written during the tumultuous second decade of the 20th century, there are many topical poems, including "al-Harb al-ʿUzmā" (The Great War). He also shows a concern for his colleagues and compatriots back in the Arab World who remained in the line of fire (e.g. "Ummah tafnā wa-antum talʿabūn", A Nation Dies While You Play). Despite such weighty times and topics, the volume also contains ex-amples of love poetry, such as "al-ʿUyūn al-sūd" (Black Eyes). Further, as in his first volume, it includes elegies such as the one he wrote for Jūrjī **Zaydān** (d. 1914). In this collection Abū Mādī continues his experiments with narrative verse (e.g. "Bāʾiʿāt al-wurūd", The Rose Sell-ers). Within the context of material culture, one interesting feature to note is that, like all of Abū Mādī's collections published in the US, the first edition of *al-Juzʾ al-thānī* is a handsome volume replete with small unattributed illustrations. However it differs from the other collections, in that it opens with a poem addressed to one of the poet's patrons—a local rug merchant named Naʿmah Tādrus (Tadross), one of the few non-elegiac panegyrics composed by Abū Mādī. A full-page photograph of the dedicatee follows the poem. Also unlike later collections, the book ends with seventeen pages of advertisements for local Arab-owned businesses.

In this second volume of poetry one can detect principles advocated by the soon to be formed Bond of the Pen (*al-Rābitah al-qalamiyyah*), of which Abū Mādī would be one of ten founding members (two of whom were Khalīl **Jubrān** and Mikhā'īl **Nu'aymah**). This is not surprising in view of the fact that the association was not formed in a vacuum. In fact, a group of the same name had been formed in New York in 1916, a few months before Abū Mādī moved there. While Abū Mādī had not participated in this earlier manifestation of the association and though some of the labor-related concerns of this early group were dropped in the second and better-known 1920 version, it becomes clear from the very fact of the earlier formation and the content of the writings of both initial and later members that the organization's ideas had been fomenting for years before its official formulation. Evidence can be found on the pages of the magazine, *al-Funūn*, founded by Nasīb 'Arīdah in 1913 that continued in circulation until 1918. In fact, Abū Mādī contributed a number of poems to that journal that would eventually appear in his second collection, such as "Fī al-layl" mentioned above.

When the organization formed again in 1920, Abū Mādī, by that time already ensconced in the New York Arabic-language cultural and press scene, signed on as one of its official members. Among the principles of the organization was the revitalization of the Arabic language and poetry through a focus on content over form. The association itself only published one volume which appeared in 1921. Abū Mādī contributed five poems to it. Continuing its activities until Jubrān's death in 1931, the group was in effect a loose affiliation rather than an actual organization. It should be mentioned here that such attempts at literary and linguistic reform were not limited to the *mahjar* poets (see, for example, the entries on Ibrāhīm al-**Māzinī** and 'Abd al-Rahmān **Shukrī** for references to their "*madrasat al-tajdīd*", School of Reform, and their journal, *al-Dīwān*, and to the entries on 'Alī Mahmūd **Tāhā** and Ahmad Zakī **Abū Shādī**

concerning the Apollo Group). While Abū Mādī was one of the founding members of the Bond of the Pen, it has been suggested that he was somewhat less radical than the group's other stalwarts, though one can certainly see a very large difference between the poem's of his second volume and those of his most famous later volume, *al-Jadāwil* (Brooks, 1927), a likely indication of the influence of its members on his thinking and writing.

Al-Jadāwil was published by *Mir'āt al-gharb* and contains 36 poems, including his most famous poem of all, "Talāsim" (Riddles). In his short preface Abū Mādī adopts a Bond of the Pen-like stance on poetry: "You are not of me if you think poetry turns on phrase and meter." In his introduction to the volume, Mikhā'īl Nu'aymah writes that he cannot believe that this is the same poet who just eight years prior penned the collection, *al-Juz' al-thānī*; only now does he feel a spiritual connection between himself and Abū Mādī. Robin Ostle states that it is the volume's first poem—"al-'Anqā'" (The Phoenix)—that marks Abū Mādī's "new departure: this poem is a long statement of doubt, urgent aspiration, mystery and constant searching. The strange legendary bird is a symbol for something people seek but which constantly eludes them." Salāh 'Abd al-Sabūr calls the poem "Talāsim" one of the "Mu'allaqāt" of the era, referring to the canonical pre-Islamic collection of poems that form a kind of historic base and standard for Arabic poetry until the 20th century; he suggests that the volume as a whole breaks new poetic ground. Tāhā Husayn would not have entirely agreed with this assessment. It should come as no surprise that what Husayn—known for his deep knowledge of classical Arabic and his pedantic stand on prosody—attacks is the form. He says that Abū Mādī may seem to be playing with the traditional meters but in fact does not know them. He goes on to generalize about the *mahjar* poets as a whole and perhaps the Bond of the Pen specifically, claiming that they have begun a whole literary school based on their ignorance of the traditional meters. Husayn did have some reserved praise for the work, however, commenting that Abū Mādī was able to get his ideas across effectively despite the work's formal deficiencies.

This volume develops on some of the philosophical and introspective tendencies that are already evident in his second collection, in poems such as "al-Shāʿir" and "al-Shāʿir waʾl-ummah" (The Poet and the Nation). Unlike his previous two volumes, this third collection is almost devoid of love and occasional poems. Instead, it is full of ponderous poems about the place of not just the poet in the world but of humans in general. Some of these poems, in addition to "Talāsim" mentioned above, are among his best-known and best-regarded works, poems like "al-ʿAnqāʾ," "al-Tīn" (Mud) and "al-Masāʾ" (Evening).

His most famous poem, "Talāsim," deserves a closer look. It is from this poem, contends ʿAbd al-Sabūr, that his generation learned that the poet does not simply sing but also introspects. An initial glance at the poem on the page tells the reader that for Abū Mādī this work is a departure; it is one of the few in the volume that abandons the traditional two-hemistich monorhyme format of classical Arabic poetry. Instead, each section is comprised of several lines in the form of a question ending in the reply, "*lastu adrī*" (I do not know). These 71 questions are divided into 7 sections including the untitled introductory one, with names like "Fī al-dayr" (In the Monastery), "Bayna al-maqābir" (Among the Tombs), and "al-Fikr" (Thought). In simple almost prose-like language, the poet poses question after question. A translation of the first two questions will give us an idea of the tone and tenor of the poem: "I came, from where I know not, but I came, and I saw in front of me a path, which I took, and I will continue on this road whether I want to or not. How did I come? How did I see my path? I do not know. Am I old or new to this world? Am I completely free or a prisoner in chains? Do I lead myself in my life or am I led? I wish I knew, but I do not know." This kind of anguished questioning is a trademark of the *mahjar* writers and romantic poets of this period in general. It is no wonder that this poem became, as Ostle calls it, a "virtual manifesto" of the movement.

The volume also largely discards the poet's concern for the physical wellbeing of humans in favor of more spiritual and philosophical concerns. Even in a poem on poverty the poor man is both literally hungry and spiritually desperate: "The fang of despair has bitten him in his soul while the tooth of hunger bites his insides." The titles of not only the volume as a whole but also many of the individual poems show an increased concern with nature, e.g. "al-Dafādiʿ waʾl-nujūm" (Frogs and Stars), "al-Samāʾ" (The Sky), "Rīh al-shamāl" (The North Wind), "al-Masāʾ," and "al-Qafr" (The Wasteland). These poems reveal a synergy with the romanticism of the day, a romanticism that in the *mahjar* poets was inextricably combined with nostalgia for the homeland. Much has been made of the influence of the Nineteenth Century European and American Romantics on these poets and not enough perhaps on the effects of the Industrial Revolution and the subsequent waves of migration and urbanization on life in general and poetry and literature across regions and time periods more specifically. In typical Abū Mādī fashion, however, just when he seems to follow Jubrān and Nuʿayma into nature-inspired rapture, he pulls back and sets himself slightly apart. In "The Wasteland" for example, he acknowledges the futility of trying to escape civilization wholly. The poem ends with the speaker informing his reader that he has learned from his retreat to the wasteland that one always remains a prisoner of the need for social intercourse. One surprising element in this collection is an absence of poems explicitly for Lebanon, for it was in the period from which these poems were culled that Lebanon was made into a modern nation state. That said, much of the above-mentioned nostalgia that one finds in this period and implicitly in this volume could well have been expressed with Lebanon in mind.

Soon after the publication of *al-Jadāwil* Abū Mādī started his own fortnightly journal, *al-Samīr*, in 1929. In 1936 it became a daily, and continued as such until the poet's death in 1957. The transformation of the paper into a daily is indicative of its great success. The motto of the newspaper was taken from one of his poems: "I do not present to you mere paper, for those other than you make do with ink and paper. I give thought to your souls which will remain even if the paper burns." Journalism was extremely important to Abū Mādī, for in addition to giving him space to publish his poetry, it provided a broader platform for him and people who shared his views and allowed him to reach a larger audience on a frequent basis. In fact, he would eventually write a daily column for *al-Samīr*. While not all of his poetry was political or nationalistic, he certainly saw his role as a journalist in such terms. In fact, as he wrote on the occasion of the loss of an Arab American journalist colleague, he considered himself to be a soldier with a pen dedicating his whole life to the cause of the nation *(watan)*, a term that could mean the Syria-Lebanon area specifically but more likely the Arab World as a whole. In fact, ʿAbd al-Karīm al-Ashtar tells us that in his prose writings Abū Mādī distinguished himself from *mahjar* colleagues like Jubrān and Nuʿaymah by his pan-Arab nationalism, which he attributes both to his time spent in Egypt and to his deep reading of classical Arabic literature. This pan-Arab nationalism often manifested itself in support for the Palestinian cause.

It is important to mention that, despite its weighty epigraph, *al-Samīr* was not a literary journal per se. A cursory look at the articles in a "typical" issue can tell us much, not only about this publication, but about journalism in the *mahjar* in general, for there is a mistaken impression that all of the journalistic output was of a literary nature. The first issue of *al-Samīr*'s second year begins with a commemoration of a full year of publication. The next article is a story about a dangerous Mexican animal referred to as "the highway robber." Then comes a report on the heat wave that hit New York that year. Its writer encourages people to wear the traditional garment known as *al-qunbāz* to better deal with the unusually high temperatures. An article entitled "How Long Does a Woman's Beauty Last" follows this. Next comes a piece about the famous people born in that month. Then there is a translated article by an Austrian writer about the city of Vienna. The issue also includes an article about the difficulty faced by those hosting mourners in an urban setting and how their houses are transformed into "restaurants" as they try to feed all of the guests. Then

comes the poetry section with a poem by Abū Mādī that would appear in his next collection of poems. Following the poem is a translated short story entitled "The Thief of Secrets" and finally a section of the pithy sayings of the writer Yūsuf Ahmad Najm. This is not to say that there was no weighty prose in the paper. We find, for example, in the May 1, 1932 issue Abū Mādī asking, in prose, questions similar to those in poems like "Talāsim": "Why do we love? Why do we hate? Why? Why do we build and construct? Why do we plant and cultivate? Why are we here?"

In the second year of publication *al-Samīr* acquired its own printing press which would print Abū Mādī's next collection of poetry, *al-Khamāʾil* (Thickets, 1940). The volume contains 67 mostly short poems. The title of the collection and the opening lines of the first poem—"Madkhal" (Entrance)—reveal that the poet is still very much concerned with nature: "A palm tree fell on the daisy, and suddenly in the wasteland there is honey. Then a worm walked along the branches, and the branch was stripped clean." While this volume seems to be as concerned with nature as was *al-Jadāwil*, at least one critic, the poet ʿAbd al-Sabūr, sees a creative decline in this and Abū Mādī's posthumous volume. He wonders if this might be connected to Jubrān's death in 1931 and Nuʿaymah's return to Lebanon in 1932. It should also be mentioned that Abū Mādī's own father died in 1931. If these were the only factors, however, one would find it hard to explain this volume's persistent optimism, a marked departure from *al-Jadāwil*. This optimism and call to happiness is most evident in poems such as "ʿIsh liʾl-jamāl" (Live for Beauty), "Ibtasim" (Smile (spoken to a man)), "Ibtasimī" (Smile (spoken to a woman)), and "al-Ghibtah fikrah" (Happiness is a State of Mind). The last poem begins by lamenting the fact that no one seems to enjoy holidays. It then urges the reader/listener to enjoy life via the power of positive thinking. *al-Khamāʾil* also has more occasional poems than did *al-Jadāwil*, which may be explained by Abū Mādī's increased fame and the concomitant increase in invitations to events that might be opened or closed with a poem, not to mention his advancing age and the increasing rate of demise of his colleagues. The volume also witnesses a return to the nationalistic poem, including his well-known poems "Lebanon" and "Palestine." Though the volume is not without poems of philosophizing and introspection (e.g. "al-Faylasūf al-mujannaḥ" (The Winged Philosopher)), al-Khamā'il has been described as lyrical and musical, perhaps a reminder that a poet who can philosophize can also sing.

Abū Mādī, in fact, has always been associated with music, so much so that in 1933 he was elected President of New York's new Arab Music Club. In the twenties several of Abū Mādī's poems had been set to music by Arab musicians in the mahjar. It was in 1944, however, that his poetry's most famous intersection with music occurred, for it was in that year that the Egyptian artist, Muḥammad 'Abd al-Wahhāb, sung some verses of "al-Talāsim"—apparently without the poet's permission—in the film Rasāsah fī'l-qalb (A Bullet in the Heart). In that same year the Syrian-Egyptian singer, Asmahān, passed away before she was to sing a song based on Abū Mādī's poem "al-Masā'" which had been set to music by the famous Egyptian composer, Riyāḍ al-Sunbāṭī.

In 1948 Abū Mādī returned to Lebanon to represent North American mahjar journalists at UNESCO's third world conference that was held that year in Beirut. This was his first trip back to Lebanon since he had moved to the US, and he was welcomed as a celebrity. The first thing he did, we are told, was to make an emotional visit to his hometown. Also one of his first acts was the recitation of one of his poems for Lebanon: "Waṭan al-nujūm" (Country of Stars), which would eventually be published in his posthumous collection. According to Abū Mādī, one of the highlights of the trip was meeting Ṭāhā Ḥusayn, despite his criticism of al-Jadāwil many years earlier. During his visit Abū Mādī received two medals from the Lebanese President, Bishārah al-Khūrī. Abū Mādī was also extensively interviewed while there. One interviewer wanted to know if it was safe to assume from the content of the poem "Talāsim" that Abū Mādī, born an Orthodox Christian, had become an atheist. To this question Abū Mādī responded, according

to his own account of the event in al-Samīr:

I have never doubted and thus I have never had faith. This because each person has his god, and the god that I believe in and worship is not that god of the long thick beard, that vengeful god. Instead my god is beauty and mercy, acceptance and love.

Also in al-Samīr Abū Mādī relates an exchange with another journalist that gives us insight into his conception of the role of the poet. When asked if he was satisfied with his own poetry, he responded in the affirmative, but went on to say that he wanted

to know people's opinions of it. I want to know if my poetry has energized a nation, wiped away a tear, created a smile on a sad mouth, or even inspired a rich man to place alms in the palm of a pauper.

Abū Mādī was also invited to make an official visit to Syria where he received a medal of honor from the Syrian President Qawwatlī and recited his poem for Syria—"Taḥayyat al-Shām" (Long Live Syria)—which would also be published in his posthumous collection.

Abū Mādī left the Levant directly from Damascus after receiving an urgent telegram from his brother whom he had left in charge of al-Samīr and who was finding the work overwhelming. Apparently the work took a toll on Abū Mādī as well, for he would spend several extended stays in the hospital before his death on November 13, 1957. His last decade was also marked by several attacks on his literary integrity, which came to nothing but nonetheless consumed much of his energy. One of the accusations surrounded the poem "al-Tīn" from his first collection. He was accused of having plagiarized it from an early 19th Bedouin poet who was said to have lived in the area of today's Jordan. He was also accused of translating Sir Walter Scott's poem "The Knight's Toast" into Arabic as his poem "Hiya" (She) from his third volume al-Jadāwil without attribution. Abū Mādī argued that he does mention the fact indirectly in the beginning of the poem though there was no clear statement as to the poem's source. One of the last things that Abū Mādī worked on was a final collection of poems to be called *Tibr wa-turāb* (Gold and Dust, 1960). After Abū Mādī's death, the collection and publication process was overseen by his friend, George Sayda, and the volume was published in Beirut in 1960. Making a pun of the title, the poet 'Abd al-Sabūr commented that the volume contains more dust than gold. Whether or not this is the case, the poems in it show a continued concern with man's place in nature and poetry's place in life. The volume contains 59 poems approximately half of which are occasional poems. There are elegies for the writers Khalīl Mutrān and Amīn al-Riḥānī, as well as poems for places like Boston and Miami. The volume also has a significant number of nationalistic poems in addition to those mentioned above, such as "Bilādī" (My Country) and "Sawt min Sūriyya" (A Voice from Syria). Abū Mādī also left behind close to 70 poems that did not appear in any of his collections but which were published in a variety of newspapers and journals in the US and the Arab World. These are primarily occasional poems but also include nationalistic, satirical and love poems.

As Jamīl Jabr writes, there are few Arab poets about whom critics disagree so much. Estimations range from the that of Fadwā Tūqān, who suggests that Abū Mādī is unique in the history of Arabic poetry, to Ahmad Zakī Abū Shādī who opines that Abū Mādī was the weakest and least original of all the *mahjar* poets. In general, Abū Mādī is considered the best poet of the North American *mahjar* community and one of the most important Arab poets of the first half of the 20th century. It should also be remembered that he played a pioneering role in the very active North American Arabic-language press of the period; a press the decline of which coincides in part with the cessation of the publication of *al-Samīr* upon his death. Considered to be one of the more traditional of the *mahjar* poets, Abū Mādī nevertheless played an important role in the move of the Arabic poem toward free verse. Though his mixing of meters was by no means new, coming from such a prominent poet it made the practice more visible and can be seen as an important step in the de-sanctification of

traditional Arabic prosody. Abū Mādī's stature has been boosted in Lebanon by nationalism's tendency to embrace its famous sons and daughters, especially those that write quotable and nostalgic lines of poetry about the homeland. This is even truer of Lebanon's relationship to Jubrān and Nu'aymah. For many critics, however, Abū Mādī's poetry has stood up to time better than theirs, both of whose romanticism, it can be argued, can seem excessive by today's standards. Abū Mādī's self-taught but firm knowledge of both the Arabic language and his literary antecedents, plus what seems to have been a healthy dose of anti-conformism, have kept his literary reputation intact outside of the Levant as well.

REFERENCES

Salāḥ 'Abd al-Sabūr, "Qirā'ah jadīdah li-Īliyyā Abū Mādī," in: Īliyyā Abū Mādī, *Tadhkār al-Mādī* (Beirut: Dār al-'Awdah, 1974), 249-81;

'Abd al-Majīd 'Ābidīn, *Bayna shā'irayn mujaddidayn: Īliyyā Abū Mādī wa-'Alī Mahmūd Tāhā al-Muhandis* (Cairo: Matba'at al-Shubukshī, 1952);

Roger Allen, *Modern Arabic Literature* (New York: Ungar Publishing Company, 1987), 11-16;

'Abd al-Karīm al-Ashtar, *al-Nathr al-mahjarī: kuttāb al-Rābitah al-qalamiyyah*: al-juz' al-awwal: *al-madmūn wa'l-sūrah wa'l-ta'bīr* (Cairo: Matba'at al-Ta'līf wa'l-Tarjamah wa'l-Nashr, 1961);

Hajar 'Āsī, *Sharh dīwān Īliyyā Abū Mādī: shā'ir al-insān wa'l-hayāh* (Beirut: Dār al-Fikr al-'Arabī, 1999);

Khalīl Barhūmī, *Īliyyā Abū Mādī: shā'ir al-su'āl wa'l-jamāl* (Beirut: Dār al-Kutub al-'Ilmiyyah, 1993);

Ahmad Barqāwī, *Talāsīm Īliyyā Abū Mādī* (Beirut: al-Dhākirah li'l-Nashr wa'l-Tibā'ah wa'l-Tawzī', 2004);

Jūrj Amīn Bū Samrā, *Jadaliyyat al-anā bayna al-dhikrā wa'l-hanīn fī shi'r Abū Mādī, Abū Rīshah, al-Jawāhirī wa-Abū Shabakah* (Beirut: J. A. Bū Samrā, 2000);

Muhammad Hammūd, *Īliyyā Abū Mādī: shā'ir al-ghurbah wa'l-hanīn* (Beirut: Dār al-Fikr al-Lubnānī, 2003);

Nāyif Hātūm, *Īliyyā Abū Mādī: hayātuhu – shi'ruhu – nathruhu* (Beirut: Dār al-Thaqāfah, 1994);

Īliyyā Hāwī, *Īliyyā Abū Mādī: shā'ir al-tasā'ul wa'l-tafā'ul* (Beirut: Dār al-Kitāb al-Lubnānī and Dār al-Kitāb al-Misrī, 1972);

'Abd al-Majīd Hurr, *Īliyyā Abū Mādī: bā'ith al-amal wa-mufajjir yanābī' al-tafā'ul* (Beirut: Dār al-Fikr al-'Arabī, 1995);

Jamīl Jabr, *Īliyyā Abū Mādī* (Beirut: Dār al-Mashriq, 1992);

Ja'far al-Tayyār al-Kattānī, *Īliyyā Abū Mādī: dirāsah tahlīliyyah* (Cairo: Maktabat al-Khānjī, 196?);

Alfrid Khūrī, *Īliyyā Abū Mādī: shā'ir al-jamāl wa'l-tafā'ul wa'l-tasā'ul* (Beirut: Bayt al-Hikmah, 1968);

Sālim al-Ma'ūsh, *Īliyyā Abū Mādī bayna al-sharq wa'l-gharb fī rihlat al-tasharrud wa'l-falsafah al-shi'riyyah* (Beirut: Mu'assasat Bahsūn, 1997);

Zuhayr Mīrzā, *Īliyyā Abū Mādī: shā'ir al-mahjar al-akbar: shi'r wa-dirāsah* (Beirut: Dār al-Yaqzah al-'Arabiyyah li'l-Ta'līf wa'l-Tarjamah wa'l-Nashr, 1963);

S. Moreh, "Free Verse in Modern Arabic Literature: Abu Shadi and His School," *Bulletin of the School of Oriental and African Studies* 31.1 (1968): 28-51;

'Īsa al-Nā'ūrī, *Īliyyā Abū Mādī: rasūl al-shi'r al-'Arabī al-hadīth* (Amman: Dār al-Tibā'ah wa'l-Nashr, 1958);

R. C. Ostle, "Īliyyā Abū Mādī and Arabic Poetry in the Inter-War Period," in: *Studies in Modern Arabic Literature*, ed. R. C. Ostle (Warminster, England: Aris and Philips, 1974), 34-45;

——, "The Romantic Poets," in: *Modern Arabic Literature*, ed. M. M. Badawi (New York: Cambridge University Press, 1992), 82-131;

Jūrj Shakīb Sa'ādah, *al-Sirā' bayna al-rīf wa'l-madīnah fī shi'r Īliyyā Abū Mādī* (Beirut: Dār al-Hadāthah, 2002);

Najdat Fathī Safwat, *Īliyyā Abū Mādī wa'l-harakah al-adabiyyah fī 'l-mahjar* (Baghdad: Matba'at al-Hukūmah, 1945);

Jūrj Dīmitrī Salīm, *Īliyyā Abū Mādī: dirāsāt 'anhu wa-ash'āruhu al-majhūlah* (Cairo: Dār al-Ma'ārif, 1977);

Nādirah Sarrāj, *Thalāthat ruwwād min al-mahjar* (Cairo: Dār al-Ma'ārif, 1973);

'Abd al-Latīf Sharārah, *Īliyyā Abū Mādī: dirāsah tahlīliyyah* (Beirut: Dār Sādir li'l-Tibā'ah wa'l-Nashr, 1961);

Mahmūd Sultān, *Īliyyā Abū Mādī: bayna al-rūmānsiyyah wa'l-wāqi'iyyah: dirāsah tahlīliyyah* (al-Kuwayt: Dār al-Qabas, 1979);

Fadwā Tūqān, "Muqaddimah," in: 'Īsā al-Nā'ūrī, *Īliyyā Abū Mādī: rasūl al-shi'r al-'arabī al-hadīth* (Amman: Dār al-Tibā'ah wa'l-Nashr, 1958), 7-12;

Fu'ād Yāsīn, *al-Shā'ir al-muhājir Īliyyā Zāhir Abū Mādī* (Cairo: al-Dār al-Qawmiyyah li'l-Tibā'ah wa'l-Nashr, 1963).

Ahmad Zakī Abū Shādī

(1892 – 1955)

ROBIN OSTLE
University of Oxford

WORKS

Andā' al-fajr ("Dew Drops of Dawn", 1910; 2nd ed. Cairo, 1934);

Zaynab ("Zaynab", Cairo, 1924);

Misriyyāt ("Poems on Egypt", Cairo, 1924);

Anīn wa-ranīn ("Moans and Laments", Cairo, 1925);

Shi'r al-wijdān ("Poetry of Emotion", Cairo, 1925);

al-Shafaq al-bākī ("The Weeping Dawn", Cairo, 1927);

al-Muntakhab min shi'r Abī Shādī ("Selections from the Poetry of Abū Shādī", Cairo, 1926);

Watan al-farā'ina ("Land of the Pharaohs", Cairo, 1926);

Mukhtārāt wahy al-'ām 1928 ("Selections Inspired by the Year 1928", Cairo, 1928);

Ashi''ā' wa-zilāl ("Rays and Shadows", Cairo, 1931);

al-Shu'lah ("The Torch", Cairo, 1933);

Atyāf al-rabī' ("Spring Phantoms", Cairo, 1933);

al-Yanbū' ("The Source", Cairo, 1934);

Fawq al-'ubab ("On the Torrent", Cairo, 1935);

al-Kā'in al-thānī ("The Second Being", Cairo, 1935);

'Awdat al-rā'ī ("The Shepherd's Return", Alexandria, 1942);

Min al-samā' ("From the Heavens", New York, 1949);

Qadāyā al-shi'r al-mu'āsir ("Issues in Contemporary Poetry", 1965).

The name of Ahmad Zakī Abū Shādī will always be associated with the Romantic style of Arabic poetry which flourished primarily in Egypt in the decades between the two World Wars, and also with the name *Apollo*, which was the title both of the literary journal which he founded and edited in 1932 and of the group of poets who gathered around the journal and in which many of their works appeared.

The appearance of the *Apollo* journal was something of an historic point of departure in that this was the first periodical devoted entirely to literature and the arts to appear inside the Arab world, although it should not be forgotten that a similar publication had been established in New York by the Syro-Lebanese emigrant poets led by Jubrān Khalīl **Jubrān** and Mīkhā'īl **Nu'aymah** (Naimy): this was *al-Funūn* which ceased publication in 1918, and which may well have been a precedent in Abū Shādī's mind when he launched the *Apollo* journal and society in 1932. This being said, it would be misleading to think of the *Apollo* society as a closely knit group or school of writers who shared ideas and had common literary objectives. While it was indeed the focal point of activity and promotion

of the Romantic style of Arabic poetry, Abū Shādī's primary aim was to promote the cause of literature in general and to foster co-operation and mutual understanding between Arab writers both inside and beyond Egypt irrespective of their stylistic affiliations. Hence the first President of *Apollo* was Ahmad **Shawqī** (1868-1932), the doyen of the neo-classical style, and when he died in 1932, he was succeeded by Khalīl **Mutrān** (1872-1949) who although responsible for significant innovations in the early stages of his career as a poet, was not a central figure in the Romantic movement. It is likely that Abū Shādī was particularly concerned to avoid the bitter divisiveness which had characterised much literary debate during the previous decade, for example in the vitriolic attacks aimed at Ahmad Shawqī and the neo-classical style in general by the so-called *Dīwān* poets, and in particular 'Abbās Mahmūd al-'Aqqād (1889-1964) and Ibrāhīm 'Abd al-Qādir al-**Māzinī** (1890-1949).

Abū Shādī's productivity throughout his career was nothing short of extraordinary both because of the sheer volume of what he wrote and for its remarkably varied nature, this being a reflection of his unusual array of talents. Born in Cairo in 1892, he completed his secondary education in 1911 and entered the School of Medicine in the recently established Egyptian University. At this time, he suffered both from ill health and from the emotional crises of late adolescence, having been much affected by an unsuccessful love affair. The object of his unrequited love appears in his poetry under the name of "Zaynab". He spent the years 1912-1922 in England where he completed his medical studies, specialising in bacteriology. He returned to Egypt in 1922 accompanied by his English wife. Apart from literature, poetry, and his professional medical expertise, other consuming interests which he maintained throughout his life included bee-keeping, painting and drawing. After his emigration to America in 1946, an exhibition of his art work was held in New York. His literary output was prodigious in the extreme: he was the author of nineteen collections of poetry, several scripts for operas, translations, and divers volumes on literature and other subjects. While one can appreciate that the quality of such a vast and varied production is inevitably uneven, nevertheless he made important contributions to the development of the Romantic style and sensibility, especially in the realm of love poetry. This was quite apart from the vital role which he played as a stimulating inspiration and patron to a whole generation of young poets inside and beyond Egypt.

In Abū Shādī's first collection of verse *Anda' al-fajr* (Dew Drops of Dawn, 1910), the author makes clear his own inclusive non-factional approach:

I was influenced by Mutrān, Shawqī, Hāfiz, Muharram, and al-Rāfi'ī in different fields, and I never once denied the merit of those distinguished men, even at the time when there arose the revolt of Shawqī's school against the poets of innovation, and I was harmed by much of the heat from their fires.   (*Andā' al-fajr*, 2nd ed., Cairo 1934, 124)

The collection appeared when the poet was only eighteen years old, and according to the author represented only selections from the all the poetry which he had composed by then. The book was re-published in 1934 containing some additional material, and with a dedication to "Zaynab"—the woman whom he had loved no less than twenty-five years ago. Most of the contents of this volume are unsurprisingly stilted and immature, revealing a talent for versification rather than poetic originality: there are traditional gloom-laden pieces bemoaning lack of success in love, poems written in honour of certain friends as well as to his mentor, Khalīl Mutrān, and also some patriotic pieces. Here and there certain poems stand out from the more mundane majority: "Banāt al-Kharīf" (Daughters of Autumn) has lines which convey simply and skilfully the swift force and movement of the leaves carried on the wind, and "Wahy al-Matar" (Inspiration of the Rain) is an exquisite piece of subtle identification between his own thirsting for his love, and the thirsting of the ground and plants for the life-giving rain with appropriate onomatopoeic effects. Unfortunately it is not possible to determine whether these poems were added to the second edition at a later stage, or whether they were precocious sign

of the major talent which was to flourish in later years.

The unhappy love affair of Abū Shādī's adolescence was undoubtedly one of the most formative experiences of his life, and the memory of "Zaynab" remained with him long after he married his English wife. This experience was also the most important source of inspiration for Abū Shādī the poet. His second collection of poetry, published in Cairo in 1924, actually bears the title *Zaynab*, and is described by its author as "breaths of lyrical poetry drawn from the verse of youth." In fact this lyrical love poetry is his most important contribution to Romantic poetry in Arabic, and even at this relatively early stage in his career he is clearly an innovative talent who anticipated much of the best of the love poetry which came into its own in Egypt in the 1930s. Of course love poetry had been one of the main themes of the work of Khalīl Mutrān and the *Dīwān* poets, but this had rarely departed from the often cliché-ridden rhetoric of old Arabic amatory verse. In his "Zaynab" poems Abū Shādī creates a new language of a simple direct emotional frankness which moves this poetry beyond the conventional range within which this subject had usually been treated. In "Zaynab" and "Yā Ilāhī" (Oh My God) one also encounters the tendency which he displayed to elevate his beloved to a level far above human weaknesses and imperfections, in a manner reminiscent of the spiritual romantic love poetry of the western tradition, or indeed not unlike the intensely platonic pieces which one finds in the *'udhrī* love-poetry of the Umayyad period (660-750CE) of early Arabic history. It is clear that the beautiful Zaynab has a divine unattainable quality, and Abū Shādī will not be able to reach her in his lifetime.

The starkly contrasting nature of Abū Shādī's poetic output is illustrated by the other collection published in 1924: this is entitled *Misriyyāt* (Poems on Egypt) which consists of patriotic poetry, interesting perhaps in that it reminds one of the admiration which he felt for Hāfiz **Ibrāhīm**, and also because it makes clear that he was deeply committed to social and political issues. It is equally clear that his poetic talent was not displayed to its best effect in these loudly declamatory pieces, most of which are about Sa'd Zaghlūl, the Wafdist hero of Egypt's transition to political independence in the early 1920s. These contrasts of quality and style continue to feature in most of Abū Shādī's subsequent work: the collection *Anīn wa ranīn* (Moans and Laments) which appeared in 1925 again has the poet looking back to his unrequited love through what he describes as "pictures from the poetry of youth," expressed in short lyrical poems about "Zaynab". But these are also accompanied by poems in which Abū Shādī appears more as a social versifier: there are pieces in honour of friends and those whom he admires such as 'Abd al-Rahmān **Shukrī** (no. 10) and poetic letters written between him and Khalīl **Mutrān**. Other poems are dedicated to Ahmad Shawqī and Hāfiz Ibrāhīm who might almost have been the authors, such is the neo-classical nature of the style. The other collection published in 1925 entitled *Shi'r al-wijdān* (Poetry of Emotion) consists largely of poems which had already appeared in previous volumes, and would not normally attract particular comment save for one feature: in addition to the poetry it contains a number of articles and critical comments on poetry and literature by Abū Shādī's friends and colleagues, to the extent that the volume almost begins to look like a number of a literary review than a volume of poetry. This and other similar volumes produced in the 1920s are the forerunners of the *Apollo* review itself which began its brief period of publication in 1932.

In 1926 the work of printing *al-Shafaq al-bākī* (The Weeping Dawn) began. Originally Abū Shādī had planned this as a two volume collection, but it finally appeared as one massive tome in 1927, containing some thirteen hundred and thirty-six pages. It maintains what was to be the familiar pattern of most of the subsequent collections in its general articles on literature interspersed amongst the poetry. Some of these provide an insight into how Abū Shādī saw his mission as a poet and in wider social terms. For him, poetry had the capacity to link together such diverse areas of human activity as science, philosophy, art and literature, and it must at the same time be firmly rooted in its society. While he subscribes to the traditional Romantic view of

the poet as something of a prophet amongst his people, he has to be a prophet who is in tune with the needs and tastes of the people. It becomes clear that Abū Shādī sees poetry as a medium which can transcend the boundaries of artistic, spiritual, philosophical and technical activities, and indeed in his own life and varied career he puts this into practice through his work as a bacteriologist, poet, painter, critic and apiarist. While it is undoubtedly the case that Abū Shādī was one of the leading figures in the development of the Romantic movement in Arabic poetry, it is equally true that he also held on to what appears as a very traditional view of the nature and function of poetry in Arabic, namely as a medium which can span the widest possible range of topics which affect the lives of individuals and society at large. The hundreds of pages of poetry in this volume reflect these very different preoccupations: the most satisfying pieces are those in which in which he concentrates on himself, his own loves and passions, while the numerous poems on politics, religion, painting, bee-keeping and a variety of social problems show Abū Shādī more in the role of a gifted versifier than an inspired poet.

In the years which preceded the appearance of the *Apollo* journal, Abū Shādī published some short collections of limited interest: *al-Muntakhab min shi'r Abī Shādī* (Selections from the Poetry of Abū Shādī, 1926), *Watan al-farā'ina* (Land of the Pharaohs, 1926), and *Mukhtārāt wahy al-'ām 1928* (Selections Inspired by the Year 1928). In 1931 the collection *Ashi''ā' wazilāl* (Rays and Shadows) provided a foretaste of how broad minded and far-ranging the *Apollo* society was to become: there are articles on figures from Greek mythology, translations from English and French poets such as Robert Bridges and Edmond Rostand, and numerous illustrations of paintings by western artists accompanied by Abū Shādī's poems on the subjects of the paintings. This had already been a feature of *al-Shafaq al- bākī*, but now becomes one of the central themes of the book. The poetry displays the by now familiar range of subject and quality: his lyrical poems of platonic love are the most significant in terms of interest and quality, and stand in sharp contrast to the numerous pieces in which the poet expresses in verse his numerous theories on life, art and science. *Al-Shu'lah* (The Torch, 1933) contains a preponderance of social and patriotic poetry, much of which had been published previously, while *Atyāf al-Rabī'* (Spring Phantoms, 1933) is dedicated yet again to his beloved "Zaynab". This volume displays excellent evidence of the cosmopolitan nature of Abū Shādī's cultural mission, both as a poet and as the driving force behind the *Apollo* society. A number of poems are dedicated to Zeus, Aphrodite and Adonis, while other are inspired by the Bible and Pharaonic civilization. The collections which appeared over the next two years continued this pattern without adding to it significantly (*al-Yanbū'* (The Source, 1934), *Fawq al-'ubab* (On the Torrent, 1935), and *al-Kā'in al-thānī* (The Second Being, 1935).

In 1934, to Abū Shādī's great distress, the literary journal *Apollo* ceased publication. While his broad-minded cosmopolitan approach to art and culture in general had been a great inspiration to like-minded contemporaries, and especially to younger poets and writers, this had also laid him and the *Apollo* society open to attack by less generous critics. Abū Shādī himself was always deeply conscious of how damaging to the cause of literature were the quarrels which concentrated more on personalities than on the texts:

Perhaps one of the most important principles which Apollo has promoted is freedom from the rivalry for the leading positions in poetry which youth used to worship, and the spreading of the spirit of truth and personal respect amongst that youth which is the hope of the present and the future, and on which we depend for the continuation of the Renaissance.

(*Apollo*, September 1934, 4)

He was particularly glad of the fact that he had opened up publishing opportunities for the poets of the younger generation, even in those conservative newspapers and periodicals which previously had rejected them. In the penultimate number of *Apollo*, he reasserted that the aim of the society had always been to defend literary opinions and points of principle, and not to descend to the level of personal attacks. Unfortunately, the opponents of *Apollo* were not so

high-minded. Without giving specific details, he says sadly in the last number of *Apollo*:

Indeed the various setbacks and numerous affronts which we have suffered from government sources and others have passed all bounds of endurance. In spite of that, we have held out and contented ourselves with complaint to his Excellency the previous Prime Minister, and we have endured until the day when the true sun of liberty will return again to light, anticipating that we shall receive the necessary justice.

(*Apollo*, December 1934, 414)

After the disappearance of *Apollo*, the previous vast output of verse from Abū Shādī was curtailed, and during the last twenty years of his life he published only two further collections. The first was *'Awdat al-Rā'ī* (The Shepherd's Return, 1942), produced in a special limited edition of which only fifty copies were printed and intended as gifts for friends and certain libraries. Perhaps unsurprisingly, the reader can detect a note of bitterness and disillusionment, as the poet sees himself as one outcast by his own society, especially in the poems "al-Mutamarrid" (The Rebel) and "'Arūs al-Zalām" (Bride of Darkness). The poem which he wrote to his beloved England, "Watanī al-thānī" (My Second Homeland) may be an indication that his thoughts were beginning to turn beyond Egypt in the light of his feelings of rejection and disappointment. After the death of his English wife, he emigrated to America in 1946. His final collection, *Min al-samā'* (From the Heavens, 1949), contains poems which he wrote in America between 1946-49, one of which is a tender and moving elegy to his wife in which he sees her death as presaging his own end.

Given the extraordinarily varied nature of Abū Shādī's career, he is not an easy figure to evaluate: he achieved distinction in most of the fields to which he devoted his considerable talents, from apiculture to bacteriology, and was one whose breadth of culture and liberal beliefs were to some degree ahead of his time and his society at large. He made a lasting contribution to the poetry of Romantic love in Arabic, although the gems of his poetic creativity are frequently obscured by the great mass of his verse which is more competent than inspired. His personal disillusionment is perhaps balanced by the lasting achievement of the creation of the *Apollo* journal and the literary society of the same name. This had an importance which extended far beyond the brief span of its existence, and through its spirit something of Abū Shādī's magnanimity and liberal culture were introduced into a society which was sorely in need of it.

REFERENCES

M. M. Badawi, *A Critical Introduction to Modern Arabic Poetry* (Cambridge: Cambridge University Press, 1975);

Ismail Ahmed Edham, *Abushady the poet: a critical study* (Leipzig: G. Fischer, 1936);

Muhammad ʿAbd al-Fattāh Ibrāhīm, *Ahmad Zakī Abū Shādī* (Cairo: Maktabat al-Shaʿb, 1955);

Salma Khadra Jayyusi, *Trends and Movements in Modern Arabic Poetry,* 2 vols. (Leiden: E. J. Brill, 1977);

ʿAbd al-Munʿim Khafājī, *Rāʾid al-shiʿr al-hadīth* (Cairo: Matbaʿat al-Munīriyyah, 1953);

Kamāl Nashʾat, *Abū Shādī wa-harakat al-tajdīd fī ʾl-shiʿr al-ʿarabī al-hadīth* (Cairo: Dār al-Kātib al-ʿArabī, 1967).

Tawfīq Yūsuf ʿAwwād
(1911 – 1989)

PAUL STARKEY
University of Durham

WORKS

al-Sabī al-aʿraj ("The Lame Boy", Beirut, 1936; Beirut: Dār al-Thaqāfah, 1963);

Qamīs al-sūf ("The Woollen Shirt", Beirut: Dār al-Makshūf, 1937);

al-Raghīf ("The Loaf", Beirut: Dār al-Makshūf, 1939);

al-ʿAdhārā ("The Virgins", Beirut, 1944; Beirut: Dār Sādir, 1966);

al-Sāʾih waʾl-turjumān ("The Tourist and the Interpreter", Beirut: Dār al-Makshūf, 1962);

Ghubār al-ayyām ("The Dust of the Days", Beirut: Dār al-ʿIlm liʾl-Malāyīn, 1965);

Tawāhīn Bayrūt ("The Mills of Beirut", Beirut: Maktabat Lubnān, 1972);

Qawāfil al-zamān ("The Caravans of Time", Beirut: Muʾassasat A. Badrān, 1973);

Matār al-saqīʿ ("Frosty Airport", Beirut: Maktabat Lubnān, 1982);

Hisād al-ʿumr ("The Harvest of Life", Beirut: Maktabat Lubnān, 1983).

Complete Works

Tawfīq Yūsuf ʿAwwād, *al-Muʾallafāt al-kāmilah* ("Complete Works", Beirut: Maktabat Lubnān, 1987).

Works in Translation

Death in Beirut, tr. Leslie McLoughlin (London: Heinemann Educational, 1976); translation of *Tawāhīn Bayrūt*;

"Le touriste et l'interprète," tr. Michel Barbot, *Orient* 36 (1965): 51-112; translation of *al-Sāʾih waʾl-turjumān*.

Tawfīq Yūsuf ʿAwwād is widely recognized as one of the leading Lebanese novelists and short-story writers of the twentieth century. His writing career was a somewhat curious one, spanning a period of some four decades but including a literary 'silence' of almost a quarter of a century, attributable mainly no doubt to the heavy demands of the author's parallel diplomatic career. Although now somewhat eclipsed by the writings of a later, more experimental generation of writers, ʿAwwād's two novels, whose publication dates are separated by over thirty years, occupy crucial positions in the development of the modern Lebanese, and indeed, of the Arabic, novelistic tradition. The first, *al-Raghīf* (The Loaf), published in 1939, may be regarded as a work in a tradition of historical novel writing that owes much to the pioneering efforts of the Lebanese-Egyptian Jurjī **Zaydān** (1861-1914), though the historical focus of ʿAwwād's own work, which centers on the Lebanese experience under the Ottomans during the First World War, is comparatively recent by comparison with most of the works of Zaydān himself. While the historical orientation of *al-Raghīf* is quite explicit, however, ʿAwwād's second novel, *Tawāhīn Bayrūt*, published in 1972 (English translation: *Death in Beirut*, 1976), has been widely read as a 'prophecy' or 'premonition' of the forthcoming Lebanese Civil War of 1975-90. A comparison of the two works is highly instructive, both in terms of the evolution of the author's own technique from the comparatively straightforward narrative of *al-Raghīf* to the considerably more complex structure of *Tawāhīn Bayrūt*, and as a reflection of the evolving political climate of the region.

Tawfīq Yūsuf ʿAwwād was born in the village of Bharsāf, in the Matn district of Mount Lebanon, on 28 November 1911, the second of seven children. His early childhood was spent under the Ottoman occupation of Lebanon, and although his own family was fairly comfortably off, he witnessed the catastrophic effects of the famine in Mount Lebanon during the later years of the First World War—an experience that was to leave a lasting impression on him and which is reflected in particular in his early writings. Between 1920 and 1923 he was educated locally, taking his elementary certificate at the village school in nearby Bikfayya, before moving to Beirut, where from 1923 to 1927 he attended the College of St Joseph run by the Jesuits. Here he came under the influence of Father Rūfāʾīl Nakhleh, who encouraged him in his literary inclinations that had already begun to become apparent. For a time, he attempted

unsuccessfully to earn a living from writing, resisting his father's attempts to persuade him to qualify as a lawyer or to set up in business. During this period he wrote for a number of newspapers and periodicals, including *al-Bayraq*, *al-ʿArāʾis* and al-*Nidāʾ*, before being invited in 1931 to serve as editorial secretary to the nationalist newspaper *al-Qabas*, based in Damascus. Here, he both registered for a law degree and married a Lebanese merchant's daughter, by whom he subsequently had four children.

Following his marriage and qualification as a lawyer, ʿAwwād returned to Beirut in 1933 and accepted a position as editorial secretary of the newly founded newspaper *al-Nahār*, which quickly established itself as a leading Beirut daily, a status that it still retains. He continued to hold this position until 1941, playing a leading part in the development of Lebanese intellectual life during this period, both through his membership of literary groups such as the al-ʿUsbah al-ʿasharah and through his writings in the periodical *al-Makshūf* and elsewhere; these embraced both poetry and prose. The publication of his first volume of short stories, *al-Sabī al-aʿraj* (The Lame Boy) in 1936 enabled him to begin to achieve a wider prominence. This first collection of short stories was followed by a second, *Qamīs al-sūf* (The Woollen Shirt, 1937).

These two early collections of short stories contain respectively fourteen and seven stories. Both collections may to a large extent be regarded as springing from the same social milieu as the novel *al-Raghīf* already discussed: both evince a natural sympathy, and empathy, with the poorer members of society, as well as an assured, if fairly straightforward, narrative technique: in both these respects, they bear comparison with the work of better known short-story writers from other parts of the Arab world, including, for example, the Egyptian writers Yahyā **Haqqī** (1905-93) and the brothers Muhammad (1892-1921) and Mahmūd (1894-1973) **Taymūr**.

In the introduction to his first volume of stories, *al-Sabī al-aʿraj*, ʿAwwād made clear that he regarded the short story as the literary form best suited to the needs of the age. Some idea of the flavour of the collections may be gained from a brief analysis of selected stories. The title story, for example, depicts an impoverished boy who is sent out by his uncle, first to beg, then to sell sweets; one day, returning home by tram, he is knocked to the ground by the conductor and loses his takings. His uncle, unsurprisingly, punishes the boy severely for his loss, but the boy takes his revenge during the night by beating the uncle with a stick; when, by chance, the oil from the lamp is spilled and the house burns down, the boy escapes and the wicked uncle dies. The moral of the tale—that virtue will eventually triumph over vice—is both clear and conventional, though it has been argued that the author would have been better advised to omit the ending, which seems unnecessarily melodramatic and detracts from, rather than adding to, the force of the message. Other tales from the same collection include "al-Maqbarah al-mudannasah" (The Filthy Graveyard), which revolves around a village girl forced to prostitute herself in the city and subsequently killed; "al-Armalah" (The Widow), a sensitive story of love and conflicting emotions; and "al-Shāʿir" (The Poet), in which a student falls in love with an Italian woman who subsequently leaves to return to her own country. None of the themes involved seems particularly out of the ordinary, though the writing is always competent, if seldom particularly innovative.

The same qualities apparent in ʿAwwād's first collection of short stories—most notably, a capacity for exploring the subtleties of human emotion through tales of "ordinary" people—are again evident in Qamīs al-sūf, the title story of which is a sensitive account of a widow's love for her son, combining the familiar "town versus country" motif with a tale of two generations. Other stories in the collection include "Tūhā", which touches on the sensitive theme of the preference for male children in many parts of the Middle East, and "Kārākhū", in which a Lebanese emigrant returns to his village from America, boasting of the wealth he has acquired, but is subsequently discovered to be penniless.

It was with the full-length novel al-Raghīf (The Loaf, 1939) that ʿAwwād was to consolidate his reputation; it was an immediate success and was quickly recognized as a landmark in the literary expression of Arab nationalism. It was inspired by the Arab resistance to the Turks during the First World War. This period had proved a particularly difficult one for the Lebanese, who had been subject to oppressive measures from the Ottoman authorities under the military governor Jamāl Pāshā, and who had suffered a disastrous famine in which up to one fifth of the population of Mount Lebanon, mainly Christian, had died of starvation or disease—an event that also provided the inspiration, for example, for Mīkhāʾīl **Nuʿaymah**'s famous poem "Akhī" (My Brother). The period also saw a strengthening of the Arab nationalist movement, however, through the Arab Revolt, led by the Sharif of Mecca, which began in June 1916, culminating in the enthusiastic reception of Faisal and his army by the Muslims of Syria and Lebanon in October 1918.

It is against this historical background that ʿAwwād unfolds his tale, which is centered on the impoverished inhabitants of the village of Sāqiyat al-Misk, dominated as they are by feudal landowners in league with the Ottoman authorities. The work is divided into five sections, each of which corresponds both to a stage in the journey of the loaf of the title, and to the progress of the Arab Revolt against the Ottomans: al-Turbah (Soil), al-Bidhār (Sowing), al-Ghayth (Heavy Rain), al-Sanābil (Ears of Wheat) and al-Hisād (Harvest). The hero of the novel, Sāmī ʿĀsim, is a fervent Arab nationalist, well educated by local standards, who belongs to a secret revolutionary organization devoted to the struggle against Ottoman rule. Hunted by the Turks, he takes refuge in a cave, where his beloved, Zaynah, brings him food and information, but the location of the hideaway is revealed and he is captured and tortured by the Turks. When the first stirrings of the Arab Revolt are felt, Sāmī is believed to be dead, along with others in the first group of Arabs who revolted against the Ottoman authorities and were subsequently executed. In revenge, Zaynah allows herself to be enticed to the Turkish commander's house where she kills the drunken officer who is trying to seduce her; she then joins a group of Arab saboteurs who have taken their lead from the Declaration of the Arab Revolt in Mecca in June 1916 and learns that Sāmī is not dead but is leading the Arab forces in their fight against the Turks. Sāmī, however, dies in the fighting and is thus unable to be with Zaynah as the victorious Arabs enter Damascus in triumph, having ousted the Turkish army, which flees northward in disarray. The rout marks a decisive victory for the Arabs, who thus win back for themselves not only their freedom but also the loaf of bread that provides the work with its title.

On one level, this novel is clearly analyzable as a representative of a particular trend in Arab novel writing which produced a number of works that may be broadly defined as 'historical-romantic'. The trend found perhaps its most prolific exponent in the works of the Lebanese Jurjī Zaydān (1861-1914), who after his emigration to Egypt produced a series of some 20 novels from 1891 on, each centered around a particular period or episode in Arab Islamic history, and usually also involving a hero and heroine in love. This trend was continued by a number of authors in Egypt and elsewhere, for example Muhammad Farīd Abū Hadīd's early work *Ibnat al-Mamlūk* (The Mamluk's daughter, 1926), set during the early years of Muhammad ʿAlī's reign during his struggle with the Mamluks.

Like many other such works, Tawfīq Yūsuf ʿAwwād's novel appears to serve a dual purpose; for, like other parts of the Middle East, Lebanon had emerged from the yoke of the Ottoman Empire at the end of the First World War only to find that one form of foreign domination had been replaced by another, in the form of the French Protectorate; thus, while looking back with pride to the struggle against the Ottomans of two decades previously, the work also contained a further relevance for the author's contemporaries. Prior to Tawfīq Yūsuf ʿAwwād, however, Jurjī Zaydān's efforts do not appear to have inspired any corresponding sequence of historical novel writing in Lebanon itself; as Hamdi Sakkut has recently noted, despite the pioneering efforts of the Lebanese pioneers of the *nahdah* ("revival") in the nineteenth century, no Lebanese authors of consequence had emerged to parallel the Egyptian generation of

Tāhā Husayn and Tawfīq al-Hakīm in the succeeding decades, and *al-Raghīf* may therefore be regarded as the first significant Lebanese novel of the twentieth century. For a work of pioneering status, however, the novel displays a considerable accomplishment of technique—to quote the Lebanese critic Suhayl Idrīs:

there is a coherent structure to the work which leads the reader through the work with a good deal of confidence. Furthermore, the framework within which the story is treated shows a good deal of focus and artistic acumen which allows the events of the narrative to be portrayed in a gradual progression of considerable subtlety.

This combination of contemporary relevance and assured artistic technique no doubt accounts not only for the work's initial enthusiastic reception but also for its continuing reputation as a significant landmark in the development of the modern Arabic novel.

In the meantime, the author had also been more directly active in the political arena, agitating for the political independence of Lebanon, which had been placed under the French mandate in 1920. As a result of his political activities, ʿAwwād, with several colleagues, was placed in detention for a month in 1941. In the same year, he resigned from *al-Nahār* and founded the weekly *al-Jadīd*, which subsequently became a daily, and continued to run this publication until 1946.

The year 1944 saw the publication of a third volume of collected short stories entitled *al-ʿAdhārā* (The Virgins), in addition to a continuation of his political activities with a call in *al-Jadīd* for "A Lebanese Beveridge" to advance the cause of social justice in Lebanon. At this point, however, ʿAwwād's career, which so far had followed a fairly conventional path of writer, journalist and political commentator, assumed a radically different direction; invited in 1946 to join the Lebanese diplomatic service, he embarked on a distinguished career which lasted some thirty years until his retirement in 1975 from the post of Lebanese Ambassador in Rome. In the meantime, he had served in a wide variety of postings, including Spain, Japan, and South America, in addition to Tunis, Cairo and

Tehran in the Middle East itself. These postings were interspersed with periods of service in Beirut itself: in 1949-50 he was Head of the Arab section in the Ministry of Foreign Affairs, and between 1961 and 1966 he served as Director of Social and Cultural Affairs in the Foreign Ministry.

Given the heavy demands of his diplomatic career, it is perhaps less surprising than it might at first sight appear that he should have published almost nothing of substance between *al-ʾAdhārā* (1944) until the early 1960s, when he produced a short play entitled *al-Sāʾih waʾl-turjumān* (The Tourist and the Guide), which won an award for the best play of 1962; a number of other publications followed, including *Ghubār al-ayyām* (The Dust of the Days), a collection of reflective essays written over an extended period and published in book form in 1963. It was not these essays, however, but rather his second full-length novel *Tawāhīn Bayrūt* (literally "The Mills of Beirut"; English translation published as *Death in Beirut*) that has guaranteed ʿAwwād a lasting and distinguished place among Arab writers of the second half of the twentieth century. The work, originally written in 1969 while the author was serving in Tokyo, reflects the anguish of the period following the disastrous Arab defeat in the 1967 war with Israel (the so-called *naksah*, "setback"), and was received with particular interest when it appeared in 1972 because of the author's long publishing silence; it proved prophetic in its depiction of the strains and tensions latent in Lebanese society—tensions that were to erupt only a few years later in the Lebanese Civil War of 1975-1990. The occasion of its publication prompted the Lebanese poet Unsī al-Hājj to remark that the author, instead of writing about history, was now engaged in making it. The work also prompted UNESCO to include the author in a list of world writers who best represented their age and to recommend the translation of his works into other world languages; the English translation by Leslie McLoughlin was made, as his preface to *Death in Beirut* makes clear, in the village of Shemlan, "overlooking Beirut and its international airport … accompanied by the sounds of modern warfare, regular and irregular, by land, sea and air".

The political and literary context of this second novel, *Tawāhīn Bayrūt (*1972), for which the Arab world had had to wait over thirty years since the publication of his first novel, is unsurprisingly very different from that of *al-Raghīf*. Perhaps most striking, however, is that, whereas *al-Raghīf* expressly looks backwards to an earlier historical period while retaining an obvious relevance to the political situation of 1939, *Tawāhīn Bayrūt*, though given a contemporary setting, has been widely read as a 'prophecy' of the future Lebanese Civil War of 1975-90. Set in the aftermath of the catastrophic Arab defeat in the so-called 'Six-Day' War of 1967, the novel, although clearly reflecting the regional context more generally, focuses on the events that took place in Lebanon (specifically Beirut) in 1968 and 1969—a period marked by student strikes and riots, by a growing Palestinian influence on the delicate structure of the country, and by international events, some of which bear an eerie resemblance to those of the events of 2006—not least, the 1968 Israeli attack on Beirut International Airport, specifically referred to in the book, when thirteen civilian aircraft were set fire to on the ground. In contrast to the comparatively straightforward oppositions with which we are presented in the earlier novel, therefore—essentially, a struggle for liberation on the part of the "good" Arabs against the "wicked" Turks—the world that the author presents to us in *Tawāhīn Bayrūt* is an infinitely more complex one: "a mosaic", as the Lebanese critic Mona Amyuni has described it, "of the cosmopolitan Beirut scene before the start of the Lebanese civil war in 1975 … made up of splinters and burnt fragments, 'as all the casseroles of the Arab world were boiling in Beirut'".

The main actions of this extremely complex novel unfold primarily through the experiences of Tamima Nassour (using the transliteration of the English translation), a Shiʿite girl from an impoverished village in south Lebanon, who comes to Beirut to study in the Teachers' Training College there—a variation on the 'town' versus 'country' theme that had already proved a popular and recurrent one in Arabic fiction (as indeed, in other literatures). In a more specifically Lebanese touch, Tamima's father has, many years before, left the village to earn a living in Sierra Leone, from where he sends monthly remittances to his family. In Beirut, Tamima becomes a lodger in the pension of Mme Rose Khoury, where her feckless brother, Jaber, is also staying, and it is through the characters that Tamima meets in Mme Khoury's establishment as well as through her participation in the turbulent student politics of the city that ʿAwwād introduces us to the disparate ideologies whose competing attractions were shortly to be played out by rival militias in the civil war of 1975-90. These characters include, among others, Ramzi Raad, a well known writer and revolutionary journalist, who seduces Tamima and subsequently becomes her lover (the seduction scene, incidentally, has been considered one of the most sexually explicit pieces of writing in modern Arabic literature); Akram Jurdi, a Shiʿite resident of Beirut who owns estates in the Bekaa Valley but is at the same time a lecherous opportunist with designs on Tamima; Mary, Tamima's Christian girlfriend and confidante, who works in the American University Hospital in Beirut; Hussein Qamooʾi, her brother's henchman, who has strong connections with the Palestinian fedayeen; and Abu Sharshur, a Palestinian labourer who serves as Tamima's protector. Most importantly, they include Hani Raʿi, an idealistic Maronite student leader, with whom she falls in love, but whom she eventually abandons to devote herself to the Palestinian struggle.

The romance between Tamima and Hani is without doubt the most crucial relationship in the book. Although all accounts of romance between a Muslim man and a Christian woman (of which there are a number of others in modern Arabic literature) raise sensitive issues because of the taboo on marriage between Muslim women and non-Muslim men, the issues acquire a particular added significance in the Lebanese context because of the social and political structure of the Lebanese state, which was (and remains) governed by the principles of confessionalism. The abortive romance of Tamima and Hani indeed may perhaps best be seen as a mirror of the Lebanese quest for identity in a

political context that had been further complicated in the previous few years by the rise of Palestinian influence. In this context, the idealistic Hani argues that it is time to throw off the relics of the past and "for the two communities to merge. Blood ties—that's the question for Lebanon". For Hani, Lebanese unity appears to be a goal in itself: he is contemptuous of the idea of espousing the Palestinian cause, claiming that "Between Lebanon and the Palestinian movement, there is a marriage of hypocrisy. The movement claims to be pure and chaste, and Lebanon claims that it will go to any lengths to die for its sake. A marriage of hypocrisy is bound to lead to such tragic deaths." Tamima, on the other hand, proves ultimately unable to accept this line of reasoning, preferring at the end of the novel to identify herself with the Palestinian cause, the only option that seems to contain any ideology clarity. The book concludes cryptically, with words taken from jottings in her notebook: "I shall never speak from this day on. From the moment I set off with the man, no more will be heard of the name of Tamima Nassour."

In the light of this ending, it is no surprise that the work has been interpreted in a variety of different ways by different critics, for whom it has raised questions not only of the author's political intentions but also of the work's "feminist" credentials, or lack of them. It is, however, arguably, in the very multiplicity of possible interpretations that the strength of the work lies, for however one chooses to interpret its central themes, it is clear that ʿAwwād's purpose was not to write a work of propaganda on behalf of one group rather than another, but rather to express in novelistic form the tensions and undercurrents latent in Lebanese society that were rapidly acquiring a dangerous momentum. In this respect, a comparison with the earlier novel al-Raghīf is instructive on several counts. In terms of the concept of identity, we may note that while al-Raghīf is primarily a novel about Arab identity (a concept that, at the time at the time of writing of the novel, at least, appeared to be a relatively straightforward one), Tawāhīn Bayrūt is concerned rather with ideas of Lebanese identity, a concept that for historical and other reasons has proved, and continues to prove, both complex and elusive. These differences are reflected in the narrative techniques employed by the author. On the one hand, *al-Raghīf* is firmly anchored in the literary conventions of the period, which seem to reflect an age when political and moral certainties still held sway: essentially, as already noted, a story of the struggle between the "good" Arabs and the "bad" Turks, its eventual outcome is never in doubt, no matter how great the sufferings of the Arabs along the way. The world of *Tawāhīn Bayrūt*, on the other hand, is an infinitely more complex one, in which moral and political certainties (with the exception of the iniquity of the Israelis, perhaps) are almost entirely absent. The increased complexity of the issues involved and the uncertainty of the outcome are reflected in the more complex narrative techniques employed by the author—even though it has to be admitted that his techniques still appear fairly conventional when set against those used by later Lebanese writers such as Ilyās Khūrī and Rashīd al-Da'īf, for whom the fragmentation of Lebanese society in the Civil War of 1975-90 entails at times an almost total fragmentation both of language and of consciousness.

It is perhaps a measure of the significance attached to 'Awwād's work in the region itself that, in an "intertextual" reference, its title was quickly appropriated by the Syrian feminist writer Ghādah al-Sammān (1942–), whose *Kawābīs Bayrūt* (Beirut Nightmares, 1976), is centered on the nightmares endured by the residents of Beirut during the so-called 'Hotel battles' of late 1975. Recent events in the area in mid-2006 suggest that the relevance of *Tawāhīn Bayrūt* as a 'prophetic' document unfortunately remains undiminished.

By comparison with his two novels and two early collections of short stories—all of which may be accounted, to a greater of lesser degree, milestones in the development of modern Arabic fiction in the Levant—much of 'Awwād's other writing may well strike the reader as somewhat "run-of-the-mill", and it is indeed undeniable that a considerable proportion of 'Awwād's output consists of the sort of routine essay and journalistic pieces that have formed the staple fare of many, if not most, Arabic writers of the twentieth century. Despite this, however, and despite the inevitable disruption to his writing activities caused by his diplomatic career, it would be unfair to dismiss the remainder of his work as of no interest or value. The appearance of 'Awwād's play *al-Sā'ih wa'l-turjumān* (The Tourist and the Guide) in the early 1960s, for example, prompted the distinguished Lebanese critic Mīkhā'īl Nu'aymah (1889-1989) to rejoice that the author had successfully returned to writing with a piece that exhibited all the qualities displayed in his early short stories; and indeed, this lively short piece, set in the ruins of Baalbek and featuring not only a local guide and an American tourist but also a man from Mars and the "voice of time", makes one wish that the author had perhaps had a less itinerant career and been able to devote more energy to the theatre. A similar sense of potential talent that might have been developed further is occasioned by a reading of his collection of two-line poems, *Qawāfil al-zaman* (1973). This form makes considerable demands on the writer through the need to encapsulate an idea in a limited number of words, a feature that it obviously shares with the Japanese *haiku*; although well known in the medieval Arabic tradition, it is tempting to speculate that 'Awwād's interest in it may have been stimulated by his recent posting to Tokyo.

'Awwād's works produced during the last years of his life include both poetry and prose but are of less interest or significance than his two novels or early short stories. *Qawāfil al-zamān* (The Caravans of Time), published in 1973, is a collection of two-line poems that represents an attempt to revive a long-neglected genre in Arabic literature. 1982 saw the publication of *Matār al-saqī'* (Frosty Airport), a fourth collection of short stories, most of which had been written some years previously. *Hisād al-'Umr* (the Harvest of Life), published in 1983, contains a collection of short pieces, as well as some short poems, and provides a commentary on phases of his diplomatic career.

During the civil war of 1975–90, 'Awwād chose to stay in Lebanon, mainly in his birthplace of Bharsāf, which escaped many of the ravages of the capital, Beirut. In 1976, however, he suffered the loss of manuscripts and correspondence when his Beirut residence was hit. He died in a bomb blast in 1989.

REFERENCES

Roger Allen, *The Arabic Novel* (Manchester: Manchester University Press, 1982; 2nd ed., Syracuse: Syracuse University Press, 1995), 52-54;

Suhayl Idrīs, "'Awwād wa-'Raghīf' al-istiqlāl", *al-Ādāb* (February 1957): 11-15;

——, *Muhādarāt 'an al-qissah fī Lubnān* (Cairo: Jāmi'at al-Duwal al-'Arabiyyah, 1957), esp. 52-64;

Elise Salem, *Constructing Lebanon: A Century of Literary Narratives* (Gainesville: University Press of Florida, 2003), esp. 80-87;

Jān Tannūs, *Tawfīq Yūsuf 'Awwād: dirāsah nafsiyyah fī shakhsiyyatihi wa-adabih* (Beirut: Dār al-Kutub al-'Ilmiyyah, 1994).

Dhū 'l-Nūn Ayyūb
(1908 – 1988)

MUHSIN AL-MUSAWI
Columbia University

WORKS

Rusul al-thaqāfah ("Messengers of Culture", Baghdad: al-Matba'ah al-'Arabiyyah, 1937);

al-Dahāyā ("Victims", Baghdad, 1937);

Sadīqī ("My Friend", Baghdad: Matba'at al-Ahālī, 1938);

Wahy al-fann ("Inspired by Art", Baghdad: Matba'at al-Ahālī, 1938);

Burj Bābil ("Tower of Babel", Baghdad: Matba'at al-Ahālī, 1939);

al-Kādihūn ("The Toilers", Mosul: Matba'at Umm al-Rabī'ayn, 1939);

al-Duktūr Ibrāhīm ("Doctor Ibrāhīm", Mosul: Matba'at Umm al-Rabī'ayn, 1939; republished, Baghdad: Sharikat al-Tijārah wa'l-Tibā'ah, 1960);

al-'Aql fī mihnah ("The Mind in Trouble", Baghad, 1940);

Humayyāt ("Fevers", Baghdad, 1941);

al-Kārithah al-shāmilah ("Total Disaster", Baghdad, 1945);

'Azamah fārighah ("Empty Pretensions", Baghdad, 1948);

al-Yad wa'l-ard wa'l-mā' ("Manpower, Land, and Water", 1948; Baghdad: Matba'at Shafīq, 1970);

Qulūb zam'ā ("Yearning Hearts", Baghdad, 1950);

Suwar shattā ("Scattered Impressions", Baghdad: Manshūrāt al-Thaqāfah al-Jadīdah, 1954);

al-Rasā'il al-mansiyyah ("Forgotten Letters", Baghdad: Matba'at al-Liwā', 1955);

Wa-'alā 'l-dunyā al-salām ("Farewell to this World", Beirut: Dār al-'Awdah, 1972);

Abū Hurayrah wa-Kūjkā: Qissat madīnatayn ("Abū Hurayrah and Kujka, story of two cities", Baghdad: 'Alī Yahyā Mansūr Publications, 1977; and Sūsah: Dār al-Ma'ārif lil-Tibā'ah wa-'l-Nashr, 1995).

Qisas min Fiyinā (Tales from Vienna Baghdad: Matba'at al-Ma'ārif, 1957)

Complete Works

al-Āthār al-kāmilah li-adab Dhī 'l-Nūn Ayyūb, 3 vols. (Baghdad: Wizārat al-I'lām, 1970).

Selections

Mukhtārāt Dhū 'l-Nūn Ayyūb ("Selections from Dhū 'l-Nūn Ayyūb's Writings", Baghdad: Matba'at al-Liwā', 1958).

Critical Works

"Adab al-qissah fī 'l-'Irāq", *Majallat al-Rābitah* 23 (28 April 1945): 581;

"Qissatī ma'a al-qissah", *al-Adīb al-Mu'āsir* 1 (December 1971): 139;

Qissat hayātihi bi-qalamih, 3 vols. (Vienna: n.d.);

——, (Baghdad: Dār al-Hariyyat (?), 1986).

Works in Translation

"The Pillar of the Tower of Babel," in *Arab Short Stories: East and West*, trans. with an introduction by R. Y. Ebied and M. J. L. Young (Leeds, 1977), 1-11.

The prolific and controversial Iraqi writer and novelist, Dhū 'l-Nūn Ayyūb al-'Abd al-Wāhid, was born in Mosul (1908) and died in Vienna in 1988. He attended primary school in Mosul between 1914 and 1922, followed by secondary school from 1922 to 1927. Although he was selected for a scholarship abroad, a so-called "medical reason" prevented him from going, something that he continued to resent for the rest of his life. Instead he went to the Teachers' College in Baghdad (1927-29) where he specialized in mathematics and natural sciences. He then embarked on a teaching career, working at secondary schools in a number of cities, but in 1933 he almost lost his job when an Iranian woman who was in love with him committed suicide. After a plea to Sāti' al-Husrī, the powerful director at the Ministry of Education, he was allowed to keep his job.

His career as a short story writer and novelist seems to have begun in 1935 when he published his first story, "Sadīqī" (My Friend), in the newspaper, *al-Tarīq* (no. 678, 25 June 1935). In it he uses his own direct manner to delineate his model character: someone with a tall, well-built body, different from other people, unique in his character, unrestrained by customs, following his own predilections and instincts. In an article published in *al-Adīb al-Mu'āsir*, the journal of the Iraqi Union of Writers (n. 1, December 1971, 129), he explains how as a writer he strives to express his views on social and political realities in a narrative mode. In the introduction to one of collections of stories, *Rusul al-thaqāfah* (Mes-

sengers of Culture, 1937), he explains that the writer's mission is to provide an exact and authentic portrayal of "their observations of exceptional events, unique characters, laws and customs—governmental or popular, including unwritten ones that influence society. They should be daring in their criticism of such things, regardless of rewards or punishments" (ibid., 3).

Ayyūb's narrative writings can be subdivided into two phases. The first includes his first seven collections: *Rusul al-thaqāfah* (Messengers of Culture) and *al-Dahāyā* (Victims), both published in 1937; *Sadīqī* (My Friend) and *Wahy al-fann* (Inspired by Art), both 1938; and *Burj Bābil* (Tower of Babel), *al-Kādihūn* (The Toilers), and the novel *al-Duktūr Ibrāhīm*, all 1939. The second comprises his collections and novels from the Second World War until the mid-fifties: *al-'Aql fī mihnah* (The Mind in Trouble, 1940), *Humayyāt* (Fevers, 1941), *al-Kārithah al-shāmilah* (Total Disaster, 1945), *'Azmah fārighah* (Empty Pretensions, 1948), *Qulūb zam'ā* (Yearning Hearts, 1950), *Suwar shattā* (Scattered Impressions, 1954), and the novel *al-Yad wa'l-ard wa'l-mā'* (Manpower, Land, and Water, 1948). His novella *al-Rasā'il al-mansiyyah* (Forgotten Letters) appeared in 1955. Later come his works written in Vienna, others written upon his return to Iraq as Director of Information and Culture in 1958 (before his appointment as the Iraqi attaché in Vienna in 1960), and still others from his subsequent years of exile following the 1963 coup against 'Abd al-Karīm Qāsim (who was executed in 1963).

He made use of a number of different works to record aspects of his own life: his veiled autobiographical short story, "Mu'āmarat al-aghbiyā'" (Conspiracy of the Dim-Wits), included in his fourth collection *Wahy al-fann* (Inspired by Art, 1938); a brief autobiographical sketch included in Yūsuf 'Izz al-Dīn's *al-Riwāyah fī 'l-'Irāq* (The Novel in Iraq, 1973); and a three-volume autobiography, *Dhū 'l-Nūn Ayyūb: Qissat hayātihi bi-qalamih* (Vienna, 1980), reprinted in Baghdad (1986). The last work is in three parts: *Dhikrayāt al-tufūlah* (Childhood Memoirs); *al-Sibā wa'l-shabāb* (Boyhood and Youth); and *Ma'a al-hayāt wa-jhan li-wajh* (Face to Face with Life). The autobiography shocked many people for being so confessional, but his friend, the Iraqi ex-Communist 'Azīz al-Ḥajj, came to his defense in *Abū Hurayrah al-Mawsilī* (1990), finding such an exposed kind of narrative sincere and in keeping with the subject's own character (Introduction, 9-15).

In "Mu'āmarat al-aghbiyā'" he depicts the principal stages in his early youth, pointing out how his interest in narrative began when he listened to story-tellers' tales in the *katātīb* (traditional Qur'an schools), then started to read tales, epics, and detective stories for himself. A teacher introduced him to Jurjī **Zaydān**'s historical novels, the chronological structure and unity of exposition of which left an abiding impression on him. Thereafter he encountered more sentimental writers like Mustafā Lutfī al-**Manfalūtī** (d. 1924), and authors of historical romances such as Rider Haggard (d. 1925). Yet more influential were Emile Zola and H.G. Wells. His writings show the clear impact of Zola, but also of Russian writers, such as Pushkin, Turgenv, Tolstoy and Dostoevsky. *Crime and Punishment* was a major influence on Ayyūb, clearly reflected in a story included in his collection, *al-Dahāyā* (Victims, 1938) that carries one of Dostoevsky's own titles. Dostoevsky's salutary impact is more effectively shown in another short story, "'Āsifah wa-sadāhā" (A Storm and its Reverberation) from his collection, *Burj Bābil* (Tower of Babel, 1939). There the protagonist's stream of associations and flashbacks gives us a personal history of the journalist, Tūmā, his opportunism and corruption, all in the cause of social and political advancement. The associations in the journalist's mind swing back and forth in response to the raging storm outside, as he waits for two ex-ministers who are due to pay him an evening visit in order to assist in the downfall of the present government and the formation of a new one in which he can be a minister. The storm mirrors the stress on the inner workings of the mind. Fear of divine retribution is further augmented by the picture of Christ that hangs on the wall, shining every now and then whenever it is illuminated by a flash of lightning. All these images help to create a psychological state that

only intensifies his sense of guilt, something that leads him to regret his career of double-dealing and opportunism. The visitors do not show up, but when the storm recedes, they call to tell him that they will be coming tomorrow. His earlier resolution no longer to be a part of this scheme dissipates as a result of their decision to see him tomorrow. This concern with social evil, corruption, and opportunism was to remain one of Ayyūb's primary preoccupations.

The ways in which Ayyūb voices these concerns in his stories made him an appealing figure for political parties, and especially the Iraqi Communist Party, which made him its leader in 1939. However he was later criticized and expelled for behaving in a way that was too free for the codes of conduct and commitment that had been established by the Party. Furthermore, the Ministry of Education reprimanded him for his collection, *Burj Bābil*, and proceeded to banish him because his story entitled "Nahwa al-qimmah" (Towards the Summit) was interpreted as a criticism of the Ministry's general director, Dr. Fādil al-Jamālī (d. 1998). In this case and others, Ayyūb endeavored to explain that, in writing the story, he had no specific person in mind. In the second edition of his novel *Duktūr Ibrāhīm* (1939; reprinted 1960), he returns to the topic, declaring on the back cover of the second edition that: "This narrative biography is not aimed at any specific person, but rather at a large group both in our country and elsewhere. It describes what I call contemporary or intellectual opportunism." He continues:

Some people have tried to link this criticism to Dr. Fādil al-Jamālī, but I have denied that previously and I do so again now; nor do I do so out of fear, since he is now in prison under a sentence of death.

All that said however, his collection, *Rusul al-thaqāfah*, does contain a story like "al-Bek al-muthaqqaf" (The Educated Dignitary), that depicts a decent official who only manages to obtain advancement when he resorts to nepotism through an influential uncle. *Burj Bābil* also contains social tracts that deal with corruption and the political scene in Iraq in the 1930s. His collection, *al-Dahāyā* (Victims) explores the status of women and criticizes both the social conditions that lie behind prostitution and enforced marriages. His other 1938 collection, *Wahy al-fann* (Inspired by Art), highlights the role of the artist in exposing social evils.

Ayyūb's short story, "Fī qāʿidat al-Burj" (The Pillar of the Tower of Babel), takes as its topic Dr. Ibrāhīm, an Iraqi who returns from study at London University and uses every possible means to obtain a position that would not be open to him by normal means. Returning to his homeland during a period of political transition, "he was," as the narrator tells us, "an active member of the Young Men's Muslim association, because he was a Muslim who was zealous on behalf of his religion; of the Young Men's Christian Association because his wife was a religious Englishwoman; of the Society of Freemasons, because he was a man of high moral principles; and of the Muthannā ibn Harithah al-Shaybānī Club, because he was a staunch nationalist." ("The Pillar of the Tower of Babel," 6). The narrator adds: "He bitterly attacked the Shiʿites and, when in the company of Sunnis, dubbed them 'foreigners' so as to win the trust of his party, while with communists he confessed that as a student he had been a communist." If somebody questioned his opportunism, he had an answer: "That was the way the Heir Apparent of Great Britain had behaved." The hybrid intellectual returns with an opportunist mind, the narrative tells us, and yet it is a mind that fits a circumstance in which the major players have no connection with the public. Landlords, officers, and prominent officials fight to consolidate their interests, while genuine political engagements are put aside.

This particular short story was to become the impetus for Ayyūb's lengthy novel, *al-Duktūr Ibrāhīm* (1939). In it we learn that the protagonist's father has made a fortune by claiming he was a descendant of the Prophet's family. Chance has led him to discover the tomb of a saint, with a sharp blade and a green piece of cloth hidden there. These have become the symbols whereby he has managed to legitimize his succession as the custodian for the tomb. Nature has helped him, too, by turning that year into one of rain and fertility and thus a sign of

his blessed presence in the village community. All this is narrated with an ironic touch, since, following the son's return after getting his doctoral degree from London University, he turns out as the novel's protagonist to be the craftiest of villains in the emerging Iraqi elite. In his particular case, acculturation is of little help. As in the earlier story, this "hybrid" intellectual finds himself operating amid Baghdad's elite, presumably a reference to the renowned nationalist club, *Nādī al-muthannā*, whose members were then advocating the cause of Arabism, the unification of all Arabs, a cause to be forwarded through a vanguard party or club whose membership would be based on purity of blood. "But as I have indicated before," he says, "my father is of a Persian extraction and my wife is English. When the club was established and members began to carry out their program, I became afraid." (2nd ed. [1960], 184-185). He continues: "Origin and marriage were to be my weakest points and exposed me to attacks. But my fears were soon dissipated when I noticed that all the grand officials were not Arabs; the ones whose fathers held high positions in the Ottoman administration belonged to the club and were even more devoted to the idea of purity of blood than others of pure Arab descent. With that in mind, I requested membership and initiated my career serving the nationalist cause."

The author's message in this novel is clear enough: The elite who ruled Iraq during the post-Ottoman colonial period were intent on developing a particular ideological framework and the preservation of elitism and power through a systematic displacement of others. In the already mentioned story, "Muʾāmarat al-aghbiyāʾ," he notes how dismayed he was to discover that ideological terms were being randomly used to satisfy the interest of the few people in power, regardless of the various socialist, nationalist, populist, and other slogans that were being bandied about. He goes on to explain how he intends to publish series of articles in order to expose corruption, an endeavor which led him to write his stories and novels. When asked by the Lebanese monthly, *al-Ādāb* (N. 2, February 1954, 9), for his thoughts about his own writings, he replied:

"Let's start with the motive: I should say it was a social one....For me it seemed only natural to write down my emotions, impressions, aspirations, and opinions in a narrative style that would edify and entertain. My stories do not deal with specific persons, but rather types and common conditions."

In each of his collections, as well as the novellas and novels, he tends to depict a particular thematic pattern or concern. In the 1930s and early 1940s his works were so popular that different political factions used to exploit his narratives, with their bold critiques of the misuse of power, corruption, and maltreatment of women, in order to indict individuals and institutions. This caused him serious trouble, not only with senior officials in the Ministry of Education (as noted earlier), journalists, and the Iraqi Communist Party, but also with the various political groupings that burgeoned during that period. Hence, as the war was drawing to an end he decided to give up his job. In 1944 he embarked on a private project, a kind of agricultural co-operative, but after just three years it closed with a loss of money and much disappointment.

While most of his representations of social or political evil were portrayed in a direct fashion, some of the stories adopt a more allegorical approach, such as those included in his collection, *al-'Aql fī miḥnah* (The Mind in Trouble, 1940). In one story, "Masra' al-'Aql" (The Slaughter of Reason), a brilliant doctor is accused of holding liberal ideas and believing in leftist ideology or western sciences. One day he decides to show the regime and its ultra-conservative entourage that he has manufactured a medicine that can eradicate a person's will and transform him/her into a machine that will accept orders and become a subservient tool. The regime and its powerful figures are overjoyed by this discovery, and the doctor is no longer harassed.

Ayyūb may well have derived a new sense of purpose from the 1948 popular uprising (*al-Wathbah*) against the Portsmouth Treaty, a pact that was intended to tie Iraq more closely to British interests. His early disappointments with political parties were forgotten, as was his disenchantment following the failure of his agricultural project. He nominated himself for parliament as representative of his hometown Mosul, but lost the campaign by just two votes. The year 1948 had served to give him a sense of closer contact with people, a feeling that was to be amply illustrated by the focus of his novel *al-Yad wa'l-ard wa'l-mā'* (Manpower-Hands, Land, and Water, 1948), which explores the ways in which corruption affects the social and economic life of the country and particularly its peasants. Dismayed by the government's pandering to the interests of influential landlords, he decided to write an expose of the feudal system and its devastating impact on the country. The novel depicts a number of educated people who are placed in charge of a project aimed at presenting the ideal model for agricultural cultivation. The protagonists put their money and energy into a project about which they know very little, one that forces them to confront actual circumstances and social demands in the countryside, but it fails as, of course, had Ayyūb's own agricultural project). In the novel scathing criticism is directed against both landlords and their subordinates in the state administration.

In 1950 he published his next collection of stories, *Qulūb zam'ā* (Yearning Hearts), one that retains a lingering recollection of the 1948 uprising. However, while the political dimension is still present, there is also a romantic side. He concentrates on individuals who, like the writer himself, found themselves facing hard times. The ten stories in the collection all focus in one way or another on thirst, whether for justice, love, freedom, or even vengeance, and seek to reveal the discrepancies between what educated minds aspire to and the realities of emotion and passion. While this collection tries to capture the personal side of life in the period following the 1948 uprising, the next one, *Suwar shattā* (Scattered Impressions, 1954), shows a mixture of concerns. Some such as "Fatat al-Jisr" (The Young Girl at the Bridge) have a very realistic background. It tells the story of the way in which a famous heroine in 1948 defies the police shooting at demonstrators crossing the Martyrs' Bridge by marching at the very head of their procession. However, the general historical context of this collection is the October 1952 uprising. Stories like "Sayd al-Bashar" (Hunting Humans) concentrates on oil companies and their abuse of natural resources and local populations, while "Kābūs" (Nightmare) seeks to expose the terms of the military pact with the British authorities.

In 1954 Ayyūb was nominated for parliament and won a seat as representative of the National Front that consisted of a number of anti-colonialist political groups; he thus became one of the twelve representatives whom the Front was able to get approved after an intense upsurge of public opinion against the regime. However, the government was equally intent on signing another treaty that would further link Iraq to Anglo-American interests, a policy implemented through the Baghdad Pact of 1955, which did indeed tie Iraq to Britain. Parliament was dissolved, and a new era of repression began. Soon afterwards Ayyūb left Iraq and settled in Vienna for four years.

This 1954 collection also reveals something else. Ayyūb had become increasingly unhappy with the attitude of certain story-writers who started criticizing his social and political narratives and making disadvantageous comparisons with stories by Western and Egyptian writers. ʿAbd al-Malik Nūrī (b. 1921), the renowned Iraqi writer of short stories, wrote an article, "Suwar khāṭifah min hayātinā al-adabiyyah" (Passing Images from our Literary Life)— published in *Akhbār al-sāʿah* weekly (n. 24, 2 April 1953), in which he first admits to being no less impressed by Ayyūb's stories than those of the rest of his generation and says that he was much influenced by Ayyūb and his commitment to social and political issues. However, he then goes on to note that it was only later that it occurred to him that Ayyūb had never dealt with the more profound aspects of his characters' minds, their intimate feelings and obsessions. Fuʾād al-Takarlī (b. 1927), another famous Iraqi writer of fiction and also a friend of Nūrī, echoes the same opinions in "al-Qiṣṣah al-ʿIrāqiyyah waʾl-Duktūr Idrīs" (The Iraqi Short Story and Doctor Suhayl Idrīs), an article published in *al-Usbūʿ* weekly (N. 20, 15 May 1953, 28-29), in which he comments on an essay by Suhayl Idrīs, the editor of the Lebanese journal *al-Ādāb*. Al-

Takarlī is equally critical of Ayyūb's tendency to write narratives as social and political tracts, with no effort to delve into the psychological depth of each character. Ayyūb was offended by the comments in Nūrī's article and published a poem poking fun at Nūrī that was published as an epigraph to a short story, "Thawrat al-ʿAbīd" (The Slaves' Revolt) that was in fact dedicated to Nūrī (*Akhbār al-Sāʿah* Weekly, N. 79, June 1954).

The Vienna years brought new life and color to Ayyūb's writing. It was there that he wrote his novella *al-Rasāʾil al-Mansiyyah* (Letters in Oblivion or Forgotten Letters) and another collection of stories, *Qisas min Vienna* (Stories from Vienna, 1957). Ayyūb tells us that he wrote the novella in 1955. While it thematically linked to a number of his more romantic stories, and especially the ones in his collection, *Qulūb Zamʾā* (Yearning Hearts, 1950), there is also a clear difference of tone, one that enables the reader to see this novella as being more in tune with existentialist writings that were very much in vogue among Arab intellectuals at the time. The male protagonist is introduced as someone in love and uncertain about his life, career, and expectations. He loves a woman whom we are only able to envisage through the perspectives and responses emerging from his own letters. She is not given a voice of her own, but we are made aware of her position, aspirations, likes and dislikes. The man claims that he is not exactly in love with her, nor is he happy with their marriage later on. He finds it binding and restrictive, and suggests an alternative arrangement whereby each of them will respect the desires and whims of the other. Both partners have the right to love and live as they wish, but we learn that the woman is unhappy with the arrangement. In the third section of the letters, he becomes more passionate, since he finds in her letters a life and warmth which he lacks in the isolated town where he works. This passion survives just as long as the physical separation lasts, but, no sooner are they together again than he starts musing about his sense of ennui and fatigue. For him love is merely a physical passion, something that can vanish the moment there are other women in his life. The novel concludes with an inevitable separation.

Ayyūb's quest for a haven in later life led him to discover such a sense in Vienna, something made abundantly clear by his collection, *Qisas min Vienna*. In his story "Jadīd tahta al-shams" (New Under the Sun), the protagonist admires everyone around him. He comes upon a young woman who appeals to him so much that he decides to settle in the city. In this story, as in a number of others in this collection, Ayyūb develops a more nuanced approach to the portrayal of women, one with more awareness and depth to it. Other stories in the collection deal with suffering, oppression, and loss, but Vienna manages to put its stamp on everything, and the particular place brings with it a more sophisticated view of life.

For almost the next ten years, no further novels or stories are published, and yet this period of personal experience and meditation materializes in later writings that focus more closely on his personal life. In his novel *Abū Hurayrah wa-Kujka: qissat madīnatayn* (1977; reissued as *Abū Hurayrah wa-Kujka: riwāyah* [The Transmitter Abū Hurayrah and the She-cat: A Novel, 1995]), Ayyub nicknames himself "Abū Hurayrah" (literally, "father of the cat"). While the she-cat (or Kujka) of the title is a reference to his wife, he himself is Abū Hurayrah, someone who happens to be a transmitter of traditions as is the case with his renowned forebear, Abū Hurayrah, the Prophet Muhammad's companion and transmitter of traditions (who was given his nickname because of his fondness for his cat).

In summary, we can say that Dhū 'l-Nūn Ayyūb was never accorded the recognition that he deserved, even though his early writings and their appeal to political parties had a considerable impact. His commitment to social and political issues and his outspokenness caused him considerable difficulties and certainly led many partisan intellectuals to criticize his works. On the other hand, the second phase of his career—the 1940s—coincided with an increasing

attention to the quality of art and a concomitant interest in more nuanced psychological approaches rather than statements of direct social or political protest. Both attitudes exacerbated his sense of disappointment, something that ironically was alleviated during his exile by his new family life and his emerging interest in themes of passion and love about which he could express himself more freely, employing his customary naturalist bent that demanded no obligations other than to one's own feelings and needs. On the other hand, his early writings, such as *Duktūr Ibrāhīm*, have been more favorably received in recent times as a result of an increasing interest in postcolonial theory (as shown in Muhsin al-Musawi's book *The Postcolonial Arabic Novel* [2003]). His works certainly deserve more critical attention, since historians and critics will find in them the materials needed in order to assess their readings of Iraqi society and politics.

REFERENCES

'Abd al-Ilāh Ahmad, *Nash'at al-qissah wa-tatawwuruhā fī 'l-'Irāq, 1908-1939* (Baghdad: Matba'at Shafīq, 1969);

——, *al-Adab al-qasasī fī 'l-'Irāq mundhu 'l-harb al-'ālamiyyah al-thāniyah*, 2 vols. (Baghdad: Wizārat al-I'lām, 1977);

'Abd al-Qādir Hasan Amīn, *al-Qasas fī 'l-adab al-'irāqī al-hadīth* (Baghdad: Dār al-Ma'ārif, 1956);

'Azīz Hājj, *Abū Hurayrah al-Mawsilī: Dhū 'l-Nūn Ayyūb wa-sīratuh* (London: Riyad al-Rayyis, 1990);

Yūsuf 'Izz al-Dīn, *al-Riwāyah fī 'l-'Irāq* (Cairo: ALECSO [Arab League Education, Culture, and Science Organization], 1973);

Muhsin J. al-Musawi, *The Postcolonial Arabic Novel* (Leiden: E. J. Brill, 2003; reprinted 2005).

Samīrah ʿAzzām

(1927 – 1967)

IBRAHIM TAHA
University of Haifa

WORKS

Ashyā' saghīrah ("Little Things", Beirut: Dār al-ʿIlm li'l-Malāyīn, 1954);

al-Zill al-kabīr ("The Great Shadow", Beirut: Dār al-Sharq al-Jadīd, 1956);

Wa-qisas ukhrā ("And Other Stories", Beirut: Dār al-Talīʿah, 1960);

al-Sāʿah wa'l-insān ("The Clock and the Man", Beirut: al-Muʾassasah al-Ahliyyah, 1963);

al-ʿĪd min al-nāfidhah al-gharbiyyah ("The Festival from the West Window", Beirut: Dār al-ʿAwdah, 1971);

Asdāʾ ("Echoes", Beirut: Bīsān li'l-Nashr wa'l-Tawzīʿ, 1997); collected and introduced by Saqr Abū Fakhr.

Works in Translation

"Still Another Year" (ʿĀm Ākhar), from her second collection *al-Zill al-kabīr* ("The Great Shadow"), in: *Arabic Writing Today: The Short Story*, ed. Mahmoud Manzalaoui (Cairo: American Research Center in Egypt, 1968), 297-303;

"A Palestinian" (Filastīnī), from her fourth collection *al-Sāʿah wa'l-Insān* ("The Clock and the Man"), in: *A Land of Stone and Theme: Anthology of Palestinian Short Stories*, ed. Nur and Abdel-Wahab Elmessiri (London: Quartet Books, 1996), 99-105;

"The Man and the Clock" (al-Sāʿah wa'l-Insān), from her fourth collection *al-Sāʿah wa'l-insān* ("The Clock and the Man"), in: *Modern Arabic Short Stories: An Anthology in Translation*, ed. and transl. Shojaa al-Anni, N. Viswanathan, and Hammed S. Muhsin (India: Emerald Publishers, 1986), 1-7;

"Bread of Sacrifice" (Khubz al-fidāʾ), from her third collection entitled *Wa-qisas ukhrā* ("And Other Stories"), in: *Anthology of Modern Palestinian Literature*, ed. Salma Khadra Jayyusi (New York: Columbia University Press, 1992), 389-399;

"Tears for Sale" (*Dumūʿ li'l-bayʿ*), from her second collection *al-Zill al-kabīr* ("The Great Shadow"), in: *An Arab Mosaic: Short Stories by Arab Women Writers*, transl. Dalya Cohen-Mor (Potomac, MD: Sheba Press, 1993), 33-39; also in: *Modern Arabic Fiction: An Anthology*, ed. Salma Khadra Jayyusi (New York: Columbia University Press, 2005).

Translations by the Author

Kāndīdā ("Candida: A Pleasant Play", Beirut: Dār al-ʿIlm li'l-Malāyīn, 1955); a play by Bernard Shaw, first published in 1926;

Janāh al-nisāʾ ("Pavilion of Women", Beirut: al-Muʾassasah al-Ahliyyah, 1956); a novel by Pearl S. Buck;

Rīh al-sharq wa-rīh al-gharb ("East Wind, West Wind", Beirut: al-Muʾassasah al-Ahliyyah, 1958); by Pearl S. Buck;

Amrīkī fī awrūpā ("An American in Europe", Beirut: al-Muʾassasah al-Ahliyyah, 1959); by Sinclair Lewis; translated together with Marwān al-Jābirī;

al-Qissah al-qasīrah fī Amrīkā ("The Short Story in America", Beirut: Dār Sādir, 1961); by Ray B. West;

Kayf tusāʿid abnāʾak fī 'l-madrasah ("How to Help your Children in School", Beirut: Maktabat al-Maʿārif, 1961); by Mary Frank and K. Laurence;

Hīna faqadnā al-sabr ("When We Lost Patience", Beirut: Dār al-Talīʿah, 1962); by John Steinbeck;

al-Qissah al-amrīkiyyah al-qasīrah ("The American Short Story", Beirut: al-Maktabah al-Ahliyyah, 1962); by Danforth Ruse;

Tūmās Wūlf: Mukhtārāt min fannihi al-qasasī ("Thomas Wolfe: A selection of his short stories", Beirut: Dār Majallat Shiʿr, 1962);

Hikāyāt al-abtāl ("Heroes' Tales", Beirut: al-

Muʾassasah al-Ahliyyah, 1963); by Alice Isabel Heseltine;

ʿAsr al-barāʾah ("The Age of Innocence", Beirut: al-Muʾassasah al-Wataniyyah, 1963); by Edith Wharton;

Fann al-tilifizyūn ("Art of Television", Beirut: al-Dār al-Sharqiyyah liʾl-Tibāʿah, 1964); by William Kaufman;

ʿAshr qisas li-Somerset Mūm ("Ten Stories by Somerset Maugham", Beirut: n.d.).

Samīra ʿAzzām played a significant role in the Palestinian fiction of the mid-20th century, in general, and in the modern Palestinian short story in particular. "There is no dispute about the fact that Samīrah ʿAzzām is the pioneer of the modern Palestinian story" (Abū Bakr, 1985: 5). Her literary contribution can be found on two different levels: original literary writing and literary translation. From an early age, Samīrah ʿAzzām showed a great interest in pieces from world literature, some of which she translated into Arabic. Being fluent in English, ʿAzzām greatly benefited from reading pieces of Western narrative fiction in their original language and used this skill to her advantage to improve her own short stories. Most of her works are assembled in books, while others are scattered throughout various journals.

Her brief life can be subdivided into three major phases: her childhood and youth in Acre (1927-1948); her life in the Diaspora, moving from one place to another (1948-1959); and her settling in Lebanon and her death (1959-1967).

Born on September 13, 1927 to an Orthodox family in north Palestine in Acre (a historical city with a Mediterranean Sea shore), she spent her childhood and the first chapter of her youth in Acre. After attending a local elementary school she received part of her secondary education in Haifa. Owing to her skill and talent, she was appointed as a schoolteacher at a girls' school in Acre in 1943 at the age of 16. Two years later, in 1945, she was promoted to a principal at the same school. It was then that ʿAzzām started to publish her first literary works, under the pen-name "Fatāt al-sāhil" (The Seashore Young Girl), in *Filastīn*, a well-known newspaper published in Jaffa (1911-1967).

After the first chapter of her life, ʿAzzām started her life in the Diaspora, moving about eight times, mainly from Lebanon to Iraq and vice versa, over a period of 19 years (1948-1967). In 1948, when Jewish militias started to conduct military actions that forced many Palestinians to leave their homeland, she fled the country, heading with her family to Lebanon. Almost every two years thereafter, she moved from state to state, reflecting the confused life of a woman who could not find a suitable place in which to settle down. After a short while, she left Lebanon for Iraq, where she spent about two years teaching at a girls' school. In 1950, she returned to Lebanon, where she spent two years writing short stories for publication in two journals, *al-Ādāb* and *al-Adīb*, as well as translating many Western literary works into Arabic.

Two years later, in 1952, she left Lebanon for the second time to go to Cyprus, where she worked in broadcasting in the Near East Radio. At the same time, ʿAzzām continued translating and publishing her own short stories in the same Lebanese journals. Two years later, in 1954, she again returned to Lebanon, where she spent some three years working in broadcasting and publishing two collections of short stories. The first collection of short stories was entitled *Ashyāʾ saghīrah* (Little Things, 1954), and the second one *al-Zill al-kabīr* (The Great Shadow, 1956).

In 1957, three years later, she left for Iraq for the second time to work in Iraqi radio. There she met Adīb Yūsuf Husn, a young Palestinian man originally from Nazareth. They traveled back to Beirut to get married before returning to Iraq for the third time. In Iraq, ʿAzzām welcomed the Iraqi revolution headed by Abd al-Karīm Qāsim in 1958. In the same year, ʿAzzām accepted a proposal to work in the radio controlled by the revolution leadership. However, in 1959, just one year later, she received notification ordering her to leave Iraq because of her oppositional attitude to ʿAbd al-Karīm Qāsim's regime. It is worth mentioning that ʿAzzām's relationships with the Iraqi pioneering poets, Badr Shākir al-Sayyāb and Nāzik al-Malāʾikah, became very close during the years from 1957-1959.

In 1959, she was compelled to return to Lebanon, where she got a job in Franklin, a translation and publishing house. In Lebanon, 'Azzām accelerated her literary writing and publishing of her short stories. She published two collections of short stories: *Wa-qisas ukhrā* (And Other Stories, 1960), and *al-Sā'ah wa'l-insān* (The Clock and the Man, 1963). At this time, 'Azzām began to write her novel, entitled *Sīnā' bi-lā hudūd* (Sinai without Borders), but was unable to complete it due to the outbreak of the 1967 war. Shocked by the total defeat of this war, 'Azzām attempted in August 1967 to go back to Palestine through Jordan, where she died from a heart attack in east Jordan at 40 years of age.

'Azzām's literary work may be subdivided into into two stages: firstly, texts written in Acre prior to 1948 (before leaving her homeland); secondly, texts written from 1948-1967 (from the day she fled Acre for Lebanon until her death). These two major stages of her literary activity parallel her life in her homeland and in the Diaspora.

In the first stage, 'Azzām mainly published short sentimental and romantic texts and stories in the newspaper *Filastīn*. *Asdā'*, the sixth collection of short stories assembled and introduced by Saqr Abū Fakhr, presented stories and other pieces written from 1945-1950 that had never previously been published. The collection was published on the thirtieth anniversary of her death in 1997. If these stories and other pieces had never been published previously, as Abū Fakhr maintains in his introduction to the collection (p. 12), that would seem to imply that there are many other texts and stories published by 'Azzām in *Filastīn* that could not be obtained and still need to be collected. However, many of the texts and stories published in *Asdā'* give us a clear picture of the themes and styles she was using in the pre-1948 stories.

It is worth mentioning that some of these texts recall the romantic themes and styles that Jubrān Khalīl **Jubrān** (1883-1931) had employed some two decades earlier. Looking closely at 'Azzām's texts written before 1948, we get the clear impression that 'Azzām imitated many texts published by Jubrān in various collections. 'Azzām refers to roses, the good earth, Jesus, different types of people, happiness, artists, bells, and other romantic themes and values, all couched in a figurative language with which we are so familiar from Jubrān's literary works.

In the second stage of her literary activity, 'Azzām wrote and published her more sophisticated short stories. In *Ashyā' saghīrah* (1954), 'Azzām showed a particular interest in women's affairs, status, and relationships with men, but surprisingly showed no interest in the Palestinian question. In addition to female subjects, this collection deals with social and human tragedies in which characters become anti-heroes facing serious problems with no apparent means of escape.

In her second collection of short stories, *al-Zill al-kabīr* (1956), 'Azzām examines all three topics mentioned above. Accurately speaking, only two stories refer to political themes associated with the Palestinian problem, while the other ten stories deal with different types of figures in a social respect, focusing primarily on women's issues. Moving from a romantic point of view in *Ashyā' saghīrah* to a more realistic one in *al-Zill al-kabīr*, 'Azzām shows a greater sophistication in her characterization, plot formation, and modes of closure. The third collection, *Wa-qisas ukhrā* (1960), deals with themes similar to those in the previous collection, as is apparent from the title. This collection includes 17 short stories, with 10 focusing on women's issues and the other stories addressing social problems and obstacles faced by Palestinians in the Diaspora.

In her fourth collection, *al-Sā'ah wa'l-insān*, 'Azzām tried her hand, for the first time in her literary career, at writing very short stories, a new experimental genre or at least sub-genre. Six out of the 14 stories in the collection are "short, short," as she herself calls them. Those short-short stories consist of about 500-600 words and have no specific title; instead there is a comprehensive and general title covering all of them: *qasīrah ... qasīrah*. Thematically, 'Azzām continues to focus in these 14 short and very short stories on the same topics, namely female, social, and political/national issues. "Filastīnī" (A Palestinian), for example, describes the terrible lives of Palestinians refugees in their camps in Lebanon. In such hostile societies, a Lebanese ID seems to some Palestinian refugees the only way of improving their everyday life in exile. In the following paragraph, the narrator emphasizes two points: the humiliating processes that Palestinian refugees have to endure in order to get Lebanese IDs, and the severe conditions and sarcastic treatment they expect to suffer if they fail to obtain those same IDs:

It was too much [two thousand liras for a Lebanese ID]... *Some years ago he had balked at paying a quarter of this amount* [*two thousand liras*] *to unearth a grandfather from a good Lebanese village or to resurrect a whole new history of his grandfather, Abu Saleh, who, as far as he knew, had been born had died, again as far as he knew, in al-Ramah. He had not quite denied him three times before the cock crew, but rather had asked his permission to make use of a geographical coincidence which would exempt him from the word 'Palestinian', a word which linked him to a breed in whom all signs of individuality had been wiped out. The word is uttered pityingly, but he refuses to be an object of pity* [...]. *A cloud of anxiety made him feel as if he, his shop, his four children and his wife were mere playthings to be trifled with by those interpreters of events. His only guarantee against the unknown of multiple deportation was for him to become naturalized. The incentive* [*to obtain a Lebanese ID*] *would* [...] *become stronger whenever something occurred to shake up his crumbling existence.*

(El-Messiri, 1996: 101-102)

In contrast with the previous collections, the fifth, *al-'Īd min al-nāfidhah al-gharbiyyah*, shows no noticeable changes on either thematic or aesthetic levels. It includes 12 short stories and 25 texts/fragments dealing with labor and national values, assembled under one title *Wujdāniyyāt Filastīniyyah*. These fragments seem to have been written immediately after 'Azzām left Acre in 1948, which would explain the presence of so many expressions of sentiments, dreams, longing, and nostalgia for Acre, where she was born and spent half of her short life.

'Azzām published most of her short stories in the Lebanese journals *al-Adīb* and *al-Ādāb* from 1951 to 1966 prior to their being assembled into books by herself and others. She also translated

many short stories from English into Arabic and published them in the *al-Adīb* journal from 1950 to 1954. It is worth mentioning that most of 'Azzām's original and translated short stories were originally published in *al-Adīb*, while only a few were published in *al-Ādāb*. As already noted, 'Azzām also published most of her early work in the newspaper, *Filastīn*. At a later stage, she also published several of her works in *al-Sha'b*, an Iraqi newspaper, and in the Lebanese journals *Sawt al-Mar'ah* (The Woman's Voice) and *Dunyā al-Mar'ah* (The Woman's World).

In total, about 96 literary pieces by 'Azzām are known to have been published: about 85 short stories; eight romantic/sentimental texts; one short play "'Indamā tamrad al-nisā'" (When Wives Get Sick); a prose-poem "'Afwan ayyatuhā al-ajrās" (Sorry, Bells!); and a single chapter of an incomplete novel. One has also to assume that there are a few additional texts that were published here and there in various journals and newspapers.

'Azzām's literary works deal in the main with three major topics: women's issues, social problems, and the Palestinian question. Those that treat women's issues account for almost 50 percent of 'Azzām's total literary work. 'Azzām was the first Palestinian writer to take a leadership role in "women's literature" by focusing on various generations of female characters and the social and economic roles they played in society. Hanān 'Awwād classifies the positions of these female characters into four categories: early stage of ripe femininity, stage of marriage, late stage of femininity, and motherhood (see 'Awwād, 1987: 55-57). In all of these categories, the female characters seem to be explicitly scared, victimized, isolated, and unable to find the appropriate and most direct way of attaining fulfillment. This may explain why female characters in 'Azzām's stories manifest a sincere fear of being a female with particular needs (Misbāh, 2000: 123). In her analysis of female characters in 'Azzām's literary work, 'Awwād rejects the notion that motherhood is the only role/status that women need in order to keep their fear under control, as argued by 'Azzām herself. Despite the fact that 'Azzām is not considered as a feminist writer in the modern sense, she undoubtedly laid the foundation for Palestinian women's literature in modern times.

The second topic, that of social problems, finds ʿAzzām focusing mostly on poor and marginalized characters. By so doing, ʿAzzām transfers them from the margins to the center; turning them into major characters, she puts them at the top of the agenda of the collective consciousness. Many of these characters are young boys compelled by severe circumstances of poverty and marginality to go begging in the streets and, at the very best, to sell newspapers. All of these characters are used by ʿAzzām to illustrate life under the shadow of "otherness," represented by various types of outsider figures.

ʿAzzām uses the third topic, that of the Palestine issue, to shed light on three interconnected stages of the question. She provides descriptions of Palestinians compelled to leave their homeland for the Diaspora, recalling many heroic cases of resistance from the past and considering a series of practical acts of resistance (Tāhā, 2004: 143). It may seem surprising that fewer than ten of her stories directly address the Palestinian problem, and yet they play a key role in reshaping the Palestinian identity of the characters presented in her literary work (Abū Bakr, 1985: 71-82).

Most students emphasize the realistic approach that ʿAzzām adopted as the foundation of her short stories. This approach applies to characters, events, and circumstances that reliably portray her immediate surroundings and environment. In her paper "Dawr al-adab fī maʿrakat Filastīn" (The Role of Literature in the Battle for Palestine, Tāhā, 2004: 199-204), ʿAzzām urges Palestinian writers to associate themselves with Palestinian disaster of 1948 ("al-Nakbah"), that is, to be in daily contact with common people who have to conduct their miserable lives in refugee camps. In that way they will become fully engaged with their reality and clearly relate to their problems. Having personally experienced the terrible life of Palestinian refugees in refugee camps in Lebanon, ʿAzzām retained in her mind many images of severe poverty and death, which she later reconstructed through many of the characters and textual realities in her stories.

Most of ʿAzzām's stories end with sarcastic closures and pessimistic destinies, in which major characters arrive at an unavoidable death. In her literary work, she reflects the trauma of being compelled to leave her homeland where she was settled with her family in peace, as well as the reality of refugee camps, through the repeated use of similar marginal characters addressing the same concerns, problems and dreams.

Students of ʿAzzām's translations distinguish two stages of this activity: 1950-1954 when she translated nine short stories from English into Arabic and published them in *al-Adīb* (a period that served as a practice stage in which she only translated shorter texts); and 1955-1964, when she translated and published 13 books from English into Arabic, many of them literary masterpieces by well-known writers, including Shaw, Pearl S. Buck, Pushkin, Chekhov, Sinclair Lewis, Tolstoy, and Oscar Wilde.

In addition to literary texts, ʿAzzām translated two books of literary criticism dealing with the American short story, from which ʿAzzām greatly benefited in improving her own literary skills.

With her particular interest in Western narrative fiction, ʿAzzām apparently sought to adapt new styles, modes, and literary yardsticks as a way of establishing new trends in Palestinian fiction. ʿAzzām was also interested in topics such as media and communication, education, and psychology. In particular, she attributed considerable significance to subjects related to the education of future generations and to the role of media and journalism in the "battle for Palestine."

In a paper delivered in the fifth conference of Arab writers held in Baghdad in February 1965, ʿAzzām presented her views on literature and its role in the Palestinian problem. ʿAzzām adopted the phrase "an unavoidable battle" *(maʿrakah)* as a way of referring to the fate of the Palestinian people in 1948, rather than calling it "an issue" *(qadiyyah)*. She was convinced that, if Palestinian people had a sincere wish for life, they had no choice but to carry out this mission of "an unavoidable battle" (Tāhā, 2004: 199). Along the lines of her distinction between *maʿ-*

rakah and *qadiyyah*, she further discriminates between *maʿrakah* and *nakbah*. While *nakbah* demands an emotional reaction, she says, *maʿ-rakah* "requires a comprehensive sense and a foreshadowing approach" in order for literature to deal with it not only emotionally, but also mentally. She is thus challenging Palestinian writers to move from a depiction of weeping victims to that of real fighters. This goal can only be achieved if Palestinian and Arab writers relate at the profoundest level to the Palestinian *nakbah* and its consequences; by becoming involved, for instance, in the life of Palestinians in refugee camps. They need to focus on the whole picture of the Palestinian people, rather than on the individual behavior of some Palestinians; they should be involving themselves in the Palestinian problem on a daily basis and not merely on specific occasions.

Thus, ʿAzzām attributed extreme significance to the engagement of writers in reality. According to her, writers should reflect collective feelings so as to guide politicians in formulating guidelines for their policies and choosing the right political battles. It was her belief that a collective effort was needed to initiate a comprehensive, conceptual, and spiritual mobilization which would address the threat that was shaking the very foundation of "the Arab being." She went on to suggest a series of steps to achieve such a mobilization: rewarding writers—Palestinians, Arabs, and foreigners—with different categories of support and employing all types of available media, including newspapers, journals, television, and cinema (Tāhā, 2004: 199-204).

ʿAzzām made a major contribution to modern Palestinian literature. She believed strongly in the power of words and in their key role in human existence, something that is particularly cogent when a people feels threatened and is deeply engaged in an endless struggle for fundamental rights and needs.

It is important to bear in mind that many of her earliest texts remain unpublished and indeed perhaps unknown. Only a few of them were published by her in the newspaper *Filastīn* before 1948. Other texts, including a chapter of an incomplete novel and a paper about the role of Palestinian literature, are assembled in Tāhā's book (2004). That acknowledged however, she managed over a period of forty years to write and publish 19 books, of which 13 were translations from English in such fields as literature, literary study, education/psychology, science, and documentation. Two of her six collections of short stories (*al-ʿĪd min al-Nāfidhah al-Gharbiyyah*, 1971; *Asdāʾ*, 1997) were published after her death.

ʿAzzām's important role in the development of the short story has its beginning and ending in two extremely significant events, particularly for Palestinian people. It begins with the establishment of Israel in 1948 (the "*nakbah*"), and ends with the bitter defeat of the Arab states and the occupation of the West Bank and Gaza Strip by Israel in 1967, the "*naksah*" (setback). Contributors to Palestinian literature during this period included only four women who had any intense involvement in the development of modern Palestinian literature: Asmā Tūbī (a playwright), Fadwā Tūqān (a poet), Najwā Qaʿwār-Farah (a writer of plays and short stories), and Samīrah ʿAzzām (a writer of short stories). Compared with the other women writers, ʿAzzām was undoubtedly responsible for the largest number of books and texts to be written and published by a Palestinian woman writer. Moreover, ʿAzzām is the only one who showed an exclusive interest in narrative fiction, especially the short story. Unlike Najwā Qaʿwār-Farah, who tried two or three genres, for instance, ʿAzzām concentrated only on a single genre (Hāshim Yāghī, 1981: 215). In this respect, ʿAzzām laid the foundation for the modern Palestinian short story both thematically and aesthetically. In less than twenty years, ʿAzzām managed to write some seven collections of short stories, in addition to many other contributions to translation and cultural activities in journalism and media. I

As the first Palestinian author to focus on female affairs, ʿAzzām is rightly considered the founder of a new trend in Palestinian literature, namely, "women's literature." However, as a realistic writer, she was clearly more concerned with her fictional characters than with historical events or circumstances surrounding them. Although politically involved, she was more focused on matters of private consciousness, feelings, dreams, and individual concerns. Overall, given Samīrah ʿAzzām's belief in words, whether original or translated, and in their power to improve our individual and collective world, she apparently dedicated her life to expressing her voice through literature and translation.

REFERENCES

Walīd Abū Bakr, *Ahzān fī rabīʿ al-burtuqāl: Dirāsah fī fann Samīrah ʿAzzām al-qasasī* (Damascus and Nicosia: al-Ittihād al-ʿĀmm li'l-Kuttāb al-Filastīniyyīn and Āfāq li'l-Dirāsāt wa'l-Nashr, 1985);

Hanān ʿAwwād, "Athar al-Nakbah ʿalā adab Samīrah ʿAzzām," *al-Mawākib* 4.7-8 (1987): 50-69;

Faysal Darrāj, "Samīrah ʿAzzām: al-Bahth ʿan al-insān wa'l-akhlāq wa'l-watan", *Shuʾūn Filastīniyyah* 120 (1981): 120-141;

Yūsuf Hittīnī, *Samīrah ʿAzzām: Rāʾidat al-qissah al-filastīniyyah* (Damascus: Manshūrāt Dār al-ʿĀʾidī, 1999);

Munīrah Misbāh, *Min fadāʾ al-hulm ilā ufuq al-ihtimālāt: Nusūs tuhājir bi-'ttijāh Filastīn* (Beirut: al-Muʾassasah al-ʿArabiyyah li'l-Dirāsāt wa'l-Nashr, 2000);

Kathyanne Piselli, *A Daughter of Palestine: The Short Fiction of Samīrah ʿAzzām* (Michigan: The University of Michigan, 1986); an unpublished dissertation;

Suhayr al-Qalamāwī, "Adībah min Filastīn: Samīrah ʿAzzām", *al-Hilāl* 73.12 (1965): 170-176;

Nādirah al-Sarrāj, "Samīrah ʿAzzām fī dhikrāhā al-khāmisah: Dirāsah fī fannihā al-qasasī", *Shuʾūn Filastīniyyah* 14 (1972): 69-82;

Salāh Tāhā, *al-Kātibah al-ʿakkiyyah Samīrah ʿAzzām* (Acre: Muʾassasat al-Aswār, 2004);

George Tarābīshī, "Samīrah ʿAzzām wa'l-unūthah al-taʾīsah", *Dirāsāt ʿarabiyyah* 7.5 (1971): 88-109;

Yūsuf Sāmī al-Yūsuf, "al-Shakhsiyyah wa'l-qīmah wa'l-uslūb fī adab Samīrah ʿAzzām", *al-Fikr al-dīmūqrātī* 9-10 (1989): 300-323.

Mahmūd Sāmī al-Bārūdī
(1839 – 1904)

TERRI DeYOUNG
University of Washington, Seattle

WORKS

Mukhtārāt al-Bārūdī ("Selections by al-Bārūdī"), ed. Yaqūt al-Mursī (Cairo: Matbaʿat al-Jarīdah, 1909-1911);

Kashf al-ghummah fī madh sayyid al-ummah ("Release From Grief Through Praising the Leader of the Community", Cairo: Matbaʿat al-Jarīdah, 1909);

Dīwān al-Bārūdī ("Collected Poetry"), ed. Mahmūd al-Imām Mansūrī, 2 vols. (Cairo: Matbaʿat al-Jarīdah, 1914-15);

——, ("Collected Poetry"), ed. ʿAlī al-Jārim and Muhammad Shafīq Maʿrūf, 4 vols. (Cairo: Dār al-Maʿārif, 1940-1975);

Awrāq al-Bārūdī ("al-Bārūdī's Papers"), ed. Sāmī Badrawī (Cairo: al-Markaz al-ʿArabī li'l-Bahth wa'l-Nashr, 1981).

Translated Works

A. J. Arberry, *Arabic Poetry: A Primer for Students* (Cambridge: Cambridge University Press, 1965), 148-155;

Mounah Khouri, *Poetry and the Making of Modern Egypt* (Leiden: E. J. Brill, 1971), 7-36, *passim*;

M. M. Badawi, *A Critical Introduction to Modern Arabic Poetry* (Cambridge: Cambridge University Press, 1975), 16-29.

Mahmūd Sāmī al-Bārūdī, born in Cairo in 1839, is easily the most highly regarded and widely admired nineteenth-century Arab poet. This has been especially true in his homeland of Egypt, but there have been few rivals to his claims in other parts of the Arab world. Literary critics, colleagues and disciples have endorsed the judgment that al-Bārūdī rescued Arabic poetry from a state of exhaustion and irresolution, marked by superficiality, traditionalism and a concern with virtuosity in form to the detriment of content, into which it was seen to have fallen in the late eighteenth and early nineteenth centuries. He did this by simultaneously drawing inspiration from the works of the best poets of the pre-Islamic and early Islamic periods—the "classical tradition" in Arabic—and capitalizing upon their precedent by consistently relating it to his own experience. Al-Bārūdī was perhaps uniquely able to successfully accomplish this transformation because he was one of the most compelling and tragic individuals among the Egyptian elite of his time, who made an impact as a soldier, diplomat, politician, revolutionary, exile and finally the blind elder statesman of literature in the salons of Egyptian society as it made its transition to the modern world. Thus his experiences were closely bound up with the progress of the Egyptian nation as it developed in the nineteenth century. His work simultaneously demonstrated the relevance of the classical tradition to modern times and enhanced the stature of the poet who successfully evoked the greatness of that past. The few voices raised against the nearly universal chorus of acclaim for al-Bārūdī have only taken him to task for not differentiating his poetry radically enough from his immediate predecessors, never questioning the value or overall quality of his writing as such.

Despite the near universal praise lavished upon al-Bārūdī his poetic legacy was not particularly well served by posterity. He devoted most of his later years—spent largely in exile on the island of Ceylon—to revising his collected poems, which he was able to finish editing shortly before his death. But publication of this manuscript proceeded only in fits and starts. A hastily prepared version of the first two volumes

appeared shortly after his death in 1915. But a more authoritative redaction of the first two volumes was only made available in 1940-42. The publication of last two volumes was delayed for over thirty years more, the last volume only appearing in 1975. A truly definitive literary biography, based on archival research and interviews with surviving friends, colleagues and family, was not written until 1969. Further hitherto-unpublished poems and papers found their way into print in 1981 and there may still be materials of considerable significance that remain in manuscript or have yet to be discovered. This relative lack of critical attention, and al-Bārūdī's own unwillingness to discuss his life in writing, means that any current assessment of his career, especially in certain periods, can only be provisional.

What is clear is that he was born into a world that had been transformed out of recognition in the lifetime of his parents, who were both members of the Turkish Circassian nobility of Egypt who had come to power in the wake of the Ottoman conquest of the country in 1517. This group, in its turn displaced when Muhammad ʿAlī took over the governorship of Egypt in 1805, gradually reconciled themselves—though in many cases with ill-grace—to the revised power dynamic instituted by their new governor who sought to remake Egypt on the model of the secularized modern states emerging in Europe in the wake of the industrial revolution.

The coup de grace for the old order occurred in 1811 when their leaders were invited to an investiture ceremony at Muhammad ʿAlī's residence in the fort known as the Citadel perched in the Muqattam Hills above Cairo. At the conclusion of the formalities, the guests left the hall, moving into a narrow defile on the ramparts of which Muhammad ʿAlī had stationed a contingent of archers. All the Turko-Circassian leaders were killed in the ensuing bloodbath, including both al-Bārūdī's maternal and paternal grandfathers.

Al-Bārūdī's father, however, wasted little time lamenting the past and promptly joined the army of his new suzerain. But he and the other members of the old gentry never completely relinquished the attitude that the ruler and his descendents were dangerous upstarts, lacking in the traditions and values that made for good governance. Although al-Bārūdī, as a loyal servant of the new order, was careful never to express himself too overtly, some of this distrust of the Muhammad ʿAlī dynasty persists as an undercurrent in his poems, especially those composed after he became involved in the events leading up to the ʿUrābī Revolution in 1882.

Al-Bārūdī's father, Hasan Husnī Beğ, belonged to one of the first graduating classes from Muhammd ʿAlī's military school, where the students were educated using a modern curriculum, designed to turn them into model soldiers, which was supported by books produced on the first printing press imported into Egypt. By the time of his son's birth a decade later, however, the Viceroy's ambitious plans had been derailed by the Ottomans with their allies the English. In 1840 they compelled Muhammad ʿAlī to sign a treaty requiring him give up many of his conquests and drastically scale back his army. Hasan Husnī al-Bārūdī was then posted to one of the few remaining territories left to Muhammad ʿAlī, the Sudan, where he died of fever in 1846, when his son was only seven years old. From that point on, it was Mahmūd Sāmī's mother who took primary responsibility for the education of her son.

Given the lack of appropriate modern schools (all closed by Muhammad ʿAlī's successor ʿAbbās, with the exception of one advanced military training academy) and his status as the scion of a wealthy upper-class family, al-Bārūdī was educated at home, by tutors, until he reached adolescence and enrolled in the government's selective military academy. He nevertheless followed the curriculum laid down by Muhammad ʿAlī's first Minister of Education, Rifāʿah al-**Tahtāwī**, which included considerable exposure to the works of the great Arab poets of the past. This feature of his early study was likely crucial in forming al-Bārūdī's literary taste, because instruction at the Select Military Academy (where he was enrolled after 1851) was, with the exception of religious subjects and grammar study necessary to understand the Qurʾān, all in Turkish, and students were disciplined for using Arabic outside of the designated classes. These Turkish classes included instruction in military drill, mathematics, and drawing (for the production of maps and the architectural plans of fortifications). There was also some elementary instruction in Persian, for this was the prestige language at the Ottoman court, and Persian literature had had a profound effect on the development of Turkish after the founding of the Ottoman state. Unfortunately, surviving records give us almost no information about al-Bārūdī's personal accomplishments, triumphs and trials during his formative years at school. Only the bare fact that he graduated in 1854, the year of ʿAbbās's death by assassination and the accession of ʿAbbās's uncle Saʿīd to the throne, is recorded.

We know, if anything, even less about the years that followed. Under Saʿīd, an amiable but not very effective ruler, the army was allowed to deteriorate even further than it had under ʿAbbās. This lack of opportunity in the profession he had been trained for may have motivated al-Bārūdī to decide to leave Egypt. At any rate, he departed his homeland for Istanbul in 1857, where he found employment as a confidential secretary in the Turkish Foreign Ministry, a position that would allow him to put the skills in Arabic, Persian, and Turkish he had acquired as a student in ʿAbbās's Select Military Academy to good use. He would remain in Istanbul, working at the Ministry, until 1863.

It has been suggested that during this time he composed poetry in Turkish and Persian, but none of this verse has been preserved. Even in Arabic, the only poem that can reliably be dated to this period is an elegy he wrote for his father when, by his own admission, he was "rising twenty" (thus, most likely in 1859). Although this is the earliest dated poem included among al-Bārūdī's collected works, it already demonstrates a finely crafted control of the requirements for successful poetic composition in Arabic. It is in no way a trial or an attempt; thus suggesting that al-Bārūdī consciously chose not to preserve for posterity the evidence of his poetic apprenticeship or any traces of his juvenalia. We can only guess at the struggles and false starts that lay behind the craftsmanship of this homage to his barely remembered father, who is celebrated as an "unsung hero" who nevertheless provides a worthy model for his son and heir to emulate.

The obscurity in which al-Bārūdī had been laboring for the nearly a decade, since his graduation from the Select Military Academy, changed dramatically in 1863. This was the year when Muhammad ʿAlī's grandson Ismāʿīl, only surviving child of his eldest and ablest son Ibrā-hīm (who had unexpectedly predeceased his father by a few months in 1848), succeeded to the rule of Egypt. As his first official act, Ismāʿīl traveled to Istanbul to offer homage to the Sultan and be confirmed in his new office. While he was there, al-Bārūdī took advantage of the occasion to offer his own homage to Ismāʿīl in the form of a panegyric poem composed to honor the young ruler, and the rest, as they say, was history. Ismāʿīl was so impressed with al-Bārūdī's poetic talent that he took him into his own entourage, and by February 1863 al-Bārūdī was back in Cairo working for the Egyptian Foreign Ministry Office and frequenting Ismā-ʿīl's private social gatherings in his off-duty hours.

Interestingly, al-Bārūdī did not automatically settle into the job of chief court poet for Ismāʿīl, producing encomia of the ruler suitable for recitation on public occasions and intended to reinforce the majesty and dignity of his sovereign's accomplishments. He produced only one more major panegyric for Ismāʿīl, composed shortly after his return. Yet this second poem is far more noteworthy than the first. The earlier poem, despite its clear impact on the trajectory of al-Bārūdī's career, has struck critics as a prefabricated work, assembled from bits and pieces of the panegyric inventory of Arabic poetry. It praises Ismāʿīl, for example, at the center of the poem (the position of prominence in the traditional ode, the place where the patron's name was often mentioned directly for the first time in the composition) for a bland catalogue of traditional virtues that have little to do with specific actions undertaken by Ismāʿīl as an individual. He is "the father of glory," "the offspring of generosity," "the companion of noble deeds," who has "gathered together in himself forbearance, valor, and generosity, with no one

to compete with him in his glory." The very repetitiveness of the catalogue indicates the impoverishment of the poet's inspiration. This impression is enhanced by the very long *nasīb*, or recollection of a past love affair, which opens this first panegyric. In the hands of a skilled poet, the meditation on unfulfilled love, or desire, that forms the core of the *nasīb* can be generalized to engage aspects of the author's relationship to his patron who can—much like a beloved—grant him recognition or withhold it. Thus, the *nasīb* can be essential in establishing the tone of the whole poem. In al-Bārūdī's first panegyric to Ismāʿīl, however, the *nasīb*, while long and elaborate, is quite disconnected from the rest of the work.

These observations would not be true of the second panegyric, which assumes a quite different character. This poem does not begin with a *nasīb* at all. It commences instead with the spread of the news of Ismāʿīl's succession to the throne, a token of change comparable, in the poet's eyes, to the reception of Joseph's shirt at his father Jacob's house in the Qurʾānic story (Sūrah 12), where it brings new hope to the old man who had believed his son was dead. Since Joseph was in the Qurʾān—as he had been in the Bible—the virtual ruler of Egypt, the relevance of the allusion to Ismāʿīl is doubly reinforced. The rest of the poem is also replete with references to Egypt and examples of the ways Ismāʿīl's rule promises to return that land to its beauty and former productivity. Most noteworthy is al-Bārūdī's personification of Egypt in the center of the poem as a beautiful woman, the ultimate object of desire. This image, while not original to al-Bārūdī (it turns up occasionally in the poetry of earlier generations, including some widely disseminated efforts by Rifāʿah al-Tah-tāwī) will become a trademark of his work, and one source of the claim that al-Bārūdī is the first poet to incorporate the concept of Egypt as a nation (countries are frequently depicted as female in modern nationalist iconography), and the object of nationalistic aspirations, into his writing.

Yet, whatever the reception may have been for al-Bārūdī's second panegyric, it remained an isolated effort that was not capitalized upon. For the rest of this decade and well into the 1870s, al-Bārūdī seems to have channeled most of his energy into enjoying himself at Ismāʿīl's pleasure-loving court, which quickly became as notable for its conspicuous consumption as for its reforms. His revels are recorded in the extensive wine and love poems that survive from this period, but they are mostly conventional and forgettable works. Only occasionally do they reflect upon the deeper questions generated by a decision to abandon oneself to a life of hedonism and self-gratification—to explore the psychology of this particular form of obsession. Not surprisingly, it is difficult to date these compositions with any precision and correlate them with real events, since they all come out of one mold. Nor do the prefatory comments al-Bārūdī attached to these poems in the process of editing them for his *dīwān* give much help, being laconic in the extreme.

This routine of court life in the 1860s and early 1870s was only interrupted twice. In 1864 al-Bārūdī was selected to participate in a mission sent to observe army maneuvers in France and England. This experience, his only trip to Europe, yielded a charming hunting poem that uses language and imagery gleaned from the examples of hunting poetry composed by the great masters of this genre in Arabic to describe al-Bārūdī's visit to an English lord's country estate for a weekend of fox hunting and socializing. His evocation of the occasion, while entirely consistent with the conventions of the Arabic tradition, nevertheless achieves an exquisitely detailed reminiscence of what is unmistakably the English countryside, first at dawn, and then again at sunset as the hunt wound its way homeward, a set of tableaux whose resonance is enhanced by al-Bārūdī's decision to frame the entire event in measured references to the swift passage of time and the brevity of human existence.

On a more prosaic note, al-Bārūdī greatly enhanced his military stature following his return to Egypt by submitting a detailed and perceptive report on these maneuvers, full of recommendations for reform in the army, and he was subsequently granted a long-standing wish and was transferred to the army full time as a lieutenant colonel in November 1864. Shortly thereafter, he was promoted again, to full colonel in command of a regiment of the elite Khedival guards. At the end of 1865, he was assigned to participate in an expedition sent by the Ottoman sultan to subdue a rebellion launched by the inhabitants of the island of Crete, then under Turkish rule. Ismāʿīl, as a vassal of the Ottoman sultan, could be called upon to supply troops for the imperial army, and on this occasion he eagerly offered to meet his suzerain's needs.

Service in this expedition to Crete was the second interruption of his career at the court and his first taste of military duty. Al-Bārūdī, though only 26, acquitted himself well as a soldier, leading his troops into battle for at least one significant victory that proved the effectiveness of Ismāʿīl's new army as a fighting force, especially in comparison to the Ottoman troops, who had nearly been ousted from the island before the arrival of the Egyptian reinforcements.

But even more significantly, these experiences were recorded in poems that marked a significant departure in his poetry from his practice up to this point, and took his work to a new level of seriousness, psychological depth and engagement with the world around him, setting the stage for what was to come. Perhaps the most famous of these is the poem that begins "Slumber has taken the corners of our eyes, and night travel has shaken the reins of the horsemen," otherwise referred to as his "Nūniyyah" (in reference to the rhyme letter used at the end of each line). It begins by describing the rebels and the Egyptian army encamped side by side in mountainous terrain, awaiting the opportunity to engage in battle when dawn arrives. The topography and the darkness prevent the poet from seeing much beyond scattered points of light from the campfires, but he can hear the enemy in the distance, singing songs and making merry to the tunes of skilled musicians. He contrasts this to his own encampment, where confusion, shouting and the moans of the wounded dominate. The horses, in particular, seem restive and nervous, and he attributes this as much to their longing for Egypt as to their anticipation of the impending battle. The recollection of his homeland moves him to a long reminiscence of the beauties of Egypt and the Edenic tranquillity that reigns there, so different from his current situation. But it also reminds him that he has recently received news that a former friend, who had remained behind, is taking advantage of his absence to slander and disparage him. He comforts himself, however, with the belief that his resolution and noble heritage will allow him to prevail both against his enemies at home and those before him on the battlefield.

This poem expresses for the first time that unique blend of ancient and contemporary, of public and personal, that becomes the hallmark of al-Bārūdī's best mature work. The vocabulary belongs to the traditional poem. The setting, however, is contemporary and includes enough individualized reference and detail to keep it from becoming merely a literary restatement of precedents composed by leading poets of the past. The sections of the poem, moreover, neatly interweave in a delicately balanced parallelism.

The first section—portraying the open enemy waiting on the battlefield—is linked to the third section—depicting the secret enemy back home—through the mediation of the middle section describing Egypt. Egypt, or more precisely the memory of Egypt, motivates the sense of duty and responsibility that impels the poet to fight both enemies. Through the poet's resolve and strength of will comes the guarantee that both will be defeated. The equation of the two enemies is never explicitly stated but it lies in the background as the hidden clock-spring that determines the poet's actions and gives the poem its coherence.

Once he had returned victorious from the Cretan campaign, newly awarded the Ottoman Medal of Merit, Fourth Class, by the Sultan, al-Bārūdī to all outward appearances relapsed into his familiar persona of staunch supporter of the monarchy and dilettante man-about-town, though with more restraint than previously. This new circumspection in his behavior may have been occasioned by his marriage in the autumn of 1867 to 'Adīlah Yakan, eldest daughter of Ahmad Yakan Pasha, who had been for many years right-hand man to the dynasty, being the son of Muhammad 'Alī's sister Zubaydah. None of al-Bārūdī's love poetry can be directly linked to his

wife, and little is known from other sources about their private feelings for each other, but they had five children over the years and she stood loyally by him during his fall from power and exile. When she died in 1885, at the comparatively young age of 37, he wrote one of his most emotional and touching elegies, where his raw feelings hover close to the surface, as he mourns her loss.

His marriage to one of Ismā'īl's cousins would have brought al-Bārūdī closer to the royal inner circle than ever before, but his public appointments reinforced this intimacy. Immediately upon his return, he was named aide-de-camp to the Khedive and was thus in constant attendance at his side. In 1873, when Ismā'īl's son Tawfīq was officially named heir to the throne, al-Bārūdī was made his chief aide-de-camp and official adviser, perhaps with the idea to better prepare him for the responsibilities of his new position. From his new vantage point, al-Bārūdī had an opportunity to get to know Tawfīq well, and he seems to have believed that Tawfīq would be sympathetic to governmental reform and be less autocratic than his father. But he also saw him, as others did, as basically a weak, indecisive and timorous figure. So, perhaps it was no surprise that when he was given the opportunity in October 1875 to return to Ismā'īl's direct employ as his private secretary, he did so.

Perhaps because of his new found entrée into the private circles of the sovereign, al-Bārūdī found out very quickly after his return that all was not well with the finances of the Egyptian government. To finish the Suez Canal and finance his reforms, as well as his luxurious life-style, Ismā'īl had been compelled to contract an increasing number of loans from British and French financiers, at ruinous interest rates.

Ismā'īl's increasingly desperate shady maneuvers to service the debt and contract new loans must have filled his aide-de-camp with severe misgivings. Al-Bārūdī seems to have been particularly alarmed by Ismā'īl's increasing reliance on two ministers known for their opportunism: Ismā'īl Siddīq al-Mufattish (a childhood playmate whose mother had been the Khedive's wet nurse) and Nūbār Pasha (a clever financier of Armenian origin who had close ties to the European adventurers flooding into Egypt at that time). At any rate, al-Bārūdī composed several biting satires about the pair, which can be confidently attributed to this time period.

Other avenues were also available for expressing his disquiet. After his return from Crete, al-Bārūdī had begun to hold a regular literary gathering, or salon, at his house, attended not only by his fellow poets, but also by government ministers and intellectuals interested in reform, including a number of the 'ulamā', or traditional scholars associated with al-Azhar. It was probably through their attendance at his salon that al-Bārūdī became acquainted with some of the foremost Muslim reformers of the time, including Jamāl al-Dīn al-Afghānī and Muhammad 'Abduh, with whom he would collaborate closely in their mutual opposition to the Muhammad 'Alī dynasty's policies.

Almost certainly for the consumption of this group, al-Bārūdī composed a poem in 1868 (usually known as his "'Ayniyyah," because of its rhyme letter 'ayn) that capitalized on the skills he had honed in his panegyrics to Ismā'īl and in his war poetry during the Cretan campaign, but would depart radically from them in its condemnation of the monarchy and its call to the people of Egypt to rise up in a revolution against it. Such an appeal, to the people to stand up against the tyranny of their own rulers and exercise sovereign power themselves, had never been made in quite this form in an Arabic poem before. It was all the more unexpected, because in his Cretan "Nūniyyah" al-Bārūdī had condemned the inhabitants of the island for rising up against their Ottoman overlords, calling them a "people mired in the temptations of Satan (al-shaytān), having slunk away from their obedience to the Sultan (al-sultān)," thus implying that rebellion was a sin for which not only secular, but religious, judgment awaited. Now, barely two years later, he depicts himself as calling out to the Egyptians: "O People, rise up! Life is but an opportunity and, over time, there are many paths abounding and chances to secure advantage." This clarion challenge, coupled with his rhetorical question earlier in the poem asking "Where are the ancient kings who mounted up to

the very heights?" followed immediately by his bitter reply: "The land is devoid of them" could hardly be read in the context of the times as anything but the most radical exhortation to his audience to rid themselves of the tyrants oppressing them. His poems composed a decade later, in the midst of the fever pitch of the 'Urābī Revolution itself, may equal but do not surpass the rhetorical intensity of this initial effort, when the troubles that were coming were but a distant blot on the horizon. And perhaps because it was so early, al-Bārūdī seems to have received no favorable response, even among his coterie of close friends, to the warnings and exhortations he embodied in this composition. On the other hand, he does not seem to have suffered any repercussions from his boldness, perhaps because Ismā'īl was kept unaware of the poem's existence, and al-Bārūdī's career continued on its upward trajectory.

Though the "'Ayniyyah" was a powerful piece of revolutionary writing, into which he had poured many of his most heart-felt emotions, al-Bārūdī did not actively seek to disseminate it widely at the time for obvious reasons. His earlier, less controversial poems, however, had another destiny in the 1870s. His contemporary, and sometime friend and ally, the educator 'Alī Mubārak, put into action in 1871 a plan he had long cherished to bring the benefits of modern education at the post-secondary level to the Egyptians and perhaps lay the groundwork for founding a secular university in the future. To this end, he sponsored a series of lectures in 1871 at a large lecture amphitheater, known as the Dār al-'Ulūm (House of Sciences) at the Darb al-Jamāmīz educational complex in Cairo. These lectures were very popular, and the following year 'Alī Mubārak, now Minister of Education, instituted a regular program of study named after the lecture hall where it all began. The new Dār al-'Ulūm started with a cohort of about 30 students, taken from the most talented graduates of al-Azhar, who were to be trained as teachers for the new state school system. This was far more economical than sending them abroad, and the cash-strapped Ismā'īl welcomed the possibility. Most of the instructors were foreign, but the teacher recruited as professor of

Arabic language and literature, Husayn al-Mar-safī, was an associate of Muhammad 'Abduh and Jamāl al-Dīn al-Afghānī and, like them, an Islamic scholar interested in reforming Egyptian society and government. He was also an old friend of al-Bārūdī, and may have even been one of his childhood tutors.

However they may have first met, al-Bārūdī always referred to al-Marsafī as "my professor" and greatly admired his literary judgment. It seems the favor was returned. When al-Marsafī was asked to turn his lecture notes into a book, he included a number of al-Bārūdī's poems in the text, as samples of stylistically exemplary works by a modern author. These included the hunting poem from al-Bārūdī's English trip, the "Nūniyyah" composed during the Cretan war, and a number of poems al-Bārūdī had written (perhaps especially for his old friend) modeled on famous poems by classical Arab authors like al-Mutanabbī (d. 965), Abū Nuwās (d. c. 813), Abū Firās al-Hamdānī (d. 968), and al-Buhturī (d. 897). Al-Bārūdī's poems, although they used the same rhyme and meter as—and frequently incorporated quotations from—their exemplars, were not so much imitations as potentially contentious re-statements, or variations on, their predecessors, where the ideas and assertions found in the originals were put to the test and their possible inadequacies explored. This variety of contrafaction (known in Arabic as *mu-'āradah*) has always been a dynamic and lively part of the poetic tradition.

That al-Bārūdī's poems became part of the curriculum early on at one of the most prestigious schools in Cairo at the time ensured that his work would attract wider interest and an audience it might not otherwise have had, since newspapers only became a common venue for the publication of literary works in the 1880s and 1890s, after al-Bārūdī had been exiled to Ceylon. Before then, the salon with its coterie audience would have been the main center of dissemination for new literary works, and this was naturally limited in scope.

Also included in the pages of Marsafī's book entitled *al-Wasīlah al-adabiyyah* (The Literary Method) were several poems that represented the product of the next stage of al-Bārūdī's

career, when he returned to the army and was sent again to aid the Ottomans, this time in a war they were fighting against Russia. In 1875, al-Bārūdī had taken up Ismā'īl's offer to return to his employ as his private secretary. One of his first important assignments in that position was to travel to Istanbul to petition the Sultan not to require the Khedive to send troops to aid him in putting down yet another revolt, this time among the Herzogovinians in the western Balkans. Al-Bārūdī spent three months in Istanbul (October-December 1876), but the Sultan would only agree to remit the obligation to money in lieu of troops. Upon his return to Egypt, al-Bārūdī was involved in a train accident that nearly cost him his life. But even more ominously, when he finally arrived in Cairo, it was to find that Ismā'īl Siddīq al-Mufattish had disappeared under mysterious circumstances (murdered, it was rumored, on the Khedive's orders) and Ismā'īl, on the verge of bankruptcy, had been forced to accept supervision of his government's activities by a pair of foreign nationals (an Englishman and a Frenchman) who held ministerial rank in his cabinet. Britain and France had insisted on this system, known as the Dual Control, to protect the interests of their nationals who had issued the bonds securing the Egyptian debt.

Given the uncertainties in Cairo, and the deepening sense of crisis there, it is perhaps not surprising that al-Bārūdī took the opportunity in April 1877 to rejoin the army when Russia declared war on Turkey, leaving Egypt once again for Istanbul. This time the fighting was much more intense than the previous year, and the Sultan insisted on troops, not money. In the summer, al-Bārūdī, by this time a full general in the Egyptian army, found himself stationed on the shores of the Black Sea, in approximately the same area where the Crimean War had been fought approximately twenty years before. As summer waned, he led his troops in several successful engagements, mostly in Bulgaria and the southern Ukraine. Between battles, al-Bārūdī found time to write at least four substantial poems, which he duly sent back to his friend Husayn al-Marsafī in Cairo, to be included in his textbook.

But in the end, despite the better-than-expected performance of the Arab and Turkish troops, the Russians prevailed and in February 1878 their armies stood at the gates of Istanbul. The new sultan, ʿAbd al-Hamīd, was forced to sue for peace and the Egyptian troops returned home.

Al-Bārūdī's Balkan poems can best be characterized as a throwback to the days of the Cretan War. They focus on the depiction of the fighting, not the causes behind it. Longing for Egypt, the distant beloved, pervades all the pieces. If anything, these odes are even more deliberately painstaking in their traditionalism than al-Bārūdī's earlier efforts, relying extensively on imagery and metaphors borrowed from early Arab poets' writing about Bedouin raids in the desert before the rise of Islam.

A much more important influence on the revolutionary poetry he would be composing upon his return, as well as for the direction his public career would take, were the contacts al-Bārūdī made among his fellow army officers while in the Balkans. First, there were the Turks. Between 1876 and 1878 leading reformers in the Empire had enacted several liberal democratic reforms in the Ottoman state, such as the adoption of a constitution and an elected parliament. While ʿAbd al-Hamīd would shortly find himself strong enough to suspend the Constitution and rule as an autocrat for the next thirty years, the example of those heady days remained. It is impossible to tell exactly how much of this new thinking al-Bārūdī would have absorbed from his fellow officers among the Turkish forces, or during his sojourn in Istanbul a year earlier, but he could hardly have been unaware of the events and the issues they raised.

More influential yet was his introduction to the members of a growing secret organization among the junior officers in the Egyptian army. These individuals, soon to become known as the Young Officers, or the Egyptian Officers (to differentiate them from the Turko-Circassian officers who made up the bulk of the upper ranks), had committed themselves initially to the cause of reform in the army, but eventually they would go beyond this to embrace the cause of liberation of Egypt from foreign tutelage, a

equitable solution to the debt crisis, and the establishment of an elected representative government based on a written constitution.

But, as before the war, when al-Bārūdī returned to Cairo in 1878, it was publicly as the loyal servant of the regime. He was almost immediately appointed governor of al-Sharqiyyah province in the Nile Delta region, and then Prefect of Police for Cairo. Barely had he settled into his new positions when he was called to negotiate with the junior army officers who were on the verge of open rebellion because of the government's tardiness in paying their salaries, which were over eighteen months in arrears. In his capacity as military governor of Cairo, al-Bārūdī persuaded his former subordinates and comrades in arms to submit a written petition instead, defusing the crisis. The ministers responsible, including Nūbār Pasha, were dismissed. Nūbār was replaced by Sharīf Pasha, a long-time civil servant of Turkish origin, who had and supported the idea of constitutional rule.

The British responded to these developments by appealing to the Ottoman sultan, demanding the deposition of Ismāʿīl and the installation of his son Tawfīq as Khedive. The Sultan, in need of British support after his defeat in the Russo-Turkish war, sent a telegram on June 26, 1879 ordering Ismāʿīl into exile. Without any supporters to come to his aid, Ismāʿīl was forced to abdicate in favor of his son.

All during this period al-Bārūdī continued to compose poetry. These poems were not like the Russo-Turkish war poems, but returned to the vein of the "ʿAyniyyah," painting a bold picture of the misery in Egypt, condemning autocratic rule, and complaining of corruption in the government. Several of the most strident are labeled in the dīwān as "protests against a tyrannical government" and some critics have suggested that they actually belong to the slightly later period when Tawfīq's administration was under fire, but the consensus is that they were written about Ismāʿīl. None of them focus as much as the "ʿAyniyyah" does on the principle of popular rule, but as a group they form a fitting prelude to the poem al-Bārūdī offered to the new sovereign upon the latter's investiture as Khedive. Although the earlier part of this poem rehearses the same complimentary recitation of Tawfīq's virtues that would be typical of these congratulatory odes, the latter half of the poem is devoted to advising the Khedive on the importance of "consultation" *(shūrā)* a code word of the time referring to representative rule. This advice is placed within the context of ascribing to the new Khedive a catalogue of customary Arab virtues, not just martial ones but also those of just dealing, forbearance, and fair-mindedness, thus demonstrating that consultation (and therefore representative government) is entirely consistent with the traditions of rule and the virtues ascribed to a heroic leader in the Arab world.

At first Tawfīq appeared to be entirely receptive to these appeals from al-Bārūdī and the other reformers. He asked Sharīf Pasha to form a new government in July. Sharīf did so, relying on close political allies of his, including al-Bārūdī as Minister of Education and of Charitable Endowments. Al-Bārūdī did not remain long as education minister, soon replaced by a more qualified technocrat. He remained longer—over two years—as Minister of Charitable Endowments *(awqāf,* sing. w*aqf).* The *waqf* was the exception to the well-defined system of Islamic inheritance, allowing the testator to direct a portion of his or her wealth to fund a particular endeavor that benefited the Muslim community as a whole. Schools, as well as mosques and hospitals, were frequent recipients of *waqf* endowments. Thus al-Bārūdī's initial twin appointments were not so unconnected as might first appear.

By Ismā'īl's time, the income from *waqf*s represented one of the few revenue streams not earmarked for debt service. Al-Bārūdī directed these monies into service projects benefiting large sectors of Egyptian society. He also thoroughly reviewed and revised the rules of operation at the Ministry. He formed a committee of experts (scholars, engineers and historians), charging them to search out *waqf*s that had escaped the Ministry's attention. Probably most important for the future of scholarly study, he ordered that any old books and manuscripts lodged in libraries attached to mosques and schools be collected together and stored until 'Alī Mubārak finished constructing Dār al-Kutub, the new Egyptian national library.

Similarly, al-Bārūdī who, like Ismā'īl, had been interested in Egyptian antiquities ever since archaeological excavation began seriously in the country in the 1860s, sought to preserve these relics while Minister. He collected what he could find together and kept them in the Hākim mosque until a special building could be built to house them. In 1879, this interest also began to surface in his poetry. He composes several poems that make use of references to the monuments of ancient Egypt—most particularly the Pyramids and the Sphinx—as evidence of Egypt's past greatness and a sign that the country and its people can be great once again. These culminate in a poem he composed to be read aloud at the inauguration ceremonies of the Cairo Welfare League (Jam'īyyat al-Maqāsid al-Khayriyyah), a literary and political association founded in 1880 by Tawfīq's son, 'Abbās Hilmī, and the disciples of Jamāl al-Dīn al-Afghānī, especially Muhammad 'Abduh. This poem begins with the declaration "By the power of knowledge, the might of nations is strengthened, and rule that persists over time is linked to the pen," and it uses as evidence of this proposition the enduring rule of the Pharaohs whose records were then being deciphered in the form of the hieroglyphics written on their monuments. Thus, the author neatly knits his twin interests in education and antiquities into one seamless whole. Al-Bārūdī was the first serious Arabic poet to show any interest in these ancient Egyptian monuments, and he inaugurated a trend that was enthusiastically continued by later neo-Classical poets. It should be noted, however, that in this he was following in the path of al-Afghānī himself, who had adopted this rhetorical position in his speeches beginning in 1878, and even before that, of Rifā'ah al-**Tahtāwī**, who had alluded in his educational works to the greatness of ancient Egypt and the lessons modern Egyptians should draw from their ancestors' example.

Al-Bārūdī was, however, soon diverted from his attentions to educational and cultural issues by a series of crises in the government where his political skills were increasingly put to the test. In August Sharīf Pasha and most of the ministers in the government resigned when Tawfīq refused to accept the draft of a new constitutional law submitted by Sharīf. He was replaced by a close ally of Nūbār, Riyāḍ Pasha, who was known for his friendliness to the European powers and his opposition to constitutional reforms. Two ministers from the old cabinet were retained: Mustafā Fahmī as Foreign Minister and Mahmūd Sāmī al-Bārūdī as Minister of Religious Endowments. Fahmī had proved himself as an expert in his position by his knowledge of European languages and his abilities as a negotiator. The reason for the retention of al-Bārūdī, however, was less immediately clear. Some, like Sharīf Pasha, took it as evidence of al-Bārūdī's opportunism and his lack of allegiance to the Constitutionalist cause. Yet all of al-Bārūdī's previous and subsequent actions would seem to belie this conclusion, culminating in the fact that he would in 1882 lose all of his property and be exiled precisely for his devotion to the principle of constitutional rule, when he could easily have renounced it and walked away free at many points during the run of events leading up to his trial. Others have claimed that he was acting as a "Trojan horse" for his military colleagues, like Ahmad 'Urābī, informing them of developments in the government and thereby keeping them from falling victim to various plots instigated by their political enemies. But this presupposes a level of organized opposition in military circles to Tawfīq, and Riyāḍ's ministry, for which there is no documentary evidence, at least not until much later in the course of developments. Perhaps it was simply that he was promised a free hand to continue his educational and cultural reforms, in concert with 'Alī Mubārak, who joined the new government as Minister of Public Works.

At any rate, Riyāḍ at first had much success in defusing the financial crisis of the Egyptian government, precisely because his good relations with the Europeans allowed him to get them to agree to the concessions necessary to reduce the interest rate on the debt and reschedule payments. But he did not respond sufficiently to the concerns of the large landowners (like Sharīf Pasha) who had supported constitutionalist reforms and, even more ominously, to the needs of the army, especially the native

Egyptian component, who continued to find themselves on the short end of the financial stick in the government budget.

The junior officers also resented the efforts of the Minister of War, Fu'ād Rifqī, to restrict the opportunities Egyptians (as opposed to Turko-Circassians) had to rise in the ranks. So, in February 1881, under the leadership of Ahmad 'Urābī, colonel of the Fourth Regiment, the soldiers staged a demonstration (as they had done in 1879) and presented a list of demands to Riyāḍ and Tawfīq. Al-Bārūdī was sent to negotiate (successfully) with the demonstrators, and on February 6 Tawfīq appointed him Minister of War. For almost seven months al-Bārūdī was able to work effectively as the intermediary between Riyāḍ and the officers, earning the respect of both for his ability to fashion compromises. However, in August Tawfīq compelled al-Bārūdī to resign for not being, in his opinion, sufficiently forceful with the officers. Within a few weeks, the officers joined forces with Sharīf Pasha and the Constitutionalists to agitate for al-Bārūdī's restoration, as well as for more fundamental reforms in the government, including the much delayed convocation of the parliament.

On September 9 Tawfīq's decision to reshuffle regimental assignments to bring troops to Cairo more loyal to him than to the Young Officers' group provoked a further demonstration in front of 'Abdīn Palace that soon turned into an armed confrontation. 'Urābī then put forward a list of three demands: 1) dismissal of Riyāḍ, 2) convocation of the Chamber of Deputies, and 3) expansion of the army to a full strength of 18,000 soldiers. After long negotiation, Tawfīq agreed to replace Riyāḍ's ministry with one headed by Sharīf Pasha, reinstating al-Bārūdī as War Minister. He asked for a longer time to consider the other demands, until the new cabinet was sworn in. 'Urābī and his fellow officers acquiesced for the moment, and by the end of the year all the proposed reforms would be enacted or well in train.

Out of this confrontation, 'Urābī emerged as a charismatic figure, an unquestioned hero to many segments of Egyptian society. Though al-Bārūdī had the more exalted title, he does not seem to have been able to appeal to the crowd in the same way as 'Urābī. Yet the two military men seem also to have worked together with remarkable effectiveness and frequently appeared together on public occasions. In recognition of this fact, 'Urābī officially became Deputy Minister of War on January 4, 1882.

But this period of harmony among all elements of the government was not to last. When the Deputies of the Chamber (the revival of an elected consultative body that had been set up early in Ismā'īl's reign and then largely ignored) were seated in December 1881, they almost immediately came into conflict with Sharīf, who wanted to limit their powers and ensure that they supported the large landowners. Tensions intensified when an official Note arrived from the French and British Foreign Offices emphasizing their unchanged support for the Khedive, who was thereby encouraged to seek a more direct role in the direction of government policy. But in the end, the army, which still held the decisive power of military force, came down in support of the Chamber, so Tawfīq and his advisors backed down, asking the deputies to put forward a nomination for Prime Minister in place of Sharīf. They chose al-Bārūdī as their candidate because they believed he understood and sympathized with their aims, while still representing the old Turko-Circassian ruling class. Thus al-Bārūdī became Prime Minister for a reluctant but cowed Tawfīq on February 3, 1882.

Al-Bārūdī's tenure in office was short—only four and a half months—but it was singularly eventful. By the 7th of February, al-Bārūdī had nominated a full slate of ministers and obtained Tawfīq's consent to a Basic Law—called by some a Constitution for Egypt—that regulated elections to the Chamber and established the procedures for orderly conduct of its business. Most significantly, the new law stated that "no law shall become valid until it is read before the Chamber of Deputies, article by article, voted clause by clause, and consented to by the Khedive," and that "no fresh tax—direct or indirect—on movable, immovable or personal property may be imposed in Egypt without a law voted by the Chamber." This paved the way for a gradual transition from the Executive to the Legislative branch of government in terms of power over taxation, which would have prevented the sort of abuses that had developed up during Ismā'īl's reign.

During this period—unlike most other times during his life—al-Bārūdī composed very little poetry that can be confidently dated as contemporary. But his sponsorship and enactment of the Basic Law constitutes, in its own way, an equally important legacy to the nation, one which shows his unwavering commitment to the constitutional rule of law.

Al-Bārūdī's relationship with Tawfīq, never easy, deteriorated sharply in May of 1882. A plot by the Turko-Circassian element in the army to remove the Egyptian Officers had been discovered and about 50 participants sentenced, largely to exile and loss of rank. Tawfīq, encouraged by the British Consul-General, Edward Malet, refused to ratify the sentence, asking the Ottoman sultan to intervene. Al-Bārūdī's government offered various compromises, none of which Tawfīq would accept, preferring to wait for word from Istanbul. In the meantime, Lord Granville, Chief Secretary for Foreign Affairs in the English Cabinet, ordered the English and French fleets, in compliance with the terms of their official Note of January, to take up positions off the coast of Alexandria. Al-Bārūdī was unable to secure support from the majority of the Chamber of Deputies, and on May 29, he and his Cabinet resigned.

Opposition to Tawfīq's plans now devolved on the leadership of 'Urābī and the army. Officially, al-Bārūdī may have retired to his country estates, but Louis Sabūnjī's letters to Wilfrid Scawen Blunt reveal that he continued to meet with 'Urābī, working closely with him and Muḥammad 'Abduh to thwart Tawfīq's designs. On June 11th 1882 an altercation between an Egyptian and a Maltese resident of Alexandria degenerated into a riot that killed around 50 Europeans and 3,000 Egyptians. On the 13th, Tawfīq went to Alexandria and placed himself under the protection of the Anglo-French fleet. Using the Alexandrian riot, the subsequent destruction of the European quarter there, and some reinforcements of the city's fortifications as a pretext, the Commander of the foreign fleet,

Lord Seymour, issued an ultimatum to ʿUrābī on July 6th to withdraw all Egyptian forces from the city or face bombardment. On July 11 and 12, Alexandria was bombarded by the British. Large portions of the city were set on fire or reduced to rubble. ʿUrābī withdrew his troops to Kafr al-Dawwār, a city south of Alexandria that controlled the rail line linking Alexandria to Cairo. Meanwhile the French government had withdrawn its support from the joint expedition, and Britain was left to re-impose khedival rule by itself. Rather than confront the Egyptian army right away, Gladstone's government gathered a 30,000-man force from England and India, which landed in Egypt at Port Saʿīd on the Suez canal, an approach poorly defended by ʿUrābī. Al-Bārūdī, along with other officers and troops, was dispatched to defend against the advancing force, but they failed to hold the line as the troops panicked and ran. Al-Bārūdī remained with some of his officers to oppose the English, but in the end he had to retreat, virtually alone, northward toward Damietta. In the midst of the fight, news arrived that his mother, who had been gravely ill the past few weeks, had passed away. Shortly after the defeat, he wrote a long elegy in her honor, in which her death is seen as part of a constellation of fateful blows, occurring virtually simultaneously, which demonstrate to her son the futility of human ambition and the power of fate.

On September 13th the Egyptian army was overrun in a morning attack at al-Tall al-Kabīr, and ʿUrābī retreated to Cairo. Al-Bārūdī heard of the attack and telegraphed ʿUrābī in Cairo, asking his permission to turn southward with his remaining soldiers, in order to cut the Ismāʿīliyyah canal and flood the approaches to Cairo, but he received a reply that ʿUrābī and the provisional government were planning to surrender to the English without any further delay. Al-Bārūdī, by this time back in Cairo himself, tried to persuade ʿUrābī and his generals to "declare Cairo an open city and retreat with the army to Upper Egypt and the Sudan," but surrender was the path that was chosen, and the deed was carried out on September 15th. Al-Bārūdī refused to surrender his sword and he returned to his house in the city, saying "if they want me, they know where to find me." Shortly thereafter, he was among the first to be arrested and put in jail.

At first, conditions in the makeshift prison were appalling, and al-Bārūdī seems to have contemplated committing suicide. Later, he occupied his free time in poetic composition, and a number of poems lamenting his personal losses and the tragedy of nation, as well as defending his role in events, survive. At first Tawfīq and his supporters wanted the prisoners executed, but in the end ʿUrābī, al-Bārūdī and five others were sent into permanent exile in Ceylon, with all their wealth and titles forfeit.

In December 1882, not quite a year since he had been named Prime Minister, he found himself bundled alone on board a steamship bound for the Indian Ocean. His children remained behind in Cairo, as did his wife, who had promised to nurse her mother in her last illness. Also, she hoped to intercede with her royal relatives and obtain a pardon for her husband. But in short order she also fell ill and died, and her husband would remain in Ceylon for seventeen years, until 1900.

Al-Bārūdī's political career was now over, but his literary career continued unabated, at least at first. He busied himself composing poems on a variety of subjects, from the beauty of nature in the public gardens to his longing for his beloved Egypt, and elaborate justifications for his actions on the public stage. Nor was he able to neglect the genre of elegy, mourning first the death of his wife and several of his children, and then, in 1889, his old friends Ḥusayn al-Marṣafī and the poet ʿAbd Allāh Fikrī who died within months of each other. He also occupied his time with learning English and promoting the study of Arabic and Islam among the local inhabitants. He became markedly more religious over the years, and one of the first works published (in 1907) after his death was his long poem, in 447 verses, *Kashf al-ghummah fī madh sayyid al-ummah* (Release from Grief Through Praising the Leader of the Community), which saluted the Prophet Muhammad as founder and ideal leader of the Muslim community. Most major poets of the later Islamic centuries had tried their hands at such works as a culmination of their poetic careers, and in doing so al-Bārūdī established his wish to be considered as part of this long tradition. But, in keeping with his desire to innovate within the framework of convention, al-Bārūdī deliberately avoided incorporating elaborate rhetorical devices within the framework of the poem (the standard practice up to this point had been to use a different rhetorical device in every verse). Instead, he chose to follow the narration of events in the Prophet's life given by his earliest biographer, Ibn Hishām (d. 833 CE). Though the result was not quite an epic poem, it foreshadowed later attempts made by al-Bārūdī's disciples (most notably Khalīl Mutrān) to introduce this genre of poetry into Arabic, where it had not been previously cultivated.

During their long banishment from Egypt, the exiles grew apart. Already during their imprisonment and trial, recriminations among the group had begun to surface. Al-Bārūdī did not break openly with his comrades, and yet, while he was in Ceylon, he did not socialize much with the three colonels who had led the Young Officers: 'Urābī, 'Abd al-'Āl Hilmī and 'Alī Fahmī. He spent much more time with the younger exiles, Ya'qūb Sāmī and Tulbah 'Ismat, who had played a more political than military role in the Revolution. In 1888, three years after his wife's death, he married one of Ya'qūb Sāmī's daughters and the combined family moved to the city of Kandy in the mountainous interior from the capital of Colombo.

Tawfīq died in 1892, to be succeeded by his eldest son 'Abbās Hilmī. But it would be eight more years before al-Bārūdī would finally be allowed to return and his estates and title restored. During his last years in Ceylon, his sight increasingly troubled him and by the time of his return he was completely blind. But this did not prevent him from correcting and polishing his *dīwān* and composing an introduction for it that in many ways anticipates the doctrines, drawn from European romanticism, that were already being adopted by the younger generation. He does not follow typical neo-Classical dicta of restraint and decorum in describing how poetry should be composed, but instead emphasizes the links between poetry and emotion, saying in a

memorable turn of phrase: "Poetry is a streak of lightning associated with the imagination, whose brilliance lights up the heavens of thought." He also stresses that the language of poetry should be simple, straightforward and easily grasped, decisively rejecting the elaborate periods and convoluted metaphors of the preceding generation. But these principles are not always observable in his poetry, and thus they should be recognized as what al-Bārūdī was seeking at the end of his life, not the rules that he always followed in the practice of composition from his earliest days.

Finally, during his exile al-Bārūdī sought to make his mark on the development of modern Arabic poetry by creating an anthology of what he felt were the most important Arab poets from the classical tradition. This was perhaps a more important task in the late nineteenth century than it would be even twenty or thirty years later, because at that time many of the *dīwān*s of influential poets had not been properly edited and existed only in manuscript. Thus al-Bārūdī was performing an important service for his fellow poets. It is interesting to note that his selection of authors agrees in many ways with that of his mentor, Husayn al-Marsafī, in the latter's *al-Wasīlah al-Adabiyyah*. The four volumes of this compilation were the first works by al-Bārūdī to reach print, being published from 1909 to 1911.

While al-Bārūdī was gone from Egypt, his influence faded from the scene and other, younger poets took his place. But when he returned, it was not entirely as a forgotten man. The day he arrived in Cairo, a crowd gathered outside his house and welcomed enthusiastically his recitation of a poem composed especially for his return, in which he lovingly recounts his desire for Egypt, depicted—as was his trademark—as a beautiful woman. The poem also contains imagery of himself as a lion springing forth from concealment within a thicket, reproducing his description of his father in his earliest preserved poem. In this way, his poetry seems to come full circle back to its beginnings. Only now it is he himself, not his father, whose place in the world he must assess and memorialize.

After his return, al-Bārūdī revived his literary

salon. There he held court for a new generation of poets—including such leading lights as Hāfiz **Ibrāhīm**, Ahmad **Shawqī** and Khalīl **Mutrān**—until his death on December 12, 1904. It was through their work that his legacy lived on into the first half of the twentieth century and influenced the next generation, especially—and rather surprisingly—two poets of the *Dīwān* group, 'Abd al-Rahmān **Shukrī** and 'Abbās Mahmūd al-'Aqqād, who were also major apostles of European Romanticism.

REFERENCES

'Abbās Mahmūd al-'Aqqād, *Shu'arā' Misr wa-bī'ātuhum fī 'l-jīl al-mādī* (Cairo: Dār Nahdat Misr, 1937);

M. M. Badawi, *A Critical Introduction to Modern Arabic Poetry* (Cambridge: Cambridge University Press, 1975), 16-29;

Dawud Barakat (ed.), *al-Thawrah al-'Urābiyyah: ru'yā sahīfat al-Ahrām* (Cairo: Matba'at Dār al-Kutub wa'l-Wathā'iq, 2002);

Wilfrid Scawen Blunt, *The Secret History of the British Occupation of Egypt: Being a Personal Narrative of Events* (Cairo: Arab Centre for Research and Publishing, 1980);

A. M. Broadley, *How We Defended Arabi and His Friends* (Cairo: Arab Centre for Research and Publishing, 1980);

Jan Brugman, *An Introduction to the History of Modern Arabic Literature in Egypt* (Leiden: E. J. Brill, 1984), 28-33;

Juan Cole, *Colonialism and Revolution in the Middle East: Social and Cultural Origins of Egypt's 'Urābī Movement* (Princeton: Princeton University Press, 1993);

Shawqī Dayf, *al-Bārūdī: Rā'id al-shi'r al-hadīth* (Cairo: Dār al-Ma'ārif, 1964);

Arthur C. Dep, *Orabi Pasha: the Egyptian Exiles in Ceylon-Sri Lanka* (Sri Lanka: Arabi Pasha Centenary Celebrations Committee, 1983);

'Alī al-Hadīdī, *Mahmūd Sāmī al-Bārūdī: Shā'ir al-Nahdah* (Cairo: Maktabat al-Anjlū al-Misriyyah, 1969);

Salma Khadra Jayyusi, *Trends and Movements in Modern Arabic Poetry*, 2 vols. (Leiden: E. J. Brill, 1977), I, 37-39;

Afaf Lutfi al-Sayyid Marsot, *Egypt in the Reign of Muhammad 'Ali* (Cambridge: Cambridge University Press, 1984);

——, *A Short History of Modern Egypt* (Cambridge: Cambridge University Press, 1985);

Salīm Khalīl al-Naqqāsh, *Misr li'l-Misriyyīn* (Alexandria: Matba'at Jarīdat al-Mahrūsah, 1884);

Alexander Schölch, *Egypt for the Egyptians: The Socio-Political Crisis in Egypt 1878-1882* (London: Ithaca Press, 1981).

Khalīl Baydas
(i.e., Khalīl Ibrāhīm al-Sabbāgh)
(1874/5 – 1949)

IBRAHIM TAHA
University of Haifa

WORKS

Al-'Iqd al-nazīm fī asl al-rūsiyyīn wa-''tināqihim al-īmān al-qawīm ("A Chronology of the Russians' Origins and their Sincere Belief", Lebanon, 1897);

Al-'Iqd al-thamīn fī tarbiyat al-banīn ("The Precious Necklace Concerning the Raising Sons", Lebanon: al-Matba'ah al-'Uthmāniyyah, 1898);

Hafalāt al-tatwīj ("Coronation Parties", Beirut, 1898);

Mir'āt al-mu'allimīn ("The Teachers' Mirror",

Beirut, 1898);

Al-Kusūr al-dārijah ("Ordinary Fractions", Beirut, 1898);

Al-Kusūr al-'ashriyyah ("Decimal Fractions", Beirut, 1898);

Al-Rawdah al-mu'nisah fī wasf al-ard al-muqaddasah ("A Description of the Holy Land", Beirut, 1899);

Tārīkh al-tayarān ("History of Flying", Cairo, 1912);

Al-Duwal al-islāmiyyah ("The Islamic States", Jerusalem, 1912);

Rihlah ilā Sīnā' ("A Journey to Sinai", Beirut, 1912);

Mulūk al-Rūs ("Russian Kings", Jerusalem, 1913);

Darajāt al-hisāb ("Stages in Mathematics", Jerusalem, 1913), two vols.;

Darajāt al-qirā'ah ("Stages in Reading", Jerusalem, 1913-1921), six vols.;

Umam al-Balqān ("The Balkan Peoples", Jerusalem, 1914);

Tasrīh al-absār fīmā tahtawīhi bilādunā min al-āthār ("Exploring the Archeology of our Homeland", Jerusalem, 1920);

Al-Wārith ("The Heir", Jerusalem: Matba'at Dār al-Aytām al-Sūriyyah, 1920);

Tārīkh al-Quds ("A History of Jerusalem", Jerusalem, 1922);

Dīwān al-fukāhah ("An Anthology of Humor", Jerusalem: Matba'at Dayr al-Rūm al-Orthodox, 1924); a collection of short stories;

Masārih al-adhhān ("Vistas of the Mind", Cairo: al-Matba'ah al-'Asriyyah, 1924);

Mukhtār al-Bayān wa'l-Tabyīn ("A selection of texts from al-Jāhiz's [book] *al-Bayān wa'l-Tabyīn*", Jerusalem: Matba'at Bayt al-Maqdis, 1924); edited together with Sharīf al-Nashāshībī;

Al-Kāfī fī 'l-sarf ("A Comprehensive Book on Arabic Etymology", Jerusalem, 1924);

Al-'Arab: Abtāluhum wa-ashhar hawādithihim ("The Arabs: Their Heroes and the Most Famous Events in their History", Jerusalem, 1942);

Nahnu wa'l-lughah ("Language and Us", manuscript);

Ahlām al-hayāh ("Dreams of Life", manuscript); collection of short stories;

Asrār al-hayāh ("Secrets of Life", manuscript); collection of short stories;

Suwar al-hayāh ("Images of Life", manuscript); collection of short stories.

[The last five items are unpublished manuscripts that were lost, along with many other manuscripts from Baydas's private library, when he left his home in Jerusalem during the 1948 war.]

Works Arabized or Translated into Arabic by Baydas

Tārīkh Rūsyā al-qadīm ("A History of Ancient Russia", Beirut, 1898);

Ibnat al-qubtān ("The Captain's Daughter", Beirut: Matba'at Jarīdat al-Manār, 1898); a long story by Pushkin;

Al-Qūzāqī al-walhān ("The Distracted Caucasian", Beirut, 1898); a novel by Tolstoy;

Al-Tabīb al-hādhiq ("The Skillful Physician", Beirut, 1898);

Shaqā' al-mulūk ("Kings' Misery", 1908; 2nd ed. Jerusalem: Dayr al-Rūm al-Orthodox, 1922); a novel by Marie Corelli;

Ahwāl al-istibdād ("The Terrifying Misfortunes of Despotism", Haifa: al-Matba'ah al-Wataniyyah, 1909; 2nd ed. Cairo, 1927); a novella by Tolstoy;

Al-Hasnā' al-mutanakkirah ("The Disguised Belle", Jerusalem: Matba'at Bayt al-Maqdis, 1911; 2nd ed. 1925); a novel by Emile Silgary;

Hinrī al-thāmin wa-zawjatuhu al-sādisah ("Henry VIII and his Sixth Wife", n.p., 1912, 1913); a novel by F. Malbach;

Al-'Arsh wa'l-hubb ("The Throne and Love", Jerusalem: Dār al-Aytām al-Sūriyyah, 1914, 1921);

Al-Shābb al-muntasir ("The Triumphant Young Man", Jerusalem, 1945);

Hannā Kārnīnā ("Anna Karenina", manuscript); a novel by Tolstoy.

Khalīl Baydas was well educated and involved himself in a wide range of activities, including pedagogy, journalism, translation/arabization, and creative literary writing. He apparently wrote some 44 manuscripts, but several of them are lost; only about 37 published books and unpublished manuscripts by Baydas on various topics are known to scholars. These may be classified under the rubrics of creative literature, historiography, works on education, and school textbooks.

His biography can be subdivided into four major stages: childhood and education in Nazareth (1874/5-1893); work in Syria and Lebanon (1893-1908); a period in Haifa and Jerusalem (1908-1948); final days outside his homeland in Amman and Beirut (1948-1949).

Baydas, known also as Khalīl Ibrāhīm al-Sabbāgh, was born in Nazareth to a Christian family originally called al-Sabbāgh before it was changed to Baydas (see al-Asad, 1963: 16-17). His elementary education was at local schools in Nazareth, where he concentrated particularly on Arabic and religion. He went on to study at the Russian seminary in Nazareth for six years from 1886 to 1892, where he mastered the Russian language.

Thanks to his skills in languages and teaching, Baydas served as principal of several Russian elementary schools in Syria and Lebanon from 1893 to 1908. In Lebanon, he married Edāl Abī al-Rūs, a teacher at the school where he was principal at the time. Another student at that school was Mīkhā'īl **Nu'aymah**, the renowned Lebanese writer. As principal, Baydas advised Nu'aymah to complete his studies at the Russian seminary in Nazareth where Baydas himself had graduated.

In 1908, after spending about 15 years in Syria and Lebanon, Baydas returned to Palestine. In Haifa he spent some three years working on his journal al-Nafā'is. In 1911, he quit his job as a teacher and at his parents' and relatives' request moved to Jerusalem to represent the Orthodox church at the Patriarchate House. In that city he participated in a mass march in April 1920 at which he held the crowd in thrall with his address censuring the Balfour Declaration of 1917. His speech resulted in several clashes between Palestinians and Jews, in which many were killed. Baydas was arrested and jailed in Acre for four months. Back in Jerusalem, he returned to teaching and worked at the English Mutrān School until his retirement in 1945.

In 1948, Baydas decided to stay at home in Jerusalem during the fighting over the city between Jewish and Arab forces. However, fear of violence by Jewish militias compelled him to walk to Silwān (a Palestinian village and a district of Jerusalem) prior to leaving for Amman. Soon after, Baydas left Amman for Beirut, where he died in February 1949.

Baydas's literary career comprises five principal domains in which he made major contributions to the development of modern Palestinian literature from late 19th century: the journal al-Nafā'is al-'asriyyah; translation; creative literary writing; literary theories; and pedagogical works.

One of Baydas's important cultural contributions involved his initiative in publishing a journal under extremely adverse conditions. Entitled al-Nafā'is (Treasures), the first volume appeared in Haifa in October/November 1908. Two years later, when Baydas moved to Jerusalem, he continued publication until the end of 1923. For various reasons, he interrupted publication twice, once (1914-1919) because of World War 1, and again (1920) when he was serving his six-month jail sentence in Acre. From 1909, with the 10th number, the title was changed to al-Nafā'is al-'asriyyah.

The journal undoubtedly had a major impact on the development of Palestinian literature in particular, and exerted some influence on modern Arabic literature in general. Credit for publication of the journal goes entirely to Baydas himself. In spite of a number of obstacles, he made enormous efforts to keep the enterprise running, continually updating and improving it. His contributions to modern Palestinian literature through this journal can be summarized as follows:

– According to Baydas himself, al-Nafā'is al-'asriyyah functioned as a convenient medium for publishing his own translations, especially from Russian, but also from European literature in general. At least one translated text appears in every issue of the journal. Baydas was the first to translate many masterpieces of Russian literature into Arabic. In this sense, al-Nafā'is al-'asriyyah was to play a key role in the translation movement in modern Arabic literature in the first decades of the 20th century. As previously mentioned, Baydas was sufficiently well-known to make this initiative possible.

– Baydas helped to accelerate the development of not only modern Palestinian literature but also and more generally modern Arabic literature, by attracting many writers from the Arab world and all over the world, including Ma'rūf al-Rusāfī (1875-1945) from Iraq, Halīm Dammūs (1888-1957) from Lebanon, Qistākī al-Himsī (1858-1941) from Syria, Wadī' al-Bustānī (1888-1945) from Lebanon, and many others.

– By publishing the journal, Baydas not only provided Palestinian writers with an accessible source whereby they could become acquainted with the works that he included in it, but also afforded them the opportunity to submit for publication their own works from within various fields of culture. Palestinian writers who indeed published through the journal include Mohammad Is'āf al-Nashāshībī, Khalīl al-Sakākīnī, 'Alī al-Rīmāwī, Iskandar al-Khūrī al-Baytjālī, 'Abdallāh Mukhlis, Būlus Shahādah, and many others.

– Baydas himself took advantage of the existence of his journal to publish not only his translations but also his own creative literary works. Most of the stories in his two collections, *Masārih al-adhhān* and *Dīwān al-fukāhah*, were originally published in *al-Nafā'is al-'asriyyah*; indeed most of the chapters of his novel *al-Wārith* were also originally published in the journal in 1919.

Being fluent in Russian, Baydas took the first steps to translate into Arabic many literary works by prominent Russian writers in the late 19th and early 20th century. Before Baydas's efforts such translation activity had been limited, chiefly involving religious texts. Baydas was the first dominant figure among Palestinian and Arab writers/translators to translate works of Russian literature into Arabic in the late 19th century (al-Asad 1963: 34). Showing a specific interest in Pushkin among the Russian writers, Baydas also translated English, German, French, and Italian literary works from Russian. He also rendered some Arabic texts into Russian.

Baydas's translation was not literal or 'pure', so to speak, but a mixture of translation and creative writing. He felt free to make major changes in the original text so that it could meet the Arab readers' expectations. This kind of translation is commonly called 'arabization', implying that translators did not merely translate, but rather recreated or rewrote. In a brief introduction to his 'translation' of Marie Corelli's novel *Shaqā' al-mulūk* (The Kings' Misery), Baydas wrote:

We have arabized it [the novel] *from Russian under the title* Shaqā' al-mulūk*, making additions, omissions, changes, alternations, classifications, etc., to conform with the* [Arab] *readers' taste.*   (Baydas 1922: 2)

The phrase "freely arabized by Khalīl Baydas" is clearly printed on the front covers of many of his 'translated' texts. One might well argue that this process of arabization from Russian and other literatures was a major factor for Baydas as he simultaneously honed his talents and skills in creative literary writing. To summarize, arabization served for Baydas as a blend of the processes of translation and creative writing. In the late 19th and early 20th century arabization had served an important function throughout the Arab world where readers were not familiar with the various genres of narrative fiction 'translated' into Arabic. In this sense, arabization played a key role by mediating between Arab readers and Western literature. The next step following arabization was independent creative writing.

At the beginning of his career, Baydas was wholly engaged in translation/arabization, but not in creative writing. After his initial exposure to the phenomenon of narrative fiction, its genres and techniques, Baydas ventured to write original stories (short and long) and novels. By the time that he published his first literary work in 1920, a novel entitled *al-Wārith* (The Heir), Baydas had already translated eight Western novels/novellas over a period of 17 years between 1898 and 1914, illustrating the major influence that 'translation' had on improving Baydas's skills in literary writing. Referring to Arab writers and Arabic literature in general in the introduction to his collection of short stories, *Masārih al-adhhān* (Vistas of the Mind), Baydas is clearly aware of the important role that Western fiction has played in the development of modern Arabic literature:

It is obvious that the genre of novel in the West is full of good attributes. Ahead of us by many stages in this field, the West has contributed hundreds and thousands of skilled novelists who are undisputed masters of this genre. By translating them or imitating their style, we can provide our literature with treasure and beauty, and our writers with style, knowledge, and art.

(Baydas 1924: 15)

Baydas translated/arabized eleven books (see list above), of which only one is a work of non-fiction, a history entitled *Tārīkh Rūsyā al-qadīm* (a history of ancient Russia). The other ten are all literary works, the last being Tolstoy's *Anna Karenina*.

Since his interests were diverse, Baydas contributed to Arab culture in a variety of forms, including literature. He wrote six books of narrative fiction: one novel and five short story collections, but only the novel and two of the short story collections were actually published; the manuscripts of the other three collections were lost.

Baydas started publishing his own literary work in 1920 at the age of 45 or 46, many years after gaining experience in translation and arabization. In that year his novel *al-Wārith* (The Heir), subtitled "a social and amorous novel," appeared. The plot concerns two 'affairs' in which ʿAzīz, the major character, plays a key role: the first is with Esther, a beautiful Jewish singer and actress who performs in famous Egyptian theaters and bars; the second is with his wife Najlāʾ, the only daughter of ʿAzīz's uncle, Nuʿmān al-Halabī, whom he marries after the affair with Esther comes to an end amid serious problems. Nuʿmān al-Halabī is a rich man originally from Syria, who has moved with his family to Cairo. Having no children except Najlāʾ, he does his best to maintain and support his nephew ʿAzīz. Dominating most of the events in the novel, ʿAzīz's affair with Esther, or more accurately his sincere love for her, costs him an enormous amount of money. Once Esther feels sure of ʿAzīz's love, she decides to exploit him for his money. When it is all gone,

ʿAzīz makes great efforts to get more. Esther decides to squeeze him for as much as she can and conspires with other Jewish characters to set numerous traps for ʿAzīz. Inevitably he falls into them. Once he finds himself in deep financial trouble, his uncle compels him to marry Najlāʾ, hoping that the marriage will succeed in putting an end to his love for Esther. However, in spite of his marriage, ʿAzīz's love for Esther does not fade; he still meets her in secret. Esther schemes to take advantage of the marriage as a means of getting yet more money out of him. As a result, ʿAzīz sinks deeper and deeper into debt. Najlāʾ does not complain but remains constant in support of her husband, standing by him unstintingly. She gives him all the money she has saved for many years so that he can settle his debts. Realizing that Esther is using him ruthlessly, while Najlāʾ is doing her utmost to support him both emotionally and financially, ʿAzīz gradually starts to push Esther out of his mind and heart, while at the same time falling in love with his wife. The novel concludes with a typically happy ending: one year after these troubles are over ʿAzīz and Najlāʾ are blessed with a male child; they call him Nuʿmān, after his grandfather, Nuʿmān al-Halabī, who begins to recover from his illness.

Being one of the first novels ever written in Palestinian literature, *al-Wārith* is of more historic than aesthetic value (al-Asad 1963: 62; Abū al-Shabāb 1998: 73). Any reading of it raises a number of questions concerning aspects of the novel's plot. This applies in particular to the unsophisticated nature of the novel's characters and narrative structure, based on the two traditional rivals, evil and good, something that makes the moral of the story seem excessively obvious and naive. Furthermore, the anticipated happy ending of the struggle between these rival values serves to restrict the reader's involvement, while the obviously unequal struggle between the two is clearly meant to influence the reader's response. The stereotypical situation, involving 'a naïve victim versus a powerful evil,' leaves the reader with just one option, namely to feel nothing but sympathy for the victim. Adding to the unconvincing aspects of the novel are the authorial interventions in the course of the events so as to express personal opinions concerning war and politics. Beyond all this, the division of the principal characters in the novel into two categories, evil, represented by all the Jews, and good, represented by victimized Arabs ('Azīz and Najlā'), bases the entire plot on naïve generalities. These reservations notwithstanding, if we evaluate this novel within its own historical context, it does have a scholarly value in that it represents an early attempt at novel writing in Palestine in the understudied period during and immediately after World War I (Abū Hannā 1994: 93-119).

In addition to this novel, Baydas published two collections of short stories. The first, *Dīwān al-fukāhah* (An Anthology of Humor), is subtitled "a collection of 24 literary, historical, amorous and social stories". The second, *Masārih al-adhhān* (Vistas of the Mind), is similarly termed "a literary, aesthetic, and fictional collection about life's truths". Baydas's three lost collections of short-story manuscripts were entitled *Ahlām al-hayāh* (Dreams of Life), *Asrār al-hayāh* (Secrets of Life), and *Suwar al-hayāh* (Images of Life). The manuscripts were lost when the writer left his home in Jerusalem during the 1948 war, and parts of his personal library disappeared in the process. Some of the 'stories' in both published collections are clearly free translations/arabizations: "Nādī Sūrāt" (Surat's Club), for example, is the arabization of a short story by the French writer Bernard de Saint Pierre (1737-1814), while "al-Malik al-saghīr" (The Little King)—in the collection, *Dīwān al-fukāhah*—is originally the work of the Anglo-Irish writer Oscar Wilde (1854-1900). Considering that many of these stories deal with foreign situations and characters from various periods in history, many questions arise concerning their originality. Both published collections, for instance, include tales and characters from ancient cultures and differing historical periods and geographical regions: Egypt, India, Greece, France, the USA, and others (al-Asad 1963: 64-65). Baydas was especially interested in social issues, such as family relationships involving husbands and wives and older and younger generations. However, the subtitles of both collections make it clear that many kinds of short fiction are present: symbolic

and historic stories, tales, fragments, and the like. Surprisingly, Baydas did not treat relationships between Palestinian Arabs and Jews in Palestine. The only work in which he does refer to Jews is his novel discussed above; even there the events are located in Cairo rather than in Palestine itself.

Generally, in his fiction Baydas takes the first steps towards highlighting the close linkage between literature and reality. Unlike many Arab writers in that period, who write in romantic and sentimental styles, Baydas, influenced by realistic Russian literature, is mostly preoccupied with various social questions. As a realistic writer, Baydas makes great use of Arab and general history to reflect contemporary issues. In this sense, he is aware in practice of the significance of intertextuality for writers as a way of enriching their work equally on the aesthetic and thematic levels. All the reservations expressed above regarding his novel *al-Wārith* hold for his short stories as well.

Within the realm of criticism Baydas is acknowledged as being the foremost Palestinian writer to attribute great significance to novels in particular and to narrative fiction in general in late 19th and early 20th century. He expressed his opinions on novels and short stories in the introduction to his collection, *Masārih al-adhhān*. Incidentally, writing about "*al-riwāyah*" (a term denoting almost exclusively the genre of the novel later on) Baydas refers to short stories and novels alike. This introduction functions as a kind of manifesto where he records his views on the role of narrative fiction and the writer's craft. Narrative fiction, he says, should involve both moralistic and aesthetic dimensions. This combination of the two facets of literary work should succeed in providing it with some form of balance between content and form.

Without doubt, the novel's value derives from the benefit it offers and the message it implies. The novelist's worth stems from the facts/truths with which she/he provides the reader, all told in an attractive and aesthetic style.

(Baydas 1924: 14)

In this manifesto, Baydas pays special attention to what novels and stories should be and do. In his view a 'real aesthetic novel/story' should introduce values and messages that lead to some sort of social reformation. Equally it should praise virtue and condemn vice (Baydas 1924: 12). He believes that narrative fiction should deal with ordinary people, their needs, dreams, and concerns. That is why the writer should maintain contact with the common people, or come from among their number, so that he can experience their life and consequently represent it in an authentic way. Furthermore, a writer should be well informed and educated.

He would not be a professional novelist if he did not read hundreds of novels and histories, become familiar with the world's events, get involved in the lives of the people; if he did not appreciate the meaning of life, its secrets and modes, did not draw his novel's purpose from life's events and human nature, and was not able to apply them to truth and reality.

(Baydas 1924: 12).

Such notions clearly show Baydas's belief in committed literature and help to explain his reasons for forcefully attacking 'commercial' novels. In his view, such novels are weak, poor, and unsubstantial, not only for their stylistic faults but also their insipid subjects, which negatively affect the roles that he wishes to see language, literature, morals, sentiments, and virtue playing in the evaluative process (Baydas 1924: 13-14). Qustandī Shūmalī believes that Baydas continued what Muhammad Rūhī al-Khālidī had done before him, namely by showing profound interest in literary theory and criticism in his book, *Tārīkh 'ilm al-adab 'ind al-Ifranj wa'l-'Arab wa-Victor Hugo* (A History of the Europeans', Arabs' and Victor Hugo's Literary Studies) (Shūmalī 1990: 43-47). Baydas was to further develop some of al-Khālidī's views on literature, such as the need to emphasize meaning and content over words/language, and the essential requirement of any writer to be well informed about foreign literatures.

As a schoolteacher, Baydas published many books on topics that were intended to respond to students' interests and needs. Among these topics are Arabic language and literature, mathematics, education, history, and geography. He published three books on Arabic language and literature: *Darajāt al-qirā'ah* (Stages in Reading); *Mukhtār al-Bayān wa'l-tabyīn* (A Selection of Texts from [al-Jāhiz's Book entitled] *al-Bayān wa'l-tabyīn*), with Sharīf al-Nashāshībī; *al-Kāfī fī 'l-sarf* (A Comprehensive Book on Arabic Morphology); three books on mathematics: *al-Kusūr al-dārijah* (Ordinary Fractions); *al-Kusūr al-'ashriyyah* (Decimal Fractions); *Darajāt al-hisāb* (Stages in Mathematics); two books on education: *al-'Iqd al-thamīn fī tarbiyat al-banīn* (The Precious Necklace of Raising Sons) and *Mir'āt al-mu'allimīn* (The Teachers' Mirror); and no less than ten on history and geography: *al-'Iqd al-nazīm fī asl al-rūsiyyīn wa-i'tināqihim al-īmān al-qawīm* (A Chronology of the Russians' Origins and their Sincere Belief); *al-Rawdah al-mu'nisah fī wasf al-ard al-muqaddasah* (A Description of the Holy Land); *Tarīkh al-tayarān* (History of Flying); *al-Duwal al-islāmiyyah* (The Islamic States); *Rihlah ilā Sīnā'* (A Journey to Sinai); *Mulūk al-Rūs* (The Russian Kings); *Umam al-Balqān* (The Balkan Peoples); *Tasrīh al-absār fīmā tahtawīhi bilādunā min al-āthār* (Exploring the Traces of our Homeland); *Tārīkh al-Quds* (A History of Jerusalem); *al-'Arab: Abtāluhum wa-ashhar hawādithihim* (The Arabs: Their Heroes and Events in their History).

In the introduction to his *al-Kāfī fī al-sarf* (A Comprehensive Book in Arabic Morphology), Baydas offers his views on school-textbooks, noting that writers of such texts should be aware of students' abilities and needs. Through his many school texts on a wide variety of topics, Baydas had a considerable impact on both sides of the literary process, namely production and consumption. According to Baydas, writers need to be fluent in their own language and well educated so that they can create good pieces of literature. But writers also require good readers, and such a goal can only be attained if special care is devoted to students. By spending a great deal of time and effort on textbooks, Baydas actually laid the foundations for emerging literary and cultural movements. When one bears in mind that most people in the Levant, particularly in Palestine, during the period under discussion were uneducated and even illiterate, the contribution that Baydas made to the development of different literary and cultural activities in the region (duly mentioned in numerous issues of his journal *al-Nafā'is al-'asriyyah*) can be readily appreciated. Contributions to Palestinian literature before Baydas are extremely rare (Abū Hannā 1994: 85-87; 'Abd al-Raḥmān Yāghī 1981: 437-439), a circumstance that undoubtedly explains the consensus about Baydas' pioneering role in the history of Palestinian literature. According to 'Abd al-Raḥmān Yāghī, Baydas laid the foundations for a literary tradition, and particularly in the realm of Palestinian narrative fiction (Yāghī 1981: 452). Al-Asad believes that Baydas was a pioneer not merely in narrative fiction, but also in other milieus (al-Asad 1963: 31).

Baydas's achievements can be summarized as follows. The journal *al-Nafā'is al-'Asriyyah*, succeeded in placing creative literature, particularly narrative fiction and translation, at the center of Palestinian interests for future generations. In so doing, it attracted the attention of a large number of Palestinian writers and readers alike. Secondly, Baydas's translations, especially those of literary works, established a foundation for the emergence of a tradition of narrative fiction, involving matters of genre, technique, and theme. In his journal the principal concern was with narrative fiction rather than other genres. This role of Baydas may be considered primarily responsible, in my opinion, for the fact that the genres and subgenres of narrative fiction were predominant in modern Palestinian literature in the first half of 20th century. According to the well-known Russian arabist Ignaz Krachkovsky,

Two of the serious translators who graduated from the Russian Seminary in Nazareth are Salīm Qab'īn and Khalīl Baydas. Although they were never in Russia, Russian became a national language for them. Both of them worked in journalism and education. Arabs will be indebted to them for being among the first to translate original Russian [literary] works before 1905, in addition to many translations of short stories. (quoted in 'Ubayd Allāh 2001: 64)

Heavily influenced by the Russian and other European novels and stories that Baydas trans-

lated from Russian, he was determined to avoid the more romantic styles and themes as far as possible. Instead, he focused on a more realistic approach, both thematically and aesthetically. This may help to explain the obvious tendency encountered in modern Palestinian literature from the outset to utilize the techniques of realism. Finally, as a teacher of such methods, he had a great influence on younger generations to emulate his example in creative writing and translation. A list of such writers would include: Jibrā'īl Abū Sa'dā, Anton Ballān, Iskandar al-Khūrī al-Baytjālī, 'Abd al-Raḥmān Bushnāq, Ibrāhīm Hannā, Rashīd Dajānī, Jubrān Matar, Philip Hannā Sā'igh, and others.

SELECTED REFERENCES

Hannā Abū Hannā, *Dār al-Mu'allimīn al-Rūsiyyah fī al-Nāsirah "al-Siminār" 1886–1914 wa-atharuhā 'alā al-nahdah al-adabiyyah fī Filastīn* (Nazareth: Wizārat al-Ma'ārif wa'l-Thaqāfah, 1994);

Ahmad Abū Matar, *al-Riwāyah fī al-adab al-Filastīnī (1950–1975)* (Beirut: al-Mu'assasah al-'Arabiyyah li'l-Dirāsāt wa'l-Nashr, 1980);

Wāsif Abū al-Shabāb, *Funūn al-nathr fī al-adab al-Filastīnī, 1900–1948* (Amman: Rawā'i' Majdalāwī, 1998);

Nāsir al-Dīn al-Asad, *Khalīl Baydas: Rā'id al-qissah al-'arabiyyah al-hadīthah fī Filastīn*, 2nd ed. (Palestine: Wizārat al-Thaqāfah al-Filastīniyyah, 2001);

M. Peled, "Palestinian Literature in 1917–1948," *Arabica* 29.2 (1982): 143-183;

Jihād Sālih, *Khalīl Baydas* (Ramallāh: al-Markaz al-Filastīnī li'l-Dirāsāt wa'l-Nashr, 2005);

Kāmil al-Sawāfīrī, *al-Adab al-'arabī al-mu'āsir fī Filastīn min 1860 ilā 1960* (Cairo: Dār al-Ma'ārif, 1979);

Ahmad 'Umar Shāhīn, *Mawsū'at kuttāb Filastīn fī 'l-qarn al-'ishrīn* (Damascus: Dā'irat al-Thaqāfah / Munazzamat al-Tahrīr al-Filastīniyyah, 1992);

Qustandī Shūmalī, *al-Ittijāhāt al-adabiyyah wa'l-naqdiyyah fī Filastīn: Dirāsah li-hayāt al-naqd al-adabī al-hadīth fī Filastīn min khilāl jarīdat Filastīn* (Jerusalem: Dār al-

'Awdah li'l-Dirāsāt wa'l-Nashr, 1990);
Muhammad 'Ubayd Allāh, *al-Qissah al-qasīrah fī Filastīn mundhu nash'atihā hattā jīl "al-Ufuq al-Ba'īd"* (Amman: Wizārat al-Thaqāfah, 2001);

'Abd al-Rahmān Yāghī, *Hayāt al-adab al-Filastīnī al-hadīth min awwal al-nahdah hattā 'l-nakbah*, 2nd ed. (Beirut: Dār al-Āfāq al-Jadīdah, 1981).

'Alī al-Du'ājī
(1909 – 1949)

WILLIAM GRANARA
Harvard University

WORKS

Jawlah hawla bārāt al-bahr al-abyad al-mutawassit ("Bar Hopping Along the Mediterranean", Tunis: al-Dār al-Tūnisiyyah li'l-Nashr, 1987);

Sahirtu minhu al-layālī ("Sleepless Nights", Tunis: al-Dār al-Tūnisiyyah li'l-Nashr, 1987);

Taht al-sūr ("Beneath the Wall", Tunis: al-Dār al-Tūnisiyyah li'l-Nashr, 1983); edited with introduction by 'Izz al-Dīn al-Madanī.

Works in Translation

Periple à travers les Bars Mediterranéens (Tunis: Maison Tunisienne de l'Edition, 1979); translated and introduced by Tahar Cheriaa;

Sleepless Nights (Carthage: Bayt Hikma, 1991); translated and introduced by William Granara.

'Alī al-Du'ājī, literary and cultural icon, is one of the pioneers of modern Tunisian literature. He was a charter-member of the "Taht al-sūr" group of artists and intellectuals who combined literary and artistic experimentation with a politics of anti-colonialism and the struggle for national independence. Although his production cut across various media, he is best remembered as 'the father of the modern Tunisian short story.'

'Alī al-Du'ājī was born to a well-to-do family in the city of Tunis in 1909. His father, al-Hājj Muhammad al-Du'ājī, traced his roots to Turkish soldiers who came with the Ottoman fleet to the shores of North Africa in the sixteenth century to combat invading Crusader forces. Not much is known of his father other than he was a wealthy merchant and landowner who died when 'Alī was four years old; he bequeathed to his wife and children a sizeable trust fund from which the family was able to live comfortably. His mother's family was from the island of Kerkenna (off the coast of Sfax). Her father was employed as a high-level administrator in the beylical government and had served for a period of time as regional governor of Jerba where 'Alī's mother, Nuzhat Bint Shaqshūq, was born and educated. She gave birth to three daughters and two sons, 'Alī being the only survivor of the two. Growing up fatherless and being the only son, 'Alī received the pampering attention and doting affections of a household of women. This may, in part, explain why his fictional world would come to be heavily populated by women characters.

The young 'Alī received his primary education in a neighborhood school where he learned both French and Arabic. His mastery of French at an early age was a source of great pride to him. That, in addition to his playful boasting of his 'Turkish' roots, contributed to his snobbish elitism that was emblematic of the *baldi* upper middle class of urban Tunisians at the time. Upon completing his primary school education, he enrolled for a short time in a local Qur'ān school *(kuttāb)* but soon discovered that this did not suit his temperament and interests. His mother desperately tried to turn him towards a career in business, and for a brief period he worked as an apprentice to a local successful merchant.

Both formal education and a career in business were not meant to be, and the independent minded and financially secure al-Duʿājī embarked upon a project to educate himself by reading and research. He devoured as much as he could, reading avidly in French literature and culture. When he made the acquaintance of ʿAlī al-Jandūbī, a prominent literary scholar whose vast library included books, manuscripts, journals and periodicals from Egypt and Syria, he discovered the wide world of medieval and modern Arabic history, literature and cultural studies.

Al-Duʿājī's emergence into the public sphere coincided with a journalistic renaissance that was exploding on both the political and artistic worlds throughout the decade of the 1930s. With the colonial government's easing up on censorship in 1936, al-Duʿājī started up his own periodical, *al-Surūr*, a gesture that, given the dizzying number of journals proliferating at the time, seems to have been the fashion among intellectuals in order to promote their own works and ideas. Several of al-Duʿājī's contemporaries have attributed the fact that *al-Surūr* lasted a mere six weeks to his lack of discipline, poor managerial skills, and cavalier attitude towards money. His predilection for alcohol and drugs, which would come to have a deleterious affect on both his literary production and his health, may also have been a contributing factor in the journal's failure.

Al-Duʿājī came to be associated with a group of artists and intellectuals who congregated nightly in the cafes of the Bab Souika neighborhood of the old madina in Tunisia to exchange ideas, argue politics, and imbibe mind-altering refreshments. Among the elite group, known as *Jamāʿat taht al-sur* (The Beneath-the-Wall Group) were the brothers Mustafā and Bashīr Khrayf, Zīn al-ʿĀbdīn al-Sanūsī, al-Tahar al-Haddād, Abū 'l-Qāsim al-**Shābbī** (health permitting) (d. 1934), Muhammad al-Saʿīdī, al-Hādī al-ʿAbīdī, and ʿAlī al-Jandūbī. They all shared a passion for politics combined with an

unflinching commitment to create a modern national Tunisian literature and culture that would simultaneously denounce European colonialism in all its forms and embrace the cause of social justice and economic and social equality at home.

The group was, for all intents and purposes, homosocial, and many of its members remained bachelors throughout their lives. Interestingly, the cause of women's liberation and equality was a dominant theme in their political and artistic ideology and writings. As was mentioned earlier, a rather large coterie of women with independent minds and strong characters populate al-Duʿājī's fiction. On the other hand, in an essay entitled "Taht al-sūr" (al-Madanī, 9-54), al-Duʿājī, in sketching people and events that marked nightly life in the cafes of the old quarter, mentions singing girls, actresses, and the occasional reference to prostitutes. The fact that there were as yet no serious female writers or intellectuals at the time suggests that their support for the women's movement may have been more in theory than in practice.

Another distinguishing feature shared by the members of this group was an aggressive pursuit of a modernist polymathy that exposed them to a wide range of inquiry and experimentation, ranging in the fields of politics and literature, history and criticism, fiction (novels and short stories), poetry, theatre, music, photography, film, sculpture and painting. Al-Duʿājī was especially known for his versatility as a sketch artist, songwriter, playwright, and short story writer, and his literary production, especially his short stories, would reflect the multi-media influences on his work.

Although the climate in which al-Duʿājī matured and flourished artistically was highly charged with anti-colonial sentiment, which at times ventured toward the violent, it seems he did not share the political and intellectual angst of many of his colleagues. He did espouse the causes for national independence and social justice, and there were aspects of his work that shared affinities with the firebrand politics of contemporary pan-Arabism, but the ideological overtones of his production could be best understood in terms of cultural assimilation and peaceful coexistence. His snobbery about his Turkish roots and his mastery of French, his bourgeois background and financial security, all played a part in crafting a vision of himself and his work as loyal products of a modern, westernized, secular nation that enjoys a long history and culture with the wider Mediterranean world. In contrast to the confrontational politics brewing between the new generation of 'neo-destourians' (adherents to the new Constitutional Party founded by Habib Bourguiba in 1934) and their more conservative and accommodating 'old-destourians' (members of the first Liberal Constitutional Party founded in 1920 by ʿAbd al-ʿAzīz Thaʿalībī) and their incessant squabbles over the merits and dangers of assimilating into French ways, al-Duʿājī's œuvre, by contrast, more often than not depicts and fantasizes east-west encounters in broad romantic strokes. Absent in his works is the biting criticism of European political and cultural imperialism as well as of his fellow countrymen who allowed themselves to be seduced by it. Against the anti-colonial discourse under which much of his work was produced, and to which most of his colleagues ascribed, al-Duʿājī's creative world may be read as a kind of escapist romanticism in which the stark realties of everyday Tunisian life, the rapid rate of change, and the alienating effects of a foreign modernity are captured at their most humane, vulnerable, and humorous moments.

In his short story "The Story of Uncle Giac-comino," al-Duʿājī constructs an imaginary of cross-cultural tolerance between east and west in the character of an elderly Tunisian of Sicilian origin who narrates to the author/narrator his quest to find his fiancée kidnapped from the small fishing village in Sicily sometime in the later part of the nineteenth century. After discovering that a group of Arab traveling merchants have taken his beloved Mariana and returned to their country, the young Giaccomino scrapes up enough money and ventures across the hostile waters of the Mediterranean in a small fishing boat to find her. In this story, which begins with all the stock images and misconceptions European traditionally held about Arabs and their preoccupations with white slavery, the plot takes an unusual turn as the

young lover encounters a series of receptive Tunisians who aid him in his quest. First, there are the fishermen who help him safely to shore. Then a local citizen takes him in and provides him with shelter and food. Several days later, he meets a captain from the Coast Guard who befriends him and leads him eventually to the beylical palace where he is met first by friendly chamberlains and finally received by the ruler himself, Muhammad Beğ. In the meantime, Captain Selim has sent out informants to scout the 'white slavery' markets, and discovers that Mariana has been bought and married to a local wealthy merchant.

The political and aesthetic messages of the short story are disseminated in the highly-charged romanticism in the resolution of the story: the bey is moved by Giaccomino's story and rules in his favor, provided that Mariana agrees to leave her Tunisian husband and return to her Sicilian fiancée; the newly united couple are married at St. Paul's Cathedral in the city of Tunis in a fairy-tale ceremony attended by Christians and Muslims, Italians and Tunisians (including Mariana's first husband); and the choice of the newlyweds to remain in Tunisia to live their marital life.

Once again, read in the context of the contemporary cross-cultural conflict exacerbated by French colonial rule in Tunisia, al-Duʿājī's story posits a politics of peaceful coexistence in which two cultures, two religions, and two races who share a common history continue to live as equals in tolerance and respect. This philosophical and aesthetic stance with regard to east-west encounters, in fact, dominated al-Duʿājī's œuvre from the earliest stages of his writing. As much as he was a Tunisian nationalist, he was at the same time a pan-Mediterraneanist, and both his fictional world and his non-fictional writings are populated with characters, plots, and settings that reflect positively this pan-Mediterranean vision.

This is certainly the case with his early trave-logue, *Jawlah hawla bārāt al-bahr al-abyad al-mutawassit* (Bar Hopping Along the Mediterranean) which he wrote during a trip along the Mediterranean shores in 1933 and later published in installments throughout 1935 in the prestigious literary journal, *al-ʿĀlam al-adabī*, edited by his friend and colleague, Zīn al-ʿĀbdīn al-Sanūsī. This composition, something between a personal diary and a travelogue, with glimmers of an attempt at a novel, remains in fragments like much of his other works. Scholars to this day are at a loss to explain why, for example, major portions, like his account of Alexandria, are missing.

It has been suggested that al-Duʿājī took this trip in the aftermath of a series of failed business ventures, or even as a possible escape from the tight grip that his overbearing mother continued to exert over him for most of his life. But the reasons for this journey and the text which follows it are more likely to be found in the intellectual culture of the time. Since the middle of the nineteen-century, upper-middle class, western-educated Arab men often topped their educations, formal or otherwise, with a journey *(rihlah)* to Europe as a *de rigueur* rite of passage to full intellectual and artistic legitimacy. The national narrative of modern Tunisian history invariably begins with reformist thinker and intellectual pioneer, Khayr al-Dīn Bāshā (1810-87), whose journey to France and his textual account of it, *Aqwam al-masālik fī maʿrifat ahwāl al-mamālik* (1867), established this tradition. Closer to al-Duʿājī's own time, eminent men of letters wrote accounts of their own journeys; those who did not travel abroad published diaries and memoirs that recounted journeys of psychological displacement, cultural assimilation, and professional accomplishment. Two prominent figures who had strong influences over the young and impressionable al-Duʿājī may very well have inspired him to produce a work such as *Bar-hopping*. One was Abū 'l-Qāsim al-Shābbī (1909-34), Tunisia's brilliant young poet who succumbed to heart disease and tuberculoses in the prime of youth and who bequeathed a diary that covered a mere six weeks of his stunning life in the cultural spotlight. The second is Mahmūd al-Bayram al-Tūnisī (1893-1961), the Egyptian born poet, essayist, and anti-colonial agitator par excellence, who wrote his memoirs in fragments that spanned nearly a decade of life in exile, beginning in 1919. When Bayram arrived in Tunisia at the end of 1932, he had already been twice expelled from his native Egypt for his vitriolic writings. After twelve years of forced exile in France, he was received by Tunisian literati as the accomplished author, poet, and journalist who espoused all the right causes, from anti-colonialism, freedom of expression, the emancipation of women, to the preservation and rejuvenation of Arabic language and literature.

According to the many friends and scholars who wrote posthumously on the life and work of al-Duʿājī, there is a consensus that he found in Bayram something of a role model and idol. Sixteen years his junior, al-Duʿājī could indeed find much to identify in the outspoken and controversial journalist, poet, and political activist. Like Bayram, al-Duʿājī lost his father at an early age, rejected all forms of conventional education, tried his hand at and failed in business, and developed a predilection for drugs and alcohol. According to contemporary Francophone journalist, ʿAbd al-ʿAzīz Laroui, al-Duʿājī affected Bayram's mannerisms; he even claims that it was Bayram who was responsible for al-Duʿājī's notorious addictions.

The personal and professional relationship between Bayram and al-Duʿājī was one that embraced a vast spectrum of contemporary political, artistic, and ideological currents that electrified the cultural scene in Tunisia during the 1930s. This relationship was built upon the shared view that while colonialism was detrimental to the development of Arab societies, many aspects of westernization were powerful and necessary antidotes against a stagnant, obsolete, clergy-controlled traditionalism that was equally—if not more—detrimental to progress. Both men shared a commitment to writing and to creating new literary and artistic modes of expression that would narrate the human condition and champion the cause of the common man. They shared an ardent passion for journalism, for the freedom of the press to lash out at the social injustice, religious hypocrisy, and economic inequity that was ravaging their societies. The impact of Bayram on al-Duʿājī's *œuvre* is evident: al-Duʿājī experimented with *maqāmāt* stories and *zajal* poetry, genres that Bayram had popularized. In fact, so much of their work shares similar themes and motifs that it has led to confusion over the authorship of some works. It is likely, therefore, that al-Du'ājī's journey to Europe and his published account of it were a process of following in Bayram's footsteps.

But that wide spectrum of currents in Tunisian political and cultural life in the 1930s generated a complex discourse with sharply conflicting points of view, with Bayram and al-Du'ājī often reacting in different ways to certain issues. For, beyond their shared brilliant sense of humor, accurate caricaturing, and refined sensitivities to human suffering and frailties, the two men were separated by life experiences, temperaments, and political expectations that influenced their responses to events taking place around them. Al-Du'ājī, who paled in comparison to Bayram in terms of production, creativity, and language, and who lacked the discipline, focus and consistency that marked Bayram as a writer, never suffered the humiliation of forced exile and the pangs of cold and hunger that Bayram had to endure throughout his years in France.

Bar Hopping Along the Mediterranean has none of the political angst nor the gut wrenching accounts of hunger and humiliation that pepper Bayram's *Mudhakkirāt fī 'l-manfā* (Memoirs in Exile). Quite the opposite, it is a picaresque account of people and episodes that al-Du'ājī happens upon on ships, cafes, and tourist sites. It is a haphazard literary text that bears all the markings of al-Du'ājī's subsequent work; above all, it illustrates the author's uncanny ability to capture the totality of the human condition through a series of snapshots and vignettes that expose the humanness and vulnerability of ordinary people living on the edges of society or struggling to make their way against the behemoth of a changing world. Drawing on a simplest physical characteristic or a quirky personality trait, al-Du'ājī at every moment of writing constructs a universe of people who connect to each other in a common—if flawed—humanity. There is the confused muezzin who sits on top of his minaret calling the faithful to prayer as he squirms uncomfortably in a western style cap ordered by Atatürk to replace the turban in order to make Turkey a modern European state. Or the

tour guide in Pompeii who parrots historical and archeological facts in a halting French, of all of which he has little command. And we meet Madame Know-it-All, the archetypal ugly tourist, who invades every conversation as she drags her speechless husband behind her on a leash. Whereas *Bar Hopping* lacks much of the anti-colonial rhetoric (as well as the intellectual curiosity and self-critical introspection) that spice modern Arabic journey texts, it does succeed in positing a world delightfully turned upside-down, where the forces of politics, religion, culture, and history are all distilled into the caricatures of these ordinary people.

Al-Du'ājī's most enduring contribution to Tunisian national and pan-Arabic literature are his short stories that were collated and published in 1969 (reprinted in 1987), twenty years after his death, into a single anthology entitled *Sahirtu minhu al-layālī* (Sleepless Nights, 2000). The short, sketchy, and at times piecemeal quality of the stories can be attributed as much to his spirit of experimentation as to the frenetic pace of the rise and fall of popular journals that flooded the cultural scene in Tunisian in the thirties and forties. Following the colonial government's proclamation lifting censorship in 1936, to cite just one example, we see an outburst of journals in fierce competition with each other to publish short stories, poems, songs, cartoons, riddles, art and music criticism, and above all, biting political commentary. By way of example, on August 31, 1936, al-Du'ājī began his short-lived *al-Surūr*; Zīn al-'Ābdīn al-Sanūsī published his *Tūnis* at the same time; Bayram al-Tūnisī left *al-Zaman* in that same year and started his own *al-Shabāb* on October 29, and then another, *al-Sardūk*, in April 1937.

Al-Du'ājī's literary influences were wide and varied. According to his contemporaries, he admired the medieval Arab belle-lettrist, al-Jāhiz (d. 869), and the poet Abū 'l-'Alā' al-Ma'arrī (d. 1057). His favorite modern writers were Chekhov, Flaubert, Mark Twain and Jack London. Such diverse interests no doubt had an impact on the eclectic styles and forms of his storytelling.

Reading the stories in his collection in sequence (assuming they were collated by chronological order), one can see both a gradual evolution from crude experimentation and borrowing to literary maturity and confidence, a progression that runs along a romantic, realistic, philosophical continuum. The opening story in the collection, "The Treasure of the Poor," is a translation of a story in rhyme written by the Italian author, Gabriele d'Annunzio (1863-1938). It is high romanticism in its most melodramatic phase, and it does suggest a process of translation, imitation, adaptation, and indigenization that informed Arabic-European literary encounters and borrowings at the time.

Al-Duʿājī tapped into popular culture as well. *"Ahlām Haddī"* (Haddī's Dreams, 1944) is a prose composition in standard Arabic (MSA) of a Bedouin woman's song that was recounted to al-Duʿājī in the Tunisian dialect. The 'picara' disguises her identity and sex by wearing men's clothing, effecting a mannish voice, riding horses through the desert, and smoking kif with the men around the campfire. It is her means of being free in a traditional Bedouin, homosocial, desert environment. On a starless night, Haddī asks that the candle be extinguished, and then improvises an imaginary tale that reveals a poetic soul: At the top of a castle by the sea, a swarthy man in a smoking jacket awaits his fair-haired lover in a marble-walled room as she prepares for bed. She is dressed in a silk robe; in her hand is the candle. Then in slow, suggestive movements, she disrobes herself limb by limb. Their lovemaking takes place as the waves crash against the walls of the castle.

The story, built on a series of binary images of masculinity and femininity, desert and sea, tender kisses and rough waves, prose and poetry, traditional values and modern liberation, emits its strongest message in the tension between the romanticism of a pristine native Arab environment and the allure of a modern romance, both offering the freedom to choose one's identity and course of existence. Haddī's character is a prototype for the al-Duʿājī heroine (or anti-heroine), a complex figure, liberated from the overdetermination that would confine the female character in Arabic literature until the emergence of women writers in Lebanon and Syria a generation later. Akin to the *scoundrel/narrator* of the pre-modern *maqāmah* tradition, Haddī,

like Shahrazād, has the ability to disguise herself in word and deed, thereby marking her own identity and assuring her survival.

"Sirr al-ghurfah al-sābi'ah" (The Secret of the Seventh Room, 1946) is similar in its mixing of the medieval and modern in creating an indigenous Tunisian short story: it is a composition of embedded stories within stories, showing signs of al-Duʿājī's growing mastery of modern narratological techniques. The story draws on an *Arabian Nights*-like tale of a young prince kidnapped by a sorcerer and taken to a castle where he is provided with everything he could want save entry into the seventh room. True to the weakness of human nature and the enticements of good story-telling, the young prince enters the room. Surrounding the medieval tale is the story of a modern physician who tells his impressionable students about a beautiful but mysterious woman whom he eventually treats for a venereal disease. The conscious choice of the young woman to leave the comforts of her bourgeois family and seek refuge in a brothel as a way of seeking her own independence may carry autobiographical echoes of the author's own dissipated life and his contempt for social and moral conventions.

Al-Duʿājī's fictional world also draws on theatre and cinema as several of his short stories suggest. *"Rāʿī al-Nujūm"* (The Star Gazer, 1944) is a theatrical dialogue between two characters, 'he' and 'she' as social outcasts. In a male-female binary, he is the unrealistic philosopher and she the cynical realist. The story bears an uncanny resemblance to [the later] Samuel Beckett's bleak *Endgame* and *Waiting for Godot* in its dark, empty surrealism, and its philosophical and psychological musing about modern man's alienation and inability to communicate. The title story of the collection, *"Sahirtu minhu al-Layālī"* (Sleepless Nights, 1946) also reads like a script for a TV melodrama about a neglected housewife and her abusive and alcoholic husband who remains voiceless in the story's background. The narrative unfolds through a bickering dialogue between the wife and her aunt who taunts her niece into leaving with their small child. But in a tender, almost, humorous, turn of plot, the story concludes with the wife's defenses of and passion for her husband.

Several stories in the collection harp on violence and revenge that follow failed relationships, real or imagined, loneliness and rejection. In *"Qataltu Ghāliyah"* (I Killed Ghalia, 1946) and *"Mujrim raghma anfih"* (A Criminal in Spite of Himself, 1945) we see al-Du'ājī's skillful use of Hitchcockesque black and white settings, foggy and deserted train stations, abandoned warehouses, and poorly lit street corners on rainy nights. The narrative techniques vary as well, with frequent flashbacks, flashforwards, ellipses, mistaken identities, sudden twists of plot, and surprise endings, accompanied by dialogue that dissolves into monologue as man pours out his soul to an unresponsive society.

Al-Du'ājī reaches his full maturity as a short story writer in *"Nuzhah Rā'iqah"* (A Pleasant Outing, 1946). It is an allegorical depiction of Tunisian life in the 1940s, a humorous tale of an afternoon outing, with farcical characters and picaresque adventures, whose simple plot is to have an ordinary picnic. Through the narrator's interior monologues, descriptions, observations, and commentaries all addressed directly to the reader audience, we hear the cacophony of a Tunisian society clashing with itself against the proliferation of technological instruments of modernity to which its characters aspire. Much of the action takes place on and off the road, between two symbolic settings. The first encompasses the action on the road, speeding on a tree-lined highway, racing with passing trucks, and wandering off onto the unpaved and unknown; or treading on brush and marshes through dark forests in search of real or imaginary streams. The second setting takes place in the car into which the seven characters are packed with picnic baskets and cooking utensils. The narrator, trapped in the front seat, conveys the tight confines of a speeding car going nowhere, as the physical discomfit and anxiety that lie beneath the humor express the human condition.

The ironic tones of the story are richly enhanced in the characters of 'Abdallāh Tūnisī (perhaps a name akin to our own John Doe), the picnic's host, and his 'quarter brother' 'Āmirah, the owner and driver of the car. In a delightful switch of the *maqāmah*'s host/guest hierarchy, it is 'Abdallāh's failed attempts at hospitality and planning which result in a spoilt lunch, and 'Āmirah, whose ignorance of the roads and the car he owns ends in a total breakdown, thus becoming the objects of derision and the focus of the satire. The incongruous descriptions of both their houses and their clothing focus our attention on the clash between European imperialism's modern materialism and the simple lives of the average North African. Cultural pretensions, migration from the village to the city, the clash of tradition and modernity, and the frantic quest for material gain, render these characters as failures of colonialism's *mission civilisatrice* and the prototype of the modern Arab misfit, the Tunisian *gu'r*, that sometimes humored, often scorned Arab who cannot seem to find his way through the maze of modern civilization as defined by Europeanism.

Perhaps no short story writer at this time in the Arab world produced such a motley collection of stories that vary in narrative techniques and experimentation. We may gain some insight into his process when he wrote in an essay entitled "The Short Story in Modern Maghribi Fiction" (reprinted in al-Madanī, 65-80):

The short story ... is in essence a believable depiction of an unusual scene. Its unusualness should be both credible and palpable to the reader. The mission of the short story writer is to show reality, pure and simple, in a clear and illuminating language. He should seize the reins of his pen and protect it from excessive comments, personal feelings, and pedantry.

'Alī al-Du'ājī died of tuberculosis in a free clinic of a public hospital on May 27, 1949. His considerable wealth had been exhausted, and the years of excessive living had taken its toll on both his health and his purse. Two photographs at the end of al-Madanī's Du'ājī anthology *(Taht al-sūr)* capture a proud but broken man sitting alone on his deathbed. By many accounts he was abandoned by many of his friends and harbored bitter disappointment for not being recognized for his work. On the tenth anniversary of his passing, Zīn al-'Ābdīn al-Sanūsī published an article entitled "al-Du'ājī's Legacy" (*Mirāth al-Du'ājī*, reprinted in al-Madanī, 98-204) which resurrected critical inquiry and public interest in his work. Al-Sanūsī reports that al-Du'ājī had written in his lifetime 163 radio sketches, and that his heirs discovered sixty more among his affects. He wrote fifteen plays, some of which he directed himself. In addition, he composed nearly five hundred songs and poems *(zajal)* in Tunisian Arabic. For some today, he is best remembered for his play *Zawba'ah fī finjān* (A Storm in a Teacup) that was part of the inaugural celebrations for Tunisian Television in 1966.

Again, in the late sixties, one full generation after his passing, 'Alī al-Du'ājī resurfaced on the national Tunisian consciousness and cultural scene, thanks in large measure to the critical reappraisals of Tawfīq Bakkār and 'Izz al-Dīn al-Madanī, along with the publication of his works into single volumes.

Al-Sanūsī writes that al-Du'ājī's œuvre emanated from an acute ability to observe everybody and everything around him, and that he observed with his heart and his conscience (al-Madanī, 198). Bakkār writes that

each of his stories is a trip where he takes you by the hand and leads you into a corner of Tunisian society to introduce you to some aspect of the Tunisian persona.   (*Tajdīd*, 1962)

Al-Du'ājī once dubbed himself as an 'artist of the downtrodden' *(fannān al-ghalābah)*, and this best encapsulates the essence of his politics, sensibilities and artistic inclinations He possessed a rare quality in his vision, his language, and his artistry to tap into the Tunisian soul. For this he is considered a major figure in modern Tunisian literature and culture.

REFERENCES

Tawfīq Bakkār, "Ali Du'ājī: Fannān al-ghalābah", *al-Tajdīd* 11 (Nov. 1962);

W. Granara, "Picaresqe Narratives and Cultural Dissimulation in Colonial North African Literature", *Arab Studies Journal* 11.2-12.1 (Fall-Spring 2003-4).

Ilyās Farhāt

(1893 – 1976)

SALMA KHADRA JAYYUSI

Cambridge, Massachusetts

WORKS

Rubā'iyyāt Farhāt ("The Farhāt Quartets", Brazil, 1925);

Dīwān Farhāt ("Farhāt's Dīwān", Brazil, 1932); introd. by George Hassūn Ma'lūf;

Ahlām al-rā'ī ("The Shepherd's Dream", São Paolo: Majallat al-Sharq, 1952);

Qāla al-rāwī ("The Narrator Speaks", Damascus: the Syrian Ministry of Culture, 1965);

Fawākih rij'iyyah ("Late Fruits", Damascus: the Syrian Ministry of Culture, 1967);

Matla' al-shitā' ("Approach of Winter", Cairo: Maktabat al-Qāhirah, 1967).

Collected Poems

Dīwān Farhāt (São Paolo, 1954); 4 vols., introduction by Habīb Mas'ūd; 1. *Rubā'iyyāt Farhāt* ("The Farhāt Quartets"); 2. *al-Rabī'* ("Spring"); 3. *al-Sayf* ("Summer"); and 4. *al-Kharīf* ("Autumn").

Ilyās Farhāt was a major Lebanese émigré poet in Latin America who flourished there in the second and third quarters of the twentieth century. Born to a poor family, Farhāt never received any formal education beyond elementary school. Dire living conditions prompted his emigration to Brazil in 1910 where he tried to eke out a living through extremely hard work in a difficult environment, never earning enough to secure the affluent life achieved by many of his émigré compatriots. He started his creative career early, while still in Lebanon, writing *zajal* in the Lebanese colloquial, a form of folk poetry far removed from the language, technique and usual content of formal poetry. In Brazil he shifted to writing formal poetry, applying himself to learning its methods and technique, and soon came to excel in the art. In 1925 he won solid acknowledgement as a poet with his first collection, *Rubā'iyyāt Farhāt* (The Farhāt Quartets), after which regular further publications in periodicals brought him to poetic prominence in Latin America and the Arab world alike.

He wrote a vivid and moving verse, one that sometimes reflects a literature of wisdom and contemplation but mainly deals with patriotic themes involving the Arab world as a whole, with constant resort to descriptions of his personal experience that possess great charm and candor. He was honored a number of times in cultural circles in both Latin America and the Arab world, which he visited on invitation during the latter part of his life. He has five collections of verse which include his four volume, *Dīwān Farhāt,* published in 1954. He also has a short biographical prose account.

The second and third decades of the twentieth century were a period of revolution in Arabic literature. In the Arab world itself literature was in great need of change; by the 1920s, the dominant neoclassical school, headed by the great Ahmad **Shawqī** (1869-1932), had outlived its once crucially needed role. Along with Shawqī, a large number of poets were now being forced to cede their place, albeit slowly, to a new spirit, romantic in the main, and to new, if mild, innovations in the technique of the poem. In this context the influence of the Arab poets of North America (who, with their southern colleagues, came to be known as the "Mahjar" [émigré] poets) was of central importance, in criticism and creative writing, in its influence on the Arab world—one that heralded a romantic mood, advocating change and innovation in both style and content, and themselves embracing these concepts with zeal.

One of the most interesting features of Mahjar poetry overall is the basically different contribution made, respectively, by the southern and northern poets. Of the two the northern contribution was the more *avant garde* and Westernised, bent on innovation and modernization. It was to have a profound influence on the technical and attitudinal course of modern Arabic poetry. The Arab poets of North America were an actual link between Western poetry and an Arabic poetry eager to modernize. Having experienced at first hand an ambience which celebrated the ideals of progress and freedom in glowing terms, they rapidly adopted these values as universal ideals, but usually failed to link them to the political aggressions that were continually being launched against their homelands. Their adoption of the values in question remained largely on the abstract and universal levels, making an appeal on the spiritual and intellectual levels. As they compared conditions at home with those in North America, the cause that motivated them the most was the generalized one of individual liberty, reform, social justice, progress, innovation in art and life. The major figures among these northern Mahjar poets (including Jubrān Khalīl **Jubrān** and Īliyyā **Abū Mādī**) had greater access to Western literature, mainly in English, than their southern colleagues. All of them were also influenced by the rapid pace of change to be found in America and its attitude towards progress and achievement, and by its material prosperity and greater opportunities for cultural exchange. They became more easily critical of their original world.

By contrast, the southern poets found themselves in an environment which was not radically different from the environment from which they had come, where sharp individualism and a slower pace of life prevailed. Most of the major poets in the southern group actively embraced actual events that occurred in the homeland, as the problems engendered by them made the news. They made use of poetry in order to play their part in the political upheavals that were engulfing the world of their origins, speaking to people's practical concerns and spontaneous feelings—anger, rejection, and hope, and to their will to strive and prevail. In general, their poetry was more aligned with the traditional school, but two southern experiments endeavored to introduce some very novel themes and treatment: that of Fawzī al-Ma'lūf (1889-1930) in his highly innovative long poem, "'Alā bisāt al-rīh" (On the Carpet of the Wind), a delightful work on an evidently abstract theme, involving the dualism of good and evil, the ultimate freedom of the soul, and life's slavery and burdens; secondly, that of Shafīq al-Ma'lūf (1905-1977) in his experimental long poem "'Abqar" in which the poet pays an imaginary visit to 'Abqar, the valley of poetic inspiration in Arabia, meets a host of exotic creatures, and listens to their exhortations against the wickedness of man. However, these two experiments seem to have made little mark on poetry at home. They were no match for the *avant-garde* experiments in the North, which exercised such an indelible influence.

The lesser degree of fervor displayed by the more avant-garde Arab poets in North America in their reactions to the major political events in their home countries, as compared with the poets in Latin America, actually provoked some criticism on Farhāt's part. As an avid nationalist, he himself considerably enriched modern Arabic poetry with his expression of the patriotic values and national zeal and leveled some direct criticism at the northern poets (who came to be known as "al-Rābitah al-Qalamiyyah" ["The Bond of the Pen"]) for what he regarded as their indifference. On this subject he has the following to say to the Syrian literary historian, 'Umar al-Daqqāq:

the quarrel between us was due to our enthusiasm [in Latin America] for the Arab world and the events that were happening there. All our poetry was patriotic and nationalistic, while all we heard from our northern friends was echoes of metaphysical ideas and whispers of spiritual thoughts. (See 'Umar al-Daqqāq, *Shu'arā' al-'usbah al-andalusiyyah fī 'l-mahjar*, Beirut, 1973, 627)

Farhāt's criticism of the North Mahjar poets was coupled with another charge: what he viewed as their penchant for writing about abstract issues, reveries, and metaphysical themes, and, above all, their introduction of what he termed unsavory changes in the technique of the Arabic poem and its language. In one of his quartets he describes the North Mahjar poets as renegades, their language as chaotic, their meaning as imprecise, their logic as faulty, their poetry as incomprehensible to earth and heaven alike.

Born in the small town of Kfarshīma south of Beirut, (the birthplace of several other eminent Lebanese men of letters), he had very scant education, leaving school when just ten years of age. The village school he attended was run by priests of his own denomination. According to his own later account of himself he learned little there, but, while still at school discovered that he had a powerful capacity for memorization and eloquent declamation of speeches. He attended two other schools, but only very briefly. Coming from a very poor family, he quickly joined the labor force. Traveling first to Beirut as an apprentice making wicker chairs, he then tried his hand at other things—including work at printing presses, which gave him the welcome opportunity to read books, something that was to prove highly beneficial to his later career as a poet.

Two events stand out in the seven years prior to his emigration to Brazil. The first was a love-affair with a young woman, Anīsah, from his own family and home town. In order to make enough money to ensure a decent life for both of them, he was prompted to emigrate to Brazil where two of his brothers had already gone. It was only after he had secured a promise from the girl to wait for his return that he entertained the idea of emigrating. However, that promise was never fulfilled; soon after his emigration the girl got married at the behest of her family. In fact, this was a not unusual story in Lebanon during the early years of the twentieth century, usually ending with the girl's marriage to someone else soon after the young man's departure; the girl would be following her family's manipulative instructions, while the young emigré usually remained in the new world. This incident, perhaps his first great shock in a life that was to be filled with frustration and disappointment, was the incentive for Farhāt to write a poem revolving around a lock of hair that the girl had given him as a token of their love. Despite its simplistic style and approach, the poem became very popular in both South America and the Arab world. It would be another forty-nine years before Farhāt saw his homeland again.

The second important event was his very early discovery of a talent for Lebanese *zajal*, a special form of colloquial poetry consisting of a kind of improvisation that stems from personal awareness of self and the other but without being necessarily a revelation of real personal experience. Although it can describe the state of mind of the poet *(zajjāl)* and is sometimes written down, good *zajal* is best extemporized. The *zajjāl* sets up a contest with another *zajjāl*; both face a live audience, and each ones does his best to convince them that he should be the winner of the poetic joust; on occasion the competition engages more than one poet on each side. The art of *zajal* usually involves oral improvisation based on the clever manipulation of language and subject matter. It can resort to puns, sarcasm (usually of a benevolent variety), negations and contradictions, competitively teasing the other poet in favor of self and what belongs to self. The main goal is to amuse the audience by improvising clever retorts, often in the same rhyme and metre. As an example, here is a typical exchange involving a famous Lebanese *zajjāl*, Amīn Ayyūb, in a contest with the young novice Farhāt:

In the beginning I was deceived
Thought you were worthwhile
But found out you're not worth
More than five piastres.

[To which Farhāt's retort was instantaneous:]

At first I took you for an equal
Then threw you far behind.
Should they give me the meanest farthing
I'd be an ass if I didn't sell you.

The young Farhāt quickly learned to excel in his *zajal* improvisations. Even at such an early age he managed to challenge some of the more prominent *zajal* poets in his region. He took this poetic gift with him to his new country, but in the new environment his *zajal* attachment was to give way to a much more consequential in-

volvement with formal poetry, a form in which he was to excel and become one of the luminaries of Arabic poetry in the Americas.

In Brazil, Farhāt quickly discovered that life was going to be very difficult for him. Many of the new Arab immigrants managed to succeed in business, some of them becoming very rich, but Farhāt was destined for a life of penury and struggle. His two immigrant brothers, with whom he initially lived and worked and who were a little later to be joined by the rest of the siblings, were working in the commercial field. They were a working class family who felt at home in the kind of life dictated by their immigrant status and their restricted abilities. However, Farhāt never felt at home in the work he had to do. He was erratic, easily drawn to rejecting anything that touched his pride, but at the same time happy to be self-dependent and not beholden to anyone. We find him moving from job to job, from raising pigs to journalism, often compelled to brave the wilderness as a traveling salesman selling goods to native Americans:

Treacherous nights have fought him, blindfolding his eyes
Squeezing poisonous despair into his mouth.
And he has passed his fortieth birthday, yet is still
Tossed hopelessly from wilderness to wilderness
("On the Deck of Irlanza", *al-Sayf*, ii [1954], 96)

His often changeable life took him eventually to San Paulo, the city in which most educated Arab immigrants lived. There he came to know several men of letters, the most famous of whom was al-Qarawī (Rashīd Salīm al-Khūrī [1887-1984]) who became his friend, someone with whom he shared a deep affinity for good poetry and a commitment to Arab nationalism.

In San Paulo he had also to confront the great divide among Arab immigrants who were often deeply split in their political opinions. Since he was an avid nationalist heavily involved in events taking place in the Arab world at large, there was a natural animosity between him and those who favored the colonial relationship with France. Speaking sarcastically he says:

But we owe her [France] a great deal
We're now safe from thieves of East and West
For she's not left a thing in Lebanon
Worth stealing.

> (*Rubā'iyyāt Farhāt*, in *Dīwān Farhāt*
> [1954], 220)

Because of his clear and unmitigated anti-colonialist stance, he was very often the butt of virulent attacks from opponents. However, Farhāt lived and died without ever accepting any compromise in his political, ethical and humanistic outlook on life.

In 1921 he married Julia Bishārah Jibrān, a young woman from an Arab immigrant family. With him she shared life's hardships and the joy of parenthood. They had five children in all, one of whom, a girl, died very young. After many years of struggle, he managed to purchase two houses. However when he received an invitation to make a return visit to his homeland in 1959, he sold both houses in order to finance his extended stay in the Middle East.

Farhāt may have had to struggle constantly to make a living, but, as noted above, he managed to transform himself from a *zajjāl* into an eminent poet. Living an insecure life in his new country and moving from one job to another, he had little hope of a ready-made live audience for *zajal* sessions in Brazil. It must therefore have become quite clear to him that there was little place for *zajal* in his life. Yet his irrepressible poetic gift needed to find a new outlet and platform, and, while it was not yet fully geared to the norms of formal poetry, he realized early on that it was indeed the new platform for him, one with which every Arab speaker could resonate. His new medium had to be the written word.

This soon led him to a further discovery: his knowledge of grammar and prosody was deficient. But such was his ambition and pride that he made up his mind to succeed as a poet. With that in mind, he began to read as many Arabic books as he could find and with a diligence that would eventually flower into an eloquent poetic expression. His reputation as a poet was finally established with the publication of *Rubā'iyyāt Farhāt* (The Farhāt Quartets) in 1925. The first edition included some hundred and sixty quartets, spread over 173 pages of very

small size, and the second of 1954 added a further seventy. The poems contained a varied commentary on his experiences and impressions on life. Some of them are personal, but most encapsulate his observations on the world and society. He expressed a vehement contempt for two things, the first of which was organized religion:

Priests love to organize rituals
All devoid of genuine faith
[True] religion has become a pearl
Buried under heaps of empty shells

> (ibid., 93)

The second was for commerce and the entrepreneurial ethic:

Bedouin philosophy, many centuries ago
Despised commerce, and they were right.
The market of commerce is a jungle
In which wolves howl at you left and right.
Thrown into it, my hands have no nails
To give protection, my jaws have no canines.

> (ibid., 109)

A third major dimension to be found in his poetry is his constant vigilance concerning political events in the Arab world. Criticizing Britain's policy in Palestine, he says sarcastically:

In Jerusalem the most just of countries tries
To revive the dead, by killing the living.

> (ibid., 119)

His highly developed moral and humanitarian outlook is reflected in verses like the following against racism:

If you judge a man by his color,
You've only judged a sheathed sword.
Perhaps beneath a dark skin a heart
as white as a dove pulsates with virtue.

> (ibid., 162)

Many of the quartets refer indirectly, or sometimes directly, to actual experiences, (mainly negative ones), yet in their general conclusions they achieve a universality. They hark back to the rich and ancient tradition of Arabic aphoristic poetry; much loved and memorized, its popularity has continued unabated through the centuries. Farhāt proved himself to be a true heir of this inherited genre of which axioms, maxims, and meditative observations on life form the core.

It seems fit that Farhāt's first attempt at formal poetry should have taken the form of such short poems. After all, this was his first experiment at writing formal poetry, far removed from the techniques, language and content of Lebanese *zajal*. He was now treading new ground, ground that for him was almost sacrosanct, and striving to find his own mode and language. As a novice, he had to align himself judiciously with the well-rooted tradition of the poetic heritage, but he was equally determined not only to prevail in the end but also to find his own voice.

The important point to note here is that these quartets contained a good measure of poetry in them. Their publication seems to have aroused great admiration, assuring Farhāt an immediate and favored place among the Arab poets of South America. His imagination was now kindled, and he gained both confidence and a greater affinity for formal verse. Once he had become his own poet, his genius contrived to find its particular medium of expression. The neo-classical form, with its terseness of language and rhetorical mode of address, was to be his principal model, but in content his authenticity regularly steered him in much of his verse away from the objectivity and formality of neo-Classicism towards the subjective and confessional. We have here a poetry that probes the intricate avenues of human experience, with great success and often charm:

The change from a poetry long dedicated to public ostentation to a poetry of experience and direct personal involvement took place at his hands easily and naturally; so easily and naturally that his service has not been clearly noticed by critics and writers on the Mahjar. They recognized that his poetry was a mirror of his life but they failed to see that this constituted a basic development in poetry, a new approach and attitude.

(Salma Khadra Jayyusi, *Trends and Movements in Modern Arabic Poetry*, Leiden: E. J. Brill, 1977, I, 81)

Following the success of the *Quartets*, he demonstrated greater interest in writing longer poems, at times composing some very long monorhymed *qasīdahs*. In 1932 a committee of men of letters in San Paolo collaborated in publishing his other poetry in a collection titled, *Dīwān Farhāt*. It contained 123 poems with varying lengths and topics, many on the subject of love, including all his youthful poetry written between 1917 and 1932.

Publication in Arabic in South America was obviously expensive: in fact it was to be many years before Farhāt saw the bulk of his poetry published. His third volume, *Ahlām al-rā'ī* (A Shepherd's Dreams) was published in 1953 by the owner of *al-Sharq Review* in Brazil and distributed free to the magazine's subscribers. It was a small book of allegorical verse in which a herd of sheep and their dog comment on the wickedness of man, focusing on the greedy rich and the clergy. Although he himself seems to have favored this particular collection, it is not his best; he excels more in his lyrical poetry. It was in 1954 that the bulk of his poetry to date was collected; after he himself had edited the poems, they were published in four volumes. The first was a republication (with additional quartets) of his *Farhāt Quartets*. The other three were a collection of the rest of his poetry, published with the titles *al-Rabī'* (Spring), *al-Sayf* (Summer), and *al-Kharīf* (Autumn).

In 1959 the government of the United Arab Republic (of Syria and Nasser's Egypt) invited Farhāt and al-Qarawī to visit their homeland. They spent a year touring Lebanon, Syria and Egypt, where they received an unprecedented welcome from their Arab compatriots in recognition of their cogent verse and the support that they had given, throughout their poetic career, to the Arab national cause. In 1967 the Ministry of Culture in Damascus published his collection, *Fawākih rij'iyyah* (Late Fruits), and in the same year a further collection, his last, *Matla' al-shitā'* (Approach of Winter) was published by Maktabat al-Qāhirah. However, there was little in these two volumes to add to the more splendid poetry he wrote earlier in life.

Aside from his poetry, his autobiographical work, *Qāl al-rāwī* (The Narrator Speaks) was published in 1965 by the Ministry of Culture in Damascus. He had initially finished writing it in 1947 and sent it as a manuscript to ʿĪsā al-Nāʿūrī, the editor of the review, *al-Qalam al-Jadīd*, in Amman, Jordan. Al-Nāʿūrī published most of it in his review in 1952-53, but then the review was closed down. Later (1957) it was published in another review, *al-Rāʾid al-ʿArabī*, in Hamāh, Syria, and in 1965 it appeared in book form from the Ministry of Culture in Damascus.

As Farhāt's poetry composed in South America became more accomplished in the third decade of the 20th century, it managed to coincide with the fertile period of innovation in literature in the Arab world, a movement that culminated in the rise of a romanticism that had arrived in the various Arab countries in an intermittent fashion. However, poetic taste does not change that radically or quickly. Even up till the present time, Arabs in the millions still enjoy a taste of the diction and rhythms of the old qasīdas. Farhāt's poetry, with its rejection of the formality and objectivity of neo-Classicism and his instinctive absorption of a good part of the new approach—notably reflected in his great penchant for writing about his personal experience, won him a large audience. He was, moreover, loyal to the well-seasoned spirit that has clung to the Arab poetic apprehension, to an extent up to the present day. That spirit, as conveyed through a poet's work, can be a decisive factor in the assessment of its poetic value. Much poetry has been immortalized, not just for its aesthetic qualities but also for the spirit conveyed by the meaning and outlook of the poet. This element is not often alluded to by critics, and yet it can be a decisive factor in the evaluation of a poetic œuvre within its own time and subsequent times, in its durability. The unchallenged popularity of the great classical poet, al-Mutanabbī (d. 965), for example, owes much to the fact—coupled in his best poetry to a perfection in technique and address—that his poetry revives, sustains and celebrates the earlier Arab spirit at its best and fullest. Ilyās Farhāt can boast of being one of the modern poets who, with great dignity, successfully celebrated the diehard Arab spirit with its indefinable allusions,

the spirit that has always brought Arabs closer together and allowed them to interconnect through their poetry. It is the major factor in an art whose motifs, technique, and outlook are all well entrenched within the poetic heritage. In Farhāt's case it is rendered during the early stages of an Arab modernity that imposed itself to a certain extent through natural compulsion, but equally through a spontaneous rejection of both alien elements and an outmoded indigenous poetic expression.

Farhāt's poetry hails from the inner recesses of the heart; no poetry should be alien to the heart's language; no poetry can rely on cerebral equations that obliterate the inner, most spontaneous apprehension of human experience. A genuine poet always senses the fine threads that bind his utterance to the experience of his times, without necessarily embracing topics in fashionable demand. For all that, Farhāt never turned his back on those topics foremost in the expectations of his audience. He did not seek a completely new approach, but rather, by voicing an ardent personal element in his verse, achieved a radical continuity vis-à-vis the classical repertoire, at once subjective and objective, mixing the externalized with the often internalized experience.

The neoclassical directness from which he never veered insured that he was never elusive and never understated, but always specific. Poetry is the one literary genre which, if handled by a good poet, can accommodate ambiguity with success. But Farhāt's poetry belongs to the age of poetic clarity. Sincere in emotion, candid in thought, almost fanatically truthful, he is always guilefully unpretentious, and his message travels, with an endearing transparency, directly to the hearts and minds of his readers.

As an Arab fully aware of his roots and attached to his history, Farhāt's verse was strongly focused on identity. He would never agree to be one of those modern poets who chose universal topics that seem to belong nowhere. Mīkhāʾīl Nu-ʿaymah's famous poem "Akhī" (My Brother)—one of the few poems which he wrote as an Arab critically aware of the state of things at home, is filled with denigration of the entire social and political panorama of his original world and devoid of any faith or vision for the future. Farhāt on the other hand specifies the ills, but blames them on the culprits who lead his good people astray. When he generalizes, it is only in order to designate the wrongdoers. He bears the Arab dilemma as a personal responsibility, as a cause of deep concern, never contrasting his people's failed experience with that of the flourishing world in the West in such a way as to make them feel responsible for their own failures rather than the victims of oppression and injustice. He certainly never participates in the self-flagellating, self-rejectionist current that begins with Nu'aymah and continues to the present day, bringing in its wake a shaken self-confidence, even despair. His inner decorum and moral sense, his positive outlook on his people and their rich culture, his constant awareness of their integrity and freedom, and his faith in their capacity to prevail, these qualities would not allow him to indulge in condemnations of this

kind—condemnations that some poets, even some of the most famous in contemporary times, have expressed with impunity.

REFERENCES

Ibrāhīm al-Kīlānī, *Shakhsiyyāt: dirāsah adabiyyah wa-nafsiyyah* (Damascus: Ittihād al-Kuttāb al-'Arab, 1973);

——, *al-'Urūbah tukarrim al-shā'ir Ilyās Farhāt* (Damascus: Ministry of Culture, 1959);

'Īsā al-Nā'ūrī, *Ilyās Farhāt, shā'ir al-'urūbah fī 'l-mahjar* (Amman: Dār al-Nashr wa'l-Tawzī' wa'l-Ta'ahhudāt, 1956);

Samīr Qatāmī, *Ilyās Farhāt, shā'ir al-'Arab fī 'l-mahjar: hayātuhu wa-shi'ruh* (Cairo: Dār al-Ma'ārif, 1971);

Muhyī al-Dīn Ridā, *Balāghat al-'Arab fī 'l-qarn al-'ishrīn* (Damascus: Maktabat al-Hadārah, 1920);

al-Thaqāfah 2.2 (July 1959), special issue on Ilyās Farhāt.

Zaynab Fawwāz al-'Āmilī

(c 1850 – 1914)

MARILYN BOOTH
University of Edinburgh

WORKS

al-Durr al-manthūr fī tabaqāt rabbāt al-khudūr ("Scattered Pearls Concerning the Classes of Cloistered Ladies", Cairo/Būlāq: al-Matba'ah al-Kubrā al-Amīriyyah, 1312 [1894-95]);

al-Rasā'il al-zaynabiyyah ("The Zaynab Epistles", Cairo: al-Matba'ah al-Mutawassitah, n.d.);

Riwāyat al-Hawā wa'l-wafā' dhāt arba'at fusūl ("Love and Loyalty in Four Acts", Cairo: Maktabat al-Jāmi'ah, [1893]);

Riwāyat Husn al-'awāqib aw Ghādat al-zāhirah ("Good Consequences, or The Maiden from [the village of] al-Zāhirah", Cairo: al-Matba'ah al-Hindiyyah, 1899/1316);

Riwāyat al-malik Qūrūsh aw malik al-Fars ("King Qūrūsh or King of Persia", Cairo: al-Matba'ah al-Hindiyyah, 1905).

Later Editions

al-Durr al-manthūr fī tabaqāt rabbāt al-khudūr (Cairo: Matba'at Būlāq, 1914);

al-Durr al-manthūr fī tabaqāt rabbāt al-khudūr (Kuwayt: Maktabat Ibn Qutaybah, n.d.); facsimile ed., lacking pp. 2-4 (*taqārīz*) and pp. 551-52, a final encomium to the khedive;

Husn al-'awāqib (riwāyah); al-Hawā wa'l-wafā' (masrahiyyah), ed. Fawziyyah Fawwāz, Min al-Turāth al-'Āmilī, no. 1 (Beirut: al-Majlis al-Thaqāfī li-Lubnān al-Janūbī, 1984).

Works in Translation

"Fair and Equal Treatment" (1891/92), in: *Opening the Gates: A Century of Arab Feminist Writing*, ed. Margot Badran and Miriam Cooke (London: Virago, 1990; Bloomington and Indianapolis: Indiana University Press, 1990), 221-26; translated by Marilyn Booth.

In company with 'Ā'ishah Taymūr ('Ā. al-**Taymūriyyah**), Zaynab Fawwāz was among the earliest generation of Arab female intellectuals to participate in public debates on the politics of the nation, gender and literature in the modern era. When she died in January 1914, Fawwāz was eulogized in the Egyptian press as a leading journalist and imaginative writer—a remarkable feat for a Shī'ī immigrant from south Lebanon in the nineteenth century who was, moreover, poor and female. Like so many of her contemporaries, Fawwāz wrote in a range of genres: poetry, mostly occasional and praise poems in the monorhyme *qasīdah* form; the novel, new at the time to writers of Arabic; a play, probably the first play by an Arab woman to be published; and nonfictional essays in the mainstream newspapers of Cairo and Beirut as well as in a few magazines directed to a female Arabophone audience. Her essays were hard-hitting, giving her a means to debate male commentators at a time and in a context where she could not or would not transgress the practices of spatial seclusion, including the wearing of the face-veil, and thus could not orally address mixed audiences in public forums. The newspaper was a substitute, and Fawwāz made the most of it. Also like Taymūr, Fawwāz has enjoyed a late-twentieth-century fame as an "early feminist," as one of many writers, women and men, who initiated a wide-ranging discourse on gender politics, social-political organization, and modernity from the 1880s on in the Arab capitals.

If Fawwāz is recognized by historians of gender and of Arabic literature for her essays and her fictional prose, she is perhaps best known for her monumental biographical dictionary of women, discussed further below. Yet, as I have remarked in a longer study of this compendium, this woman who compiled and constructed so many other women's lives in print was utterly reticent on her own life experience. Though her novel *Husn al-'awāqib* (Good Consequences) draws from the scenery of her youth, and though some of her essays touch upon her own acquaintances and social life as an adult in Cairo, we are dependent on others for information, and there are several narratives, each with its own store of mystery and romance. We do not even know Fawwāz's birth date: sources give dates ranging from 1846 to 1860. The sources do agree that she was born into a Shī'ī family of limited means in the town of Tibnīn in the heavily Shī'ī region of Jabal 'Āmil, which had long been a center of Shī'ī intellectual activity. Indeed, in her adulthood Fawwāz would be hailed from afar by the publisher of the venerable south Lebanese magazine *al-'Irfān*, which published one of her poems and, in 1959, featured a multi-part biography of Fawwāz by Muhammad Yūsuf Muqallid, who was able to rely partly on interviews conducted in the area and in Damascus.

As a young girl, it seems, Zaynab was taken into the local ruling household of 'Alī Bek al-As'ad, as a domestic employee or client of some sort, probably working under the supervision of 'Alī Bek's consort, Fātimah bint As'ad al-Khalīl, who was born somewhat before Fawwāz (1840-41/1256). Somewhat unusual for her time, Fātimah was not only a literate woman but a poet herself, and she taught Zaynab at least the rudiments of reading and writing. If only we could know more about this first mentoring relationship! Fātimah is one of the few women featured in Fawwāz's biographical dictionary who was still living when it was composed, and Fawwāz emphasizes her learning in *fiqh* (jurisprudence) and poetry (as well as, of course, her memorization of the Qur'ān). If Fawwāz was born as early as 1846, then her mistress would have been only a few years older; if as late as 1860, Zaynab was young enough to be Fātimah's daughter (according to her biography of her mentor, Fātimah did not marry until the age of eighteen), and surely that would have made a difference in their relationship.

There is more disagreement concerning Fawwāz's marriage(s) and the circumstances under which she moved first possibly to Beirut, then to

Alexandria and ultimately to Cairo. According to Muqallid, she was married in Tibnīn to another al-Asʿad retainer, a groom and falconer who was possibly her relative, but they were divorced; she went to Egypt, this source speculates, in search of more learning and because of "family presence" there. (Her brother was a lawyer in Egypt, but we do not know when he first arrived there or who immigrated first. That he was a lawyer suggests that these siblings' birth family did in some sense foster intellectual and professional achievement.) Other sources have suggested that she fled a betrothal or a consummated marriage in Tibnīn (possibly to a relative who approached her after her divorce from the retainer) by going to Beirut and finding employment, then immigrating to Alexandria with her employers, who may have been members of the aristocratic Yakan family. But another narrative has her moving to Alexandria with her birth family when she was about ten years old.

Whatever the case, in Egypt Fawwāz soon became a protégée of newspaper publisher and littérateur Hasan Husnī Pāshā al-Tuwayrānī (1849/50-1896 or 1897/98, 1266-1315), whom she may have met through the Yakans, if she did indeed work for them. It was in his newspaper *al-Nīl* (The Nile) that she published many of her most famous essays beginning in the early 1890s. This was her most productive decade, for most of her essays appeared in the press during it, as did her biographical dictionary and, at the end of the decade, her first novel and her sole play.

Her essays in *al-Nīl* and in other periodicals as well as a few poems were collected and published in *al-Rasāʾil al-Zaynabiyyah* (the Zaynab Epistles; the volume is labeled "Part One" but a second volume never appeared). Undated, this volume must have appeared no earlier than very late 1905, for the latest essay contained therein had been published 18 Jumādā II 1323 [20 Aug. 1905], but no later than late 1906, for the volume had been given to at least one reader by the time the fourth issue of *Fatāt al-sharq* (Young Woman of the East), one of the early Arabic women's magazines, with a publication date of 15 January 1907, went to press. The magazine's

editor (and a sister novelist), Labībah Hāshim, mentioned that Fawwāz had given her a copy, praising its author for her "fine writing... and no wonder, for she is among the excellent lady writers *(afāḍil al-sayyidāt al-kātibāt)* in whom the East takes pride ... we urge everyone to read it and enjoy the pearls of its benefits and its themes. It can be obtained from the writer at Sūq al-Silāh Street in Cairo."

In her magazine, Hāshim constantly exhorted young women to read "beneficial" works and to model themselves upon the paragons of womanhood whom she featured in her magazine's biographical sketches, Fawwāz among them. What a young woman would have learned from reading Fawwāz's essays drawn from *The Nile* and other newspapers was the benefit of scrappy and persistent challenges to those commentators—whether women or men—who thought women should submit to the dictates of patriarchal family arrangements concerning choice and age of marriage (not to mention the necessity of marrying) and that girls' education should center solely on providing a healthy and educative upbringing to their children. Like many men writing in the press, Fawwāz inveighed against practices that she saw as exploitative of people and wasteful of resources (such as the *zār*, which referred to a range of spirit-exorcism ceremonies), and also rejected the uncritical westernizing agenda of some of the literati, in particular those in close communication with Europeans, such as some (but by no means all) elite Levantine Christians. But she took to heart the needs and interests of the powerless, whether girls forced into marriages they did not want or older wives faced with the presence of young co-wives (and indeed, in these essays she seems to speak from the heart!), or victims of famine in Algeria. She is sensitive to human psychology and its uses by those with power. In her very first essay in *al-Rasāʾil al-Zaynabiyyah* (The Zaynab Epistles), first published in the Beirut newspaper *Lisān al-hāl* on 28 April 1892, she argues that husbands have learned how to convince a woman that "shutting the doors of education [to her], her not leaving the home, and prohibiting her from attending public women's occasions" are crucial to "the system"; that she "came to imagine that such deeds were grave offenses... that would violate the system of her honor and the law of her protection." Fawwāz applies her characteristically caustic language here:

The husbands' argument ... is that if woman was to learn the true essence of the society ... she would become—or so they claim—malcontent with her life, detesting the rule of her despotic husband; knowledge and learning would compel her to break the rod of obedience and leave the noose of slavery for the arena of freedom.

Her use here of the language of public politics, introducing it at the end of a discussion of marital psychological politics, is breathtaking: at once she demolishes the patriarchal argument for keeping women secluded from education and social participation (even as she is careful not to argue for mixed public gatherings, although there is a story extant that she herself attended one of the nationalist leader Mustafā Kāmil's speeches), and links it to public politics by her choice of diction. This is not an accident: close analysis of Fawwāz's diction throughout her essays reveals a consistently sly juxtaposition of the "domestic" and "political" realms, more pointedly, I would argue, than is true of many other writers of the time. And, by extension, the interrelation of private and public politics is implicated in anticolonial nationalist politics: a forthright challenge to imperial interests across the Arab world can be easily read into her writings, both in what is there and in the silences.

Fawwāz's fiction parallels and explores the thematic contours of her essays. Her first novel, *Husn al-ʿawāqib aw Ghādat al-Zāhirah* (Good Consequences, or The Maiden of al-Zāhirah) is considered by the Syrian critic Buthaynah Shaʿbān to be the first novel in Arabic, though this is contested by the presence of other fictional narratives in that era, even if the novel was written in 1885 and its publication delayed, as some have claimed. The story draws from the author's early life in Lebanon; indeed, Fātimah Asʿad al-Khalīl may be one model for the heroine, and the fortress of Tibnīn, dating from the Crusader period, is itself a player in the plot. More important than referential links, though, is the fact that this story traces the far-flung wanderings of the heroine, Fāriʿah, as she eludes one importunate cousin who wants to marry her even as she (respectably) encourages another cousin, against the wishes of her mother and eldest brother. (This heroine's father, like Fātimah's, died when she was young, and so it is the less prominent representatives of the patriarchy whom Fāriʿah must resist.) That *ghādah* means "young woman" underlines the "everywoman" quality of the message here. In addition to melodramatic adventure and a huge cast of traditional supporting characters, the novel provides a sensitive analysis of gender politics and their centrality to the politics of public rule. And as the heroine faces eastward—seeking refuge at one point in the opulent Persian-rug covered tent of a Bedouin leader's female household—the silence on "western influences" speaks loudly indeed. Young Arab women do not need "the West" to mark out their own futures, in their own voices.

Fawwāz herself was quite astonishingly unconventional in managing her own marital history (such as we know it!). At some point—probably not long before al-Tuwayrānī returned to Istanbul, where he died—Zaynab received an offer of marriage from the Syrian newspaper editor, belletrist, and Ottoman civil servant Adīb Nazmī al-Dimashqī (c1840-1915?), who had apparently read something of hers, leading to a correspondence. But when Zaynab arrived in Syria—Nazmī was at the time in a tiny village in the Hawrān, as an official of the government—she discovered three co-wives and a lack of Egyptian newspapers, and a combination of family tensions and intellectual boredom seems to have propelled her back to Egypt after initiating a divorce with Nazmī. Back in Cairo again, Fawwāz is said to have married an officer in the Egyptian army, but nothing is known about this match (even the sequence is in doubt: Muqallid places this marriage before that to Nazmī). With such an independent trajectory, it seems no wonder that Fawwāz gave attention in her writings to the issue of family pressures affecting marriage choices among young women and men. Not only her first novel but also her one play centered on this theme. But it was not just a question of life experience: this was a theme that many of the earliest modern Arabic fictions treated, for it seemed a central issue to young intellectuals of the time both in itself and as a symbolic field with resonance for questions of communal and national freedom of choice as well.

If only she had written about herself among those "Scattered Pearls" *(al-Durr al-manthūr)* whom she commemorated in biography! She tells us in her introduction what sources she used; and she gives us a sense of her outlook as she reproduces essay after essay by her contemporaries, to prove to the reader that in 1894, a critical mass of writing Arab women already exists. She even publishes an essay by Hannā Kūrānī, with whom she had a vociferous running debate about the proper sphere of women's activities, in the pages of *al-Nīl*. (There is possible evidence that some signatures of the book were published considerably earlier than the publication date of 1894; did Fawwāz want to have Kūrānī included or, by the time of their debate, did she have no choice?). And the 550-odd biographical sketches in the book, as much as they follow the diction and emphases of pre-modern Arabic biographical dictionaries in the qualities they emphasize and the anecdotes they tell, allow certain themes to emerge through repetition across the lives of women of discrete times and places, from pre-Islamic Arabia to classical Greece and Persia to medieval Europe to the modern moment of Fawwāz's own turn-of-the-century. One prominent theme is that women have always been intimately involved in ruling large populations, and not simply through "women's wiles" but rather through their strong and judicious decision-making. As Fawwāz says of Fāṭimah al-Asʿad, "She had firmly in hand the reins of matters [of state], not to mention having firm possession of her husband's heart." A second and pointed message to readers, demonstrated in entry after entry, is that learning has been the province of women, who have excelled in intellectual arenas, and women have been teachers throughout history. Third, women have not been timid about pursuing their goals. Fourth, women have participated in and contributed to collective social goals, whether commer-

cial, intellectual or political, peaceful or violent. The collective impact of these sketches is to break down the notion of essential or "natural" gender roles. And finally, Fawwāz offers that leitmotif of Arabic (and other) biographical sketches of women from a consciously modern perspective: women's intellectual work doesn't detract from their *home*-work! This was a theme that editors in the women's press would repeat and repeat through their biographical sketches, many of which (especially in *Young Woman of the East*) were drawn partially or wholly from Fawwāz's *Scattered Pearls*. Fawwāz's volume is also important in juxtaposing Arab and Muslim women with women of other cultural areas or heritages. This has the effect of decentering "the West"; while Fawwāz's portraits of European and American women are mostly positive, they are no more so than those of Arab and/or Muslim women, and the latter outnumber the former. The points are subtly made that Arab and Muslim women have their own profound female heritage on which to build, that the colonial accusation of "Islam holding back society by repressing women" is flimsy indeed when faced with the claims of history, and that women can find—and have found—their ways to self-fulfillment and creative power (as well as repressive power!) by means of their own cultural tools. This becomes an especially resonant message when one remembers that Fawwāz corresponded with Berthe Honoré Palmer in Chicago to offer her biographical dictionary as a contribution to the Women's Library that was a signal project of the Women's Building at the 1893 Chicago Exposition, one of the most famous and ambitious of nineteenth-century World's Fairs. Here was an Arab woman writing the lives of Western women for the edification of her compatriots, a version of Western lives that most women visiting the Women's Building would not have been able to read. There is no evidence, sadly, that Fawwāz's book actually was part of the Women's Library: the list of acquisitions does not include it. Yet the gesture itself was important, locally as well as in Chicago, and Fawwāz recognized that: her exchange with Palmer was published in *al-Nīl*. For local readers, this might have acted as both a source of pride—Arab women demonstrating to American women their own intellectual activisms—and as an exhortation to view cultural exchange as emphatically not unidirectional.

Fawwāz as a writer was squarely within her own time: she was not an innovator in prose (or poetry). But she dared to put conventional forms to new uses, and old usages to new effects. She dared to put a female signature on genres that had been entirely or almost entirely the province of male authors (notably, biography). She dared to challenge other writers in the public forum of the press, unveiling her name and her views if not her face. In her own life, she dared to try new experiences; she also dared to leave behind unsatisfactory marriages and stultifying places, even though she did not have the financial security to guarantee an easy life.

REFERENCES

Zaynab Nubuwwah Bahbūh, *Zaynab Fawwāz: Rā'idah min a'lām al-nahdah al-'arabiyyah al-hadīthah, 1846–1914* (Damascus: Manshūrāt Wizārat al-Thaqāfah, 2000);

Marilyn Booth, "Exemplary Lives, Feminist Aspirations: Zaynab Fawwaz and the Arabic Biographical Tradition," *Journal of Arabic Literature* 26.1-2 (March-June 1995): 120-46;

——, "Fiction's Imaginative Archive and the Newspaper's Local Scandals: The Case of Nineteenth-Century Egypt," in: *Archive Stories: Facts, Fictions, and the Writing of History*, ed. Antoinette Burton (Durham, NC: Duke University Press, 2006), 274-95;

——, *May Her Likes Be Multiplied: Biography and Gender Politics in Egypt* (Berkeley and Los Angeles: University of California Press, 2001);

Fawziyyah Fawwāz, "Sīrah wa-hayāh," in: Zaynab Fawwāz, *Husn al-'awāqib (riwāyah); al-Hawā wa'l-wafā' (masrahiyyah)*, Min al-Turāth al-'Āmilī no. 1 (Beirut: al-Majlis al-Thaqāfī li-Lubnān al-Janūbī, 1984), 11-34;

Muhammad Yūsuf Muqallid, "Zaynab Fawwāz," *al-'Irfān* 47.2-10 (1959-60);

Hilmī Namnam, *al-Rā'idah al-majhūlah: Zaynab Fawwāz, 1860-1914* (Cairo: Dār al-Nahr li'l-Nashr wa'l-Tawzī', 1998);

Joseph T. Zeidan, *Arab Women Novelists: The Formative Years and Beyond* (Albany: State University of New York Press, 1995).

Tawfīq al-Hakīm
(1898 – 1986)

DINA AMIN
Villanova University

WORKS

Plays

Ahl al-kahf ("People of the Cave", Cairo: Matba'at al-Hilāl, 1934);

Shahrazād ("Scheherazade", Cairo: Dār al-Kutub al-Misriyyah, 1934);

Prāksah ("Praksah", Cairo: Maktabat al-Tawakkul, 1939);

Masrahiyyāt Tawfīq al-Hakīm ("Tawfiq al-Hakīm's Plays"), 2 vols. (Cairo: al-Nahdah al-Misriyyah, 1939);

Pygmālyon ("Pygmalion", Cairo: Maktabat al-Tawakkul, 1942);

Sulaymān al-hakīm ("Solomon the Wise", Cairo: Maktabat al-Ādāb, 1943);

al-Malik Udīb ("King Oedipus", Cairo: Maktabat al-Ādāb, 1949);

Masrah al-mujtama' ("Theater of Society", Cairo: Maktabat al-Ādāb, 1950);

al-Aydī al-nā'imah ("Soft Hands", Cairo: Maktabat al-Ādāb, 1954);

Izīz ("Isis", Cairo: Maktabat al-Ādāb, 1955);

al-Masrah al-munawwa' ("Varied Theater", Cairo: Maktabat al-Ādāb, 1956, 1966);

al-Safqah ("The Deal", Cairo: Maktabat al-Ādāb, 1956);

Lu'bat al-mawt ("Death Game", Cairo: Maktabat al-Ādāb, 1957);

al-Sultān al-hā'ir ("The Perplexed Sultan", Cairo: Maktabat al-Ādāb, 1960);

Yā tāli' al-shajarah ("O Tree Climber", Cairo: Maktabat al-Ādāb, 1962);

Rihlat al-rabī' wa'l-kharīf ("Journey in Spring and Autumn", Cairo: Dār al-Ma'ārif, 1964);

Bank al-qalaq ("The Bank of Anxiety", Cairo: Dār al-Ma'ārif, 1966);

Masīr sursār ("Fate of a Cockroach", Cairo: Maktabat al-Ādāb, 1966);

al-Wartah ("The Dilemma", Cairo: Maktabat al-Ādāb, 1966);

al-Hubb ("Love", Beirut: Dār al-Kitāb al-Lubnānī, 1973);

al-Hamīr ("Donkeys", Cairo and Beirut: Dār al-Shurūq, 1975);

'Imārat al-mu'allim Kandūz ("Boss Kanduz's Apartment Building", Cairo: al-Dawliyyah li'l-Intāj al-Thaqāfī, 1981);

Imsik harāmī "Grab the Thief", Cairo: al-Dawliyyah li'l-Intāj al-Thaqāfī, 1981);

Rusāsah fī 'l-qalb ("A Bullet Through the Heart", Cairo: Maktabat al-Ādāb, 1985);

Rajul bi-lā rūh ("A Man with No Soul", Cairo: Dār al-Hilāl, 1998); introduction by Alfred Farag.

Other Works

'Awdat al-rūh ("Return of the Spirit", Cairo: Matba'at al-Raghā'ib, 1933); autobiographical novel;

Yawmiyyāt nā'ib fī 'l-aryāf ("Diary of a Country Prosecutor", Cairo: Matba'at Lajnat al-Ta'līf wa'l-Tarjamah wa'l-Nashr, 1937); novel;

'Usfūr min al-sharq ("A Bird from the East", Cairo: Matba'at Lajnat al-Ta'līf wa'l-Tarjamah wa'l-Nashr, 1938); autobiographical novel;

'Ahd al-shaytān ("Pact with Satan", Cairo: Lajnat al-Ta'līf wa'l-Tarjamah wa'l-Nashr, 1938); collection of short stories;

Arinī 'llāh ("Show Me God", Cairo: Maktabat al-Ādāb, 1953); collection of short stories;

Adab al-hayāt ("The Literature of Life", Cairo: al-Sharikah al-'Arabiyyah li'l-Tibā'ah, 1956); literary essays;

Nazarātī fī 'l-dīn wa'l-thaqāfah wa'l-mujtama' ("My Views on Religion, Culture, and Society", Cairo: al-Maktab al-Misrī al-Hadīth, 1979);

Ahādīth al-arba'ā' ("Wednesday Talks", Cairo: Maktabat al-Ādāb, 1983); theological reflections;

Qālibunā al-masrahī ("Our Dramatic Form", Cairo: Dār Misr li'l-Tiba'ah, 1988); dramatic criticism.

Works in Translation

The Maze of Justice (London: Luzac & Co., 1947); translation of *Yawmiyyāt nā'ib fī 'l-aryāf*, tr. by Aubrey Eban;

"The River of Madness," in: *Islamic Literature* (New York: Washington Square Press Inc. 1963); translation of *Nahr al-junūn*, tr. by Najib Ullah;

The Tree Climber (London: Oxford University Press, 1966); translation of *Yā tāli' al-shajarah*, tr. by Denys Johnson-Davies;

Bird of the East (Beirut: Khayats, 1966); translation of *'Usfūr min al-sharq*, tr. by R. Bayly Winder;

Fate of a Cockroach: Four Plays of Freedom (London: Heinemann, 1973); translation of *Masīr sursār*, tr. by Denys Johnson-Davies;

"The Sultan's Dilemma" and "The Song of Death", in: *Arabic Writing Today: Drama*, ed. Mahmoud Manzalawi (Cairo: American Research Center in Egypt, 1977); translation of *al-Sultān al-hā'ir* and *Ughniyyat al-mawt*;

"Tender Hands," in: *Plays, Prefaces and Post-scripts of Tawfīq al-Hakīm*, vol. 2: *Theater of Society* (Washington, DC: Three Continents Press / Boulder, CO: Lynne Rienner Publishers, 1984); translation of *al-Aydī al-nā'imah*, tr. by William M. Hutchins;

Muhammad (Cairo: al-Adab Press, 1985); translated by Ibrahim Hassan El-Mougy;

Return of Consciousness (New York and London: New York University Press, 1985); translation of *'Awdat al-wa'y*, tr. by Bayly Winder;

People of the Cave (Cairo: Elias Modern Publishing House & Co., 1989); translation of *Ashāb al-kahf*, tr. by Mahmoud-El Lozy;

Return of the Spirit (Washington, DC: Three Continents Press/Boulder, CO: Lynne Rienner Publishers, 1990); translation of *'Awdat al-rūh*, tr. by William M. Hutchins;

The Prison of Life: An Autobiographical Essay (Cairo: American University in Cairo Press, 1992); translation of *Sijn al-'umr*, tr. by Pierre Cachia;

In the Tavern of Life & Other Stories, translated by William Maynard Hutchins (Boulder: Lynne Rienner Publisher, 1998);

"The Mailman," in: *Modern Arabic Fiction*, ed. Salma Kh. Jayyusi (New York: Columbia University Press, 2005), 86-89; translation of *al-Būstagī*, tr. by Roger Allen.

Tawfīq al-Hakīm (1898-1986) is a giant literary figure in Egypt and the Arab world. Many consider him the founder of modern Egyptian and Arab drama. He was born to a middle class family in Alexandria on October 9th; the exact year of his birth is under dispute; among the suggested dates of his birth are: 1897, 1899, 1902 and 1903. Even though al-Hakīm wrote numerous short stories, novels, poems, autobiographies and essays, he is chiefly known for his dramatic writing as he wrote over seventy plays of exceptional variety. Throughout his life and after his death, al-Hakīm has been repeatedly described as artistic, cynical, cautious, a devout lover of modern art and music, anxious, and curious about anything new or unfamiliar. He is also occasionally labeled as misogynistic and miserly. From his formative years, al-Hakīm had a passion for music and world literature in translation, and thus it is not surprising that his initial experiments at writing for the theater were mainstream musicals, named "operettas," as well as melodramatic adaptations from European plays and farces.Unlike the older generation of playwrights or his contemporaries, for many years al-Hakīm did not emulate the oral traditions, improvised street performances, puppet or shadow theaters of the pre-modern Arab dramatic performances in his drama. Instead his ideal theatrical form as a young theater artist

was based on the French paradigm which he studied and was exposed to while studying law in France (1925-1928). Later in his career he changed his mind about the effectiveness of western theatrical form and called for a return to indigenous forms. Throughout his dramatic writing career, Tawfīq al-Hakīm focused on two objectives: to produce a dramatic heritage of Arabic plays, thus filling a literary gap which the non-textual origins of Arab dramatic performances before him did not fulfill; and to present a broad variety of dramatic writing styles on the Arab stage.

When al-Hakīm was born, Egypt had been under British occupation since 1882. Local resistance to colonialism had been growing increasingly vehement. Musical theater, farces, and translated melodramas (mostly from the French nineteenth century dramatic tradition) were the thriving theatrical models throughout his childhood and boyhood. Western theatrical forms, based on texts and assuming a fourth wall, had been introduced to Egyptians by the Syrians Mārūn al-**Naqqāsh** (1817-1855) and al-**Qabbānī** (1833-1902) who had fled their homeland as a result of religious persecution and settled in Egypt where literature and art were both flourishing. Once settled in Egypt they had found a tolerant political atmosphere and a wide audience for their art. Until the second half of the nineteenth century, Egyptians, as most other Arabs, had been used to the less formal dramatic performances of local street players, whose acts were based on improvisations, stock characters and familiar plotlines. The new theatrical conventions demanded of its audience different viewing habits that were unlike those established throughout the pre-modern period. The pre-nineteenth century Arab performers followed the politics of anti-realism in street performances by recreating stock characters and improvising comedic situations, and by men playing women's roles. Since their performances were mobile and unrealistic in its overall approach, sets were not required and the *mise-en-scène* (scenery) was imagined by the viewers rather than actually being constructed. Great emphasis was also placed on the audience's interactive participation with the players. However, with the arrival of the 'imitation of life' dramas in the Arab world (borrowed from western theatre), the dramatic performance experience was transformed and the rituals of spectatorship were reformulated. As performances moved from their previous outdoor and simple spaces into elaborate indoor and darkened auditoriums, the audience was forced to reshape its viewing behavior as they were now expected to accept the fourth wall and its implicit constraint on their previous interaction with the actors.

Egyptians, being inured to traditional street performers who would come to them, soon developed the habit of going to the theater, and it rapidly became a favorite pastime. Furthermore, women's participation in theatrical performances became imperative as well as the incorporation of realistic stage sets, costumes and lighting. Most importantly, by the mid-nineteenth century the advent of "theater" based on the western paradigm—as opposed to the premodern "dramatic performances" by street performers, dancers, epic poets, puppeteers and shadow theater, marked the rise of dramatic textual hegemony over oral and improvised performances.

In 1870, the 'father' of Egyptian theater, Jewish Egyptian nationalist Ya'qūb **Sannū'** (1839-1912), established the first professional theater troupe and presented a repertoire of both stage-adaptations of French farces and his own original texts. He was the first director/manager to present women on stage. Although initially a favorite of Khedive Ismā'īl, Sannū''s theater was closed down after his plays were declared subversive by the British for criticizing their occupation of Egypt.

While Sannū''s theater established an enduring theatrical tradition, it did not lay the foundation for a dramatic literary heritage. Hence, theater in Egypt remained within the realm of entertainment until Tawfīq al-Hakīm and a few others of his generation created a body of dramatic works that were both thought-provoking dramatic literature and well-constructed stage scripts.

In Egypt, during the first two decades of the twentieth century, three major theatre companies were in competition: George Abyad's company (1912) produced stage adaptations of world literature and translated western theatre classics; Najīb al-Rīhānī's company (1916) was the most successful of all, producing primarily comedies and a new trend of drama called Franco-Arab pieces (which were in effect Arabized comedies that included long segments of dance); and Ramsīs company (1923), established by two theatre greats, Yūsuf Wahbī and 'Azīz 'Īd, which produced both original Egyptian melodramatic texts as well as western classics in translation. Many other small theatre companies also thrived during that same period as well as musical theatre companies, such as that of Sayyid Darwīsh and Salāmah Hijāzī, which were already big successes. Then there was the 'Ukāshah troupe, which inherited some of the plays by Salāmah Hijāzī and with which al-Hakīm started a career of writing for the theater.

In 1919 a nationwide revolt, led by Sa'd Zaghlūl, broke out, and the streets were crowded with rallies against the British occupation in Egypt. As the nascent feminist movement was on the rise, the leader of the Arab Feminist Union (established in 1923), Hudā Sha'rāwī, led her countrywomen alongside the men in those rallies. A build-up of the spirit of nationalism swept the nation and the people were united in their hatred to the British occupation.

With the same intense dislike towards the British as the rest of the nation, al-Hakīm wrote his first full-length play while still in secondary school. The play was called *al-Dayf al-thaqīl* (The Unwelcome Guest, 1918-1919), an allegory of the British occupation of Egypt. The plot revolves around a guest who overstays his welcome and behaves maliciously. The play was never staged because of its blatant satire of the British and in any case would never have escaped the censors' attention.

Among the main reasons why al-Hakīm's early plays were not performed was the nature of his family situation and the restrictions that his education and class imposed on his career path. The eldest of two sons, he was born into a financially secure middle-class family. His father, Ismā'īl al-Hakīm, was a strong, miserly, autocratic man with an eccentric character, but also a strong sense of responsibility and duty towards his family. He was a lawyer who worked as a prosecuting agent in the judiciary branch of the government. His work in the legal section forced the family to travel frequently, since he was constantly being transferred. As a result of this perpetual traveling during al-Hakīm's childhood, his schooling was repeatedly interrupted. His mother, a rebellious, aggressive, dominant, and hard-headed woman, inherited a small fortune from her father, and was thus determined not only to manage her own money but also to have all her assets put in her name alone and not shared with her husband.

When al-Hakīm was still a child, his mother came down with a mysterious malady and was bedridden for a long period of time. Determined to find the cause of his wife's illness, Ismāʿīl al-Hakīm devoted much of his time to reading and researching French medical textbooks. This long ailment was beneficial to the young Tawfīq, since his mother, who had taught herself to read and write, read to him and other members of the family many tales from *A Thousand and One Nights* and other collections of folktales as a means by which to pass time. Al-Hakīm himself tells us in one of his many autobiographical works, *Sijn al-ʿumr* (The Prison of Life, 1964), that his mother's skillful storytelling flair represented his earliest exposure to and enthusiasm for literature. Upon her recovery she stopped reading to him those stories, but by that time he had already become so attached to that sort of mental stimulation and entertainment that he started reading them for himself.

At school al-Hakīm was never an exemplary student and had particular problems with mathematics. However, with the help of private tutoring in certain subjects and through personal perseverance, he managed to continue his education without massive interruptions. In secondary school his love for classical Arabic poetry and prose increased with the support of one teacher, and it was from this time that his attachment to Arabic literature became permanently embedded in his soul.

Al-Hakīm's earliest artistic awakenings, we learn, occurred at the age of ten, when a *shaykh* (teacher) was hired to help him memorize the Qurʾan. That shaykh had a beautiful voice when reciting the Scriptures or calling to prayers. Al-Hakīm's admiration for his teacher's voice led him to imitate the shaykh's chanting and recitation. His next artistic experience took the form of observing the colorful banners, decorated caravans, and attractive entertainments that used to pass by beneath his window in the provinces where he lived as a child and which used to take place during the *mawlid*s (birthday celebrations of holy men) of Sīdī Ibrāhīm al-Disūqī. Another early artistic awakening took place when his mother and grandmother befriended a band of *ʿawālim* (belly-dancers and entertainers) who had come from Cairo to entertain the guests for his youngest uncle's wedding. This friendship resulted in frequent visits of the mistress of that troupe to their house. Al-Hakīm's admiration for her musical talent represents his earliest attraction to music and popular forms of song and dance. It is thus not surprising that his first attempts at writing for the theater would be musical drama. Furthermore, as a child his father took him to watch *Shuhadāʾ al-gharām*, a musical version of *Romeo and Juliet*, by the famous troupe of Salāmah Hijāzī. Al-Hakīm reports that he was totally dazzled by the cast's elaborate costumes and sword-fighting scenes.

During his first year of secondary school, al-Hakīm's parents sent him to Alexandria to continue his education. There he became an avid enthusiast of the cinema, something that he had never seen before. When Ismāʿīl al-Hakīm learned of his son's cinema-going habits, he punished him and made him swear never to go to the movies again. It is during this time that al-Hakīm turned his attention from cinema to Arabic literature. He attributes this turning-point to a new teacher who had joined his school that year and who determined to challenge outdated curricula and allow his students to read pre-Islamic and pre-modern love poetry. More importantly, he encouraged al-Hakīm to experiment with his prose writing and advised him that the best kind of rhetoric was one that did not try to be rhetorical. Al-Hakīm was never to forget that advice.

The following year, al-Hakīm moved to Cairo, where he continued to live with two paternal uncles and an aunt until he finished school and attended university. Unchaperoned and unsupervised in the big city, al-Hakīm was introduced and became drawn to the theater. He was a constant attender at theatrical performances until the point was reached when he himself joined the profession. As his love for theater increased, he became eager to read examples of it as well as attend it. At that period Arabic theatrical scripts were not usually published in printed versions, and western drama was not readily available either in original language or in Arabic translations. Even so, he managed to read whatever he could find in the bookstores of Cairo.

As a Law undergraduate al-Hakīm's commitment to the theater became even stronger. Between 1920 and 1925, he wrote four plays to be performed by the 'Ukāshah Brothers troupe. In writing plays at this initial stage in his career, al-Hakīm decided to use a pseudonym, Husayn Tawfīq, since theater was considered a disreputable field, most especially by his own parents, who regarded it as an unsuitable career or even hobby for a serious young lawyer. Three of these early plays were adaptations or Egyptianizations—an emerging new term at that time—from the French. These plays were: *Aminūsah* in 1922, an adaptation of Alfred de Musset's *Carmosine*, which was never performed; *al-Mar'ah al-jadīdah* (Modern Woman, 1923), inspired by the Egyptian women's liberation movement; *al-'Arīs* (The Bridegroom, 1924), based on a French play entitled *Arthur's Surprise*; and *Khātim Sulaymān* (The Seal of Solomon, 1924), written in collaboration with a friend, which was also an adaptation from a French play. These plays were never published, except for *al-Mar'ah al-jadīdah*, which was published in the 1950s after many revisions.

It is important to note that at this early stage in al-Hakīm's career, one of the most significant theatrical influences on him were the plays that were both produced and acted by George Abyad. According to al-Hakīm himself, Abyad's stage productions were the closest paradigm of high culture at that time, in that he presented serious storytelling on stage; before and after him there was only comedy and melodrama. Having broken away from the musically-inclined Hijāzī's troupe, Abyad went on to present serious drama

and tragedies on stage. At that time the term *masrahiyyah* (play) was not yet known to the Egyptian audience; rather, a stage production was known as *riwāyah* (story, or narrative). Abyad was the first to produce non-musical and non-comedic *riwāyāt* (stories) on stage, thus inspiring in al-Hakīm the notion that serious stories/dramas could be appreciated and well-attended by the Egyptian audience.

After earning his baccalaureate al-Hakīm was sent to Europe to continue his education. His father, Ismā'īl al-Hakīm, was exasperated by his son's involvement with the theatrical and literary circles and consulted with Ahmad Lutfī al-Sayyid (d. 1963), famous littérateur, journalist and politician, and an old family friend, about his son's future. Advised by the latter to send him abroad and away from the theater to study, Ismā'īl al-Hakīm decided to accept the suggestion. In 1925 he sent his son to France to obtain a Doctorate in Law. Once settled in Paris, Tawfīq al-Hakīm was surprised to find himself turning away from the popular theatre, farces, vaudevilles and operettas to which he had become accustomed in Cairo and developing instead an overwhelming interest in the French avant-garde theatre of the time. The highly intellectual content of such works was soon to inspire him to write what became known later as his 'Theatre of Ideas.' Instead of concentrating on the legal studies, al-Hakīm found himself enthralled and fascinated by western culture. Much to his father's dismay, he became devoted to the study of the western literary tradition, especially drama. Most of the three years in France were spent reading books on the history of western philosophy, history and art. Needless to say, he frequently went to the theater. At the beginning of his stay he would go to watch popular farces, revues and vaudevilles, but eventually found himself drawn very strongly to Realism and the more cerebral theater of Ibsen, Pirandello, Chekhov and Shaw, which constituted the French *avant-garde* at the time. Al-Hakīm, who had been fairly well-read in Arabic literature and culture, had virtually no knowledge of Western culture prior to his stay in France, except for the few French and English plays he had read in Cairo. He documented his deep fascination with the artistic and intellectual life in France in his various autobiographies. This contact with the west widened his creative consciousness and shaped his ideas, making him a well-rounded and culturally aware intellectual whose dramatic vision would thereafter combine and capture Egyptian concerns within western forms. Al-Hakīm's natural curiosity and literary enthusiasm led him to undertake research on western culture and history with the same eagerness he had earlier applied to the survey of the Arab literary tradition. He was to bring that same zest to the examination of texts throughout his life.

As a result of his concentrated study of Western culture and diligent observation of French theater, al-Hakīm redefined his relationship with the theater in Egypt on the one hand, and found his literary *raison d'être* on the other. He came to realize that rather than an ephemeral activity, theater should be a serious branch of literature. From that moment on, he turned his back on musical theater forever and focused on literary dramatic texts.

While in France, al-Hakīm did not break away from the theater scene or milieu in Egypt altogether. In fact, he finished writing a play which he had started in Cairo, entitled *'Alī Bābā*. He mailed the play back to Cairo to be performed by the 'Ukāshah Brothers troupe. The play is based on a French opera-comique by Albert Vanloo and William Brusnach entitled *Ali Baba et les quarante voleurs*. In France he also wrote his reality-based novel, *'Awdat al-rūḥ* (The Return of the Spirit, 1927), a fictional portrayal of the life of his paternal uncles and aunt in Cairo, with whom he had lodged while completing his undergraduate education.

When al-Hakīm failed to obtain his doctorate, he was summoned back to Cairo by his irate father. For a few years afterwards he was employed as a public prosecutor, occupying posts in different parts of the country. Living in the provinces of Egypt provided him with material and experiences for his creative writing. It inspired him to write one of his finest prose works, namely *Yawmiyyāt na'īb fī 'l-aryāf* (English translation: *Maze of Justice*, London 1937), as well as a number of plays.

Al-Hakīm's literary production during and immediately after his sojourn in France constitutes his formative years. After his return to Egypt his dramatic writing veered away from farces and musicals and evolved into intellectual drama. However, during his absence the general condition of Egyptian theater had changed. A number of famous troupes had disbanded, including the 'Ukāshah Troupe. As a result the farces of Najīb al-Rīḥānī and the melodramas of Yūsuf Wahbī were the only form of theater prospering at that time. Even though al-Hakīm realized that his new writing style would not appeal to popular taste, he did not feel discouraged from continuing to write plays; it merely resigned him to the fact that they might not be performed. The plays he wrote immediately after his return were: *al-Khurūj min al-jannah* (Expulsion from Paradise, 1928); *Ba'd al-mawt*, or *Sirr al-muntahirah* (After Death, or The Suicide's Secret, 1928); *Hayāh tahattamat* (A Wrecked Life, 1930); *Rusāsah fī 'l-qalb* (A Bullet in the Heart, 1931); and *al-Zammār* (The Piper, 1932). He wrote the first two in classical Arabic and the others in the colloquial. A common thread running through these plays is that they combine philosophical ideas, social satire and lighthearted comedy, and are all set in contemporary society. As a group they represent the introduction of intellectualism to the Egyptian stage, presenting social themes by way of psychological realism and metadramatic elements such as play-within-a-play or role-playing. He also examines gender relationships in the form of plays that portray a series of battles of the sexes, a tendency that with him would last a lifetime. Al-Hakīm's flair for depicting human folly burgeons at this stage and is manifested in the form of brutal criticism of social customs and depictions of gender idiosyncrasies as well as through satire and comedic twists.

al-Khurūj min al-jannah is essentially a dialectical drama about what constitutes happiness. Al-Hakīm draws from the story of Adam and Eve. The play sentimentalizes the female character who perceives that love is volatile and that the only way to make it eternal is by walking out of it. Thus, she sacrifices her deep love for her husband by leaving him. In expelling herself from her paradise of domestic bliss with the man she loves, she appeases herself by knowing that sacrifice is the greatest expression of love. The husband on the other hand becomes a victim of her grand sentimental ideas. In the course of the play he fails to understand her actions since she never explains them to him. Giving in to his fate, he idealizes his wife and converts his anguish over losing her into art, the manifestation of the eternal, by writing a play by the same title. The play makes him a great dramatist, but he sinks deeper into loneliness and as such he lives the rest of his life, expelled from paradise. Through suffering he becomes the ultimate artist-recluse.

Another example of intellectualism occurs in *Ba'd al-mawt*. Written in four acts, the play is centered around an older doctor who is under the impression that ʿAzīzah, his beautiful young patient, is madly in love with him. When she commits suicide from his clinic window, he assumes it is a result of her immense love for him. Her death however results in a surprising burst of life in the old man. He feels rejuvenated, and his self-confidence is regained. His clinic becomes crowded with society ladies who are now curious about the Don Juan-type doctor. His relationship with his wife is ruined when he snubs her and calls her 'an old hag' even though she is fifteen years his junior. For revenge, the wife sets out to discover the truth about the young woman's death. Iqbāl, the wife, finds out that the young woman had been in love with her driver, who jilted her for another woman. To retaliate, the young woman killed herself and made sure it was known to be for the sake of the famous doctor, who happens to have the same name as the young chauffeur, Mahmūd. Brutally, Iqbāl faces her husband with those facts and basks in her pleasure as he loses his newly found flamboyance. In no time Mahmūd is again an aging doctor with nothing to look forward to, as he is now the one to be snubbed by both his wife and society. The title *After Death* could refer to either the resurrection that takes place in the doctor's life after the metaphorical death of aging or it could simply refer to the incidents that ensue after the death of the young woman.

Choosing to write plays in the colloquial dialect was quite a daring decision for a playwright who wished to present his drama to society as literature. Until then—and for many years thereafter—classical or literary Arabic was considered the only appropriate medium for anything to be termed "literature." Works composed in colloquial dialect were ignored and excluded from serious consideration or critical evaluation. Realizing this fact, al-Hakīm abandoned his use of the colloquial in the next phase of his career and reverted to the classical language.

After failing to reach a broader public with his previous set of plays, which combined the philosophical with the entertaining, al-Hakīm focused his attention during the next stage on writing dramas that were unabashedly intellectual. In doing so, he had no qualms in describing those plays himself as *al-masrah al-dhihnī* (drama of ideas), works composed to be read and not performed. According to him, those texts were more dramatic literature than theatrical pieces, but al-Hakīm's critics have always chosen to construe that as a failure on his part to create plays that contain adequate dramatic action. Still others have considered them good material for the stage, provided that some editing could be exercised on them. Those plays are: *Ahl al-kahf* (People of the Cave, 1933); *Shahrazād* (1934), *Pirāksā* (1939, enlarged in 1954), *Pygmālyon* (1942), *Sulaymān al-Hakīm* (Solomon the Wise, 1943); and *al-Malik Udīb* (King Oedipus, 1949).

To a large extent, "theater of ideas" (also labeled "theater of the mind") was a phase of intellectual fusion for al-Hakīm. Within its framework he integrates history and international classics with contemporary and local concerns in order to integrate western form and Egyptian thought. According to al-Hakīm at the time (1930s and '40s), the best dramatic formula was "to ladle water from the spring, then to swallow it, digest it, and assimilate it, so that we can present it to the public tinged once more with the color of our own thought and imprinted with the stamp of our beliefs." This definition was al-Hakīm's own description of the Greek-Qur'an-folklore-inspired dramas that he wrote in the 1940s.

At a time when there was a heated debate on what constituted *asālah* (authenticity or closeness to one's historical roots) and *turāth* (heritage), and how to protect local tradition from the invasion of western ideas, al-Hakīm took a moderate stand alongside the towering figure in Arab literature and culture, Tāhā **Husayn**. The latter believed that "the study of literature should be a mixture of the two methods, the traditional [pre-modern Arab] and the European," and took to task the Arab scholars of his days for their "ignorance not only of Latin and Greek authors but also of the great writers of the West, from the Renaissance onwards." Moreover, Husayn insisted that language is an essential criterion in the decision of what constitutes "good" or "bad" literature, and al-Hakīm aided him on that front as well.

In an attempt to debunk on the one hand traditionalists who wished to revive the poetic diction and themes of Arabic literature by emulating the great poetry of the earlier Abbasid period (8th–13th centuries CE), and, on the other hand, their extreme opponents—modernists— who condemned everything that was classical and traditional and demanded a literature that could be of service to contemporary society, al-Hakīm wrote *Ahl al-kahf*, a play that is particularly significant not only in terms of his own artistic development, but also as a benchmark for the development in the Arab dramatic genre as a whole in the 1930s.

The play tells the story of the seven sleepers of Ephesus ("The Sleepers of the Cave") to be found in Sūrah 18 of the Qur'an. A group fleeing from a ruthless and non-believing king determined to kill them for having converted to Christianity fall asleep in a cave while waiting for time to pass and only wake up some three hundred years later to a world of which they cannot be a part. Al-Hakīm makes use of the story as a parable for the question of modernity and tradition that preoccupied much intellectual, political and social discourse during the first half of the twentieth century. The play ends with the three sleepers choosing to go back to die in the cave since they are unable to acclimate themselves to the changes that have taken place while they have been in their deep slumber. Along with them goes the beautiful princess, Pirāksā, who, having fallen in love with one of the three sleepers, Mishlinya, decides that she would prefer dying with him in the cave to facing life without him. She symbolizes young artists who must make a choice of either advocating the traditional way and thus confining their art to the past, or accepting the dictates of change and expressing themselves in accordance with the needs of their time.

Written in the literary language, *al-fushā*, the play was widely welcomed by the intellectual elite; it was accorded the special prestige of being the first play staged at the newly established Egyptian National Theater (inaugurated in 1930). However, while it was praised in the cultured circles, it failed as a performance, being unable to capture the hearts of the broader public. Even though it is written in four lengthy acts and in classical Arabic, neither of them elements that would work for a popular success at the time, the play has still managed to sustain its existence until today as a highly admired piece of dramatic literature.

Al-Hakīm had clearly subscribed at this juncture to Tāhā Husayn's view of Arab literary history as having fallen into a decline for some five hundred years and then risen to a cultural renaissance in the nineteenth century. Thus the parallelism between this historical paradigm and the message of al-Hakīm's play seems very clear: the people of the cave *(Ahl al-kahf)* represent the Arabs, who wake up from a state of cultural stupor to discover an advancing world all around them. The implicit moral lesson is that they should either decide to keep up with modernity or else, like the protagonists in the play, regress once again into a decline.

Another example of intellectualism is apparent in al-Hakīm's Greek-inspired play *Pirāksā*, an adaptation to the Egyptian stage of Aristophanes's anti-war comedy, *Lysistrata*. Naming his play *Praxa, or How to Govern*, al-Hakīm urges his readers to examine the original first, as he deviates significantly from the Greek text. While Aristophanes' play is a comedy about the revolt of women against their war-mongering husbands, al-Hakīm's is a serious drama about the uprising of women against their corrupt husbands who have failed to govern fairly. The play contemplates the fantasy of an all-women government.

Since al-Hakīm was known for his quick responses to the socio-political issues of his time, it is not surprising that he reacted to the nascent feminist movement of that era by writing a play about the power of women. His project was however completed in two distant installments: the first part of the play in 1939 appeared in three acts, the second part in the 1950s expands the play by three more acts. While al-Hakīm chose to parry questions as to why he chose to write the play in two separate parts—with a gap of some fourteen years between them that straddles two utterly different political systems—a study of Egyptian social history and the development of the feminist movement in particular during the first half of the twentieth century makes it clear that he was in fact commenting on actual events that occurred simultaneous with the composition of the two parts.

Part I of the play reflects the feminists' stance against reactionary elements in government. In 1931, Ismā'īl Sidqī, the conservative prime minister, suspended parliament in order to suppress liberal voices within it and then called for new elections, a move that was regarded as unconstitutional by nationalists, both men and women. With the liberals not allowed to vote in parliament, the national outcry engendered a women's protest, even though at that juncture they themselves had still not been given suffrage. Unable to vote themselves, nationalist feminists realized that they could still influence the votes of their male relatives. By preventing their male family members from participating in the political process as part of a struggle against reactionary elements in government, their actions closely resembled those of the women in Aristophanes' *Lysistrata*.

In an introduction to the revised version of the play, al-Hakīm declares that he "had to stop at three acts [in 1939] for reasons of sheer prudence, even though [he] had much more to say. The 1952 revolution gave [him] the opportunity to express what [he] had to say in full." It is important to mention here that, in the process of drafting a new post-revolutionary constitution, another movement was initiated by women when they sensed that their rights were about to be overlooked. To appease feminists, the government included mention of women, albeit in a cursory fashion, but still failed to grant them suffrage rights. In 1956 Dorreya Shafīq, a staunch feminist, led a group of women in a hunger strike until women were given their democratic rights in full. In response, Gamāl 'Abd al-Nāsir (Nasser), the President of Egypt at the time, granted Egyptian women suffrage. It is quite obvious that the two historic and revolutionary movements in women's politics instigated by Egyptian feminists, first in the 1930s and then again the 1950s, evoked images from Aristophanes's *Lysistrata* that inspired al-Hakīm to amend his initial view. While he saw a democratic government including women's involvement as an impossibility in the 1930s, judging by his portrayal of Praxa in the first part as an inefficient ruler, in the 1950s he revised his stance. In the second part he expresses the opinion that the only sound and democratic recourse to government is a collaboration between genders as well as the intelligentsia.

Generally speaking, the end of the 1940s and 1950s represent a major turning-point in al-Hakīm's playwriting; it is also his most prolific period. The success of the 1952 revolution in Egypt which transformed the country from a monarchy into a republic, and the rise of Socialist Realism as a prevalent literary mode of expression, which, like the revolution itself, focused on the working classes and the underdogs of society, combined to prompt al-Hakīm to follow the principles of Realism in his own writing. During this period he shifted his attention from intellectualism to real-life issues, criticizing a number of social institutions and ancient customs that, in his opinion, needed to be questioned and changed. The result of this new interest was his production of three major collections of plays, mostly one-acts, under three broad titles: *Masrah al-mujtama'* (Theater of Social Themes, 1950), *al-Masrah al-munawwa'* (Theater of Diverse Themes, 1956) and *al-Masrah al-hādif* (Politically Committed Theater, which are plays written throughout the 1950s). The last collection was a direct response to the 1952 revolution and reflective of its principles. The premise of social commitment is most apparent in *al-Aydī al-nā'imah* (Soft Hands,

1954), which discusses the value of work and pokes fun at the outmoded class structure of the pre-Revolutionary society that divided the population into an aristocracy and a working class. The message of the play is supportive of one of the revolution's principal goals, that of redistributing wealth so as to create social equality between the rich and poor.

In recent years, *Masrah al-mujtama'* has become al-Hakīm's most popular and widely produced collection, and one of the most closely analyzed; it is also the work that scholars and feminists use the most frequently to indict him of misogyny. His portrayal of women in this collection is certainly excessively critical, if not downright negative. His female characters are repeatedly presented as small-minded, irrational and materialistic human beings in a constant search for husbands. In many of the plays a recurrent theme are irreconcilable differences between married couples; al-Hakīm consistently paints an unhappy picture of both the institution of marriage itself and of wives. Other plays provide grossly exaggerated (mis)representations of female characters such as *Urīd hādhā 'l-rajul* (I Want This Man), *al-Nā'ibah al-muhtaramah* (The Respectable Lady Member of Parliament), *Urīd an aqtul* (I Want to Kill), *Ashāb al-sa'ādah al-zawjiyyah* (The Happily Married) and *Sāhirah* (Enchantress). While mostly centered around social satire, not all the plays in the collection fall into that category. *Mawlid al-batal* (A Hero is Born), for instance, is a story about Arab nationalism and patriotism. Furthermore, most of the dramas in these three collections condemn government corruption and deride social pretentiousness and materialism. This is apparent in *'Imārat al-mu'allim Kandūz* (Boss Kandūz's Apartment Building), when Kandūz, a *nouveau riche* butcher who owns a building, tries to swindle suitors into marrying his daughters by promising them apartments along with the marriages. In a sort of Molière-type humor as in *The Would-be Gentleman*, the play starts with Kandūz pretending to be genteel when a young man and his mother come to visit. A funny misunderstanding takes place when Kandūz believes that the young man is there to ask for his daughter's hand in marriage whereas all he wants is to rent an apartment in the building.

The most artistically seamless play included in *Masrah al-mujtama'* is *Ughniyyat al-mawt* (Song of Death). While neither a satire of the social urban scene nor a deliberately negative portrayal of women (although it depicts dimensions of wickedness within the female character), it is still a scathing critique of brutal village customs. The play presents a tragic portrayal of an upper Egyptian mother seeking revenge for the murder of her husband who has been killed by his family's enemies seventeen years before the events of the play. In order to protect her infant son from the wrath of the enemy family, she sends him to be raised by a relative in Cairo; she announces to the village that he is dead. When he becomes a teenager, she sends him to work in a butcher's shop so he can learn the art of killing and grow up to be a cold-blooded murderer capable of handling his family's enemies single-handedly. But instead, her son, 'Ilwān, goes to study theology at al-Azhar University, the oldest Islamic university in the world, and comes of age with an enlightened outlook that refuses to accept time-honored village customs which he now regards as criminal, regressive and barbaric. Thus, when his mother summons him back to the village, he complies, but returns with a different agenda in mind.

The play starts with the mother, 'Asākir, eagerly awaiting her son's return. She has asked his cousin to wait for him at the train station and sing a certain tune when 'Ilwān arrives. A superb dramatic exposition takes place as 'Asākir and her sister impatiently wait to hear the song indicating his arrival. When 'Ilwān finally arrives at home, she is surprised to observe that he has not donned traditional attire, but is wearing modern western clothes. As the mother urges her son to take revenge, she hands him the bloodstained knife with which his father was murdered. After keeping it for him for all those years, she now demands that he use it. 'Ilwān refuses and instead proposes seeking a peaceful resolution with the enemy family. He also suggests that the punishment of those who had killed his father be left to the police authorities to handle. Appalled by such suggestions, hurt and enraged, his mother vehemently refutes his

suggestions and tells him to leave at once, vow-
ing that she never wants to set eyes on him
again. As he heads back to the train station, she
asks his cousin to kill him and sing a tune when
the deed has been done.

The last scene of this long one-act play is
identical to the first, in that the mother is waiting
to hear a song in both. The last song, however, is
a prognosticator of her own son's death. The
moment she hears the dreadful song of death,
she utters the words "my son", thus becoming a
quintessential tragic figure possessed of an
excessive desire for revenge that in the process
destroys her. The metaphors incorporated into
this play are numerous; they include a direct
attack on brutal country traditions and a reap-
pearance of one of al-Hakīm's favorite dichoto-
mies, that of modernity versus tradition. This
play has acquired a special poignancy in the
wake of the Camp David Accords between
Egypt and Israel on the one hand and the tragic
events of September 11th 2001 on the other, in
that a number of directors have chosen to stage it
as a metaphor that calls for an end to the continuing cycle of revenge and violence.

Apart from the above plays, Tawfīq al-Hakīm
wrote a further series of plays in the 1950s that
reflect his new found interest in Realism. *Al-
Safqah* (The Deal, 1956) is arguably his most
important play during that decade. In composing
it he used a level of language, which he called
"the third language," that he argued could work
as a language of both entertainment and literature. *Al-Safqah* depicts a real life situation turned
into fiction. A group of villagers tries to purchase some land from a foreign company that is
selling its landholding by auction. When a rich
landowner stops in their village by accident
because his car breaks down, the sale is interrupted. Not knowing the reason for his detour in
their village, they all assume that he is there to
outbid them. They collect money and attempt to
bribe him out of the deal. Not understanding at
first why they are offering him money, he is
confused by the proposal. However, once he
figures it out, he turns out to be a tough negotiator; not only does he demand higher compensa-
tion, but also insists on taking the beautiful
young woman, Mabrūkah, with him back to

Cairo. Naturally this is not well received by the
village community. However, Mabrūkah too
insists on going. Once in Cairo, she pretends to
have contracted cholera, which means quarantin-
ing everyone in the house and taking her to
hospital. Two days later she is released, thus
allowing the villagers enough time to win the
bid for the land. The polarity implicit in this
portrayal of rich and poor, city and country, and
urban and country folk manners, is certainly
reminiscent of al-Hakīm's earlier interest in
engaging his characters in dialects, but in this
play he also manages to create dynamic dramatic
action.

In the preface to the play, which he entitles
"Manifesto," al-Hakīm outlines his new vision
for the Arab stage. In drawing attention to the
difficulties that theater has encountered in attracting mass audiences he focuses on both
language and subject matter. Concerning language, he explains that a "third" language is
needed to bridge the unfamiliarity of standard
Arabic on the one hand and the incompatibility
of colloquial registers with the writing of dramatic literature on the other. This third language,
which he uses in composing *al-Safqah*, provides
entertainment without sacrificing beauty of
expression; it also allows for trans-Arab understanding in that it transcends the limits imposed
by local dialects. On the other hand, since the
subject matter is inspired by a real-life situation,
it is akin to a "slice of life," that can reflect a
layperson's fears and dreams. Al-Hakīm also
expresses the need for simplicity in production
values applied to stage productions (a principle
that he reiterates in the 1960s). In his opinion
this simplicity can facilitate the production of
plays in any theatrical space available and within
any budget. Al-Hakīm's speculations proved to
be accurate; the play was his most successful to
date on both the critical and financial levels.

The last play written by al-Hakīm in the
1950s is *al-Sultān al-hā'ir* (The Sultan's Dilemma, 1960). It borrows its atmosphere and
tone from *A Thousand and One Nights* but also
reflects contemporary issues such as the question
of legitimacy of ruling. The premise of the plot
is quite unusual: the social order of the play's
imagined world is in an uproar when it is dis-

covered that the Sultan is still technically a slave and thus ineligible for the post of sultan; the only lawful recourse is to have him sold in a public auction in the hope that his new owner will thereafter manumit him. When this procedure is carried out, everyone in the city is shocked to learn that the person who has outbid everyone else and purchased the Sultan is the most notorious courtesan in town. The Sultan honors the deal and makes his way to her residence as her property. Much to his surprise, it turns out that all she wants is to have a conversation with him. He discovers that she is a lover of art and has enjoyed men's (not women's) company neither for sexual pleasure nor for money but rather for their knowledge, experience and wisdom. Thanks to her late husband she herself is wealthy and has no need of their money; what she seeks is only their friendship. He obliges her, and they spend the evening conversing. In the process she becomes smitten with him, and he in turn harbors great respect for her. After spending the night engaged in an intellectual exchange of ideas, she honors her promise in the morning and manumits him.

The play is well structured and combines some of al-Hakīm's best writing qualities: humor, witticism, intellectualism (albeit watered down), excellent plot and insightful themes that reflect contemporary political controversies, as well as an exemplary character construction. However, it presents a skewed portrayal of woman through the disappointing development (or regression) in the courtesan's character. Though the drama starts with her as a strong, assertive and independent woman who dares to single-handedly challenge patriarchy, she progressively loses her power as the plot unfolds. More and more smitten by the charisma of the Sultan, she succumbs to the stereotypical polarization of gender roles that assumes men to be powerful (thus better) and women weak (thus inferior), both emotionally and physically. By the end of the play, al-Hakīm manages to reduce the courtesan's stature from that of owner of a slave-king to one of a woman in love, who is willing to give up her rational faculties and intelligence now that she is emotionally involved.

While the form and structure of *al-Sultān al-hā'ir* abide by the Aristotelian dramatic paradigm, al-Hakīm deviates radically from that traditional format in his next stage and departs from the dictates of Realism. The 1960s was a period of great fervor in Egyptian theater as a new generation of playwrights emerged; some of the best modern plays were products of this period. Following seventy years of occupation the British had evacuated Egypt in 1956, and thus the 1960s were the first post-colonial decade in Egypt. The excitement engendered by the achievement of independence pervaded every facet of life and culture. In theater, a movement towards independence from western art forms and dramatic conventions followed the country's political sovereignty, and the quest for an authentic identity for Egyptian theater and culture, autonomous from western forms, became an incessant discussion in critical discourse. As a playwright who had been inspired by western theater for some thirty years and frequently borrowed from it, al-Hakīm did not shy away from that debate. On the contrary, he was responsive to it in two distinctive phases; in the early 1960s he adopted Absurdism, a certified western dramatic form, and argued that it had existed for centuries within the folk life of Egypt before it found its way to Europe. During the second half of that decade, he deviated again by attempting to reconstruct pre-modern Egyptian dramatic art forms on the contemporary stage and defended that choice in a study entitled *Qālibunā al-masrahī* (Our Dramatic Form, 1967).

Adopting Absurdism emerged primarily from al-Hakīm's "creative panic;" a self-descriptive phrase which, he explained, did not allow him to subscribe to a single writing style, and always drove him to new experiments and territories. It was this artistic propensity that propelled him to introduce Theater of the Absurd to the Arab stage in the 1960s in spite of the genre's many detractors. Theatre of the Absurd is one of the most important theatre movements of the twentieth century in Europe, closely related to existentialism, whose pioneers are Sartre and Camus. Since Absurdism is a direct outcome of the experience of war and genocide in Europe, many

scholars and critics considered its introduction to
the Arab world during the wars of independence
from western colonialism to be inappropriate.
After all, the early 1960s were still a period
marked by a certain political and social optimism. And yet, in spite of criticism, Tawfīq al-
Hakīm wrote a number of plays in that dramatic
style throughout the 1960s; they were more
appreciated in subsequent years than at the time
in which they were written and produced.
Among those plays are: *Yā tāli' al-shajarah* (O
Tree Climber, 1962), *Rihlat sayd* (Hunting Trip)
and *Rihlat qitār* (Train Journey); two one-act
plays written in 1964; and *al-Wartah* (The Dilemma), *Masīr sursār* (Fate of a Cockroach),
and *Kull shay' fī mahallih* (Not a Thing Out of
Place), all written in 1966.

In the preface to his first play written in the
Absurdist style, *Yā tāli' al-shajarah*, Tawfīq al-
Hakīm mentions that Theatre of the Absurd had
started to appear when he lived in France. However, at that time he chose not to bring it to
Egypt for fear that the Egyptian audience, which
in his opinion was still untrained to appreciate
experimental theater projects, would fail to comprehend it. However, this reluctance to present
Absurdism to the Egyptian audience did not last
long, for after his second visit to France in 1959,
al-Hakīm finally decided to write his first play of
that style. Since Theater of the Absurd relies
heavily on abstraction and symbolism, and
consciously deviates from the Aristotelian uni-
ties of time, space, and plot, al-Hakīm explains
that the most important unity in a work of that
genre is the artistic vision, which, in his opinion,
is what holds the work together and aids in
comprehending its ambiguities and symbolism.

According to al-Hakīm, Theater of the Absurd is the presentation of "reality without realism; reaching for the absurd and the illogical in
every form of artistic expression; and finding
abstraction in order to reach new rhythms and
meanings." As such he used it as a model in his
dramatic writing for a few years. In the same
preface he expresses his philosophy regarding
Absurdism, noting that ridiculous and nonsensi-
cal artistic forms have existed at the heart of
Egyptian folk traditions for centuries; thus the
voice of Absurdism as an expression of the

illogical and inexplicable had been known to
Egypt before the West took heed of its importance. Al-Hakīm explains that

*when a play consciously departs from realism, it
loses any justification for using realistic language through its characters. Therefore, what
becomes more suitable for its unrealistic events
is an unrealistic language, in other words a
language other than the language of conversation...*

From this point of view he argued that the resort
to classical Arabic in order to represent everyday
conversation, where typically characters would
not use it or even have knowledge of it, automatically introduces an element of the "absurd"
to the scenes that are designed to imitate everyday life on stage.

Those principles are reflected in *Yā tāli' al-
shajarah*, which takes its title from an ancient
folk limerick. The play consists of two acts and
revolves primarily around the relationship between Bahādīr and his wife Bahānah. One day
she disappears, and, since he is the one who is
held accountable for her disappearance, he is
interrogated and imprisoned. In the second act
she reappears, and he is released. Back at home
Bahādīr asks Bahānah about her disappearance.
When she refuses his initial simple question,
"Where were you all that time?" he does actually kill her.

In the play there are two instrumental characters, an elderly maid and a dervish. The old
servant plays an important role in the dramatic
structure of the play. During the police interro-
gation following Bahānah's disappearance, the
maid mentions that the couple had a loving and
caring relationship and that, in general, they
were happy together. She also mentions that
before Bahānah met Bahādīr, she was married
and widowed, and that she was pregnant with a
daughter whom she aborted in the fourth month.
The maid also mentions that Bahādīr was very
attached to an orange tree in their garden and a
green lizard that resided underneath it.

The dervish is another pivotal character in the
play. He is the closest person to Bahādīr and was
the one to inspire the latter with the notion of an
ideal tree that produced four different kinds of

fruit year round. This idea is what drives Ba-hādīr to confide in the dervish about his desire to bury his wife under the tree in order to fertilize it and enhance its growth.

The play displays a variety of features of the Theater of the Absurd genre: the staccato speech pattern that characterizes communication (or lack thereof) between characters; various metad-ramatic techniques, whereby the reenactment of the past (and sometimes of the future) occurs within a scene taking place in the present; the play's dreamlike atmosphere combining realistic elements with surrealistic ones; and, especially typical of Absurdist drama, the temporal and spatial organization of the play that do not fol-low the linearity of Realism, with scenes simul-taneously linking multiple spaces and time-frames. Furthermore, the play does not focus on stage action but rather emphasizes cerebral ideas that are shrouded in symbolism, a method whose aim is not to engage the spectators or readers emotionally with the play, but instead to connect them intellectually with a certain philosophical debate. This aspect is certainly in congruence with al-Hakīm's former propensity for intellec-tualism, which he seems never to have aban-doned.

After a period in which he was preoccupied with Absurdism, al-Hakīm's intellectual rest-lessness and continuous search for innovative dramatic expressions led him to engage with the critical debates of the time. Throughout the 1960s the catchphrase was the quest for the real 'iden-tity' of Egyptian theater. Eventually he too began participating in those polemics, resulting in his advocacy of the concept of cultural continuity. In *Qālibunā al-masrahī* (Our Dramatic Form, 1967) he argues that, while the employment of western forms was inescapable, Arabic drama and literature never lost their link with the spirit of classical Arabic literature and pre-modern performance arts. He emphasizes that there is an older dramatic art form, which, according to him, best captures the spirit of Arab dramatic performances and outlines the characteristics of that art form, noting:

It is undoubtedly the stage at which we [Egyp-tians'] were very far from the idea of 'acting' or 'imitating.' It is the period in which we knew no

other [dramatic art form] than that of the haka-wātī *[storyteller, narrator],* maddāhīn *[panegy-rists] and* muqallidīn *[impersonators].*

According to al-Hakīm those art forms were by-and-large solo performances that involved the audience in a different way than that of western theater. While those dramatic presentations are best described as storytelling or epic-poetry recitation, they were much more than just that, for they addressed and involved the audience directly. The dramatic form proposed by Tawfīq al-Hakīm is an audience-centered one that de-pends on (re)telling the stories of world classics without relying on recreating a "text." Instead it relies solely on the oral skills of the storyteller or performer. To demonstrate his point, al-Hakīm applies the narrator/impersonator criteria to a few world classics such as *Agamemnon, Hamlet, Don Juan* and *Six Characters in Search of an Author*. In adapting such classics to the narra-tor/impersonator theater, he has, in effect, trans-formed them from their fixed textual form to stories that are open to embellishments and alterations in order to suit the sensibilities of the target audience.

Tawfīq al-Hakīm did not produce any further dramas of great import in the 1970s and thereaf-ter, a situation that continued until his death in 1986. However, he continued to produce weekly critical commentaries and essays for the Egyp-tian newspaper *Akhbār al-Yawm*. Up until the end he remained active on the cultural and po-litical fronts. The best description of al-Hakīm may be the one proposed by the prominent drama critic 'Alī al-Rā'ī who notes that "a care-ful study of al-Hakīm's dramatic career shows clearly that inside the dramatist there were two artists, one a thinker, the other a clown, with neither leaving the other alone."

REFERENCES

Roger Allen, "Drama and Audience: The Case of Arabic Theater", *Theater Three* 6 (1989): 25-54;

——, "Egyptian Drama after the Revolution," *Edebiyat* 4.1 (1979): 97-134;

——, *The Arabic Literary Heritage: The Devel-opment of its Genres and Criticism* (Cambridge & New York: Cambridge University Press, 1998);

—— and Salma Khadra Jayyusi (eds.), *Modern Arabic Drama: An Anthology* (Bloomington: Indiana University Press, 1995);

Gaber Asfur (ed.), *Tawfīq al-Hakīm: hudūr mutajaddid* (Cairo: al-Majlis al-Aʻlā liʼl-Thaqāfah, 2001);

Luwīs ʻAwad, "Yā Tāliʻ al-Shajarah," in: *Dirāsāt fī ʼl-naqd waʼl-adab* (Cairo: Maktabat al-Anglo al-Misriyyah, 1964), 229-243;

M. M. Badawi (ed.), *Modern Arabic Literature*, The Cambridge History of Arabic Literature series (Cambridge: Cambridge University Press, 1992);

M. M. Badawi, *Modern Arabic Drama in Egypt* (Cambridge & New York: Cambridge University Press, 1987);

——, *Modern Arabic Literature and the West* (London: Ithaca Press, 1985);

Pierre Cachia, *An Overview of Modern Arabic Literature* (Edinburgh: Edinburgh University Press, 1990);

Fuʼād Dawwārah, *Masrah Tawfīq al-Hakīm: al-masrahiyyāt al-majhūlah* (Cairo: al-Hayʼah al-Misriyyah al-ʻĀmmah liʼl-Kitāb, 1984);

William Maynard Hutchins, *Tawfīq al-Hakīm: A Reader's Guide* (Boulder & London: Lynne Rienner, 2003);

Richard Long, *Tawfīq al-Hakīm, Playwright of Egypt* (London: Ithaca Press, 1979);

ʻAlī al-Rāʼī, "Tawfīq al-Hakīm: Birth of a National Playwright in Egypt," in: *Modern Arabic Literature*, ed. M. M. Badawi, The Cambridge History of Arabic Literature series (Cambridge: Cambridge University Press, 1992), 368-383;

——, "Arabic Drama since the Thirties," in: *Modern Arabic Literature*, ed. M. M. Badawi (Cambridge: Cambridge University Press, 1986), 358-403;

Hamdī Sakkūt, *Taufiq al-Hakīm: Bibliography* (Cairo: Egyptian Supreme Council for Culture, Limited Review Edition, 1998);

Ghālī Shukrī, *Thawrat al-muʻtazil: dirāsat muʼallafāt Tawfīq al-Hakīm* (Beirut: Dār al-Āfāq al-Jadīdah, n.d.);

Paul Starkey, "The Four Ages of Husayn Tawfīq: Love and Sexuality in the Novels of Tawfīq al-Hakīm", in: *Love and Sexuality in Modern Arabic Literature*, ed. Roger Allen et al. (London: Saqi Books, 1995), 56-64, 231-2;

——, *From the Ivory Tower: A Critical Analysis of Tawfiq al-Hakim* (London: Ithaca Press, 1987).

Yahyā Haqqī
(1905 – 1993)

MIRIAM COOKE
Duke University

WORKS

Qindīl Umm Hāshim ("The Lamp of Umm Hashim", Cairo, 1944);

Sahh al-nawm ("Wake Up", Cairo, 1954);

Dimāʼ wa-tīn ("Blood and Mud", Cairo, 1955);

Umm al-ʻawājiz ("Mother of the Aged", Cairo, 1955);

Fajr al-qissah al-misriyyah ("Dawn of Egyptian Fiction", Cairo, 1957);

Khallīhā ʻalā ʼllāh ("Leave it to God", Cairo, 1959);

Khutuwāt fī ʼl-naqd ("Steps in Criticism", Cairo, 1960);

ʼAntar wa-Juliyāt ("ʻAntar and Juliette", Cairo, 1961);

Fikrah fa-ʼbtisāmah ("A Thought and a Smile", Cairo, 1962);

Damʼah fa-ʼbtisāmah ("A Tear and a Smile",

Cairo, 1962?);

Haqībah fī yad musāfir ("Suitcase in a Traveler's Hand", Cairo, 1969);

'Itr al-ahbāb ("Perfume of the Loved Ones", Cairo, 1971);

Nās fī 'l-zill ("People in Shadow", Cairo, 1971);

Yā layl, yā 'ayn ("Oh Layl, Oh 'Ayn", Cairo, 1972);

Unshūdah li'l-basātah ("An Anthem to Simplicity", Cairo, 1973);

al-Farash al-shāghir ("The Empty Bed", Cairo, 1986);

Madrasat al-masrah ("The School of Theater", Cairo, 1986);

Min fayd al-Karīm ("From God's Grace", Cairo, 1986);

Safhah min tārīkh Misr ("A Page from Egyptian History", Cairo, 1986);

Turāb al-mīrī ("Government Mud", Cairo, 1986);

'Ishq al-kalimah ("Love of Words", Cairo, 1987);

Fī 'l-sīnimā ("On the Cinema", Cairo, 1988);

Hādhā 'l-shi'r ("This Poetry", Cairo, 1988);

Kunāsat al-dukkān ("Shop Sweepings", Cairo, 1991);

Ta'ālā ma'ī ilā 'l-kūnsīr ("Come with me to the Concert", Cairo, 1980).

Works in Translation

The Saint's Lamp, and other Stories, translated by M. M. Badawi (Leiden: E. J. Brill, 1976);

Good Morning! And other Stories, translated by Miriam Cooke (Washington: Three Continents Press, 1984);

Blood and Mud: Three novelettes, translated by Pierre Cachia (Pueblo, Colorado: Passeggiata Press, 1999).

Translations by the Author

Jules Romains, *Duktur Knuk* (1960); translation of *Dr. Knock, or The Triumph of Medicine* (1923);

Maurice Maeterlinck, *al-'Usfūr al-azraq* (1966); translation of *L'Oiseau bleu* (1909);

Edith Saunders, *al-Ab al-dalīl* (1971); translation of *The Prodigal Father* (1951);

Mihail Sadoveanu, *al-Balātah* (1972); translation of *Baltagul* (1930), through the English translation *The Hatchet* (1961);

Stefan Zweig, *Lā'ib al-shatranj* (1973); translation of *Schachnovelle* (1944);

Thomas Mann, *Tūnyū Krūjir* (1973); translation of *Tonio Kröger* (1903).

Yahyā Haqqī once complained that people seemed to think that he had written nothing other than his most famous work, the novella *Qindīl Umm Hāshim* (a thought that he shared with this writer in Cairo, May 1979). This was far from the case. In fact, he was a prolific writer who in his long literary career produced a novel and over twenty volumes of stories, essays and literary criticism. His subjects ranged widely from life in rural Egypt to travels around Europe and Turkey, from forbidden love to the dangers of technology and necrophilia, from Egyptian fiction to the fights among the poorest of the urban poor.

Haqqī was born on 7 January 1905 into a literary family of Turkish descent. During his childhood, they lived in Hārat Mida, an alley close to this same shrine of Umm Hāshim in the heart of popular Cairo. The falafel stands, the Sufis reciting their *dhikr*s, the Muslim holidays, the saints' tombs, the craftsmen, the merchants and the beggars were all to play their part in his writings. Haqqī's love for these people is filled with anger and bitterness and sometimes humor. Yet even while smiling at their eccentricities, he never lost sight of the wretched who eke out their miserable lives in circumstances few care to imagine.

Yahyā Haqqī grew up during the era when Egyptians were chafing under the dual yoke of British and monarchic rule. The end of World War I brought the first waves of resistance to colonial rule in the region. They were quickly quashed when the British and the French met in Versailles and then in Lausanne to draw new boundaries around emerging nation-states in the Middle East and then to divide the region between them. Sa'd Zaghlūl's Wafd Party, that had demanded and been denied a role in the European deliberations, led the charge against British rule in Egypt for over thirty years. Between 1919 and 1952 the call for independence was on many lips. Although as a student Haqqī did not participate in political campaigns, he and his family supported Zaghlūl.

The young Haqqī became active in the literary movements of the 1920s. This was a period of transition not only in political but also in cultural sensibility in the Arab world. Literary schools were emerging with the mission to embed the generally European genres of "scientific" literary criticism, the short story and the novel, in local realities. The so-called Woman Question was challenging preconceived notions about the role of women in society. The Egyptian Feminist Union under the leadership of Hudā Shaʿrāwī drew the attention of Arabs everywhere to women's rights to education, employment and uncovered faces. Writers took up women's cause and wrote angrily about the ways they were treated. They were particularly outraged by the general tolerance for honor killings. It has been suggested that intellectuals' early engagement with feminist issues contributed to the development of a local literature that was no longer so imitative of European models.

Haqqī associated himself with *Jamāʿat al-madrasah al-hadīthah* (The Modern School) under the leadership of Ahmad Khayrī Saʿīd. In several essays he reminisces about the meetings at Café al-Fann where they used to discuss European and Russian writers. The Europeans fed their minds; the Russians their souls. They published *Fajr: sahīfat al-hadm waʾl-bināʾ* (Dawn: The Destruction-Construction Journal) that promoted socially responsible stories and decried the current trend to copy western literary models (see for example *Fajr al-qissah al-misriyyah*, 76-81). It was members of this "Modern School" that introduced peasants and ordinary people into literature, and gave Egypt its own literature (*ʿItr*, 129; *Fajr*, 257). In 1926 Haqqī published "al-Dars al-awwal" (The First Lesson) in the newspaper *al-Siyāsah al-Usbūʿiyyah* (published later in *Umm*). His first mature story, it indicts the progress project that ignores the price poor people pay for the comfort of the rich. A little boy, living alone with his father, the stationmaster of a remote milk-train stop, and his pious Nubian assistant, await the train that will take him to his first day of school. Under the boy's horrified gaze the train drags the Nubian off the platform and mangles him under its wheels. The assignment of the first lesson is to write about the benefits of the train. In Haqqī's writings the train (sometimes the tram) becomes emblematic of the evils of modernization (see below).

Haqqī wrote "al-Dars al-awwal" while studying at the Sultāniyyah Law School in Cairo where the playwright Tawfīq al-**Hakīm** was also a student. In 1927, he graduated and was appointed Administrative Assistant, a vaguely defined job that allowed him to do as much or as little as he pleased. He was posted to Manfalūt, a small town in Upper Egypt, where he lived for two years. There he met people like the Nubian, the boy and his father. For the first time he came into contact with fellaheen (Arabic *fallāhīn*, peasants, sg. *fellāh*) whose legal cases he had to adjudicate. Despite all attempts to come close to them, he was kept at a distance. They would have nothing to do with this man who came from Cairo to represent the government.

This distance, however painful, was instructive. It allowed Haqqī to theorize authenticity in stories like "Hasīr al-jāmiʿ" (The Mosque Mat, in *Umm*). Far from the international circles of intellectuals in Cairo he thought about the fellaheen who had always lived outside the purview of the center that foreigners had dominated for two thousand years. The fellaheen's distance from him was no more than a reenactment of their millennial resistance to colonial rule. Ergo, the fellaheen remained uncontaminated; they were the last scions of the Pharaohs whose profiles painted in the tombs in Luxor could be seen in the fields flanking the River Nile; they were the true Egyptians. To be a true Egyptian was to be connected to the Pharaohs—a theme that was to be taken up by Najīb Mahfūz in a trio of early novels: *ʾAbath al-aqdār* (Mockery of the Fates, 1939; translated by Raymond Stock as *Khufu's Wisdom*, 2003), *Radūbīs* (Rhadopis, 1943; translated by Anthony Calderbank as *Rhadopis of Nubia*, 2003) and *Kifāh Tībā* (The Struggle of Thebes, 1944; translated by Humphrey Davies as *Thebes at War*, 2003).

This mapping of the contemporary on to a great civilization of the past was also a trope in colonizers' description of their projects. The countries they subjected had no "history" because history entails change and evolution, but they did have the glorious civilizations that made them worthy of conquest. Without history they could not change unless an agent with History and Civilization intervened, and that was the role of the colonial enterprise, the so-called civilizing mission. In *Qindīl Umm Hāshim*, written almost twenty years after he left Upper Egypt, Ismāʿīl's English professor praises him not for his individual talent but for his cultural heritage, saying:

I bet the soul of a Pharaonic priest transmigrated into you, Mr. Ismāʿīl. Your country needs you because it is the land of the blind.

(*Qindīl*, 83)

This is the colonizers' universal project: to revive an ancient civilization in their subjects who lack history. In the process of bringing civilization to their benighted world, they are in turn enriched by the civilizations they resuscitate.

This romantic idealization of a pure pre-Islamic past coincided with comparable theories that kept popping up in the 1930s and 1940s in other Muslim countries under European domination. The current failure was due to the stunting influence of Islam; to regain their past greatness they needed to go back to a time before Islam and revive their ancient civilization that was so much greater than the Europeans' younger attempts to overcome barbarism.

When his two years in Upper Egypt were over, Haqqī, now aged 23, entered the Foreign Service. He was sent first to Jeddah, then Istanbul, Rome, Paris and Ankara. While working abroad he continued to write. Serving as secretary in the Egyptian consulate archives in Jeddah in 1930, he published some literary criticism. For example, in the daily newspaper *al-Balāgh*, he published several reviews, including one of Ahmad **Shawqī**'s acclaimed drama *Masraʿ Kalyūbatrah* (Death of Cleopatra, 1929), a piece that was later published in *Khutuwāt*). He had feared that the poetry would spoil the play, but in fact, as he notes approvingly, it managed to enhance the nationalist message. In *Majallat al-Rābitah al-Sharqiyyah* he published his essay "White and Non-White" (also published in *Khutuwāt*) about the British colonizers in India.

Despite their apparent sophistication, he suggests, they are morally no better than the Ku Klux Klan. He deplores what he calls the primitive racism of Europeans and Americans and their intolerance of Islam.

His posting to Istanbul between 1931 and 1933 was a particularly fertile period. He was in the land of his ancestors and of the Sufi poet Jalāl al-Dīn Rūmī (d. 1273). Haqqī was always interested in Sufism even as he affirmed his faith in mainstream Islam (although without the emphasis on meat and animal slaughter!). In *Damʿah* (1965), he ascribed to the soil of Turkey the power to open the soul to mystical experiences. He lamented the secular revolution of Atatürk that closed down Sufi monasteries and criminalized individual Sufis whose whirling, Haqqī felt, was so much more dignified than the ecstatic practices of Egyptian Sufis (16-18). On one occasion he accompanied some diplomats to the Hagia Sofia—that he described as an impressive but cold museum-like mosque/church—to watch Muslims at prayer during the "Night of Power" (the night of the month of Ramadan when the Qur'anic revelations are believed to have begun). How odd it was, he felt, to watch when he would have preferred to be among the watched; never before had he witnessed such joy and humility in a crowd, such piety and vulnerability. The place was a sea roaring with prayers (30-42). In closing, he wondered whether Atatürk had created this spiritual fervor when he banned religious practices. In Turkey he continued to read Russian literature in English translation. He was particularly drawn to the rivals Tolstoy and Turgenev who gave him faith in the power of literature to influence politics. For, despite their very different approach to literature, they both wrote as patriots. This connection to the country, this nationalist commitment was vital to Haqqī; in praising Tawfīq al-**Hakīm** he wrote that people cut off from the spirit of their country could not write good literature (*Khutuwāt*, 97). Through literature, they worked for the liberation of the serfs. Whereas Turgenev was a realist with his feet firmly planted in the ground, Tolstoy was an idealist, a mystic, with his eye to the sky. Their struggle for the rights of the disenfranchised in a society of privilege helped Haqqī to understand his own society in transition into modernity (article later published in *Khutuwāt*).

This time spent in Turkey was to prove problematic in that it intensified Haqqī's awareness of his Turkish ancestry. He began to entertain doubts about his ability to speak for Egyptians (*Dam'ah*, 129). Who had this right, he asked? Was attachment to the land of birth enough for one to become a national of that land? Was it a matter of living close to the Nile, the lifeblood of Egyptianness? Or, was it commitment to a burning nationalist cause? If the latter, then his uncle, Mahmūd Tāhir Haqqī (d. 1964), was thoroughly Egyptian. His powerful telling of the celebrated Dinshaway incident, *'Adhrā' Dinshawāy* (The Virgin of Dinshaway, 1906; translated by Saad El-Gabalawy as *The Maiden of Dinshway*, 1986), a work that launched the resistance to the English at the turn of the 20th century, must have naturalized him. Haqqī praises his uncle for humanizing and even glorifying the fellah (claiming that he was the first to write about them), and for making the people aware of the enormity of the crime that the English were perpetrating against them.

Haqqī never answered these questions to his complete satisfaction, probably because he actually valued the role of outsider. He realized that a position on the margins granted him an invaluable perspective as participant-observer and that this marginality did not necessarily preclude him from being fully Egyptian. In an autobiographical piece, "Ashjān 'udw muntasib" (The Sorrows of an Associate), he writes uncertainly:

Even though I am of Turkish extraction, I still feel that I am absolutely part of the soil and the people of Egypt.   *(Qindīl, 56)*

It was in Turkey also that he began to write his *Sa'īdiyyāt*, the stories about the Sa'īd, or Upper Egypt, that he published in 1955 in his first two collections, *Umm al-'awājiz* (Mother of the Aged) and *Dimā' wa-tīn* (Blood and Mud).

Three of the five stories from Upper Egypt— "al-Bustagī" (The Postman), "Qissah min al-sijn" (A Story from Prison) and "Abū Fūda"— were published in *Dimā'*; the other two—the already mentioned "Hasīr al-jāmi'" (The Mosque Mat) and "'Izāzat rīhah" (The Perfume Bottle)—were published in *Umm*. Made into a successful film by Husayn Kamāl, one of his best known stories from this period is "al-Bustagī" (in *Dimā'*). True to the expectations of the Modern School, the story is politically engaged, in that it presents a critique of the practice of honor killings. This story is also considered to be the first instance in which an Egyptian writer made use of the technique of flashback. In *Umm* he also published two Cairo stories. "Al-Ihtijāj" (The Protest) is about the one brief moment in the life of a maid when she can no longer stop herself from protesting at her cruel treatment. The title story, "Umm al-'awājiz" (Mother of the Aged), follows a beggar who is fighting other beggars down the ladder of life; thinking that he has reached the bottom rung, it turns out that there is more below.

Haqqī spent some of the war years (1939-45) in Italy and Germany where he witnessed the fascist regimes of Mussolini and Hitler. In Libya he watched from close at hand a fierce struggle to rid the country of its Italian occupiers. Yet he rarely refers directly to these violent years. It is during this same period that he is to publish the already mentioned *Qindīl Umm Hāshim* (translated into English as *The Saint's Lamp*). The work appeared in 1944, a year before the end of World War II, and tells a narrative of two civilizational failures that can be overcome by bringing them together. The inter-cultural themes and characters of this superb contribution to Arabic fiction can be summarized as follows:

The first light of dawn awoke him from his fitful sleep. He rushed out on deck and peered into the distance. Finally, after days at sea they were about to arrive. Alexandria was spread out on the horizon, her arms spread wide to welcome home a native son. Ismā'īl was returning to Egypt after seven years of study in England. Dr. Ismā'īl, the ophthalmologist, was eager to see his family and betrothed to start to cure Egyptians of their many diseases. How was it that the departing ship seven years ago had sailed so swiftly and this homecoming boat was so slow? But the trip did finally end, the ship docked, and the freshly minted doctor disembarked. He took a train to Cairo, and there the adventure began. The idealized Egypt of his dreams in the cold North quickly separated from the reality of the people that he was seeing as though for the first time. All he could see was their faults. How dirty and superstitious they were! How in need of the talents he brought back from the lands of modernity and civilization.

Beginning his medical revolution at home, he took over the treatment of Fātimah, his cousin and fiancée. Ever since he could remember she had quietly submitted to a traditional cure. Daily, her aunt had infused into her weak eyes drops of oil from the lamp of Umm Hāshim. The oil was thought to have miraculous powers because its lamp hung in the sacred shrine of Sayyidah Zaynab (aka Umm Hāshim), the granddaughter of Muhammad, the Prophet of Islam. Watching the daily ritual that had not changed over the course of the years, Ismā'īl was incensed. He rushed to the shrine and broke the lamp. The shrine custodian saved him from the mob's fury and Ismā'īl escaped. Fātimah was to be his first patient who would show the people the power of the medicine he had brought from the West. They would see with their own eyes the vanity of their superstitious beliefs and practices. Fatima, however, deteriorated under his care until she was almost blind. Ismā'īl despaired until on the Night of Power, the most important day in the fasting month of Ramadan, he saw a light flood the square in front of the shrine. He returned to Umm Hāshim, humbly took of her oil and mixed it with his western medicines. Fātimah thrived and Ismā'īl opened a clinic for the poor.

So ends Yahyā Haqqī's most famous story. It is not only the Egyptians' blind traditionalism that Haqqī is criticizing; he is not a knee-jerk modernist after all. He is also pointing to the weaknesses at the source of the colonial system that has dominated his country for over sixty years. The scientific prowess that lay at the heart of its claims to civilizational superiority was inadequate. Through his hero Ismā'īl, Haqqī suggests that neither science nor religion is effective alone, but that each needs the other: "There is no sight without insight" (*Qindīl* [1975], 72). The play on blindness, sight and insight runs through the novella.

In an almost schematic manner, Haqqī lists the virtues of both societies. The West values the individual, love and self-reliance; the East prioritizes community, commitment and reputation. Each of these values considered alone might constitute a fault but together they create a fully human society. *Qindīl Umm Hāshim* takes on the modernist project of gauging the distance between one part of the world and another in terms of progress: how far are Asia and Africa from Europe, how far is Egypt from England? Haqqī interrogates the assumption that modernity is Europe's gift to the rest of the world that, because of its lack, is backward. What he suggests is that modernity is a time in which all live, however differently, in mutual need. The word "progress" is empty when it does not contribute to the health of the people. Progress is not merely material but also spiritual. In such a scheme, religion is not an opiate for the people, it is indispensable to their total health.

The subtleties at work in this seemingly unsubtle story passed many by. Most famously, the literary critic and religious fundamentalist Sayyid Qutb (executed in 1966) hailed Haqqī as an Egyptian nationalist and a pious Muslim (Qutb 1946). The rejection of the West and the embrace of Islam was what counted and not the questioning and then valorizing of both Eastern and Western belief systems. For Qutb Western modernity and all who aspired to it were no better than idolaters from the *jāhiliyyah*, the time of ignorance before Islam.

Fu'ād Dawwārah, the man who devoted years to finding all of Haqqī's writings in publications however obscure and then arranging them into several volumes, remembers the first time he read Ismā'īl's story. He loved it and showed it to some friends who were just then discovering Najīb Mahfūz, insisting that they read it. He wrote an enthusiastic review only to incur the author's displeasure. Dawwārah had not noted Ismā'īl's Sufi inclinations, because it was not his religion but rather his mystical bent that had allowed Ismā'īl to reconcile these opposite social systems (al-Mu'ātī 1995, 45, 50). It was in Sufism that the dynamism of Islam might be located.

Was this, one wonders, Haqqī's way of rebuking Qutb for his simplistic assessment of the novella?

In 1949, five years after the publication of *Qindīl*, Haqqī was sent to Paris where he worked as First Secretary to the Egyptian Embassy. The two years he spent in the French capital provided him with ample material for his reflections on Western society that he later published in *Haqībah fī yad musāfir* (Suitcase in a Traveler's Hand, 1969). By this time the West, so programmatically presented in *Qindīl*, has become a reality. Essays from this period are often humorous accounts of his surprised encounters with people and places that he admires and also criticizes. Praise and condemnation alternate with dizzying speed. He begins with an encomium to the western mind, one that is orderly and independent. Egyptians will be surprised to learn, he states, that French women work in every sphere of life and contribute to the general welfare. However, these "superior" people are not always happy; they are lonely in their concrete piles; they long for nature, something they can only find in animal and plant shops. Then, as though catching himself in too negative a stance, he lauds the exquisite city parks whose very existence makes him rue their lack at home. As for the proliferation of machines that perform human tasks, they are about to make people redundant. By 1969 he was already forecasting the increasingly dominant role of the computer in everyone's life. After praising museums in Paris for cherishing Egyptian treasures, he roundly condemns them for not giving enough space to his great ancestors. And what are these vile things they eat?! Horses, pigs, snails and frogs' legs, these cannot be food for civilized people. But then again, "They are governed by their own conscience, while we rely on other people's opinions. They are clean, we are dirty" (*Haqībah*, 92). Why are Egyptians not more like them? But then, on reflection, why should they want to be like the French, the English and the Italians (latter-day Crusaders) who have made of Rome and Athens a universal civilization that they are imposing on others? This is not an act of civilization, but rather of barbarism. Arabs should mount a self-defense by proving the superiority of their own civilization or else counter-attack by exposing the shortcomings of European civilization. They should not buy into the Europeans' global civilization. The further people are from Rome and Athens, the less veneration they feel (72-78).

The vacillation between the virtues and vices of East and West that marked *Qindīl* continues here. But what has changed in the interim is the intensification of the *double critique*, a concept elaborated some fifteen years later by the Moroccan philosopher Abdelkebir Khatibi. To be critical of one system does not imply the espousal of another; it is possible to see the failures in two problematic social conditions without falling into cultural betrayal. Indeed, if they are to improve, it is necessary to remain vigilant to the faults that exist in communities to which one wishes to belong (Khatibi 1983).

Haqqī's mind is teeming with contradictory images that he wants to share with his reader, but he does not resolve their dynamic into a simple matter of one civilization's superiority to the other. Strangers must remain open to each other so that they may begin to appreciate different norms and values without judging them. Civilizations cannot be imposed; they must be allowed to do their own work:

Islam's role is to spread its principles throughout the world by letting people see its advantages and not by proselytizing. This is the role that history has imposed on our countries today (101).

Three years after the 1952 Free Officers' Revolution brought independence and euphoria at the prospect of the first indigenous rule since the Pharaonic era, Haqqī followed up on "al-Dars al-awwal" with his one and only novel, entitled *Sahh al-nawm* (Good Morning!). It was his favorite work ('Abdallāh 1990). Divided in two parts, between Yesterday and Today, it details—from the perspective of the Narrator who is from but not of the village—the destruction wrought by the introduction of the train and its station into a remote village. The first part of the story revolves around the wine-bar that is the villagers' favorite meeting place, their shelter in times of trouble. Each night the main characters, none of whom is given a name but only a function, like "Butcher," or an adjective, like "Lame," present a colorful scene. But then, during the Narrator's protracted absence, the station is built. Now the train passes through the village, sometimes stopping to discharge a passenger and dump its waste on what used to be pristine farm land. In the second section, Haqqī shows how tragic the life of each of his characters has become. The person responsible for the transformation is the Ustādh, the Professor. A local boy educated in Cairo, he believes that his experience and training have uniquely equipped him to decide what is best for his people: contact with the world, modernization and the welfare of an abstract collective rather than the happiness of a few individuals. A transparent allegory, the Ustādh represents the arrogance of the new government and the dangers Haqqī foresaw in Gamāl ʿAbd al-Nāsir's (Nasser) assumption of power in 1954. He was not afraid to publish his critique. In fact, he was so concerned that it should come out uncensored that he financed the publication himself (Cooke 1987, 7-8). Already in the early days of Egyptian independence, Haqqī was practicing *double critique*.

In 1960, the author published his third collection of short stories, *ʿAntar wa-Juliyāt* (ʿAntar and Juliet). Like the two earlier collections, it brought together stories that he had published earlier in newspapers and magazines. The introduction gives a sense of Haqqī's understanding of short story writing developed over more than thirty years. As he does in so many of his writings, he insists on the use of the colloquial dialect in dialogue: it is the language of the people and will draw them into the story in such a way that they will not feel the writer's pain but only their own pleasure with the text. Next, he turns to the formal aspect of short fiction, suggesting that ideas are less vital than intricate descriptions of life and human nature. No observation is too trivial to be drawn out and elaborated with a simile, a metaphor or a digression. He terms his stories *lawhāt qalamiyyah* (pen sketches) where ideas do not march blindly along a straight line but rather jump around in their search for truth and elegance of expression. Pen sketches do not tell a story but rather take the reader into a moment in an individual's life. And this is exactly what Haqqī often does. The reader is thus forced to yield to his rambling and enjoy the language without worrying about the logical sequence of ideas. The title story of *ʿAntar*, for example, is a Marxist allegory told through the lives of two dogs. Juliet is a nervous Pekinese who is imprisoned in the lap of luxury, while ʿAntar is a happy mongrel from a poor peasant's hut down the road from Juliet's villa. One day both are out alone, and a dog-pound truck picks them both up. For a moment their lives converge on the dog-pound's straw that feels like silk to ʿAntar and thorns to Juliet. But this reduction of the rich does not last long. Juliet's owner is there within the hour, whereas Antar's owner cannot afford the three pounds that would free his mutt. The happiness of the poor is always under threat.

Haqqī seems to have written constantly, yet it was only in the second half of the 20th century that he started to collect his essays into volumes. In some cases, he might publish an essay in more than one volume, perhaps because of the positive reception it received or else because he wanted to make sure that the article be read. Many of his essays read like philosophical meditations on life, always highly literate, and often invoking great works of world literature. Essays combine vivid descriptions with laughter. His humor has been much noted.

"Curious people like me have trifling questions" (*Fikrah*, 214). Yes, he was a very curious man, and it is this very curiosity that leads him into the nooks and crannies of life. In the text itself it produces exuberant asides that may elaborate on the topic at hand or, as though he were in conversation with his reader, wander off the subject and in a new direction never to return to the interrupted thought. The essays in *Fikrah* (1962) range over a wide array of topics. With obvious pleasure in the writing act, yet also with pain at what he is obliged to witness, he allows his pen to record whatever catches his eye. He watches as police chase beggars away from those areas of the city visited by foreigners. At that point the fighting beggars (like those in *Umm*) are united so that they all seem to meld into one, into something that looks like a single pile of garbage (56). Interspersed with his criticisms of the unjust conditions in which so many Cairenes live are remarks that reveal his own attitude. Despite his love for *fūl* (a cheap dish made of fava beans, onions and garlic), he tells us that he sometimes has to stop at the door of a *fūl* shop, fearful that he may have to take on the worries of the world. How, he asks in bewilderment, can anyone possibly eat in the head-meat shop where the tears of the boy who has to chop the onions mingle with the food that then stinks and sticks in the throat! Sardonic comments about tourists and their identical quests for sites to visit slip easily into meditations about God's love and the power of beauty to render us fully human. Then out of the blue seemingly he will ask whether it is ever acceptable to lie, to cheat and to exact revenge. He writes romantically and apolitically about art and the joy of the artist who creates for himself and not for others. This is a sampling of Haqqī's effervescent observations.

Khallīhā 'alā 'llāh is a volume of semi-auto-biographical essays about his time in Manfalūt that sometimes recalls Tawfīq al-Hakīm's *Yaw-miyyāt nā'ib fī 'l-aryāf* (Diary of a Country Prosecutor, 1937; English translation: *The Maze of Justice*, 1947). He writes vividly about the people and the odd, amusing incidents he witnessed. He describes several of the prostitutes from Manfalūt's busy brothel in keen detail. But there are also macabre moments, like the time a corpse is dragged out of the Nile with its swollen belly and black and blue nails. The sightless eyes stare at him, filling him with the cold dread of death. He expatiates on the pain he feels when the fellaheen keep their distance from him. This leads him to develop his thesis on the separation of the fellah from the Cairo administrators and hence their uncontaminated connection with the great Pharaonic past. Although colleagues had warned him before he left for Upper Egypt that he would find the fellaheen to be obstinate, unchangeable and untrustworthy, he has thought these men were wrong. In such a world individuals do not have control over their destiny and so all they can do is "Leave it to God"! The book ends with him reading an advertisement in a newspaper for the worst job in the whole diplomatic corps: secretary in the Jeddah consu-

late archives. Things are so bad in Manfalūt that he decides to apply. The next thing he knows, he is in the Red Sea city. Of *Khallīhā* Nur Sherif writes:

the man no less than the artist is clearly revealed through his style.... In his approach to his material, whether he is discussing criminals... or circus animals... he is without affectation and, above all, compassionate.... Haqqī is an artist with a sense of vocation, apparent in the sincerity and truth of his work as well as in its disciplined form. (Sherif 1970, 19-20)

Nās fī 'l-zill (1971) is a collection of journal essays that represents well his real interests: the little people who have not made it on to the big stage. These are life's extras who were Haqqī's concern "because they are the real producers of life with all its headlong movement" (Hafiz 1971, 36-37). Their hearts have not been poisoned by bitterness at not having had access to the limelight. Indeed, were it not for the shadows there would be no light, just as without old age there would be no youth. Although many of the vignettes are of city folk, he writes here most urgently about the fellaheen, their language and their role in the development of Egyptian literature. The fellah

used to be outside literature, virtually ignored... The great challenge now is to introduce the case of the fellah into the general human sphere without restricting oneself to material problems but rather to dwell on spiritual values. (Nās, 50, 52)

Haqqī hopes that a young fellah who has been educated will some day write about the fellaheen because outsiders can only fumble in their clumsy attempts to enter this closed world.

In 1960 he started to collect his essays that dealt with literature and popular culture. In that one year he published both *Fajr* and *Khutuwāt*. In 1927, the year he left Cairo for the sticks of Upper Egypt, he published his first literary essay in *Kawkab al-Sharq* using the pseudonym "La-bīb" (intelligent). It was about Mahmūd Tāhir **Lāshīn**'s "Sukhriyyat al-nāy" (Irony of the Flute), one of the first stories to be published in the Modern School's journal, *Fajr*. Haqqī credits Lāshīn with bringing the sketches of the Taymūr brothers to maturity (*Fajr*, 83). He particularly appreciated Lāshīn's use of humor, particularly fellah humor, an element so crucial to his own writing. He republished his review in *Fajr al-qissah al-misriyyah* (Dawn of Egyptian Fiction).

Fajr al-qissah al-misriyyah is generally a historical volume that surveys the rise of modern literature. Literature, he asserts, first appears like the drop that precedes the gush of the oil well. He begins his literary history in 1908, the year the great nationalist Mustafā Kāmil died. He tells the story of the emergence of Egyptian literature out of the combined influences of western literary genres and an ancient cultural heritage. It is here that he gives a history of the Modern School, with a special focus on Mahmūd Tāhir Lāshīn and 'Īsā 'Ubayd, and its role in the dawning of an authentic Egyptian literature. For Haqqī this literary Egyptian dawn lasted from 1914 to 1934, from Muhammad Husayn **Haykal**'s *Zaynab* (1914) to Tawfīq al-**Hakīm**'s *'Awdat al-rūh* (Return of the Spirit). Indeed, Haqqī may be one of the first to make the now disputed claim that *Zaynab* was the first Arabic novel. He praises Haykal for writing so vividly about the lovely Egyptian countryside while dazzled by the beauty of Switzerland. Despite his usual advocacy of realism, Haqqī applauds the romanticism of the writing and disagrees with critics who thought Haykal had spent too much time describing nature. He provides detailed analyses of some stories, particularly those of Muhammad Taymūr (d. 1921), whom he dubs the pioneer of the short story because he was able to bring eastern and western literatures together through his love of Egypt, thus proving to doubters that Egypt provided ample material for fiction. Alas, however, his stories remained scattered flowers that never quite made a bouquet (59-75). Another pioneer, this time of theater, is Tawfīq al-Hakīm who is credited with professionalizing playwriting. Betraying no western influence, his plays were able to be both Egyptian and universal.

In *Khutuwāt* Haqqī writes that he had decided to collect his essays into single volumes because he was getting old (in fact, he was to live for a further 32 years) and wanted to accomplish this task "before the great sleep closes my eyes" (4). He wants the book to be a testament to the progress made in literary criticism over the past 25 years in the Arab world; serious critical assessment of literature had allowed it to progress and writers had cultivated maturity of reflection. From a political point of view, the Egyptian revolution had galvanized literary production because during revolutionary periods writers are concerned to understand themselves through their writing. They are not interested in merely repeating what has already been said and written. He reviews many Egyptian stories, following the lead of members of the *Dīwān* literary school (especially 'Abbās Mahmūd al-'Aqqād and Ibrāhīm al-**Māzinī**) who criticized the tendency to praise friends however bad their writing and to attack enemies however excellent their prose. Even before his enchantment with patriotic Russian writings, Haqqī dreamt of a political, truly national literature that might acquire the stature of world literature. The *Khutuwāt* essays like his other literary reviews treat their subjects from an impressionistic perspective. Haqqī with all his quirks generally situated himself as the ideal reader, the individual whose reaction becomes the barometer for general reception of the text. Windows to both East and West should be kept open even though he disapproves of western imitations, "even if we would like to live in their atmosphere here in our country among our people" (197, 204). His constant quoting of western influences while insisting on authenticity is an attempt to situate Egyptian literature in an international context. Some of the essays veer from the purely literary to general commentary about the world. Two examples were written in 1959, the one in Syria and the other about the Algerian war of independence. His lecture at Damascus University during the 1958-61 union of Egypt and Syria (the United Arab Republic) is entitled "Our Need for a New Style." The richness of the Arabic language must be exploited and renewed and precision of expression must be cultivated in order for precision of thought to be possible. He ends with a didactic paean to the revolutions in both countries and a call for unity against Israel (236). This political tone is struck in another essay from that same year, also later published in *Khutuwāt*, about the Algerian Muhammad

Dīb's story "In the Café." Written in the middle of the war it articulates the spirit of the noble Algerian people who have suffered so much injustice. Dīb had not confined himself to local problems but had situated them in a global context of human tragedy; he had thus rendered the local more intense (245). Haqqī also looks at popular culture, calling for a serious critique of songs.

The third literary collection to be published was *'Itr al-ahbāb* (Perfume of the Loved Ones, 1971), a wide-ranging philosophical meditation on the life of the mind and a call for a language that will not be split between the heart and the tongue. Literature should have an emotional impact. The writers' task, he asserts, is to remove veil after veil of fog that shrouds meaning until they finally reach the perfect picture that the soul had intuited without really seeing (112). One of the loved ones whose perfume he cherished was Najīb Mahfūz with whom he had worked for a while in the Arts Council. He was able to observe Mahfūz's emotional state during the writing of *al-Liss wa'l-kilāb* (1961; English translation: *The Thief and the Dogs*, 1984). He noted his obsession with Mahmūd Amīn Sulaymān, the Egyptian whose criminal career inspired the fictional character of Sa'īd Mahrān in the novel. Haqqī commented approvingly that Mahfūz struggled to be the good civil servant he was not born to be. Mahfūz's œuvre gives Haqqī the opportunity to develop his thesis of static versus dynamic writing. Haqqī praises the art of *al-Liss wa'l-kilāb* that, unlike the more famous but static *Trilogy*, is a dynamic text, it can be read and then re-read for its multiple layers of meaning (113-22). His hope in this book is that readers will get to know and like those whom he has loved, including members of the Modern School, Najīb Mahfūz, Mahmūd Tāhir Lāshīn, Tawfīq al-Hakīm and Umm Kulthūm.

Unshūdah li'l-basātah (1973) is, as its title indicates, an "Anthem to Simplicity". It collects essays about style, especially in the short story and also in poetry, all with a didactic edge. It is almost a manual for the budding writer who is told more than once to read world authors like Homer, Flaubert, Balzac, Pasternak, Dickens and Twain, but also the Indian Mirzā Asad Allāh

Ghālib and classical Arab writers like 'Umar ibn Rabī'ah. They should also study the paintings of Rembrandt and Van Gogh. Haqqī introduces *Unshūdah* by writing that he had heard that some fellaheen might be reading this book and so he was going to use their language. When some intellectuals complained that the colloquial language makes literature artificial, he responded that the writer who deserves to survive has to merge with his own people so that his style will naturally flow from this experience and the other will become the "I" (131). That is how the Arabic language whose potential is abused by so many writers can be enriched without succumbing cliché and conformity; that is how a story survives rather than dying after its first reading. The ideal writer "feels that all the words in the language are calling to him to bring them into presence" (36). Surprise the reader, advises Haqqī, be like the

flower you pick that makes you feel it has just been born, just opened its eyes. It is still bending low to the ground because of the sweet vertigo that has overcome it when its creator has surprised it into life. (75)

Among the other literary collections are: *'Ishq al-kalimah* (Love of Words) that focuses on the works of young writers whom he has encouraged throughout his career; and *Hādhā 'l-shi'r* (This Poetry) which contains essays on Muslim poets both in and outside the Arab world. Throughout his literary career he kept coming back to some writers and texts as though they were friends that you are not done with after they have said good-bye.

After the 1967 war with Israel, Haqqī did not write any more fiction, although he did publish the *Qindīl* collection in 1975. Like many of his literary peers, he was deeply shocked by the defeat and could not turn despair into literature. However, he continued his involvement in literature through his leadership of the magazine *al-Majallah*. Several writers acknowledged their debts to Haqqī who between 1962 and 1970 served as editor-in-chief of this literary magazine, a post that enabled him to promote young talents that might otherwise have remained obscured. Salāh al-Dīn al-Mu'ātī remembers how

Haqqī helped him to publish his first short story that launched him on his literary career (al-Muʿātī 1995, 5). Naʿīm ʿAtiyyah also praises Haqqī for welcoming "many young intellectuals and opening opportunities for them and for me" (87). Sāmī Farīd narrates his first meeting with Haqqī: the latter asked him to read his story out loud; when he had finished, Haqqī asked him to read it again. Haqqī told him quite simply that he would publish the story. Farīd said that Haqqī "created intellectuals and writers in the most self-effacing way" (98).

Haqqī's achievements were acknowledged during his own lifetime. In 1969 he was awarded the State Appreciation Prize. In 1990, he received the prestigious International King Faisal Prize for lifetime achievement in Arabic culture. He was called the "greatest writer of the short story in the Arab world.... And like all great writers [he] did not search out the limelight" (Kāmil 1990, 16). The quiet little man who had spent his life observing individuals and noting their faults, quirks and virtues had at last gained the recognition he had thought would always be reserved for writers such as Tāhā **Husayn**, Najīb Mahfūz, and Tawfīq al-Hakīm. He may not have written the grand autobiography, play or novel of the 20th century but his penetrating intellect, his consummate command of the languages of the Qurʾān and of the Egyptian backstreets and his deep sympathy for his fellow humans were finally acknowledged.

He died three years later at the age of 87. In his honor Salāh al-Dīn al-Muʿātī edited a volume of essays by and about intellectuals who had been marked by their meetings with Yahyā Haqqī. "Even if he is gone," al-Muʿātī wrote, "his perfume lingers among us, sweetening the fragrance of following generations" (al-Muʿātī 1995, 10). This commemorative volume pays hommage to Haqqī's extraordinary care for the right word. All praise the precision and economy of his language—goals he had set himself throughout his life. For him, Arabic was "a language of genius in its ability to be powerful both in concision and in allusion" (34). Mahmūd Muhammad Shākir from the Arabic Language Academy recollects Haqqī's passion for words and his search for their secrets (31). Naʿīm

ʿAtiyyah marvels at his unhurried pursuit of the *mot juste*, and he recounts an illuminating incident. In French, the genre of *still life* is rendered *nature mort*, but Haqqī rebelled against both English and French terms, and he came up with his own translation *al-lawhah al-shayʾiyyah* or a "painting containing things" (84).

The right word was sometimes a colloquial expression, and Haqqī justified his use of the language of the streets by pointing out its richness that defied translation into the high idiom of *fushā*. He was full of admiration for the popular poet Bayram al-Tūnisī (d. 1961), a man who made the Egyptian colloquial sing. Haqqī narrates stories about their relationship in *Kunāsat al-dukkān* (Naqqāsh 2005). Throughout his essays, the reader will find repeated discussions of the literary merits of the colloquial. Some colloquial words and phrases are so precise that their meaning defies translation, even with many classical words. To find this magical language authors should go to songs and proverbs that emerge out of the people's everyday practices; his greatest ambition was for the reader to say:

When I read you I don't feel I'm reading. My other ambition is that there will not be a single expression in Arabic that my pen will not have written.   (al-Muʿātī 1995, 140-145)

20th century intellectuals throughout the Arab world have addressed this problem of the colloquial: how to render the language of the common person in a literary text. Some denied the colloquial any place in the august company of *fushā*; the specificity of each dialect was such that it complicated understanding across borders. If Arab writers wanted to reach readers outside their nation-state they would have to stick to the lingua franca. Others agreed with Haqqī that there was too much meaning and allusion in the colloquial for it to be absent in Arabic literature; they trusted their readers who, they believed, could guess at the meaning of the few words that were strange to them. The colloquial question that preoccupied Haqqī and others from the end of the 19th century remains unanswered.

Others noted Haqqī's limitless patience in finding just the right image and that allowed him to *write and re-write a sentence up to thirty or forty times until I reach the appropriate expression that the meaning demands, but only on condition that the words do not betray the sweat and toil of the writer. The style must seem to be absolutely simple.* (Kamil 1990, 16)

This lifelong commitment to precision and the power and the beauty of language earned Haqqī the title of *sā'igh al-lughah:* the Arab Wordsmith of the 20th century.

REFERENCES

ʿAbdallāh Ahmad ʿAbdallāh, "Bānūrāmā sarīʿah ʿanhu wa-ʿan ibdāʿātih: musawwir al-hārāt al-shaʿbiyyah" (A Quick Panorama about Him and His Creative Writings: Photographer of the Popular Districts), *al-Sharq al-Awsat*, 23 April 1990;

Miriam Cooke, *Anatomy of an Egyptian Intellectual: Yahyā Haqqī* (Washington D.C.: 3 Continents Press, 1984);

Rashād Kāmil, "Milaff taqdīrī bi-munāsabat fawz sāhib ʿQindīl Umm Hāshim' bi-jāʾizat al-Malik Faysal al-ʿālamiyyah" (A Dossier of Appreciation at the occasion of the International King Faysal Award being granted to the Author of 'The Lamp of Umm Hāshim'), *al-Sharq al-Awsat*, 23 April 1990;

Abdelkebir Khatibi, *La Memoire tatouée* (Paris: Union générale de l'édition, 1983);

Salāh al-Dīn al-Muʿātī, *Wafāʾ sāhib al-Qindīl* ("Death of the Author of the Lamp", Cairo, 1995);

Rajāʾ al-Naqqāsh, "Li-mādhā ghadiba Bayram al-Tūnisī min Yahyā Haqqī?" (Why was Bayram al-Tūnisī Angry with Yahyā Haqqī?), http://by4fd.bay4.hotmail.msn.com/cgi-bin (accessed 6.6.2005);

Sayyid Qutb, *Kutub wa-shakhsiyyāt* ("Books and Personalities", Cairo?, 1946);

Nur Sherif, *About Arabic Books* [Beirut, 1970], in: *Modern Arabic Literature*, ed. Roger Allen (New York: Ungar, 1987).

Muhammad Husayn Haykal
(1888 – 1956)

MICHELLE HARTMAN
McGill University

WORKS

La dette publique égyptienne ("Egyptian Public Debt", Paris: A. Rousseau, 1912);

Zaynab: manāzir wa-akhlāq rīfiyyah ("Zaynab: Rural Scenes and Morals", Cairo: al-Jarīdah, 1913);

Jān Jāk Russū: hayātuh wa-kutubuh ("Jean Jacques Rousseau: His Life and Works", 2 vols., Cairo: Matbaʿat al-Wāʿiz, 1921);

Fī awqāt al-farāgh: majmūʿat rasāʾil adabiyyah tārīkhiyyah akhlāqiyyah falsafiyyah ("In Leisure Times: A Collection of Literary, Historical, Ethical, and Philosophical Essays", Cairo: al-Matbaʿah al-Misriyyah, 1925);

ʿAsharat ayyām fī 'l-Sūdān ("Ten Days in the Sudan", Cairo: al-Matbaʿah al-ʿAsriyyah, 1927);

Tarājim misriyyah wa-gharbiyyah: Kliyūbātrah ("Egyptian and Western Biographies: Cleopatra", Cairo: Matbaʿat al-Siyāsah wa'l-Siyāsah al-Usbūʿiyyah, 1929);

Waladī ("My Son", Cairo: Matbaʿat al-Siyāsah, 1931);

Thawrat al-adab ("The Literary Revolution", Cairo: Matbaʿat al-Siyāsah, 1933);

Hayāt Muhammad ("Muhammad's Life", Cairo: Matbaʿat Misr, 1935);

Fī manzil al-wahy ("In the Abode of Inspiration", Cairo: Matbaʿat Dār al-Kutub al-Misriyyah, 1937);

al-Siddīq Abū Bakr ("Abu Bakr, the Righteous",
Cairo: Matba'at misr, 1943);

al-Fārūq 'Umar ("'Umar, the Legislator", Cairo: Matba'at Misr, 1945);

Mudhakkirāt fī 'l-siyāsah al-misriyyah: 1912–1937
("Memoirs on Egyptian Politics: 1912–1937", 2
vols., Cairo: Maktabat al-Nahdah al-Misriyyah,
1951-1953);

Shakhsiyyāt misriyyah wa-gharbiyyah ("Egyptian and
Western Personalities", Cairo: Dār Rūz al-Yūsuf,
1954);

Hākadhā khuliqat: qissah tawīlah ("Thus Was She
Created: A Long Story", Cairo: al-Sharikah al-
'Arabiyyah li'l-Tibā'ah wa'l-Nashr, 1955).

Posthumous Publications

al-Imbrātūriyyah al-islāmiyyah wa'l-amākin al-
muqaddasah ("The Islamic Empire and the Holy
Places", Cairo: Dār al-Hilāl, 1961);

al-Sharq al-jadīd ("The Modern East", Cairo: Maktabat al-Nahdah al-Misriyyah, 1962);

al-Īmān wa'l-ma'rifah wa'l-falsafah ("Faith, Knowledge, and Philosophy", Cairo: Maktabat al-Nahdah
al-Misriyyah, 1964);

'Uthmān ibn 'Affān: bayn al-khilāfah wa'l-mulk
("'Uthmān ibn 'Affān: Between Caliphate and
Monarchy", Cairo: Maktabat al-Nahdah al-
Misriyyah, 1968);

Qisas misriyyah ("Egyptian Tales", Cairo: Maktabat
al-Nahdah al-Misriyyah, 1969);

al-Hukūmah al-islāmiyyah ("Islamic Government",
Cairo: Dār al-Ma'ārif, 1977);

al-Adab wa'l-hayāh al-misriyyah: dirāsāt fī shi'r al-
Bārūdī wa-Shawqī wa-Hāfiz ("Art and Egyptian
Life: Studies on the poetry of al-Barudi, Shawqi,
and Hafiz", Cairo: Dār al-Hilāl, 1992).

Co-Authored Works

M. H. Haykal, Ibrāhīm 'Abd al-Qādir al-Māzinī and
Muhammad 'Abd Allāh 'Inān, al-Siyāsah al-
misriyyah wa'l-inqilāb al-dustūrī ("Egyptian Politics and the Constitutional Revolution", Cairo:
Matba'at al-Siyāsah, 1931).

Works in Translation

The Life of Muhammad (Philadelphia: North Ameri-
can Trust Publications, 1976); translation of
Hayāt Muhammad, tr. by Isma'il Ragi A. al-
Faruqi;

Mohammed Hussein Haikal's Zainab: the first
Egyptian novel (London: Darf, 1989); translated by John Mohammed Grinsted.

Muhammad Husayn Haykal is a major figure in
the intellectual life of early twentieth century
Egypt. Like many turn-of-the-century intellectuals of his background, he was devoted to modernizing his country. What makes Haykal stand
apart among his contemporaries is the broad
range of his contributions to modern Arabic
letters and journalism. Trained as a lawyer, he
played a prominent role in Egyptian politics as a
supporter of the Liberal Constitutionalist Party
which acted as a counter to the influence of the
more successful Wafd Party, especially after
Egypt's independence from Britain in 1922.
While he was strongly attached to the promotion
of a Pharaonic identity for Egypt, Haykal also
wrote on religion, penning what many consider
to be the first modern biography of the Prophet
Muhammad. Hayāt Muhammad (The Life of
Muhammad) is probably his most successful
work, but it is his first novel that won him a
place in the annals of Arabic literary history.
Zaynab: manāzir wa-akhlāq rīfiyyah (Zaynab:
Rural Scenes and Morals), a romantic story of
the interrelated lives of a number of men and
women living in the Egyptian countryside, was a
significant early contribution to the development
of the novel genre in both Egypt and Arabic
literature as a whole. It is frequently cited by
critics as being the first full-fledged novel written in Arabic. Though critical opinion is divided
about both the quality of this work as a novel
and its place as the "first" novel, there is no
doubt that Haykal's Zaynab inspired a generation of writers of fiction in Egypt, particularly in
taking up the lives of the fallāhīn (peasants) as a
subject worthy of attention. Haykal's work had a
crucial role in spurring interest in the modern
Arabic novel that would take on great proportions even during his own lifetime.

Though it is Zaynab, and also Hayāt Muhammad (Muhammad's Life), for which Haykal is
best-known in literary historical terms, arguably
his greatest contributions to Arabic letters were
his essays. Haykal's dedication to improving and
modernizing Egyptian society in the twentieth

century is clear not only in his role as the editor of the Egyptian daily, *al-Siyāsah*, and its weekly literary supplement, *al-Siyāsah al-Usbū'iyyah*, but also as one of its most frequent contributors. He was known to have been intellectually and ideologically devoted to the project of modernizing Egypt, changing the lives of the poor, and reforming the political system to the extent of using his own financial resources for publication of his paper. Haykal's literary and journalistic production clearly addresses pressing social concerns and the enlightenment of his fellow Egyptians.

Muhammad Husayn Haykal was born on 20 August 1888 into a landowning family in the village of Kafr Ghannam located in the Delta governorate of Daqahliyyah. His birth, early childhood and summers spent in this rural milieu seem to have had a great impact on his life, even after he had long left behind his rural origins and moved to the city. Richer than other local families in this small rural village in the Egyptian countryside, the Haykal family built up their wealth partly through holding the prestigious position of village *'umdah* (local leader). Tracing their roots in Kafr Ghannam back to the eighteenth century, Haykal males had passed down this inherited position through their family for about seventy five years when Muhammad was born. The family lived in a grand house by village standards and also were the benefactors of many aspects of the village's institutional framework, most importantly schools.

Muhammad's father, Husayn, like his father and grandfather before him, evinced a great interest in education and in particular the education of his son. It is known that he sent his son at an early age to the local *kuttāb*, or traditional religious school, where the young Muhammad memorized one third of the Qur'ān. Husayn Haykal was also known for his interest in modern ways and the improvements this would bring to people in Egypt. Thus, at the age of only seven, the young Muhammad was sent to Cairo to receive a high quality education in one of the government schools proliferating in Egypt around the turn of the century. Lodging with his uncle who taught at the prestigious al-Azhar, the premier Islamic university not only in Egypt but

the entire Arab world, Muhammad studied at the primary school in the popular Gamāliyyah quarter. Returning to Kafr Ghannam only for summers, he later wrote about the impact the separation from his family and village had on him as such a young boy.

Living between the city and the countryside is a theme that recurs throughout Muhammad Husayn Haykal's personal life, as well as that of many of his fictional characters. Clearly, this double life influenced his formation as a young man and adolescent. Anecdotes about him report his longing for the material comforts of the city when he was in the village and his nostalgia for the village when in the city, themes that will recur in his fictional works. When he was a young man, for example, Haykal printed up a small newsletter to inform people in his tiny rural village about the issues he and his family cared about and were concerned with, including modernization, education and public health. Such activities, at an early age, foreshadowed his later career as a professional journalist, intellectual and modernizing politician with a major impact on Egyptian thought in the twentieth century.

Haykal graduated from the respected Khedival secondary school in Cairo only five years after Egypt welcomed the new century. Reports hold that he was dissuaded from his original plan of pursuing an engineering degree in the United Kingdom upon graduation by the prominent intellectual figure known as the "Teacher of a generation," Ahmad Lutfī al-Sayyid (d. 1963), who was also a distant relative by marriage. Lutfī al-Sayyid's suggestion took hold and Haykal remained in Egypt, receiving a law degree from the Khedival law school in 1908. It was during this three-year period that Haykal solidified his relationship with Lutfī al-Sayyid and demonstrated his interest in the latter's journal, *al-Jarīdah*. The group of people involved in the publication and production of *al-Jarīdah* formed an intellectual school of sorts and it was through this school that Haykal began to develop his ideas more fully about how modernization should be implemented in Egyptian society.

Like many other young educated men of his generation and intellectual persuasion, Haykal left Egypt to further pursue his studies after his graduation from law school. On 7 July 1909 he sailed for Paris to take up a scholarship place in order to pursue a doctorate in law at the Sorbonne. During his three years in Paris, Haykal continued meeting his fellow Egyptian modernists and reformists and discussing plans for the improvement of a society on the verge of independence. He would maintain lifetime friendships with some of these Egyptian colleagues who, like him, became prominent figures in Egyptian life, such as Mustafā ʿAbd al-Rāziq (d. 1947) and Bahī al-Dīn Barakāt, in addition to Lutfī al-Sayyid. His doctoral dissertation, dealing with economics, which he defended and published in 1912 as *La dette publique égyptienne* (Egyptian public debt), shows his continued commitment to working on some of the most important social issues to Egyptians in the period. It is in this same year that he returned from Paris and opened a law office in al-Mansūrah.

Haykal did not remain in al-Mansūrah for long, however, and began work in the Court of Cairo in 1913. For several months in 1912-1913, during his period of transition from France to Egypt and then from the country to the city, Lutfī al-Sayyid appointed Haykal interim director of al-Jarīdah. It is in this very same year that the novel *Zaynab: manāzir wa-akhlāq rīfiyyah* (Zaynab: Country Scenes and Morals), the work which established Muhammad Husayn Haykal's position within Arabic literary history, was published in al-Jarīdah as a series of instalments. It should be noted that there is a discrepancy in the criticism as to the accurate date of Zaynab's serial publication, with many writers—including later on even Haykal himself, in his memoirs—listing its initial date of publication as 1914. As a number of critical articles discussing the novel appear in journals throughout the end of 1913, it seems that this is the more accurate date of publication. Its first publication as a full, independent volume comes in its second edition in 1929, a point discussed briefly below.

Zaynab's claim to Arabic literary fame is that it is considered by many critics to be the first full-length Arabic novel. As in all cases of claims to 'firsts,' there are some detractors to this position who for various reasons prefer to

award this distinction to a variety of earlier works or to view the process of generic development in a broader context. There is no doubt, however, that at the time of its publication it contributed to the development of the novel as an important genre within Arabic literary production. *Zaynab* is undisputedly one of the genre's pioneering works in Arabic and its originality in a number of regards has won it acclaim and renown.

It is perhaps partly because of its innovations and difference from other literary works that preceded it, in both form and to some extent also content, that at first Haykal chose to publish it anonymously on the pages of *al-Jarīdah*. He signed this tale of people looking for love and earning their livelihood in the countryside with the symbolically-laden pseudonym, *misrī fallāh* (a peasant Egyptian). Haykal's choice of name to stand in for his own is meaningful on a number of levels. He has chosen an expression that underlines both the rural origins of the author, and his Egyptian identity over others. This is reinforced by the informal, colloquial expression with the reverse syntax of the spoken idiom. Identifying himself as a peasant, while perhaps not the most accurate of descriptions of his origins strictly speaking because of his *ʿumdah* background, lends the book a certain authenticity. Whether or not its reader believed that a "*fallāh*" (peasant) could produce such a sophisticated piece of literature, it evinces solidarity with the ordinary people in the countryside. This claim to share the toils and concerns of people like the book's characters also reinforces the implicit emphasis on improving the lives of the rural poor as one of the most important issues facing modern Egypt in the early twentieth century. As critics have pointed out, an author drawing upon an expression like *misrī fallāh* in this period also claims a space in intellectual and literary production for Muhammad Husayn Haykal himself. Son of the rural landowning elite, he and others like him vied for power against sons of the ruling Turkish-Circassian elite. In this period when Haykal and his contemporaries actively engaged in the project of shaping the modern destiny of Egypt, these were crucial concerns.

Reflecting its pseudonymous Egyptian "peasant" author's concerns, *Zaynab* is very much a novel of the Egyptian *rīf* (countryside). There is a strong idealization of the countryside and its beauty, with numerous long, rambling passages about the splendors of this landscape. Many have attributed the novel's nostalgia for rural life to the fact that Haykal wrote the novel while abroad in Paris, where he was known to have been very lonely, despite his contacts with Egyptian friends and colleagues. Critics are divided on the success of the numerous sections of the novel where the land and countryside of Egypt is portrayed. Some have described them as a lyrical homage to peasants and the Egyptian homeland; others find them excessive and distracting, to the extent that they detract from the work's overall literary merit.

The plot of the novel is somewhat complex, intertwining several love stories that involve the inhabitants of an Upper Egyptian village. The characters are all rural folk, but they represent a range of social and economic positions. The eponymous Zaynab is a working peasant woman who sells her labor daily to the owner of the land she works. The scion of this landowner is Hāmid, and they have a brief, but ill-fated, flirtation—both are aware that the difference in their social positions cannot be overcome. The love story of Zaynab and Hāmid is short-lived, but each of their later romantic entanglements demonstrates the subtleties of differentiation between classes and statuses in the rural Egypt of the novel. Zaynab next falls deeply in love with Ibrāhīm who is the manager of Hāmid's family's lands, but this relationship ends when she is married to the less well-off Hasan. Both Ibrāhīm and Hasan are located slightly above Zaynab on the scale of social strata in the novel. But though locally Ibrāhīm has a certain position in relation to the other peasants, he complains bitterly that he is not wealthy enough to buy out his position as the sons of richer families consistently do. Much of Hasan's hesitations about marrying the beautiful, kind and generous Zaynab center around questions of social status as well: should he marry a woman who has laboured in the fields all her life and would have to adjust to caring for his family? Her beauty

overcomes these doubts, and he asks for her hand in marriage. In the end these choices prove fatal to Zaynab. Because she can neither prevent Ibrāhīm's departure (he is called up for military service in the Sudan), nor turn down Hasan's proposal against the wishes of her family, she is destined to wither away in an unhappy marriage constantly pining in secret for Ibrāhīm. Desiring to be a good wife to the kindly Hasan, she never reveals her secret to anyone. Only her mother witnesses the true reason for Zaynab's death from consumption, when she calls out Ibrāhīm's name on her death bed.

In many ways Zaynab's story dominates the work; she is clearly a symbol for Egypt. However, Hāmid is the character who frames the narration. He is similarly entangled in impossible love affairs, first by fancying Zaynab—a woman clearly below his station—and then his cousin ʿAzīzah, who is married off to someone else. Much like Ibrāhīm's complaints about his financial situation, which forces him into an undesired military career, ʿAzīzah's love letters to Hāmid reveal the depths of her misery as she lives the life of an elite woman, sequestered from society to the extent that she laments never breathing fresh air or seeing the sun. The description of her feelings of shame for being shy with Hāmid during the one time they are able to meet in person, after her prolonged confinement to her home upon puberty, poignantly and pointedly critiques the social practice of extreme gender segregation and the lack of opportunities for elite women who are cloistered from society. In these ways, the lives of peasants in general and women of different classes are shown in parallel in *Zaynab*; both groups are oppressed and treated unfairly. Class, social status and gender are all exposed as destructive and devastating to both individuals and Egyptian society as a whole through the multiple plots explored in the novel.

What then does *Zaynab* succeed in doing that makes it stand apart as what many critics have referred to as the first Arabic novel? As its subtitle and pseudonymous authorship indicate, it writes an Egyptian story with Egyptian characters drawing on an Egyptian literary past to offer a generically experimental work. In this way it not only offers a view into the Egyptian country-side, but also a certain future for Egyptian society and Egyptian literature. Moreover, *Zaynab* can be read as an applied experimentation with the philosophical and theoretical ideas that Haykal explored in his many essays on literature in this period. The notion of a national literary production, texts that would be truly Egyptian, is one which fascinated Haykal and many of his intellectual contemporaries.

Reading *Zaynab* as the exemplary product of a period of nascent national novelistic experimentation can also be connected to some of its formal features. One example is the way in which the Arabic language is used within the text, a subject treated by a number of scholars interested in this work. Haykal's use of modern Arabic and his experimentation and integration of 'Egyptian' elements within this are also innovative features of this novel. The straightforward literary style of the work, appropriate to a text penned by "a peasant Egyptian," makes it accessible to a range of readers. Interestingly, Haykal does not incorporate his more simple language through extensive sections of dialogue, but rather within the narration. This in itself makes *Zaynab* a contribution to some of the new ways of thinking about Arabic literary language, one of Haykal's concerns in his work on modernization and education, which recurs as a theme in his later political career.

Another reason why some critics have claimed that it is a very Egyptian novel is because of its relationship to traditional Arabic literary traditions. Clearly *Zaynab*, like other Arabic literary productions of its day, is influenced by the European generic norms and models and draws upon the classic ideas of Romanticism. In particular, it betrays its heavy debt to the thinking of Jean Jacques Rousseau, a thinker who influenced Haykal greatly as will be discussed in more detail below. However some critics have shown how elements of the stock characters and themes characteristic of traditional 'Udhri lovers of the earliest period of Arabic poetry, for example, are reflected in Haykal's telling of these interlinked and ill-fated love stories.

Moreover, in the way that it treats many of the pressing social issues of the early twentieth century—women's education and autonomy, the lives of the rural poor, social mobility among others—*Zaynab* is very much a novel of its time and place. In these ways also, it has a major influence on a number of other writers who begin to create novels in its wake. According to critics, the features that echo *Zaynab* in later novels include: using autobiographical elements in the narration; showing the lives of peasants and workers; representing 'authentic', everyday Egyptians; and the desire to ameliorate the conditions of the poor by showing the squalor of their lives to the reading public. Though Haykal's work was much praised for his depictions of the countryside and rural people, critics concur that it is more than a little nostalgic. Some have carried this even further to suggest that *Zaynab* is a work not primarily interested in social justice, or the customs and habits of the working peasants, but rather the complications of gender roles in a time of social flux. This reading points out the relative lack of attention to the inner life and thoughts of the working woman Zaynab, in favour of those of the land-owning Hāmid. In this view, the romanticized portrayal of nature contrasts with the wretched lot of peasants, reflected in much of Haykal's essay writings which eschew the notion of a noble peasant life, rather looking down on them as people who need to be civilized in and by a modern nation.

With all of the attention within Arabic literary critical circles paid to *Zaynab*'s foundational position in the history of the Arabic novel, it is often overlooked that its more concrete impact likely followed the publication of its second edition in 1929 rather than its initial serialized appearance in *al-Jarīdah*. Not only in 1929 does Haykal abandon his anonymity and sign the novel with his own name, but it is also after this that the important works usually understood to have been directly influenced by *Zaynab* were published. Many seminal works betray the marks of *Zaynab*'s project, including Ibrāhīm 'Abd al-Qādir al-**Māzinī**'s *Ibrāhīm al-Kātib* (Ibrāhīm the Writer, 1931), Tawfīq al-**Hakīm**'s *'Awdat al-rūh* (The Return of the Spirit, 1933), and even Najīb Mahfūẓ's *'Abath al-aqdār* (Mockery of the Fates, 1939). Though these dates of publication do not indicate that it was necessarily the 1929 version of *Zaynab* that inspired and influenced this wave of Egyptian novelistic production, certainly the proliferation of the genre beginning in the 1930s suggests that perhaps Haykal's willingness to attach his name to it and also its extremely enthusiastic reception in Egyptian literary circles may have induced others to pursue their publications. Moreover it was after the second edition that it became better known popularly in Egypt as well, particularly after being adapted for cinema and made into a motion picture.

In the period between the serial publication of *Zaynab* in *al-Jarīdah* in 1913 and the appearance of the second edition in 1929, there was something of a lull in Muhammad Husayn Haykal's literary output. In this period, he threw himself wholeheartedly into his political work, much of which he pursued through journalism and in particular essay writing. These included some of his most important essays on Arabic literature, in particular the idea of national literature and the notion that there could and should be something produced in Egypt called Egyptian literature. Haykal's reputation as a Pharaonist was built through his essay writing in this period.

His essays would no longer appear, however, in the review to which he had contributed so much and which in many ways launched his career as a writer and intellectual. The end of the First World War saw the demise of *al-Jarīdah*. Along with his friend from his days in Paris, 'Alī 'Abd al-Rāziq (d. 1966), and the well-known littérateur Tāhā **Husayn**, Haykal then started a new paper, *al-Sufūr*, which took up many of the issues and themes that he had worked on previously. This period also saw changes in Haykal's personal life; in 1918 he married a woman called 'Azīzah. Over the next thirty-seven years they built a family together, raising eight children, one of whom died in infancy.

The next major milestones in Haykal's career came in 1921. In this year, he broke with the ruling Wafd party, which held a monopoly on power in Egypt throughout most of his life. He also published his two-volume study of the great

French thinker Rousseau, titled simply *Jean Jacques Rousseau*. This was a momentous year for Muhammad Husayn Haykal, but it was immediately followed by one which was even more remarkable. The lasting impact that his intellectual contributions were to have on Egyptian politics and society and his own life were only to increase in 1922. After turning down an offer to become editor at the important Egyptian newspaper *al-Ahrām*, Haykal started a new paper called *al-Siyāsah* (Politics). This paper was founded to be the mouthpiece for the newly founded Liberal Constitutional Party, which was in opposition to the ruling Wafd. In his role as the party's leading spokesperson, Haykal made use of its columns as a platform for the announcement and promotion of his own opinions. At the time, founding a newspaper in direct confrontation with the Wafd party was a dangerous enterprise financially, if not in other respects too, and Haykal was often required to lend it support from his own resources.

It was in the heady political climate of the early 1920s that Haykal assumed directorship of *al-Siyāsah* and later its weekly literary supplement, *al-Siyāsah al-Usbū'iyyah*. He would never again practice law. After 1922, Haykal's vocation was solely journalism and politics, and he only engaged in literary activities from time to time, mainly through the publication of short stories, and eventually writing his second and last novel. In this enterprise Haykal was not alone; the *al-Siyāsah* group consisted of a number of other men in their thirties, who belonged to the so-called "young generation." Most of his colleagues were educated in France, as Haykal himself had been, and were linked to Lutfī al-Sayyid. One of the major goals of this project was to promote modernization and science in order to create a scientific elite in Egypt. This group of people would then promote their ideas about reform in Egypt and the need for modernization through articles on a range of issues and topics.

As is clear from his collection of essays, *Fī awqāt al-farāgh* (In Leisure Times, 1925), Haykal's frequent articles addressed these questions in detail and from a number of angles; among the most important were his reflections on literary topics. The collection includes Haykal's early essays published in diverse locations and dating back as early as his days in Paris. Some of his finest and most important literary studies appear in this volume, particularly those discussing the need to develop an Egyptian national literature. Many of the contributions to this volume are clearly marked by the influence of the work of the prominent French literary historian, Hippolyte Taine (d. 1893), which led him to embrace the notion of "objective criticism." Haykal builds on his readings of Taine to develop a theory of national literature for Egypt, encouraging Egyptian intellectuals and critics to analyze the works of other Egyptians in terms of their history and national life, tracing ideas and texts to their Egyptian origins. It is in this context that Haykal's well-known advocacy of the idea of Pharaonism comes to the fore; he argues for a greater awareness of and pride in ancient Egyptian history, especially in comparison and contrast to Europe. Essays in this volume on Haykal's contemporaries in Egyptian intellectual circles, figures such as Tāhā **Husayn** and Qāsim Amīn, are examples of how he put these theoretical ideas into practice.

Following the publication of *Fī awqāt al-farāgh*, Haykal continued to write essays and actively participate in Egyptian political life. He went on a trip to the Sudan in this period in order to examine irrigation projects and published a book on this topic in 1927, titled ʿ*Asharat ayyām fī 'l-Sūdān* (Ten Days in the Sudan). This book had a certain amount of commercial and financial success, in contrast to literary works and essays collections which had more modest success in this regard, though critically acclaimed in his time. The year 1927 was particularly difficult for Haykal and his family on a personal level as his infant son died around this time. Haykal and his wife ʿAzīzah traveled to Europe together as a way to deal with their grief over this loss. Several years after their return, Haykal published his moving tribute to their son entitled simply *Waladī* (My Son, 1931). Like his study of Sudan, this work also enjoyed some commercial success and both appear to have been written for this purpose.

After his return from Europe Haykal contin-

ued his political and intellectual work. In 1929, he published a comprehensive study of Taine's philosophical and critical works, titled *Tarājim misriyyah wa-gharbiyyah* (Egyptian and Western Biographies). As noted above, Taine's work had a major impact on Haykal's intellectual development and more specifically his analysis of art, literature and cultural production. Taine's geographical and social determinism led directly to Haykal's elaborations on objective criticism. Haykal advocates a positivistic method of literary and artistic analysis which would allow the critic to appreciate a work's true historical and aesthetic significance freed of taste or subjective understandings.

All of these ideas are worked out even more thoroughly in relation to Arabic and Egyptian literature in Haykal's second important collection of literary essays which was to become one of his major books, *Thawrat al-adab* (The Literary Revolution, 1933). The writings in this volume, which brought together essays published in diverse locations, largely support and develop Haykal's notion of national literature *(adab qawmī)*. This indeed is the title of one of the most important essays contained in the volume, "al-adab al-qawmī", in which he develops his argument that national literature is a historical imperative. Haykal argues that there is a continuity in Egyptian literary production from ancient times to the present. These works propose a genealogy for Egyptian literature which is more specifically elaborated than in his previous Pharaonic writings. Importantly, the essays in this book also begin to point to a transformation in the way that Haykal's Pharaonism relates to Islam. Within his previous system, Islam and religion are downplayed significantly. The essays in *Thawrat al-adab* mark a shift in Haykal's position that allows Islam to be conceived in a positive way in relation to national literature. Indeed Islam is shown here to be compatible with a notion of national literature, in particular because it encourages the linking of the past to the present. The seeds of Haykal's interest in reconciling Egypt's ancient past with its Islamic past and present in this period become all the more important in his next phase of literary and intellectual production.

In the early 1930s, Haykal was deeply involved with his newly founded political party, the Constitutional Liberals, who were vying for power not only with the Wafd but also with Muslim parties who were enjoying increased successes. One of the issues that Haykal became devoted to exploring was how to reconcile his deeply held notions of personal freedom, social progress and modernization with the teachings of Islam. At the same time, Christian missionary attacks on Muhammad led Haykal to want to defend Islam's prophet. The nineteenth century legacy of representing the Prophet Muhammad as a fraud or an epileptic provided a spur for Haykal to embark on writing a work which would make a lasting impact on Egyptian letters. The book resulting from his study was published in 1935 as *Hayāt Muhammad* (The Life of Muhammad). Just as *Zaynab* is regarded as a pioneering work in the development of the Arabic novel, *Hayāt Muhammad* is considered by scholars and critics to be the first "modern" study of the prophet Muhammad. Indeed Haykal himself intended this and planned to apply what he considered modern, scientific scholarship to the study of Muhammad in order to produce not merely an apologetic work but one which would contribute to scholarship.

Haykal struggled with the writing of this book at a time when he was also experiencing a return to his faith. Long a secular reformer and modernizer, he sought in this period and through this work to reconcile the worlds of Islam and modern Egyptian political life without alienating one from the other. Some of the ways in which he framed his modern biography are familiar to us today, but at the time his work was seen as a brave departure both from the classical *sīrah* (biography of the Prophet Muhammad) with its role in the religious and literary establishment and also from other types of books about the prophet written in the same period by authors and contemporaries such as 'Abbās Mahmūd al-'Aqqād, Tāhā **Husayn**, Najīb Mahfūz (b. 1911), and 'Abd al-Rahmān al-Sharqāwī (d. 1987). Though this book was published amidst a wave of Egyptian production of biographies of the prophet, Haykal's *Hayāt Muhammad* stands out in many ways. His work is distinguished by its stated purpose to present a "historical-critical" study of the prophet's life, in confrontation with orientalist literature, which would be a genuinely new, modern *sīrah*, with all of the religious connotations that this Arabic expression conjures.

Like *Zaynab* before it, *Hayāt Muhammad* began as a serial publication. The first instalment appeared in the pages of *al-Siyāsah al-Usbū'iyyah* on 26 February 1932. The series of articles which became the book started off as an extended review of Emile Dermenghem's French language study of the life of the Prophet Muhammad, *La vie de Mohamet* (The Life of Mohamet). Six articles in direct response to Dermenghem were published, and then in the seventh instalment Haykal announced his decision to begin researching elements of the prophet's life and career untouched by the French biography. From then on he continued with fifteen additional articles which came out at the rate of about one per month until 1934, the last of which dealt with the question of the so-called "Satanic Verses."

In 1935, the revised essays appeared in a single book, the first edition of ten thousand copies of which sold out within three months. It has since gone into many editions and is still widely available today. This book is certainly Haykal's best-selling one and, like his more commercially-oriented ventures before it, must have brought him some financial success. It also solidified Haykal's reputation as a serious scholar and man of letters. Moreover, the way in which the book was packaged and produced also allowed him entry into a far wider range of circles than he would have previously been able to penetrate. For example, the rector of al-Azhar at the time, al-Shaykh Mustafā al-Marāghī, supplied a generous foreword praising the work, an act which gave Haykal—the first littérateur to produce such an extensive study of the prophet, previously the prerogative of al-Azhar scholars—some credibility in religious and conservative circles. This stamp of approval by Islam's most respected institution undoubtedly helped the work's success, not only in Egypt but throughout the Arabic-speaking countries, and beyond to the rest of the Muslim world. It has been translated into a number of languages, including not only English, but also Chinese, Turkish, Urdu and others.

Though of course the extensive content in this biography of the prophet Muhammad is a crucial aspect of its value, the method of study is what Haykal himself, as well as later readers of the work, have underlined as its most important contribution. The positions that the work adapts are not unheard of or unique by any means; it is how Haykal arrives at them through a method which he deemed scientific that merits mention. As in his political, literary and social essays, it is clear, for example, that Haykal is advocating the need for Egyptians and Muslims to turn to their history and understand it better in order to build a modern society. His biography of the prophet would allow them to answer missionary attacks with responses built on modern techniques of understanding the world and not merely on blind faith. Moreover, writing a work of this nature based on extensive research and ostensibly defending Islam against Christian denigration allowed Haykal to attack the corruption of the religious authorities and the *'ulamā'* (religious scholars). For example, the entire basis of his scientific argument and pursuit is that the Qur'ān provides a complete picture of God and the prophet's ideas and intentions. All principles, according to Haykal, therefore must be derived directly from the Qur'ān itself and not from interpretations by the religious establishment. This premise allows Haykal to build on the kinds of arguments for social reform he had made previously in secular settings, but here with the backing of religion.

Haykal's discussion of the prophet's treatment of women and his view on polygamy is exemplary. He interprets polygamy on the basis that no man could ever treat four women equally, so the Qur'ānic verse allowing men to have up to four wives under the provision that he do so was meant to show its impossibility. But despite this he answers charges against the Prophet for taking even more than the four wives allowed by this verse, by arguing that at a certain time in early Islamic history, military campaigns caused a shortage of marriageable men and these marriages were thus necessary.

Similarly, he defends other attacks on the Prophet's marriages to many women both by offering counter-narratives to received accounts (such as his marriage to Zaynab) and also by allowing leeway to the Prophet because of his unique social position. This justification which gives certain social exemptions to men of influence is consistent with his general outlook, assuming that the man in question acts in a generous and upright way—which of course is what the Islamic tradition records the Prophet Muhammad as always doing.

Another example of his rational approach includes the understanding that the Prophet Muhammad's night journey to Jerusalem was undertaken by his soul and not his physical body. His rejection of miracles is one of the bases upon which he was often challenged in the less positive reviews that the work received. *Hayāt Muhammad* has received all manner of reviews and scholarly attention, both positive and negative. Some readers saw it as an attack on Islam informed by Western attitudes, others as an apology for religion against modernity. Sorting through all of these responses to the work, a few elements shine through. Haykal wanted to produce a study that would allow him to argue for the reforms and modernization of the social order in Egypt while respecting the underlying bases of Islam that he found in the Qur'ān and the exemplary life of the Prophet Muhammad. His arguments for human independence, individuality and rights were structured through the sanction of Islam. The world view that emerges therefore completely supports Haykal's political and social projects for Egypt and the leadership of men like himself in bringing them to fruition.

In the period following the publication and initial success of *Hayāt Muhammad*, Muhammad Husayn Haykal was becoming increasingly pious. He went on the pilgrimage *(hajj)* to Mecca in 1936 and began to emphasize the role of religion in modern society increasingly in his writings and engagements in intellectual and political life. Haykal followed the publication of his biography of the prophet with a sort of sequel that recounts his travels to Mecca and Medina as a pilgrim. *Fī manzil al-wahy* (In the Abode of Inspiration) appears in 1937. It is, of course, more than simply a travel account; and Haykal uses this work as a platform for his ideas about how to reconcile his modernist, reformist ideals for Egypt with a role for religion. In particular he argues that the individual must develop a direct connection and relationship with God, that a person has a specific place within the religious system. Moreover, this relationship also provides a template for the way in which society should engage religion, an engagement that Islam in particular applied as a system for the running of an orderly society—something that, according to Haykal, is fully consistent with the goals of his modernizing projects.

This turn to religion did nothing to stop Haykal's active engagement in politics. On the contrary, in the late 1930s and early 1940s, he held no less than seven cabinet positions, including that of Minister of Education in 1937, and was President of the Senate in 1945-1950. In the former role, Haykal was able to combine his political savvy with his lifelong interest in education and modernization, fueled by his family background—the generations of Haykal men committed to this issue. He advocated many reforms in the educational system in Egypt, particularly the focus on "national culture" (al-thaqāfah al-qawmiyyah) including an emphasis on the Arabic language. One of the more controversial reforms that he pursued was to stop the teaching of English and other foreign languages at the elementary level so that children could concentrate on learning Arabic. His initial proposals were modified, and the curricular changes effected under Haykal included study of European culture and arts together with the national culture and arts. During this same period he was also responsible for the establishment of the College of Arts and Law in Alexandria.

Muhammad Husayn Haykal's biographers have noted that it is in the early 1940s that a public portrait of this man truly emerged in Egypt. Politician and journalist, as well as novelist and biographer of the Prophet, he was known to have been a rather formal man. He was always dressed in a jacket, tie and tarbūsh, even on informal occasions, and is known to have always signed his name with the title "doctor" added in front and to have preserved a careful

relationship with family and friends alike. However his political personality somewhat contrasts with what seems a sombre portrait. In these circles he was known to have been a rather jolly man, always laughing, talking and smoking. Some have suggested that his reserve made him a nervous man and his public mannerisms were simply a way of concealing those insecurities.

Just as his public persona was becoming better known within Egyptian society more generally, Haykal published two more books, revealing that his commitment to the religious question had not waned. He began a series of biographies of lives of the four rightly-guided caliphs (al-khulafā' al-rāshidūn) who succeeded the prophet Muhammad for the leadership of the Islamic community upon his death. The first of the series, al-Siddīq Abū Bakr (Abū Bakr, the Righteous) appeared in 1943, followed two years later by al-Fārūq 'Umar ('Umar, the Legislator, 1945). He never completed the fourth book, though the third on the caliph 'Uthmān appeared posthumously in 1964. These works reconfirmed many of the ideas that he had begun elaborating in his biography of the prophet Muhammad, such as the corruption of the 'ulamā' and the purity of the original messages of the Prophet himself. For example, he praises Abū Bakr for his continuation of the work of Muhammad, whereas his evaluation of 'Umar is more equivocal, although he emphasizes his crucial positive role in developing the institution of ijtihād (independent legal reasoning)—praised by Haykal for promoting freedom for the individual.

In the 1950s, Muhammad Husayn Haykal started publishing his memoirs which appeared in two volumes under the title Mudhakkirāt fī 'l-siyāsah al-misriyyah (Memoirs of Egyptian Politics). The first volume covers the years between 1912 and 1937, and the second volume treats his life from 1937 to 1952. They appeared between 1951 and 1953. Much of the information that we have about Haykal's political positions and intellectual development is derived from these memoirs. Like most works of this genre published in Arabic at this time, Haykal's memoirs are a very deliberate and conscious presentation of particular aspects of his life which document his public life. There is little or no mention of his personal life, childhood and formation that is characteristic of such works. Rather, as their title indicates, they are full of information and reflections about Haykal as a politician, journalist, intellectual and man of letters in turn- of-the-century Egypt.

In a sense, Haykal's literary career came full circle with the very last work he published in 1955, the year before his death. Like his first major book, *Zaynab*, his last was also a novel, *Hākadhā khuliqat* (Thus Was She Created). Also like *Zaynab*, this novel is ostensibly about a woman's life but uses her to stand in for the nation itself. As such it is an allegory for the ways in which Egypt and the lives of ordinary Egyptians have changed in the twentieth century because of its immense challenges, including Western encroachment. It treats social and political questions pressing in Egyptian society at the time, particularly restricted and constrained gender roles for women and the need for modernization.

The story of *Hākadhā khuliqat* revolves around the difficulties in life faced by its unnamed heroine who is intelligent, educated and cultivated but is ultimately destroyed and destroys others because of her lack of opportunities to fulfil herself. Married and divorced twice in the novel, she lives on the margins of her society unable to integrate within it or accept its conservatism. Part of the protagonist's difficulty is that she was sent to school as a girl, but her father decides to stop her education before she has reached her full potential. Within the logic of the novel, this prevents her from being fully rational and able to respond to the multiple demands she faces in her life. This is one way in which critics have connected Haykal's own social and political projects, indeed his own life choices, to the novel. It is well-known that all of his five daughters were highly educated, three of them earned doctoral degrees and the other two masters.

Critics have often read this novel as a reflection on his own ideas about the workings of life and society, coming as it did, just at the end of his full life and career. When the heroine describes her betrayal of her first husband, a doctor of peasant origins, he is portrayed very much as a victim. Some have read Haykal's

sympathetic portrayal of this male character of peasant origins as a reflection of his personal stake in the issues dear to such a man. Moreover, the novel's tone is full of disillusionment, anger and cynicism about the difficulties people have in controlling their own destinies and lives. *Hākadhā khuliqat* bluntly portrays family arguments and how people's relationships are torn apart by power struggles and materialistic concerns. The novel shows how people that you love may betray you, because of their desire for power and control and their own personal greed.

Hākadhā khuliqat is almost always read as a pessimistic novel and often as one which reveals a certain amount of self-pity on the part of the author himself. The end of the novel finds the protagonist seeking solace in Islam, perhaps much as Haykal did later in life. But then her conversion turns out to be a fraud; the novel ends with her totally alone, with nowhere to turn. Many have written that Haykal himself felt alone and alienated in 1950s Egypt, at home neither in the countryside of his birth nor in the ever-expanding urban terrain that was Cairo. Though his son collected and published a number of his works posthumously, particularly short stories and essays he had written as an elderly man, this novel was the final work completed and published in his lifetime—a testament to his long dedication to the modernization of Egypt.

Muhammad Husayn Haykal lived a life dedicated to Egypt and to Egyptian politics, fighting first for Egypt's independence and then, throughout his career, for a way to build a modern nation true to its own historical roots, religious traditions and values, in addition to its ancient past. The date of Muhammad Husayn Haykal's death is perhaps symbolic. Only sixty-eight years old, he died in Cairo on 8 December 1956. His last days came at the beginning of the Suez invasion, when Britain and France landed on Egyptian shores, in collaboration with Israeli attacks, in a bid to control the Egyptian port. He would not live to see their evacuation, just two weeks after his death, but Egypt's development as a modern nation in the following years continued to build upon many of the ideas proposed and elaborated by Muhammad Husayn Haykal.

REFERENCES

Ibrāhīm ʿAwad, *Muhammad Husayn Haykal adīban nāqidan mufakkiran islāmiyyan* ("Muhammad Husayn Haykal as an Islamic Littérateur, Critic and Thinker", Cairo: Maktabat Zahrāʾ al-Sharq, 1998);

Ahmad ʿAbd al-Muʿtī Hijāzī, *Muhammad wahāʾulāʾ* ("Muhammad and These People", Cairo: Rūz al-Yūsuf, 1971);

al-Sayyid Ahmad al-Makhzanjī, *Nazrah tahlīliyyah fī kitābāt Muhammad Husayn Haykal* ("An Analytical Investigation of Muhammad Husayn Haykal's Writings", Cairo: al-Hayʾah al-Misriyyah al-ʿĀmmah liʾl-Kitāb, 1987);

Muhammad Sayyid Muhammad, *Haykal waʾl-Siyāsah al-Usbūʿiyyah* ("Haykal and [the newspaper] *al-Siyāsah al-Usbūʿiyyah*", Cairo: al-Hayʾah al-Misriyyah al-ʿĀmmah liʾl-Kitāb, 1996);

Hamdi Sakkut, *The Arabic Novel: Bibliography and Critical Introduction, 1865–1995*, translated by Roger Monroe (Cairo: AUC Press, 2000);

Samah Selim, *The Novel and the Rural Imaginary in Egypt, 1880–1985* (New York/London: Routledge and Curzon, 2004);

David Semah, *Four Egyptian Literary Critics* (Leiden: Brill, 1974);

Charles D. Smith, *Islam and the Search for Social Order in Modern Egypt: A Biography of Muhammad Husayn Haykal* (Albany, NY: SUNY Press, 1983);

Antonie Wessels, *A Modern Arabic Biography of Muhammad: A Critical Study of Muhammad Husayn Haykal's Hayāt Muhammad* (Leiden: E. J. Brill, 1972).

Tāhā Husayn

(1889 – 1973)

ROGER ALLEN
University of Pennsylvania

WORKS

Dhikrā Abī ʾl-ʿAlāʾ ("In Memory of Abū ʾl-ʿAlāʾ", Cairo: Maktabat al-Wāʿiz, 1915);

Hadīth al-arbiʿāʾ ("Wednesday Talk", 3 vols., Cairo: Dār al-Maʿārif, 1925, 1926, 1945);

Fī ʾl-shiʿr al-jāhilī ("On Pre-Islamic Poetry", Cairo, 1926);

Fī ʾl-adab al-jāhilī ("On Pre-Islamic Literature", Cairo: Matbaʿat al-Iʿtimād, 1927);

al-Ayyām ("The Days", 3 vols., Cairo, 1929, 1940?, 1972);

ʿAlā hāmish al-sīrah ("On the Margins of [Prophetic] Biography", Cairo: Dār al-Maʿārif, 1933);

Hāfiz wa-Shawqī ("Hāfiz and Shawqī", Cairo: Matbaʿat al-Iʿtimād, 1933);

Duʿāʾ al-karawān ("The Call of the Curlew", Cairo: Dār al-Maʿārif, 1934);

Adīb ("Adīb" [used as personal name, but meaning "littérateur" at the same time], Cairo: Lajnat Tarjamat Dāʾirat al-Maʿārif, 1935);

Maʿa ʾl-Mutanabbī ("With [the medieval poet] al-Mutanabbī", Cairo: Lajnat al-Taʾlīf waʾl-Tarjamah waʾl-Nashr, 1936);

al-Qasr al-mashūr ("The Enchanted Palace", Cairo, 1937); co-authored with Tawfīq al-Hakīm;

Mustaqbal al-thaqāfah fī Misr ("The Future of Culture in Egypt", Cairo, 1938);

Maʿa Abī ʾl-ʿAlāʾ fī sijnih ("With [the blind medieval poet] Abū ʾl-ʿAlāʾ [al-Maʿarrī] in His Prison", Cairo: Matbaʿat al-Maʿārif, 1939);

Shajarat al-buʾs ("The Tree of Misery", Cairo: Dār al-Maʿārif, 1944);

Sawt Abī ʾl-ʿAlāʾ ("The Voice of Abū ʾl-ʿAlāʾ [al-Maʿarrī]", Cairo, 1944);

Fusūl fī ʾl-adab waʾl-naqd ("Chapters on Literature and Criticism", Cairo, 1945);

al-Fitnah al-kubrā ("The Great Schism", Cairo, 1947);

al-Mu'adhdhabūn fī 'l-ard ("The Tortured of the Earth", Cairo: Dār al-Ma'ārif, 1949);

Alwān ("Hues", Cairo, 1952);

Khisām wa-naqd ("Contumely and Criticism", Cairo, 1955);

Min adabinā al-mu'āsir ("From Our Contemporary Literature", Cairo, 1958);

Khawātir ("Thoughts", Cairo, 1967).

Works in Translation

An Egyptian Childhood (London: G. Routledge, 1932); translation of *al-Ayyām*, I, tr. by E. H. Paxton;

A Stream of Days (Cairo, 1943); translation of *al-Ayyām*, II, tr. by Hilary Wayment;

A Passage to France (Leiden: E. J. Brill, 1976); translation of *al-Ayyām*, III, tr. by Kenneth Cragg;

The Call of the Curlew (Cairo: The American University in Cairo Press, 1980); translation of *Du'ā' al-Karawān*, tr. by A. B. al-Safi;

The Dreams of Scheherazade (Cairo: General Egyptian Book Organization, 1974); translation of *Ahlām Shahrazād*, tr. by Magdi Wahba;

The Future of Culture in Egypt (Washington: American Council of Learned Societies, 1954); translation of *Mustaqbal al-thaqāfah fī Misr*, tr. by Sidney Glazer.

Tāhā Husayn was, without any doubt, a very significant, perhaps the most significant, cultural figure in the Arab world during the 20th century. There are so many ways in which his life and the influences that affected him and that he exerted on several generations of Egyptian and Arab intellectuals and writers are emblematic of an entire era in Arab literary life. In purely spatial terms we follow him from his early days in an Upper Egyptian village to the capital city of Cairo, thence to France for graduate studies and a return to his homeland where he was to become professor, critic, novelist, university rector, Minister of Education, and permanent controversialist. The causes he espoused, the works he wrote, the cultural and political arguments in which he involved himself with such stubborn gusto, these were all symptomatic of several decades during which Egyptian society found itself confronted by processes of rapid change. It is perhaps the most visible symbol of the very rapidity of those cultural and social transformations that Tāhā Husayn, the reformist radical of the 1920s and '30s and hero of a whole generation of younger writers, was later in life to become one of the most conservative forces in the context of those further changes that were the natural consequence of the processes of revolution and the achievement of independence from colonial rule during the 1950s and beyond, thereby becoming something of a *bête noir* to the younger generation of that era.

Tāhā Husayn was born on the 14th of November, 1889, in the village of 'Izbat al-Kīlū, near the Central Egyptian town of Maghāghah (which lies half way between Banī Suwayf [Soueif] and Minya. At the age of three Tāhā Husayn suffered the tragedy that was to change his entire life. Afflicted with one of the fly-borne eye diseases that are endemic to the region, he was "treated" by the local barber—a regular practice at the time. As a result, he became almost totally blind, a scene that is graphically captured in 'Ātif Salīm's film devoted to his life, with the appropriate title of *Qāhir al-zalām* (Overcoming Darkness, 1979). Like most children he attended the local *kuttāb* (Qur'ān school) at which the sacred text would be memorized by rote. The first volume of his renowned autobiography, *al-Ayyām* (The Days, 1929, available in English as *An Egyptian Childhood*) contains a memorable account of his experiences in this environment: the way in which the "Master" would consign the task of rehearsing the younger pupils to elder ones, the initial triumph when Tāhā Husayn memorized the entire text of the Qur'an, the all too easy process of forgetting it through lack of practice, and the eventual success at convincing his father that he was indeed a genuine *hāfiz* (someone who had memorized the entire Quranic text).

The next phase of his life is one that takes him away from this provincial village to the capital city of Cairo. One of his elder brothers was already studying at the al-Azhar mosque-college in Cairo; he was charged with taking the 13-year old Tāhā Husayn back with him to Cairo in 1902. The second volume of *al-Ayyām* (1939, available in English as *The Stream of Days*) contains details of the demanding life into which the young boy was inserted. Initially awed by such hallowed surroundings, Tāhā Husayn conveys through the autobiographical voice his rapidly growing sense of disappointment at the pedagogical methods and the faulty learning of many of the shaykhs. In this scenario two figures stand out as exceptions. One is Shaykh Sayyid al-Marsafī, who aroused in his young pupil a strong love for the early literary tradition of the Arabs, and most especially for its pre-Islamic poetry. The second figure was to play an equally important role in Tāhā Husayn's educational development, although not through direct instruction but rather through the profound influence that he exerted on an entire generation of Egyptian reformers, namely Muhammad 'Abduh (1849-1905), one of the most significant intellectual figures in the history of modern Islam.

By the time Tāhā Husayn had spent some time studying at al-Azhar in Cairo, he was already beginning to realize the rapidity of the changes within Egyptian society at the turn of the century that were transforming the intellectual and cultural environment all around him. Closely following upon the establishment of a secular University in Cairo in 1908, Tāhā Husayn began to commute across the city to attend lectures there. For a while, he participated in the intellectual life of both institutions, but he gradually distanced himself from his attachments to al-Azhar and its intellectual environment.

This decision is, of course, the most obvious sign of this realization on his part, and it was to prove the first phase in a process that changed the course of his intellectual development. At the new university he was exposed to the ideas of prominent orientalist scholars, two of the most renowned of whom were Carlo Nallino and Enno Littman. In assessing the impact that these teachers had on the young and precocious blind student, we can cite his own words as recorded in the third volume of his memoirs (ably translated by Kenneth Cragg):

In due course, new professors came who called forth my entire devotion and found pride of place in my heart. There was Professor Carlo Nallino, the Italian Orientalist, who lectured in Arabic on the history of literature and poetry in the Umayyad period... Then there was a German professor, Dr. Littmann, who lectured on Semitic languages and their relationship to Arabic... Nothing made me sadder than when classes came to an end, and my most eager longing was for the time when the next would begin.   (*A Passage to France*, 1976, 35-6)

By this stage in his career as a student, Tāhā Husayn had already made the acquaintance of Ahmad Lutfī al-Sayyid (1872-1963), the editor of the newspaper, *al-Jarīdah*, who was clearly attracted to this young and potentially brilliant blind student from the Egyptian provinces. Lutfī al-Sayyid's influence on Tāhā Husayn was enormous, as it was on many younger and emerging intellectual figures in Egypt; to such an extent that he was regularly dubbed *ustādh al-jīl* (professor to a generation). While Tāhā Husayn continued his studies at the King Fu'ād University (later, the University of Cairo), including courses on history, geography, literary criticism, and philosophy, he also wrote articles on a variety of topics that were published in *al-Jarīdah*, the first of them appearing as early as 1908.

The new methods of literary analysis that Tāhā Husayn was learning at the secular university clearly mark an important transitional stage in the development of his ideas. He determined to adopt a method that would make use of the same critical yardsticks to evaluate each period within the heritage as a whole and not to rely on the pre-modern critical predilection for regarding the earliest phases in the tradition in particular as somehow superior because of their anteriority. When the time came to select a topic for what was to be the first doctoral dissertation at the university, Tāhā Husayn selected the one poet from the Arabic literary heritage with whom he could closely identify: the blind poet Abū 'l-'Alā' al-Ma'arrī (973-1058). The work was defended in May 1914 and—typically, one might suggest—Tāhā Husayn used the occasion to argue fiercely with one of his teachers, Shaykh Muhammad al-Mahdī, over the interpretation of certain lines of the poet.

Dhikrā Abī 'l-'Alā' (Recalling Abū 'l-'Alā' [al-Ma'arrī], 1915), as the published version of Tāhā Husayn's first PhD dissertation is entitled, is an expression of developing sense of the methods of literary analysis. The study seeks to place the renowned blind poet into his time period and society, no doubt in a desire to underline the "objective" nature of this new approach to literary research. There are lengthy chapters on the political circumstances of the time and on the events in the life of al-Ma'arrī. A further chapter examines his philosophical beliefs, focusing especially on his firm convictions regarding predestination and the absence of free will. It is only in the final chapter that Tāhā Husayn turns to literary texts *per se*, and even there the concentration is on one work, the so-called *Luzūmiyyāt*, a collection of poetry (the original title is *Luzūm mā lā yalzam*, The Requirement of What is Not Required) in which al-Ma'arrī demands of himself that he use a system of end-rhyming that is more rigorous than that established by the critical community of prosodists. Later in his lengthy career Tāhā Husayn returned to the theme of the blind poet with whom he so clearly identified. Both *Ma'a Abī 'l-'Alā' fī sijnih* (With Abū 'l-'Alā' in His Prison, 1939) and *Sawt Abī 'l-'Alā'* (Abū 'l-'Alā''s Voice, 1944) reflect the shift in his critical priorities that becomes evident through the works that he wrote in the late 1920s and 1930s.

Armed with a doctorate degree and a grant for further study, Tāhā Husayn was on the point of sailing for France when the First World War began in 1914. However, after a year's pause he sailed for Southern France in 1915 and took up residence at the ancient university of Montpelier in 1915. However, his time there was to be short, and yet it was to prove extremely significant on at least one count. He had employed a young French woman named Suzanne Bresseau to act as his reader and helper during his studies, and the two fell in love; they were married in August 1917. Subsequently they had both a son and daughter. Following a brief return to Egypt, he again responded to the siren call of a capital city and enrolled at the Sorbonne in Paris. He was to stay there for four years of concentrated study, devoting himself to courses on Philosophy (with Durkheim and Levi-Bruhl), History, Psychology, and Literature (with Gustave Lanson, whose works on literary criticism and history were to have a profound effect on him). At the same time, Tāhā Husayn also undertook to study the classical languages and ancient history. His *magnum opus* however was to be a second doctorate, this time on the renowned historian Ibn Khaldūn (1332-1406), "La philosophie sociale d'Ibn Khaldoun."

When Tāhā Husayn returned from France armed with a second doctoral degree and a diploma in Classical Studies, he was clearly a much transformed individual. Not only that, but his arrival coincided with a period of considerable political tension. The treatment by the British occupying forces of the popular nationalist leader, Sa'd Zaghlūl (1857?-1927), had led to a popular uprising (often referred to as the 1919 Revolution). On the 22nd of February 1922 a declaration was issued setting out the terms under which Egypt would henceforth be considered an independent sovereign state, and the ensuing years were to witness much public debate and controversy, as the monarchy, political parties, and religious establishment sought to redefine their relative roles and lines of authority in the light of the circumstances created by the new configuration.

It was during the aftermath of such fraught circumstances that Tāhā Husayn was given his first university appointment, as Professor of Ancient History and Classics. He now began to implement his ideas regarding the Arabic literary heritage by penning a series of articles that were published on Wednesdays in the newspaper, *al-Siyāsah*; it is for that reason that they are entitled *Hadīth al-Arbi'ā'* (Wednesday Talk). The earliest articles are actually to be found in the second volume. In a series of articles entitled "Ancients and Moderns" (*al-qudamā' wa'l-muhdathūn*) Tāhā Husayn deals with a number of the most important poets from the Umawī (660-750) and 'Abbāsī (750-1258) Caliphal periods—including Abū Nuwās (d. c. 813) and Bashshār ibn Burd (d. 783)—who had been the topic of the lectures by Nallino that he had attended before his departure for France. However, it is the contents of the first volume that exhibit the greatest shift in critical focus, in that they concentrate on the poetry itself—something that is obvious from the extent of citation to be found in the texts of the individual articles by comparison with the earlier ones. However, when the Egyptian University became a state institution in 1925, he took up the new post of Professor of Arabic Literature (at the time, Ahmad Lutfī al-Sayyid, was President of the institution). It was in this overall educational and political context that he chose to insert his direct challenge to traditional beliefs. He had in fact already been delivering a series of lectures to students on pre-Islamic poetry, and in 1926 he published his readings of the texts and their relationship with the language and content of the Qur'ān in book form, *Fī 'l-shi'r al-jāhilī* (On Pre-Islamic Poetry). From the very first sentence of this book, the reader is confronted with an author who is completely confident of his own method and prepared to face the consequences of his controversial findings. It is worth citing:

The kind of research on the history of Arabic poetry presented here is completely new, unfamiliar to people in our milieu. I am virtually certain that there will be a group of people who will greet this work with anger, while others will completely disassociate themselves from it.

The same kind of sentiment is also expressed at the beginning of a later chapter in the book (p. 125) where we read:

We assume that the adherents of the old school would not wish us to alter the realities of things or to term such truths by names other than those which are already applied to them, all that with the goal of keeping them happy and not causing them aggravation. However, even though we are assiduous in our desire to please them and not make them angry, our desire to satisfy the truth is yet more cogent and our distaste for anything that toys with truth and learning is equally strong.

The reader of *Fī 'l-shi'r al-jāhilī* does not have long to wait before the central conclusions are explicitly stated (p. 7):

The majority of what we refer to as pre-Islamic poetry is not pre-Islamic at all; it was fabricated after the advent of Islam. It is Islamic, and reflects the life, passions, and intentions of Muslims more than it does the life of people before Islam. I am virtually certain that very little remains of the vestiges of genuine pre-Islamic poetry. It neither represents nor demonstrates anything. In any attempt to obtain an authentic picture of the pre-Islamic era we should not place any reliance at all on this collection of poetry.

Ever the polemicist, Tāhā Husayn was now taking on the hallowed corpus of early Arabic poems that served as the precedents for the language of the Qur'ān itself; not only that, but he was also suggesting that the Quranic stories of Ibrāhīm and Ismā'īl (Abraham and Ishmael) were in fact myths.

In view of the fracas that ensued after the publication of this small book, it is worthwhile at this point to pause and consider what some of the ramifications of this thesis were and are. The revelation of the Qur'ān in oral form to the Prophet Muhammad in the 7th century presented the incipient Muslim community with a set of utterances that were delivered in Arabic. In the context of Islam, the Qur'ān, and the Arabic language at that particular time, the collected corpus of pre-Islamic poetry thus became hugely important precisely because of its anteriority; it was and is *the* example of Arabic as it existed before the revelation of the Qur'ān to Muhammad beginning in the early 7th century. Thus, any attempt such as that of Tāhā Husayn to call that anteriority into question was by implication an assault on the entire system whereby the discourse of the Qur'ān had been ratified and authenticated since the earliest days of Islam. And he is quite explicit on the subject (p. 9-10):

We should not cite this poetry as a means of explicating the Qur'ān and interpretation of hadīth, *but rather the exact opposite: the Qur'ān and* hadīth *should be used as sources for interpreting this poetry.*

Whatever may be said about the academic

and critical aspects of this work and its impact on Egyptian intellectual life, it has to be acknowledged that Tāhā Husayn's timing was clearly intended to be as provocative as possible. Assuming that such was his intention, he was not disappointed. Once again, al-Azhar stepped in and declared Tāhā Husayn an apostate. Not content with that, they went on to demand that he be dismissed from his chair at the university, but Ahmad Lutfī al-Sayyid invoked academic freedom in standing beside his protégé and refusing to accept Tāhā Husayn's resignation. The first version of the book was withdrawn. A year later (1927), the work was reissued as *Fī 'l-adab al-jāhilī* (On Pre-Islamic Literature), with the offending passages about the Qur'ān removed, but a great deal else added. Tāhā Husayn's Foreword is brief, accurate, to the point, and completely unapologetic:

This is last-year's book, with one chapter removed, another chapter inserted in its place, and still more chapters added. The title has been slightly altered.

Among the new material is a section on pre-Islamic prose and on contemporary attitudes to poetry and its study. However, the most significant new addition is a lengthy introductory "book" (*kitāb*) in which he considers, or more accurately reconsiders, the criteria that need to be applied in the analysis of literary works, and specifically poetry. There is now a clear retreat from the more deterministic approach that he had advocated in his earlier study of al-Maʿarrī that was analyzed above. While objective and "scientific" methods have an important role to play in the contextualization of literary creativity, they cannot, in Tāhā Husayn's opinion as expressed in 1927, serve as a substitute for the personal assessment of the critic with all its subjective aspects. Furthermore, in the wake of this outcry, Tāhā Husayn wrote a letter to the newspaper, *al-Siyāsah*, in which he stated that he was a Muslim but that his studies and his quest for truth required that he deal honestly with issues as he saw them.

In 1929, another work of Tāhā Husayn appeared, one whose rootedness in the provincial culture of his homeland may be seen in part as an attempt to quell some of the wilder accusions against him. The already mentioned *al-Ayyām* (The Days; English translation: *An Egyptian Childhood*), which had initially been published in the journal, *al-Hilāl* (beginning in December 1926), takes the form of a childhood autobiography. It opens in an atmosphere of uncertainty. The first source of such a mood is memory: the text begins with the words "he cannot remember." This very first phrase is important for two reasons: it underlines the fallibility (and selectivity) of memory, a primary feature in the composition of autobiography as a genre; and secondly it is in the third person ("he" rather than "I"). The second source of uncertainty is more subtly expressed; it has to be inferred by the reader. This narrator feels a breeze on his face and is unable to discriminate between light and dark. The boundaries of his childhood world are not clearly delineated; their limits are described in tactile terms rather than visual, spatial ones. Our narrator, we soon discover, is blind.

The bulk of the first volume of *al-Ayyām* is set in Tāhā Husayn's village. We learn about his family and the simple rural existence that they live. There are a large number of children in the household, and the blind son feels at once different and isolated.

The process begins in the village *kuttāb* (Qur'ān school) where the sacred text is learned by rote. This is to be "our friend's" (as the narrator calls his child-topic) introduction to the Egyptian educational system and its pedagogical methods, something to which the adult Tāhā Husayn is later to devote a good deal of attention, much of it highly critical. As "our friend" enter his teenage years, the return visits of his elder Azharite brother to the village become times of hope, hope that he will be allowed to accompany his brother to the capital city of Cairo in order to achieve his great goal, to be educated at al-Azhar, the renowned institution of Islamic higher learning. It is with the news that this year (in fact, 1902) he is indeed to travel with his brother that the first volume concludes. Almost immediately from its publication, this work became one of the most popular narratives in modern Arabic and it has retained that popularity ever since. The style, the gentle level of irony in the relationship between the author and his narrator, the account of a terribly deprived childhood in the provinces in Egypt, these features have endeared the work to generations of Egyptians and to many others beyond the bounds of that country.

Bearing in mind the uproar that had been created by the publication of *Fī 'l-shi'r al-jāhilī*, it is hardly surprising that Tāhā Husayn's academic career continued to be fraught with controversy. Appointed the first ever Egyptian Dean of the Faculty of Arts in 1929, he allied himself with the Wafd party in order to oppose the regime of Ismā'īl Sidqī, the Prime Minister, and was soon dismissed from his position as Dean. The challenges to Tāhā Husayn's status as a Muslim believer that had been thrown down in 1926 and his subsequent dismissal from his senior academic post clearly lend an interesting extra dimension to his decision to participate as an active member of a group of Egyptian intellectuals who, during the 1930s, wrote works that took Islam and the early stages of its development as a primary topic. They include such figures as Muhammad Husayn **Haykal**, Tawfīq al-**Hakīm**, 'Abbās Mahmūd al-'Aqqād, and Tāhā Husayn. It has been suggested on occasion that this "turn" in the 1930s marks some kind of "reversion" to Islam or even an intellectual "crisis." However, it seems reasonably clear from the above account of controversies that had erupted in the 1920s that the fires kindled during the initial confrontation between new analytical modes and traditional attitudes had produced more smoke than light. The writings of the above-named scholars (and others) are much more accurately viewed as attempts at reconciling viewpoints that had initially come into confrontation within a fraught political arena but that clearly needed to be examined within a less heated and more reasoned environment. One might suggest that the writings of Tāhā Husayn and others during the 1930s were the beginnings of what has been an ongoing debate surrounding the question as to the relationship between Islam and the concept of modernity, the religious hierarchy and the nation-state, and the individual as both believer and member of a modern society.

The first volume of Tāhā Husayn's *'Alā hāmish al-sīrah* (On the Margins of [Prophetic] Biography) appeared in 1933, and subsequent volumes were published in 1937 and 1938 (along with the later *al-Wa'd al-haqq*, The True Promise, 1950). Anyone who may have been anticipating another installment in the ongoing confrontation between the "scientific" modernists and traditional beliefs and methods was going to be disappointed by this first volume and its successors, in that Tāhā Husayn specifically announces in the prefatory material to the volume that it is intended for a general public and that he will not be applying the critical methodology that had been characteristic of his earlier (and more controversial) studies. Now officially banished (at least for a while) from the realms of academe, the Tāhā Husayn of the early 1930s is, it would appear, taking his role as public educator very seriously. The first volume of *'Alā hāmish al-sīrah* takes another look at the myths and stories surrounding the life of the Prophet Muhammad. Even though the audience and method of this study may be different from that of his previous investigations, the import of his remarks remains much the same: that such tales are part of the accretion of myth surrounding any predominant figure in history and need to be treated (and respected) as such.

The same decade (the 1930s) also saw a rise of interest in the writing of novels, a process—it must be admitted—that had already been much stimulated by the publication of Tāhā Husayn's *al-Ayyām* in 1929. All of the authors just mentioned as contributors to the series of works on religious themes were also novelists; of them, Tawfīq al-**Hakīm**, 'Abbās Mahmūd al-'Aqqād, and Tāhā Husayn wrote one or more novel during the 1930s. Tāhā Husayn's initial venture into the new fictional genre was *Du'ā' al-karawān* (English translation: *The Call of the Curlew*, 1980). It represents a significant shift towards fictionality on Tāhā Husayn's part in that it is no longer concerned with the tensions of cross-cultural confrontation or indeed with the narrative strategies of the autobiographical element in fiction. To be sure, there is much tension in this novel, but it is situated firmly within the confines of Egyptian society. The narrator, a woman named Amīnah, invokes the historical present to recount a tale of abuse and revenge, all set against the backdrop of the tense relationship within Egypt between the settled inhabitants of provincial towns and the nomadic Bedouin with whom they often come into contact.

Amīnah's father (like her mother, unnamed) was a notorious philanderer. Early in the narrative we learn that he has been murdered during the course of one of his sexual escapades. As a result, the mother and her daughters, Amīnah and Hanādī, are forced to flee the community. The three women find a new town in which to live, but each of them is placed in a different household. Amīnah works in the home of the local official, the *ma'mūr*, but the youngest of the women, Hanādī, finds herself in a household where the son is working as an engineer. He seduces the impressionable young woman, and she becomes pregnant. Forced to move again in search of help, the women return to their own folk, but during the journey Hanādī is killed by her uncle. It is now that Amīnah's retrospective narrative begins to gather strength as she recounts her systematic campaign for revenge on her sister's behalf. Returning to the *ma'mūr's* house, she first ensures that plans for an engagement between the culprit engineer and the *ma'mūr's* daughter, Khadījah, are scuppered, and then manages to arrange matters so that she herself is hired as a maid in the engineer's own home. However, Amīnah herself narrates for the reader the shift from an initial master-servant relationship and, on her part, a desire to seek some kind of revenge for her sister's death to something far more complex than that. As the engineer declares his love and desire for marriage, Amīnah finds herself compelled to reveal to him the entire story that has been recounted in the novel. The work ends, as it begins, with the invocation of the curlew's bird-song, "bird of my heart" as Amīnah terms it, always at hand during life's crucial moments.

With this novel Tāhā Husayn is certainly contributing to the process of developing the necessary crafts in order that the novel in Arabic can address itself to social issues. As suggested above, this is a highly dramatic tale, replete with tension and both overt and suppressed violence

(and it was made into a highly successful film, with the renowned Fātin Hamāmah in the major role [1959]). Typical of Tāhā Husayn and his broader cultural and educational priorities however is his use of language in this work. While other novelists may have been essaying a variety of different levels of language in order to replicate the realities of dialogue in their fictions, Tāhā Husayn here maintains a language-level that is a model of literary Arabic; indeed, it often rises to the level of poetry, as the English translator points out in his introduction. The unique style that many commentators had found so bewitching in the first volume of *al-Ayyām* is once again invoked here.

Many critics have suggested that Tāhā Husayn's next venture into fiction, the novel *Adīb* (1935), which appeared between the publication of the first and second volumes of *al-Ayyām*, was itself a further segment of Tāhā Husayn's personal narrative. Considering what might be termed the "spectrum of fictionality," it seems reasonable to suggest that *Adīb*, especially in the first half of the narrative, contains a number of autobiographical elements but that several strategies adopted by the author place it more firmly in the realms of fiction.

Adīb is a student at the Egyptian University who hails from the same area of Upper Egypt as the narrator, holds the same disdainful views towards the educational system at al-Azhar, has the same fondness for citing the names of classical Arab poets, and is intent on studying in France. While he hails from the same region as the narrator, he comes from a much wealthier family, and his feelings towards his childhood home are complex, a blend of nostalgia and resentment. Adīb's relationship with his parents, however, displays all the tensions brought about by an enormous gap in educational background and adherence to traditional norms. This is particular so when Adīb decides that, since he cannot travel to France for study if he is married, he will repudiate his wife, a decision that he asks his father (in a letter, of course) to communicate to his wife. He has also written a letter to her, but, since he cannot bring himself to send it, he instead gives it to the narrator (and thus it too finds its way into the narrative). Adīb's time in

France and his confrontation with cultural differences bring initial success as he does well at his studies. However, the differences that he observes in such detail begin to weigh him down; he gradually neglects his studies, develops an ongoing relationship with a French woman, and sinks into depression.

The narrator of "Adīb's" tale is, as we noted above, living with his brother in Cairo while he attends both al-Azhar and the secular university; he is preparing a study on the poet al-Maʿarrī; and he spends some time in Montpelier before returning to Egypt during the First World War. Adīb's lengthy disquisitions on his traditional background and the glaring contrasts between it and the secular and imported values of the West that character and narrator were to explore in the culture itself link this narrative to the tradition of the epistolary novel, with its overtly didactic intentions and relatively simple structure.

As an extension of this spirit of fictional experimentation, it is interesting to note that Tāhā Husayn involved himself in another unusual project, in that he spent a summer vacation in Switzerland in 1936 co-authoring a novel with his illustrious compatriot, Tawfīq al-Hakīm (d. 1987). The resulting narrative, entitled *al-Qasr al-mashūr* (The Enchanted Palace) involves the two writers in a discussion with the greatest story-teller of them all, Shahrazād. Each writer gets a chapter, and the other writer has to pick up where the previous one left off. The instigation for the project was apparently a desire on the part of both writers to patch up a quarrel that had arisen after Tāhā Husayn had made some critical remarks about al-Hakīm's plays. It would appear that the two men were reconciled, but neither seems to have regarded the resulting novel as a significant part of their œuvre.

In addition to these activities in the realms of fiction and religious studies, Tāhā Husayn also continued his involvement in literary criticism. He published another study on the poet al-Maʿarrī, *Maʿa Abī 'l-ʿAlā' fī sijnih* (With Abū 'l-ʿAlā' in His Prison, 1930), and in 1937 published one of his finest works of criticism, *Maʿa 'l-Mutanabbī* (With al-Mutanabbī, 1937), a study of the Arabic literary tradition's most celebrated poet, al-Mutanabbī (d. 956), "he who claims to

be a prophet". The importance of this study lies in its change of critical approach. He had decided to respond in book-form to a study on the poet by the great French Arabist Régis Blachère. Tāhā Husayn's study approaches al-Mutanabbī's *Dīwān* (collected poetry) systematically, implying in this case an analysis of the different stages in his development as a poet. In his opinion, it is the period spent at the court of the renowned ruler of Aleppo, Sayf al-Dawlah (d. 967), which stimulates the poet to produce his greatest contributions to the tradition of Arabic poetry. He analyzes with admiration some of the panegyric odes that the poet addresses to his patron, but seems to join with some of the more traditional of al-Mutanabbī's critical contemporaries in disapproving of some of the poet's innovations in the elegies that he composed for senior members of the ruler's family.

As a further contribution to this incredibly productive decade, he set himself the task of applying his acquired European learning, particularly that involving the classical languages, to the complex issues of Egyptian national identity and the role of education in fostering such ideas. His increased involvement in the broader inter-cultural aspects of this process of modernization and social transformation is reflected in the publication in 1938 of one of his most significant works, *Mustaqbal al-thaqāfah fī Misr* (The Future of Culture in Egypt). The work opens with a discussion of Egypt's placement in a broader cultural configuration. The focus of the argument is whether it needs to trace its cultural roots more in the "East" or the "West." Tāhā Husayn argues forcibly that Egypt has never been linked to the regions of any entity dubbed the "East," such as India and the regions beyond it. Its earlier heritage is linked far more closely to the Greco-Roman world; Alexandria was, after all, home to one of the world's greatest libraries which served for many centuries as a center for Hellenistic learning. Egypt's encounter with Islam did not change this essential orientation towards European culture, and, even during the period of Ottoman suzerainty, Egypt resisted any tendency to realign its sense of self-identity in a more easterly direction. It needs to be pointed out at this juncture that Tāhā Husayn's attitudes towards the Turks and their dominant role in many of the regions of today's Middle East over a period of several centuries is a direct reflection of the approach to cultural change and its reflection in the writing of literary history that he had learned so well at the hands of his French teachers. Here as elsewhere, Tāhā Husayn and many of his literary-historical contemporaries seem all too ready and willing to leapfrog over several centuries of cultural interaction in order to arrive more speedily at the 19th century, with its importation of many modern European conveniences which have benefited the Egyptian people. The notion of "backwardness" is introduced, and unfavorable comparisons are made between Egypt's pace of change and the recent history of Japanese culture in its relationship with the "West." In a word, Egypt must strive to imitate the ideals of Europe.

Having indulged in this cultural sweep across large swathes of time and space, Tāhā Husayn devotes the rest of the work to a highly detailed analysis of the educational system: its structure and goals, the need for teacher-training, the role of higher education, and the place of al-Azhar in a newly revised system. He opens with a general section in which he addresses some of the major issues confronting his nation at this crucial transitional period in its modern development. Education should be the responsibility of the state, and particular care should be taken to insure that the language of that state, Arabic, is properly taught. In a second section he examines the goals of education in more depth. Rather than the inevitability of government service as the goal of higher education, he wishes to see a broader and more intellectual set of objectives. Students should learn foreign languages so that they can become more effective world citizens. Latin and Greek are the focus of particular concern—hardly surprising in view of Tāhā Husayn's training in Paris and subsequent appointment as Professor of Classics.

Two final sections (sections 40 et seq.) are devoted to the training of teachers and the goals of university education. For Tāhā Husayn, universities should try to combine the research and applied aspects, thus meeting the needs of a variety of potential clienteles. The purpose of

university education should not be merely the acquisition of knowledge, but also the development of an enlightened outlook and a clear sense of moral conduct. A final section (50) is devoted to a consideration of the role of al-Azhar and of religious education in general (he includes Christian education and the Copts in his discussion).

This astonishingly variegated career as educator, editor of newspapers and journals, literary critic and historian, and creative writer continued into the 1940s, a period when Egypt found itself once again involved in the political tensions associated with a World War. A second volume of his already popular autobiography, *al-Ayyām*, was published in 1940 (English translation: *A Stream of Days*, 1942). It is primarily concerned with a highly critical account of his teenage years spent as a student at the al-Azhar mosque-university in Cairo, and reflects not only a different period in Tāhā Husayn's career and in the development of modern Arabic narrative, but also a different approach to autobiographical narrative. The gentle irony that characterized the narrator's sense of distance from the blind young Egyptian child of the first volume has now disappeared, to be replaced by the more strident and polemical tone of someone who feels that much closer in both time and sensitivity to the subject being portrayed.

During this same decade, Tāhā Husayn made two further contributions to the developing tradition of Arabic fiction. The setting of his next novel, *Shajarat al-bu's* (Tree of Misery, 1943 or 1944), which many critics consider his best, is once again the rural village, and, as is the case in the first volume of *al-Ayyām*, the life of the family whose generations are followed in the plot are directly and radically affected by the influence of Sufi shaykhs. In this case, a shaykh persuades two of his devotees, one of whom lives in Cairo, the other in the same village, to marry their children to each other. The daughter of the Cairene devotee, named Nafīsah, is proverbially ugly, and, while the groom himself—Khālid—seems content to obey the shaykh's injunction, his mother objects violently, stating that "a tree of misery" has been planted in the family. Thus is the scene set for a multi-generational narrative that follows the fortunes of the succeeding generations as they are forced to deal with the consequences of their elders' decisions.

The central figure in the narrative is Khālid, at the outset the son of ʿAlī who orders him to marry Nafīsah, and at the conclusion the aging elder of a complex web of intermarried siblings and cousins. Initially accepting without question the dictates of the Sufi shaykh and his father that he marry, he becomes the father of two daughters, the beautiful Samīhah and Gulnār, whose appearance replicates that of her mother. As envy and resentment worm their way into the hearts of the two generations, Khālid is persuaded to repudiate his wife and to remarry. This introduces another family, that of Hājj Masʿūd, also a follower of the Sufi shaykh, an illiterate but prosperous merchant who marries his daughter, Munā, to Khālid. This marriage is especially fruitful, producing a whole series of beautiful boys and girls. As Nafīsah's resentments smolder on and Gulnār, her daughter, remains unmarried, the "tree of misery" continues to bear its bitter fruit.

Towards the end of the 1940s, Tāhā Husayn published his only collection of short stories, *al-Muʿadhdhabūn fī 'l-ard* (The Tortured on the Earth, 1949), in which his commentary on the harshness of life in the Egyptian provinces as reflected in these novels, is expressed in even starker terms. The collection was initially published in Lebanon, since the contents were considered by the Egyptian regime of the day (of which Tāhā Husayn was himself a member) to be too controversial. Following the 1952 revolution however, the work became, in Nur Sherif's words, "a social document of the pre-revolutionary era."

The 1930s and '40s had seen Tāhā Husayn appointed to a variety of positions in academe and publishing, only to be dismissed as party elections brought new governments to power. In 1942 however, a government formed by the Wafd party was imposed upon the Egyptian people through the use of British tanks, and Tāhā Husayn's career took a new turn. Not only was he appointed Rector of the University of Alexandria, but also his acknowledged status as the doyen of Arabic letters led to his further appointment as a counselor to the Ministry of

Education, a position from which he would be able to implement reforms that would correct many of the problems that he had illustrated in his important 1938 work, *Mustaqbal al-thaqāfah*. As World War II raged on for three more years, Tāhā Husayn found himself fulfilling multiple roles: government adviser, university administrator, and from 1945-48 editor of a publishing house. For a short term he served as editor of the Wafdist newspaper, *Kawkab al-Sharq*, and in 1945 he became editor of the prominent literary journal *al-Kātib al-Misrī*. All these activities reached a culminating point when, in 1950, the blind child from the provinces of Egypt who had risen to become one of its brightest cultural stars was appointed Minister of Education. This post, needless to say, finally gave him the full discretion he needed to implement the ideas that he had laid out in such detail in his 1938 blueprint for the future. He was in the process of implementing many of those ideas and reforms (including compulsory elementary education for all children) when political events in the form of the 1952 Egyptian revolution overtook him.

The decade of the 1950s was one in which many of the countries in the Arabic-speaking world went through processes of revolutionary change of one kind or another and negotiated their independence from former colonial powers. Such events were inevitably reflected in the cultural milieu of the times. In particular, following the translation of a number of European works into Arabic—with Sartre's *Qu'est-ce que la littérature* at the head of the list—the literary world found itself concentrating heavily on the notion of "commitment" (*iltizām*), thus placing creative writers into a position whereby they could serve as potentially important contributors to the political and social agenda of the new regimes that emerged in the wake of independence from the colonial powers and a whole series of revolutions. Looking back on Tāhā Husayn's career as a critic—the historical moment to which he belongs and the principles that he followed, it is easy to understand why these new trends were ones that he bitterly resisted. Having initiated his professional career by establishing the possibility of identifying principles through which literature could be evaluated and having later shifted from a rigidly "scientific" approach to one that emphasized a more subjective and "artistic" one, he now saw that the very parameters of critical evaluation and estimates of the nature of the target readership for literature were being radically changed. In 1954 this debate, one that pitted the "traditionalists" of the older generation—Tāhā Husayn and his equally feisty contemporary, ʿAbbās Mahmūd al-ʿAqqād—against the proponents of committed literature, Mahmūd Amīn al-ʿĀlim and ʿAbd al-ʿAzīz Anīs, burst into print in Cairene newspapers. Within the context of a new and untried post-revolutionary government in Cairo (and to be replicated elsewhere in the Arab world), one that was anxious to sweep away the influence of the corrupt *ancien régime* and to develop an entirely new kind of society, Tāhā Husayn and his illustrious colleague were clearly swimming against a very strong tide by defending the esthetic bases of literature and its evaluation and adopting what many of his opponents in both newspaper columns and debates were terming an "elitist" or "ivory-tower" attitude.

The final two decades of Tāhā Husayn's life, roughly coterminous with the era of Gamāl ʿAbd al-Nāsir (Nasser) as President (1954-70), saw a continuing recognition of the enormous debt that Egyptian cultural life owed to him; he was indeed the "grand old man" of Egyptian (and, many would say, Arab) letters. He was the first recipient of the newly established State Prize for Literature, and in 1963 his lifelong love of the Arabic language and his stalwart defense of its central position within Arab society was acknowledged through his appointment as President of the Majmaʿ ʿIlmī, the Arabic Language Academy, responsible like its French counterpart for the preservation of those principles and values that carried the heritage of the past through the present into the future. He died in his home on the road to the Pyramids on the 28th of October, 1973.

Tāhā Husayn's career as author, teacher, and critic in the field of literature and its study would always have been guaranteed a particular public impact, but his personal demeanor and rugged determination were such as to insure that he would move beyond that to become a major public figure during the course of his lifetime. Many of the public debates in which Tāhā Husayn participated with both vigor and conviction, were set against the background of the clashes between the religious and the secular, the traditional and the modern, the conservative and the liberal, which, in Egypt as elsewhere, were the inevitable consequence of the processes of cultural confrontation and social transformation in which his own homeland—itself in the course of becoming a "nation"—was involved.

The one element about which he was more passionate than anything else was the Arabic language itself. Throughout his life, he was a stalwart defender of the most rigorous application of the standard written language to all walks of life; not merely the "high style" of literary texts, but in every conceivable environment. He makes his views of this topic abundantly clear in his major essay on education, *Mustaqbal al-thaqāfah fī Misr* (discussed above): the colloquial language, the language of the street and of day-to-day communication throughout the Arabic-speaking world, is a corruption of the pure, classical language of the Arabs, and every effort should be made to encourage the use of the classical form, especially through the implementation of programs within the educational sector. This attitude on his part was no mere posture. His own style—mostly involving dictation in view of his blindness—was, as virtually all critics will acknowledge—a model for emulation; beautifully cadenced, with balanced phrases, it was described with a phrase that had earlier been employed to characterize one of Arabic's great classical models of elegant style, al-Jahiz (d. 969), *sahl mumtani'* (simple, yet inimitable). Whether he was writing novels, critical articles, educational planning documents, or histories of literature, the same clear and mellifluous style would be there. What is perhaps even more remarkable and unique is that, as many of Tāhā Husayn's interlocutors were to discover, he would talk in the same level of language—adamantly refusing to use the colloquial dialect, and indeed often correcting the "faulty" syntax of those who wished to discuss topics with him. In a country like Egypt, where the colloquial dialect is considered an appropriate communication medium in a large number of public milieus, this insistence on the use of a grammatically accurate classical language on all occasions made him a unique figure in public life.

Throughout Tāhā Husayn's career there is an abundance of evidence to show that nothing delighted him more than a good argument. But, while he was a polemicist by nature, it would appear, his entire life was devoted to ways of finding paths for confluence, for fusion, for adaptation, and—indeed—for reasoned change. His forthright, highly learned, and critically astute forays into the history of the Arabic cultural heritage and his confrontations with the forces of conservatism made him a cultural icon early in his career. One might ask how it could be otherwise with the blind former Azharite scholar from the provinces who now spoke about the past, both Arab-Islamic and Greco-Roman, in such mellifluous terms? It is a cogent symbol of both the nature and pace of change that has so powerfully affected Egypt, as other nations of the non-Western world, that the popular firebrand of the 1920s, '30s, and even '40s was later to be viewed as such a conservative force.

REFERENCES

Jābir 'Asfūr, *al-Marāyā al-mutajāwirah: dirāsah fī naqd Tāhā Husayn* (Cairo: al-Hay'ah al-Misriyyah al-'Āmmah li'l-Kitāb, 1983);

J. Brugman, *An Introduction to the History of Modern Arabic Literature in Egypt* (Leiden: E. J. Brill, 1984);

Pierre Cachia, *Tāhā Husayn: His Place in the Egyptian Literary Renaissance* (London: Luzac & Co., 1956);

Muhammad al-Khidr Husayn, *Naqd kitāb Fī 'l-shi'r al-jāhilī* (Cairo: al-Maktabah al-Azhariyyah fī 'l-Turāth, 1988?);

Abdelrashid Mahmoudi, *Tāhā Husayn's Education: From al-Azhar to the Sorbonne* (Richmond: Curzon Press, 1998);

Fedwa Malti-Douglas, *Blindness and Autobiography: al-Ayyām of Tāhā Husayn* (Princeton: Princeton University Press, 1988);

Tetz Rooke, *In My Childhood: A Study of Arabic Autobiography* (Stockholm: Almquist & Wiksell International, 1997);

David Semah, *Four Egyptian Literary Critics* (Leiden: E. J. Brill, 1974);

Charles D. Smith, *Islam and the Search for Social Order in Modern Egypt: A Biography of Muhammad Husayn Haykal* (Albany, New York: SUNY Press, 1983);

"Tāhā Husayn," *Encyclopedia of Islam*, 2nd ed. (Leiden: E. J. Brill, 1954-2005).

Bibliography

Hamdi Sakkut and Marsdon Jones, *A'lām al-adab al-mu'āsir fī Misr: 1. Tāhā Husayn* (Cairo: American University in Cairo Press, 1975).

Hāfiz Ibrāhīm
(1872? – 1932)

MICHELLE HARTMAN
McGill University

WORKS

Complete Poetry Collections

Dīwān Hāfiz: Nazm Hāfiz Ibrāhīm wa-sharh Muhammad Hilāl Hāfiz Ibrāhīm ("Hāfiz's Complete Poems: Composed by Hāfiz Ibrā-

hīm and explained by Muhammad Hilāl Hāfiz Ibrāhīm", Cairo: al-Tamaddun, 1901);

al-Juz' al-thānī min dīwān Hāfiz: ta'līf Muhammad Hāfiz Ibrāhīm ("The Second Part of Hāfiz's Complete Poems: Composed by Muhammad Hāfiz Ibrāhīm", Cairo: al-Islāh, 1907);

Dīwān Ḥāfiz li-nāzim 'iqdih Muhammad Ḥāfiz Ibrāhīm ("Ḥāfiz's Complete Poetry: Works by the Great Poet Muhammad Ḥāfiz Ibrāhīm", Cairo: al-Islāh, 1911);

'Umar: manāqibuh wa-akhlāquh ("'Umar: His Exploits and His Character", Cairo: al-Sabāh, 1918);

Dīwān Ḥāfiz min hayātih ilā wafātih ("Ḥāfiz's Complete Poems from his Birth to his Death", 2 vols., Cairo: al-Hilāl, 1935);

Dīwān Ḥāfiz Ibrāhīm ("Ḥāfiz Ibrāhīm's Complete Poems"), ed. Ahmad Amīn et al. (2 vols., Cairo: Dār al-Kutub, 1937, 1939).

Individual Prose Publications

Layālī Satīh ("The Nights of Satīh", Cairo: al-Islāh, 1906);

Kutayyib fī 'l-tarbiyah al-awwaliyyah ("A Little Book on Elementary Education", Cairo: al-Ma'ārif, 1911-1912);

Kutayyib fī 'l-iqtisād ("A Little Book on Economics", Cairo: al-Ma'ārif, 1913).

Translations by the Author

Victor Hugo, *al-Bu'asā'* (Cairo: al-Rahmāniyyah, 1903; reissued Cairo: Abī 'l-Hawl, 1922); translation of *Les Misérables*;

al-Mūjaz fī 'l-iqtisād ("Excursions in the Study of Economics", 5 vols., Cairo: al-Ma'ārif, 1913); translated with Khalīl Mutrān from a work by Paul Leroy-Beaulieu.

Works in Translation

Salma Khadra Jayyusi (ed.), *Modern Arabic Poetry: An Anthology* (New York: Columbia University Press, 1987), 77-78.

Ḥāfiz Ibrāhīm (?1869/1872 - 21 July 1932) was known as the *Shā'ir al-Nīl* (Poet of the Nile). It is often remarked that he earned this nickname because the Nile runs through his poetry. Certainly, there are many mentions of the Nile and other features of Egypt's natural geography in Ḥāfiz Ibrāhīm's works. His nickname, however, reveals what is probably the most important feature of his reputation—that he was an Egyptian nationalist poet, more specifically one whose writings espoused the cause of the Egyptian common people. Writing at the turn of the 20th century, Ḥāfiz Ibrāhīm was considered to be, and to this day is referred to as, the "Poet of the People." He is understood to be a person who expressed in his poetry that he cared about the lives and struggles of ordinary Egyptians. In this regard, it is important to note that Ḥāfiz Ibrāhīm himself was a man of a modest background. In contrast to most other poets and littérateurs of his day, who tended to hail from less humble families and origins, he was reportedly born on a houseboat on the Nile and had very little formal schooling. Despite these obstacles, he became one of the great neo-classical poets of his day. Like the other major Arab neo-classical poets, Ḥāfiz Ibrāhīm's reputation was built by composing traditional, finely-crafted verse. It is important, however, that his poetry seems to have particularly appealed to the Egyptian populace because of its ironic commentary on the political and social problems of his era.

Ḥāfiz Ibrāhīm's importance as a neo-classical poet is almost always paired with the achievements of his contemporary, and sometimes rival, Ahmad **Shawqī**. Both of these men, like many other poets of their generation, were very much influenced by the pioneer of neo-classical verse innovations in Egypt—Mahmūd Sāmī al-**Bārūdī**. Bārūdī's formative influence can be seen in Ibrāhīm and Shawqī's traditional and carefully-worked poems, which draw heavily on themes, imagery and language of their classical predecessors. Though perhaps not the most creative or innovative of the neo-classical poets, Ahmad Shawqī and Ḥāfiz Ibrāhīm are the two names which are most commonly associated with this poetic movement. And both poets retain their popular appeal and literary reputation in Egypt to this day. As poets these two had a greadt deal in common, but their lives, careers, outlook on life and even their poetic output were markedly different. Shawqī's aristocratic background, and role as a court poet, could not be more different than Ḥāfiz Ibrāhīm's struggle to overcome his modest beginnings, become a poet and support himself. Shawqī's more elite production can be contrasted to that of Ḥāfiz Ibrāhīm, who is best known for his embrace of popular causes and his commentary on issues such as poverty and the struggle for Egyptian independence. The divided allegiance of Egyptians to each of these poets reflects their opposed social and intellectual backgrounds. Though Shawqī is the more prolific and better-known of the two, Ḥāfiz Ibrāhīm's special appeal seems to reside in his rise from an impoverished background to becoming such an important Egyptian literary figure and the fact that throughout his career he never abandoned his embrace of the issues close to the hearts of ordinary people.

Ḥāfiz Ibrāhīm's early biography is a very Egyptian story of perseverance in the face of adversity, as appropriate for someone carrying the title "Poet of the Nile." Ḥāfiz Ibrāhīm's birth on a Dayrūt houseboat is thought to have taken place sometime between the years 1869 and 1872. His family home floating on the Nile far from the capital city coupled with the lack of certainty as to his exact date of birth is an indication of his poor and disadvantaged background. Moreover, Ḥāfiz Ibrāhīm was only four years old when his father died. This tragic death had a major impact on his young life, and a series of moves to different cities in Egypt soon faced him. After his father's passing, he was forced to begin a new life with his mother and thus they moved first to Cairo and then to Tanṭā, another provincial Egyptian city, in order to live with his mother's brother and his family. Ḥāfiz Ibrāhīm therefore grew up under the care of his maternal uncle, and this involved not only living in the same household, but also this man's financial support and sponsorship. These events interrupted the boy's formal education and he stopped attending school regularly at a young age. He worked in a series of jobs in order to contribute to family expenses, including as a clerk in a legal office. Though his schooling was not completed, it is reported that Ḥāfiz Ibrāhīm did attend classes, at least sporadically, at the local Aḥmadī mosque and shrine of Aḥmad al-Badawī. In addition to studying classical religious texts and the Arabic language, he became familiar with the classical Arabic poetic traditions through his studies with the mosque's 'ulamā'.

It is in this period of his adolescence that Ḥāfiz Ibrāhīm is said to have developed a particular fondness for the classical verse of the 'Abbasid period, considered the golden age of classical Arabic poetry. His gift for the memorization and recitation of poetry, and rapid mastery of classical forms, provided him a firm foundation for his later poetic output as a neo-classicist. It is also believed that this is when Ḥāfiz Ibrāhīm first became acquainted with the works of Bārūdī that would so inspire him later. The young man thus built up his literary and poetic education while, at the same time, working as an apprentice in several law offices in Tanṭā. Eventually in 1890 he quit this city in order to pursue his fortunes in Cairo. Some have attributed his move to Cairo to his inability to pursue a successful career as a lawyer. Others have emphasized his desire to strike out on his own and start a new life, rather than continuing to live at his uncle's expense in Tanṭā. With this important move to the capital his nascent poetic career would begin to develop further and gain momentum.

After his arrival in Cairo, Ḥāfiz Ibrāhīm decided to pursue a military career, a practical choice for a young man of his background. With the encouragement of his sister's husband who was himself an officer he enrolled in military college in Cairo. He looked forward to the promise of a stable career upon completion of his studies there, and one which at the same time would allow him time to pursue his literary interests. Ḥāfiz Ibrāhīm completed his course at the military academy in 1891 and graduated as a second lieutenant in the artillery. Upon graduation, he worked for a time in government service as a police officer, for both the Ministry of the Interior and the War Ministry. It was the latter which sent him to Sudan as a soldier in 1895.

In the Sudan Ḥāfiz Ibrāhīm served, unhappily, in the military under Lord Kitchner's command. There is no doubt that young Ḥāfiz's sojourn in Sudan was an extremely bitter experience, and he complained ruefully about it in his frequent letters home. All reports of his time there point to the many miseries and hardships he endured and emphasize his loneliness in particular. The author spend a period of five years in the Sudan, and it was in this period that he composed his earliest poems, though some lines of his verse compositions have been preserved from before this date. Moreover, his experiences in Sudan influenced him enough that references to them appear in later prose works like his narrative in the *maqāmah* style, *Layālī Satīh*. He sent a number of these poems back to Egypt in letters to his family and friends; they are included in his *Dīwān* (collected works). Many of these early poems first appeared in the year 1900. The poems that Hāfiz Ibrāhīm composed in Sudan and sent back to Egypt were representative of the breadth of his talents and poetry that he would later write. For example, he wrote poems to friends such as Muhammad Bēg Bayram, celebrating his virtues. At least one 'wine poem'—celebrating an evening drinking with friends—is extant. Other poems on the subject of Sudan, British rule there and in Egypt, and of course complaints against life in Sudan are also included in his collected works and prefigure the major output of poetry which would flourish upon Hāfiz Ibrāhīm's return to his homeland.

One poem from this early period in Hāfiz Ibrāhīm's career, published in 1900, shows his use of humor and allegory to inscribe stinging social critiques. The poem titled *Wasf kisā' lahu* (Description of a Suit of His) is on one level an ode written in a high style in honor of a suit but also can be read as an ironic commentary on modernity. This composition gently mocks those who feel that they are important because they wear suits—here a symbol of the west and western influence on Egypt—and strut about in them as though they have somehow transcended their formerly lowly status. The poem provides a fine example of the layered meanings that Hāfiz Ibrāhīm was able to encode in seemingly traditional poems in a classical format. This particular poem was deemed important enough to be chosen as the representative sample of Hāfiz Ibrāhīm's poetry in the major anthology of modern Arabic poetry translated into English, *Modern Arabic Poetry: An Anthology*.

Hāfiz Ibrāhīm's stint in the Sudan came to an end, as did that of a number of his colleagues, when he was sent down to the army reserves in 1900. He was part of a group of eighteen officers, all of whom were charged by the authorities with having participated in a mutiny against the British leadership in the Sudan. Those accused of having been engaged in this 1899 uprising—allegedly inspired and masterminded by the Khedive—were then relieved of active duty and sent back to Egypt. Both general accounts of this mutiny and accounts of Hāfiz Ibrāhīm's specific participation in it are sketchy. However, it can be said with certainty that he was removed from active duty at this point and returned to Egypt.

The poems that Hāfiz Ibrāhīm had been composing while in the Sudan and publishing in Egypt began to bring him greater fame after 1900. In 1901 his first *Dīwān* (collected works) was published, and a number of important poems and other works followed shortly after this. For example, he continued to publish poems in praise of friends, public figures and other poets. One example is his poem in honour of the man whose works so inspired him, Mahmūd Sāmī al-**Bārūdī** (d. 1904). Another such poem was written to a man he greatly respected, the Lebanese poet and lawyer Dā'ūd 'Ammūn (1902). 'Ammūn reciprocated by writing a poem back to him which appears alongside it in some versions of Hāfiz Ibrāhīm's collected works. He published a number of other notable poems in this period just at the turn of the century. For example, despite his negative estimation of the British colonial project in Egypt and the Sudan, he wrote two well-known poems dedicated to British royals: a *rithā'* (elegy) on Queen Victoria in 1901 and a congratulatory poem to Edward VII on his coronation in 1902. Even in this early period, it can be noted that Hāfiz Ibrāhīm's reputation as a nationalist, like that of many of his contemporaries, was built less on a specific political platform and more on a general sense of discontent with British rule and aspects of the Ottoman Empire. A poet like Hāfiz Ibrāhīm was therefore able to write some poems to celebrate members of the British royal family or the Ottoman sultan, while composing others that severely critique both governments. Thus Hāfiz Ibrāhīm wrote a number of more directly and explicitly political poems in this period, including several which were published in the

years between 1901-1902 on the need to remove
the khedive from office. Later in his career he
was to become famous for his political poems
and embrace of nationalist ideas; in this earlier
period, only the early stirrings of such writings
can be detected.

In 1903, three years after Ḥāfiz Ibrāhīm's
return to Cairo, he took early retirement.
Altogether, he had done fourteen years of
government service by this time. Ḥāfiz Ibrāhīm
remained unemployed for eight further years
after this, existing off his meager retirement
pension. It seems that during this period he was
unable to find work despite the intervention of a
number of people on his behalf, especially as he
became an increasingly important poetic figure
and had more and more contacts with people
who themselves held positions of importance.
Some of the people with whom he was known to
meet during the period after his return were
well-known public figures, including political
leaders like Muhammad ʿAbduh, Qāsim Amīn,
Mustafā Kāmil, and Saʿd Zaghlūl, among
several others who were influential in Egypt at
the time. Many have attributed the increasingly
nationalist bent of Ḥāfiz Ibrāhīm's poems in the
period after 1903 to these friendships, which
would last a lifetime. Some of the finest elegies
Ḥāfiz Ibrāhīm produced later in his career were
written in commemoration of the deaths of these
men.

It should be noted, though, that Ḥāfiz Ibrāhīm's contacts with important government
figures and nationalist leaders like ʿAbduh, his
aristocratic colleagues like Ahmad Shawqī, and
other literary figures like Khalīl **Mutrān**, did not
lead him to abandon friends and colleagues who
shared his humble background. It is well-known
that Ḥāfiz Ibrāhīm was an extremely sociable
and personable man and that, upon his return to
Cairo in 1903, he did not turn his back on old
friends and associates. The fact that he continued to mix with people of all backgrounds
and classes further reinforced his populist image
as the "Poet of the People." Moreover, there is
no doubt that Ḥāfiz Ibrāhīm's many and varied
experiences of life in Sudan and Egypt, Cairo
and the countryside, gave him a perspective on
social and political issues that he incorporated

into his poetry, known for its reflection of the
real-life experiences of Egyptian people.

Despite the financial hardships that he faced
during this period of retirement and unemployment between 1903 and 1911, critics agree that
it was during these eight years that Ḥāfiz Ibrāhīm produced his finest verse. Perhaps because
of the difficult situations that he continued to
confront in his own life, he was better able to
relate to the economic difficulties of the
millions of Egyptian common people and
therefore to hone his critiques of government
corruption and British rule over Egypt. Ḥāfiz
Ibrāhīm's poetry in this period was infused by
a nationalist spirit, and he linked his call for the
improvement of society to a stronger Egyptian
leadership. These nationalistic poems are what
brought him fame and made him so popular.
He is well-known both for the wistful and
melancholy tone of many of his poems and also
for his stinging criticism of social injustices.
Critics often emphasize Ḥāfiz Ibrāhīm's
attention to content while remarking on the
greater prowess of Shawqī in formal terms.
Ḥāfiz Ibrāhīm's formal achievements and
mastery of the neo-classical form should not be
ignored, however, and he is known as a stylist
with full control over his art.

Ḥāfiz Ibrāhīm was a meticulous poet whose
verse compositions are models of the neo-
classical style in its more traditional manifestations. During the course of his career he
made few innovations or changes to the long-
established classical poetic forms; for example,
he rarely deviates from monorhyme or conventional metre. He took great care over the
writing of each individual poem and was
extremely concerned with how they would
sound when recited aloud. Therefore, as he
composed his verses he would sing out each line
to determine its effect on the listener. Ḥāfiz
Ibrāhīm's concern with the effect and sound of
his poems is clear not only in reading his poetry
but also from a consideration of some of the
themes and issues that he addresses in them.

The preservation of the Arabic language, in
particular, the formal language of literature, and
its prestige and importance to Arabs and
Egyptians is an issue Ḥāfiz Ibrāhīm wrote about

consistently throughout his career. His often-cited 1903 poem "al-Lughah al-ʻarabiyyah tanʻā hazzahā bayn ahlihā" (The Arabic Language Laments its Fate Among its (own) People) is a well-known example of this position. As the title indicates, in this work the poet proclaims the need for the preservation of the Arabic language. One issue that he takes on is the protection of the formal language against the corrupting influences of the colloquial. This poem was written specifically, however, in response to the threat to Arabic from British educational policies privileging English. The main thrust of this poem, therefore, is that the Arabic language must be defended against increasing encroachments of the west in order to preserve Arab culture and heritage.

Alongside his poetry, one of the first literary works that Ḥāfiz Ibrāhīm undertook upon his retirement from government service was his translation of Victor Hugo's *Les Misérables*, titled in Arabic *al-Buʼasāʼ: muʻarrab ʼan Victor Hugo* (The Wretched: an Arabic Version of Victor Hugo's Work, 1903). The turn of the century was a period in Arabic literary history that witnessed something of a "boom" in translations of European literary works. Many of these "translations" were rather what we might consider "adaptations"—works loosely based on the original works that convey their main ideas, plots and themes, but adapted to a variety of local circumstances and contexts, and often bearing only a passing resemblance to the original works. Whether *al-Buʼasāʼ* was more of a translation or an adaptation on the part of Ḥāfiz Ibrāhīm, and how much of it he actually completed on his own, has been debated by his critics and biographers. There is some disagreement about the author's knowledge—or lack of knowledge—of French, and of foreign languages more generally. Some of these critics point out that he never once in his life left the Nile valley to go beyond Egypt and Sudan and that it is therefore implausible that he could have a knowledge of French, especially given his intermittent schooling. Others propose that he completed this translation by consulting others and with a rudimentary knowledge of French, much as many other "translators" of this era did. In any case, Ḥāfiz Ibrāhīm's work, like many such others, was less "translated" in the sense that we understand it today, but rather composed as a new and original Arabic version of stories, based on loose translations which already existed.

The Arabic version of *Les Misérables* is much like other translations/adaptations of Ḥāfiz Ibrāhīm's era in other ways as well. It is written in an extremely ornate prose style, as one might expect from a neo-classical poet like Ḥāfiz Ibrāhīm. Its style suggests that at least the final version that we have today, *al-Buʼasāʼ*, was written by Ḥāfiz Ibrāhīm alone as attributed. The title of the work is unlike some others of its era in its simplicity and close resemblance to the original French title. Though published in 1903, soon after Ḥāfiz Ibrāhīm's return from the Sudan, it is notable that it was considered important enough to be reissued in 1922. It met with attention and some acclaim after the appearance of this second edition—one sign of its currency is that no less a critic than Tāhā **Husayn** reviewed it in the Egyptian daily newspaper *al-Siyāsah* in that same year.

Ḥāfiz Ibrāhīm's poetic works and translations in this early period of his career show an interest in exploring some of the contacts and conflicts between East and West, in the context of social justice and injustice. His critique of British educational policies and the need to preserve the Arab heritage fits with these overall concerns, just as the translation of this particular text by Victor Hugo seems very much in line with Ḥāfiz Ibrāhīm's concern with issues such of poverty. Two further poems show a different angle of his embrace of a general feeling of affiliation with the "East" as opposed to the "West"—those he wrote celebrating the Japanese victory in their war with Russia. His poem "Ghādat al-Yābān" (A Young Woman of Japan) and another "al-Harb al-Yābāniyyah al-Rūsiyyah" (The Japanese-Russian War) both commemorate this victory. As with other Arab nationalists of his day, Ḥāfiz Ibrāhīm saw this war as symbolic of the victory of an Eastern power over the West. Within these poems, therefore, Ḥāfiz Ibrāhīm uses Japan as a symbol that could serve as a possible model for later action by other Easterners, such as the Egyptians, in their struggles against the British.

The year 1906 saw developments in Hāfiz Ibrāhīm's personal life as well as his poetic and literary career. It was in this year that he was married for the first and only time—to a local Cairene woman. The marriage lasted for less than four months, however, and the couple separated. Hāfiz Ibrāhīm never married again and had no children. His literary output was not slowed in this period at all and in addition to writing the poetry that would make him famous, he also published his only original prose work in 1906. His narrative written in the neo-classical *maqā-mah* style, entitled *Layālī Satīh* (The Nights of Satīh), was the only work (other than the translation of *Les Misérables*) that he wrote in prose that would attract critical or popular attention.

Hāfiz Ibrāhīm was not alone amongst his neo-classicist contemporaries in seeking to try his hand at this difficult genre. The influence of Muhammad al-**Muwaylihī**'s well-known neo-classical *maqāmah*-style narrative, *Hadīth 'Īsā ibn Hishām*, is clear in *Layālī Satīh*, which similarly is a modern revival of this classical genre. Hāfiz Ibrāhīm's closest colleague, Ahmad Shawqī, also published a neo-classical work in the same *maqāmah* style. Unlike the attempts of many of his counterparts, however, Hāfiz Ibrā-hīm's *maqāmah* has been deemed a critical success and is regarded as better than most others, including that of Shawqī. It is particularly striking that such a difficult, and in some ways esoteric, work was reprinted as recently as 1964. In addition, it even has received some modern critical attention, primarily for its social commitment and trenchant commentaries on the ills of Egyptian society in this period.

Such a positive reception so many years after the heyday of Arabic neo-Classicism points to the likely reason for the enduring interest in Hāfiz Ibrāhīm's contribution to the genre. His focus on issues and topics of importance rather than primarily on clever manipulations of symbolism or complex verbal trickery distinguish this text. The work is not without its allusions and complexity however. The name of the character Satīh, after whom the work is titled, for example, invokes the pre-Islamic legendary figure of the same name. Satīh is a mythical personage dating

back to pre-Islamic Arabia who is traditionally represented as a diviner or judge.

The framework for *Layālī Satīh* is also that of a classical *maqāmah*—a series of meetings and conversations which form the "stages" required by the genre. In this particular work, these meetings are between the narrator, Satīh, and Satīh's son. The bulk of the text therefore consists of a series of meditations on a variety of issues, held together by the conceit of the conversations held between these three figures on a series of successive evenings. In *Layālī Satīh*, people bring grievances against the state of affairs in Egypt and then these troubles are answered by a mysterious narrative voice which intervenes in the conver-sations with lengthy discourses and expositions on a number of topics.

In many cases, the answers to the various complaints that people bring up lead to extensive analyses and digressions. Situations are discussed in some detail and remedies are suggested. This engagement with the most important issues and problems of his day is likely why Hāfiz Ibrāhīm's *Layālī Satīh* is considered a work of social criticism. Some examples of the topics addressed in *Layālī Satīh* include: the presence and position of Syrian émigrés in Egypt, the capitulations (extra-territorial laws for foreigners in Egypt), the British presence in Egypt and rule in Sudan, and women's rights. All of these issues were among those most debated in Hāfiz Ibrāhīm's Egypt; this willingness to engage with issues of social importance so directly gives this contribution to the revival of the *maqāmah* genre its special flair. In addition to these issues, the text also makes commentaries on poetry, including that of Hāfiz Ibrāhīm's friend and rival Ahmad Shawqī. Another particularly important issue of the time, especially for writers such as Hāfiz Ibrāhīm, was the influence the press had on the development of Arabic language and literature. *Layālī Satīh* once again takes on the issue of the preservation and maintenance of the Arabic literary language as well. Though a work like this might not be considered humorous today, it does nonetheless contain a number of droll and witty elements. One way in which it achieves this effect is by employing a verbose style and recherché words in places. Like most examples of the *maqāmah* genre, the bulk of this work is written in verse and rhymed prose. Some sections of the text, however, become quite conversational, and Ḥāfiz Ibrāhīm then makes use of unrhymed prose in these sections.

The year 1906 is also important to Ḥāfiz Ibrāhīm's literary production, as it is the year in which one of his most famous and emotionally charged poems was published. 1906 is the year of the infamous Dinshaway incident in which, after a conflict with some British officers in the Delta town of the same name that originally left one of their soldiers and several Egyptians dead, a number of Egyptian peasants were executed in retribution. The cruelty of the punishment and summary manner in which it was inflicted en-raged Egyptians. No poet writing at the time could remain silent about this incident, and the Poet of the Nile did not. Indeed, his first poem about Dinshaway—he was to write several—has been favorably compared with the one that Aḥmad Shawqī composed about the same event. One reason for this praise is that Ḥāfiz Ibrāhīm responded so quickly to the situation in verse; his poem appeared in July 1906. Moreover, he is lauded for the empathy which the poem showed towards the people of this village. "Ḥādithat Din-shawāy" (The Dinshaway Incident) addresses the British in a scornful and sarcastic tone, accusing them of valuing the life of the Egyptians no more than that of ordinary animals. Later in the same poem he asks whether they were seeking punishment or revenge and com-pares these ruthless killings to the Inquisition and the time of Nero. In another poem on the incident published in October the same year his description of the hanging and flogging is a moving account of the tragic situation. This poem clearly invokes the responsibility of the British Consul-General, Lord Cromer, for the incident. It is clearly this type of poem that attracted common people to Ḥāfiz Ibrāhīm's poetic output and vision. The publication of these poems earned him another appellation, one that rhymes in the original Arabic, "The nationalist poet and publicist of Dinshaway in the world" (shāʿir al-waṭaniyyah wa-mushahhir

Dinshawāy fī 'l-barriyyah). Some critics have pointed to these poems as part of what lead people throughout Egypt to regard the humiliation of the Dinshaway incident as a national issue and one which could rally the people of the nation together.

The events of Dinshaway had a major impact on British governance in Egypt, in particular, it certainly hastened Lord Cromer's resignation from his position as Consul-General of Egypt in 1907. That provided yet another occasion to be marked by many poets in verse. Ḥāfiz Ibrāhīm's long contribution to this corpus, "Widāʿ al-Lūrd Krūmir" (Farewell to Lord Cromer), is another of his better-known compositions which advances the kinds of criticisms upon which his reputation relies. The complexity of this farewell poem and the way in which Ḥāfiz Ibrāhīm addresses Cromer reveal particular and unusual elements con-cerning the poet's approach to such critiques, no matter what his reputation. The poem, for example, begins with praise of Cromer for what he has done for Egypt, citing his contributions to Egypt, partly through improving the lives of poor people. According to this poem, it is only Dinshaway and Cromer's cold response to it that prevents Egyptians from feeling great sadness at his departure. The poem then goes on to list in some detail the achievements of Cromer's policies—agricultural reforms, freedom of ex-pression, alleviation of poverty, for example— and some of their shortcomings—educational policy, hostility to Arabic, attacks on Islam and so on. At the end of the poem, Ḥāfiz Ibrāhīm professes his neutrality: he is after all a poet, not a politician. What is so interesting here is that to a certain extent there is something for everyone in this poem—both a critique of the British and praise of their accomplishments. To be sure, many of Ḥāfiz Ibrāhīm's other poems demonstrate a much more critical and intensely nationalistic response to the British. But this poem is indicative of a stance that he often adopted and that can be seen as a link to that of his liberal nationalist colleagues such as ʿAbduh. These Egyptian nationalists were often cautious and balanced in discussing and critiquing the British and were generally in favor of constructive engagement with them. This constitutes a partial response to critics who have expressed amazement that a nationalist poet like Ḥāfiz Ibrāhīm should never have been forced to leave Egypt, while others such as al-Bārūdī and Shawqī, who seemed less of revolutionary in their writings, spent several years in exile outside Egypt. In many poems, Ḥāfiz Ibrāhīm manages to couch his strident criticisms and reproaches within and in conjunction with more conciliatory verses. This becomes all the more relevant in his later poems—those composed after his period of unemployment ends and he becomes a government employee once again.

After eight lean years of unemployment, Ḥāfiz Ibrāhīm was awarded with a prestigious job as a civil servant in 1911. He was hired to be the head of the literary section of the Dār al-Kutub, the Egyptian National Library, a position befitting his status as one of Egypt's most important poets at the time. This office job seemed to suit his personal interests, and it finally brought him financial stability. In this later period of life, Ḥāfiz Ibrāhīm was known for frequenting local cafés and holding court in his office at Dār al-Kutub. He remained ever friendly and engaging and was known to maintain contacts with people from the wide variety of backgrounds and different lives that he had led. From his important government contacts and his aristocratic fellow poets to his less fortunate countrymen and friends from earlier times before his rise to fame, Ḥāfiz Ibrāhīm was reputed to be a charming and eloquent man with a wide circle of people around him.

There is a debate among critics over the poet's literary output in this period. Some claim that as his financial and material situation improved, his poetry suffered. They suggest that his poetic output slowed and his verse lost some of the flair for which he had become famous. They go on to point out that the tone of his poems becomes more restrained and cautious— with fewer powerful statements in verse decrying corruption in Egypt and the plight of the poor. The implication here is that, after being hired by the government and working for it, Ḥāfiz Ibrāhīm no longer felt such criticism to be

appropriate or necessary. Other critics disagree, pointing out that Ḥāfiz Ibrāhīm did continue to write poetry after this period; indeed some of his finest verse was composed while he was working at the library. It is important to recall again that, despite his nationalist reputation, Ḥāfiz Ibrāhīm did manage to write poetry throughout his career that was balanced; in some ways even his strongest critiques were often mediated by other more cautious statements. Moreover, at the beginning of this period, Ḥāfiz Ibrāhīm managed to publish three other non-poetic works, two of them in collaboration with his friend and colleague, the poet Khalīl Mutrān. His *Kutayyib fī 'l-tarbiyyah al-awwaliyyah* (A Little Book on Elementary Education) appeared in 1911-1912. His second "little book", this one on economics, appeared in 1913, *Kutayyib fī 'l-iqtisād* (A Little Book on Economics), as did his translation of Paul Leroy-Beaulieu's study of economics, which is listed as a co-translation with Mutrān, *al-Mūjaz fī 'l-iqtisād* (Excursions in the Study of Economics).

Whether or not it can be determined objectively that there was a decline in Ḥāfiz Ibrāhīm's poetry, some of his finest and best-known verse compositions did indeed appear after he was employed at the National Library. Perhaps the most important of these is his 1918 poem "al-'Umariyyah" (Poem for 'Umar). As the title indicates, this is a *madīh* (praise poem) written in honor of the second caliph 'Umar ibn al-Khattāb. The poem is extremely long. It is divided into sections and has both a panegyric and epic quality to it. Though it honors one of the important figures of early Islam, it would be misleading to classify this poem as one written out of piety. Though Ḥāfiz Ibrāhīm certainly would have identified himself as a Muslim, he was not known to be particularly pious; the poem is better understood as celebrating a central figure in Islamic history rather than as a devotional piece. It is also a particularly good example of Ḥāfiz Ibrāhīm's adherence to the standard and traditional neo-classical style. It begins with a standard *nasīb* or prelude, includes no innovations or deviations, and maintains its monorhyme on the syllable *-hā* throughout the entire poem.

The following year, 1919, witnessed a revolution in Egypt, and in that year too Ḥāfiz Ibrāhīm penned a number of interesting poems. They included another *madīḥ*, this time a poem in praise of his colleague Aḥmad Shawqī, "Tahiyyat Aḥmad Shawqī Bēğ" (A Salute to Aḥmad Shawqī Bēğ), written in honor of his colleague's return to Egypt from exile. After the revolution, he wrote a poem "Muẓāharat al-sayyidāt" (The Women's Demonstration) in which he celebrates the nationalist sentiments and actions of Egyptian women. The piece was first published in nationalist broadsheets; because of the political sensitivities of the era it only appeared in the mainstream press in 1929. The poem pokes fun at British soldiers for attacking a women's demonstration. In it, the poet encourages women to take part in such nationalist demonstrations— a theme which was to recur in other poems of the period. Indeed at this time he writes several poems to his friend and colleague, Qāsim Amīn, the well-known defender of the rights of women and author of books such as *Taḥrīr al-mar'ah* (The Liberation of Women, 1899).

Though not many details of Ḥāfiz Ibrāhīm's personal life appear in his biographies, one that is often mentioned is his first trip to Europe in 1923 when he spent three months in Northern Italy, Austria and Paris. A number of impressions are recorded in his poems; among other things it emerges that he visited Victor Hugo's home, Napoleon's grave, and climbed high into the Alps. In the poetry some of the most striking comments concern the different customs and traditions, as he perceived them, in the dress and behavior of European women in comparison with Egyptian women.

Ḥāfiz Ibrāhīm's literary relationship with Aḥmad Shawqī continued throughout his life. A further example of this is his long panegyric addressed to his fellow poet, "Tahni'āt Aḥmad Shawqī Bēğ" (Congratulations to Aḥmad Shawqī Bēğ). Ḥāfiz read this poem to the assembly gathered to honor Shawqī at the Cairo Opera, on 29 April 1927, when the title "Prince of Poets" was bestowed upon him. Ḥāfiz Ibrāhīm was one of many of the great poets of the era who composed poems on this occasion to be declaimed to the crowd. His contribution is a traditional *madīḥ* of over one hundred lines, rhyming on the consonant *'ayn*, which celebrates the achievements of his illustrious contemporary.

In the final years of his life and as his fame spread, Ḥāfiz Ibrāhīm was himself celebrated on a number of occasions. In response to invitations he used to travel abroad to read and present his poetry and listen to readings held in his honor. For example, he visited Damascus in 1928 to attend one such occasion, and in the following year made a summer trip to Beirut where he was feted at the American University of Beirut, followed by yet another visit to Damascus. On these occasions he recited his long poem in praise of the region, "Tahiyyat al-Shām" (A Salute to Syria, 1929). His connections to Syria and Lebanon were strong, and he maintained close contacts with a number of Syrian and Lebanese poets, writing about the connections between Egypt and these two countries on a number of occasions.

Early in 1932, four years after these travels and celebrations, Ḥāfiz Ibrāhīm retired from his post at Dār al-Kutub which at that point he had held for a little more than twenty years. Just four months later in June of the same year, he died at his modest home in the suburbs of Cairo.

Just as their poetic careers were linked in life, Ḥāfiz Ibrāhīm and Aḥmad Shawqī are also remembered together in their death. The two men passed away within several months of each other in 1932, prompting many expressions of grief that bemoaned the loss of two such great poets and important Egyptian literary figures in such a short space of time. Seventy years later, in 2003, Cairo's *al-Ahrām* (The Pyramids) newspaper ran an article commemorating this loss with the title "The Summer the Poets Departed." The newspaper recalled the memories of both men for their illustrious poetic careers and devoted space to their obituaries and a commemoration of their poetic contributions. In both these commemorations, those of 1932 and of the memorial review in 2003, Shawqī was celebrated more lavishly and in greater detail than Ḥāfiz Ibrāhīm, all in accordance with the greater acclaim that the former poet had generally received. Even so, a good deal of attention was also devoted to the role and status of Hāfiz Ibrāhīm. Even many years after their deaths the names of the two poets remain as a linked pair in the history of modern Arabic poetry.

In 1937, five years after Hāfiz Ibrāhīm's death, a posthumous collection of his complete poetry was published, consisting of two volumes. This hefty publication attests to the range of poems Hāfiz Ibrāhīm produced during his long career. From his poems to friends, colleagues and important figures, to wine poems, to political and social commentary to elegies, the breadth and depth of the author's poetic output is striking. Although clearly influenced by the tradition of classical Arabic poetry and not a great innovator in form, Hāfiz Ibrāhīm nonetheless helped to spearhead a neo-classical movement which was to play such an important role in breathing new life into Arabic poetry. His collection demonstrates what has come to symbolize the traditional school of neo-classical poetry. Of course, the collection also shows that, though strongly influenced by the classics, Hāfiz Ibrāhīm had a strong interest in content as well as form. His commitment to addressing social and political issues through his poetry, shines through in these poems, at times directly as in his poem about the Dinshaway incident, and at times ironically or allegorically, as in the poem he wrote to his suit.

The importance and influential role of the "Poet of the Nile" is thus due in no small part to the fact that he wrote about the concerns of ordinary Egyptians in a form and language that paid homage to the great tradition of classical Arabic poetry. His mastery of the techniques of classical poetry and the beauty of his verse according to these standards conveyed a genuine concern with real problems and issues of common people in Egypt. His relationship and association with the great neo-classical poet of his day, Ahmad Shawqī, is part of what contributed to his fame. Shawqī was the Poet of the Princes before becoming the Prince of Poets;

Hāfiz Ibrāhīm was and still is seen as the Poet of the People. This contrast serves to remind people how Hāfiz Ibrāhīm overcame his less than aristocratic background, how he had to work to support himself and how in spite of all the odds he became a great poet and national icon. His interest in the issues of the people and his embrace of national aspirations are taken to be more genuine than those of other poets. Though he himself was as concerned with the form, sound, resonance and effect of his poetry as with its content, it is fair to say that Hāfiz Ibrāhīm has remained so beloved until today because of the way he embraced the concerns and plights of the Egyptian people.

REFERENCES

A. J. Arberry, "Hāfiz Ibrāhīm and Shauqi", *Journal of the Royal Asiatic Society* 1937: 42-58;

Jan Brugman, *An Introduction to the History of Modern Arabic Literature in Egypt* (Leiden: E. J. Brill, 1984), 45-51;

H. A. R. Gibb, "Studies in Contemporary Arabic Literature", *Bulletin of the School of Oriental Studies* 7.1 (1933): 1-22;

Salma Khadra Jayyusi, *Trends and Movements in Contemporary Arabic Poetry* (Leiden: E. J. Brill, 1977);

Mounah A. Khouri, *Poetry and the Making of Modern Egypt* (Leiden: E. J. Brill, 1971);

Umberto Rizzitano, "Hāfiz Ibrāhīm", *Encyclopedia of Islam*, 2nd ed. (Leiden: E. J. Brill, 1954-2005);

Paul Starkey, "Ibrāhīm, (Muhammad) Hāfiz", in: *Encyclopedia of Arabic Literature*, ed. J. S. Meisami and P. Starkey, 2 vols. (London & New York: Routledge, 1988), 386;

Abdus Subhan, "Muhammad Hāfiz Ibrāhīm Bek: The Poet of the Nile Valley", *Islamic Literature* 1955: 621-62.

Shakīb al-Jābirī
(1912 –)

WALID HAMARNEH
Swarthmore College

WORKS

Novels

Naham ("Gluttony", Damascus, 1937);
Qadar yalhū ("Destiny's Play", Damascus, 1939; repr. Damascus: Dār al-Yaqzah al-'Arabiyyah 1947?); revised ed. with the title *Qadar yalhū: siyāghah jadīdah* (Beirut: Dār al-Nahā, 1980; repr. Damascus: Dār Tlās, 1988);
Qaws quzah ("Rainbow", Damascus: Dār al-Yaqazah al-'Arabiyyah, 1946);
Wadā'an yā Afāmiyā ("Goodbye, Apamia", Damascus: Dār al-Hilāl, 1960; repr. Damascus: Dār Tlās, 1988).

Other Works

Ta'thīr al-uzūn fī mushtaqqāt al-bitrūl ("The Effect of Ozone on Petroleum Derivatives", Damascus, n.d.);
Al-Jiyūlūjiyyah ("Geology", Damascus, n.d.);
Jābir ibn Hayyān ("Jabir ibn Hayyan", Damascus, n.d.).

Al-Jābirī was born into one of the richest aristocratic families of Aleppo in Northern Syria in the year 1912. His father, Murād, divorced his mother the day he was born which resulted in some childhood suffering. He was sent to private schools in 'Ālayh and Beirut in what is today Lebanon but was then still a part of Syria under French mandate. He went to Geneva to study chemical engineering and continued his post-graduate studies in Berlin where he received his Ph.D. While in Europe he also worked for the League of Nations. Upon returning to Syria in 1943 he became the Director General of Information and Publishing for the new independent government, and in 1945 Director General for Metallurgy, a post in which he was also responsible for supervising indigenous industries as well as foreign companies that were looking for ores and oil in Syria. During that period he was also active in Syria's cultural and literary life, founding a periodical, *'Ālamān* (Two Worlds), then another, *Asdā'* (Echoes). In 1952 he was appointed ambassador to Iran with the rank of minister; upon his return to Syria in 1955 he was appointed Director of the Glass industry. He held other positions in Syria and other Arab countries, but was also involved in the cultural sphere as the head of the Syrian Society for the Arts and the Arab Writers Union. Following his retirement in 1963 he moved to Beirut, but still spends his summers in Blūdān in Syria where he has been active in preserving the natural beauty of the place and the environment.

Although al-Jābirī had studied chemical engineering, he was very much engaged in politics during his period of study in central Europe. Being from a family that gave Syria a number of its political leaders, he aspired to become a major political influence in his country upon his return. However, while in Switzerland and Germany, he was exposed more to German culture and literature rather than the French cultural tradition which he had mostly encountered as a student in Syria. German classical writers, especially Goethe, were to have a lasting influence on him; it was also through Goethe's prism that al-Jābirī's literary and artistic conceptions were formed, to the extent that his reception of even some of the classics of English literature such as Shakespeare was mediated through Goethe's interpretation.

He published his first novel *Naham* in 1937 and followed it with three others, the last of which was published in 1961. He also wrote and published a few short stories in periodicals, but did not collect them. As a chemical engineer, he also published scientific books.

Historians of Arabic literature in Syria tend to agree that the novels of al-Jābirī are the earliest manifestations of the modern artistic novel in that country. It may be no coincidence that the publication of his first novel, *Naham*, in 1937, coincided with the formation of the modern state of Syria. Throughout its long history, Syria had been either a part of a larger political entity or was itself divided into smaller units. After four centuries as part of the Ottoman Empire and following a short period of independence under King Faisal, Syria was occupied by the French. In 1936 the French divided their mandate into what are now known as the two states of Syria and Lebanon.

If *Naham* (Gluttony) is analyzed for its subject matter and themes, it has very little to do with either Syria or the Arab World. Only two aspects connect it to the region: it was written in Arabic; and its protagonist (though Western) is somewhat similar to the kind of character that will become the typical protagonist of some of al-Jābirī's later novels.

The central character in *Naham* is a certain Ivan Kozarov, about whom we learn a good deal by way of letters sent by no less than seven women who have had a variety of relationships with him. The first letter comes from Evelyn, a nun who hates him because he had an affair with her, then left; second is Gretel, who, while still a virgin, would love to give him her body and remain his forever, but who is still conflicted between the demands of heart and mind; third is Herta, who reminds him that he had promised to visit her and her family in the hope of establishing a more formal relationship with him; fourth is a seventeen year-old girl, unnamed, who admires Ivan as a writer, especially his last novel and its chapter on jealousy; a fifth letter comes from Dorothea, who regrets her sexual relationship with him since it has been reduced to something merely physical with no spiritual dimensions; sixth is Hildegard, who challenges him with the information that she has fallen in love with another man and demanding that he stop contacting her; seventh and last comes Alice, who, watching him develop a relationship with another

woman, acknowledges deceiving him and thereby taking her own revenge.

This information provided, the plot moves on to a masked ball. There a young man named Pietro Dakovich flirts with the host, Hildegard; after dancing and playing the piano he steals a kiss from her. No sooner have they separated than she discovers that the supposed Pietro is none other than Ivan. She first sends him a furious letter, but then follows it with another in which she apologizes for the cruel language she has used. She reminds him that the fault is his, not hers.

The final chapter transports us from Germany to the Spanish civil war where Ivan is now a barely recognizable figure fighting on the republican side. He meets Alice again; even though she recognizes him, he insists that he is Pietro Dakovich.

From this brief summary of the novel it is clear that the structure is not based on plot but rather on a single male character, a kind of romantic hero surrounded by women who are linked with him in different ways. And yet the character of Ivan remains unconvincing and sometimes even shallow; while he is cultured and able to mingle seamlessly with the upper classes of German society, his name strongly suggests that he is a white Russian, something that makes it difficult to believe that he would side with the republicans in Spain. But, in spite of weaknesses in plot structure and characterization, the novel is carefully composed from a linguistic perspective. It has a highly elevated style, with lots of references to motifs in European literature, a feature that is further emphasized by the novel's epigraph taken from Goethe, namely that the "eternal feminine" attracts us. It is the exaggerated craving for that ideal that provides the causality for Ivan's motivations. Since sexuality is such an important aspect of the relationships in the novel, psycho-analytical references abound. However, they are not in themselves capable of accounting for Ivan's character-traits; rather they seem to reflect the anarchic and rebellious romantic spirit to be found in many European works that may have served as models. Yet, what weakens the effect in this novel is that it is derived from an early nineteenth century romanticism that is transposed on to Germany of the inter-war period where it no longer existed. However, despite the stark contradiction between the romanticized idealization of Ivan and attempts at a deep psychological characterization of his character, the novel has many strengths when compared with other examples of the genre being written by contemporaries in the Arab world, especially in its more structured attempts at characterization.

Naham came as a surprise to many readers in the Arab world because of its openly physical themes and its language. But probably more interesting was the challenge that it posed to previous attempts at novel writing in Arabic. Despite its many shortcomings, it nevertheless presented the most extreme example yet in Arabic fiction of the ideology of the modern autonomous individual. In that sense it is extremely modern and revolutionary, in that it constructs an autonomous individual who functions as the centre of its fictional world, someone who is (and this is what is most significant) conscious of his own subjectivity and centrality within the world in which he is he living. It is that feature that imbues him with an agency unheard of at this stage in the development of modern Arabic fiction.

Al-Jābirī's next two novels, *Qadar yalhū* (Destiny's Play, 1939) and *Qaws quzaḥ* (Rainbow, 1946), are linked in terms of both plot and character. *Qadar yalhū* tells the story of 'Alā', a Damascene student in Berlin, who, having met a girl (Else) on the street at night, realizes that she is in distress, invites her to his place and lets her stay with him. It emerges that she has left her widowed father's home because of problems with her step-mother. Berlin has not been kind to her, and she has used up all the money she had taken from her father; penniless and homeless, she has been sleeping in public parks and is starving. 'Alā' embarks on an affair with her and offers her help; she in turn tries to convince him to change his ways, but to no avail. He loves women, life, dancing, music and fun, while she is mostly depressed and morose. She falls in love with this young Syrian man who is being so kind to her, but for

him she is just a passing fancy. She becomes pregnant but keeps the news to herself; while still in love with him, she is well aware that for him their relationship is simply one among many. Once he has completed his studies and is about to take the train back to Syria, a friend hands him a letter from Else in which she tells him that she is pregnant. She promises to take care of their child and to instill in him a pride in his father and his father's tradition, religion, and culture. While in Europe, 'Alā' has always felt an enormous nostalgia for his homeland, but once he is back he finds that he cannot cope with his changed circumstances, terming himself an outcast from two civilizations.

At this point the novel jumps in both time and place. It is twelve years later, and 'Alā' is in Beirut. A friend of his is a habitué of the city's nightclubs where he regularly consorts with the women who work there. He convinces 'Alā' to accompany him to one of these nightclubs where he has become infatuated with a German woman; he wants 'Alā' to translate for him. When they meet the woman (named Else), she is immediately attracted to 'Alā' and completely ignores his friend. Such unusual behavior on the part of a woman working in these establishments, coupled with her name, seems enough to provoke suspicions, and yet 'Alā' seems completely oblivious. However, after a while the woman confesses to 'Alā' that she is indeed his Else. In a gesture so characteristic of romantic novels she tells him that she is dying from tuberculosis and that his son (whom she had named Muhammad 'Alī) also died of the disease as a child. She gives him a wooden box containing her journals and what remains of his son's possessions. Pursuing the same romantic mode to its conclusion, she does indeed die. As her funeral procession makes its silent way to her grave, the wind is howling, the skies are cloudy, and rain is falling in torrents.

Else thus emerges as a typical romantic character—frail, loving and decent, and yet characteristically tragic, but 'Alā' may also qualify as one, although the novel's ending does not reflect that of a romantic hero. His character is more plausible than Ivan, but it still suffers from many weaknesses. 'Alā' informs us that, as a 23 year-old man, he is extremely emotional, filled with that sickness that Western writers had written about a great deal, what he terms the sickness of the times. He can also be viewed as a typical Don Juan figure, a man for whom women easily fall but who is never satisfied with a single relationship. But 'Alā' is a more credible character than *Naham*'s Ivan, since some of these same characteristics can be justified through the lack of love and habitual solitude he suffered as a child deprived of his father's love. When these features are added to the effects of culture-shock in the Western context, his character-traits seem more easily justified.

The character of 'Alā' resembles many protagonists in early Arabic novels, traveling to the West and being strongly affected by the experience, one that engenders infinite contradictions. This theme will remain central to many fictional works in the Arab world.

With regard to 'Alā' what is significant is that, despite his great love for his own culture and religion, he also greatly admires European values, although he seems for the most part to be completely detached from the actualities of the relationship between his homeland and the West. At the symbolic level, the novel inverts those actualities; whereas Syria as a colony was actually the weaker partner, the relationships with Else and the other German women manage to portray 'Alā' as the stronger party, whereas Else herself is depicted as weak and romantic. One might perhaps interpret this inversion of the actual power relationship at a symbolic level by suggesting that the two characters represent al-Jābirī's personal view of their respective cultures, one in which the East (in this case Arab culture) is superior to that of the West (which is seen as moribund).

The second of these novels, *Qaws quzah*, narrates the same story of 'Alā' and Else, but from the latter's perspective; additional information is provided to clarify what we have already learned from *Qadar yalhū*. After meeting him on that fateful night, falling in love, and getting pregnant, she leaves him but arranges things so that their meetings seem coincidental. Following his departure, she works

for a well-to-do Austrian family who have been negatively impacted by the Anschluss (the unification of Austria with Hitler's Germany). They let Else and her son, Muhammad 'Alī, live in a small place in the countryside; the boy is brought up by his mother to love Islam and the Arabs (a section that is full of affectation and rather unconvincing). When Else is forced to leave to Berlin, her son suffers a lot, contracts tuberculosis (mostly due to malnutrition), and dies. She decides to return to her family in Hamburg, only to find that her father has migrated to the United States. Else meets an old childhood friend who works as a dancer in a nightclub; she convinces Else to do the same, and thus she ends up in Beirut. The third part of the novel narrates her encounter with 'Alā' in the Beirut nightclub; how she lets him know who she is, that she is sick and dying, and that their son is also dead.

This novel conveys much the same mood as its sister novel, *Qadar yalhū*. Indeed, as a kind of addendum, it is clearly replete with attempts to rationalize many aspects of *Qadar yalhū* that remain ambiguous—a goal in which it is not particularly successful (even if we bear in mind that the author is rewriting the text many years later). While Else describes how she becomes attached to 'Alā' and the kind of love she feels for him, she loses her own personality almost completely, becoming even more nationalistic (Arab) than 'Alā' himself. But in a kind of corrective gesture she regrets having experienced the realities of the East's poverty and affectation, whereas she would have preferred to preserve the imaginary East that 'Alā' had described to her, one where materiality is looked down upon and moral values and spirituality reign supreme.

In these two novels we clearly see the writer developing a better technique and language than is evident in *Naham*. Despite the contradictions between romantic and idealized themes on the one hand and realistic ones on the other, the two novels are more successful in their characterization. Even so, there remain two fundamental aspects that weaken them: the adoption of ideological stances that are not congruent with the characters themselves, especially the many rhetorical encomia of the East; secondly, the author's failure to utilize the many contradictions and tensions involving characters and their social contexts as devices for the further development of both character and plot.

Al-Jābirī's final novel, *Wadāʿ an yā Afāmiyā* (Goodbye, Apamia, 1960), published almost 14 years after *Qaws quzah*, was originally hailed by critics as a great innovation in the Syrian and Arabic novel, but such initial enthusiasm has subsequently subsided somewhat. Even so, it is a finer artistic achievement than the author's other works and stands out as his most technically developed novel; indeed it differs from the majority of Arabic novels published during the two decades following WW II, most of which were written in a realistic or naturalistic paradigm, including the early works of Mahfūz such as the renowned *Trilogy* (1956-7). Since discourse is one of its central features rather than story (the mode of exposition rather than the plot), we will provide a summary that adheres as closely as possible to the mode of exposition in the novel itself, thus also affording some insights into its structure.

The opening pages of "Goodbye, Apamia" present the main characters and their relationships in the manner of dramatis personae in drama. The narrator then informs his readers that they need to be familiar with Apamia, the location where the action is to take place. A detailed historical description now follows, tracing its long history from Greek to Arab times and emphasizing its beauty. The description closes with a sentence foreshadowing the overall romantic and pessimistic atmosphere of the novel; misery, it says, is the ultimate fate and things always end in tears.

The scene now shifts to the ruins of Apamia where a group of peasants sit waiting for the return of a Belgian archaeological expedition that is to continue its excavations after a year's gap. Two women peasants are foregrounded: Nujūd, a symbol of purity, and Nadā, who symbolizes egotism. Once the expedition has arrived, we learn that Alberto Scarpa, the Italian painter, is emotionally and spiritually attached to Nujūd, even though he has already

had an affair with Nadā. We also discover that everyone on the expedition admires Nujūd, but especially its leader, Mayanas. Each member of the expedition is now described, including Lacoste, an architect who no longer believes in anything; and Mayanas, who is infatuated with Apamia as place and wishes to replicate it in Brussels.

Nujūd's father is also introduced, and no opportunity is lost to describe Nujūd's purity and beauty, and to juxtapose the almost sacrosanct nature of rural and Bedouin life with the corrupt but seemingly civilized Europe.

The plot develops with Nujūd's father marrying Nadā and the departure of the entire expedition for the winter, leaving behind Scarpa who is eager to paint more pictures of Apamia. Although Nadā tries to rekindle her previous relationship with him, he rejects her; the more she presses him, the less he wants her and the more he wants Nujūd.

With chapter eleven we reach a central point in the conflict between the contrasting values represented by Nadā and Nujūd. While the entire village is attending a wedding celebration, Nadā sneaks into Scarpa's lodging and notices a painting of a native girl whom she immediately recognizes as Nujūd. Hearing Nujūd approach, she quickly hides in the kitchen. Nujūd loves the painting and kisses it, thus arousing Scarpa who tries to kiss her. When she resists violently, he becomes even more aggressive, but at this point Nadā appears. In spite of Nujūd's pleas she rushes to the village to announce to everyone that Scarpa and Nujūd are having an affair. In spite of her innocence Nujūd now feels that her honor has been forever tarnished, and runs away into the woods where she is attacked by a wild animal. Thereafter she makes her way to the closest city, the seaside town of Latakia, providing yet another opportunity for description of the mountains and woods of the region.

The description of her trip through the woods is juxtaposed with another situated in Latakia where a group of affluent urban characters are celebrating in the city's Casino. They include a poet (Nawfal Ilyās), a political leader (Saʿd), Muhammad Dīb, and the beautiful

Helena, with whom Sa'd is flirting. These shifts in scene provide the reader with a vivid contrast between nature and affluent culture, something that is emphasized by the description of the casino and its complete detachment from its surroundings. Once Sa'd returns to his cottage in the woods, he discovers Nujūd bleeding in front of the door, takes her inside and tends to her wounds. As they begin to heal, he falls in love with her. She also is in love with him and expresses her affection by serving him as best she can, remaining with him even when his other friends leave because he refuses to join their plans to cheat in the process of prospecting for ores. One day he sees her bathing in the stream, but manages to restrain his emotions, but, when he spots her again on her way back to the cottage, his passions are again aroused. She too seems willing to give way to such emotions, but then all of a sudden his ethical self intervenes to prevent him from acting. Nujūd's reacts in shame and runs off into the woods. Chasing after her, he professes his genuine love, but to no avail. This separation has an even more ironic twist, in that the reader now learns that Sa'd has already asked a religious shaykh to come to his house on that very day to marry them. Finally he has to acknowledge that destiny is too strong; now he will never be able to win back the "bearer of his children."

The novel's basic structure is clearly dramatic, but not in the Aristotelian sense so much as the Shakespearean. It possesses what critics since the romantics have termed Shakespearean irony, implying an interplay between parallelism and antithesis, similarities and contrasts, especially through direct juxtaposition within the work. Among al-Jābirī's techniques we would list: the scenic structure and division of the narrative, much influenced by the cinema; an emphasis on dualities and their juxtaposition, to the extent of exaggerating such oppositions in the presentation of characters; and the use of space montage as a way of heightening

suspense as well as achieving ironic effects. At the time of publication these more developed techniques were new for the Arabic novel, but beyond that al-Jābirī uses them to good effect.

While in his earlier works al-Jābirī may have failed to resolve basic contradictions, specifically those between the ideology of romantic idealization and the urge to be realistic and credible, in *Wadā'an yā Afāmiyā* he is more successful in functionalizing those contradictions, using them as a means of developing the novel's plot and action. Despite some weaknesses, from the perspective of both structure and technique it was the most interesting novel written in Syria up to that time.

Al-Jābirī thus emerges as the most prominent pioneer figure in the long process of development of a tradition of modern Arabic fiction in Syria. As is the case with his analogues in other regions of the Arabic-speaking world, the difficulties encountered in the process of introducing a complex fictional genre to a new cultural context are evident in his works, but the changes and developments in his fictional technique are equally evident. He was a pioneer who laid the groundwork on which future generations of Syrian writers have been able to build.

REFERENCES

Eros Baldissera, "Šakīb al-Jābirī, pioniere del romanzo siriano", *Quaderni di Studi Arabi* 4 (1986): 117-128;
——, "Syrian Narrative and the Topic of Sex: Šakīb al-Ğābirī and Muḥammad al-Naǧǧār via Zakariyyā Tāmir", *Quaderni di Studi Arabi* 10 (1992 [publ. 1993]): 99-108.
Encyclopedia of Arabic Literature, ed. Julie S. Meisami and Paul Starkey, 2 vols. (London: Routledge, 1998), I, 404-5.
Ibrāhīm al-Sa'āfīn, *Tatawwur al-riwāyah al-'arabiyyah al-hadīthah fī bilād al-Shām* (Baghdad: Wizārat al-Thaqāfah wa'l-I'lām, 1980).

Muhammad Mahdī al-Jawāhirī

(1901 – 1997)

MUHSIN AL-MUSAWI

Columbia University

WORKS

Halbat al-adab ("The Literary Domain", Baghdad: Matba'at Dār al-Salām, 1921);

Bayna al-shu'ūr wa'l-'ātifah ("Between Feeling and Passion", Baghdad: n. p., 1928);

Barīd al-ghurbah ("Mail from Exile", n. p.: n. p., 1965);

Barīd al-'awdah ("Mail of Homecoming", n. p.: n. p., 1968);

Ayyuhā al-araq ("Oh Insomnia", Baghdad: Mudīriyyat al-Thaqāfah al-'Āmmah 1971);

Khaljāt ("Sentiments", Baghdad: Mudīriyyat al-Thaqāfah al-'Āmmah 1971);

Dhikrayātī ("My Memoirs"), 2 vols. (Damascus: Dār al-Rāfidayn, 1988).

Collected Poetry

Dīwān al-Jawāhirī, ed. 'Alī Jawād al-Tāhir, Ibrāhīm al-Sāmarrā'ī, Mahdī al-Makhzūmī, and Majīd Biktāsh, 7 vols. (vols. 1-6: Baghdad: Matba'at al-Adīb, 1973-1977; vol. 7: Baghdad: Dār-al-Rashīd, 1980; whole edition repr. London: n.p., 2000); ed. 'Adnān Darwīsh, 5 vols. (Damascus: Ministry of Culture and National Information, 1979-1984); 4 vols. (Beirut: Dār al-'Awdah, 1982); ed. Yūsuf Hādī, 5 vols. (Beirut: Bīsān, 2000).

Works in Translation

"Come down, darkness," translated by Christopher Tingley, and "Lullaby for the Hungry", translated by Issa J. Boullata, in: *Modern Arabic Poetry: An Anthology*, ed. Salma Kh. Jayyusi (New York: Columbia University Press, 1987), 79-81;

"A Lullaby for the Hungry," translated by Terri DeYoung, in: *Iraqi Poetry Today*, ed. Daniel Weissbort and Saadi A Simawe (London: King's College, University of London, 2003), 94-99.

The renowned Iraqi poet Muhammad Mahdī al-Jawāhirī was born in 1901 in the holy city of Najaf in Iraq (the site of the shrine of Imam 'Alī ibn Abī Tālib, the cousin of the prophet Muhammad). As one of the greatest neo-classical poets in the Arab world, al-Jawāhirī has drawn wide recognition, but his output and life record remain controversial. He himself used to complicate things by providing several versions of the same story, beginning with his date of birth: 1901 to the committee formed by the Iraqi Ministry of Information in 1969-1970 to supervise, edit, and publish his poetry; 1900 in an earlier submission to the same committee; 1898 according to a biographer, Ja'far Bāqir Mahbūbah (1955); a specific date, 26 July 1899, will also be encountered. This propensity for skipping or altering details can be offset by the record of his publications which serve as correctives to many other versions.

Al-Jawāhirī is acclaimed by critics and scholars such as Jabrā Ibrāhīm Jabrā (quoted by Altoma 1979, iv), as the poet who is closest to the Iraqi conscience. Jabrā also speaks of his poetry as

part of the emotional, intellectual and political experience of the entire people, even though the attitude of individuals toward the poet may vary.

As part of a memorial commentary included in the special issue of the Syrian-Iraqi quarterly *al-Madā* (1998), the Palestinian poet Mahmūd Darwīsh suggested that al-Jawāhirī is the most important classical Arab poet in the 20th century. This critique places the poet and his poetry in an adequate frame of reference in both biographical and literary terms.

Muhammad Mahdī al-Jawāhirī's career as poet is well-documented both in his own poetry and in the records of friends and opponents. His poetry was collected, at times with annotation, in

Dīwān al-Jawāhirī (7 vols.), published by the Ministry of Information in Iraq. This definitive edition was supervised by a committee consisting of three prominent professors: 'Alī Jawād al-Tāhir, Ibrāhīm al-Sāmarrā'ī, and the linguist and grammarian Mahdī al-Makhzūmī, assisted by Majīd Biktāsh. In the Syrian edition, 'Adnān Darwīsh included the rest of the poet's quartets, along with appendices and indices, a fifth volume. In 1988, al-Jawāhirī published his memoirs, *Dhikrayātī*, in two volumes (Damascus: Dār al-Rāfidayn).

The early life of the poet is solely connected with Najaf, a city of great literary and cultural reputation, where *majālis* (assemblies) were renowned for their literary and political discussions; they were attended by many of the most illustrious names in literature, not only in Iraq but also in the Middle East as a whole. No less influential was al-Jawāhirī's own family, with its famous poets and scholars, especially his grandfather, Shaykh Muhammad Hasan al-Jawhar, the author of *Jawāhir al-kalām fī sharh sharā'i' al-islām* (The Jewels of Speech in Explicating Islamic Laws). In those times the family name was Āl-Jawhar. The poet's uncle, Shaykh Jawād, also had an abiding influence on his growth and initial emergence, first in Najaf, then in Baghdad of the 1920s.

Al-Jawāhirī's development as a poet and his intellectual journey can be followed through reference firstly to his early upbringing, followed by his move to Baghdad, especially after the emergence of national rule in 1921; then to his participation in the *Wathbah* (literally: leap) or popular uprising, 5-27 January 1948, the most explosive event to follow the 1920 popular revolt against the British; and lastly his lengthy period of exile, 1961-1997, interspersed with brief homecomings (the longest of which saw him return to Baghdad from 1969 till 1976). A different way of considering his literary biography is through the thematic patterns that permeate his poetry and poetics throughout his career and that are closely linked to his own life-circumstances. While his personal history and the history of Iraq and, to some extent, of the Middle East region at large, colored and shaped his vision and vocation as poet and public figure,

they need to be viewed in conjunction with his many other concerns; they include his ideas about poetry, his views of East and West, his national poetics, orations on solidarity, exile and alienation, others on love and blame, elegies, celebrations of nature, defense of women's rights, and friendly tributes. Every theme shows a personal touch and relates to his vocation as public intellectual, for even his ideas on poetry draw on the Arabic tradition of *mu'āradah* (contrafactions), the process whereby a poet would endeavor to invoke and outdo the poetry of strong precursors and contemporaries.

The poet's childhood was a varied one. His family sent him to religious schools in Najaf, as was the tradition until very recently. His father believed that every day his son should memorize an oration from *Nahj al-balāghah* (The Path of Rhetoric) by Imam 'Alī Ibn Abī Tālib (d. 661), a poem by Abū 'l-Tayyib al-Mutanabbī (d. 968), along with foundational texts in Qur'ānic studies, philology, and grammar. Having passed a rigorous daily test, he was allowed to join his father at the evening sessions where literary and philological topics were discussed. At this early stage he displayed an inclination towards literature, reading the works of al-Jāhiz (d. 868/9), Ibn Khaldūn's (d. 1406) *Muqaddimah* (Prolegomena), and poetry collections. He also showed a prodigious memory; on one occasion he was able to recite a poem of 450 lines after being absent from the session for eight hours. His father was keen for him to specialize in science, but that wish was not fulfilled. After his father's death in 1917, the son began to read even more in the fields of rhetoric, logic, and philosophy.

In 1920 he participated as a poet in the uprising against the British occupation, although his first published poems only appeared in 1921. In his collected poetry of that year, one poem, "Munā shā'ir" (A Poet's Hope, *'Irāq* daily, no. 367, 8 August 1921, reprinted in the Baghdad ed., I, 117-18), shows an early awareness of his vocation as a poet with strong national and personal leanings, someone committed to both his nation and his personal aspirations. In another poem, "al-Thawrah al-'irāqiyyah" (The Iraqi Revolution; Baghdad ed., I, 491-92), he invokes a strong polemic that was to dominate his poetry ever after. In this poem he sees Iraq as inevitably free from domination, noting that in Egypt and India signs of liberation and national awareness were already visible. Here al-Jawāhirī is looking at the Middle East as a set of nations in turmoil, yet with strong prospects of revolution and change. Other issues proved no less engaging, in that in 1929 he dedicated a poem to Palestine, "Filastīn al-dāmiyah" (Bleeding Palestine), and wrote many other poems on national, Arab, and international issues. He dedicated other poems to the renowned Egyptian poets, **Shawqī** and Hāfiz **Ibrāhīm** ("Shawqī wa-Hāfiz," *al-Najaf* daily, no. 29, 2 January 1926). In this poem he allies himself with these two great neo-classical poets, for, as he puts it,

Oh, Shawqī and Hāfiz, none but you can feel the pulse of verse, and none other can preserve it.
(Baghdad ed., I, 301-02).

Promised the post of secondary-school teacher in Baghdad, he moved there in 1927. He was disappointed when, in spite of the promise made by the Minister of Education, Sayyid 'Abd al-Mahdī al-Muntafjī (a tribal shaykh and descendant of the Prophet's family), his appointment was changed by the King's powerful advisor, Sāti' al-Husrī, to a primary school in the Kāzimiyyah district of Baghdad. Upon the request of the Minister of Education, the King put al-Jawāhirī in charge of chancery and reception at the palace, an honorary gesture intended to counteract the decision of Sāti' al-Husrī who seemed determined to humiliate al-Jawāhirī because of his alleged Iranian origins. Al-Jawāhirī kept his post at the palace until 1930.

This incident seems to have been part of an ongoing feud between the poet and Sāti' al-Husrī, who, apparently unfamiliar with Iraqi politics, sentiments, religions, and sects, thought that al-Jawāhirī's identity card, with its declared Iranian affiliation, was accurate, whereas it was in fact a gesture of sectarian opposition to the Ottomans. Thus when Syrian teachers were fired from their jobs in spite of demonstrations by both Shī'ite and Sunni students against the decision and sent back to Syria, al-Jawāhirī viewed the decision as a blow to al-Husrī. He composed a poem, "Tahiyyat al-wazīr" (Greet-

ings to the Minister, 1927; Baghdad ed., I, 389-90), in which he congratulated 'Abd al-Mahdī, the minister involved in the dismissal. Even this poem finds a precedent in 1926. The poet had been spending the summer in Iran and enjoyed himself so much that he published a poem, "Barīd al-ghurbah" (A Letter of Homesickness, published in *al-Fayhā'* daily, no. 10, 31 March 1927; Baghdad ed., I, 357-58).

This latter poem was to remain close to his heart since its aftermath proved to be a major turning-point in his life, one from which he never recovered; the same was the case with his adversary, Sāti' al-Husrī. Al-Jawāhirī re-published the poem in his own newspaper *al-Furāt* (no. 19, 2 June 1930), along with a foreword in which he says:

To you, Ministry of Education, who trace the mote or speck in the eyes of some, while being blind to the thorn in the eyes of others; to you, a Ministry that is so sluggish.
(Baghdad ed., II, 357).

The director, Sāti' al-Husrī, read the poem as being xenophobic, an elevation of Persia and its people at the expense of the Arabs. As a consequence, he decided to fire the poet from his position. The particular lines that angered him run as follows:

It is 'Persia', its wind is a north-west breeze, and its sky is a canopy of branches and leaves;
Its lovers are infatuated, and infatuation is heartbreaking for being so.

He adds:

In Iraq, I have a clique, without whom Iraq cannot be so loved,
Without them the Tigris, though sweet, matters not, nor is the Euphrates worth tasting.
(*Dīwān*, Baghdad ed., I [1972], 359-60).

Sāti' al-Husrī was not a littérateur, but an educator and an ideologue. His own interpretation of the poem (included in his memoirs) insisted on confusing a sense of joy and rapture with racial and religious affiliation. The Minister of Education, obviously aided by the poet himself, tried to explain the metaphorical implications of the poem, but Sāti' al-Husrī persisted in his rejection of such a reading, in that, for him at least, the poem only managed to underline his belief that the poet was of Iranian descent and unfit for teaching in Iraq. The poet tried many times to argue against this attitude, pointing out to the director the requirements of Iraqi identity-registration under the Ottomans. He even drew a comparison with the Arab teachers who were hired to teach in Iraq. "But they are Arabs," was Sāti' al-Husrī's answer, as he himself notes in his memoirs (*Mudhakkirātī*, I, 588-599).

This particular event was to become central to al-Jawāhirī's life, and he returned to it on a number of occasions. In a chapter included in his memoirs he collaborated with the Iraqi exile Hādī al-'Alawī, in examining and denouncing Sāti' al-Husrī's position. When his Syrian nationalist and intellectual friends chided him for it, he claimed the chapter had been written solely by Hādī al-'Alawī, a claim denied by the latter (*al-Madā*, 21). However, the rift between these two men, the poet and the formidable educator and nationalist ideologue, has deeper roots that are based on the poet's view of his own upbringing, status, and career, and his sense of being the inheritor of a great Arab poetic tradition, one with which cultural borrowings from Europe were unable to come to terms. This facet of his poetic persona shows in his many dedications to forebears and precursors. Upon the death of the great Egyptian poet Ahmad **Shawqī** (d. 1932), he recited a poem (11 November 1932) at a memorial meeting convened by the Arab Office at the American School in Baghdad. The poem, published in the proceedings of the festival, is exceptional for its focus on poetic talent. Al-Jawāhirī regards the deceased poet as being uniquely gifted in the context of an Arab nation that has been suffering through a prolonged era of decline. While celebrating Shawqī's achievement and poetics, he does not forget to mention his own role as the bearer of the same tradition. The same celebration of the Arab poet as a dynamic force is also to be found in his poem composed upon the death of the great Iraqi poet al-Zahāwī (d. 1936), published in *al-Bilād* (The Homeland) daily (no. 798, 25 February 1936). In this poem al-Zahāwī

is portrayed as the "father of poetry," one who "has stirred dead hearts" and filled them with "light and power."

He now became a regular participant in the Iraqi press. At a later stage he became editor of some major newspapers in Iraq, such as *al-Furāt* in 1930 (banned after 20 issues), *al-Inqilāb* in 1936, *al-Ra'y al-'āmm*, *al-Awqāt* and *al-Thabāt* from the late 1930s to the early 1950s. In 1931 he was appointed as a teacher in the Ma'mū-niyyah school in Baghdad, then was transferred to the Prime Minster's office as chancery clerk. By this time, his first collection of poetry, *Halbat al-adab* (The Literary Domain, 1921), had already appeared; in it he contrafacted a number of poets from among precursors and contemporaries. In the introductory note to this edition, he wrote:

As part of my involvement in the field of literature, I have pursued a particular path; it is one that I have not forsaken, nor will I do so. It involves the following: Whenever I witnessed a great littérateur possessed of a special talent, I followed his line and intended purpose. I would exert myself to the utmost to remain as close to him as possible, as though I were making it possible for him to see himself through me, as though I were uncovering his deepest poetic secrets.

In 1928 another collection appeared, *Bayna al-shu'ūr wa'l-'ātifah* (Between Feeling and Passion), and in 1935 his *dīwān* (collected works) appeared under the title *Dīwān al-Jawāhirī* which continued to expand through many editions until his complete collected works appeared.

Newspapers afforded him daily contact with Iraqi politics. In 1936, after the coup led by Bakr Sidqī, he began publishing the daily newspaper *al-Inqilāb*. However, as soon as he realized that Sidqī was a mere dictator, he began to write articles against him and his administration, a move that led to his imprisonment for three months and the newspaper's closure for a month. After Sidqī's regime had fallen, he changed the paper's name to *al-Ra'y al-'āmm*, but the paper continued to suffer many setbacks because of its oppositional stance. After the failure of the March 1941 revolution against the British domination of Iraq, he joined many intellectuals in leaving for Iran, but returned later in the same year to resume the publication of *al-Ra'y al-'āmm*. In 1944 he participated in the poetry festival in Damascus that celebrated the memory of the great poet Abū 'l-'Alā' al-Ma'arrī (1057).

No matter what the occasion, al-Jawāhirī's dedications have a personal touch. By invoking the names of precursors or forebears, al-Jawāhirī always has a particular purpose in mind. For instance, in 1929 while staying in the Iraqi city of Sāmarrā', the erstwhile abode of the caliph al-Mutawakkil (d. 861), he is reminded of the Syrian-born poet al-Buhturī (d. 897) and his festive poetry. And yet he uses the occasion of his poem "One Hour with al-Buhturī" (*'Irāq* daily, no. 2899, 21 November 1929) to refer to rulers who build palaces and castles at the expense of their people. The caliph al-Mutawakkil who resided there was one of those rulers "who vaingloriously reigned over their people and treated them as cattle." In a comparison with his invoked precursor, al-Jawāhirī bewails the fact that "had al-Buhturī been Iraqi-born, he would have suffered neglect" like the rest of the Iraqi people. While continuing to bewail such neglect, the poet also has another contemporary poet in mind, the then destitute Ma'rūf al-**Rusāfī** (d. 1945). In 1944, al-Jawāhirī published a poem in his newspaper, *al-Ra'y al-'āmm*, that is dedicated to al-Rusāfī (no. 1008, 15 May 1944). Al-Rusāfī responded (no. 1019, 27 May 1944) with another poem in which he addresses al-Jawāhirī as follows: "Through you, not me, poetry has flourished/ though, like you, I was once a poet." In this poem al-Jawāhirī recognizes al-Rusāfī as a talented poet who, in spite of his dire poverty, remained rigorously committed to what his conscience and nationalist sentiment dictated. Five years after al-Rusāfī's death, al-Jawāhirī published another poem in *al-Awqāt al-baghdādiyyah* daily (no. 22, 20 March 1951), the newspaper where we worked after the closure of *al-Ra'y al-'āmm*. As an elegy, the poem celebrates the dedicatee, but its concluding four lines identify the speaker with that dedicatee. Both live in poverty but possess ideas in abund-

ance and vigorous minds; "how similar we are to each other/ and how close my fate to yours." He adds: "As fated would have it, both of us descend into a pit" of need and neglect.

There are many other poems in this same vein. After the poet, Muhammad Sālih Bahr al-'Ulūm (Abū Nāzim), an ardent communist and national figure, had been imprisoned in 1963, the poet wrote a poem in 1965 in memory of the 1948 *Wathbah* (discussed below), which he recited in Prague. It concluded: "O Abū Nāzim, your imprisonment is my imprisonment, for I belong to you as you belong to me" (Baghdad ed. 5: 227-34). In 1952 when Iraq suffered yet more political repression under military rule, al-Jawāhirī published his "Lullaby for the Hungry" in the same newspaper (no. 28, 28 March). It was later republished several times in his *dīwāns* of 1953, 1961, and 1969, and the collected works. This latter poem is a scathing satire on the entire political, social, and cultural situation, drawing attention to the many pitfalls of the dominating discourse and hegemonic practices.

The poet had already been involved in many controversies with the government, the most renowned of which is probably "Dhikrā Abī 'l-Timman" (In Memory of Abū 'l-Timman), the great Iraqi national leader and the major influence in Iraqi national politics. On the fortieth day after his death in 1945, the poet recited the poem to an enormous gathering. It was no less critical and satirical than the other poems discussed here, but it managed to inflame national feelings and characterized the regime as a puppet. "Who could imagine," he asks, "that a system built on such shaky foundations could survive so long?" he asks. The people perpetuating the regime were participants in "a drama of distorted roles, whose parts were woven by time." But who are those people, he asks; and the answer is: bad actors or puppets instructed what to do by the showman, the colonizer and performing factional roles according to the colonizer's plan (Baghdad ed., IV, 142). Moreover, "bewildered people question this anomaly, for who are the owners of this land?" The government's reaction to this poem was to sue him, so he responded with an article published in *al-Ra'y al-'āmm* (no. 1443, 1 February 1946), from which the censor deleted many passages, replacing them with comments such as "eight lines deleted here by the censor" (Baghdad ed., IV, 135-138). In another poem, "al-Maqsūrah" (The Balcony), published in his own newspaper (no. 1910, 11 August 1948), the poet confronted unnamed opponents who were bent on soiling his reputation; they are described as representative of "a group in Iraq driven to its destiny like cattle," one that subordinates itself to foreign powers and plays an opportunistic role—"the hand saying 'yes' while pretending to say 'no'." Worse still are those who "assume the airs of littérateurs," wearing such a pose as "garb" while using café-corners as their refuge. In contrast the poet profiles himself as being genuine, committed, and ready to risk his career and life for his "conscience."

Such double invocation of both the ruling elite and second-rate littérateurs who serve as their lackeys is no mere passing reference. The same theme appears in a major poem, "Akhī Ja'far" (My Brother Ja'far), recited on 14 February 1948 to an enormous gathering at the Haydarkhānah Mosque, days after the martyrdom of his brother, Muhammad Ja'far, and many others in Ma'rakat al-Jisr (Battle at the Bridge), a reference to clashes that occurred when police cut off demonstrators on a bridge and massacred some 300-400 of them. In issue no. 1833 of al-Ra'y al-'Āmm, (11 February 1948), the poet had provided an introduction to the poem's publication with a foreword that emphasized two things: first, memories of the martyr and his colleagues are forever preserved in Iraqi hearts; second, the government and ruling clique are in disarray, fully aware that the Iraqi people will take their revenge. He adds:

those among your Iraqi people who have stained the name of literature and poetry with shame and who are the lackeys of the 'bastard' [referring to either the premier, Sālih Jabr, or the powerful figure, Nūrī al-Sa'īd] *have noticed, without being even slightly moved by the occasion, how the hearts of Iraqis bleed poetry and prose in your memory.*

(Baghdad ed., IV, 255-56).

The poem itself begins:

Are you aware or not, that the wounds of martyrs are a mouth, / a mouth not of the pretentious or the supplicant / it calls on the downtrodden hungry to spill your blood to feed yourself / and it shouts at the subservient few, insult your perfidious clique to obtain mercy.

The poem appeared initially in the poet's newspaper (no. 1836, 15 February 1948) and was republished many times in his *dīwāns* of 1949, 1957, 1960, 1967, and 1968; it was to become one of the most important poems in the poet's entire corpus. This Bridge Battle was to become the cornerstone event for the historic *Wathbah* (Uprising), and the bridge itself has been known as *Jisr al-shuhadā'* (The Martyrs' Bridge) ever since.

The period of the 1948 *Wathbah* against the Portsmouth Treaty (an alliance between Iraq and Great Britain that subjected Iraq to British military and economic control) was the most productive period in al-Jawāhirī's life and poetic output. He had already been involved in organized politics as a founding member of the leftist National Union Party, originally established in 1946 (with 500 members of different ethnicities, religions, and professions) but forcibly closed by the government in 1947. The Party's leader was 'Abd al-Fattāh Ibrāhīm, a pioneer in Iraqi democratic politics. But the *Wathbah* itself had a very powerful impact on al-Jawāhirī's frame of mind; it placed him at the center of Iraqi politics, a virtual poet-laureate acknowledged by all. On 14 April 1948 (soon after the *Wathbah*), he attended a student congress organized by the Iraqi Communist Party with the intention of forming an Iraqi Student Union and mobilizing students "in the service of independence and democracy in opposition to imperialism." For the occasion the poet recited an ode in Lions' Square in east Baghdad where the congress of 5,000-6,000 people had gathered.

Until 1948, al-Jawāhirī had been a member of the Iraqi parliament, representing Karbalā'. However his decision to resign from his parliamentary position as a gesture of protest against the terms of the Portsmouth Treaty (described above) highlights many of the contradictions in his personal life while at the same time drawing attention to the implications of his role in relation to both the government and leftist powers in Iraq, especially the Iraqi Communist Party (ICP). For, even though the Independence Party was behind the initial demonstrations of 5-7 January 1948, the Iraqi Communist Party took over and undertook a great deal of organization, especially after its Secretary General, Yūsuf Salmān (Fahd), urged his colleagues to do so from his prison cell. Yet, while the poet was a friend of Fahd (who was executed in the same year), he never considered himself a communist. He certainly composed poems hailing the role of the ICP, but denied any involvement in its politics. On 7 September 1959, he was elected as President for the Association of Journalists in his capacity as the editor of *al-Ayyām* (The Days). Still later, after the 1963 coup in Iraq and the massacre of communists and their allies, he was closely allied with the IPC. He was in charge of the Higher Committee of the Movement Abroad for the Defense of the Iraqi People, founded on 22 March 1963 in Prague where he had settled as an exile since 1961. In general however, he cannot be easily compartmentalized; even during the late 1940s, he had tried to sustain some independence. He denounced the government, but still visited the Prince-Regent to thank him for his condolences upon his brother, Ja'far's, murder.

1948 was also important for al-Jawāhirī in that it enabled him to participate fully in Iraq's cultural and political life. The events of that year had made it possible for Iraqis to witness their own sense of unity, one that involved all political and social forces, as well as their ability to organize public demonstrations and meetings. Cultural cafés and clubs proliferated, and the publication industry became very active. People came to expect much from him, and his brother's martyrdom proved to be a major catalyst for his political opposition. At the memorial event held forty days after the death of his brother, he recited another poem, "Yawm al-shahīd" (Martyr's Day). He tied the date of the event, 27 January 1948, to the national political calendar: "Greetings and Peace on you, martyr's day/ you and the struggle make our history." He adds: "You sanctioned the resurrection of the

generation that will inevitably be resurrected / and you set the Day of Judgment for the oppressors." Other poems are dedicated to martyrs, but 1948 also witnessed a decline in expectations. The government applied new repressive measures against not only the press but also nationalist groups and political organizations. One year later, he wrote a poem in remembrance of the uprising entitled "Atbiq Dujā" (Gather, O Darkness) and followed it in 1951 with "Tanwīmat al-jiyā'" (Lullaby for the Hungry).

In other poems he paid homage to public figures. One such was dedicated to the dean of the College of Medicine, Hāshim al-Witrī, in 1949, recited at a celebration held in the Masbah Club on the River Tigris in Baghdad. Here he associates himself with the great classical poet al-Mutanabbī (d. 968) and rephrases his forebear's famous verse extolling his own poetry: "If I recite a poem, time becomes its rhapsody." al-Jawāhirī also refers to the regime's efforts to silence him:

They claim that all the openings and outlets are closed in the face of a mounting wave / they lie, for time's mouth is filled with my poems which traverse the earth to east and west.

He concludes with a line that ever since has served as one of the most celebrated poetic expressions of defiance and protest: "I am their terrible destiny, raiding their homes. / I encourage baby and chamberlain alike to insult them." The regime had regarded the poem as an explicit statement of opposition, but there was no printed copy available to incriminate him. As the Lebanese communist Karīm Muruwwah had noted, al-Jawāhirī had been so incensed by this reaction that he tore the poem to pieces and discarded it under a table at the club. Karīm, the Lebanese leftist intellectual and historian Husayn Muruwwah, and his son, Nizār Muruwwah, collected up the scraps of paper; once back in Lebanon, they managed to piece them all together and sent the poem to the *Telegraph* daily newspaper in Beirut, where it was first published. As Karīm Muruwwah notes (*al-Madā* 19.1 [1998], 12), the poem's publication led to al-Jawāhirī's imprisonment in 1949.

The later phases of the poet's life were closely linked to his periods of exile. In 1951 he left for Egypt, but following the Iraqi Revolution of 1958, he returned to Iraq and spent several years of cordial relations with the revolution's leaders. However, once again he began to feel the pressures of censorship and to sense the anti-leftist tendencies of the government of General 'Abd al-Karīm Qāsim who had befriended him for the first two years of the Revolution. In 1961, he left for Lebanon, then traveled to Prague as guest of the Czech Union of Writers. He was to remain there for seven years. It was there that he wrote his next collection, *Barīd al-ghurbah* (Mail from Exile), published in 1965. In 1968 he was invited by the new Iraqi government to return to his homeland, and in the following year he published another poetry collection, *Barīd al-'awdah* (Mail of Homecoming). He served as president of the Union of Iraqi Writers; in 1971 he represented Iraq in the eighth conference of Arab writers in Damascus. In the same year, the Iraqi Ministry of Information issued two further collections of his poetry: *Ayyuhā 'l-araq* (O Insomnia), and *Khaljāt* (Sentiments). In 1973 he headed the Iraqi delegation of writers to the ninth conference of Arab writers in Tunisia. He was on very good terms with the Iraqi President, Ahmad Hasan al-Bakr (d. 1980), and wrote one of his most moving elegies upon the death of al-Bakr's son, Muhammad. However in 1977 pressures on his family, based on sectarian, religious and other motives, once again forced him into exile, along with many other leftists and communists. After another stay in Prague, he moved to Damascus in 1994 and was greeted with great acclaim by the Syrian President Hāfiz al-Asad. It was there that he died.

Three separate trends can be identified in his poetry of exile. The first speaks of his longing for Iraq, with a strong nostalgia that becomes even more intense for expressing the impossible. The second relates to an innate desire for natural-ness and spontaneity, while the third derives self-aggrandizement from exile, thereby evoking a sense of affinity with important ancestors who suffered similar troubles and were unduly neglected. A representative poem of the first trend is "Yā Dijlata 'l-khayr" (O Tigris of

Plenty), written in Prague in 1962, where he maintains a tacit opposition to the current Premier of Iraq, General Qāsim. Recollecting dead or murdered members of his own family (including his mother and brother), he complains of his enforced estrangement and of the general air of neglect, pretentiousness, hypocrisy, and corruption which he sees as characteristic of his country at the time. He also criticizes comment-ators who disparage his poetry or evaluate it in terms of modernist classifications and standards (Baghdad ed., V, 81-107). Of the second trend his poem entitled "Zorba," written in Prague in 1969 (Baghdad ed., VI, 371-378), is a good example, in that, besides the clear affinity with the protagonist of Kazantzakis's (1883-1957) novel, it also shows how his readings of other works at times managed to influence his own sentiments.

Typical of the third trend are the poems he delivered at Poetry Festivals, especially the one held in Baghdad in April 1969. It was there that he recited his renowned poem, "Yā 'bna 'l-Furātayn" (O Son of the Two Euphrates), pub-lished in the Kurdish leader Jalāl al-Tālabānī's newspaper *al-Nūr*, no. 221, 13 July 1969). Here al-Jawāhirī uses the occasion to identify himself with the great classical poet al-Mutanabbī: both hail from the same region; furthermore, al-Jawā-hirī's birthplace, Najaf, is near al-Mutanabbī's Kufa, hence the title of the poem. The poem maintains this identification, as the phantom of his poetic forebear appears to the speaker as if fresh from the latter's last battle at Dayr 'Āqūl. Even so, the phantom renders time luminous, "a shiny yesterday and a becoming," with a "face like a dawn beam" and "glittering eye like a twinkling ember." He is a combination of "the dove and the eagle." The speaker and the dedicatee are alike in a world of many Kāfūrs, a reference to the regent of Egypt, Kāfūr al-Ikhshīdī, a black eunuch servant, who ruled the country after his master's death. Adopting this analogy, al-Jawāhirī deplores a present that oppresses the talented and decent. Both men are *gharīrān* (innocent and good) in "a corrupt world, which they are too sublime to accept" (Baghdad ed., V [1975], 357). As the strong poet, al-Jawāhirī invokes his powerful precursor, al-Mutanabbī, in order to counter the oblique criticism aimed at his poetry by Suhayl Idrīs, the editor-in-chief of the literary journal *al-Ādāb*: "A friend of mine, whose talent I will not deny," says al-Jawāhirī referring to Suhayl Idrīs, "means to 'deny' the old generation any poetic achievement, as though he were the 'arbiter' of the entire poetic scene" (Baghdad ed., V [1975], 358). The poet is well aware that Idrīs is singling him out for such criticism, so he foregrounds his response by relying on posterity, in that the traditional poetic form of the *qaṣīdah* had not been rendered obsolete by time nor is its reliance on a fixed rhyme scheme regarded as a negative. The continuing popularity of al-Mutanabbī, al-Jawāhirī argues in the same poem, indicates that poetry in the classical mode has an enduring appeal.

This particular feature points to the constant presence of prominent poetic forebears in al-Jawāhirī's poetry from his earliest collections of poetry. In another poem (1935) that was recited in absentia in Damascus, al-Jawāhirī retraces al-Mutanabbī's personal history and career (Baghdad ed., II [1973], 279-286). Here soothsayers inform al-Mutanabbī's father about his son, a wonder and a genius, "who has signs of immortality"; "What a soul is this that regards life without challenge as worthless?" The emphasis on this aspect of al-Mutanabbī's life fits well into al-Jawāhirī's advocacy of leftist politics and his advocacy of the underprivileged and downtrodden. In a celebrated poem from 1944, even his poetic ancestor, al-Ma'arrī (d. 1057), is depicted as a poet and intellectual of great acumen and modesty: "seated on a mat ... with a jug of water to sustain him, a mind, and shelves of books" (Baghdad ed., III [1974], 91). Yet this old man is able to surprise and destabilize attitudes and habits of thought in a world "about which he ponders with compassion and care" (ibid., 84). Al-Ma'arrī is seen as a great dissolver of habit, tradition, and conformity, another Messiah in culture's terrain. "The revolt of the intellect has a long history which speaks of a thousand Messiahs who have been crucified for its cause" (Baghdad ed., III [1974], 84). Upon listening to al-Jawāhirī recite his poetry, the great Egyptian critic Tāhā Husayn (d. 1973)

concluded:

al-Jawāhirī stunned me with his enchanting eloquence, in itself the surviving remnant of the genuine Arabic literary heritage.
                              (Baghdad ed., III [1974], 91).

Yet, the new generation of Iraqi poets in the late 1940s, such as 'Abd al-Wahhāb al-Bayātī (d. 1999) and Badr Shākir al-Sayyāb (d. 1964), criticized al-Jawāhirī's classical poetics. Karīm Muruwwah, the editor of *al-Tarīq* quarterly (the intellectual platform for the Lebanese Communist Party), expressed a different point of view: in a special issue of the journal *al-Madā* 19.1 (1998), he stated that

al-Jawāhirī's poetry is a register of a long period of Iraqi and Arab history, covering almost three quarters of the 20th century. At the same time, it serves as a record of a personal life, one that is unique and rebellious in its passions and contradictions.   (ibid., 5)

In summary then, Muhammad Mahdī al-Jawāhirī's life and poetic career manages to evoke contradictory opinions, but we are left with a strong and enduring sense of the power and effectiveness of his poetry and his prominent role as a modern poet grounded in a classical past that he uses with great eloquence to express the aspirations and agonies of the Iraqi people. While he expected a more favorable critical reception, al-Jawāhirī was aware that he was widely admired by the reading public throughout the Arab world. His poetry of social and political protest, as well as his outpourings of love and passion, make him a unique voice, one that is able to establish appropriate linkages to the great predecessors of the classical tradition.

REFERENCES

Salih Altoma, "In Memoriam: Muhammad Mahdi al-Jawahiri", *Arab Studies Quarterly* 19:4 (Fall 1997): iv-viii;

Mahmūd Darwīsh, "Ahamm shā'ir klāsīkī fī 'l-qarn al-'ishrīn" (The Most Important Classical Poet in the Twentieth Century), *al-Madā* quarterly, Damascus, 19.1 (1998): 69;

Sāti' al-Husrī, *Mudhakkarātī*, 2 vols. (Beirut:

Dār al-Talī'ah, 1967), I, 588-99;

Sulaiman Jubran, "The Old and the New: al-Jawahiri's Poetic Imagery", *Asian and*

African Studies 26 (1992): 249-262;

Ja'far Bāqir Mahbūbah, *Mādī al-Najaf wa-hādiruhā* (Najaf: Matba'at al-Ādāb, 1955).

Jubrān Khalīl Jubrān
[Kahlil Gibran]*
(1883 – 1931)

SUHEIL BUSHRUI
University of Maryland

WORKS

al-Musīqā ("Music", New York: al-Mohajer, 1905);

'Arā'is al-murūj ("Nymphs of the Valley", New York: al-Mohajer, 1906);

al-Arwāh al-mutamarridah ("Rebellious Spirits", New York: al-Mohajer, 1908);

al-Ajnihah al-mutakassirah ("Broken Wings", New York: Mir'āt al-Gharb, 1912);

Dam'ah wa-'btisāmah ("A Tear and a Smile", New York: Atlas, 1914);

The Madman (New York: Alfred A. Knopf, 1918);

al-Mawākib ("Processions", New York: Mir'āt al-Gharb al-Yawmiyyah, 1919);

al-'Awāsif ("Tempests", Cairo: al-Hilāl, 1920);

The Forerunner (New York: Alfred A. Knopf, 1920);

al-Badā'i' wa'l-tarā'if ("Beautiful and Rare Sayings", Cairo: Maktabat al-'Arab, 1923);

The Prophet (New York: Alfred A. Knopf, 1923);

Sand and Foam (New York: Alfred A. Knopf, 1926);

Jesus, the Son of Man (New York: Alfred A. Knopf, 1928);

The Earth Gods (New York: Alfred A. Knopf, 1931);

The Wanderer (New York: Alfred A. Knopf, 1932);

The Garden of the Prophet (New York: Alfred A. Knopf, 1933).

Collected Works (Arabic)

The Collected Works: al-Majmū'ah al-kāmilah li-mu'allafāt Jubrān Khalīl Jubrān, 4 vols. (Beirut: Dār al-Jadīd, 1994); vol. 1: *al-'Arabiyyah* (Arabic Works), introduced and edited by Jameel Jabr; vol. 2: *al-Mu'arrabah* (English Works translated into Arabic), ed. and introduced by Jamīl Jabr; vol. 3: *al-Rasā'il* (The Letters), ed. Antoine al-Qawal; vol. 4: *Nusūs khārij al-majmū'ah* (Additional Collected Papers), ed. introduced by Antoine al-Qawal.

Collected Works (English)

The Treasured Writings of Kahlil Gibran (Secaucus NJ: Castle Books, 1980); there are several anthologies, both small and large, that include Arabic pieces in translation. Many of these overlap. This specific volume includes the largest collection of Arabic pieces translated into English.

Art Works

Twenty Drawings (New York: Alfred A. Knopf, 1919); introduced by Alice Raphael;

Wahib Kayrouz, *'Ālam Jubrān al-rassām* ("Jubrān's Art World", Beirut: Dār Sādir and Lajnat Jubrān, 1984);

Wahib Kayrouz, *Gibran in His Museum* (Bsharri: Bacharia, 1995);

Annie S. Otto, *The Art of Kahlil Gibran: Visions of Life as Expressed by the Author of "The Prophet"* (New York: Citadel Press, 1965).

Works in Translation

Nymphs of the Valley (New York: Alfred A.
Knopf, 1948); translation of *'Arā'is al-murūj*,
tr. by H. M. Nahmad;

Spirits Rebellious (New York: Alfred A. Knopf,
1948); translation of *al-Arwāh al-mutamarridah*, tr. by H. M. Nahmad;

The Broken Wings (New York: Citadel Press,
1957); translation of *al-Ajnihah al-mutakassirah*, tr. by A. R. Ferris;

A Tear and a Smile (New York: Alfred A.
Knopf, 1950); translation of *Dam'ah wa-
'btisāmah*, tr. by H. M. Nahmad;

The Processions (New York: The Wisdom
Library—a division of the Philosophical Library, 1958); translation of *al-Mawākib*, tr.
and ed. with a biographical sketch by George
Kheirallah.

[*NB: Jubrān's (Gibran's) full name in Arabic
was Jubrān Khalīl Jubrān (or Jibrān Khalīl Jibrān), the middle name being his father's. It is a
convention among Arabs to use the father's
name after one's first name. He always signed
his full name in his Arabic works, but he
dropped the first name in his English writings.
He did not only that but also changed the correct
spelling of "Khalil" to "Kahlil" at the instigation
of his English teacher at the Boston school he
attended between 1895 and 1897. Another reason for this change may have been a bureau-
cratic decision to Americanize what seemed too
foreign a name for public usage. The family
name Jubrān/Jibrān/Gibran is related to the
Arabic word *jabara*, which means "to restore to
harmony, to bring unequal parts to unity, as in
algebra."]

Among twentieth-century Arab writers, Jubrān
Khalīl Jubrān (Kahlil Gibran) occupies a special
place in that his corpus is bilingual and includes
Arabic as well as English works which were,
and still are, widely read. His best known work,
The Prophet, and some of his Arabic works have
been translated into some forty different languages, enabling him to be read and appreciated
throughout the world.

Iconoclastic in many ways, Khalīl Jubrān was
a revolutionary poet in every sense of the word.

In Arabic, he rejected traditional, restrictive
literary conventions in favor of new forms and
themes that maximized the scope of artistic
expression. He infused the language with the
rhythms of everyday speech, borrowing from the
colloquial whatever suited his artistic designs.
He endorsed social reform and championed individual freedom. He was innovative and creative in his treatment of the perennial subjects of
love, nature, religion, and the individual's relationship to society and to others. Intellectually,
Jubrān exercised a notable and enduring influence on the world of Arabic letters as the
founder and leading proponent of what later
critics called the Romantic school of Arabic
literature. He and his fellow poets, known as
shu'arā' al-mahjar (the immigrant poets), were
largely responsible for shaping the fortunes of
modern Arabic poetry and literature.

In his English writings, he attempted to blend
the riches of Arabic mythology and poetry with
the English Romantic literary tradition. Though
he promoted the reconciliation of traditions and
cultures more strongly in his English works than
in his Arabic œuvre, in both languages he passionately defended the environment, human
rights, women's rights, religious unity and interfaith dialogue. He espoused unity as a prerequisite to laying the foundation for the creation of a
culture of peace. His entire output stands as
proof of that unity which informed his broad
vision of a world in which human rights and the
physical world would be secured and respected,
releasing the peoples of the world to live a new
life free from acrimony and conflict. Above all,
he was an ardent advocate of change. In the
West, he believed he had a mission to challenge
materialistic values and revive spirituality. In the
East, particularly the Arab World, he called for
an awakening to the realities of the modern
world, and for a radical transformation in the
political, social, religious, and cultural life of
Christians and Muslims alike.

Although Jubrān's artistic output never
matched his literary creativity in terms of popular appeal or professional influence, for him the
canvas represented another form in which his
poetry could be expressed. By the time of his
death, his artworks numbered more than 2,000 in

various mediums: oil, watercolor, pencil, and ink. Today, these works are widely scattered in public galleries and private collections in the United States; a small number are in Paris, and some 500 others are held by the Bisharri Museum in Lebanon.

Khalīl Jubrān was born on 6 January 1883, in the town of Bisharri, Lebanon, close to the holy grove of cedar trees—on the edge of Wādī Qadīshah (The Holy or Sacred Valley)—which would become a prominent symbol in his writings as an emblem of all that was sacred and numinous in his native land.

Jubrān's mother, Kamileh Istiphan Rahme, was a widow with a six-year-old son when she married her second husband, Khalīl Jubrān, father of the poet.

Lebanon's geography, religious demographics, and history informed Jubrān's humanistic world view, as seen in his writing and artwork. During his lifetime, Jubrān came to see Lebanon as a crossroads between the modern and the ancient worlds, and as a geographic meeting point between Islam and Christianity. In this locale, Jubrān saw the dangers of factionalism and sectarianism, and more specifically, the exploitation of religious divisions for narrow political purposes. On the other hand, he was inspired by Lebanon's rich tradition of inter-religious harmony while recognizing that it was sometimes shattered by internal and external political forces.

Even as the Lebanese struggled to overcome their internal divisions by upholding their best traditions of religious tolerance, they were also subject to the stirrings of pan-Arab nationalism. By the time of Jubrān's birth in the late nineteenth century, the Arabs had been subjected to domination at the hands of the Ottoman Empire for almost five hundred years (Lebanon was under Ottoman control for exactly four centuries, from 1516 to 1916).

The circumstances surrounding the decision of the Jubrān family to emigrate to America and leave the father behind in Lebanon are murky, to say the least. The important fact is that on 25 June 1895, Kamileh arrived in the United States accompanied by Jubrān, his half-brother Boutros (Peter), and his two sisters Marianna and Sultana

in search of a better life and a more promising and secure future.

Life for the immigrant family in Boston's Chinatown entailed a series of challenges. It was through the industry of Jubrān's mother, Kamileh, that the family survived in its new environment. It was she who held the family together through the precarious years of her son's childhood and adolescence.

For his part, the young Jubrān arrived in the New World possessing no English and with only a bare minimum of elementary education. He spent the years of 1895 to 1897 in Boston learning English. In 1897, his family decided that he should return to Lebanon in order to begin an intensive course of studies at the Madrasat al-Hikmah (also called the Collège de la Sagesse) in Beirut. During the two years he spent at al-Hikmah, he studied a wide variety of subjects even going beyond those prescribed in the curriculum; his main interests were Arabic, French, and creative writing. He immersed himself in ancient and modern Arabic literature. He also familiarized himself with contemporary literary movements in the Arab world. This interval of study equipped Jubrān for his first experiments as a writer in Arabic.

Later, in 1902, when Jubrān was in Lebanon serving as a guide and interpreter for an American family on a tourist excursion, he was forced to return to Boston after receiving news of the death of his sister, Sultana, from tuberculosis, and of his mother's cancer. The next year, his half-brother died in March from tuberculosis followed by his mother, Kamileh, in June. Thus, in a short span of time, Jubrān suffered the loss of his immediate family members. The death of Jubrān's mother was an especially grievous blow for a young man of twenty with a sensitive and gentle nature. The loss was deeply felt and was echoed years later in *al-Ajnihah al-Mutakassirah* (The Broken Wings, 1912):

He who loses his mother loses a pure soul who blesses and guards him constantly.

(Translated by A. R. Ferris)

After Kamileh's death, Marianna, Jubrān's surviving sister, kept house and cared for him devotedly. Never marrying, she supported herself and Jubrān by working as a seamstress, thus enabling Jubrān to pursue his literary and artistic ambitions with a single-minded determination.

His teachers, and eventually, members of the artistic community of Boston, began to discern Jubrān's artistic talents some time after his return from Lebanon in 1902. Jubrān's most important early artistic connection was with the avant-garde photographer Fred Holland Day, who befriended Jubrān and introduced him to the wider creative circles in Boston. In January 1904, Day held an exhibit of Jubrān's paintings and drawings at his studio in Boston, the first such public exposure Jubrān received. A month later, a second exhibition was held at the Cambridge School, a private educational institution owned and operated by Mary Haskell (1873-1964), who became an important figure in Jubrān's personal and artistic life.

According to accounts left by those who knew Jubrān, he was always shy and ill at ease in the company of women. Although he never married, he nevertheless had an intense and passionate relationship with Mary Haskell, who became his patroness, mentor, collaborator, and sometime fiancée. During the summer of 1899 while he was on vacation in Bisharri, before he met Mary Haskell, Jubrān fell desperately in love with a beautiful girl. Although there has been much conjecture as to the nature of this relationship and over the identity of the young woman, it is certain that Jubrān found this, his first love affair, both frustrating and disappointing. In the autumn he returned to Boston by way of Paris, and several years later described the unhappy dalliance in *al-Ajnihah al-Mutakassirah*. Despite whatever romantic troubles he experienced, one of the themes which emerges from Jubrān's personal life and from his writings and art, is his deep connection to women. As he wrote in a 1928 letter to May Ziadeh (Mayy Ziyādah):

I am indebted for all that I call "I" to women, ever since I was an infant. Women opened the windows of my eyes and the doors of my spirit. Had it not been for the woman-mother, the woman-sister, and the woman-friend, I would have been sleeping among those who seek the tranquility of the world with their snoring.

In Jubrān's family life, his father played a largely negative role until his death in 1909. The relationship between father and son was troubled, disrupted as it was by the older man's lack of responsibility towards his family. The separation of Jubrān's father from his family, which arose after the latter's emigration to the United States, merely confirmed in physical terms the emotional chasm between father and son that had arisen much earlier. Even the opportunity afforded by Jubrān's return to Lebanon between 1897 and 1899 did not lead to reconciliation.

Instead of paternal backing, Jubrān received the wholehearted support and succor of his mother and his sister, Marianna, in both practical and emotional terms. Jubrān witnessed the industry and practicality with which his mother and sister combined the daily business of running a home with earning a living, and this furnished him with a deep respect for women's capabilities. His attitude towards women was influenced by the important friendships he forged with the young Boston poetess Josephine Preston Peabody; with the journalist, novelist, and suffragette Charlotte Teller; and with a group of exceptionally talented women that included Marjorie Morten, Adele Watson, and Juliet Thompson. Mary Haskell's important influence on Jubrān's life was perhaps only second to his mother's. Jubrān's connection to Mary Haskell, however, was critical to his development as a writer at a time when he was feeling his way towards fluency and facility in the English language.

Another significant female figure in Jubrān's life was the Lebanese writer May Ziadeh (Mayy Ziyādah, 1886-1941), perhaps the most distinguished Arab woman-author of that time. Ziadeh's work as a reviewer of new literary publications introduced her to Khalīl Jubrān, whose influence on her thought and style can be seen everywhere in her writings. In 1912, she reviewed Jubrān's *al-Ajnihah al-mutakassirah*, and thus began a unique literary and love relationship carried on through correspondence. Although they never met in person, they maintained their relationship for twenty years. Jubrān and Ziyādah achieved a rare intimacy and harmony of understanding which was broken only by Jubrān's death. They also exchanged ideas on art and literature, as well as their belief that a woman had the right to take control of her life and destiny.

A commitment to women's equality with men and a belief in their right to similar privileges, duties, and opportunities informed Jubrān's thinking on social issues, and he explored these topics extensively in his writings, condemning misogyny and arranged marriages. Over time, Jubrān became widely known as an ardent proponent of women's rights. On 15 December 1914, the American newspaper *The Buffalo Times* reported Jubrān's views on women in an article headlined "Set Womankind Free, and There'll Be No War." In addition to reporting Jubrān's views on gender relations, the article reproduced a piece of Jubrān's artwork called "The Great Solitude," which symbolized, according to the newspaper, "the 'oneness' of mankind."

Jubrān's literary career falls into two distinct phases. The first extends from 1905, when his first work in Arabic, *al-Musīqā* (Music), was published, to 1918. The second opens with the publication of his first English work, *The Madman*, in 1918, and continues to his death in 1931. Although Jubrān wrote exclusively in Arabic throughout the first period, from 1918 onwards, he used English as his main form of expression, producing eight books between that year and 1931, two of which came out after his death.

Jubrān's preferred medium in his earliest Arabic works was the short narrative. As he developed as a writer, he gradually adopted the forms of parable, apothegm, didactic essay, aphorism, allegory, and "prose epigram," all of which later became characteristic of his English writings. In both his Arabic and English works, he employed a highly personal style which contains strong echoes of the Song of Solomon, the Psalms, the Book of Isaiah, and the sayings and parables of Jesus; thus, the lifelong influence of the Bible on his creative development and poetic language can be discerned.

Jubrān's prose-poems, the medium in which he expressed himself with the greatest fluency and flexibility, are markedly idealistic without any sense of embarrassment, an unusual quality to be found in a Western author during this period of history. The West had become preoccupied with the ideas of Charles Darwin (1809-1882), Friedrich Nietzsche (1844-1900), and Karl Marx (1818-1883), and found itself ravaged by cynicism, a sense of anxiety, and a feeling of guilt and abject despair. Jubrān's fresh and new Romanticism enabled him to express himself in a manner which would have been more in harmony with the European climate of a hundred years earlier, retaining the freshness of discovery without the Western veneer of ennui and disillusionment which characterized the early twentieth century.

The almost audible tone of Jubrān's early Arabic works is a pronounced bitterness and frustration arising from his perception of the unreformed ills of society which he ardently wished to see reformed. In particular, he opposed injustice against women, the greed and covetousness displayed by religious figures, and the narrow, traditionalist outlook of a prejudiced society long overdue for change. It is also in these early writings that we encounter the attitudes which established Jubrān's reputation as a firebrand and a revolutionary intent on destroying the institutions of church and state, a reputation that continues to follow him today and which the publication of his later mystical works only partially mitigated.

The piece regarded by many as Jubrān's first attempt at writing an Arabic book was entitled *Nubdah fī fann al-musīqā* (On Music, 1905); it was published by the newspaper *al-Mohajer* in New York. "A lyrical eulogy betraying all the characteristics of neophyte apprenticeship" (Bushrui/Jenkins 1998, 72), *al-Musīqā* nevertheless displays the passion and imaginative prowess of its author. In subject matter and in style it was innovative, not withstanding Khalīl Hāwī's comment that "[i]t is evident that we can hardly claim for this piece the definiteness of form which would enable us to assign it to any one literary genre."

The publication of *al-Musīqā* excited the imagination of Jubrān and filled him with enthusiasm to publish his next book, *'Arā'is al-murūj* (Nymphs of the Valley, 1906). This was followed two years later with *al-Arwāh al-muta-marridah* (Spirits Rebellious, 1908). Both of these works are important documents which advocate the reform of religious, political, and social institutions. But in neither of these books does Jubrān articulate a clear strategy for overcoming the ills of society as he assesses them. In short, Jubrān's assessment is accurate, but his solutions are utopian.

'Arā'is al-murūj consists of three short narratives: "Ramād al-ajyāl wa'l-nār al-khālidah" (Dust of the Ages and the Eternal Fire), "Martā al-Bāniyyah" (Martha of the Town of Ban), and "Yuhannā al-majnūn" (John the Madman). In the first story, Jubrān develops his concept of reincarnation, which would become one of the predominant elements of his thought in years to come. The second story is about the plight of women who find themselves the victims of a corrupt social system, while the third is an open attack on a greedy and avaricious clergy.

al-Awrdāh al-mutamarridah is a collection of four short stories: "Wardah al-Hānī" (story of a woman by the same name), "Surākh al-qubūr" (Cry of the Tombs), "Madja' al-'arūs" (The Bride's Couch), and "Khalīl al-kāfir" (Khalīl the Heretic). These four short stories examine in outspoken and defiant terms Lebanon's oppressive social conditions, reflecting also similar conditions throughout the Arab world. In this collection, Jubrān is particularly severe in his judgment of the misuse of ecclesiastical power.

Two stories in particular, "Wardah al-Hānī" and "The Bride's Couch," focus on the rights of women victimized by a corrupt and ruthless social system upheld by an equally corrupt religious establishment. To support his plea on behalf of women, Jubrān also shares his own conception of God as He who gives men and women alike "spirit wings to soar aloft into the realms of love and freedom" and a faith which "makes us all brothers equal before the sun."

"Khalīl al-Kāfir" is very similar to the earlier story "Yuhannā al-majnūn" in *'Arā'is al-murūj*, but in "Khalīl al-kāfir" the sense of defeatism expressed in "Yuhannā al-majnūn" transforms into a refusal to accept tyranny, religious or political. Jubrān's style begins to acquire new poetic power and a passionate intensity as is expressed in the following oration by Khalīl the Heretic, which demonstrates the new vigor and vibrancy with which Jubrān infused his language:

From the depths of these depths
We call you, O Liberty—hear us!
    From the corners of this darkness
We raise our hands in supplication—turn your
    gaze towards us!
On the expanse of these snows
We lay ourselves prostrate before you, have
    compassion upon us!
...
From the sources of the Nile to the estuary of the
    Euphrates
The wailing of souls surging with the scream of
    the abyss rises;
From the frontiers of the peninsula to the mountains of Lebanon
Hands are outstretched to you, trembling in the
    agony of death;
From the coast of the gulf to the ends of the
    desert
Eyes are uplifted to you with pining hearts—
Turn, o Liberty, and look upon us.
                    (Translated by Suheil Bushrui)

Jubrān's ambition was not restricted only to the realm of literary creation. He felt deeply that he had another gift to develop, and he wanted very much to study art and become a painter. Thanks to the generosity of his patroness, Mary Haskell, Jubrān went to Paris towards the end of 1908 to study art at the Académie Julien and at the École des Beaux-Arts. During his stay in Paris, he came into contact with European literature, especially the works of contemporary English and French writers. He also became particularly interested in the work of William Blake, who greatly influenced his thought and art. For a time, Jubrān fell under the spell of Friedrich Nietzsche's *Thus Spake Zarathustra*; but Nietzsche's influence, unlike that of Blake, was short-lived and Jubrān soon rejected Nietzsche's philosophy of nihilism and destruction.

Jubrān discovered Nietzsche in Paris and found that *Thus Spake Zarathustra* had captured the imagination of everyone in the literary and artistic worlds in France. Nietzsche had achieved wide, controversial popularity in Europe because of his vehement opposition to traditional Christian beliefs and values. Yet to concentrate only on this aspect of his thought is to distort his message. There is no evidence that Jubrān read any of Nietzsche's works except *Thus Spake Zarathustra*. This book alone, however, is wholly in tune with Jubrān's own conviction that true wisdom and a closer approach to God involves the rejection of conventional wisdom and institutionalized religious practice. These serve only to draw the soul away from God in the service of man-made conventions through a social coercion which perverts the spirit of genuine religion. Paradoxically, according to Mary Haskell, Jubrān even went so far as to compare Nietzsche to Jesus Christ. Possibly, Jubrān made this comparison because he found the German philosopher's refreshing, incisive style to be close in spirit to the trenchant and uncompromising sayings of Christ. At the height of his infatuation with Nietzsche, he wrote the following from Paris to Adele Watson:

Yes, Nietzsche is a great giant—and the more you read him the more you will love him. He is perhaps the greatest spirit in modern times, and his work will outlive many of the things which we consider great. Please, p-l-e-a-s-e read, "Thus Spake Zarathustra" as soon as possible for it is—to me—one of the greatest works of all times.

These words may appear to be excessively adulatory, but they mirror the admiration for Nietzsche's work which, as noted, was then widespread throughout Europe. Jubrān's assessment also reflects his delight in finding a writer whose views on the weakly sentimental image of Christ (which Jubrān himself forcefully rejected in *Jesus, the Son of Man*), and on the hypocrisy of organized religion, paralleled his own.

Throughout his adolescence and maturity, Jubrān absorbed and assiduously reworked a wide range of Western and Arabic literary and artistic influences and crafted a style which combined the best of both traditions. Alongside the obvious affinities with Blake, Wordsworth, Shelley, and Keats, his work can be compared

with that of the American Transcendentalists, Emerson, Thoreau, and Whitman. Much of what he came to absorb from European and American literature convinced him of the universality of great literature and reinforced those values he had already encountered at al-Hikmah School a few years earlier. At al-Hikmah, he was guided to immerse himself in the Arab literary classical tradition, and encouraged to acquaint himself with the masterpieces of classical Arabic literature such as *Kalīlah wa-Dimnah*, Abū 'l-Faraj al-Isfahānī's (d. c. 972) great poetry collection *Kitāb al-aghānī*, The *Prologemena* of ibn Khaldūn (d. 1406), The *Epistles* of Badī' al-Zamān al-Hamadhānī (d. 1008) and to read the poets al-Mutanabbī (d. 965), al-Bahā' Zuhayr (d. 1258), as well as the Sufi masters of Arabic poetry.

During Jubrān's studies in Paris, he came into contact in 1909 with Yūsuf al-Huwayik, a classmate from his days at the Beirut school Madrasat al-Hikmah. The two men became close friends, and together they sought to connect with modern trends in painting. They found, however, that they had no sympathy with Cubism, which they regarded as a "lunatic revolution." Jubrān decided to leave his teacher, Maître Lawrence, whose work Jubrān detested immensely, and began to work on his own. It was during this period that Jubrān met the sculptor Auguste Rodin (1840-1917), and although this meeting lasted only a few moments, Rodin was to exert a powerful influence on Jubrān's art.

From his European vantage point in Paris, Jubrān forged a connection in 1910 with Amīn al-Rīhānī (1876-1940), a fellow Lebanese-American thinker and writer who was to have a profound influence on Jubrān's intellectual and creative development.

On the last day of October, 1910, Jubrān returned to Boston from Paris. The two years he had spent in Paris were crucial for his development as a poet and as a painter. "Paris," as he later told Mary Haskell, "was [for him] a time of self-discovery." Shortly after his return, Jubrān proposed marriage to Mary Haskell, who was ten years his senior, but she gently and altruistically declined his offer. Meanwhile, events in the Arab region captured an increasing amount of Jubrān's attention as he and his fellow Arab-Americans witnessed, and became involved in, the stirrings of Arab sentiments against Ottoman rule. In 1911, at a time of intense political activity occasioned by the freeing of Arab territories from Ottoman rule, Jubrān founded *al-Halaqah al-Dhahabiyyah* (The Golden Circle), one of many semi-political Arab societies which sprang up in Syria, Lebanon, Constantinople, Paris and New York. The Golden Circle, however, was not popular among Arab immigrants and was dissolved after its first meeting.

In 1911, Amīn al-Rīhānī published *The Book of Khalid*, his first English-language novel and perhaps the first novel ever published in English by an Arab. Rīhānī had commissioned Jubrān to illustrate *The Book of Khalid*. Jubrān—who in his circle referred to Rīhānī as *al-mu'allim* (lit. "teacher"), in recognition of his mentorship and leadership—along with Mīkhā'īl **Nu'aymah** [Naimy] (1889-1988), another Lebanese-American writer and colleague, was deeply influenced by *The Book of Khalid*. It left an indelible impression on him and may have encouraged him to start writing in English. Rīhānī's work contains echoes of the Christian-Muslim synthesis that also found expression in Naimy's *Book of Mirdad* and Jubrān's *Prophet*. Although Jubrān was to achieve the greater fame through his poetry and art, he always looked up to Rīhānī, who was seven years his senior, as a kind of elder brother.

Jubrān's Paris experience widened his intellectual and artistic horizons. Boston seemed on his return too narrow and stifling to accommodate his dreams. Again with Mary Haskell's help, in 1912 he moved from Boston to New York, where he rented a studio at 51 West Tenth Street, between Fifth and Sixth Avenue. "The Hermitage," as Jubrān called his studio, remained his home until his death. Ultimately, Jubrān found New York to be a dynamic centre of Arab immigrant cultural activities and a haven for new artistic talent.

After settling into this new environment, Jubrān published *al-Ajnihah al-mutakassirah*, an autobiographical novella on which he had been working since 1903. The book follows the story of Salmā Karamī, a Lebanese girl who is com-pelled to marry the nephew of an influential Maronite bishop. Jubrān describes Lebanon as a society where a woman "is looked upon as a commodity, purchased and delivered from one to another," and where men view women "from behind the sexual veil and see nothing but externals." Apart from being the love story of a young couple and a spirited defence on behalf of true love, *al-Ajnihah al-mutakassirah* defines Jubrān's belief in the sanctity of our Mother Earth, and illustrates how Jubrān saw in nature "a life that influences the kinship of all men," and how nature supplied Jubrān himself with a rich store of symbols that provided both the emotional and intellectual apparatus of his poetry.

Everything in nature bespeaks the mother. The sun is the mother of earth and gives it its nourishment of heat; it never leaves the universe at night until it has put the earth to sleep to the song of the sea and the hymn of birds and brooks. And this earth is the mother of the trees and flowers. It produces them, nurses them, and weans them. The trees and flowers become kind mothers of their fruits and seeds. And the mother, the prototype of all existence, is the eternal spirit full of beauty and love.

(Translated by A.R. Ferris)

Whether the corpus of writing left by Khalīl Jubrān constitutes a coherent whole, does not in any way affect the unifying factor that indisputably holds his work together—namely his unity of vision. The overriding theme of all Jubrān's work is unity; it is the ancient vision of the one-ness of the universe and the unity of humanity.

Such a vision of unity had permeated all he had done, and he had finally found this vision fully manifested in the person and the teachings of 'Abdu'l-Bahā' (1844-1921), the son of the founder of the Bahā'i Faith. In 1912, 'Abdu'l-Bahā' was conducting a speaking tour across North America, and that same year Jubrān had the opportunity to meet him in New York City. The poet was deeply impressed by 'Abdu'l-Bahā''s teachings and bearing, and in many ways, according to Jubrān, he provided the template for Jubrān's portrayal of Jesus in *Jesus, the Son of Man*. Jubrān said of 'Abdu'l-Bahā', whose portrait he sketched: "For the first time I saw form noble enough to be a receptacle for the Holy Spirit." Jubrān's views on women's rights found confirmation and support in 'Abdu'l-Bahā''s lectures throughout the United States in 1912. The Bahā'i teachings concerning the oneness of religion and interfaith harmony also struck a chord with Jubrān as this had long been one of his central concerns.

Jubrān's abiding concern for the theme of unity appeared in *Dam'ah wa-'btisāmah* (A Tear and a Smile, 1914), a collection of stories, didactic tales, poems, and prose pieces—fifty-seven pieces in all. Most of the materials collected in this book were written between 1903 and 1908, and were published in the newspaper *al-Mohajer*. The main themes of *Dam'ah wa-'btisāmah* seem to fall into four major categories: society and its reform (for example, "Fī madīnat al-amwāt" [In the City of the Dead], "al-Ams wa'l-yawm" [Yesterday and Today], and "al-Kūkh wa'l-qasr" [The Palace and the Hut]); the sanctity of nature (for example, "Amām 'arsh al-jamāl" [Before the Throne of Beauty], "Unshūdat al-zahr" [The Song of the Flower], and "Hayāt al-hubb" [The Life of Love]); universal love (for example, "Munājah" [A Soliloquy], "al-Tifl Yasū" [The Child Jesus], and "Bayn al-kharā'ib" [Among the Ruins]); and the unity of being including the unity of all religions (for example, "Nashīd al-insān" [The Hymn of Man], "al-Nafs" [The Spirit], and "Sawt al-shā'ir" [The Poet's Voice]). This last theme occupied Jubrān's attention throughout his life. In the piece entitled, "Sawt al-shā'ir," he expresses this concept in the following words:

You are my brother and I love you.
I love you when you prostrate yourself in your
     mosque,
and kneel in your church, and pray in your
     synagogue.
You and I are sons of one faith—the Spirit.
                                    (Translated by H.M. Nahmad)

With the publication of his first English book, *The Madman* (1918), Jubrān began what in retrospect is clearly the second phase of his creative life. Although the author was to publish three more books in Arabic—*al-Mawākib* (The

Processions, 1919) and two collections of previously published items, *al-'Awāsif* (The Tempests, 1920) and *al-Badā'i' wa'l-tarā'if* (Beautiful and Rare Sayings, 1923)—for the remainder of his life he worked and published primarily in English.

The Madman states the themes of social criticism and the primacy of the outsider/poet/seer which recur throughout Jubrān's mature writings. It is significant that this book was first published just as the First World War ended, and sounds a note of growing pessimism in Jubrān's work from that period. *The Madman* illustrates Jubrān's masterful use of wisdom stories, or parables, a format in which he successfully married Eastern and Western elements. Wisdom stories are an important part of the Sufi tradition, which uses the themes of paradox and illusion to illustrate the spiritual immaturity or blindness of ordinary human beings who are attached to the transient world and its deceptive appearances. The book in general demonstrates a command of the paradox that reveals the truth. In the first of these stories, he explains how he became a madman:

One day, long before many gods were born, I woke from a deep sleep and found all my masks were stolen,—the seven masks I have fashioned and worn in seven lives,—I ran maskless through the crowded streets shouting, "Thieves, thieves, the cursèd thieves."

Men and women laughed at me and some ran to their houses in fear of me.

And when I reached the market place, a youth standing on a house-top cried, "He is a madman." I looked up to behold him; the sun kissed my own naked face.... my soul was inflamed with love for the sun, and I wanted my masks no more. And as if in a trance I cried, "Blessed, blessed are the thieves who stole my masks."

Thus I become a madman.

What appears to be a disaster—the theft of the masks—leads the narrator to discover a blessing in the loss of his false appearance and spurious protection and the revelation of the truth. The thirty-five parables which follow possess a flavor of irony which once again recalls Blake, and suggest the subjects of the sermons to be preached by Almustafa in *The Prophet*: malevolence, hypocrisy, injustice, ambition, unthinking conformity, moral and spiritual blindness and the narrow Puritanism so detested by Blake as well as by Jubrān. Several contain descriptions of the madman himself, with his attributes of darkness and constant searching, and a note of plangent pessimism in the final cry to the "God of lost souls."

In sum, *The Madman* demonstrates a sense of renewed energy, for the poet has managed to overcome his negative attitude and his inability to act; he finally accepts life with its evil and good and now blessed with a Divine Vision he dares to seize the Eternity of life as opposed to its ephemerality.

In 1919, Jubrān published his first and only collection of drawings, *Twenty Drawings*. The book included an introduction by Alice Raphael, a respected art critic, and contained works considered by some critics to be his best visual art up to that date. The pieces included in *Twenty Drawings* clearly demonstrate the mystical qualities Jubrān imbued in all his works, whatever the medium.

Al-Mawākib represents the only major attempt by Jubrān to create a lengthy Arabic poem in which he observed certain traditional principles of metrical patterns and rhyme. A mystical poem of two hundred and three lines, *al-Mawākib* is rich in its use of poetic image, metaphor, and symbol. Its tone is moral and its subject matter philosophical. It is a dialogue between two characters on the border of a forest, a youth and an old man, and portrays two aspects of life as "seen by man in two selves—the self of civilization… and the spontaneous simple self" or the natural self. The most powerful metaphor in the poem is the "Forest" or the "Wood" recalling the words of Wordsworth ("The Tables Turned"):

One impulse from a vernal wood
May teach you more of man,
Of moral evil and of good,
Than all the sages can.

In fact, *al-Mawākib* as a whole evokes that ancient feeling of the mystery of Nature:

Have you taken to the forest,
Shunned the palace for abode?
Followed brooklets in their courses,
Climbed the rocks along the road?
Have you ever bathed in fragrance,
Dried yourself in sheets of light?
Ever quaff the wine of dawning,
From ethereal goblets bright?

        (Translated by George Kheirallah)

In the midst of the intense heat of Jubrān's creative work in English, the writing of a long poem in traditional Arabic verse indicated the poet's desire to remain connected with his Arab poetic tradition. On its publication, *al-Mawākib* was bitterly attacked by the purists and traditionalists; the most vehement criticism, among others, came from the pen of 'Umar Farrūkh in *al-Amālī* magazine. Against a barrage of negative criticism and outright denunciation of Jubrān's attempt at vivifying a language and a literary tradition that had become stagnant, fifty years later two distinguished critics, Iḥsān 'Abbās and Muḥammad Yūsuf Najm, considered the poem as a landmark in the legacy of the *mahjar* poets, and took it as a yardstick against which to measure the entire corpus of the Arab literary renaissance in America. Whatever the merits or shortcomings of *al-Mawākib*, the poem was seminal in the development of modern Arabic poetry in the early twentieth century. Thus, Jubrān's reputation and fame placed him in a position of leadership to become *ustādh al-mahjariyyīn* (the mentor or master of the immigrant poets). The large group of Arab poets and writers who were active in creating the new literature were in need of guidance and direction, which Khalīl Jubrān seemed suited to provide.

On 20 April 1920, at Jubrān's studio in New York, Jubrān and Mīkhā'īl Nu'aymah joined with other Arab-Americans to found *al-Rābitah al-Qalamiyyah* (the Bond of the Pen), which was also known as "Arrabita" (its name transliterated into English). The Bond of the Pen was a literary society composed of Arab émigrés, including distinguished personalities such as 'Abd al-Masīḥ Ḥaddād, Nadrah Ḥaddād, Nasīb 'Arīdah, Rashīd Ayyūb, William Catzeflis, Īliyyā **Abū Mādī**, and Wadī' Bahūt. Amīn al-Rīhānī, although not a member of the Bond of the Pen, served as a supporter and occasional advisor to the group.

According to the minutes of the first meeting of the Bond of the Pen, as recorded by Mīkhā'īl Nu'aymah, the goal of the association was

... to lift Arabic literature from the quagmire of stagnation and imitation, and to infuse a new life into its veins so as to make of it an active force in the building up of the Arab nations.

At the second meeting of the group held one week later, its leadership was selected from among its ranks. In a development which reflects the stature Jubrān had by then attained even among a distinguished group, he was appointed as the Bond of the Pen's president, or "Chieftain" as the office was more poetically called. Mīkhā'īl Nu'aymah, who was selected as the Bond of the Pen's secretary, or "Counsellor," wrote the by-laws for the group.

Figures associated with the Bond of the Pen and the *mahjar* school would exert a powerful influence on both the Arab cultural renaissance and interfaith and intercultural relations between the West and the Arab world. This group of artists, essayists, poets and thinkers acted as cultural ambassadors between the East and the West at a significant historical moment when modernity and an early form of globalization were being thrust on the Arab world as a result of its newly found oil wealth and when America was emerging as an advanced industrial power. Jubrān and the others in his group served, through their incisive pens and poetic vision, as oracles that foresaw with piercing clarity the nature of the spiritual challenges confronting both America and the Arab world.

Even as Jubrān assumed leadership of the Bond of the Pen, he continued an active cycle of publishing. His *al-'Awāsif* was a collection of short narratives and prose poems which had originally appeared in the journals *Mir'āt al-Gharb* and *al-Funūn* between 1912 and 1918. At the heart of this collection of thirty-one pieces is his anguished cry in defence of his beleaguered people in Lebanon, who had been destroyed by famine and smothered by tyranny and injustice—powerfully expressed in his piece entitled

"Māta ahlī" (Dead Are My People). Also in 1920, Jubrān published his second English book, *The Forerunner*. In the story called "God's Fool" appears a character who is a dreamer. Being a stranger in a foreign land, knowing neither its language nor customs, the dreamer assumes the sordid behavior he witnesses as divine behavior. In fact, the fool sees God's image in everything. So that even when he is punished for his behavior, the dreamer accepts this reprimand as an honor.

The Forerunner is most significant because it paved the way (appositely, in view of its title) for *The Prophet.* It draws on the tradition of animal fables—as familiar to the Arab reader of *Kalīlah wa-Dimnah* as to the European reared on Aesop or the mediaeval tales of Reynard the Fox and his fellow beasts—to reveal universal truths with a simplicity and directness worthy of the best traditional tales. Animals serve in like fashion to demonstrate the littleness of their (and by inference, human) perceptions of the world in the face of the greatness of reality, as in the tale of a frog who is angrily pushed into the river by his comrades for telling them that they are correct in their speculations about the forces which move the log on which they are floating downstream. This semi-humorous story hides a deeper truth, that of the visionary seer whose understanding only earns him contempt from the common people until he couches his message in language acceptable to them, as in the final parable, that of the forerunner himself, who is only received when he actually denounces them:

From the housetop I proclaimed you hypocrites, pharisees, tricksters, false and empty earth-bubbles... . It was love lashed by its own self that spoke... . It was my hunger for your love that raged from the housetop, while my own love, kneeling in silence, prayed your forgiveness.

But it is this disguise

that opened your eyes, and my seeming to hate that woke your hearts.

The work ends on a note of hope and the possibility of redemption.

Some time after he published *The Forerun-*

ner, Jubrān's health, which had always been somewhat fragile, began to deteriorate. Nevertheless, he did not slow the pace of his work, and in 1921 Jubrān published *Iram dhāt al-'imad* (Iram, City of Lofty Pillars), a thematic play in the form of a discourse on mysticism. Though weak in dramatic interest, *Iram dhāt al-'imad* expresses some of Jubrān's most profound and abiding convictions, such as the following speech by its central character, Amīnah al-'Alawiyyah:

All things in this creation exist within you, and all things in you exist in creation; there is no border between you and the closest things, and there is no distance between you and the farthest things, and all things, from the lowest to the loftiest, from the smallest to the greatest, are within you as equal things.

(Translated by A.R. Ferris)

Amīnah al-'Alawiyyah is modeled on the great Sufi woman-poet Rābi'ah al-'Adawiyyah (714-801), a legendary figure, universally regarded as the most eloquent voice expressing divine love. The Sufi masters Ibn al-'Arabī (1165-1240), Ibn al-Fārid (1180-1234), and al-Ghazzālī (c. 1059-1111), had already taught him about the Unity of Being and inspired in him a deeper vision of the nature of the universe. Such a perspective is clearly reflected in the passage quoted above, which emphasizes the interdependence of the whole of creation.

In 1923, *al-Badā'i' wa'l-tarā'if*, a collection of Jubrān's previously published material in Arabic, was edited and published by the owner of Maktabat al-'Arab publishing house in Cairo. Jubrān was never given the opportunity to approve the title chosen for the book or the articles selected for inclusion. Much of the material in *al-Badā'i' wa'l-tarā'if* is of a mystical nature, especially the pieces entitled "Nafsī muthqalatun bi-athmārihā" (My Soul is Heavy-Laden with its Fruits), "Wa'azatnī nafsī" (My Spirit Advised Me), "al-Ard" (The Earth), "al-Kamāl" (Perfection), and fourteen short poems, some of which are composed in the tradition of the Andalusian poetic genre, the *muwashshah*. Included also are several pieces in which Jubrān expresses his ideas on politics (for example, "Lakum Lubnā-

nukum wa-liya Lubnānī" [You Have Your Lebanon and I Have Mine] and "al-Istiqlāl wa'l-tarābīsh" [Independence and the Fez]; on language (for example, "Mustaqbal al-lughah al-'arabiyyah" [The Future of the Arabic Language]; on culture (for example, "al-'Ahd al-jadīd" [The New Era]; and on philosophy and spirituality (for example, "Ibn Sīnā wa-qasīdatuhu" [Avicenna and His Poem], and two very short articles—one on "al-Ghazzālī" and the other on "Ibn al-Fārid." *al-Badā'i' wa'l-tarā'if* is most notable because it included imaginative sketches which Jubrān had drawn when he was seventeen years old of some of the greatest Arab historical figures such as Hārūn al-Rashīd and some of the most famous philosophers and poets in Arab history such as Ibn Sīnā (Avicenna), al-Ghazzālī, al-Khansā', Ibn al-Fārid, Abū Nuwās, Ibn al-Muqaffa' and others.

1923 was an especially important year in Jubrān's literary career because it was in that year that he published his most famous work, *The Prophet* (originally entitled *The Counsels*). It is not surprising, given the primacy of *The Prophet* in Jubrān's works, that all those preceding it have been described as exploratory, or even as rudimentary, the products of "an extremely sensitive soul groping its way towards a goal whose contours are as yet wrapped in mist." Despite its phenomenal popularity throughout the world, *The Prophet* holds an ambiguous position in English literature, or rather literature in English—a position which has so far largely debarred it from receiving serious critical attention in the West.

The words of Jesus Christ in the New Testament provided the inspiration for the message and spirit of *The Prophet*, while the influence of Nietzsche's *Thus Spake Zarathustra* was limited to shaping the format of the book. By the time Jubrān began working on *The Prophet*, he had pared his style down to a streamlined simplicity in a determined search for the most effective means of expressing his spiritual message, consciously modelled on the clarity and purity of Biblical diction.

The Prophet expresses Jubrān's message through experiences based on many varieties of human relations. The work conveys, above all, its author's impassioned belief in the healing and restorative power of Universal Love, in the Unity of Being, and in a mystical tradition in which love is the key to all things, as well as a liberating force for healing and reconciliation.

The Prophet presents twenty-six poetic sermons preached by Almustafa on a wide range of human subjects, including Love, Joy and Sorrow, Freedom, Good and Evil, Prayer, Religion, and Death. He delivers these homilies as he prepares to depart for his native island. Almustafa clearly experiences a tinge of regret at leaving those to whom he has given so much of himself. The female seer, Almitra, his soul-mate, knows that his departure will signify his return to the unborn state to repeat the cycle of reincarnation, which he promises to undergo ("A little while, a moment of rest upon the wind, and another woman shall bear me"), as a means of reaching those who have yet to be taught the truth. She senses his deep loneliness ("In your aloneness you have watched with our days…"). At the close, Almustafa explains the necessity of this "aloneness:"

And some of you have called me aloof, and drunk with my own aloneness… .
How could I have seen you save from a great height or a great distance?
How can one be indeed near unless he be far?

In these words he expresses the paradoxical duality of joy and sorrow, mutuality and solitude, the desire to remain and the longing to depart which Almitra recognizes in Almustafa and Mary Haskell sees in Jubrān himself—in the words of *The Prophet*:

Deep is your longing for the land of your memories and the dwelling place of your greater desires… .

Implicit in this view of the prophet and teacher is also the creative isolation of the artist, familiar from the Romantics and, in Jubrān's own time, from the writings of Thomas Mann, including his *Tonio Kröger*, whose main character cannot fulfill his mission unless, like Christ in the Garden of Gethsemane, he moves apart from his disciples to confront the trials of his calling in solitude.

Almustafa's views on Love are a synthesis of Muslim and Christian mystical teachings. These views have much in common with both the Sufi masters and mediaeval Christian mystics such as Julian of Norwich (1342-1416), St. Teresa of Ávila (1515-1582), and St. Catherine of Siena (1347-1380) in their perception of love's dual nature as a source of searing ecstasy and profound pain:

To be wounded by your own understanding of love;
And to bleed willingly and joyfully.

Jubrān emphasizes the essential identity of love, joy, sorrow and pain, and finds unity within these apparently irreconcilable differences: "The righteous is not innocent of the deeds of the wicked," and "You cannot separate the just from the unjust and the good from the wicked." Although these statements seem at first to run counter to the recorded words of Jesus, Jubrān probably intended them to be interpreted as a counterbalance to the dualistic, or even Manichaeistic, approach to Christianity which led to sectarianism and schism within the Christian community. Prayer, too, is treated with a similar concern to dispel religious hypocrisy, though in a subtle and skilful manner rather than by overt condemnation:

You pray in your distress and in your need; would that you might pray also in the fullness of your joy and in your days of abundance.

In these words can be found the spirit of Jubrān's earlier Arabic writings carried on in a more profound form. Once again, the insistence on the healing power of Universal Love as the source of true wisdom is emphasized. It cannot be contained in words because of its infinite nature: "Who among you does not feel that his power to love is boundless?"

The great appeal of *The Prophet* rests not so much in its philosophical construction as in the compelling nature of its language and the simplicity of its message. Avoiding the crude vitalism or labored didacticism which could so easily have reduced its message to bathos, it speaks to the reader in a positive, uplifting tone, encouraging rather than hectoring, couching its criticism in words of inspiring exhortation rather than crushing the spirit with harshness. For Jubrān himself, *The Prophet* constituted his "first work" in that it was a mature effort which expressed his philosophy in its clearest and purest form. With the possible exception of his last great work, *Jesus, the Son of Man*—which was written with a somewhat different purpose in mind—none of his writings would ever achieve the same level. He was aware, however, that it could not be the full summation of all he had to share with the world.

Jubrān's next published work after *The Prophet* was *Sand and Foam* (1926), a book of aphorisms. Some of the materials in *Sand and Foam* were originally written by Jubrān in Arabic and were translated into English for inclusion in this book. Certain of the sayings in *Sand and Foam* echo the voices of both Almustafa and William Blake in their gnomic, pithy forms. The proverbial utterances on love, for example, and on religion, are a case in point: "Love and doubt have never been on speaking terms." And the love that does not "renew itself every day becomes a habit and in turn a slavery." The sermon on Religion in *The Prophet* is almost surpassed by two aphorisms in *Sand and Foam*:

Many a doctrine is like a window pane.
We see truth through it, but it divides us from the
*   truth.*
Our God in His gracious thirst will drink us all,
*   the dewdrop and the tear.*

Alongside these we may set the wise words on the relationship between men and women:

Men who do not forgive women their little faults
*   will never enjoy their great virtues.*

Jubrān sought to give lasting form to his vision of Jesus in his longest and most ambitious work in English, *Jesus, the Son of Man* (1928). In this work, Jubrān portrays Jesus through the eyes of seventy-eight of his contemporaries, and through "His words and His deeds as told and recorded by those who knew Him." Most of those contemporaries are real, historical figures mentioned in the Gospels. A few, however, are the creation of Jubrān's imagination. Once more, Jubrān rejects the mawkish portrayal of Jesus which had

appeared in other sources. Jubrān has one of his characters reflect on Jesus with these words: "He was far from being lowly and meek. Lowliness is something I detest; while meekness to me is but a phase of weakness." These phrases have a markedly Nietzschean ring and are a manifestation of Nietzsche's continuing influence on Jubrān. Jubrān's Jesus, then, is far from a weak and pitiful figure; he is not a Man of Sorrows lacking any spark of vitality or resistance.

Jubrān explains the title of his 1928 book in words he attributes to the disciple John, son of Zebedee and brother of James:

Now you would know why some of us call Him
the Son of Man. He Himself desired to be called
by that name, for He knew the hunger and the
thirst of man, and He beheld man seeking after
His greater self. The Son of Man was Christ the
Gracious, who would be with us all.

The frontispiece to *Jesus, the Son of Man*, drawn by Jubrān himself, depicts Jesus as a man whose steeply-angled forehead, thick eyebrows, determined chin, full mouth, and strong neck combine to give an antidote to any idea of a piously resigned half-man. Jubrān's Jesus comes closer to contemporary portrayals of Christ such as those in Nikos Kazantzakis's *The Last Temptation*: fully human and entirely male as well as divine. This is mirrored by the description given by Jubrān's Nathaniel:

... It is the mighty hunter I would preach, and
the mountainous spirit unconquerable.

Because Jubrān kept to a rather hectic work schedule, he neglected his health, which deteriorated steadily. The pace of Jubrān's output is demonstrated by the fact that in 1931 he published *The Earth Gods*, shortly before his death. *The Earth Gods* seems to be a fragment rather than a complete work. Whether Jubrān began writing this piece as a play as early as 1915 or earlier is not clear. The finished product, however, lacks dramatic unity while each of the three characters is used by the author as a mere mouthpiece. The poem is full of gloom and despair, perhaps reflecting the mood of a man facing his own mortality. *The Earth Gods* is a symbolical poem in which three gods represent three tendencies in man's nature: boredom with power, the relishing of power, and faith in the power of love. It is this last element that is the key to the message of *The Earth Gods*: man must aspire to acquire the attributes of the Divine if he is ever to reconcile the duality that is his curse. It is only through love that confusion, anxiety, and restlessness can be overcome. Peace in the world will only come in dance and song and a newly found humanity: "And let love, human and frail, command the coming day."

Jubrān died on Friday 10 April 1931, at St. Vincent's Hospital in New York after a long and painful illness, described in the autopsy as "cirrhosis of the liver with incipient tuberculosis in one of the lungs." For two days his body lay in a funeral parlor, where friends, colleagues, and thousands of admirers came to pay their last respects. Jubrān's body was then taken to Boston, where a funeral service was held in the Church of our Lady of the Cedars. Jubrān's remains were then taken to a vault to await transfer to Lebanon. Jubrān's body arrived at the port of Beirut on 21 August. It was then carried to its final resting place, his hometown of Bisharri, where it was interred in the old chapel of the Monastery of Mar Sarkis. Today, not far from Mar Sarkis, a permanent Jubrān museum has been established by The Jubrān National Committee.

Following his death, two more works by Jubrān appeared: *The Wanderer* (1932) and *The Garden of the Prophet* (1933).

The Wanderer is a collection of fifty parables reflecting an Eastern flavor of the perennial philosophy. In this work, Jubrān promotes an ethic of compassion that stands in opposition to the legal and political hypocrisies created by man to protect vested interests. This ethic is a means for overcoming that duality which exists between word and deed. In *The Wanderer*, Jubrān amplifies religious themes he explored in earlier works. Here, he denounces the strain within Christianity which condemns all those souls who have not been baptized as Christians. Once again, Jubrān displays a trademark scepticism about the fruits of so-called civilized life— in the words of the parable entitled "Peace and

War:" "For God's sake, run for your lives. Civilization is after us."

The Garden of the Prophet, conceived by Jubrān as the second part of a trilogy planned to conclude with the unwritten *The Death of the Prophet,* remained unfinished at the time of Jubrān's death. *The Garden of the Prophet* was put together by Barbara Young, an American poet who served as Jubrān's amanuensis during his last years. Barbara Young not only collated scattered manuscript materials but pieced them together with many of her own words, drawing on Jubrān's Arabic works of a mystical nature, especially the piece entitled "Nafsī muthqalatun bi-athmārihā" from *al-Badā'i' wa'l-tarā'if* (published in 1923). *The Garden of the Prophet* does not rise to the level of Jubrān's finest work, lacking its clear vision and sincerity, and is of lesser literary value, although it does in places recall his characteristic style and thought; in the final analysis, it in no way diminishes or depreciates his previous work or his stature.

In celebration of its sixtieth anniversary in 1995, the prestigious Penguin publishing company named Jubrān as among the most important authors of the twentieth century, and included him in the anniversary series in honor of those authors. Today, there is every indication that Jubrān's worldwide readership continues to grow. His stature and importance increase as time passes, for although he died in 1931 and his first book was published one hundred years ago, his message remains as potent and meaningful today as when he was writing. With its emphasis on the healing process, the universal, the natural, the eternal, and the timeless, his work represents a powerful affirmation of the human spirit.

The need for Jubrān's voice to be heeded remains strong. In the seventy-five years since he died, the Arab world has been transformed beyond recognition by the oil riches that have come its way. Whilst this phenomenon has not been without its benefits, bringing progress in place of stagnation, among some of the wealthier Arabs it has engendered a materialistic approach that runs counter to their spiritual heritage. Religious intolerance, too, thrives in the Middle East as it does elsewhere in the world. These are subjects on which Jubrān has much of value to say, and throughout his English and Arabic writings, he reminds us of the sanctity of our Mother Earth and the need to protect the natural environment. But it is as the voice of reconciliation and consolation that Jubrān needs most of all to be heard.

Khalīl Jubrān was truly a citizen of the world: a man from the East who brought a much-needed element of spirituality to the West; and eventually a man of the West as well, benefiting from an environment in which freedom, democracy, and equality of opportunity opened doors for him. His work remains a shining example, on an individual level, of the inspired results that can be forthcoming when cultures merge in a spirit of unity and goodwill.

REFERENCES

Ihsān ʿAbbās and Mohammad Y. Najm, *al-Shiʿr al-ʿarabī fī ʾl-mahjar* ("Arabic Poetry in North America", Beirut: Dār Sādir, 1967);

S. B. Bushrui (trans.), *Unpublished Gibran Letters to Ameen Rihani* (Beirut: Rihani House for The World Lebanese Cultural Union, 1972);

—— and A. Mutlak (eds.), *Fī dhikrā Jubrān Khalīl Jubrān: Abhāth al-muʾtamar al-ʿawwal liʾl-dirāsāt al-Jubrāniyyah* ("In Memory of Khalīl Jubrān: The First Colloquium on Jubrān Studies", Beirut: Maktabat Lubnān, 1981); commemorating the 50th anniversary of Jubrān's death;

—— and Joe Jenkins, *Khalil Gibran: Man and Poet: A New Biography* (Oxford: Oneworld, 1998);

—— and S. H. al-Kuzbari (eds. and trans.), *Gibran: Love Letters* (Oxford: Oneworld, 1995);

Wadīʿ Dīb, *al-Shiʿr al-ʿarabi fī ʾl-mahjar al-amrīkī* ("Arabic Poetry in America", Beirut: Rihani House, 1955);

Rose Ghurayyib, *Jubrān fī āthārihi al-kitābiyyah* ("The Writings of Khalīl Jubrān", Beirut: Dār al-Makshūf, 1969);

J. Gibran and K. Gibran, *Kahlil Gibran: His Life and World* (Boston: New York Graphic Society, 1974; New York: Avenel Books, 1981; New York: Interlink Books, 1991);

Kahlil Gibran: Essays and Introductions (Bei-

rut: Rihani House, 1970); anthology of criticisms compiled for the Gibran International Festival, May 23-30, 1970;

K. S. Hawi, *Khalil Gibran: His Background, Character and* Works (Beirut: American University of Beirut, 1963; Beirut: Arab Institute for Research and Publishing, 1972; London: Third World Centre for Research and Publication, 1982);

V. Hilu (ed.), *Beloved Prophet: The Love Letters of Kahlil Gibran and Mary Haskell and her Private Journal* (New York: Alfred A. Knopf, 1972);

Y. Huwayik, *Gibran in Paris* (New York: Popular Library, 1976); trans. and intro. M. Moosa;

Wahīb Kayrūz, *ʿĀlam Jubrān al-fikrī* ("Jubrān's Intellectual World", 2 vols., Beirut: Bacharia, 1983);

M. Naimy, *al-Ghirbāl* ("The Sieve", Beirut: Naufal, 1998); first published 1923;

——, *Kahlil Gibran: His Life and His Work* (Beirut: Khayāt, 1964; Beirut: Naufal, 1974); includes twenty seven letters written to the author;

A. S. Otto, *The Art of Kahlil Gibran* (Port Author: Hinds Printing Company, 1965); includes four letters;

Alice Raphael, *Twenty Drawings* (New York: Alfred A. Knopf, 1919);

William Shedadi, *Kahlil Gibran: A Prophet in the Making* (Beirut: American University of Beirut, 1991); book based on the manuscript pages of *The Madman, The Forerunner, The Prophet,* and *The Earth Gods,* including four hitherto unpublished manuscripts: *Lullaby, The Last Guest, Untitled, Poverty & Sundry Aphorisms;*

George Syidah, *Adabunā wa-udabāʾunā fī ʾl-mahājir al-amrīkiyyah* ("Our Literature and Men of Letters in the Americas", Tripoli: al-Saʾih Books, 1999);

Robin Waterfield, *Prophet: The Life and Times of Kahlil Gibran* (Harmondsworth [UK]: Penguin, 1998);

Martin L. Wolf, "Preface" to *A Treasury of Kahlil Gibran* (New York, The Citadel Press, 1965); translated from the Arabic by A. R. Ferris and edited by Martin L. Wolf;

Barbara Young, *This Man from Lebanon: A*

Study of Kahlil Gibran (New York: privately printed by the Syrian American Press, 1931; New York: Alfred A. Knopf, 1945, 1981).

Bibliographies

Suheil Bushrui (ed.), *Khalil Gibran: Selected*

Bibliography (Beirut: Gibran International Conference, 17-21 August 1983); Arabic and English;

Yūsuf 'Abd al-Ahad (ed.), *Jubrān fī āthār al-dārisīn* ("Jubrān in the Writings of Scholars", Damascus: Ittihād al-Kuttāb al-'Arab, 1981).

Mahmūd Tāhir Lāshīn
(1894 – 1954)

SABRY HAFEZ
University of London

WORKS

Sukhriyyat al-nāy ("The Flute's Irony", Cairo: Matba'at al-Shabāb, 1926); collection of short stories;

Yuhkā anna ("Once Upon a Time", Cairo: Dār al-'Usūr, 1930); collection of short stories;

Hawwā' bi-lā Ādam ("Eve Without Adam", Cairo: Matba'at al-I'timād, 1933/1934); novel;

al-Niqāb al-tā'ir, wa-qisas ukhrā ("The Flying Veil, and Other Stories", Cairo: Matba'at Halīm, 1940).

Collected Works

al-A'māl al-kāmilah ("The Collected Works"), ed. Sabry Hafez (Cairo: al-Majlis al-A'lā li'l-Thaqāfah, 1999).

Works in Translation

"Village Small Talk", in: Sabry Hafez, *The Genesis of Arabic Narrative Discourse* (London: Saqi Books, 1993), 262-68; translation of "Hadīth al-qaryah", tr. Catherine Cobham.

The arrival of Lāshīn on the Egyptian literary scene in the 1920s marked a turning-point in the history of modern Arabic narrative discourse in general and the short story in particular. He was an outstandingly vigorous pioneer who developed the genre and brought its formative

years to a close. His writings represent the culmination, in both form and content, of the work of previous writers and of his contemporaries. He was also the most gifted and relatively more prolific writer of a versatile literary group, *Jamā'at al-Madrasah al-Hadīthah* (The Modern School, 1922-27), which played a decisive role in developing modern Arabic narrative discourse, extending its reading public, and shaping the characteristics of the new sensibility of that period.

Lāshīn was born on 7 June 1894 in a middle-class family living in one of Cairo's popular and most overcrowded quarters, al-Sayyidah Zaynab, where he spent his childhood. From the outset, his life was intermingled with the attempts to establish new literary discourses and root them in Arabic culture. This is because his father, Husnī Lāshīn, was a widely read army officer, fond of literature and interested in cultural issues in general, a fact that provided our writer from the start with a rich library at home. His elder brother, Muhammad 'Abd al-Rahīm Lāshīn, also played an important role in educating and inspiring his younger brother. The life of Muhammad 'Abd al-Rahīm Lāshīn strikingly resembles that of another eldest son of a prominent literary family, Muhammad Taymūr (d. 1921, cf. entry on Mahmūd **Taymūr**). Muhammad 'Abd al-Rahīm Lāshīn graduated from Madrasat al-Mu'allimīn al-'Ulyā (Teachers Training School), then was sent to England to study history. When he was in London, he fell under the spell of the vibrant English theatre scene in the West End and Covent Garden. The great actors of the early years of the twentieth century impressed him, and when he returned to Egypt in 1914, he devoted the rest of his short life (he died in 1916) to improving both the standard of theatre and of acting and actors. He established a theatre troupe, for which he wrote or translated the necessary texts, and acted and directed most of the group's productions. His fondness for literature, and his artistic activities and ideas had a seminal influence on his younger brother, Mahmūd Tāhir Lāshīn, and on many of his friends who later formed *Jamā'at al-Madrasah al-Hadīthah.* Although his premature death affected the family, his enthusiastic spirit propelled his younger brother, Mahmūd Tāhir Lāshīn, to step into his shoes and pioneer another genre of modern literature and art.

Before his elder brother's death, Lāshīn enjoyed a solid education both at home and at school. He went to the prestigious Muhammad 'Alī Primary School, then on to the Khidīwiyyah (Khedival) Secondary School, from which he obtained his Baccalaureate in 1912. He then went to the High School of Engineering (Cairo) from which he graduated in 1917 as a civil engineer, one year after the death of his brother. On 17 July 1918 he was appointed at *Maslahat al-Tanzīm* (City Planning Department) and worked as an urban planning officer, a job that acquainted him with the inner details of the life in Cairo's different districts and classes. He continued to work in this department until his retirement in 1953, and died after few months' illness on 17 April 1954.

Lāshīn commenced writing short stories as early as 1921 or 1922, but he refrained from publishing any of his early attempts and continued to improve on them until late 1924. From then on, he wrote and published frequently in *al-Fajr* and, after its closure, in several other magazines (including *al-Jadīd, al-Hadīth, Shahrazād, al-Majallah al-Jadīdah,*

and *al-Hilāl.* He was, in fact, the first member of the group to write short stories to any significant extent, and was the most profound of them. He was also the only one with the courage to collect his works in book form, for, despite the fact that many of his colleagues (e.g. Ahmad Khayrī Sa'īd, Husayn Fawzī and Yahyā **Haqqī**) wrote and published a number of relatively mature and coherent stories, they did not at the time collect them in book form. His first collection, *Sukhriyyat al-nāy* (The Flute's Irony), appeared in 1926, and his second, *Yuhkā anna* (Once Upon a Time), in 1929/1930, bringing most of his work within the context of the Modern School, which was already going into decline by the end of the 1920s.

The Modern School did not start as a proper literary school, as the name might seem to imply, but rather as a gathering of enthusiastic young writers whose common dream of issuing a paper of their own, one in which they could express their views and publish their unconventional works, took almost a decade to materialize. As early as 1917, the nucleus of this group had already been formed as a small and zealous study group. It consisted of only four members: Lāshīn, who was a student at the High School of Engineering; Ahmad Khayrī Sa'īd and Husayn Fawzī, who were students at the School of Medicine; and Hasan Mahmūd, who was a student at the Faculty of Arts.

The group soon succeeded in attracting new members, and over the next eight years developed and shaped their ideas. Those eight years, 1917-1925, were to be of special significance in the nationalist struggle in Egypt and the growth of its aspirations for independence. By the end of 1924 they had managed to reach a degree of uniformity of ideas, justifying the claim to be a literary school. A most important stage in the life of this school was reached when the first issue of its weekly, *al-Fajr: sahīfat al-hadm wa'l-binā'* (The Dawn: The Paper for Destruction and Construction), appeared in January 1925. The title and subtitle of this journal emphasize the intention to break with previous practices and herald a new dawn, to dismantle the edifice of the old canon in order to construct new modes of literary thought.

Like many avant-garde literary movements, the Modern School held their meetings in a pavement café or in the private homes of their members (e.g. Lāshīn and Ibrāhīm al-Misrī). Their cultural views and artistic visions were developed and shaped through fervent discussion. They were influenced mainly by European culture and literature. Yahyā Haqqī, a member of the group, divided their cultural development into two stages. During the first and less significant stage, they read mainly French, British, American and Italian authors. These included French writers such as La Fontaine, Balzac, Hugo, Dumas père and fils, Baudelaire, Flaubert, de Maupassant, and Rimbaud; British writers such as Shakespeare, Scott, Carlyle, Thackeray, Dickens, Stevenson, and Wilde; American writers such as Poe and Mark Twain; and Italians such as Dante, Boccaccio, and Pirandello. The influence of these authors was largely a theoretical one; it may have increased their knowledge of artistic devices but in general it failed to give them inspiration.

During the second and crucial stage, which Haqqī calls *marhalat al-ghidhā' al-rūhī* (the stage of spiritual nourishment), they fell entirely under the influence of Russian literature until it became the *primum mobile* behind their movement and the main source of their inspiration. They identified easily with the world of pre-revolutionary Russian literature and read Pushkin, Gogol, Lermontov, Turgenev, Dostoevski, Tolstoy, Chekhov, Gorky, and Artsybashev. The impact of these authors' works upon them was enormous. Some of the leading members of the group went as far as to deny any influence but that of Russian literature; one asserted that Russian literature and music were the closest to "our spirit and our problems," and others devoted a great deal of time and effort to introducing and translating Russian literature. Indeed, there is hardly an issue of *al-Fajr* without one or more Russian writers studied or translated in it. There is also some evidence to suggest the group's acquaintance with the work of the Palestinian author Khalīl **Baydas** and the translations of Russian short-stories in his collection *al-Nafā'is al-'asriyyah* in Palestine.

Indeed, Baydas's collection was published in Cairo a few months before the launching of *al-Fajr.*

The group was to play a crucial role in creating a favorable atmosphere through the spread of its critical concepts and ideas, which made it easier for Lāshīn himself to omit the lengthy introductions that his predecessors had felt compelled to write. In contrast to his predecessors, Lāshīn (surrounded as he was by the other members of the group who were naturally critical as well as supportive) realized the necessity of rewriting and revising his work in order to refine, compress, and improve its structure and style. This enabled him to provide the modern Arabic short story, in the early stage of its development, with a rich world of experiences and characters. In his few works, he was able to create a coherent artistic vision and to put the new ideas of his group into practice. As well as the works of his elder brother, who ignited his enthusiasm for literature, Lāshīn read the short stories of his predecessors and assimilated their more significant achievements. He especially tried to avoid treating their themes or dealing with their character types. Nevertheless, he did adopt in his own way some of the 'Ubayds' and Muhammad Taymūr's themes, but did not overwork them, as they had done. He clearly intended to achieve a wide modulation in theme, character, and structure.

Lāshīn, himself a son of the middle class, naturally focused his work on its characters and values. Yet he does not side with this class at the expense of art or reality, nor does he offer the reader his own views about it. The people who matter in Lāshīn's world represent the whole spectrum of middle-class life: for example, a lawyer who comes home, after studying in France, with ambitious dreams in his mind and tuberculosis in his body which annihilates both his life and dreams, in his first published collection, *Sukhriyyat al-nāy* (1926). Another lawyer brings home from France, along with his excellent qualifications, a foreign wife who erodes his happiness, wealth, fame, stability, and honor. The wife fails to adjust her life or habits to those of Egypt, and when she dies she leaves behind a miserable daughter who is unable to feel at home with either the Egyptian community or the ghetto of alien Europeans ("al-Witwāt," The Bat). A third lawyer falls for the widow of his dearest friend and soon turns a discussion of the complicated problem of her inheritance to maudlin talk and kisses ("Wa-lākinna-hā 'l-ha-yāh," But That's Life). In "Fī qarār al-hāwiya" (In the Bottom of the Abyss) a teacher of geography and calligraphy who is dismissed from his job descends into alcoholism and forces his wife into prostitution. "Manzil li'l-ījār" (A House to Let) tells the story of a civil servant who has risen from the working class and gets married to the domineering daughter of his previous master, who is now bankrupt. In "Jawlah khāsirah" (A Lost Round) another civil servant pours scorn on the guttersnipes of the overcrowded slums of the city. Most of these civil servants spend a great deal of their time in pavement cafés, chatting over a cup of tea and a hubble-bubble pipe about their fears, interests, and superstitions (as in "Qissat 'ifrīt," A Story of a Ghost), or venting their feelings about their sexual frustrations (in "al-Fakhkh," The Trap).

Apart from these civil servants and pro-fessionals, there are also other characters from different sections of the middle class: a poly-gamous, self-made cloth merchant who treats his children badly ("al-Infijār," The Explosion); a foreign salesman who is rejected by the profess-ionals of his class ("al-Witwāt"); and a wicked, educated dropout from the upper class who secures his future by marrying rich old women and fleecing them of their money ("Bayt al-tā'ah," The House of Obedience). There are also many others, such as the rich widow who ensnares young men through her wealth and her sensually plump figure, in "al-Kahlah al-maz-huwwah" (The Coquettish Old Woman); the widow who fights at all costs for the future of her children ("al-Qadar," Destiny); and the rejected wife who jealously keeps up with the news of her former husband with his new wife ("Mādhā yaqūl al-wad'," What Does Fortune Say?). A student comes from the countryside to complete his higher education in the capital and seduces the wronged wife of his next-door neighbor, in "Bayt al-tā'ah"; yet another one allows his childish curiosity to ruin his neigh-bor's life ("al-Shabah al-māthil fī 'l-mir'āh," A Ghost in the Mirror). Corrupt clerics are repre-sented—two Muslims and one Christian—taking advantage of the veneration in which their robes are held. Although Mahmūd Taymūr's stand vis-à-vis religious sheikhs was almost identical with Lāshīn's, one cannot say that Lāshīn's excori-ation of these religious figures was influenced by Taymūr's work because some of Lāshīn's work was published before those of Taymūr. Lāshīn was the only writer to attack both sheikhs and clergymen. His story "Mintaqat al-samt" (District of Silence) in which he gave Christian clergy-men the same severe treatment, had no pre-cedent and no successors for many years to come.

In addition to all these, there are two other characters that are particularly significant, not only because they offer the reader the first coherent presentation of the frustrated and thwarted individual in modern Egyptian litera-ture, but also because they have momentous political implications. The first is the protagonist of "al-Zā'ir al-sāmit" (The Silent Visitor), a brave soldier in Ahmad 'Urābī's army who is dragged down by the disastrous rout of the revolutionary forces in 1882; his children are brought up by a defeated and socially frustrated father and subsequently meet with extreme misfortune. The second is one of the activists in the 1919 Egyptian revolution; his fate, described in "Taht 'ajalat al-hayāh" (At Life's Mercy), is no less tragic than that of his predecessor. He also has a dramatic fall, from being a brilliant student at Cairo University, a revolutionary activist, and a far-sighted intellectual to become a frustrated man filled with despair and vague fears. Without a clear understanding of what the failure of 'Urābī's uprising meant to Egyptians, or what the ramifications were of the brutal destruction of Egypt's aspirations during the 1919 revolution, it is difficult to comprehend fully the significance of these two short stories or to appreciate some of their various levels of meaning. It is not merely a coincidence that Lāshīn chose a soldier to portray the deep suffering and humiliation of Egypt's defeat by the occupying British forces and a clever student to portray the far-reaching effect of the crushing of the country's hopes for independence, nor that his treatment of the second story is more convincing and artistically more coherent than the first one. After all Lāshīn was himself one of the intellectuals who were involved in the 1919 revolution and suffered from the dissipation of its hopes.

All but one of Lāshīn's stories take place in the city, where he focused on two main scenes: the first domestic, inside the houses of the urban middle class, and the second public, in cafés, government offices, and the streets and alleys of the poor quarters of Cairo. This does not mean that Lāshīn offers his reader limited scope of movement in the location of his action. Within the city he introduces a wide range of common and interesting places, achieving thereby a kind of spatial survey. There are variations on the internal scene in the middle-class house, with its multifarious degrees of poverty and wealth, tidiness and disorder, cleanliness and filth. When he takes his characters outside, he accompanies them to a wide variety of locations: pleasant pavement cafés, gloomy bars, the hall of a canonical court, a boat on the Nile, the cemetery, or the tram stop. He also mentions Alexandria, the seaside, and Upper Egypt, without departing from Cairo, which remains the centre of his world. For him, anywhere else exists only verbally and not factually.

In his *mise en scène* Lāshīn uses three methods. The first is romantic representation, dealing with the location of the action through the emotional and sometimes sentimental moods of the characters involved and denying it any objective, independent existence. The second is photographic representation, where he tries to achieve verisimilitude and describes the setting in the minutest detail, regardless of its function in the work. The third is realistic representation, in which the scene, described in a condensed and functional manner, becomes integral to the action without denying the location its independence from both action and character; in this case the main concern is to attain integration and harmony between the various aspects of the work. These three methods do not correspond to three stages in Lāshīn's literary career, but coexist, mainly because of the brevity of the period in which he

wrote the bulk of his work. With this wide range of urban characters and locations, Lāshīn succeeds in providing his readers with a comprehensive social survey of Egyptian life in the 1920s. He deals with a range of themes and issues in his attempt to base the short story in the life of the middle class that formed the major part of the new reading public.

Among Lāshīn's themes, three were inherited from previous writers and the rest were new. Like 'Abdallāh Nadīm before him, he exploits the theme of alcoholism and without managing to free himself entirely from his predecessor's overtones. Even so, his treatment of the theme is more plausible since he delineates some of the reasons why men drink, treats the consequences of alcoholism and how it leads to the tragic disintegration of the family, and describes how drinking can be a symptom of a state of grave anxiety and remorse and often a prelude to insanity. Lāshīn also introduces some illuminating variations on the brothers 'Ubayds' favorite theme, that of incompatible spouses. Even though he too emphasizes the problem of cultural gap between the spouses, he manages to avoid repeating their opinions on the subject. He shows his appreciation of marriage as an institution which has enabled civilized man to channel and control his natural craving for sex and companionship, but still attacks marriages established on feeble foundations and raises a variety of issues concerning the causes and consequences of such marriages. He criticizes laws and conventions that grant husbands rights that they certainly do not deserve and impose heavy burdens on the wife. He delineates the grave consequences of resorting to the matchmaker, whose very existence typifies the regressive habits and customs within the framework of which marriage takes place, and blames the age-gap between partners in a marriage for its effects on their social and psychological well-being. The third theme that Lāshīn derives from the work of his predecessors (such as al-**Shidyāq** and **Jubrān**) is that of corruption and hypocrisy among religious leaders. He criticizes what he regards as their unjustified status. He shows how their religious pretensions are wholly insincere and self-interested and how they exploit religion to facilitate their sinful behavior. His treatment of this theme adds depth to the representation of the evil nature of such people, adding ignorance, deception, pimping, and greed to their vices.

In addition to these three themes which Lāshīn inherited but which he was able to revitalize and give further depth through mature representation and narrative structure, there are a number of new ones: polygamy and the ways in which it militates against the polygamist's children and inflicts evils on the whole family; the lack of healthy accommodation, especially for those on limited incomes; and the need to adapt to new cultural influences properly and carefully (especially the ones coming from occidental civilization) and to be constantly aware of their possible consequences. He also exposes quack doctors ("Jawlah khāsirah"), faith healing ("al-Zā'ir al-sāmit"), the closed horizons of civil servants who have many aspirations they are unable to fulfill ("al-Fakhkh," The Trap), and corrupt policemen who make decisions according to the size of the bribe they are offered ("al-Shāwīsh Baghdādī," Sergeant Baghdādī). He also treats the dramatic effect of superstition on family life ("Qissat 'ifrīt" and "al-Zā'ir al-sāmit"), and illustrates the suffering of helpless widows in a world without adequate security ("al-Qadar" and "Madhā yaqūl al-wad'"). He criticizes the annoying, yet traditional interference of mother-in-laws in the life of newly-weds, and scorns the greed of those who use marriage as a bridge to wealth in "Ālū" (Hello) and "Bayt al-tā'ah".

Lāshīn's desire to control the form and content of his work demonstrates itself in his stand *vis-à-vis* human character and women in particular. Apart from being heavily influenced by the Turkish criteria of female beauty, it seems at first glance that Lāshīn supports women's emancipation, but deeper exploration shows this not to be the case. There is evidence to suggest that he considers women to be the origin of malice, vice, evil and anxiety. Even in those stories which seem to defend the wronged woman, such as "Bayt al-tā'ah" and "Fī qarār al-

hāwiyah", he fails to vindicate her on the basis of her own intrinsic merits (for instance, for being a sensitive, cultured, attractive person like women in the stories of the 'Ubayd brothers), but rather because she is victim of man's tyranny. In these same stories, alongside the victims, there are other women who play the villain, plan adultery carefully and skillfully, and take revenge promptly when ill-treated. With a number of Lāshīn's female characters fidelity is in short supply; revenge is more important than loyalty; and a justification for their deeds is readily available. Women can, and do, easily turn their husbands' life into hell, impoverishing them without the slightest compunction, betraying their memories with their closest friends, or using influential lovers to impose their will upon their spouses. When serving as a mother-in-law, the female character is wicked and unbearable; as a mother, she can offer nothing but hollow sympathy, and may indeed harm her daughter by her naïve good intentions. She can also be the cause of many crimes committed by men and plays an active role in prostituting her fellow women. However, in spite of the nature of these female characterizations, there is as much justification for calling him a misanthropist as a misogynist, since his male characters are often no less degenerate. In his works the male character can be a ruthless drunkard who compels his young daughter to go out into the severe cold of midnight to buy him drink, or who treats his wives malevolently and relieves them of their money. When he himself makes some money, the first idea to cross his mind is that of marrying another wife and being parsimonious with his own children. If he occupies a religious position, he exploits people's confidence in order to satisfy his lust and greed; if he attains a public position, he accepts bribes. He never hesitates to betray his friends with their wives or to marry women out of avarice.

And yet, however dark his portraits of men and women, Lāshīn is by no means a moral preacher; indeed, among Arab short-story writers up to the 1930s, he is the least didactic. He tries to bring about reform not through exhortation, but instead through the provocative effect of his art. His posture towards the characters that deserve to be criticized is indicative of a sarcastic and satirical attitude that he adopts towards certain social phenomena in his society. Some of his contemporaries realized the provocative nature of his satires but failed to see his point (in his introduction to *al-Niqāb al-tā'ir*, for example, Husayn Fawzī blames this satirical attitude for the critics' neglect of Lāshīn's work and for their deliberate attempt to hide it from the European orientalists so it would not deface their spotless image of Egyptian social life; see *al-Niqāb al-tā'ir*, 8). Though Lāshīn presents a gloomy picture of Egypt's social life, it is difficult to maintain that his way of expressing his disaffection with dominant social values is based purely on distortion. His candor in stripping both character and situation to the bone is supported by sensitive artistry, a fine sense of humor, and a deep understanding of the undercurrents of Egyptian life.

In his sense of structure he is the strongest among his contemporaries, a feature well illustrated by an analysis of one of his mature stories, "Hadīth al-qaryah" (Village Small Talk). "Hadīth al-qaryah" demonstrates the degree of maturity and sophistication which Arabic narrative discourse had attained by 1929. Its primary theme is the very process that brought the new narrative discourse into existence: the search for modes of development and progress. It tells the story of a visit to a village by two city-dwellers and their encounter with its folks and their leader, the village *imām*. During this visit, shaykh Muhsin (the village *imām*), relates another story about a *mu'āwin* (a government official) who comes to visit the village from the city, spots the beautiful wife of 'Abd al-Samī', offers her husband a job in the city, and asks him to bring his wife with him to help with the domestic chores in the *mu'āwin*'s house. 'Abd al-Samī' soon discovers that they are having an affair; surprising them in bed, he kills them both and then goes to the police station and confesses. This story is related to the two urban visitors as part of the nightly chat, which gives the story its title. Lāshīn calls his story "Hadīth al-qaryah" in order to draw attention to the nightly gathering which forms the core of the story, and to

emphasize that the story is not in fact entirely about 'Abd al-Samī''s tragedy of adultery and revenge (which occupies no more than one-third of the entire work), but rather concerned with the more general talk which has preceded, accompanied, and followed it, including the telling of 'Abd al-Samī''s story.

The work is rich in meaning, economic in style, and pertinent in its profound analysis of the clash between the various contradictory views. It maintains a delicate artistic balance between the various narrative elements, and uses words to their full poetic value. It employs suggestive symbols that manage to draw upon the different shades of light in order to illuminate both scene and characters. This use of light imagery in the text is not merely a gratuitous description of nature; rather it constitutes a code, whose code words permeate the text and operate in both the frame and the enframed stories.

Lāshīn's contributions to modern Arabic fiction were not confined to the maturation of the genre of the short story, but extended to the novel through his sole contribution to the genre, *Hawwā' bi-lā Ādam* (Eve without Adam, 1933). The novel has been widely acknowledged as major step on the Arabic novel's road to literary and convincing narrative, for, as Hilary Kilpatrick notes, "the author's degree of technical maturity has enabled him to create a work of fiction in which, for the first time in modern Arabic literature, the outcome appears as a natural development from the interaction of characters and their environment, and the themes gain from the skill with which he treats them" (*The Modern Egyptian Novel*, 51). The novel tells the story of an educated, sensitive young woman, Hawwā', who has developed her modern outlook against the traditional background of her family. In telling the story of Hawwā''s maternal family and how she was brought up by her maternal grandmother, the novel roots her upbringing in a history of women's suffering and patriarchal injustices. The grandmother, though superstitious and illiterate, is keen to educate Hawwā' and showered her with love, care and affection, and Hawwā' flourishes under this care and develops into the complete opposite of her grandmother: educated, rational and ambitious. She is the top of her class, but soon after her graduation and beginning of her career she receives a devastating blow, when she is passed over in the selection process for study abroad. Because of her lower middle class background, Hawwā' is deprived of this opportunity; instead, the educationally inferior, but socially rich and well connected Saniyyah is selected. However, this harsh injustice fails to cripple Hawwā', it motivates her to work even harder in order to change her society by joining a reformist association and call for changes in her society through education. Her persuasiveness, eloquence and brilliant argument in the advancement of her cause enable her to rub shoulders with the aristocracy; she attracts the attention of a certain Farīdah Hānim who invites her to her manor house, and introduces her to her husband, Nāzim Pāshā, and her son, Ramzī.

Although Hawwā' now becomes a regular presence in Farīdah Hānim's manor house, her position remains precarious and ambivalent. The more Hawwā' is integrated in the life of the manor house, the more she feels that she is culturally, educationally and emotionally more than equal to its family members. She becomes attached to Ramzī, even though he is clearly younger than her and does not view her as a possible match in spite of his admiration for her cultural education and her ongoing quest to overcome her situation. The more she loves him and attempts to overcome their class differences, the more she becomes aware of the social gulf that separates them. She tries desperately to overcome the obstacles that stand in their path, but her attempts fail. Eventually Ramzī is betrothed to a rich girl from his own class, whereupon Hawwā' falls ill and dies.

This sad story symbolizes the distressing situation faced by Egypt's intellectuals at the time where ideas of reform and social change were exacting a heavy personal price. Like the narrator of "Hadīth al-qaryah" who is left behind, flabbergasted and abandoned, Hawwā''s dilemma stems from her love for her people and her inability to bring about change. As the novel ends, she emerges as an alienated and lonely person in a text inhabited by less educated and certainly less cultured characters, people who even so constitute the majority in the society and the textual space that represents it. The death of Hawwā' at the end of this novel is a damning statement regarding a callous society that crushes its most sensitive cultural citizens and progressive individuals while continuing to allow its more mundane and regressive citizens to flourish. By making his protagonist a woman, Lāshīn is also championing the cause of women's emancipation within an intolerable context. It was to take Egypt several more decades before adopting his vision and changing the situation that he is criticizing in this novel.

Although he tried to write after the breakup of the Modern School group, it would appear that the very process of working within the group was an important stimulus, for thereafter he found it extremely difficult to continue. Nevertheless, he published intermittently more short stories which appeared with his novelette "al-Niqāb al-tā'ir" (The Flying Veil), in his third book *al-Niqāb al-tā'ir* (1940). He also serialized his novel *Hawwā' bi-lā Ādam*, which appeared in book form in 1934. After his third collection he published only one short story, "Mā lam aqul-hu li-ahad" (What I've Never Told Anyone, in *al-Hilāl*, Nov. 1945), and spent the last years of his life in isolation suffering from literary neglect.

Lāshīn's career was both short and chequered. Like that of his colleagues in the Modern School, his work is clearly influenced by Russian literature in general, and by Chekhov's short stories in particular. Although he could not completely eschew the dramatic, he managed to downplay it in most of his works. He introduces ordinary men who are leading normal lives. He accentuates the noble and naïve qualities of his lone, proud characters by setting them in coarse and repugnant surroundings. Like Chekhov, he is fond of contrasting the savage, crude blindness of vulgarity with the delicate, vulnerable, perceptive grace of refinement. He uses both comic and poetic irony to portray such contrasts in a subtle and effective artistic manner. His remarkable sense of comedy sharpens the effectiveness of his racy description and provides his language with suggestive power.

Apart from his attempt to avoid his predecessors' technical shortcomings, Lāshīn was fully aware of his readers and was eager to win their support. This awareness accounts for the simplicity of his language and the frequent occurrence of preambles, in some of which he attempts to address his reader directly. In the sphere of language, as Yahyā Haqqī notes, Lāshīn's style "succeeds in shedding the trappings of archaic traditional prose, inherited from the epoch of Ibn al-Muqaffa' and al-Jāhiz to the era of Tawfīq al-Bakrī, yet it fails to escape from the influence of al-**Manfalūtī** and al-**Muwaylihī**" (introduction to *Sukhriyyat al-nāy*, 2ⁿᵈ ed., 1). He uses many Qur'ānic expressions and traditional or highly classical verbal structures, but for different purposes. By grafting these expressions on to his language, Lāshīn kills two birds with one stone: he assures his reader that he can write in the traditional manner if he likes (in fact some of his critics swallowed the bait and praised his elegant classical style), while at the same time demonstrating the absurdity of writing in such an undisruptive language. Lāshīn turns what has been for too long a highly respectable style into the subject of mockery; ironically, he juxtaposes highly classical expressions, with their inherent wordplay and metonymy, with vernacular or transcribed foreign words, a feature that reveals another facet of his dilemma. However, his use of language is more sensitive, skilful and aware of the nature of narrative linguistic demands than that of any other short-story writer in the Arab world before 1930.

In conclusion, Lāshīn, together with the pioneering literary group of the Modern School developed a new narrative discourse, participated in delineating its genres, and brought it to maturity, a process which had started sixty years earlier with the first works of Salīm al-Bustānī and 'Abd Allāh Nadīm. Although he is widely acknowledged as the prime figure in the process of maturation of the short story, his novel *Hawwā' bi-lā Ādam* and that of Ahmad Khayrī Sa'īd, *al-Dasā'is wa'l-dimā'* (Blood and Conspiracies, 1935), played as important a role in the maturation of the novel genre. The strength, both in quality and quantity, of his writing established and broadened the base of the new narrative discourse and gained for it the respectability it needed in order to flourish. The impact of his work upon the intelligentsia and the reading public could be seen throughout the next three decades and in the works of other writers from the same generation including Yahyā **Haqqī**, Tawfīq al-**Hakīm**, Tāhā **Husayn**, and Mahmūd **Taymūr**, and many authors in the succeeding generation, one of whom (Najīb Mahfūz) was the first Arab writer to win the Nobel Prize for literature, primarily for his realistic narrative work.

It is rather ironic that the man who is now universally credited with bringing modern Arabic narrative discourse to the peak of its maturity, died unnoticed, and had to wait for nearly a decade to be widely acknowledged and his early works reprinted.

REFERENCES

'Abd al-Muhsin Tāhā Badr, *Tatawwur al-riwāyah al-'arabiyyah al-hadīthah fī Misr, 1870-1938* (Cairo: Dār al-Ma'ārif, 1963), 260-77;

Stephan Guth, "The Modern School and Global Modernity: The Example of an Egyptian Ghost Story of the mid-1920s (Mahmūd Tāhir Lāshīn, *Qissat 'ifrīt*)", *Middle Eastern Literatures* 10.3 (Dec. 2007): 231-250;

Sabry Hafez, *The Genesis of Arabic Narrative Discourse: A Study in the Sociology of Modern Arabic Literature* (London: Saqi Books, 1974);

Hilary Kilpatrick, *The Modern Egyptian Novel: A Study in Social Criticism* (London: Ithaca Press, 1974), 51-58.

Mustafā Lutfī al-Manfalūtī

(1877 – 1924)

PAUL STARKEY
University of Durham

WORKS

al-Nazarāt ("Views", vol. 1: Cairo, 1910; vol. 2: Cairo, 1912; vol. 3: Cairo, 1921); numerous editions, reprints and abridgements;

Mukhtārāt al-Manfalūtī ("Selections of al-Manfalūtī", Cairo, 1912);

al-'Abarāt ("Tears", Cairo, 1915); numerous editions and reprints;

al-Qadiyya al-misriyyah min sanat 1921 ilā sanat 1923 ("The Egyptian Question From 1921 to 1923", n.p., n.d.); reissued in: *The Unknown Works of Mustapha Lutfi al-Manafaluti*, ed. 'Alī Shalash (Silsilat al-A'māl al-Majhūlah, London, 1987).

Complete Works

al-Mu'allafāt al-kāmilah ("Complete Works"), 2 vols. (Beirut: Dār al-Jīl, 1980, 1984).

Translations / Adaptations

Mājdūlīn, aw Taht zilāl al-zayzafūn (Cairo, 1917; various later editions); translation of Alphonse Karr, *Sous les Tilleuls*;

Fī sabīl al-tāj (Cairo, 1920; various later editions); adaptation of François Coppée, *Pour la Couronne*;

al-Shā'ir, aw Sīrānū dī Birjarāk (Cairo, 1921; various later editions); translation of Edmond Rostand, *Cyrano de Bergerac*;

al-Fadīlah, aw Pūl wa-Virjīnī (Cairo, 1923; various later editions); translation of Bernadin de St-Pierre, *Paul et Virginie*.

Mustafā Lutfī al-Manfalūtī (1877-1924) is recognized as a pivotal figure in the evolution of a modern style of Arabic prose writing at the beginning of the twentieth century. His published works occupy the transitional period that separates Muhammad al-**Muwaylihī**'s *Hadīth 'Īsā ibn Hishām* (1907) from the resurgence of the new prose style exemplified by the works of a new generation of Egyptian authors, such as Tāhā **Husayn**'s *al-Ayyām* (1926-1928) and Tawfīq al-**Hakīm**'s *'Awdat al-rūh* (1933). Al-Manfalūtī's career and works embody a number of contradictions, not least the fact that, unlike Tāhā Husayn and Tawfīq al-Hakīm, for example (who both knew French well), he knew no European language properly, and indeed is never known to have travelled outside Egypt; despite this, however, his works reveal a fascination both with European ideas and indeed with Western literature, and he translated, or adapted, a number of works of Western literature into Arabic. Despite al-Manfalūtī's pivotal position in the evolution of modern Arabic prose, his ideas and outlook—like his prose style—remained for the most part essentially conservative and seem today in many respects to belong to another age; despite their slightly anachronistic feel, however, they have remained popular among the Arab readership.

Mustafā Lutfī al-Manfalūtī was born in al-Manfalūt, in the governorate of Asyūt (Upper Egypt), probably on 30 December, 1877. His father was a judge, from a family claiming descent from the Prophet's cousin 'Alī, and his mother was of Turkish origin, but they divorced when Mustafā was a young boy. Mustafā received a traditional Islamic education in Manfalūt, before being sent at the age of around thirteen to Cairo, where he studied at the Islamic al-Azhar University. During the latter part of his stay in Cairo, he attended classes with the Islamic religious reformer Muhammad 'Abduh (1849-1905), whom he greatly admired as a teacher and who in turn was impressed with al-Manfalūtī. The extent of Muhammad 'Abduh's support for him may be judged from the fact that, when al-Manfalūtī penned a poem in 1897 in *al-Sā'iqah* magazine criticising the Egyptian Khedive, he was sentenced to a year in prison, but released after six months after a plea from his teacher on his behalf. When Muhammad ʿAbduh died in 1905, al-Manfalūtī returned to Upper Egypt for two years before he had completed his *ʿālimiyyah* (diploma).

Al-Manfalūtī's first literary productions were in the field of poetry, but in 1907, he began writing for the Cairo newspaper, *al-Muʾayyad*, owned by ʿAlī Yūsuf and associated with the names of Muhammad ʿAbduh and the Egyptian nationalist leader Saʿd Zaghlūl. Although he professed not to like journalism, the remainder of his professional life, like that of many other Egyptian writers of his generation, was effectively divided before journalism and a career in the Egyptian civil service. In 1909, he was appointed as *muharrir ʿarabī* (Arabic editor) in the Ministry of Education. His subsequent appointments included posts in the Ministry of Justice, the Secretariat of the Legislative Assembly, the Secretarial Department of the Royal Court, and the Egyptian Parliament. Although this progression of appointments may give the impression of a model civil servant's seamless career, the reality appears to have been considerably less straightforward: the period in question was a difficult one for Egypt, which had had to endure a series of humiliating episodes in its relationship with Britain, which had occupied the country since the ʿUrābī revolt of 1881/82; popular resentment at British rule, personified in the autocratic rule of the governor-general, Evelyn Baring (later Lord Cromer), finally spilled over in the popular revolt of 1919, which was followed by a series of negotiations with Britain led by the nationalist leader Saʿd Zaghlūl. The Egyptians were, however, by no means united among themselves. In 1921, al-Manfalūtī was dismissed by the Prime Minister ʿAbd al-Khāliq Sarwat (Tharwat) Pāshā for an article in which he had defended Zaghlūl, but he was subsequently reinstated; this pattern of events was to be repeated on at least one further occasion.

Al-Manfalūtī's first contributions to *al-Muʾayyad* appeared under the title "al-Usbūʿiyyāt" (Weekly Articles), but he later adopted the title "al-Nazarāt" (Views, Reflections) for his articles, selections of which were later republished in book form (together with some additional material) in three volumes in 1910, 1912 and 1921 respectively; they remain the best known and most enduring of his works, and have been reprinted innumerable times. These works are best regarded as examples of journalism rather than imaginative literature, though ironically, al-Manfalūtī professed not to like journalism himself, advising someone seeking his advice on the subject not to enter the profession and telling him: "you won't be able to be successful as a journalist, unless you're a lying one" (*Nazarāt*, 2, 190). Be that as it may, from an early age he had also shown an enthusiasm for imaginative literature—an enthusiasm that had indeed led to conflict with his teachers at al-Azhar—and had read widely not only in the field of medieval Arabic literature but also in the field of European literature (mainly French) in translation. It is therefore perhaps unsurprising to find that, with the exception of the political tract entitled *al-Qadiyyah al-misriyyah min sanat 1921 ilā sanat 1923* (The Egyptian Question from 1921 to 1923), all his subsequent publications were of a literary nature. What is more surprising, in view of al-Manfalūtī's well-known lack of competence in any European language, is that the majority of these works rely heavily on translation or adaptation from French (or in one case, apparently, on English). This fact has inevitably led to a considerable amount of speculation about the precise processes that al-Manfalūtī used to produce his text, and although in the case of both *Mājdūlīn* and *al-Shāʾir*, for example, the author has offered some explanation in his introduction to the works, many questions remain unanswered. Be that as it may, these works fall into two groups: the first, published under the title *al-ʿAbarāt* (Tears, 1915), consists of a collection of some eight short stories, of which four are described as *mawdūʿah* (original) and four are translated; the collection has remained popular until today and may be counted the author's best-known work after *al-Nazarāt*—the two works indeed often being mentioned together. The second group consists of four longer translations or adaptations from French works, entitled *Mājdūlīn*, *al-Shāʾir*, *Fī sabīl al-tāj*, and *al-Fadīlah aw Pūl wa-Virjīnī*, respectively; all these works were published between 1917 and 1923, during the last few years of al-Manfalūtī's life.

Al-Manfalūtī died in Cairo on 12 July 1924. His death failed to attract as much immediate local attention as might have been expected, as it coincided with an attempt on the life of the nationalist leader Sa'd Zaghlūl, but he was soon being widely mourned, not only in Egypt but indeed throughout the Arab world. Eulogies were delivered at a large public gathering in the Ezbekiyya Gardens in Cairo by prominent members of the literary establishment including Ahmad Shawqī and Hāfiz Ibrāhīm; their tributes, together with a number of other tributes paid to the author, are reprinted by 'Alī Shalash in *The Unknown Works of Mustapha Lutfi al-Manafaluti*.

Writing in 1929, the British scholar Hamilton (later Sir Hamilton) Gibb noted that al-Manfalūtī's essays "(had) survived the furious attacks of both conservatives and modernists, and remain down to the present the most widely read work in modern Arabic literature." As the numerous reprints since that date demonstrate, al-Manfalūtī's works continue to be widely read, and although the extent of his longer-term contribution to the development of Arabic literature is rather doubtful, he has continued to be respected until this day as a leading figure in the Egyptian literary movement of the first decades of the twentieth century.

The textual history of the three parts of *al-Nazarāt* (1910, 1912, 1921) is a little complicated. The majority, though not quite all, of the essays and articles published in the collection had originally appeared in al-Manfalūtī's column in the magazine *al-Mu'ayyad*, but the collections also include a small amount of other material, some of which was previously unpublished. The popularity of the collection has also led to the appearance of numerous editions and reprints, not all of which contain precisely the same selections in the same order. This, however, is a theoretical rather than a real difficulty, since the essays were in any event never intended to form a unified literary work or to be read from cover to cover. In a standard edition, the three volumes contain respectively

some 49, 48, and 35 articles and essays, a total of some 132 items, and, as might be expected in view of the origin of most of them as magazine articles, they are all short, none of them extending over more than ten pages or so.

The first volume is preceded by an introduction by al-Manfalūtī himself, which, despite its rather long-winded nature, is of some interest for the light it throws on the author's approach to the writing of literature. Al-Manfalūtī begins by saying that he is often asked how he goes about composing his *rasā'il* ("epistles") by people who seem to want to imitate them. Al-Manfalūtī, however, regards this as the wrong approach, for despite his omnivorous reading (he seems to like nothing better than to shut himself up alone in his room with a book), he himself, so he claims, has never tried to imitate previous writers—an attitude in which he has been assisted by his poor memory. The exposition that follows lays considerable stress on a rather vaguely defined concept of "beauty", and on the "heart" as a key value in the composition of literature; identifying three sorts of discourse, "the discourse of the tongue, the discourse of the intellect and the discourse of the heart", he expresses a preference for the discourse of the heart, which he describes as "prose or poetry that you listen to and feel that the author is sitting beside you".

The subject matter of the essays themselves is extremely varied, as befits an author who needs to retain the attention and loyalty of his readers through a regular column extending over several years. Social, political and religious themes of various sorts form the author's staple diet, but there are also essays on purely literary themes, on the Arabic language itself, and several inspired by events or situations in the writer's own life. A few essays are based on translated material. Some idea of the range covered may be gleaned from the titles of the first few essays in the first volume: "al-Ghad" (Tomorrow) is a reflective piece on the impossibility and undesirability of knowing the future; "al-Ka's al-ūlā" (The First Cup) a moralistic piece on the evils of drink; and "al-Dafīn al-saghīr" (The Young Boy Buried) a moving lament for his own dead son. Later essays in the same volume include, by way of example, "Ayna 'l-fadīlah?" (Where is Virtue?); "al-Ghanī wa'l-faqīr" (Rich and Poor); "al-Intihār" (Suicide) and "al-Madaniyyah al-ghar-biyyah" (Western Civilisation). In terms of the views expressed, the essays represent a curious mixture of attitudes, which seldom give the impression of having been worked into a coherent philosophy; in this respect, they again betray their origins as short pieces written for immediate reading. At times, his writing is explicitly anti-Western: in "al-Madaniyyah al-gharbiyyah", for example, he satirises his fellow-countrymen who ape Western habits, warning his fellow writers, and the leaders of Egypt, that there is nothing in the personal morality of the Westerners for them to envy;

so let them not dress up this Western civilisation in such a way as to deprive (Egypt) *of its spiritual independence after politics has deprived it of its personal independence* (p. 120).

At the same time, many of his essays reveal the obvious influence not only of the ideas of the progressive Syrian intellectual Farah Antūn and his school, but also those of European writers such as Rousseau and Victor Hugo—an interesting indication, in view of al-Manfalūtī's ignorance of French, of the extent to which such influences had permeated the Egyptian society of the day. In "Madīnat al-saʿādah" (City of Happiness), for example, he describes a vaguely socialist vision of an ideal state with no ruler and no ruled. In his treatment of Islam, he in general emerges as a supporter of the religious reforms advocated by his former teacher Muhammad ʿAbduh, attacking, for example, both the arch-conservatives of al-Azhar and the Sufi orders—though at other times, he could be critical of Muhammad ʿAbduh. Al-Manfalūtī's liberalism in any event did not extend to the ideas of Qāsim Amīn, the Egyptian reformer who in two books, *Tahrīr al-mar'ah* (The Liberation of Woman, 1899) and *al-Mar'ah al-jadīdah* (The New Woman, 1900), had advocated measures for the emancipation of women, including reforms in education and the abolition of the veil; the latter in particular al-Manfalūtī decisively rejected.

Perhaps the most obvious impression to be derived from a reading of *al-Nazarāt* in terms of its subject matter, however, is not so much the specific ideas that the author advances, as the distinctive mix of compassion, sadness and pessimism that runs through all three volumes of the work. Al-Manfalūtī's vision of life does indeed appear to have been of a "vale of tears". To a large extent, this attitude doubtless had its origins in his own experiences: he himself describes how

he has never forgotten the misery he has encountered in life, the time when his mother was divorced and married another man after his father, the time when he lived in a humble room, leading a life of hardship, having to put up with people who were trying to separate him from his books and his literature, making him feel persecuted and oppressed, until he fled from them, then death snatched from him his children one after another, piling sorrow upon sorrow.

This well of personal unhappiness finds expression in the subject matter of *al-Nazarāt* in the number of pieces devoted to subjects such as poverty, unfaithfulness, prostitution, suicide and the like, together with an obvious sympathy for the weak, the poor and the generally unfortunate—a category that, at times at least, seems to include all women. Al-Manfalūtī seems peculiarly aware not only of the evil of poverty and the gap between rich and poor, but also of the need to respond to it through both personal and institutional charity. In this respect, the personal misfortunes he had himself endured may be said to have had a positive, inspirational effect on his writing; but they were also undoubtedly responsible for the tone of almost mawkish sentimentality and self-pity that too frequently creeps into his work. This strand of his make-up finds particularly obvious expression in the final essay in the third volume of the collection, a lament for lost youth in which al-Manfalūtī speaks of having reached the top of the "pyramid of life"; the essay, entitled simply "Arbaʿūn" (Forty), was written when the author had reached that age—by no means an advanced one—and reads like a premonition of death.

If the subject matter and views expressed in *al-Nazarāt* seem at times to suffer from an inconsistency of vision, the same may be said to apply to the style in which the essays are written. As already noted, al-Manfalūtī himself expressed the view that good style had its origins in the heart rather than the tongue or the intellect. Both this view and *al-Nazarāt* itself, however, need to be assessed against the background of the developments taking place in Arabic literary expression at the turn of the century. In this context, it is salutary to recall that the first volume of *al-Nazarāt* appeared only three years after the first publication in book form of Muhammad al-Muwaylihī's *Hadīth 'Īsā ibn Hishām*, probably the last great work in Arabic to be written using the form of the medieval Arabic *maqāmah* ("place of standing", an episodic narrative genre probably originating in the 10th century AD), and involving the copious use of *saj'* (rhymed prose). Despite the obvious brilliance and attraction of al-Muwaylihī's work, however, and his success in utilising the traditional form in a work relevant to contemporary Egypt, parts of *Hadīth 'Īsā ibn Hishām* at least remain characterised by the over-elaborate word play that had become a feature of the genre during the previous centuries and that not infrequently threatened to elevate the form of expression above the ideas themselves. There can be little doubt that one of the attractions of al-Manfalūtī's work to his contemporary readers was that, in terms of the progression of ideas, his style is straightforward and transparent—fully in keeping, indeed, with his own philosophy, which held that good style came from speaking the truth from the heart. A more detailed analysis of his prose style suggests, however, that despite his obvious awareness of the need to evolve a more modern style, and despite his attacks on writers who imitated the style of the *maqāmāt*, his own writing is by no means free of many features of *saj'*: these include, for example, the use of various sorts of rhyme; the deliberate repetition of phrase patterns; "padding" the text with synonyms or near-synonyms that add little or nothing to the sense; and the use of word-plays that involve words derived from the same Arabic root. In this respect, as in many others, al-Manfalūtī's work, both in *al-Nazarāt* and else-

where, represents a curious synthesis of medieval and modern outlooks.

The slim volume of fiction entitled *al-'Abarāt*, first published in 1915, contains eight short stories, of which four ("al-Yatīm", The Orphan; "al-Hijāb", The Veil; "al-Hāwiyah", The Abyss; and "al-'Iqāb", The Punishment) are described as *mawdū'ah* (composed, i.e. original), while the remaining four ("al-Shuhadā'", The Martyrs; "al-Dhikrā", Remembrance; "al-Jazā'", Requital; and "al-Dahiyyah", The Victim) are described as *mutarjamah* (translated). One "original" story ("al-'Iqāb") is described in a footnote as having been composed "in the manner of an American story", a description that raises more questions than it answers; at the very least, however, it presumably indicates an acquaintance, on the part either of al-Manfalūtī himself or of one of his collaborators, with one or more collections of American short stories, either in Arabic translation or, in the case of a collaborator, in the English original.

Of the "translated" stories, two derive from works by the French writer and diplomat Chateaubriand (1768-1848). Of these, "al-Shuhadā'" is based on the French original *Atala* (1801), a story in which the theme of the "noble savage", so beloved of the French Romanticists, plays a prominent part, while the second, "al-Dhikrā", is based on an original entitled *Les aventures du dernier Abencérage* (1826); this story, with its historical setting during the period of the collapse of Islamic rule in Spain, seems to sit slightly uneasily in the collection as a whole. A third story, "al-Dahiyyah"—the last and longest in the collection—is derived from Alexandre Dumas fils's *La dame aux camélias* (1848), a story that was subsequently to reappear as the libretto for Verdi's *La Traviata*, and that has been aptly described both as a "four handkerchief tale" and as exemplifying G. K. Chesterton's category of "good bad books".

Insofar as the collection possesses a unity, what links these stories together is a pervasive sentimentality and pessimism that makes the volume title *al-'Abarāt* (already used by the author as the title of a piece in *al-Nazarāt*) a particularly apt one. The mood is set with the work's "Dedication", in which the author speaks of shedding his tears before the wretched of the world, "in the hope that they will find some comfort and solace in my weeping over them." Scarcely a page of the collection lacks some reference to some form of sadness or unhappiness. A particularly common pattern in the narrative is the descent of an individual, or individuals, into illness, death, or some other form of misery, evoking the narrator's, and by implication, also the reader's, reflections and compassion. Thus, all of the first four stories in the collection end in graveyards; the conclusion of the fifth finds the narrator's friend confined to a lunatic asylum, having lost his reason; while at the end of the final story,

they all went to Marguerite's grave before leaving, and wept profusely as they stood around it. But Suzanne wept more than anyone else, even though she was unaware that she was weeping for the woman who had sacrificed herself for her sake.

A link to some of the themes of *al-Nazarāt* is provided by "al-Hijāb", which relates the progressive disintegration of a man who has spent several years in Europe to return a changed man; here, al-Manfalūtī casts his story in the form of a moral tale intended to represents a warning to the reader about the lax morals of the West and the dangers of their intruding into Egypt. Reflections on a period of residence in the West, either in fictional or non-fictional form, had not unnaturally provided one of the standard *topoi* for Arab writers during the nineteenth century, and they have continued to provide productive subject-matter until this day; for al-Manfalūtī, however, who had not only not visited Europe but had almost certainly never left his native Egypt, the theme—far from providing the opportunity to expand intellectual horizons that it had for other writers—seems to be merely another excuse to rehearse the anti-Western and anti-feminist sentiments already evident in *al-Nazarāt.*

Despite its popularity with some groups of readers, it is hardly surprising that *al-'Abarāt* has generally found a cool reception from the critics. Although the narrative generally flows easily, the stories almost entirely lack the wit

and sparkle of the best pieces of *al-Nazarāt*, and the range of subject matter and emotional experience to which al-Manfalūtī apparently has access are so limited that the collection almost seems designed to reveal the limitations of the author rather than his capabilities. Most readers will probably find it hard to put the book down without the feeling that "enough is enough".

The majority of al-Manfalūtī's other works fall into the category of extended translations or adaptations from French originals, and are of varying degrees of interest. The first of these, *Mājdūlīn, aw Taht zilāl al-zayzafūn*, which appeared in 1917, is an Arabic version of *Sous les Tilleuls*, by Alphonse Karr (1808-90), a journalist and author of a number of minor sentimental and humorous novels, of which *Sous les Tilleuls*, an "autobiographical romance" published in 1832, was the first. Al-Manfalūtī's own work was preceded in the first edition by a note explaining that the French text had been first translated for him by Fu'ād Kamāl, and it is thus explicitly marked as a "twice removed" version of Karr's original.

The second work, *Fī sabīl al-tāj*, published in 1920, is an adaptation of a historical verse drama entitled *Pour la Couronne* by the dramatist and poet François Coppée (1842-1908), first published in 1895. As in the case of Alphonse Karr, there seems to be an obvious affinity of outlook between al-Manfalūtī and Coppée, who was known as the "poet of the humble", because of his sentimental treatment of the poor—a description that could equally appropriately have been applied to al-Manfalūtī himself. In making his Arabic version of this work, al-Manfalūtī took considerable liberties, not only substituting prose for the verse of the original, but at the same time converting the drama into a novel—a procedure which he also adopted for *al-Shā'ir, aw Sīrānū dī Birjarāk*, published in 1921, and to which we now turn.

Al-Manfalūtī's version of *Cyrano de Bergerac* (to which he added the supplementary title *al-Shā'ir*, The Poet) is of considerably more interest than his first two adaptations, not only in itself but also for the reaction it provoked in Egyptian literary circles. The work is an Arabic adaptation of the play *Cyrano de Bergerac* by the French playwright Edmond Rostand (1868-1918), originally published in 1897. Rostand's play was in turn based on the colourful seventeenth-century soldier and writer Cyrano de Bergerac (1619-55), whose life had subsequently acquired a legendary quality; essentially a moral tale of gallantry cast in the form of a romantic drama, Rostand's play relates how the swashbuckling but ugly Cyrano, who loves his cousin Roxanne, continues to support her despite her love for another man; the general sentiment of the story may perhaps best be described as that of a man dying of thirst offering his cup to someone else. It is easy to see the appeal of this story to the sentimental al-Manfalūtī, not only for the theme itself, but also (more speculatively) because the larger-than-life Cyrano seems to have about him something in common with the heroes of popular Arab tradition. Be that as it may, in addition to "polishing" the Arabic version of the play that had been translated from the French by Muhammad ʿAbd al-Salām, al-Manfalūtī decided, as with *Fī sabīl al-tāj*, to recast it in the form of a novel. This led to a heated exchange of views in the pages of *al-Ahrām* (then, as now, the leading Cairo daily newspaper) in which Mansūr Fahmī, who praised the work, clashed with Tāhā Husayn, the "dean" of modern Arabic literature, with whom al-Manfalūtī did not see eye to eye and with whom he had already embarked on a literary feud. On one level, the exchange, in which Tāhā Husayn described al-Manfalūtī's transformation of the play into a novel as an "abomination" and a "crime against the author", may be read as a debate on the philosophy of translation and adaptation—a topic of considerable relevance in the context of the Arabic literature of the period, the development of which had been to a large degree stimulated by the nineteenth-century translation movement. So heated was the language employed, however, that it is difficult to resist the impression that personal factors also played a major part in the exchange.

For his final extended adaptation, *al-Fadīlah aw Pūl wa-Virjīnī* (1923), al-Manfalūtī again retained the title of his original source, while adding an "alternative" title, *al-Fadīlah* (Virtue). The work is based on the novelist and naturalist

Jacques-Henri Bernadin de St Pierre's (1737-1814) *Paul et Virginie* (1788), a *pastorale* that both looks back to a lost golden age of human happiness and forward to an ideal republic of justice and equality (a theme touched on elsewhere in al-Manfalūtī's writing, as we have seen). The story tells of Paul and Virginie's upbringing on Mauritius, of their separation when Virginie is sent to Paris, and of her drowning on her return when, shipwrecked, she refuses to surrender her virtue to a sailor. This tale, with its overtones of the "noble savage", and its echoes not only of Daniel Defoe's *Robinson Crusoe* but also of the Arabic medieval writer Ibn Tufayl's *Hayy ibn Yaqzān*, seems to have struck a particular chord with Arab writers of the period, for it had already been translated into Arabic by the Syrian Farah Antūn; the fact that al-Manfalūtī should nonetheless have felt moved to produce another version (described on the title page as *mulakhkhasah*, "abridged") is an indication of the overwhelming appeal of the theme.

Although many commentators have been critical of the quality of al-Manfalūtī's "translations", comparing them unfavourably with those of other translators such as Farah Antūn and Muhammad ʿUthmān Jalāl, their popularity during the 1920s is not only an interesting indication of readers' tastes at the time, but also, perhaps, a salutary reminder that concepts such as "fidelity to the text" and "accurate translation" so beloved of the literary specialist have never been of much concern to the consumers of popular fiction.

REFERENCES

Ahmad ʿAbd al-Hādī, *al-Manfalūtī: hayātuhu wa-muʾallafātuh* (Cairo: al-Hayʾah al-Misriyyah al-ʿĀmmah liʾl-Kitāb, 1981);

Muhammad Abū ʾl-Anwār, *Mustafā Lutfī al-Manfalūtī: hayātuhu wa-adabuh*, 3 vols. (Cairo: Maktabat al-Shabāb, 1981-85);

ʿAbbās Bayyūmī ʿAjlān, *al-Manfalūtī waʾl-Nazarāt* (Alexandria: Muʾassasat Shabāb al-Jāmiʿah, 1987);

——, *al-Manfalūtī wa-atharuhu fī ʾl-adab al-hadīth: fikran wa-uslūban* (Alexandria: Dār

Lūrān liʾl-Tibāʿah waʾl-Nashr, 1977);

ʿUmar al-Disūqī, *al-Manfalūtī: dirāsah naqdiy-yah tahlīliyyah* (Cairo: Dār al-Fikr al-ʿArabī, 1976);

H. A. R. Gibb, *Studies on the Civilization of Islam* (London: Routledge & Kegan Paul, 1962), 263-9.

Mahmūd al-Masʿadī
(1911 – 2004)

MOHAMED-SALAH OMRI
Washington University, St. Louis

WORKS

Mawlid al-nisyān ("The Birth of Forgetfulness", *al-Mabāhith*, April-July 1945);

al-Sudd ("The Dam", Tunis: Dār al-Nashr li-Shamāl Ifrīqiya, 1955);

Haddatha Abū Hurayrah qāl... ("Abū Hurayrah Told Us...", Tunis: al-Dār al-Tūnisiyyah liʾl-Nashr, 1974);

Taʾsīlan li-kiyān ("The Authenticity of a Being", Tunis: Muʾassasat Ibn ʿAbd Allāh, 1979);

Essai sur le rythme dans la prose rimée en arabe (Tunis: Muʾassasat Ibn ʿAbd Allāh, 1981);

al-Īqāʿ fī ʾl-sajʿ al-ʿarabī: muhāwalat tahdīd wa-tahlīl ("Rhythm in Arabic Rhymed Prose: Essays in Definition and Analysis", Tunis: Muʾassasat Ibn ʿAbd Allāh, 1996); Arabic version of the *Essai* (1981);

Min ayyām ʾImrān wa-taʾammulāt ukhrā ("Days in the Life of Imran, and Other Medita-tions"), ed. Mahmūd Tarshūnah (Tunis: Dār al-Janūb liʾl-Nashr, 2002).

Complete Works

al-Aʿmāl al-kāmilah ("The Complete Works", 4 vols., Tunis: Dār al-Janūb, 2003).

Publications in Periodicals

"Bi-zāhir al-Qayrawān" ("On the Outskirts of Kairawan"), *al-ʿĀlam al-Adabī* (March 1930): 22-24;

"Le rêve et l'oriental ou victoire sur le temps", *Afrique Littéraire* 2 (December 1940);

"al-Sindabād waʾl-tahārah" ("Sindabad and Pur-ity"), *al-Mabāhith* 42-43 (September-October 1947): 8-9;

"Hadīth al-qiyāmah" ("The Resurrection"), *al-Mabāhith* 5 (August 1944): 7;

"Hadīth al-baʿth al-awwal" ("The First Awaken-ing"), *al-Mabāhith* 6 (September 1944): 9;

"Hadīth al-kalb" ("The Dog"), *al-Mabāhith* 8 (October 1944): 9;

"Hadīth al-ʿadad" ("Multitude"), *al-Mabāhith* 8 (November 1944): 10;

"Hadīth al-ghaybah tutlab fa-lā tudrak" ("Ab-sence Sought but never Achieved"), *al-Fikr* (March 1956);

"Cultural Development in the Arab States", in: *Cultural Development: Some Regional Ex-periences* (Paris: UNESCO, 1981), 283-369.

Works in Translation

Nos lo contó Abù Hurayra (UNESCO, 1996); translation of *Haddatha Abū Hurayrah qāl...*, tr. by Santiago Martinez de Francisco;

De Geboorte van het Vergeten (Amsterdam: In de Knipscheer, 1995); translation of *Mawlid al-nisyān*, tr. by Marcelle van de Pol;

La Genèse de l'oubli (Tunis: Bayt al-Hikmah, 1993); translation of *Mawlid al-nisyān*, tr. by Taoufik Baccar;

Le Barrage (UNESCO: Vega Press, 1981); trans-lation of *al-Sudd*, tr. by Ezzeddine Guellouz;

J. C. Bürgel, "*Der Damm*: Ein modernes arabi-sches Drama von Mahmūd al-Masʿadī", *Die Welt des Islams* 21 (1981): 30-79; translation of *al-Sudd*.

Mahmūd al-Mas'adī was Tunisia's most important prose writer in the 20th Century, winning
praise from such authorities in Arabic literature
as the Egyptian Tāhā **Husayn** (1889-1973), the
Sudanese writer al-Tayyib Sālih, and the Egyptian novelist Jamāl al-Ghītānī. Outside Tunisia,
he was the country's best known cultural figure
for decades. Yet his fiction has been difficult to
classify or place within the mainstream of the
Arabic novel. His work has been seen as
contemplative; vanguard; heritage model; poetic
fiction; mediator between pre-modern narrative
and the novel and experimental. Roger Allen
recognizes that the writer's work has had lasting
appeal due to "the extreme elegance of its
language, a factor which seems to have ensured
it an enduring place in the history of modern
Maghribi fiction". Robin Ostle notes al-Mas-
'adī's role in bridging the gap between tradition
and modernity, turning the perceived limitations
and the archaisms of Arabic into "highly creative elements of a work of literature which
sacrifices nothing of the modernity and relevance of its message". In Tunisia he had had an
unchallenged status, became a canonical author
and influenced many writers. Al-Mas'adī was
also one of the architects of the nationalist
movement in French-occupied Tunisia from
1934 to 1956, and a key figure in the independent Tunisian State from 1956 to the early
1980s. He founded the modern university system,
and ran the cultural policy of his country,
maintaining the broadly secularizing agenda set
by the country's first president Habīb Bourguiba
(1903-2002), with close ties to Europe, particularly France, and moderate politics, which often
favoured the interests of the nation-state against
pan-Arabist tendencies.

Al-Mas'adī's career and fame as writer started
in the late 1930s with most of his fictional
writing done before 1950. But several of the
writer's best known texts were not published in
full or in book form until much later. He lists his
three main fictional texts in this order: *Haddatha
Abū Hurayrah qāl* (written before June 1940),
al-Sudd (September 1939 – June 1940), *Mawlid
al-nisyān* in the early 1940s. He later added rare
chapters or occasional stories, such as the collected narrative *Min ayyām 'Imrān* (The Days of

Imran) which includes aphorisms in Arabic and
in French, which were published for the first
time in 2003. At the level of genre, he explored
drama in *al-Sudd* and partially in *Mawlid al-
nisyān*, the novel in *Haddatha* and shorter narrative form in the remainder of his work. But
regardless of date and genre, al-Mas'adī is
identified with a particular style and a distinctive
set of themes. It seems that time, even when it
involved changes as dramatic as the end of
colonialism, did not really affect his work in any
significant manner, making a chronological
treatment of his work misleading. Works published 50 years apart still bear the same stamp.
For this reason, dates of publication do not really
show a progression but mark stages in the writer's
career and show his impact on the literary scene
in his native country and abroad.

Al-Mas'adī was born in the coastal village of
Tāzarkah in the North East of the country on
January 28, 1911. He attended the most influential institutions of learning of his time at
home and in France. After a primary education
in the prestigious modern school al-Madrasah al-
Sādiqiyyah, founded by the reformer Khayr al-
Dīn Pasha, between 1921 and 1932; he studied
at the French school Lycée Carnot in 1933, the
Zaytūnah Islamic University and al-Khaldūniy-
yah. In France, he attended the Sorbonne from
1933 to 1936, then in 1939, and in 1947. These
institutions positioned al-Mas'adī to become
prominent among a company of elites and local
leaders. Later on he had the opportunity to affect
these very institutions, as a teacher at Lycée
Carnot (1936-38) then at Sādiqiyyah (1938-48),
and as the architect of Tunisia's educational
policy between 1958 and 1968. Al-Mas'adī also
taught simultaneously at the Centre d'Etudes
Islamiques at Paris University (1947-52) and at
the Collège d'Etudes Supérieures in Tunis
(1948-55) where he became Chair of the Arabic
Literature Department.

Al-Mas'adī's role in the outlook of the
emerging society in Tunisia cannot be under-
estimated. As a key policy maker in the educational system, the reforms he put together
affected all Tunisians and set the course for the
type of education, language competence and the
intellectual training of generations. As Secretary

of State for Education, Youth and Sports, he supervised the conception and implementation of "The Project for Educational Reform of 1958," which aimed at universal access to elementary education in ten years, the development of secondary education and the establishment of a modern university system. Among the most prominent aspects of this reform were integration of the Islamic institution al-Zaytūnah within the university system as a college for religious studies and maintaining bilingual education in Arabic and French. These two bold moves ended the domination of religious institutions over the educational system in the country, setting Tunisia apart from most of the Islamic world in this area. Al-Mas'adī's legacy in this field had wide implications on the society at large and continues to be debated today. He was also minister of Cultural Affairs from 1973 to 1976 and founder of a key monthly cultural magazine, which continues to be published today. He was Member of Parliament from 1959 until he became Speaker between 1981 and 1986.

As public figure, al-Mas'adī was the product of institutions and conditions where most of the leaders of the nationalist movement and the ensuing Tunisian state were formed. During the colonial period, there were two conceptions of what Tunisia was and how it should be. While the French settlers sought to take root, native intellectuals wanted to recover their own. The settlers had the support of the colonial machine while al-Mas'adī and his compatriots had to rely on modest local means. The journal *al-Mabāhith* was the writer's forum and his organized intervention in the process of elaborating a 'national culture' in Tunisia in the 1940s. It was also through the journal that he would establish himself as a writer.

Yet, while it may be obvious to locate al-Mas'adī's position in the politics of culture in Tunisia, his own cultural politics was not defined solely by the national cause or by his role as native intellectual. Some of his essays and personal involvement show intense commitment to the constitution of a national culture; he had a wider view of literature and the role of Islam in the world. He insisted that nationalism

and literature were not always compatible. At the height of tensions between the Tunisians and the French in the 1940s and 50s, and during the heyday of pan-Arab nationalism, he argued for the freedom of the writer to choose whether to support nationalism or not. He warned against the pitfalls of pan-Arab nationalism in the late 1950s (advocating an outright rejection of the West and a reductive view of the role of nationalism which sidelines the role of Islam). Al-Mas'adī's legacy in the development of the educational system in his country is highly valued. But his role in the development of Tunisian culture after independence, particularly as Minister of Cultural Affairs, remains unstudied. While this period witnessed significant developments in theatre, cinema and literature, it was also marked by an increase in limitations on rising political resistance and contestation, as part of the overall politics of the Tunisian state at the time. Was al-Mas'adī, the "responsible militant" as his colleague in *al-Mabāhith* termed him, perhaps too bound by the state line to heed and defend his own call of 1957 for the complete freedom of writers and artists?

Al-Mas'adī was also a scholar of Arabic literature and language. His own academic work bears kinship to the tradition of Islamic studies in France during one of its most brilliant periods. His mentors included the eminent scholars Gaudefroy-Demombynes, Levi-Provinçal, Henri Massignon and Regis Blachère. His complementary doctoral thesis, *Essai sur le rythme dans la prose rimée en arabe* (An Essay on Rhythm in Arabic Rhymed Prose), which was written in 1939 but published as a book only in 1981, is a meticulous numerical study of rhythmic patterns in Arabic prose with focus on the *Maqāmāt* of Badī' al-Zamān al-Hamadhānī (d. 1008). This research was considered "groundbreaking" and "pioneering" by Gully and Hindle in their recent work on rhythm in medieval Arabic epistolary literature. Other published research includes articles on the theory of knowledge of the mystic and theologian, Abū Hāmid al-Ghazālī (d. 1111), the philosophical poet Abū 'l-'Alā' al-Ma'arrī (973-1058), the poet of asceticism, Abū 'l-'Atāhiyah (d. 848), several pieces on literary criticism and cultural issues, and short translations from French.

With such a profile, al-Mas'adī became a major player on the cultural scene in Tunisia before and after independence. In the colonial period, his most significant impact was during the crucial years when he was Editor in Chief of *al-Mabāhith* (1943-47), the most important Tunisian journal of its time and forum for a collective academic project to construct a national culture in Tunisia. Al-Mas'adī's most involving anti-colonialist activities were in the arenas of labour unionism and politics. He was President of the Teachers Union in Tunisia and Member of the Secretariat General of the International Teachers Federation from 1951 to 1955 and Assistant Secretary General of the powerful General Union of Tunisian Workers from its foundation in 1948 until 1955. When the Union leader, to whose memory al-Mas'adī dedicated his book *al-Sudd* (The Dam), was assassinated, the writer was put in charge of the Union. But as a result of a crackdown by the French authorities, he was exiled to the south of the country from September 1952 until May 1953. In the political field, al-Mas'adī played an important role as member of the Neo-Constitutional Party of Tunisia from the time of its foundation in 1934. He participated in the negotiations with the French that lead to self-rule in 1954 and was reportedly instrumental in keeping Tunisia out of the Axis alliance during the German occupation of the country in 1942.

Outside the country, al-Mas'adī was Tunisia's best-known cultural figure. He was the country's representative at the UNESCO for 10 years (1958-68) before becoming Member of its Executive Council (1977-8 and 1980-85). In this capacity, he contributed to several UNESCO studies on education and culture including *Cultural Development: Some Regional Experiences* (1981), with the comprehensive essay, "Cultural Development in the Arabic Cultural Region" as well as expert essays on the state of education. Until his death, he was Member of Advisory Board of the Arab League's Educational, Cultural and Scientific Organization (ALECSO); of the Editorial Board of the Syrian project *al-Mawsū'ah al-'arabiyyah al-kubrā* (The Great Arabic Encyclopaedia) from 1978, and of the

Jordanian Academy of Arabic Language from 1980. Al-Mas'adī was also the spokesperson for Tunisian writers and often represented them abroad.

Al-Mas'adī's earliest work is a one-act play published in 1930 and inspired by the history of the Islamic city al-Qayrawān. But his first significant work of fiction is *al-Musāfir* (The Wayfarer), which was initially written in French as "Le Rêve et l'oriental" and published in 1940 and then in Arabic in 1942. The story was later reprinted in *al-Sudd*'s first edition in 1955, under the title *Min rūh al-sharq* (From the Spirit of the East) with a short introduction by the author and an epigraph by the tenth century prose master Abū Hayyān al-Tawhīdī (d. 1023). The story marks a key stage in al-Mas'adī's conception of the East and the West. However, in a lecture delivered in 1975, he tried to dismiss the story by suggesting that it reveals what he "thought at the time was the Oriental (Eastern) conception of life and existence" and "the conception of Western civilization of the role of Man and his existential responsibilities." "The Wayfarer" represents a submissive self, a view that the writer himself questions in his book *al-Sudd*, for instance. Even so, this retrospective reading, which may have been made under a perceived pressure to provide some keys to an opaque text, does not detract from the importance of *al-Musāfir* in al-Mas'adī's work as a whole.

In the story, a man who is identified only as "al-Musāfir" (The Traveler) stands on a mountain outside a city, recalling his travels in search of "serenity and dream". He is advised to "interrogate the East," but two years of search have been spent to no avail. The serenity he seeks is not the "serenity of the Greek Apollo whose apparent calm hides internal pain and anguish". It is rather akin to marble, "like Eastern music and the lines in Eastern sculpture where the end meets the beginning, where there is no movement, change or transformation. Serenity is not cowardice and resignation to fate or belief in pre-determination. Rather, it is the great stillness." The Easterner, like marble, has defeated time. For time pertains to movement: time originates in movement and movement is measured by time. "Movement is change, corruption and finitude". The traveler finds manifestations of the East's victory over Time in the Pyramids, Buddha, the prophets and "even the serenity of Tunisians who remain unshaken amidst a world torn by wars and rebellions". The East does not experience the loneliness of Dionysus in his attempt to reunite with the origin from which he was severed because he "did not lose ties to the Absolute whole". This tie shields the Easterner against the pain of the limitation inherent in the human self. He is like the mystics, al-Hallāj (d. 922), al-Ghazālī (d. 1111) and others, who shunned the human condition in search of the world of God, but only to be confronted with human limitations which compel the wanderer to take refuge in "transcendental truths". The Traveler thinks he has found serenity in the East but he realizes that the "gift was deceptive". He knows he has not yet attained such wisdom. He then recalls the latest stages of his journey and contemplates the town of Kisra, built on rocks from which springs clear water but where the land is barren and the sky is empty. The Traveler visits the town of Makthar (the Roman Maktaris), where he reads the Roman arch as a "door for ascension to the sky," reminding him of his own ascent. But he denies that this has actually happened because the ascent has seemed too easy, almost natural. At this point, he realizes that the serenity of the Easterner cannot be attained through reason or thought. Harmony and union with the universe can only be attained through other means: "The self must open up to the universe, be alert and attentive to it; it must then accept it, trust it and surrender to it" (133). At this point in his journey the Traveler opens up to the city and descends to it, alert and at ease.

The theme of East and West does not dominate al-Mas'adī's other work but the search and the metaphysical questioning remain a constant. A full exploration of the human experience through the life of one character is the subject of the writer's earliest fictional book, *Haddatha Abū Hurayrah qāl*. The narrative is divided into 22 sections called *hadīth*s (discourses or narratives) that vary in length from three short sentences ("Hadīth al-shaytān", The Devil) to 14 pages ("Hadīth al-ghaybah tutlab

fa-lā tudrak", Absence Sought but Never Attained). The life and experiences of the main character, Abū Hurayrah, are told in the form of anecdotes or stories reported by a variety of narrators, including Abū Hurayrah himself, who narrates four tales. The events take place in Islam's holy cities of Mecca and Medina and other neighbouring areas during the early period of Islam. Abū Hurayrah's journey begins at age twenty and lasts two decades. It covers a wide variety of experiences often alluded to in the titles of *hadīth*s. For example, "Hadīth al-ba'th al-awwal" (The First Awakening) is an account of Abū Hurayrah's awakening to the pleasures of life; "Hadīth al-ta'āruf fī 'l-khamr" (Acquaintance over Wine) describes his first encounter with his lover, Rayhānah; "Hadīth al-'adad" (Multitude) is devoted to Abū Hurayrah's experience of society and life among the community; "Hadīth al-hikmah" (Wisdom) describes his encounter with a philosopher. Abū Hurayrah's journey exposes him to a cast of characters and situations where he learns more about himself and the meaning of the world around him. He moves on in pursuit of higher understanding of life and being until he reaches a revelation. The story ends with him crying: "Truth, here I come," whereupon he disappears in the darkness of night atop a mountain.

The book was not published in full until 1973 after an eventful and telling history, which reveals the cultural and religious climate in the Arab world at the time. A letter dating from the early 1940s states that al-Mas'adī had given the manuscript to a Lebanese writer for safe keeping, fearing that his ship could be attacked during the journey from Marseilles to Tunis in the aftermath of the German occupation of Paris. But the latter was unable to locate the owner of the manuscript until the early 1970s. It is, however, certain that there must have been a second manuscript. For while this copy was in Lebanon, four sections of the book were published by the journal *al-Mabāhith* in Tunisia in 1944.

One significant discrepancy between sections published in 1944 and the 1973 edition pertains to the name of the main character. He is called Abū Durayrah in the earlier version and Abū

Hurayrah in the later text. However, letters written in 1947-48 clearly indicate that the original name was Abū Hurayrah. In more recent interviews, al-Masʿadī has commented that he chose the benign Abū Durayrah, a diminutive form of his step-daughter's name Durra, because he was deterred by the fate of his compatriot, al-Tāhir al-Haddād, the advocate of women's rights, who was vilified and shunned for ideas that were considered anti-religious in the 1930s. To use the name of the revered companion of the Prophet, Abd al-Rahmān Abū Hurayrah (d. 678), in a work of 'secular' and impious fiction would have raised the wrath of the religious establishment at the time. Furthermore, and in addition to changing the name, al-Masʿadī chose to publish the chapters which contained "less contentious" material first. And even by the middle of the 1950s, the writer did not feel he could publish the book without major difficulties. For this reason, he started with *al-Sudd* (The Dam), a book he considered less controversial, delaying publication of *Haddatha* until 1973 when he himself had the authority of the post of Minister of Cultural Affairs and a considerable weight across the Arab world.

Outside Tunisia, opposition to *Haddatha* was no less vehement. Al-Masʿadī's letter to Tāhā **Husayn** (dated October 17, 1947) notes that the prominent French Islamicist, Levi-Provençal, has given the manuscript to Husayn for evaluation and set up a reading committee for the same purpose. A year later, al-Masʿadī reports that the book was rejected on the same grounds, namely that the main character should not be named Abū Hurayrah. He wrote to Tāhā Husayn on December 14, 1948, complaining of "various opponents, both material and *ʿimāmiyyah*," the latter being a sarcastic reference to turbaned religious sheikhs. He also deplores the limitations imposed on Arab writers in the name of blasphemy and respect for the past, pointing out that no one seems to have the freedom to

invent an imaginary person bearing the same name and that no writer can put down an Arabic word without being drawn into an uneasy confrontation with the turbaned sheikhs.

It is small wonder then that Tāhā Husayn,

who was himself the subject of a serious controversy two decades earlier, appears to have withheld his endorsement of the book,

In fact, al-Masʿadī's narrative and literary choices were not without major risks.

For in addition to recalling the revered figure of ʿAbd al-Rahmān Abū Hurayrah, the title itself, *Haddatha Abū Hurayrah qāl*, alludes to the sacred tradition of the Prophet's sayings and deeds known as *hadīth*. This convention is central to Islamic culture as a whole, and hence to Arabic literature. Using it as a blueprint in a work of fiction in the twentieth century is an act which involves significant implications and risks. For *Hadīth* is the second most important source of Islam as discourse and as practice, at least for Sunnis. It is both the first exegesis of Qurʾan and the first application of it in Islamic history. Together with the Qurʾan itself, it constitutes the fundamental sources of the religion. Since the Prophet's word as revealed in *hadīth* was meant to guide the Muslim community, its veracity had to be beyond doubt. For this reason, the process of its compilation and analysis has been scrupulous and rigorous, resulting in a well-regulated academic discipline where the narrators of *hadīth* play a particularly significant role. These reports of the Prophet's words and deeds were, of course, susceptible to manipulation, alteration or even fabrication and forgery in order to serve sectarian, political or personal motivations. But in a largely oral culture, it was inevitable that the primary source for such information was the memory of those who had had direct contact with the Prophet, most notably his companions and wives. Transmitters were thus subjected to intense scrutiny which often exceeded the examination of the *hadīth*. Therefore, Abu Hurayrah is a key figure in this tradition, being one of the most trusted and most prolific transmitters of *hadīth* as well as a faithful close companion of the Prophet. Knowing this, one begins to appreciate why the mere use of his name in a context which inspires doubt and impiety would be a significant challenge to Islamic culture, even a punishable offence. To use the formula and the transmitter in a fictional account involves playing with the reader's expectations. But it is this very reference which constitutes one key element in al-Masʿadī's particular pathway to the Arabic narrative tradition. The other element is his use of the Arabic language.

This language first came to wider public attention in 1955 when al-Masʿadī published the play *al-Sudd*, the book which really made his reputation outside Tunisia and remains his most recognized text in the Arab world and abroad. It has been translated in full into French and German, and partially into Russian, Spanish and English. *Al-Sudd* is, in part, a dramatization of the conflict between a strong-willed man, Ghaylān, and Sāhabbāʾ a goddess with a fully institutionalized religion, including a gospel, a prophet, priests, worshippers and rituals. Sāhabbāʾ's power is overwhelming. She dominates the people of the valley and controls the forces of nature. In the opposite camp stands Ghaylān, a human being with limited power but a set of strong ideas and ambitious goals. His philosophy in life is based chiefly on the autonomy of individual willpower and freedom of action. He draws his strength largely from his own determination but benefits from relative control over his workers and the unconditional support of a reliable "spirit" named Mayārah. Among Ghaylān's most outspoken sceptics is his companion Maymūnah, who fears the power of the goddess.

The two sides live in a state of physical as well as ideological conflict. The conflict is introduced through Voices; some of these speak on behalf of man, others represent the goddess. Ghaylān pokes fun at the local religion, accusing its prophet of speaking gibberish. He believes that the people of the valley are incapable of action and creativity because they are in the grip of a religion that deprives them of their will. In order to correct this, he decides to build a dam, irrigate the land and create a prosperous life in the valley. Rituals of Sāhabbāʾ's religion in the form of incantations, songs and dance are performed by a chorus of monks who dance around a water bowl and "call for water to turn into fire, for dams to crumble and for Ghaylān's hands to be amputated". Sāhabbāʾ gives a sign of her power, and the water catches fire. The ritual ends with signs of gratitude to the goddess.

In Scene Three, Maymūnah dreams that the dam has crumbled in a devastating quake. "I had a frightening and awesome vision of untold horror!" she says. "I saw a dam made up entirely of skulls arranged in perfect order". She describes water gushing through holes previously filled with human eyes, noses and mouths. In the dream she calls to Ghaylān for help, but a voice replies: "You're calling for him, but his skull has not yet arrived." The awesome quake shakes the mountain and swallows the river and the entire valley. In Scene Four, the Three Stones are transformed into three young women who muse about the purpose, vanity and arrogance of human beings. "Humans are fond of gathering and collecting," the Second Stone says. "It is as though they were narrators or storytellers." She goes on to claim that the real aim of their effort may be the search for themselves.

As work on the dam progresses, conflicts sharpen and tensions increase. Maymūnah accuses Ghaylān of a fruitless attempt to hide his inability to confront the truth. A glimpse of the battle between Ghaylān and his "enemies" emerges from Maymūnah's account of the setbacks that befall the construction of the dam during the intervening months: tools have been stolen; a fever has killed half of the work force; a flood has carried away two whole months' worth of work; a shipment of iron poles has vanished; and Ghaylān has been temporarily disabled by a fever. But Ghaylān remains defiant, insisting that the "story" is not over yet. Nevertheless, in spite of his open defiance, Ghaylān is gradually driven to impatience and anxiety. Both he and Maymūnah have recourse to stories from the tradition to support their divergent visions. His precedent is the story of Āsāl and Nāʾilah in which Āsāl leaves his lover at the height of their love in order to seek a higher experience. Maymūnah in turn cites the story of Hāmān whose search for perfect existence drives him to madness. At this stage, Mayārah makes her first appearance and lends new impetus and energy to Ghaylān. With this, the play reaches its climax and the conflict its height.

With the help of Mayārah, Ghaylān forces the people of the valley, their prophet and the stones to accede to his will. Later the same afternoon, songs and voices are heard coming from the valley as a devastating storm breaks out. Phrases from Sāhabbā's gospel, first recited in Scene Four, are repeated here as if to confirm that the gospel was an oracle. However, the conflicting visions of the dam remain unchanged; while Maymūnah sees it in ruins, Ghaylān perceives it rising to the sky. At this stage, the dam is destroyed and the goddess seems to have the final word, but the play takes one more turn when Mayārah declares that, amidst the chaos, she sees a light beckoning her and Ghaylān. Both of them decide to reach for it. Maymūnah stays on the ground while the Mule remains chained to a rock.

With the publication of al-Sudd, Tunisian critics heralded the birth of a major work of art and the rise of Tunisian literature. Abroad reaction to al-Sudd was enthusiastic, but circulation was very limited. In his 1957 reviews Tāhā Husayn praised the book for attempting a new genre, the symbolic story, and declares that he was impressed by the writer's command of Arabic. Yet, despite this intervention from the "Dean of Arabic Letters" at the time, al-Mas'adī and his book did not make any real headway among readership in the Arab East. In Tunisia, on the other hand, it was not long before the book became part of school curriculum, which guaranteed its readership and effect on generations of Tunisian students and a number of writers. Ghaylān became one of the nation's icons, and his author secured his place as the leading cultural figures in the country. Critics have studied the play from various angles and in several languages; and a full translation appeared in French in 1981 as part of the UNESCO series of representative writers.

Ironically, however, al-Sudd was not the writer's first book to be published in full. Mawlid al-nisyān (Genesis of Oblivion) appeared in its entirety as instalments a decade earlier, in 1945. In this story, told in seven chapters, Ranjahād seduces the "wise" physician, Madyan, into giving up his search for a drug which would help him defeat Time, abandoning his companion and the hospice he runs and accepting her lead on a journey of self-discovery. When they near the ultimate goal,

Ranjahād unmasks her true identity. At the gate of Salhawa, the spring which gets its name from a plant called salhawah, known to bring nisyān (oblivion) and salwā (consolation), Ranjahād "explodes with laughter, falls apart and vanishes." Madyan raises his head to find himself alone in the dark forest. When he returns home, his companion, Laylā, inquires about his trip, but he says nothing. Madyan is silenced by the turn of events, struck dumb by the realization that what he thought was an epic journey through the far reaches of the soul was no more than a staged comedy of fate. Madyan eventually discovers a medicine, tests it and experiences a moment of timelessness, but he soon realises that "Time cannot be forgotten" and that the body is transient. Mawlid was a success both in Tunisia and abroad. It has been translated into French (1993) and Dutch (1995).

The most recent of al-Mas'adī's works to be published is Min ayyām 'Imrān (The Days of Imran, 2002). However, it does not really stray far from the writer's already established style, tone and themes. Like Haddatha, al-Sudd and Mawlid, it is the story of a man, Imran, and a woman, Dānyah, who meet up in order to seek company, fight off solitude and search for a meaningful existence. They go through various experiences and states, questioning belief, life, love, society, death. The narrative ends with their story transformed into the originating myth of a water spring gushing out from the cliff of a mountain that borders the sea at the spot where they have both met their death. Min ayyām 'Imrān is told in short segments, likened by critics to prose poems. Some of these take the form of dialogue, others narratives or meditations. The book was most likely conceived in the late 1940s but was written over a very long period of time in sporadic bursts. The earliest section appeared in 1954 but the complete text was not compiled and published in book form (along with the writer's aphorisms) until 2003 by the al-Mas'adī scholar, Mahmūd Tarshūnah.

The opacity of al-Mas'adī's texts and the fact that they tackle touchy issues in Islamic culture, such as the nature of faith and the limits of human power, have divided critics of his work since the mid-1950s. It is true that each of his

books puts accent on a different aspect of his
thought and style; but there is a unifying tone
and overarching themes that have led critics to
view the writer's work as a unified whole. His
writings have been largely interpreted in relation
to the colonial situation in Tunisia, the struggle
of Arab writers to revive the Arab and Islamic
cultural heritage, and the relationship of Arabic
literature to the literary traditions of the West.
Al-Masʿadī's style has been seen by some as a
successful adaptation of Arabic to modern
concerns and by others as precious and archaic.
Ghaylān has been hailed both as a hero who
resists foreign occupation and a revolutionary
who attempts to redress the backwardness of his
society. Abū Hurayrah in turn has been regarded
as a revolutionary figure who questions blind
belief and shakes off the inherited values of his
society. Yet both have also been criticized for
being elitist figures, disconnected from the
people and offering idealistic solutions to real
problems. Much has also been made of the
meaning of the death of al-Masʿadī's characters
at the end of the stories. Some critics have seen
this as failure to provide solutions and positive
models for a society in need of both. Others
have explained these endings as the natural
outcome of the impossible goals that characters
set for themselves. Yet other critics have also
pointed out the spiritual and metaphysical nature
of the stories and read the endings accordingly,
as sublimation or transformation of human existence on earth into a higher form of being,
regardless of whether the stories are interpreted
in light of Western philosophy or Islamic ideas,
and particularly Sufism.

In fact, the presence of mystical elements in
al-Masʿadī spans all his work but functions in
different ways in each of his key texts. Ghaylān's experience is not as varied as Abū Hurayrah's or as overtly mystical as Madyan's. It
nonetheless highlights specific instances of the
Sufi journey experienced by neither of the latter
character. As the play al-Sudd progresses, it becomes clear that the dam Ghaylān is constructing has more to it than the declared
purpose of collecting water for irrigation. The
completion of the dam, he claims, will be a
moment "of perfect creation. The transcendence

of his "earthly" project to a search for self-
fulfilment is guided by Mayārah, who begins the
story as an outsider and then lends guidance and
support to Ghaylān when she judges that he has
earned them through his individual effort. It is
through her that the dam can be interpreted as a
test of Ghaylān's capacity and real aims. Unlike
Abū Hurayrah, Ghaylān does not engage in
ritualistic practice, but focuses instead on
making rather than meditating. In the case of
Abū Hurayrah however, reaching the goal involves going through the stations of the Sufi way
and experiencing states, shunning temptation
along the journey to knowledge of sclf and the
world. In the case of Madyan, there is a debate
as to whether spiritual knowledge is attainable
through science or intuitive revelation.

As far as foreign sources are concerned,
there is agreement that al-Masʿadī's work bears
strong affinity to and clearly engages with
seminal texts from European modern literature
as well as Greek tragedy. There is a specific
affinity between Goethe's Faust and al-
Masʿadī's two characters Madyan and Ghaylān.
The Faust myth is most evident in Mawlid,
where Madyan, like Faust, is a physician
searching for a potion; Ranjahād combines the
sorceress and the devil, Mephistopheles; Madyan's soul flies away to join the "world of the
dead" just like Goethe's Faust. Also like Faust,
al-Masʿadī's main characters realize that
forgetfulness and freedom from the past only
come at the expense of life itself and that
man's reward is in trying. Al-Sudd in particular
recalls Prometheus Bound by Aeschylus and
Ibsen's Master Builder, in that they show the
desire of the main characters to teach fellow
humans productive life and skills.

Haddatha Abū Huraryah qāl has been likened
to Nietzsche's Zarathustra. Both texts take the
form of discourses and raise the question of the
limits of human will and power. Both are
episodic in structure and appear to stem from a
desire to explore other paths to knowledge
beyond reason. Al-Masʿadī, however, considers
this to be the result of Eastern influences on
Nietzsche rather than the other ways around.
From twentieth century sources one can draw
attention to the affinity between al-Masʿadī's

ideas and the work of the French existential philosophers, Jean-Paul Sartre and Albert Camus, particularly the sense of existential anguish and the absurdity of human suffering. However there is in al-Masʿadī a desire to recast these myths and characters in an 'Islamic' context and an Arabic style of thinking, linking these ideas to antecedents in Islamic culture such as the philosophical writings of sceptics like al-Maʿarrī and to Sufi writings and thinking, such as the work and life of Abu Mansūr al-Hallāj (d. 922). Al-Masʿadī's theory of human position in the universe may explain this blending. According to him the human self is limited on side and unlimited on the other. While it may appear powerless in the face of the universe and by comparison to God's power, it is nonetheless privileged since it is extracted from the divine self. This origin endows the human self with attributes of the Absolute Self. This is the meaning of the human being as vice regent of God. Tragedy is therefore the record of human beings as they

oscillate between man and beast; enduring the pain and powerlessness or the feeling of power-lessness in the face of face of fate, death, life, the unknown, the gods, himself.

No matter the interpretation, however, it seems there is consensus that al-Masʿadī's work remains a seminal experiment in reworking the Arabic language and narrative tradition into modern texts where issues of concern to the Islamic writer of the post-colonial period are treated in a daring manner. For this reason perhaps, there is a serious disjunction between the main stream of national literature in the Arab world and al-Masʿadī's writings. On the face of it, writing seems like the sphere where al-Masʿadī took refuge from political activity, the pressures of trade unionism and the bureaucracy of his government positions. Intellectually, writing was a space where he could express his inner tribulations as public intellectual. It was an area where he could explore the narrative tradition, the potential of the Arabic language, and world literature, away from the need for representing the national struggle and the social circumstances of the nation; and away from the

clarity and immediacy demanded by activist discourse. Yet, in the Arab world, the communities of readers who received his work have been largely shaped by nationalism and moderniz-ation as the two dominant paradigms among his critics, which led to both accusations that he betrayed his people and the glorification of his work as pioneering and unique. The reception of al-Masʿadī's fiction is perhaps indicative of the lack of a 'horizon of expectations' within which he might be read. His work frustrates the desire among foreign critics for local colour, facile political readings of Arabic literature and a practical literary history focused on genres and trends. In Tunisia he enjoyed a wide influence as a stylist, but little effect when it came to his engagement with tradition or language. He seems, however, to have become somewhat trapped in two separate spheres, so enclosed in his style and outlook that he remained un-changed throughout his career. He was also perhaps too much of a canonical figure, trapped in his image and a success that would be hard to emulate. His stature as prominent public official made him bound by the institution in his country and prevented him from free creative work.

Al-Masʿadī was a bilingual intellectual who early on made a conscious choice to separate the two languages. He published his research in French and Arabic, but wrote his fiction in Ara-bic. He was guided by the ideas and aesthetics learned from close knowledge of Western literature and through deep academic and personal experience of the Arabic literary and linguistic tradition. Al-Masʿadī was also deeply influenced by the ideas of freedom and the humanism prevalent among intellectuals in France at the time. The desire to be part of world literature and the drive to make a lasting contribution to Arabic, as well as world, culture marks his theory of literature and finds ex-pressions in his fiction. Unsystematic as it was, his attempt to identify with the foundational role that Islam and Arabic literature played in the elaboration of the very concept of a world literature, at least in its early formulations by Goethe, but he reveals a search for analogues and common ground rather than models and points of emulation.

Al-Mas'adī died on December 16, 2004, at age 93, having experienced and affected one of the most dramatic centuries in the history of Tunisia and the Arab world as a whole. His death came in the aftermath of a flurry of public activities related to his work and gave further momentum to interest in his life and writings. The year before, 2003, was marked by the publication of his complete works in both Arabic and French, national and international colloquia organized to celebrate the events, and renewed interest among translators. After his death, numerous commemorative events took place, ranging from reading his work in daily slots on state television, to colloquia around the country, interviews with those who knew him closely, special supplements in newspapers and magazines and an outpouring of expressions of admiration from writers and poets. Al-Mas'adī's death was in reality the passing of an era. For some, it ended his dominance over Tunisian literary history, giving room for other voices to be heard. For others, it was the passing of the last of the 'great Tunisians', an event akin to the death of the poet al-**Shābbī** seventy years earlier; hence calls to commemorate al-Mas-'adī's achievements in a museum, a library, literary prizes and even a dedicated website. But unlike al-Shābbī and the pioneer of Tunisian short story, 'Alī al-**Du'ājī**, who lived in relative obscurity and were honored only posthumously, by the time of his death al-Mas'adī had been an icon for Tunisians for almost half a century.

REFERENCES

Fātimah al-Akhdhar, *Khasā'is al-uslūb fī adab al-Mas'adī* ("The Features of Style in al-Mas'adī", Tunis: Hannaba'l Publishing, 2002);

Tawfīq Bakkār, "Mahmoud Messadi: Une métaphysique de l'homme et une esthétique de l'écriture", *Echanges* 2.3 (1980): 211-227;

J. C. Bürgel, "Tradition and Modernity in the Work of the Tunisian Writer al-Mas'adī", in:

Tradition and Modernity in Arabic Language and Literature, ed. J. R. Smart (Surrey: Curzon Press, 1996), 165-185;

Khālid al-Gharībī, *Jadaliyyyat al-asālah wa'l-mu'āsarah fī adab al-Mas'adī* ("The Dialectic Relationship between Authenticity and Contemporaneity in al-Mas'adī's Writings", Tunis: Sāmid, 1994);

Adrian Gully and John Hindle, "Qābūs ibn Washmagīr: A Study of Rhythm Patterns in Arabic Epistolary Prose from the 4th Century AH (10th Century AD)", *Middle Eastern Literatures* 6.2 (2003): 177-197;

Boutros Hallaq, "Exile et créativité: Quatre œuvres majeurs de la modernité littéraire", *Asiatische Studien/Études Asiatiques* 62.4 (2008): 1147-65.

Hafnāwī al-Mājirī, *al-Mas'adī: min al-thawrah ilā 'l-hazīmah* ("al-Mas'adī: From Revolution to Defeat", 2nd ed., Tunis: al-Dār al-Tūnisiyyah li'l-Nashr, 1985);

'Abd al-Salām al-Misaddī, *al-Mas'adī bayna al-ibdā' wa'l-īqā'* ("al-Mas'adī Between Creativity and Rhythm", Tunis: 'Abd al-Karīm ibn 'Abd Allāh, 1997);

Mohamed-Salah Omri, *Nationalism, Islam and World Literature: Sites of Confluence in the Writings of Mahmūd al-Mas'adī* (London and New York: Routledge, 2006);

R. C. Ostle, "Mahmūd al-Mas'adī and Tunisia's 'lost generation'", *Journal of Arabic Literature* 8 (1977): 153-66;

Krystina Skarzynska-Bochenska, "Mahmūd al-Mas'adī and Philosophy of Life and Death in his Existential Novels", *Quaderni di Studi Arabi* 10 (1992): 109-120;

Mahmūd Tarshūnah, *al-Adab al-murīd fī mu'allafāt al-Mas'adī* ("Literature of Will in al-Mas'adī's Writings", 5th ed., Tunis: al-Maghāribiyyah, 1997);

——, "Mahmūd al-Mas'adī", *Dā'irat al-Ma'ārif al-Tūnisiyyah* ("Encyclopaedia of Tunisia", Tunis: Bayt al-Hikmah), ii (1991): 62-70.

Ibrāhīm ʿAbd al-Qādir al-Māzinī

(1890 – 1949)

WILLIAM MAYNARD HUTCHINS

Appalachian State University

WORKS

al-Shiʿr: ghāyātuh wa-wasāʾituh ("Poetry – Its Aims and Devices", Cairo, 1915);

Fī shiʿr Ḥāfiz Ibrāhīm ("On Ḥāfiz Ibrāhīm's Poetry", Cairo, 1915);

Dīwān al-Māzinī, 2 vols. (Cairo, 1913 & 1916); collected poetry;

al-Dīwān ("Collected Poetry", Cairo: Maktabat al-Saʿādah, 1921; 3rd ed. Cairo: Dār al-Shaʿb, 1972); co-author ʿAbbās Mahmūd al-ʿAqqād;

Hasād al-hashīm ("Harvest of Chaff", Cairo, 1924; Cairo: al-Dār al-Qawmiyyah li'l-Tibāʿah wa'l-Nashr, 1961; Cairo: al-Shaʿb, 1969; Beirut & Cairo: Dār al-Shurūq, 1976);

Qabd al-rīh ("Grasp of the Wind", Cairo: Elias Antūn, September 1927; Cairo: al-Dār al-Qawmiyyah li'l-Tibāʿah wa'l-Nashr, 1960; Cairo: Dār al-Shaʿb, 1971);

Sundūq al-dunyā ("Peep Show", Cairo: Matbaʿat al-Taraqqī, 1929; Cairo: Matābiʿ Jarīdat al-Misrī, 1948; Cairo: al-Dār al-Qawmiyyah, 1960; Beirut & Cairo: Dār al-Shurūq, 1980);

Rihlah ilā 'l-Hijāz ("Journey to the Hijaz", Cairo: Matbaʿat Fuʾād, 1930; Cairo: al-Hayʾah al-Misriyyah al-ʿĀmmah li'l-Kitāb, 1973);

Ibrāhīm al-kātib ("Ibrahim the Writer", Cairo: Matbaʿat al-Taraqqī, 1931; Cairo: Dār al-Maʿārif, 1943; Cairo: al-Dār al-Qawmiyyah, 1960; Cairo: al-Shaʿb, 1970);

al-Siyāsah al-misriyyah wa'l-inqilāb al-dustūri ("Egyptian Politics and Constitutional Revolution", Cairo: Matbaʿat al-Siyāsah, 1931); by al-Māzinī, Muhammad Husayn Haykal, and Muhammad ʿAbd Allāh ʿInān;

Hukm al-tāʿah ("Rule of Obedience", Cairo, 1932; Cairo: al-Dār al-Qawmiyyah li'l-Tibāʿah wa'l-Nashr, [1963]);

Khuyūt al-ʿankabūt ("The Spider's Web", Cairo: Matbaʿat ʿĪsā al-Bābī al-Halabī, 1935; Cairo: al-Dār al-Qawmiyyah li'l-Tibāʿah wa'l-Nashr, 1960);

Fī 'l-tarīq ("On the Way", Cairo: Maktabat al-Nahdah, 1937; Cairo: Dār al-Hilāl, 1953; Cairo & Beirut: Dār al-Shurūq, 1980);

ʾAwd ʿalā bad' ("Back to the Start", Cairo: Dār al-Maʿārif, 1943; 2nd ed. 1953; Cairo: al-Dār al-Qawmiyyah li'l-Tibāʿah wa'l-Nashr, 1963 [?]; Beirut: Dār al-Shurūq, 1979);

Ibrāhīm al-thānī ("Ibrahim II", Matbaʿat al-Maʿārif, 1943; Cairo: Matābiʿ al-Dār al-Qawmiyyah, 1962[?]; Cairo: Dār al-Shaʿb, 1970);

Mīdū wa-shurakāh ("Midu and Company", Cairo: Matbaʿat al-Nahār, 1943);

Qissat hayāt ("Story of a Life", Cairo, 1943; Cairo: Dār al-Shaʿb, 1971);

Thalāthat rijāl wa-ʾmraʾah ("Three Men and a Woman", Cairo: Matbaʿat Maktabat Misr, 1943; Cairo: al-Dār al-Qawmiyyah li'l-Tibāʿah wa'l-Nashr, 1961; Cairo: Dār al-Shaʿb, 1971; Beirut: Dār al-Shurūq, 1981);

ʾA-'l-māshī ("Right on!", Cairo: Maktabat Misr, 1944; Cairo: al-Dār al-Qawmiyyah li'l-Tibāʿah wa'l-Nashr, 1961; Beirut: Dār al-Shurūq, 1975);

Bashshār ibn Burd ("Bashshār ibn Burd", Cairo: Matbaʿat Mustafā al-Halabī & Lajnat Tarjamat Dāʾirat al-Maʿārif al-Islāmiyyah, 1944; Cairo: Dār al-Shaʿb, 1971);

Min al-nāfidhah ("Through the Window", Cairo: Dār al-Maʿārif, Iqraʾ series no. 83 [Oct. 1949]; Cairo: al-Dār al-Qawmiyyah li'l-Tibāʿah wa'l-Nashr, [1961?]);

Aqāsīs ("Stories", Cairo: Matbaʿat Maktabat Misr, n.d. [before 1956]); by al-Māzinī et al.;

Ahādīth al-Māzinī ("al-Māzinī's Talks", [Cairo?], 1961); preface by ʿAbd al-Wāhid al-Wakīl;

Mukhtārāt min adab al-Māzinī ("Selections from al-Māzinī's Literature", Cairo: al-Dār al-Qawmiyyah li'l-Tibāʿah wa'l-Nashr, 1961);

Sabīl hayāt ("The Course of a Life", Cairo: al-Dār al-Qawmiyyah li'l-Tibāʿah wa'l-Nashr, 1962; Beirut & Cairo: Dār al-Shurūq, 1979).

Collected Poetry

Dīwān al-Māzinī, ed. Mahmūd 'Imād, 3 vols. (Cairo: al-Majlis al-A'lā li-Ri'āyat al-Funūn wa'l-Ādāb wa'l-'Ulūm al-Ijtimā'iyyah, 1961).

Translations by the Author

al-Tarbiyah al-tabī'iyyah, aw Īmīl al-qarn al-'ishrīn ("Natural Education/Upbringing, or: 20th Century Émile", Cairo: al-Bayān, 1912-1914); translation of *Émile* by Jean-Jacques Rousseau;

Sānīn, aw Ibn al-tabī'ah ("Sanin, or: The Son of Nature", Cairo, 1920; Cairo: Dār al-Sha'b, 1970); translation of *Sanin* by Mikhail Artsybashev;

al-Kitāb al-abyad ("The White Book", Cairo, 1922); translation of the *Correspondence Respecting Affairs in Egypt by Great Britain, High Commissioner for Egypt and the Sudan*;

al-Shāridah ("The Fugitive", Cairo: circa 1932); translation of *The Fugitive* by John Galsworthy;

Mukhtārāt min al-qasas al-inglīzī ("Selections from English Fiction", Cairo, 1939); stories by Oscar Wilde and others;

Alan Kwatirmayn ("A. K.", Cairo, n.d.); translation of *Allan Quatermain* by Sir Henry Rider Haggard;

Hukm al-miqsalah ("Gallow's Verdict", Cairo, 1944); translation of *In the Shadow of the Guillotine* by Rafael Sabatini;

[Arabic Title unkown], (Cairo, n.d.); translation of *The Time Machine* by H. G. Wells;

Jarīmat al-Lurd Sāfīl ("Lord S.'s Crime", Cairo, 1944); translation of *Lord Arthur Savile's Crime* by Oscar Wilde;

Rubā'iyyāt 'Umar Khayyām ("The Quatrains of Omar Khayyam", Cairo, n.d.); translation of the English translation by Edward Fitzgerald;

Madrasat al-wishāyāt ("School of Scandals", Cairo, n.d.); translation of *The School for Scandal* by Richard Brinsley Sheridan;

al-Ābā' wa'l-abnā' ("Fathers and Sons", Cairo, n.d.); translation of *Fathers and Sons* by Ivan Sergeevich Turgenev.

Works in Translation

Ibrahim the Writer (Cairo: General Egyptian Book Organization, 1976); translation of *Ibrāhīm al-kātib*, tr. Magdi Wahba, rev. Marsden Jones;

Ten Again and Other Stories (Cairo & New York: The American University in Cairo Press, 2006); translation of *'Awd 'alā bad'* and other stories, tr. William Hutchins.

Ibrāhīm 'Abd al-Qādir al-Māzinī, the Egyptian author famed for his humor and his elegant prose, wrote primarily autobiographical short stories, novellas, novels, and was also a poet, critic, and translator. He was an influential figure in Egyptian letters during the first half of the twentieth century, and his first novel, *Ibrāhīm al-kātib* (1931; English translation: *Ibrahim the Writer*, 1976), was an important milestone in the development of the Arabic novel. Although his reputation has been somewhat eclipsed by his death at a relatively young age and by suggestions that he had appropriated phrases from other authors, he was significant in helping to define an Egyptian self-image, in pioneering a modern Arabic style that is at once clear and elegant, in launching writing as a career in Egyptian society, and in setting the bar very high for comic prose.

Although al-Māzinī himself was one of his own favorite characters and although the scholar Sayyid Hāmid al-Nassāj is certainly not the only scholar to say—as he does in his "Panorama of the Modern Arabic Novel" (1980)—that al-Māzinī was a confessional author who was unable to establish an appropriate aesthetic distance between himself and his subject matter, al-Māzinī's autobiographical statement, which is quoted by Hamdi Sakkut and Marsden Jones in *Ibrāhīm 'Abd al-Qādir al-Māzinī* (1979) is terse:

I was born August 19, 1890, and my father ... was named Muhammad 'Abd al-Qādir al-Māzinī. He was a lawyer ... . I studied in elementary and secondary schools and university-level institutions, graduating in 1909 from the Khedival Teacher Training Institute. The Ministry of Education appointed me a translation teacher... .

In the posthumously published work *Ahādīth al-Māzinī* (al-Māzinī's Talks, 1961), a collection of talks and stories at least some of which were prepared for broadcast, al-Māzinī says his father was a student at al-Azhar, a colleague there of the renowned reformer Muhammad ʿAbduh (d. 1905) and a student of the equally famous Jamāl al-Dīn al-Afghānī (d. 1897). In his work *Mukhtārāt min adab al-Māzinī* (Selections from al-Māzinī's Literature, 1961) he says that both his father and grandfather were members of the *'ulamāʾ*, the Muslim religious scholars. In *Sabīl hayāt* (The Course of a Life, posthum 1962) he says that his father, who was polygamous and fond of Turkish women, died when he was nine and when his mother, who lived for thirty-two more years, was in her thirties.

Al-Māzinī's *Dīwān* (Collected Poems, 1961) contains two couplets from a 1913 elegy for a deceased daughter. He taught in a variety of secondary schools and at al-Nāsiriyyah School for Teachers until 1914 when he resigned from service to the Ministry of Education, although he continued to teach English and translation until he was swept up in the Egyptian nationalist movement that appeared full blown with the 1919 Revolution. His entry into political activism went hand-in-hand with a career in journalism. He was, for example, in 1922 an editor at the *al-Akhbār* newspaper. According to Niʿmāt Ahmad Fuʾād in *Adab al-Māzinī* (al-Māzinī's Literature, 1961) he remarried after the death of his first wife. Each wife delivered a daughter who died young. *Fī 'l-tarīq* (On the Road, 1937) was dedicated to the memory of the second daughter, Mandūrah, and contains a fantasy with her. He was survived by three sons, including Muhammad ʿAbd al-Qādir al-Māzinī (who transcribed his name as Mohamed Abdel Kader El Mazni).

Whereas al-Nassāj criticizes al-Māzinī for emphasizing the individuality of his characters in his novels *Ibrāhīm al-kātib* (1931; *Ibrahim the Writer*, 1976) and *Ibrāhīm al-thānī* (Ibrahim II, 1943) so strongly that they appear to live outside of any society or community, Sakkut and Jones (1979) say that it was precisely because authors of al-Māzinī's generation in Egypt emphasized the sensitive and imaginative emotional fulfillment of the individual, that literature was able to develop in Egypt during the first half of the twentieth century. Muhammad Mandūr in his work *Ibrāhīm al-Māzinī* (1954, as excerpted and translated by Roger Allen, 1987) says of al-Māzinī:

I do not think we would be going too far if we suggested that he is the hero of the majority of the stories he wrote. He continues: *indeed, we can say that al-Māzinī's œuvre consists wholly of poetry, prose, stories and literary articles of a personal nature.*

As a young poet, al-Māzinī was associated with Egyptian Romanticism but was perhaps less influential for his verse than for his theorizing, the most famous example of which was *al-Dīwān* (1913, 1916), which he wrote with ʿAbbās Mahmūd al-ʿAqqād (d. 1964). Salma Kh. al-Jayyusi (1977) explains that al-Māzinī's poetry appeared more Romantic (as "poetry of the self") than it actually was, since "[h]is diction, his phraseology, [and] his general poetic structure" were reminiscent of traditional poetry. She explains also that it "failed to influence in any important way the Romantic trend in Arabic poetry." Then she declares that, since al-Māzinī as a young man fell under the influence of the poet ʿAbd al-Rahmān **Shukrī**, he "took to poetry and poetic criticism, his true talent—he became later the best humorous writer in modern Arabic literature—remaining dormant until the mid-twenties."

Sakkut and Jones (1979), however, do not consider al-Māzinī's poetry a youthful misstep and discuss some of his poems at length. They comment that his poetry shows his "intense longing for what he terms a conformity with nature." This conformity or congruence would entail an emotional and loving relationship with the natural world as a person attempts to be a good fit. M. M. Badawi (1975) says,

Mazini defines poetry as an art "of which the end is emotion, the means imagination or a stream of related ideas directed by emotion."

He also provides a translation ("Where's your Mummy?—a Dialogue with my son Muhammad") of a poem from the third volume of al-Māzinī's *Dīwān* (Collected Poems, 1961):

I did not speak to him, but the look in my eye
said
'Where is your mummy? Where's your
mummy?'
While he was prattling away, as was his wont

Every day since she has gone.
He turned to me trying to smooth the furrows in
*   my forehead,*
But how could that be done, I thought. How
*   indeed?*
When his hand had passed over my face I said
Do you know of aught, aught that might help?
Help to do what, he asked. What do you mean,
*   Dad?*
'Nothing,' I replied and I kissed him instead.

Badawi also praises al-Māzinī's long poem "The
Conflict" in which an ageing poet debates with
his own soul the appropriateness of his lust for
young women.

Al-Māzinī's career as a translator began in
the classroom when he taught translation and
paralleled his other literary pursuits over the
course of his life. One of his earliest translations
was also his most notorious: *Sanin* by Mikhail
Artsybashev (d. 1927). This was considered quite
a spicy book in its day; Vyacheslav Zavalishin
in *Early Soviet Writers* (1958) says of *Sanin*
(1907) and two other early novels by Artsybashev: "It is true that in these novels there is a
racy, ostentatious sexiness which robs them of
esthetic value." Zavalishin does admit that "his
sometimes offensive naturalistic descriptions are
accompanied by keen psychological insight and
sociological analysis." In his introduction to a
recent translation of *Sanin*, Otto Boele observes:

In Artsybashev's view modern society is not
simply imperfect or oppressive; it is a distortion
of a more natural way of life that needs to be
and can be restored through the removal of
everything artificial.

The fact that al-Māzinī translated *Sanin* in 1920
and then allegedly sold four thousand copies
before he published *Ibrāhīm al-kātib* is significant in terms of both the two novels' exploration of the psychology of human attraction
and their emphasis on the need for human
conformity with nature. Al-Māzinī's translation
was also controversial later for alleged similarities to *Ibrāhīm al-kātib* although these may
have been partly the result of a creative streak in
the translator. In any case, the free adaptation of
a foreign work *(iqtibās)* was a known entity in
Egypt at the time.

Sakkut and Jones in their bibliography (1979)
list 1995 newspaper pieces that al-Māzinī published between 1911 and his death August 20,
1949. These include, for example, an article
entitled "Siyāsat Ingiltirā wāhidah fī 'l-Hind wa-
Irlandā wa-Misr" (England's Policy is the Same
in India, Ireland, and Egypt), which was
published in *al-Akhbār* (September 13, 1921),
"Masāʿī al-Inglīz li-fasl al-Sūdān ʿan Misr"
(Efforts by the English to Separate the Sudan
from Egypt) which was published in *al-Akhbār*
(June 1, 1924), "'Awdat al-rūh li'l-ustādh Tawfīq al-**Hakīm**" (*Return of the Spirit* by Tawfīq
al-Hakīm), which was published in *al-Balāgh*
(The Report, June 25, 1933), and "Filastīn al-
thā'irah" (Revolutionary Palestine) published in
al-Shabāb (Youth, September 16, 1936). This
section of their book does not count literary
sketches or stories that were published in newspapers.

The bibliography of Sakkut and Jones also
gives two examples of al-Māzinī's literary criticism in the form of glosses for lines of poetry.
Al-Māzinī says of a line of poetry by al-
Mutanabbī (d. 965) that after reading it, he tore
up one of his own poems. They explain:

al-Mutanabbī says that death is the reason for
admiration of courage, generosity, and patience.
If not for it, a person would not be able to
perceive the meaning of many of the virtues.

Of a line by Ibn al-Rūmī (d. 896) about a child
crying on first encountering the world, al-Māzinī
admits that it is impolite on our part to meet the
world with such a din, but that our excuse is that
we are callow. Sakkut and Jones say that it is
central to al-Māzinī's approach to think that
humor and paradox can instruct us and form a
new spirit. Al-Māzinī's book *Bashshār ibn Burd*
(1944), about the pre-modern poet of that name,
has, in addition to an introduction and a conclusion, only three chapters, of which one is
"Bashshār wa'l-mar'ah" (Bashshār and Women).
He says of Bashshār that from his youth on he
was known for his satirical poems. This emphasis may be appropriate for the poet but also
reveals something about al-Māzinī.

Ibrāhīm al-kātib, which was al-Māzinī's first
and longest novel and which he dedicated to

himself, won a novel-writing competition in Egypt. While praising aspects of the work, Allen (1982) has criticized the novel as

a rather disjointed account of the love of a man for three different women: a Syrian nurse, Mary, who helps him through his convalescence from illness; his cousin, Shushu; and Layla, a girl whom he meets in Luxor…

Salāḥ ʿAbd al-Sabūr, however, says in *Mādhā yabqā minhum li'l-tārīkh* (Their Lasting Value, 1968, as translated and excerpted in Allen, 1987): "Some people may imagine that the three love stories make up the core and essence of the story." He contends to the contrary, "it is not a love story" but "a psychological one, which sheds light on a particular type of person". In fact, this seems to have been one of al-Māzinī's favorite approaches to portraying a character: to show the development of the character through his/her love with several different characters, thus bringing out different dimensions of the protagonist's personality.

Most people who know al-Māzinī's works remember him first and foremost as a humorist. He complains in *Sundūq al-dunyā* (Peep Show, 1929) of being typecast as the author of humorous essays, but in *Khuyūt al-ʿankabūt* (Spider's Webs, 1935) he quotes his mother as saying to him, "By God, I have *never* been able to tell whether you are serious or joking." Hāmid ʿAbduh al-Hawwāl (1982, as excerpted and translated in Allen, 1987) says pointblank: "Indeed, sarcasm is the essence of his style." Sakkut and Jones (1979), however, say that al-Māzinī differentiated between sarcasm or irony *(al-sukhriyyah)* and humor *(al-fukāhah)*: "Sarcasm [or irony] depends on the comparison of reality with an image of perfection." Humor is, instead, relatively sympathetic to human failings and does not involve a comparison with some standard of perfection. Humor's bedfellow is paradox, not irony. Allen (1982) has referred to al-Māzinī's "unique brand of humour." He mentions an "almost farcical sense of fun which typifies so many of his stories." Al-Māzinī's younger contemporary Tawfīq al-**Hakīm** (d. 1987) had a background in theatrical farce and was a renowned humorist too. Compared to al-

Hakīm, though, the special comic genius of al-Māzinī was to take a shtick that could have been a vaudeville routine and to make it resonate within the human psyche—as he does, for example, in "Laylah wa-lā ka-'l-layālī," (1935, "A Night Unlike Any Other", in: al-Māzinī, *Ten Again*, 2006) when a drunken "sailor", who has been imbibing with friends in a boat on the Nile, wanders into the apartment below his by accident and is chastised by a parrot. He mistakes his neighbor's wife for a dream maiden before he sobers up when she mentions her husband. In a story in *Khuyūt al-ʿankabūt*, the narrator is trapped in an elevator with a young woman who had chatted at length within his earshot at the beach about his hideous looks. Al-Māzinī's humor usually retains a tragic core, as is appropriate for someone who as a child watched a friend burn to death, an experience which is recounted in *Qissat hayāt* (Story of a Life, 1943). Al-Māzinī used his humor to explore the complexities of the human psyche, as in *ʿAwd ʿalā bad'* (1943; *Ten Again*, 2006) when the adult hero who has become a boy again is humiliated by his two sons who sneakily drape orange, lemon, and banana peels over him at his tenth birthday party: "Even my buttonholes had strips of peel tucked in and tied in bows." Worse still, he finds, "[a] rose had been fastened to each side of my head, which was even decorated with a sprinkling of blossoms." The hero knows he looks ridiculous, feels outraged, and loves his two naughty sons, all at once.

In a delightful comment, Niʿmāt A. Fuʾād (1961, as excerpted and translated in Allen, 1987) compares the extensive use of dialogue in prose fiction by both al-Māzinī and al-Hakīm:

With al-Hakīm's dialogue you are presented with a wonderfully cooked meal. Al-Māzinī, on the other hand, gives you a fresh piece of fruit that looks, tastes, and smells marvelous… . Al-Māzinī's dialogues are really poetic tableaux using simple language.

Badawi (1973) also praises al-Māzinī's dialogue, in this case with reference to *ʿAwd ʿalā bad'* (1943; *Ten Again*, 2006):

The dialogue, all written in literary Arabic, is a model of what dialogue in the Arabic novel should be like: here the problem of the duality of the Arabic language has virtually vanished, for while remaining faithful to the spoken idiom to the point of reflecting its minute rhythms, it has the polish and elegance of literary Arabic.

Badawi says here that this novel "ranks among the great works of humour in any literature."

The year 1943 was a productive one for al-Māzinī, since it saw the publication of some of his finest short novels: *'Awd 'alā bad'*, *Ibrāhīm al-thānī* (Ibrahim II), *Mīdū wa-shurakāh* ("Mīdū and His Accomplices," in *Ten Again*, 2006), *Thalāthat rijāl wa-'mra'ah* (Three Men and a Woman), and *Qissat hayāt*. *Thalāthat rijāl wa-'mra'ah* is, whether by design or not, a feminine remake of *Ibrāhīm al-kātib*, since here one woman is courted by three men, whereas in the earlier novel the hero diverts himself by courting three women. The progressive emancipation of women from traditional roles was part of Egypt's social history during al-Māzinī's lifetime. It is thus hardly surprising that it figures in his novels and short stories, but he was also part of a generation influenced by Freud. The hero in *'Awd 'alā bad'* explores his juvenile sexuality when he finds that his wife in his new life has become his mother. There is also a rather amazing—at least for its day and society—surrogate love scene between two women, each of whom is in love with the other's brother, in *Mīdū wa-shurakāh*. There is an abortion each in *Ibrāhīm al-kātib* and *Ibrāhīm al-thānī*, and a story about a young woman's abortion in *'A-'l-māshī* (Right On!, 1944); this seems a daring literary subject for the era.

In *Ibrāhīm al-kātib* al-Māzinī attempted to create a "modern" novel with love interests, and that required men and women to meet in non-traditional settings. Of it and its pseudo-sequel *Ibrāhīm al-thānī*, Hilary Kilpatrick (1974) remarks that women "are pawns at the mercy of the hero and have no existence independently of him." She says that what al-Māzinī prized in a woman was her "education and consequent ability to follow an intelligent conversation ..." but that "when it comes to the structure of personal relationships ... there is little change from the old ways." That the two heroes—

Ibrāhīm I and Ibrāhīm II—are concerned about a mutually fulfilling love and the best interests of each of the women with whom he is involved does not seem to count for Kilpatrick. Similarly in two separate stories in *Khuyūt al-'ankabūt*, a husband who has wronged his wife while fooling around with another woman, resolves of his own accord to mend his ways. Sakkut and Jones (1979) suggest that al-Māzinī's sexism was based not on an assumption of female inferiority but of a feminine tendency toward conformity, which was alien to the experimental individualism he advocated.

Ibrāhīm al-thānī, which is the introspective tale of the hero's midlife crisis, by its very title invites comparison with *Ibrāhīm al-kātib*, and both titles suggest that Ibrāhīm al-Māzinī is this writer/author. In an initial note for *Ibrāhīm al-thānī*, al-Māzinī says that both characters are the same person, since the second one is the development of the former, but that the character had changed enough that they would require someone to introduce them, were they to meet. *Ibrāhīm al-thānī* is perhaps his most undervalued novel. There is nothing especially flashy about it, although in a subplot Sādiq threatens Mīmī with a gun. It is rather the story of a man who is restless in his marriage and who experiments with falling in love with two other women—Mīmī and ʿĀ'idah—who eventually prove more problematic than his wife. This is an excellent example of al-Māzinī as a great psychological author, prefiguring the work of the preeminent psychologist of Egyptian letters, the Egyptian Nobel laureate Najīb Mahfūz (Naguib Mahfouz, 1911-2006). Part of the interest of *Ibrāhīm al-thānī* is the maturity of the relationship between the husband and wife. Tahiyyah is willing to allow Ibrāhīm to experiment with younger women, but not from desperation or submission. He, in turn, is unwilling to love his wife merely because he has married her. Once he discovers that he no longer needs the flattery of young beauties to polish his virile self-respect, he falls in love with his wife all over again, and she becomes pregnant after many childless years. Sakkut and Jones (1979) emphasize the importance of personal experimentation, which al-Māzinī believed to be the firm foundation for every admirable value.

In *Mīdū wa-shurakāh* family intrigues revolve around an unwavering core of family solidarity. A handsome young military officer, Mīdū, falls in love with a woman he sees on the street. She turns out to be a physician and the sister of a friend, who is also falling in love with the officer's sister. None of this sits well with the hero's mother, who wants to marry her daughter to a stolid cousin. The de facto pater familias is the mother's brother, who is a pedantic but athletic bookworm, who cannot deny the attraction of the young woman doctor, and so forth.

Thalāthat rijāl wa-ʾmraʾah is a parody of the typical love story. Thus it contains all the elements of a love story, including love at first sight and torrid embraces by the sea. The heroine Mahāsin has an abortion courtesy of her gluttonous father's crony Halīm and then must work as a secretary, because her father ʿIyād is spending household money on his mistress. Her fiancé Mahmūd is a government engineer who freelances as a racetrack reporter. A third interested male is Nasīm Beğ, whom she meets at work. And then there is Hamdī, too. Although this novel is comic, it does not eschew the senseless, futile, and sad aspects of life. Of the first Ibrāhīm, ʿAbd al-Sabūr asks in *Mādhā yabqā minhum liʾl-tārīkh* (1968, as translated and excerpted in Allen, 1987): "So why does Ibrāhīm reject love, which symbolizes home and family?" Then he answers, "because he is rejecting life itself". *Thalāthat rijāl wa-ʾmraʾah* is at least a life-affirming work.

Qissat hayāt was described by al-Māzinī as the reminiscences of a person like himself, rather than an autobiography. In a touching scene, the young hero is so ill that his mother is afraid he is dying. In her nervousness, she knocks a jug off the windowsill so that it falls into the courtyard several floors below. She rushes down, sure that, if it has broken, her son will die. The jug has fallen in the soft dirt, and her son's fever breaks. Later, the narrator's wife dies in childbirth, because—the narrator suspects—the doctor was drunk. He then seeks solace by editing the poems of Ibn al-Rūmī (d. 896). What might have been a set of cute auto-

biographical vignettes resonates instead with a certain gravitas.

The settings for al-Māzinī's fiction were those of middle-class Cairenes of his era: a suburban garden, the banks of the Nile, a watermelon patch—that was about it. They might venture into the countryside for a holiday or to a working-class area of Cairo on an errand but would feel uncomfortable there. Being too foreign in any way—whether too European, Turkish, or African—was grounds for discomfort. Drawing on this relatively coherent world, al-Māzinī helped define through his newspaper sketches and collections an Egyptian identity, according to which, for example, it is important to have a good sense of humor, to be level-headed but light-hearted.

Al-Māzinī created for himself a literary counterpart who was a naïve trickster. Thus he combined the two characters of the medieval Arabic genre of the *maqāmah*, in which typically the ingénue is tricked out of his money by a silver-tongued rogue in some new disguise. The naïve trickster is also an important feature of Middle Eastern folk culture and appears under such names as Juhā and Mullā Nasr al-Dīn. In "Rajul Sādhij" (A Simple Man), included in *Sundūq al-dunyā*, al-Māzinī even compared himself to the proprietor of a peep show, since both collect and show off entertaining images of the world. In this persona he indulges himself by playing jokes on the reader with deliberately ambiguous pronouns, unusual combinations of images, and visually arresting typographical displays of stuttering. Sakkut and Jones (1979) offer the genial idea that al-Māzinī wrote as if befriending the reader. One example of this phenomenon is the series of ingratiating introductory notes that al-Māzinī provided for some of his books.

Al-Māzinī, who was the father of two lively young sons in 1935—ʿAbd al-Hamīd ʿAbd al-Qādir al-Māzinī, four, and Ridā ʿAbd al-Qādir al-Māzinī, six—was unusually interested in children as characters and in allowing children to be children and not miniature adults. Sakkut and Jones (1979) say that the child was a favorite symbol for al-Māzinī and stood for the adult's attainment of the difficult goals of "combining intentional action with coincidence and chance." They explain that the author's use of the child as a symbol demonstrated that he understood his job to be "the creation of a new man." In the struggle between the adult mind in the child's body in *'Awd 'alā bad'*, the child's body frequently wins out over the man's mind. Despite sarcastic comments about children's brutish nature, al-Māzinī showed concern for children's rights and personalities, and the good-humored malice of his portraits of children adds to their verisimilitude. In a sketch called "al-Sighār wa'l-kibār" (Children and Adults, in *Sundūq al-dunyā*), the narrator suggests to a young son that they should write a book to manifest the wisdom of children. Roles will be reversed so that adults go to school in silly clothing and climb in bed by 8 p.m. In a piece called "al-Tufūlah al-gharīrah" ("Innocent Childhood") in the same collection, al-Māzinī complains that Egyptian children of four and five years are unable to think for themselves, since they lack the opportunities to exercise and explore. In his story "Fī 'l-hulm" (The Dream) from *Khuyūt al-ʿankabūt*, al-Māzinī narrates the dream conversation between an unmarried woman and her unborn (and unconceived) daughter, who is growing impatient. There is not surprisingly a generational contrast between the two women, much as there is in many works by al-**Hakīm**. Al-Māzinī's character, who never marries or conceives, remembers this conversation as a shining moment in her life. If the reader smiles or laughs, he does so out of admiration for the character's humanity.

Hamilton A. R. Gibb (1962) refers to al-Māzinī's "defiant cyncism" but also notes the especially Egyptian blend of "humor and sympathy" in *Ibrāhīm al-kātib*. M. M. Badawi (1973) comments that al-Māzinī's best humor is of enduring value, because it is so "deeply rooted in social reality." He refers to al-Māzinī's "great humanity, his affection and tolerance, his irony and urbanity of spirit" and says—in a comment as elegant as al-Māzinī's prose—that, in *'Awd 'alā bad'*, his "characters are all alive, sketchily but sensitively drawn, as in a Rembrandt etching". In short, al-Māzinī was a poet, critic, translator, teacher, journalist, and novelist who is best remembered today as a distinguished humorist with a graceful Arabic prose style.

REFERENCES

Roger Allen, "al-Māzinī, Ibrāhīm ʿAbd al-Qādir (1890-1949)," in: *Encyclopedia of Arabic Literature*, ed. Julie Scott Meisami and Paul Starkey, 2 vols. (London & New York: Routledge, 1998), II, 521-522;

——, *Modern Arabic Literature*, A Library of Literary Criticism series (New York: The Ungar Publishing Company, 1987);

——, *The Arabic Novel: An Historical and Critical Introduction* (Syracuse: Syracuse University Press, 1982);

Mikhail Artsybashev, *Sanin: A Novel*, translated by Michael R. Katz (Ithaca & London: Cornell University Press, 2001);

M. M. Badawi, *A Critical Introduction to Modern Arabic Poetry* (London, New York, & Melbourne: Cambridge University Press, 1975);

——, "al-Māzinī the Novelist," *Journal of Arabic Literature* 4 (1973): 112-145;

Issa J. Boullata (ed.), *Critical Perspectives on Modern Arabic Literature* (Washington, D.C.: Three Continents Press, 1980);

Niʿmāt Ahmad Fuʾād, *Adab al-Māzinī*, 2nd ed. (Cairo: al-Khānjī, 1961);

Hamilton A. R. Gibb, *Studies on the Civilization of Islam*, ed. Stanford J. Shaw and William R. Polk (Boston: Beacon Press, 1962);

Hāmid ʿAbduh al-Hawwāl, *al-Sukhriyyah fī adab al-Māzinī* ("Irony in al-Māzinī's Literature", Cairo: al-Hayʾah al-Misriyyah al-ʿĀmmah li'l-Kitāb, 1982);

John A. Haywood, *Modern Arabic Literature 1800-1970* (London: Lund Humphries, 1971);

William M. Hutchins, al-*Māzinī's Egypt* (Washington, D.C.: Three Continents Press, 1983);

Salma Khadra al-Jayyusi, *Trends and Movements in Modern Arabic Poetry*, 2 vols. (Leiden: E. J. Brill, 1977);

Hilary Kilpatrick, *The Modern Egyptian Novel: A Study in Social Criticism*, St Antony's Middle East Monographs, no. 1 (London: Ithaca, 1974);

Mustafā Nāsīf, *Ramz al-tifl: dirāsah fī adab al-Māzinī* ("The Child as a Symbol: A Study in al-Māzinī's Literature", Cairo: al-Dār al-Qawmiyyah li'l-Tibā'ah wa'l-Nashr, 1965);

Sayyid Hāmid al-Nassāj, *Bānūrāmā al-riwāyah al-'arabiyyah al-hadīthah* ("Panorama of the Modern Arabic Novel", Cairo: Dār al-Ma'ārif, 1980);

Hamdi Sakkut, *The Arabic Novel: Bibliography and Critical Introduction 1865-1995* (Cairo

& New York: The American University in Cairo Press, 2000); six vols.;

——, *The Egyptian Novel and its Main Trends from 1913 to 1952* (Cairo: The American University in Cairo Press, 1971).

—— and Marsden Jones, *Ibrāhīm 'Abd al-Qādir al-Māzinī* (Cairo: The American University in Cairo Press and Dār al-Kitāb al-Misrī and Beirut: Dār al-Kitāb al-Lubnānī, 1979); bibliography.

Khalīl Mutrān

(1872? – 1949)

TERRI DeYOUNG

University of Washington, Seattle

WORKS

Dīwān al-Khalīl (Cairo: Dār al-Ma'ārif, 1908);

Ilā 'l-shabāb: arājīz fī ahdath wasā'il al-najāh min al-akhlāq wa'l-ādāb ("To Youth: Poems in the *Rajaz* Metre about the Newest Ways to Success With Reference to Ethics and Morals", Cairo: Dār al-Ma'ārif, 1951);

Min yanābī' al-hikmah ("From the Springs of Wisdom", Harīsah (Lebanon): Imprimerie Būlusiyyah, 1952);

Marāthī al-shu'arā' li-nābighat 'asrih wanādirat dahrih, faqīd al-sayf wa'l-qalam al-marhūm Mahmūd Sāmī al-Bārūdī ("Elegies of the Poets for the Genius of his Age and Prodigy of his Time, the Deceased One of the Sword and the Pen, the Late Mahmūd Sāmī al-Bārūdī", Cairo: Matba'at al-Jawā'ib al-Misriyyah, 1904).

Standard Editions

Dīwān al-Khalīl, 4 vols. (Cairo: Dār al-Hilāl, 1948-1949);

——, 4 vols. (Beirut: Dār al-Kitāb al-'Arabī, 1967).

Editions and Collections

Khalīl Mutrān: qasā'id, edited with an intro-duction by Ahmad 'Abd al-Mu'tī Hijāzī (Beirut: Dār al-Ādāb, 1979);

Translations by the Author

Victor Duruy, *L'histoire universelle*, Arabic title: *Mulakhkhas al-tārīkh: mir'āt al-ayyām fī 'l-'āmm*, 2 vols. (I: Cairo: al-Bayān, 1897; II: Cairo: al-Jawā'ib al-Misriyyah, 1905);

Paul Leroy-Beaulieu, *Précis de science économique*, Arabic title: *al-Majāz fī 'ilm al-iqtisād*, 4 vols. (Cairo: Dār al-Ma'ārif, 1913);

Jules Payot, *L'éducation de la volonté*, Arabic title: *Tarbiyat al-irādah* (Cairo: Dār al-Hilāl, 1918, 1924-1925);

William Shakespeare, *Othello*, Arabic title: *Utayl* (completed and staged 1912; first printed edition: Cairo: Dār al-Ma'ārif, 1950);

——, *Macbeth*, Arabic title: *Makbith* (1915; Cairo: Dār al-Ma'ārif, 1950);

——, *Hamlet*, Arabic title: *Hamlit* (1920; Cairo: Dār al-Ma'ārif, 1950);

——, *The Merchant of Venice*, Arabic title: *Tājir al-Bunduqiyyah* (Cairo: Dār al-Hilāl, 1922);

Pierre Corneille, *Le Cid*, Arabic title: *al-Sayyid* (1930s; Harīsah: Imprimerie Būlusiyyah, 1951);

Pierre Corneille, *Cinna*, Arabic title: *Sīnnā aw*

hilim Awghustus (Cairo: Dār al-Ma'ārif, 1933);

Victor Hugo, *Hernani*, Arabic title: *Hirnānī* (Cairo: Matba'at Wizārat al-Ma'ārif al-Wataniyyah, n.d.).

Translated Works

A. J. Arberry, *Arabic Poetry: A Primer for Students* (Cambridge: Cambridge University Press, 1965), 162-163;

Mounah Khouri, *Poetry and the Making of Modern Egypt* (Leiden: E. J. Brill, 1971), 134-172, *passim*;

—— and Hamid Algar, *An Anthology of Modern Arabic Poetry* (Berkeley: University of California Press, 1974), 40-43;

Salma Khadra al-Jayyusi, *Modern Arabic Poetry* (New York: Columbia University Press, 1987), 82-84.

On April 24, 1913, Khalīl Mutrān—just past the age of forty—was honored in Cairo with a literary festival. The first of its kind in the Arab world in modern times, the gala occasion was designed to pay tribute to Mutrān's achievements in poetry, drama and journalism and to serve as a framework for the presentation to him of a Medal of Honor from the Egyptian government. Thus, at a relatively early age, he found himself already an institutional figure, a cultural icon who was henceforth generally referred to as *shā'ir al-qutrayn* (The Poet of the Two Lands). Unusual in his time, when few authors traveled far from their birthplaces for long, Mutrān had been born and grew up in Lebanon, but after 1892, when he emigrated to Egypt, that land became his new home.

No other poet active in the first two decades of the twentieth century articulated the changing sensibility in the educated classes throughout the Arab world more clearly than Mutrān. He has been considered by most critics to "bridge the gap" between the neo-Classical school of al-**Bārūdī**, **Shawqī**, Hāfiz **Ibrāhīm** and Nāsīf al-**Yāzijī** (who dominated nineteenth-century Arabic poetry), and the Modernizing *(mujaddid)* school, who saw themselves as apostles of European Romanticism and emerged to dominate the Arab literary scene between the end of World

War I and the end of World War II. Mutrān himself was one of the first Arab intellectuals to immerse himself completely in, and assimilate, French literature (he was fluent in the language and spent two years in Paris between 1890 and 1892), and many—though not all—of even his earliest poems bear the marks of a Romantic sensibility shaped by his favorite French authors, Alfred de Musset and Victor Hugo. He is often credited with introducing into Arabic the concepts of organic (structural) unity, an emphasis on the importance of content (over form), a concern with the emotions and the individual (as opposed to man as a social being), and with the deployment of descriptions of nature as reflective of human feelings (the "pathetic fallacy").

Somewhat less convincingly—since there are a number of other possible candidates for the honor—he is labeled as the originator of narrative poetry in Arabic (whose poets had not traditionally practiced this genre). Certainly it can be justly said that he did demonstrate, through his experimental poem "Nayrūn" (Nero)—consisting of 327 monorhymed lines—that the traditional structure dominating Arabic poetry was ill-suited to narrative verse, thus paving the way for more radical experiments in form following World War II. He has also been recognized for his achievements in drama (having translated a number of Shakespeare's plays into Arabic) and journalism (he worked for many years for the premier Egyptian newspaper, *al-Ahrām*, and published two papers of his own in the first decade of the twentieth century).

Though most critics today are agreed about the innovative nature and importance of Mutrān's work, during his lifetime the case was not so clear. Poets of the *Dīwān* School, and other intellectuals associated with that group, went out of their way to emphasize on a number of occasions that Mutrān's poetry had no influence on their own work. Even as late as 1938, when the Egyptian government formed a committee to revise the literature curriculum for its secondary schools, poems by the Egyptians Ahmad Shawqī and Hāfiz Ibrāhīm—contemporaries of Mutrān—were generously represented but Mutrān himself, though resident in Egypt for more than fourty years at this time, was not honored with a single citation. These ambivalent reactions—extravagant adulation vs. indifference—have left traces discernable on the assessment of Mutrān's work even today.

The exact year of Mutrān's birth cannot be determined with precision. Uniform procedures for birth registration did not exist at the time. Mutrān himself may not have known the date with any exactness, as he is credited with several different versions of his birth. Most scholars now believe the year to be 1872, but a substantial minority (including members of the poet's family) have clung to the position that it was 1869. Other dates mentioned include 1871 and 1873.

Mutrān grew up in a large (eight children) family in a spacious house located in the town of Baalbek in north-eastern Lebanon. The family of his father, ʿAbduh, had been in the area for centuries, controlling estates and villages in the Bekaa valley. They traced their lineage back to the earliest rulers in the area, the pre-Islamic dynasty of the Ghassanids, a fact that Mutrān treated with some pride on several occasions. This is consistent with his interest in the theme of temporality, the contrast between past and present, in his poetry. His sense of a personal connection to a pre-Islamic royal house was probably initially more important to Mutrān than the awareness of history fostered by living in a town built on the ruins of important religious shrines going back to the Phoenician period. In Mutrān's childhood, Baalbek was scarcely more than a village and its magnificent Roman-era temples—which today form the spectacular backdrop to a prestigious annual cultural festival sponsored by the Lebanese government—were overgrown and buried. Restoration work on the site would not begin until 1898, long after Mutrān had left. Later in life, however, he found this connection to the ancient heritage of the Mediterranean region more inspiring.

Mutrān's mother Malakah hailed from an equally prominent family, the Sabbāghs, who had been established in the town of Haifa for generations. By the standards of her day, she was a cultivated woman who was known to have composed poetry and she encouraged her son in his ambitions. It is likely that his fond memories of her accomplishments influenced his enthusiastic support for the Egyptian feminist movement in the early years of the twentieth century.

His father was more a practical businessman than a creative dreamer like his wife, but he, too, was fond of poetry, and once presented his son with the *dīwān* (collected works) of the great thirteenth-century mystical poet from Egypt, Ibn al-Fārid (d. 1235). This canonical Muslim poet from the immediately preceding literary epoch became the first inspiration for Mutrān. He tells us that he immediately composed a poem imitating the famous religious poem by Ibn al-Fārid, the *Rā'iyyah* (Poem Rhyming on "R"), adapted as a poem of praise to his father. His father's reaction, however, was not what he expected. He wrote him a letter telling him to cease and desist from this foolish ambition "because we have never met a poet with a shirt on his back!" The result was that his son abandoned further attempts at poetry for a number of years during his adolescence.

By the time Mutrān reached his early teens, he had exhausted the educational opportunities in Baalbek. His father sent him for preparatory studies in Zahlah (Zahle), the regional capital of the Bekaa valley, a town famed for its natural beauty, its fine cuisine, and its lively intellectual atmosphere. We have few details about Mutrān's school activities there, but he retained a fondness for it throughout his entire life, mentioning in a much later poem that it was his "spiritual birthplace."

In the mid-1880s, Mutrān left Zahlah for Beirut, where he enrolled in the Catholic Patriarchal College. From this point, we know a great deal more about his education. The College had been founded in 1866, to focus on providing modern training to the local elite. The classes centered on developing the student's skills in both French and Arabic.

Particularly noteworthy was the Arabic program, which was staffed by Ibrāhīm and Khalīl al-Yāzijī, the rigorously trained sons of Nāsīf al-**Yāzijī** (d. 1871), who had been an instrumental figure in establishing a neo-Classical Arabic revival in Lebanon. Mutrān soon became their star pupil, and in 1889, when Khalīl al-Yāzijī succumbed to tuberculosis, Mutrān replaced him as teacher in some of the Arabic classes. Ibrāhīm, besides being a classically trained scholar of the Arabic language, was also an advocate of political reform and the modernization of Arabic culture and society. Mutrān undoubtedly picked up some of this revolutionary enthusiasm from his revered teacher.

Mutrān also seems to have developed a certain literacy in French by the time he arrived in Beirut, so he had probably begun to study the language in Zahlah, or even before. But his anonymous French teacher at the Patriarchal College—perhaps inadvertently—steered him away from too great an interest in developing true written facility in his second language. He called the young student into his office shortly after the latter's arrival to discuss the poor mark he had received for his first French composition. He told him that his style was too flowery, too turgid, and that he must work toward greater simplicity. But he also went on to say that Mutrān would have to make a choice between honing his Arabic or his French, and that the work he did on one would inevitably be to the detriment of the other. Upon hearing this, Mutrān tells us, he decided that, from then on, Arabic would be his focus. This decision is reflected in his later writings, such as the preface to his *dīwān*, where he vigorously defends his mastery of the traditional idiom of Arabic poetry and downplays the influence of foreign models. To do otherwise would be, based on what he had been taught, to denigrate his Arabic language skills.

In his last year at the Patriarchal College, as Mutrān would later describe the situation to friends, he was both a teacher and a student. He was asked by the administration to teach classes in both Arabic and French, but he had also begun to take lessons in English and Turkish. Two years before this, he had also returned to writing poetry and had had one of his compositions published in a local magazine, *Lisān al-Hāl* (The Spokesman), edited by his friend Khalīl Sarkīs. This poem, titled "1806-1870," was preserved—with extensive revisions—as the first poem in the first edition of Mutrān's *dīwān*, published in 1908 (the *dīwān* is arranged roughly in chronological order). It has been recognized by critics as somewhat above the norm for juvenalia, and may owe something in its finely detailed scenes of war and battle to the poetry of Mahmūd Sāmī al-Bārūdī, the pioneering nineteenth-century Egyptian poet, whose work was being disseminated to an Arab audience outside Egypt around this time. Many years later, Mutrān would become a close friend and disciple of al-Bārūdī, the driving force behind organizing the ceremonies commemorating the older poet's death in 1904.

What is most striking about "1806-1870," however, is not its style but its subject matter. It deals, not with events of local interest in the Arab world, but the fortunes of the French and German nations between the battle of Jena in 1806, when Napoleon I crushed the Prussian armies and occupied Berlin as a conqueror, and 1870 when the newly united Germans defeated Napoleon III and occupied Paris. Despite Mutrān's Francophone educational background, Napoleon is depicted in the poem as something of a tyrant and the sufferings of the German people under occupation are treated with considerable sympathy. It is easy to read Mutrān's picture of Napoleon here as an indirect expression of the youthful poet's rebellion against the rule of the Ottoman sultan, ʿAbd al-Hamīd, whose administration of the non-Turkish Ottoman provinces, including Syria and Lebanon, had become increasingly repressive in the years following his accession in 1876. Mutrān's uncompromising attitude would shortly land him in political trouble and end in his abrupt departure for Paris and eventually Egypt, where he would make his home until his death in 1949.

This rebellious attitude soon led to Mutrān's flight from Beirut. There are two versions of these events. The more immediately credible is based on a first-person account by Mutrān, in which he writes that he had become involved, during his first year of teaching at the Patriarchal College, in anti-Ottoman activities and had composed a poem intended to encourage his fellow students to oppose the repressive policies of the local Turkish governor. The governor heard of the poem, which had not been published and was circulating orally among the young men of the town. He visited Mutrān at the College when he was teaching and threatened to send him to prison in Acre if he persisted in his subversive activities. Since Mutrān feared not only for himself but for possible retribution against his family, he left Lebanon secretly in 1890 on a steamship bound for Paris by way of the Egyptian port of Alexandria, determined to settle in France.

The second version of events has Mutrān returning to his rooms in Beirut one summer evening to find his bed riddled with bullets, ostensibly fired by agents of ʿAbd al-Hamīd in an attempt to assassinate him. Though this story has all the hallmarks of youthful melodrama and exaggeration, it was independently confirmed by members of Mutrān's family to later biographers. Nor are the two accounts necessarily mutually exclusive.

Whatever the truth may be, by August 1890, Mutrān found himself in Alexandria, where he briefly met with an old acquaintance from Beirut, Salīm Taqlā. Formerly Mutrān's teacher at the Patriarchal College, and a friend of his father, Taqlā was now—with his brother Bishārah— editor of the newspaper al-Ahrām which had made a name for itself reporting on the British occupation of Egypt in the wake of the ʿUrābī Revolution in 1882. Squiring Mutrān around town during the ship's three-day layover before its departure for Paris, Salīm introduced his former pupil to various distinguished individuals summering in Alexandria at the time, including the Egyptian ruler, the ageing Khedive Tawfīq, who would soon be replaced by his son ʿAbbās II Hilmī, later the sponsor of the ceremony honoring Mutrān for his achievements in 1913.

Mutrān spent almost exactly two years in Paris, between the summers of 1890 and 1892. While in France, he does not seem to have pursued formal studies or preparations for a career, but immersed himself in anti-Ottoman political activities together with other Turkish and Arab political exiles. He joined the Young Turks organization there under the leadership of Ahmad Ridā. He also briefly considered emigrating to Chile, as some of his friends and relatives had done because of Chile's liberal immigration policies and the tax remissions it offered to new emigrants, so he began to study Spanish. Then the French government, at the behest of the Ottoman embassy, abruptly declared him *persona non grata* on account of his clandestine political activities and Mutrān suddenly found himself on the steamship bound back to Alexandria. When he arrived, he found that his friend Salīm Taqlā had just died a few days before, but Salīm's brother Bishārah offered the young man a position on the newspaper as his Cairo correspondent. Thus began a period of approximately seven years when Mutrān worked for al-Ahrām, learning the newspaper business from the ground up, while also continuing to write poems and hone his poetic skills.

In 1899, Bishārah Taqlā decided to move the head editorial offices of al-Ahrām to Cairo. Mutrān, after a brief period working as an editor for the paper under his superior's closer supervision, decided to make a change. He left for a lengthy visit to Lebanon, which he had not seen for ten years, and it was probably at this time that he composed his descriptive poem "Qalʿat Baʿlabakk" (The Citadel at Baalbek), which fuses the element from the Arabic literary tradition that uses the poet's meditation upon a past love affair (called in Arabic the *nasīb*)— occasioned by his happening upon the abandoned camp site where it took place—with the nineteenth-century French Romantic fascination with abandoned ruins as a site for poetic inspiration.

The poem begins within the conventions of the Arabic tradition, with a salutation to the ruins at Baalbek, calling upon them to help the poet remember his childhood. It then moves on to describe the speaker's youthful attraction to a young woman named Hind—the name most frequently used for the poet's beloved in the tradition of the *nasīb*—which blossomed into love as they wandered and played together among the ruins of pagan Phoenician and Roman temples in Baalbek. This idyll was abruptly terminated when he decided he must leave to seek his fortune. Years later, in composing the poem, he is overwhelmed by a sense of loss reinforced by his return to the site of the temples, visible reminders of time's ravages and destruction. He uses here imagery reminiscent of French Romantic poets meditating on the lessons to be learned from the contemplation of ruined landscapes. He concludes by finding solace and new strength by countering his melancholy with the vibrancy and vitality of his memories of Hind, the real girl he still loves.

Upon his return to Cairo in late 1900, Mutrān began a new phase in his professional life, as editor and publisher of *al-Majallah al-Misriyyah* (The Egyptian Review), a general interest periodical that initially appeared twice a month. In this he was following in the footsteps of a number of Lebanese emigrants to Egypt who had established several successful newspapers and periodical journals in the last two decades of the nineteenth century. These included not only the Taqlā brothers, with *al-Ahrām*, but Ya'qūb Sarrūf and Fāris Nimr, who had brought their journal *al-Muqtataf* (The Selection)—emphasizing mostly scientific articles and descriptions of modern inventions along the lines of the American magazine *Popular Science*—to Egypt from Beirut in 1885. Slightly later, Jūrjī Zaydān founded the monthly magazine *al-Hilāl* (The Crescent) that catered to a wider audience interested in history and events, ideas and modern thought, along with accounts of the latest technical innovations. After the turn of the century, Mutrān's work would mainly be found on the pages of these Lebanese Egyptian publications, especially *al-Hilāl*.

Al-Majallah proved successful, and in 1903 Mutrān replaced it with the daily newspaper *al-Jawā'ib al-Misriyyah*. But he also continued to write poems. It was during this extremely busy period of his life that he wrote what is probably his most famous single lyric poem, "al-Masā'" (The Evening). In 1902, as a consequence of the emotional turmoil he suffered in the wake of an unhappy love affair, he became ill and was advised to recuperate at the seaside in Alexandria. In the poem, he depicts himself as sitting by the ocean's edge at sunset on the beach at a popular resort called Mex, not far from the city, reflecting on how his brush with illness did not cure him of his feelings, as he had expected, but only intensified them. After a thorough examination, and mapping, of his inner feelings, done with a directness unusual, if not unprecedented, in Arabic poetry, Mutrān turns to a detailed description of the sunset tableau, the blood red sun shrouded in dark, ragged clouds,

concluding that it is the perfect reflection of his inner turmoil. The tears dropping from his eyes, as he looks at them dancing on the rock where he sits, blend seamlessly with the breaking wave crests glittering on the horizon, and pronounce a wordless elegy on both his life and his love, announcing that both are at an end in the final lines of the poem. Unlike "Qal'at Ba'labakk," which attempts to fuse elements of both the Arabic and the Western Romantic traditions, this poem is thoroughly modern and owes little, if anything, to Arabic literary conventions. In this it prefigures tendencies that would become pronounced in Arabic poetry of the 1920s and 1930s, leading to the wholesale revaluation of the poet's relationship to the traditions of Arabic literature that would seize center stage in Arabic critical writings following World War II. But the revolutionary aesthetics of "al-Masā'" did not have an immediate impact on other Arab poets. Its effects would only begin to be felt after the poem's publication as part of the first volume of Mutrān's *dīwān* in 1908, and similar works would not be produced until after World War I, not becoming common until the heyday of the Apollo Group in Egypt in the 1930s.

In the short run, Mutrān grew increasingly disenchanted with the more commercial aspects of publishing. He had become more and more often the recipient of commissions for translations of French works from various customers, including the Egyptian Education Ministry, which supplemented his income. More importantly, he became involved in commercial investment and speculation, earning, at least at first, handsome returns on his transactions in the local stock market. This financial success allowed him to follow his inclinations when he became embroiled in a nasty confrontation with a supposed friend over a subscription fee, and abruptly terminated the publication of *al-Jawā-'ib* at the end of 1904.

However, he did not cease his literary activities. In 1908 the first volume of his poems, entitled *Dīwān al-Khalīl* (The Faithful Friend's Collection)—a play on the literal meaning of his first name—appeared in Cairo. It was generally favorably received, and the long review in *al-Hilāl* by his friend and fellow Lebanese exile,

Antūn Jumayyil (also rendered as "Jamīl"), gave the first lengthy and informed account of his aesthetic agenda. Jumayyil, basing himself on Mutrān's own introduction, emphasizes the role of personal experience, imagination, and emotion (all tempered by the mental activities of re-collection and analysis) in the production of the poet's distinctive style. This formulation, of course, recalls Wordsworth's definition of poetry as "the spontaneous overflow of powerful feel-ings recollected in tranquility," but Jumayyil prefers to trace it back to ancient Greece. Those philosophers, he says, depicted the poet as being carried away in a chariot drawn by two runaway horses, who could only be calmed and brought under control by the reins being placed in the "hands of reason, or the logical intelligence *('aql)*." This discussion of the significance of Mutrān's work represents a notable departure from custom by being one of the first, if not the very first, times that Arabic poetry is analyzed solely through the lens of Western critical theory, without reference to the Arabic tradition.

Dīwān al-Khalīl, which would be reissued with three additional volumes following the poet's death in 1949, contains over 130 poems of varying lengths almost equally divided be-tween more personal lyrics along the lines of "Qal'at Ba'labakk" and "al-Masā'," on the one hand, juxtaposed with poems composed for public occasions and commemorations. The personal lyrics reveal that Mutrān had begun to demon-strate a substantially Romantic sensibility in his work from the 1890s—very different from the style of his friends and colleagues Shawqī and Hāfiz Ibrāhīm. This distinctive "Mutrānian" style would not change substantially in the poems following 1908.

His occasional poems, however, do continue to evolve and probably reached their apogee with the publication of the poem "al-Muqāta'ah" (The Boycott), published in the revived *al-Ja-wā'ib* in 1909. At that time, the British Consul-General in Egypt, Sir Eldon Gorst, successor to Lord Cromer, had insisted on the re-imposition of the Egyptian Press Law of 1881, which pro-vided for strict censorship of newspapers and journals in Arabic as well as foreign languages. Mutrān strenuously, and unsuccessfully, opposed

this action, and "al-Muqāta'ah" was an important part of this campaign. It relies, like most success-ful occasional poems in the Arabic tradition, more on rhetorical figures of parallelism and antithesis than on the complex pictorial imagery so characteristic of Mutrān's early lyric poems like "al-Masā'."

The poem itself is brief, only six lines long. In the first line, the poet, defiant, orders his persecutors to go ahead and kill his fellow lovers of liberty "free man by free man" because—as he goes on to declare in the second line—"good will remain good, … and evil will remain evil." This is the only simple declarative statement in the poem and contains the essence of the poet's belief: there is a set of unalterable truths that cannot be changed to suit the requirements of circumstance. Lines 3-6 revert to the im-perative mode of the first line, the poet each time telling his tormentors, in perfectly balanced and measured periods, that no matter what they do—destroy their pens, cut off their hands or their tongues—he and his allies will find another means to express themselves. But when the poet reaches the point where he tells the authorities to go ahead and choke him to death if they wish, he suddenly changes his tack, acknowledging that they can indeed prevent him from speaking out. But, he says, destroying his body is the limit of what they can accomplish, and his spirit will remain free. In fact, by killing him, they will have proved his point—that true goodness can-not be corrupted by evil, and on that note he ends the point with an ironical expression of "thanks" for their support of his contention.

This uncharacteristically short piece has prob-ably been the most memorable and frequently anthologized of Mutrān's political poems. But as early as 1901, with "Maqtal Buzurjmihr" (The Murder of Bozorgmihr), Mutrān had begun to compose narrative poems with a strong political element. Though the tale ostensibly takes place in the reign of the Sassanian Persian Shah Khosrow, it is a thinly disguised narrative of contemporary despotism in the Ottoman Empire and the Arab provinces of that empire. In direct contrast to earlier nineteenth-century Arab poets, Mutrān here adopts a decidedly cynical attitude toward change by his dismissal of "the people" as a naturally revolutionary force.

Mutrān's distrust of popular revolutionary fervor as a constructive force—as opposed to the power of an individual—will be a theme that resurfaces in the mid-1920s, after the sobering experiences of World War I and the failures of the 1919 Egyptian revolution (as well as its successes). Just prior to the war, however, a purely personal crisis intervened to sideline his literary concerns, at least temporarily. In 1912, he lost everything he owned in the stock market. This financial blow came on the heels of the failure of a new literary venture he had embarked upon early in the year, the translation of a number of William Shakespeare's dramas for performance at the Cairo Opera House under the auspices of his friend, veteran actor and impresario, George Abyad. The first two, *Othello* and *The Merchant of Venice*, had been such commercial failures that publication of the texts was delayed for a number of years.

In shock from this double blow, Mutrān shut himself up away from all human contact in tiny rooms in the Cairo suburb of Heliopolis and seriously contemplated suicide, according to those who knew him best. When his friends finally persuaded him to return to Cairo and normal life, he published two poems written during these dark days, "al-Asad al-bākī" (The Weeping Lion) and "al-'Uzlah fī 'l-sahrā'" (Solitude in the Desert). Though both poems clearly reflect a time of travail for their author, the references in each to the events that gave rise to them are oblique and masked with learned allusions to the literary tradition and archaic vocabulary. There are brilliant individual lines, as when the poet starkly declares at the end of the first work: "I am the weeping lion, the mountain sorrowing, a tomb walking bloody over a field of tombs." But both, like many of his other personal poems during this period, lack the unified design that had made poems like "al-Masā'" and "Qal'at Ba'labakk" such striking innovations, and do not reflect bold exploration of new poetic territory.

When Mutrān's financial straits became generally known, the Khedive 'Abbās II Hilmī intervened and saw to it that the poet was offered the job of assistant secretary of the Khedival Agricultural Society, which gave him a small regular income until his death. He also continued to receive regular translation commissions, along with small sums for poems and short opinion pieces published in newspapers and literary journals like *al-Hilāl*. The literary gala held in 1913 can be seen in this context as just one more example of how his many friends rallied around him to show him he was not forgotten during this difficult time.

Following World War I, the Revolution of 1919 disrupted the routine of cultural life, of which Mutrān had been an integral part, and a sense of national normality only returned to the country following the achievement of limited independence in 1922. Mutrān did not compose any notable poems directly tied to the events of the 1919 Revolution, but upon its successful outcome, he celebrated the dawn of Egypt's new age in poems like his 1923 memorial, "Madrasat Mustafā Kāmil" (The School of Mustafā Kāmil), dedicated to his old friend the revolutionary thinker, who had died prematurely in 1908, or his elegy for Sa'd Zaghlūl, the leader of the opposition to the British, who died in 1927.

Elegies could be said to dominate his poetry in the postwar period, partly due to his public prominence, but also partly due to the fact that he was aging and the friends and mentors of his youth were passing from the scene. His old teacher Ibrāhīm al-Yāzijī died, for example, in 1924, and Mutrān composed one of his best remembered tributes for him. It has also been noted that Mutrān's elegiac style alters during this decade. He gradually abandons the traditional form of Arabic elegy for a new approach. No longer content to simply enumerate a list of virtues to be attributed to the departed, he begins to retell the subject's entire life history in chronological order, thus adding depth to the portrait of the deceased, as well as imparting to his subject a more human sense of growth, development and change.

Such a concern on Mutrān's part was consistent with his earlier interest in narrative poetry, displayed in the first volume of his *dīwān* in such poems as "Maqtal Buzurjmihr," "Fatāt al-Jabal al-Aswad" (The Maid of Montenegro), "al-Janīn al-shahīd" (The Martyrdom of an Unborn Babe), or even his very first composition, "1806-1870." It is thus not surprising to see it re-surface in his elegies or, even more importantly, in what many consider the last great effort of his poetic career, the epic-length narrative poem "Nayrūn" (Nero), that he composed in 1924.

The immediate impetus for "Nayrūn" was an invitation to visit some of the haunts of his youth in Syria, Lebanon and Palestine. In larger literary terms, the poem was a response to controversy over the role of epic poetry in Arabic literature. Epic has always been the poetic genre most revered by Western literatures. Historically, Arab poets had never cultivated this genre and this had been the source of criticisms leveled against the "genius" and value of Arabic poetry by Western orientalists in the nineteenth century, most notably by the influential French academic Ernst Renan, in his monumental early work on Semitic philology, *Histoire générale des langues sémitiques*, in which he had cited lack of the epic genre as evidence for a corresponding lack of creative imagination among speakers of Semitic languages. Arab authors like Mutrān became increasingly aware of this indictment in the late nineteenth and the early twentieth centuries and they, of course, responded by vigorously trying to counter this contention. The responses took a variety of forms. Mutrān's Lebanese countryman Sulaymān al-Bustānī made an important contribution to the debate by translating Homer's *Iliad* into Arabic for the first time in 1904, but even before that neo-Classical poets like the Egyptians Maḥmūd Sāmī al-Bārūdī and Aḥmad Shawqī had attempted to produce poems that, within a native Arabic context, incorporated narrative, as well as the sort of grandiloquent language and conventions associated with Western examples of epic.

Mutrān took a different approach. His aim in composing "Nayrūn"—which he makes abundantly clear in a prose introduction affixed to the text of the poem in the third volume of his *dīwān*—is not to show that an Arab poet can compose a respectable epic poem, but that s/he cannot, for reasons that have nothing to do with the innate resources of Renan's "Semitic mind." His purpose was to show that the peculiarities of Arabic poetic structure—primarily the con-

vention of ending every line with the same rhyme, known as *waḥdat al-qāfiyah*, or monorhyme—prevented the poet from naturally presenting an extended treatment of a single subject, such as epic requires. This obstacle could only be overcome by a radical overhaul of the poetic structure.

According to eyewitness accounts, his recitation of "Nayrūn" in the newly completed main auditorium of the American University of Beirut abundantly proved his point. He chose to rhyme the poem in the syllable *rā'* and, as he neared the end of the 327-line composition, the audience grew increasingly distracted from the content of the work as they tried to guess what archaic word or unfamiliar technical term the author would find to end his line, since it was considered a stylistic defect to repeat rhyme words. This virtuoso performance demonstrated, more than any learned argument, the validity of Mutrān's position, and the next generation of writers would respond by enacting the kind of radical reforms Mutrān advocated. "Nayrūn," however, has generally been seen as more than simply a *tour de force*, and is appreciated for its own indictment of the social costs of tyranny as exemplified in the character and story of the feckless Roman emperor that is its subject.

Triumphant after his tour of the Levant in the summer of 1924, Mutrān returned to the theater, then beginning a period of relative vitality in postwar Cairo. Drama, like other literary fields in this period, was beginning to feel the impact of commercialization, and was uncomfortably caught between the conflicting demands of the cultural elite and the popular audience. On the one hand, earnest and idealistic intellectuals like Mutrān, his friend, the poet Aḥmad **Shawqī**, and the young playwright Tawfīq al-**Ḥakīm**, allied with producers like the French-trained actor and manager George Abyad, sought to create a theater that would both produce works in Arabic that reflected culturally authentic attitudes and values, and make dramatic masterpieces of world literature available in translations of the highest artistic standard. In this way, to their minds, theater could be mobilized in the service of revitalizing Arabic culture and society, and making it the equal of other major world literatures.

Opposed to this were more practical-minded entrepreneurs like Muhammad Taymūr, Ibrāhīm Ramzī and Antūn Yazbak, allied with critics like Muhammad ʿAbd al-Quddūs, who wanted to produce plays that would inspire, but would also accurately reflect the experience of audiences, thus filling the theaters and turning a profit.

The implementation of these differing aims was most noticeably played out in the arena of language. Mutrān and his allies advocated using a modified version of standard Arabic—used universally in writing, but only in limited, formal, spoken contexts. Their counterparts among the entrepreneurs, in contrast, chose to use Egyptian colloquial in their works, the language really employed in everyday conversation.

The debate over whether—and when—to use standard Arabic or colloquial is one that continues to this day, especially in drama, film, and television productions. In the mid-1920s, however, the Egyptian government intervened on behalf of the intellectuals, and in 1925 the Ministry of Public Works created the Advisory Dramatic Council, to which Mutrān (and Shawqī) were appointed. The Council was given funds to promote competitions for writers of new plays and to stage productions.

Even after the failure in 1912 of George Abyad's production of *Othello*, Mutrān's first effort in the field of drama, he had continued at irregular intervals to translate plays by Shakespeare into elegant standard Arabic. *Macbeth* was completed in 1915, *Hamlet* in 1920, and *The Merchant of Venice* appeared in 1923. Mutrān appears not have worked from the English originals, however—at least not exclusively—but to have relied heavily on French translations of the plays. This charge was made originally as early as 1923 in a widely disseminated review of the translations by the Arab American author Mīkhāʾīl **Nuʿaymah**, and has been verified by numerous other literary critics over the years. Perhaps this questioning of his methods was a factor in Mutrān's decisive turn toward the translation of French dramatists after his appointment to the Advisory Dramatic Council.

Mutrān had attended a performance of Victor Hugo's drama *Hernani* while living in Paris in 1891. He had also been initially attracted to Shakespeare's works because the English playwright was Hugo's favorite dramatist. It is no surprise, then, to find Mutrān turning to a translation of *Hernani* once his fascination with Shakespeare had waned. He also translated Corneille's dramas *Cinna* and *Le Cid* in the late 1920s and early 1930s. There may have been other translations as well—at least they are mentioned in contemporary articles about Mutrān's activities—but the manuscripts have never surfaced.

In 1935 Mutrān's sustained efforts to invigorate Arabic drama through translation were rewarded when he was appointed Director of the new Egyptian National Theater Troupe. The formation of this company was part of an effort by the government to resuscitate the theater after it had fallen into a prolonged slump during the economic depression of the 1930s. Given official financial support, Mutrān was faithful to his ideal of making drama a vehicle for the improvement of cultural standards. He made a dramatic gesture by opening his first season with *Ahl al-kahf* (The People of the Cave), an original work by the outspoken young intellectual Tawfīq al-**Hakīm**.

Mutrān followed *Ahl al-kahf* with several salutary translations of Western works by prestigious authors, including his own translation of *Merchant of Venice* (Tājir al-Bunduqiyyah) and Tāhā **Husayn**'s translation of Sophocles' *Antigone*. Even though these were not commercially successful productions, they raised the standards of the Egyptian stage, and Mutrān continued to occupy the position of Director for the Troupe until 1942, when age and changing public tastes dictated his resignation.

Nor did he abandon poetry in this last two decades of his life. Probably his most public act was his acceptance of the presidency of the Apollo Group. This group of young artistic rebels against restrictive social customs, who took as their heroes the European Romantic poets (especially those like Shelley and Byron, influenced by Hellenism), began publishing an iconoclastic new journal in 1932 and formed themselves into a literary society at the end of the year. They first chose Ahmad Shawqī, who had recently been publicly proclaimed "Prince of Poets," as their president but Shawqī passed away just after the first meeting in October. To replace him, the Apollo members chose Mutrān, whose Romantic leanings were in fact more sympathetic to their own aesthetic views. Mutrān's function in the Society was mainly as a figurehead, but the attention it generated kept him and his poetry in the public eye in the early 1930s. Apollo was shortlived and soon disbanded, in 1933, but its members carried through to its logical end the revolution begun by Mutrān so many decades before.

After the beginning of World War II and his resignation from the National Theater Troupe, Mutrān began to withdraw more and more from public life. In 1947, he rallied when the Government again organized a literary gala in his honor, and he was awarded the rank of Beǧ. But he soon fell ill with asthma and severe gout and passed away peacefully in his sleep on June 30, 1949.

REFERENCES

M. M. Badawi, *A Critical Introduction to Modern Arabic Poetry* (Cambridge: Cambridge University Press, 1975), 68-84;

Jan Brugman, *An Introduction to the History of Modern Arabic Literature in Egypt* (Leiden: E. J. Brill, 1984), 56-62;

Mounah Khouri, *Poetry and the Making of Modern Egypt* (Leiden: E. J. Brill, 1971), 134-172;

Salma Khadra Jayyusi, *Trends and Movements in Modern Arabic Poetry*, 2 vols. (Leiden: E. J. Brill, 1977), I, 54-64;

Mihrajān Khalīl Mutrān, edited with an introduction by Yūsuf al-Sibā'ī (Cairo: Dār al-Qalam, 1960);

Mīshāl Juhā, *Khalīl Mutrān: bākūrat al-tajdīd fī 'l-shi'r al-'arabī al-hadīth* (Beirut: Dār al-Musīrah, 1981);

Antun Jumayyil (Jamīl), "Dīwān al-Khalīl: bahth shi'rī", *al-Hilāl* 16.9 (June 1908): 531-39;

Mikhā'īl Nu'aymah (Naimy), "Shāksbīr Khalīl Mutrān", in: M. N., *al-Ghirbāl* (Cairo: al-Matba'ah al-'Asriyyah, 1923), 195-205;

R. C. Ostle, "Khalīl Mutrān: The Precursor of Lyrical Poetry in Modern Arabic", *Journal of Arabic Literature* 2 (1971): 116-126;

Nicolas Saadé, *Halīl Mutrān* (Beirut: Librairie Orientale, 1985);

Tahir Ahmad al-Tanāhī, *Hayāt Mutrān* (Cairo: al-Dār al-Misriyyah li'l-Ta'līf wa'l-Tarjamah, 1965).

Muhammad al-Muwaylihī

(1858 – 1930)

ROGER ALLEN
University of Pennsylvania

WORKS

Individual Works

Hadīth 'Īsā ibn Hishām ("'Īsā ibn Hishām's Tale", Cairo, 1907, 1912, 1923, 1927, 1935, 1943, 1947, 1959, 1964, 2002);
'Ilāj al-nafs ("Cure of the Soul", Cairo, 1932, 1962).

Complete Works

al-Mu'allafāt al-kāmilah ("Complete Works"), ed. Roger Allen, 2 vols. (Cairo: al-Majlis al-A'lā li'l-Thaqāfah, 2002).

Works in Translation

A Period of Time (Reading: Ithaca Press, 1992); translation of *Hadīth 'Īsā ibn Hishām*, tr. by Roger Allen.

Muhammad al-Muwaylihī (1858-1930) is best known for a single work of prose narrative, *Hadīth 'Īsā ibn Hishām*, long since recognized as one of the foundational works in the emergence of a tradition of modern Egyptian (and therefrom, Arabic) narrative. However, before turning to a consideration of the author's life and the work itself, I would like to contextualize the process of its evaluation by suggesting that in recent years the very criteria within which the work of al-Muwaylihī and other early pioneers of modern Arabic literature have been judged are themselves in need of re-examination. I will identify two factors in particular as illustrations of this trend.

Firstly, in the period following the June War of 1967—an unmitigated disaster for the Arab states—there was a profound re-examination of the nature of the relationship between present and past and of the role of traditional Arab values (as seen in the cultural heritage of the region). In fictional terms this led, among other things, to a resort to the texts of the past as readily available means of illustrating the dilemmas of the present, a trend that in Western narratology has been termed "trans-textuality." In recent decades many writers have come to exploit the potential of pre-modern narrative genres, including historical ones, as a mode of expressing modernity in fictional writing. Secondly (and somewhat linked to the first), changing attitudes towards the past and a developing realization of the sheer variety that characterizes the nations of today's Arab world have led to an increased focus on elements of difference, of "particularity" (*khusūsiyyah* in Arabic). As a consequence, each region or nation within the larger Arab world has sought to "particularize" its pre-modern history and to investigate the intrinsic qualities that illustrate the relationship between their notion of modernity and what came before it. It is within this intellectual climate that al-Muwaylihī's great narrative needs to be viewed and re-assessed.

Muhammad al-Muwaylihī was born in 1858, a mere fourteen years after the birth of his father, Ibrāhīm al-Muwaylihī, in 1844. The significance of these dates is that the lives of father and son were linked by a relationship that was more characteristic of a single generation rather than two. The al-Muwaylihīs had been an illustrious family of silk merchants that had come to Egypt in the early nineteenth century from the Arabian Peninsula. Muhammad's early life was inextricably linked to that of his father, who seems to have relished the opportunities for involvement in political activities, not to say intrigue. Ibrāhīm, the father, for example, chose to ally himself with the Khedive Ismā'īl at the time when an Anglo-French financial oversight committee decided to send him into exile in 1887. Muhammad al-Muwaylihī was left on his own in Cairo and found himself arrested for distributing one of his father's subversive pamphlets during the revolt triggered by the Egyptian army officer, Ahmad 'Urabī, in 1882, an event which resulted in British occupation of Egypt (and that was not finally terminated until 1955). Muhammad himself was now expelled from Egypt and joined his father and the Khedive in Italy.

Father and son were now heavily involved in the print-politics of Egyptians in exile. During stays in Paris and London they helped collea-gues such as Jamāl al-Dīn al-Afghānī (d. 1897) and Muhammad 'Abduh (d. 1905), both re-nowned for their role in advocating reforms in Islam, in editing Arabic newspapers. Having expressed support in one such article for the Ottoman sultan, 'Abd al-Hamīd, Ibrāhīm al-Muwaylihī found himself invited to Istanbul, but, being wary of the Sultan's intentions (not to mention, the efficacy of the latter's spy-system), he sent his son, Muhammad, to conduct a check on the situation in the Ottoman capital. As a result, both al-Muwaylihīs found themselves residing in Istanbul in 1885. Muhammad al-Muwaylihī returned to Egypt in 1887, and his father followed in 1895. The latter immediately published his impressions of the Ottoman capital and its atmosphere of intrigue, initially in the Cairene newspaper, *al-Muqattam*, but soon afterwards as a book entitled *Mā hunālik* (Over Yonder, 1896). No one, it appears, was deceived by the anonymous author ("A Worthy Egyptian"), and Ibrāhīm al-Muwaylihī was ordered to send all copies of the book to Istanbul for burning.

Since I myself have a copy of the work (which I have now published in both Arabic and English translation), some copies clearly escaped notice.

On the 14th April 1898, both al-Muwaylihīs began publication of their own newspaper, *Misbāh al-Sharq*, which soon established a high reputation for its political insight and style. It was in this newspaper that Muhammad's most famous work initially appeared in the form of a series of articles under the heading, *Fatrah min al-zaman* (A Period of Time) They were an immediate success; at the instigation of colleagues and friends, Muhammad al-Muwaylihī substantially revised them in preparation for publication as a book. In the process the sequence of episodes was often altered, and, when the material was considered too ephemeral or controversial, it was omitted. The book was published as *Hadīth 'Īsā ibn Hishām* in 1907.

The first of this long series of episodes, "Fatrah min al-zaman," finds the narrator, a young Egyptian named 'Īsā ibn Hishām, wandering around the cemetery of the Imām al-Shāfi'ī in Cairo and contemplating on matters of fate and death. Behind these details lie two important features of al-Muwaylihī's text. Firstly, he had already been making use of a narrator of this name in previous articles published in the newspaper, in which he had commented on current Egyptian politics. The readership was thus "prepared" for further articles which would be similarly topical and critical, but, one suspects, neither they (nor the author himself) were aware of quite how important a work was in its initial phases. Secondly, the eventual title of the completed work, *Hadīth 'Īsā ibn Hishām*, is not present. In fact, it was first used in an announcement in the newspaper, in which readers were informed that Muhammad al-Muwaylihī would be resuming publication of his episodes after a gap. It would appear however that this second title "caught on," since that was and has remained its title ever since its publication in book form in 1907 (although the original title remains as a subtitle).

'Īsā ibn Hishām then is an Egyptian living in Cairo at the end of the 19th century; in other words, an Egypt that has been occupied by the British army and varieties of civil servants and that is struggling to cope with the pressures of local and international politics (involving Ottoman and French interests as well as British) and their multifarious ramifications within everyday life. During 'Īsā's contemplative stroll in the cemetery, a tomb opens and he finds himself facing a Pāshā from a very different period in Egyptian history, the era of Muhammad 'Alī, Egypt's ruler from 1811 till 1837. Indeed, it emerges that Ahmad Pāshā al-Manīkalī was Minister of War during Muhammad 'Alī's reign. Unaware that he has been resurrected into an entirely different era in Egypt's modern life, the Pāshā starts issuing orders and listens incredulously as 'Īsā ibn Hishām explains the realities of *fin de siècle* Cairo to him. A whole series of episodes now follows in which the Pāshā is subjected to the Egyptian system of justice. It is triggered by the fact that he assaults a donkeyman who is unfortunate enough to offer the Pāshā a ride and who encounters the blunt end of the latter's highly developed sense of his own importance. Al-Muwaylihī is now able to paint a wonderfully accurate, yet sarcastic portrait of a legal system, based on French principles (the Code Napoléon) and overseen by a British administration, and the entire tissue of illogicality and venality that accompanies it. Via attorneys, prosecutors, a variety of courts, the Records Office, and the Court of Appeals, the Pāshā is eventually acquitted. The Pāshā has been made ill by the strain of this experience, and consults a variety of doctors, each of whom recommends a different cure, disparages the expertise of his colleagues, and charges a great deal of money. At the central part of the narrative, the two men decide to leave Cairo and seek some relief in contemplating nature and its expression in literary form.

Upon their return to Cairo the two men are seated in one of Cairo's most renowned parks at the time, the Ezbekiyyah Gardens, when they encounter two other Egyptians, a thoroughly Westernized dandy (*khalī'* in Arabic) and a merchant. They themselves have just met a '*umdah*, a village-headman, a figure from the Egyptian countryside and holder of an office that is a by-word for venality and corruption. The remainder of the Egyptian segment of the story of

Hadīth 'Īsā ibn Hishām is taken up with a series of episodes in which 'Īsā and the Pāshā follow this trio as they visit a number of institutions that form part of the newly invigorated night-life of Cairo: a tavern, a restaurant, and a theater, along with other forays to a wedding and the day-trip to the Pyramids. In these episodes, in which the town-country contrast is linked to debates on the relative virtues of tradition and modernity—all within the framework of the rapid importation of Western mores and institutions—al-Muwaylihī's brilliance at portraying the clash of inter-cultural values reaches its height. These episodes involving the 'Umdah have always been the favorites of Egyptian readers and served as models for other explorations of the potential for social criticism in a number of artistic genres. The narrative closes with a short chapter in which 'Īsā reflects on the wisdom of the uncritical importation of Western ideas into Egyptian society and expresses the desire to explore that Western society in more detail.

In 1899 that desire expressed by the narrator of *Hadīth 'Īsā ibn Hishām* became a reality when Muhammad al-Muwaylihī was sent to Paris by his father so that he (or rather, his narrator, 'Īsā ibn Hishām) could comment for readers of *Misbāh al-Sharq* on the Great Exhibition being held in the city that year. The episodes that were sent back contain many of the features of the "Egyptian" set, most particularly the virtuoso use of the literary Arabic language, but, such was al-Muwaylihī's distaste for what he saw at the exhibition—most especially the Egyptian pavilion which displayed a traditional Qur'ān school with the students learning by rote—that the episodes contain little of the sarcastic detail that makes of the earlier episodes a clear precedent for the emergence of a tradition of realistic fiction in Arabic.

The textual history of *Hadīth 'Īsā ibn Hishām* is a complicated one. While what I might term the narrative's "plot sequence" that has just been essayed can be found in any version of the text, there are nevertheless significant variations that have a particular impact on its interpretation and historical significance. In fact, one might suggest that there exist three different versions of the text. The most widely available is, unfortunately, the

least satisfactory in many ways: the fourth edition of 1927 and the several reprintings that have been based on it. In that year, just three years before al-Muwaylihī's death, *Hadīth 'Īsā ibn Hishām* was chosen as a school textbook. The author must have been delighted to be given the opportunity to include in his text the episodes describing his visit to Paris, a project that had remained an aspiration ever since the publication of the first edition in 1907. He must have been less than delighted in acceding to the request that, for the publication of the narrative as a school textbook, he omit three entire chapters, devoted to trenchant analyses of the morals of the young princes of the Royal Family (who spend their time discussing the stock market and horse racing), the shaykhs of the renowned Azhar mosque-university and the habits of Muhammad 'Alī, the founder of the royal dynasty. As a result of these changes to the fourth and subsequent editions, we are faced with two somewhat different works: the first three editions (1907, 1912, and 1923) focus solely on Egypt, while the later editions include a section on a visit to France, thus linking *Hadīth 'Īsā ibn Hishām* to a number of earlier accounts on the same topic. The third version of the text is one that I myself published in Cairo in 2003 as part of a project to make the complete works of al-Muwaylihī available in modern editions. That version reconstitutes the contents and sequence of the original series of newspaper articles, "Fatrah min al-zaman" (1898-1902), upon which *Hadīth 'Īsā ibn Hishām* (the book) is based. The sequencing of episodes is different, the length of each segment is considerably shorter, and several more complete episodes that were never included in the book version of the narrative have been restored to their original placement in the sequence of episodes. In addition, other newspaper articles in which al-Muwaylihī made use of the same narrator, 'Īsā ibn Hishām, are also included as appendices. What emerges from this process of restoration is again a work with different emphases, one that concentrates to a much greater degree than the book version on contemporary events at the turn of the 19th century (the war in the Sudan, for example, and Franco-British rivalries in both Egypt itself and the Sudan).

Since the project of writing literary histories

of modern Arabic fiction, and especially the novel, began in the first half of the 20th century, *Hadīth 'Īsā ibn Hishām* has regularly been invoked as a crucial phase in the process. Critics have often depicted it as a kind of narrative "bridge," one that links past and present. To some commentators it is "modern *maqāmah*" (that being one of the most characteristic narrative genres of the pre-modern era of Arabic literature, tracing its history back to the emergence of a new kind of picaresque episodic narrative genre in the 10th century CE), while to others it marks the initial stages of an Arabic "novel."

The linkage to the *maqāmah* genre in particular is amplified by the fact that 'Īsā ibn Hishām, selected by al-Muwaylihī for his narrator of a 19th century Egyptian narrative, invokes a name that is already well known in Arabic literary history. He is the narrator (and sometimes protagonist) in the earliest examples of this particular kind of picaresque narrative, those of al-Hamadhānī (d. 1008) whose artistry was so admired that his contemporaries and successors dubbed him "Badī' al-Zamān" (the Wonder of the Age). In choosing such a name for his narrator (and later as part of his book's title), al-Muwaylihī is clearly making a conscious attempt to arouse in his readers' minds memories of the Arabic narrative heritage. In the series of newspaper articles, "Fatrah min al-zaman," many of the features of such earlier narratives are very evident. The narrative is extremely episodic; indeed, as comments included in the newspaper early in the publication sequence of the series make clear, the continued composition and publication of the series was entirely dependent on the readers' reaction to them—an interesting echo, one might suggest, of the publication history of some of Dickens's novels. And, while we are making such comparisons, it is also useful to draw attention to the similarly episodic nature of another foundational work of Western fiction, Cervantes's *Don Quixote*, itself the product of developments in the Spanish picaresque genre that counts the Arabic *maqāmah* as one of its antecedents. A second prominent feature of *Hadīth 'Īsā ibn Hishām* that links it to pre-modern Arabic narrative is its delight in all sorts of inter-textual and trans-

textual reference: lines of poetry by renowned Arab poets and a wide variety of pastiches of genres and styles.

Al-Muwaylihī's narrative then certainly looks back into the past, and consciously so. But, as we consider its position within the development of a modern tradition of Arabic narrative and specifically the novel genre, its placement into an appropriate context is rendered more complicated by the one-sided approach that has characterized the majority of studies of cultural developments during the 19th century, most often subsumed under the heading of *al-Nahdah*, implying "revival." Within such a frame of reference, the problem is essentially twofold: firstly, some previous narrative trends and works are conveniently overlooked; secondly, from a 21st century (and certainly post-1967) perspective, the literary history needs to be reconsidered in any case.

The second half of the 19th century witnessed a number of developments in narrative writing. The Lebanese writer Nāsīf al-**Yāzijī** (d. 1871) composed a series of neo-classical *maqāmāt* under the title *Majma' al-bahrayn* (Meeting-Place of the Two Seas) that represented the latest stage in a narrative tradition that had continued uninterrupted from al-Hamadhānī's beginnings in the 10th century. However, another Lebanese author and al-Yāzijī's contemporary, Ahmad Fāris al-**Shidyāq** (d. 1887), adopted a somewhat different approach. Using the elevated prose style of earlier narratives (indeed penning four of the most lexicographically challenging *maqāmāt* ever composed) he turned his attention to some of the issues of his time and the best modes of expressing them. Combining elements of the autobiographical, the female voice, and the exploration of the unfamiliar European environment, he used his famous work *al-Sāq 'alā 'l-sāq fī-mā huwa al-Fāryāq* (a punning title, utilizing parts of his own names—Fār- and -yāq—which translates as either "One Leg Over Another Concerning *Fāryāq*," or else "The Pigeon on the Tree-branch…," 1855) to turn Arabic narrative, albeit couched in traditional stylistic form, in entirely new directions, thus laying some important foundations for the emergence of a socially aware tradition of modern Arabic fiction. Alongside these trends, the same period also sees the emergence of a number of novels, initially those translated from Western literary traditions and later imitations of them. Fénélon's *Télémaque* and Dumas's *Le comte de Monte Cristo* are merely two among many such translated works, to which Arab authors add incipient essays in fiction such as Fransīs Marrāsh's (d. 1873) *Ghābat al-haqq* (Forest of Truth, 1865), Salīm al-Bustānī's (d. 1884) *al-Huyām fī jinān al-Shām* (Passion in Syrian Gardens, 1870), and Sa'īd al-Bustānī's (d. 1901) *Dhāt al-khidr* (Lady of the Boudoir, 1884). These works and others exploited the publication opportunities that were now being offered by the rapidly expanding press tradition, especially in Egypt where an indigenous public-ation movement had been bolstered by the arrival of a number of Lebanese émigrés who had fled the civil wars that had wracked the Syrian region during the 1850s and '60s. One of those émigrés was Jūrjī **Zaydān** (d. 1914) who made use of the magazine *al-Hilāl* that he himself had founded to publish a whole series of historical novels that, in an era of emerging nationalist sentiment, served to remind his readers of the significant events and periods of their past. And in 1907, the same year in which al-Muwaylihī published his much revised "Fat-rah min al-zaman" episodes in book form as *Hadīth 'Īsā ibn Hishām*, another Egyptian writer, Mahmūd Tāhir Haqqī, published his novel *'Adhrā' Dinshawāy* (The Maid of Dinshaway; translated by Saad El-Gabalawy as *The Maiden of Dinshway*, 1986), based directly on a notorious incident in the previous year (1906) in which British occupying forces had wreaked a terrible revenge on some Egyptian villagers who had objected to having their pet pigeons shot at.

Hadīth 'Īsā ibn Hishām's publication thus occurs in the midst of a period in which, in a curious twist, the majority of attempts at novel writing (with the obvious exception of *'Adhrā' Dinshawāy*) seem to favour philosophical and historical themes—albeit leavened with some romantic interest—that are somewhat removed from the concerns of contemporary society, whereas two of the major attempts at engaging with problems of modernity and cultural con-frontation, those of al-Shidyāq and al-Muway-

lihī, choose to revive textual features that are more characteristic of earlier pre-modern narra-tives. It is within this interesting mélange of generic purposes and styles that Muhammad Hu-sayn **Haykal**'s (d. 1956) novel *Zaynab* (1913) has traditionally been heralded as the first real Arabic novel. Bearing in mind the number of novels that we have cited above, the question that needs to be answered is thus: What are the particular features that make Haykal's work an "advance" on its many predecessors? The usual answer is that *Zaynab* places authentic Egyptian characters into a setting that is recognizably Egyptian. It is certainly the case that Haykal makes use of his novel to criticize the lack of education for women in his homeland, but, when we recall that this novel was in fact composed in Europe, it is hardly surprising that its overall effect is heavily tinged with nostalgia and not a little romanticized. In the context of al-Muwaylihī's *Hadīth 'Īsā ibn Hishām* and the literary history of the Arabic novel, what is significant is that Haykal's *Zaynab* points to a future that is heavily dependent on European precedents. That is particular true of the series of novels that appeared in Egypt in the 1930s. Indeed it was in that very decade that a young Egyptian writer named Najīb Mahfūz (trans-literated into English as Naguib Mahfouz, b. 1911)—became interested in the potential of fiction as a medium of social transformation and set himself to study John Drinkwater's *An Outline of Literature*. Having undertaken to read as many of the European novels listed in Drinkwater's work as possible, Mahfouz then began his own novel-writing career; its first phase reaches its acme with the publication of his renowned *Trilogy* in 1956-57. The timing of the publication of these novels was well matched with the post-independence era in Egyptian (and Arab) life, and the work was much praised at the time. Three decades later it was again praised, this time by the Nobel Committee in awarding Mahfouz the Nobel Prize in Literature in 1988. Mahfouz, dubbed by many Western critics as the "Dickens of Cairo," had now brought the process initiated by Haykal many decades earlier back to its purported progenitor culture.

However, as I noted at the beginning of this

article on al-Muwaylihī, the period after the June 1967 War had seen many changes within Arab societies, most particularly in their attitude to their past. During the 1970s the re-examination (and invocation) of Arab history and its implications were manifested within the fictional domain in the appearance of two works of major significance: Jamāl al-Ghītānī's *al-Zaynī Bara-kāt* (1971; English translation, *Zayni Barakat*, 1988) and Emil Habībī's *al-Waqā'i' al-gharībah fī 'khtifā' Sa'īd Abī 'l-Nahs al-Mutashā'il* (1972, 1974; English translation, *The Secret Life of Saeed the Ill-Fated Pessoptimist*, 1982). Al-Ghītānī uses extracts from the 16th century historian Ibn Iyās and pastiches of other types of record to paint a picture of a terrorized society that may be set in an earlier era but was clearly intended as a portrait of Egypt during the 1960s; Habībī's work is directly indebted to the *maqā-mah* genre in its episodic, non-linear structure, its plethora of intertextual reference, and its exploitation of narrative devices, as it paints a tragi-comic picture of the life of Palestinians in the State of Israel. The varied narrative examples provided by these two authors were to be followed by many other writers: a short list would include Naguib Mahfouz himself (who even invokes the name of 'Īsā ibn Hishām in his story "Ra'aytu fī-mā yarā al-nā'im" (I Saw in a Dream; collection of the same name, 1982, p. 154), 'Abd al-Rahmān Munīf (d. 2004), Ibrāhīm al-Kūnī (b. c. 1954), and BenSālim Himmīch (b. 1949). And, when the Lebanese novelist and critic Ilyās Khūrī (b. 1948) asks a rhetorical question as to how one is supposed to write logically based, linear narratives in the context of the civil war in his homeland, he is, among other things, pointing away from the predictable structures that had characterized what might be termed the "first phase" in the development of the modern Arabic novel and proclaiming the modernist virtues of fractured narratives. One is reminded here that it was the great English critic Thomas Carlyle (d. 1881) who, in an infamous remark, criticized the Qur'ān for the fractured and illogical nature of its text.

It is precisely when one looks back into the past from these recent essays in Arabic fiction that al-Muwaylihī's *Hadīth 'Īsā ibn Hishām*

(and before it al-Shidyāq's *al-Sāq 'alā 'l-sāq*) need to be seen in a different light. While, as was noted above, they certainly invoke the narrative traditions of the past, their concern with an accurate portrayal of the present (more accurate, one might suggest, than that of many novels composed during the same period) *and* their narrative strategies make them important precedents for the emergence of an Arabic fictional tradition that, once established as a valid "indigenous" genre, began the search for alternative texts and textual strategies that would reflect local and regional particularities. Al-Muwaylihī's work, always regarded as an important bridge-gesture, can indeed be seen as looking forwards as well as backwards.

After the initial set of "Egyptian" episodes of "Fatrah min al-Zaman"—the ones set in Egypt—had been published in the family newspaper, Muhammad al-Muwaylihī embarked upon the publication of a very different set of articles. They were published in the same venue under the title "Naqd Dīwān Shawqī" (1900, Criticism of Shawqī's Collection of Poetry). Ahmad **Shawqī** (d. 1932) was Egypt's most re-nowned poet and was certainly regarded as "court poet" to the Egyptian monarchy; he was to be dubbed "Prince of Poets" *(amīr al-shu'arā')* by his contemporaries. Undaunted by these facts, al-Muwaylihī launched into a fierce attack on the poet. The initial focus is on entirely non-critical matters: Shawqī's strong connections with the court and the egotistical nature of his introductory comments. The third article in the series opens with a reminder that there is an ancient adage suggesting that one should be very cautious when using the word "I". Al-Muwaylihī then proceeds to analyze some of the poet's composition on a line-by-line, word-by-word basis. The series of five articles aroused a furore in Cairene literary circles, and from a distance both physical and chronological it seems a pity that al-Muwaylihī chose to begin the series with a fierce *ad hominem* attack, since it was that feature that most pleased Shawqi's enemies and angered his friends, whereas the interesting issues concerning poetic criticism were initially sidetracked. However, when Egypt's most popular poet, Hāfiz **Ibrāhīm** (d. 1932), published the introduction to his collected poems one year later (1901), it became the trigger for a whole series of arguments and retorts over the essence and purpose of poetry that were published in *Misbāh al-Sharq* under the title, "Munāqashāt al-udabā'" (Literature Scholars Debate).

Both al-Muwaylihīs contributed to these debates, and the resulting articles were also published in later collections (notably the *Mukhtārāt*, Selections, published by Mustafā Lutfī al-**Manfalūtī**).

Towards the end of his life, al-Muwaylihī was invited by the Egyptian Ministry of Education to prepare a series of philosophical articles that he had previously published in *Misbāh al-Sharq* for publication in book form as a school textbook. He was working on their revision at the time of his death, and they were published posthumously in 1932 under the title, *'Ilāj al-nafs* (Cure of the Soul). The pedagogical intent of the volume is made clear by the inclusion of full voweling in the texts themselves (something that is normally omitted save in educational textbooks and the Qur'ān itself). The essays display their author's wide reading, with references not only to Arab poets (as is the case in *Hadīth 'Īsā ibn Hishām*) but also to European philosophers ranging from Socrates to Voltaire and Schopenhauer. The initial chapter focuses on the essence of philosophical thought; the topic can be divided, he says, into three categories: the divine, the natural and mathematical, and the ethical. There follow chapters on a variety of ethical issues: anger, courtesy, sympathy, and the abuse of prestige. Bearing in mind the vigorous antipathy towards the hated topic of philosophy that is displayed by the traditionalist shaykhs of the Azhar mosque-university in al-Muwaylihī's portrait of them within the text of *Hadīth 'Īsā ibn Hishām*, we can perhaps regard this later and much lesser known work as an attempt (fostered by the more modernizing elements within the Ministry of Education) to provide young Egyptian readers with a more nuanced and rationalized approach to the general topic and its application within a rapidly changing society.

In 1902, Muhammad al-Muwaylihī had found himself embroiled in an embarrassing social incident during which he was slapped in the face by a young nobleman (an event that some of the many political enemies of the al-Muwaylihīs then dubbed the "Year of the Slap", *'Ām al-kaff*). Muhammad al-Muwaylihī had a chronic stammer and was extremely shy in any case, but this incident seems to have somewhat traumatized him. He closed the family newspaper in August 1903, and thereafter rarely appeared in public. Most especially following his father Ibrāhīm's death in 1906, he withdrew from society. It was only a few weeks after finishing the editorial work on the above-mentioned *'Ilāj al-nafs* that he died in Hulwān (a town to the South of Cairo) on 28 February 1930.

REFERENCES

Roger Allen, "*Hadīth 'Īsā ibn Hishām* by al-Muwaylihī: Thirty years later", in: *Arabic and Islamic Studies in Honor of Marsden Jones*, ed. Thabit Abdullah et al. (Cairo: American University in Cairo Press, 1997), 117-124;

——, *A Period of Time* (Reading: Ithaca Press, 1992);

——, "Poetry and Poetic Criticism at the Turn of the Century", in: *Studies in Modern Arabic Literature*, ed. R. C. Ostle (Warminster/England: Aris and Phillips, 1975), 7-17;

——, "Some new al-Muwailihi materials or the unpublished Hadīth 'Īsā ibn Hishām", *Humaniora Islamica* 2 (1974): 139-180;

——, "Writings of Members of the Nazli Circle", *Journal of the American Research Center in Egypt* 8 (1971): 79-84;

Ahmad Ibrāhīm al-Hawārī, *Naqd al-mujtama' fī Hadīth 'Īsā ibn Hishām li-'l-Muwaylihī* (Cairo: Dār al-Ma'ārif, 1981);

Ibrāhīm al-Muwaylihī, *al-Mu'allafāt al-kāmilah* ("Complete Works"), ed. Roger Allen (Cairo: al-Majlis al-A'lā li-'l-Thaqāfah, 2007);

——, *Spies, Scandals, & Sultans* [a translation with commentary by Roger Allen of *Mā Hunālik*], (Boulder and New York: Rowman and Littlefield, 2008);

Yūsuf Ramitch, *Usrat al-Muwaylihī wa-atharuhā fī 'l-adab al-'arabī al-hadīth* (Cairo: Dār al-Ma'ārif, 1980).

Mārūn al-Naqqāsh

(1817 – 1855)

PHILIP SADGROVE

University of Manchester

WORKS

Arzat Lubnān ("The Cedars of Lebanon", Beirut: al-Matba'ah al-'Umūmiyyah, 1869); this post-humous collection, edited by the author's brother, Niqūlā al-Naqqāsh, contains in fact also the latter's speech on the opening of the theatre (c. 1869), a biography of Mārūn, Mārūn's speech on presenting the first play, a "chapter talking about theatres and plays and how to perform them in general," Mārūn's plays *Riwāyat al-Bakhīl, Riwāyat Abū 'l-Hasan al-mughaffal aw Riwāyat Hārūn al-Rashīd*, and *Riwāyat al-Salīt al-hasūd*, with a prayer by Mārūn sung by the actors *(lā'ibīn)* at the beginning of the first performance in his new theatre, a chronogram, poems in praise of his works *(tafārīz)*, a poem *(urjūzah)* on prosody and rhyme, his poetic fragments and, at the end, also elegies to him; two of the plays saw later editions:

Abū 'l-Hasan al-mughaffal wa-mā jarā lahu ma'a Hārūn al-Rashīd ("Abū 'l-Hasan the Simpleton, and What Happened to him with Hārūn al-Rashīd", Alexandria: Jurjī Gharzūzī Press, 1909);

al-Bakhīl: riwāyah mudhikah mulahhanah: dhāt khamsat fusūl ("The Miser: a Comedy Set to Music: in Five Acts", São Paolo: Matba'at al-Jadīd, 1914);

[NOTE: Mārūn's plays are collected, with an introduction by his brother, , Niqūlā's].

Editions

Muhammad Yūsuf Najm, *al-Masrah al-'arabī: dirāsāt wa-nusūs*, 1. *Mārūn al-Naqqāsh* ("Arab Theatre: Studies and Texts, 1. Mārūn al-Naqqāsh", Beirut: Dār al-Thaqāfah, 1961); without the introductory material and the extensive footnotes of the 1869 edition;

Arzat Lubnān ("The Cedars of Lebanon", Cairo: Wizārat al-Thaqāfah, al-Markaz al-Qawmī

li'l-Masrah wa'l-Mūsīqā wa'l-Funūn al-Sha'-biyyah, 1996).

The Syrian Mārūn ibn Ilyās ibn Mīkhā'īl al-Naqqāsh was one of the first Arabs to attempt playwriting in the Arabic tongue following European models. He is rightly considered the father of modern Arabic drama, in the sense that the Arab theatre movement began in Syria (modern Lebanon) as a result of his activities. Before the nineteenth-century the only drama for the entertainment of Arab audiences was shadow theatre (karākūz < Turkish *Karagöz*), puppet theatre and itinerant players of crude comedies. An Algerian writer, Abraham Daninos, totally unaware of al-Naqqāsh, had published a primitive play on European lines, *Nazāhat al-mushtāq wa-ghussat al-'ushshāq fī madīnat Tiryāq fī 'l-'Irāq* (The Pleasure Trip of the Enamoured and the Agony of Lovers in the City of Tiryaq in Iraq) in Algiers in 1847, the same year as Mārūn's first play, quoting heavily from *Alf laylah wa-laylah* (The Thousand and One Nights) and 'Izz al-Dīn al-Muqaddisī's (d. 1279) *Kashf al-asrār 'an hikam al-tuyūr wa'l-azhār* (The Revelation of the Secrets of the Wisdom of Birds and Flowers). There is no evidence that Daninos's play was performed or indeed had any impact on literary life in Algeria.

A Maronite Christian, Mārūn was born in Sidon in Syria. He grew up in Beirut, where his family had moved in 1825; his father was a member of the municipal council in 1850. Mārūn had a traditional education; he studied Arabic grammar, became absorbed in morphology, mastered logic, the rules of versification, and the branches of Arabic rhetoric. He learnt and perfected Turkish, French and Italian. At 18, surpassing his peers, he composed some poems, considered graceful, free of complication and far from colourless. He mastered and taught book-keeping on foreign principles. People sought his advice on commercial law, a subject which he had also studied with great success. Possessed of a beautiful voice, he mastered the art of music, disassociating himself from its lighter side. He became chief customs clerk in Beirut and was also a member of the Chamber of Commerce and of the Jesuit Oriental Society (al-Jam'iyyah al-Sharqiyyah) founded in Beirut in 1850. At that time Beirut was developing as a new commercial and intellectual centre in Syria. Fond of travelling, he journeyed to Aleppo, a leading centre for Arab music, Damascus, and other regions and towns of Syria.

In 1846 he traveled to Alexandria and Cairo in Egypt, then continued his journey to Italy, where he became acquainted with European theatres *(marāsih* or *tiyātrāt)* and was amazed at the wisdom and information that the theatrical medium provided for the benefit of the public. From the 1830s foreign missionaries had presented plays on the birth of Christ and other biblical subjects in schools they had opened in the Lebanon; in the 1840s Italian missionaries had built a wooden theatre in Beirut, in which plays with a religious stamp were performed. Inspired by his trip to Italy, al-Naqqāsh returned to Beirut and trained some young friends of his to perform his first play in his house in Beirut at the end of 1847. He invited all the foreign consuls accredited to Beirut and local dignitaries to the performance. This play in rhymed prose *(saj')* and verse was the five-act *al-Bakhīl* (The Miser), inspired by Molière's *L'avare*. It was neither a translation nor an adaptation, as some sources have claimed. For the most part a competent piece of work, the whole of the dialogue, entirely in verse of a rather indifferent quality and not metrically regular, was intended to be sung to the accompaniment of music, "a comedy *(riwāyah mudhikah)* wholly set to music."

Set in contemporary Beirut society, the names of the *dramatis personae* are Arabized. An old man, al-Tha'labī, wishes to marry his beautiful daughter, Hind, to an old miser, Qarrād, for his wealth; Qarrād is in turn attracted by Hind's wealth. Her brother, Ghālī, determined to prevent such a disastrous union, introduces another suitor, the young 'Īsā, a relative of her dead husband and someone she likes; 'Īsā, being a relative, can meet her, a concession by the author to the customs of Levantine society. In Act II Ghālī and 'Īsā succeed in preventing the marriage. Qarrād renounces the idea of the marriage, and tries to dissuade Hind. In Act III al-Tha'labī, believing he will be murdered, agrees that his daughter can marry 'Īsā. The final two acts are redundant to the plot. In Act IV 'Īsā, disguised as a Turkish dignitary and Ghālī, as his Egyptian clerk, support Qarrād in the case he intends to bring against al-Tha'labī for the wrongs he has suffered. In Act V the two, still in disguise, continue to plot to get money from Qarrād. When the young people reveal themselves, Qarrād forgives them; a transformed character, he joins the final chorus in singing the play's moral message: "Let every miser consider this to be the end".

The influence of Molière here is obvious enough; the same characters appear in both plays. In Molière the miser Harpagon is courting Marianne, a girl engaged to his son; his desire to marry is financial. In the Arab piece it would not have been appropriate to have the rivalry between father and son. There are the same efforts to dissuade Harpagon from the marriage, and in the end he allows his son to marry her. There are a number of identical scenes: al-Naqqāsh was obviously familiar with both *L'avare* and *Le bourgeois gentilhomme*. In the latter play Covielle and Cléante disguise themselves as Turkish princes and speak in an incomprehensible jargon. When al-Naqqāsh's characters don their disguises, Ghālī speaks in poor Arabic with a Turkish accent, while 'Īsā uses Egyptian dialect. Umm Rīshā, the servant of al-Tha'labī, is the only character to talk in the Lebanese dialect; in a footnote Niqūlā al-Naqqāsh notes that the language adopted should be suitable to the person playing the part. As in Molière the presence of servants is integral to the development of the bourgeois comedy. In the later play *Abū 'l-Hasan al-mughaffal*, 'Urqūb, the scheming servant of Abū 'l-Hasan, named after a proverbially famous liar, will do anything if it is to his own advantage, going to the extreme of betraying his master. In yet another feature drawn from Molière al-Naqqāsh frequently uses soliloquy and the dialogue follows alternate lines of verse.

Al-Naqqāsh's leading characters all reflect a particular dominant trait: avarice in Qarrād, naïvety and simplicity in Abū 'l-Hasan, and contempt and envy in Samʿān (from the play al-Salīt al-hasūd). The name al-Thaʿlabī is derived from the Arabic word "fox", and Qarrād from qird "monkey." In a feature taken from European opera, the play begins with the entrance of the chorus, "not less than six persons who appear always together, friends of Ghālī and ʿĪsā who help the two of them with their objectives;" in Acts IV and V they appear disguised as officers. Careful not to offend local customs, Mārūn adjusts the plot and the contacts between the sexes as necessary to guard the sanctity of the Arab harem.

The theatrical experiment was continued into a second year (1848/49) with a play by Mārūn's brother, Niqūlā, al-Shaykh al-jāhil (The Ignorant Shaykh). Encouraged by the public response, Mārūn wrote an original, more mature work, the three-act Abū 'l-Hasan al-mughaffal aw Hārūn al-Rashīd (Abū 'l-Hasan the Simpleton, or: Hārūn al-Rashīd), taking its story from the Thousand and One Nights (Alf laylah wa-laylah), specifically from the tale al-Nāʾim wa 'l-yaqzān (The Sleeper and the Awake) as narrated by Sheherazade. This tale discusses the theme of dream and reality, taken from two smaller tales in Alf laylah, the tale of Abū 'l-Hasan al-Khalīʾah, who falls victim to the ruses of the caliph, and of his humorous exploits at the caliph's court. Al-Naqqāsh keeps to the framework and the main outlines, retaining the characters of Abū 'l-Hasan, the caliph Hārūn, Jaʿfar, and Masrūr, the executioner, and creating a sub-plot of love and marriage. Al-Naqqāsh adds characters of his own such as the young lovers, Daʿd, Saʿīd, Salmā, and ʿUthmān, the servant ʿUrqūb, and the Mamluk Ishāq. The play gives the impression of being composed in a high Arab style, but al-Naqqāsh had tried to simplify the language. The heavy rhyming prose used throughout the play seems very artificial and makes it difficult for the dialogue to seem natural, though there are moments when it is considered highly expressive. There are passages of verse intended

for musical accompaniment, but it is not fully sung.

The caliph Hārūn al-Rashīd and his minister, Jaʿfar tour the city disguised as dervishes, Dādā Mustafā and Dādā Mahmūd, in order to find out directly about the lives of the people. They make frequent visits to a once rich merchant, Abū 'l-Hasan, who has lost his entire fortune. In Act I the Caliph learns of the wish of Abū 'l-Hasan, discontent with his lot, to sit on the throne, if only for one day. The Caliph decides to satisfy this wish. He slips Abū 'l-Hasan a sleeping pill, then has him transported to the palace. In Act II Abū 'l-Hasan wakes up in the Caliph's bed. Thinking he is dreaming, he ends by believing he really has become the caliph. As such he now receives ʿUthmān and Saʿīd, who tell him that a certain Abū 'l-Hasan is trying to prevent the marriage of his brother, Saʿīd, to ʿUthmān's sister, Daʿd; she is in love with Saʿīd, Abū'l-Hasan's more handsome brother. Abū 'l-Hasan wants to marry Daʿd, and ʿUthmān wants to marry Abū 'l-Hasan's daughter, Salmā. When Abū 'l-Hasan asks Saʿīd what he thinks of marriage in general, Saʿīd discovers that Abū 'l-Hasan wants to marry Daʿd; this conversation parallels a similar conversation in L'avare between Harpagon and Cléante about Marianne. Hind al-Hijāziyyah, a slave, persuades Abū 'l-Hasan to allow the marriage of Saʿīd and Daʿd and ʿUthmān and Salmā. When Jaʿfar spreads the rumour that Persian soldiers are attacking the city, Abū 'l-Hasan decides to flee. In Act III Abū 'l-Hasan wakes up at home once again; for a while he still believes he is caliph, but he finally accepts the reality of his return to his own house. Hārūn and Jaʿfar come to visit Abū 'l-Hasan's house. Amused by the trick they have played, they now reveal their true identities to Abū 'l-Hasan. They scatter money over the stage, and ʿUrqub rushes to pick it up. Abū 'l-Hasan meanwhile remains perplexed by everything that has happened.

On 13 January 1850 (and perhaps also at the end of 1850), this play was performed before a number of Ottoman ministers and officials resident in Beirut at the time, all the consuls and notables of the town, amongst whom were two muftis, the cadi/judge, and Wāmiq Pasha, Governor of the Province of Sidon. Al-Naqqāsh was praised for his role in bringing theatre to the country. David Urquhart, an English traveller, attending the performance, described it as "the opening of the first Arab theatre", performed by members of Mārūn's large family.

The acting was awkward, the singing abominable, but the piece was evidently managed with considerable art. It was an earnest of the resources now slumbering, and of the facility with which the Arabian spirit may be touched and awakened.

The theatre was constructed in the front of Mārūn's suburban house, the backcloth of the house imitating the scenery in European theatres. The stage was a raised platform, and spectators were seated in the courtyard, protected from the weather by a sail cloth. Men and boys, dressed as women, played the female parts; there were "no women on the stage, so were there none in the court, and not even at the windows which opened on the stage." Even though the performance was "long, very long, no one went away," and everyone seemed content. Author and actors were frequently applauded. At the end of the play Ja'far, continuing to embody his role as vizier, threw handfuls of coin amongst the audience, whilst they threw showers of roses onto the stage.

In the interval between the second and third acts a short farce was performed, on the theme of a cuckolded marriage. An ex-mufti in the audience, identifying with the action, kept informing one party concerning the activities of the other, as if playing the role of the ancient chorus. Finally the husband notices his wife's treachery. To roars of laughter the mufti kept on criticising both the guilty wife and the extremely stupid husband. This unsolicited participant in the acting contributed to the unbounded success of the farce. Such audience participation became a standard part of performances, on occasion leading to actual plot changes.

When Mārūn realized how much people liked this art, he was encouraged to continue his efforts by the Governor of Sidon, Amīn Mukhlis Pasha, and obtained a *firmān* (edict) permitting the construction of a theatre for his students. He built a large theatre beside his house outside the walls of Palace Gate in al-Jumayzah quarter in Beirut. In his will he instructed that the theatre be turned into a church, bought subsequently by the apostolic delegate. The church, Terra Santa, is there today on Rue Gouraud.

After *Abū 'l-Hasan al-mughaffal*, Mārūn next presented a drama, *Riwāyat Rabī'at b. Zayd al-Mukaddam*, composed by his brother Niqūlā. Then in 1851, some four years after his first work, he used his own new theatre as the venue for his last and weakest play, the three-act *al-Salīt al-hasūd* (The Envious, Impertinent One), in rhymed prose and verse and partly set to music; Niqūlā felt it was by far Mārūn's best work. In Act I the central character, Sam'ān, is in love with Rāhīl, daughter of Abū 'Īsā al-Shāmī, a teacher of Arabic language and literature, and asks for her hand. The subplot is the love interest of Abū 'Īsā's servant, Barbāra. Abū 'Īsā owes Sam'ān money and hopes by the marriage to annul the debt. When a Jerusalem merchant, Ishāq al-Qudsī, planning to marry Rāhīl, presents Abū 'Īsā with a costly necklace, Abū 'Īsā accepts the new suitor. Jealous and overwhelmed by doubts, Sam'ān reproaches Rāhīl for having betrayed him for another. In Act II Sam'ān decides to commit suicide. Rāhīl agrees to flee with him and marry in secret, but rather than getting closer, the two start arguing. Exasperated by his fits of temper and his drunken behaviour Rāhīl realises that she is no longer in love. In Act III when Rāhīl marries his rival, Sam'ān offers the new couple a box of poisoned sweets, but the ruse is discovered. Sam'ān is forgiven and allowed to leave, though he reaffirms to the others his perpetual hatred. In the chorus all the characters ask the spectators if they agree to the ending of the play.

Al-Salīt al-hasūd is clearly inspired by Molière's *Tartuffe, Le bourgeois gentilhomme* and *Le misanthrope*. With his pessimism, contempt and sarcastic spirit Sam'ān comes close to Alceste in the latter play. The dialogue in Act I, Scene 4, between Abū 'Īsā and Jirjis about the meaning of prose almost replicates that in *Le bourgeois gentilhomme* between Monsieur Jourdain and the Maître de Philosophie; Abū 'Īsā tries to teach Arabic prosody to his pupils, by reading aloud a poem. The fact that the servants in this play (Jabbūr, Bashārah, and Barbāra) speak classical Arabic could have resulted from criticism by conservative elements of Mārūn's use of dialect in *al-Bakhīl*.

After presenting this play, Mārūn produced some other plays that are described by Niqūlā as not worth mentioning. In fact, he may have been the author of these other plays; Niqūlā mentions in his foreword to his brother's plays that unfortunately most of his work has been lost.

All the actors in these productions were drawn from his family or friends, and included his brother Niqūlā and friends, Habīb Misk, who played the role of 'Urqūb in *Abū 'l-Hasan al-mughaffal*, 'Abd al-Ahad Nakhlah Khadrā and Hannā al-Tayyān, who played the roles of Ishāq and of Abū 'l-Hasan in the same piece. The role of Jabbūr, Sam'ān's servant, in *al-Salīt al-hasūd* was masterfully interpreted by Mārūn's friend 'Abd Allāh Kumayd; Mārūn wrote the role for him, inspired, we are told, by his politeness and charm. When the play was presented c. 1868, the role of Sam'ān was played by his nephew, Bishārah Mirzā, another actor of great talent.

Abandoning further theatrical experiments at this juncture, Mārūn left Beirut on the 19 September 1854 and went on business to Tarsus in Cilicia, an agricultural centre in south-central Anatolia. Settling there, in a short time he became a respected and popular member of the community. Ill with fever he died there on 1 June 1855, aged 38. Much lamented by the people of Beirut and Mount Lebanon, his body was buried at the beginning of June 1856 in the Maronite cemetery in Beirut.

Pandering to public taste Mārūn's three plays are all in the form of an operetta, filled with music, song and humour that were to become the staple diet of Arabic drama for decades to come. Singing and recitation of poetry, both ingredients of shadow theatre, were retained in Mārūn's new dramatic genre. Much of the dialogue is intended to be sung to specific tunes; *al-Bakhīl* has one hundred and five well-known Arabic melodies, *Abū 'l-Hasan al-mughaffal* ninty-three, and *al-Salīt* sixty-four. An index of the tunes is supplied at the end of each text. The airs are variations on well-known popular tunes, inspired by the local folklore of Egypt, Syria and Iraq. Two popular French airs are also used: *Marlbrough s'en va-t-en guerre*, known to the Arabs as "A Mamluk travelled to war", and *Peuple français* (French People), also called *La Parisienne* by Casimir Delavigne, with music by François Aubert, the anthem of the French revolution of 1830. Mārūn may have borrowed dramatic elements, such as farce, avarice, love, elopements, comic effects, disguises, hair breadth escapes, intrigues, duels, attempted murder, and music, from the stories and shadow theatre of popular entertainers in Arab streets and cafes. As in shadow theatre and performances of itinerant players, many comical situations in his plays result from double entendre, beatings and burlesque dances. Mārūn incorporated these traditional itinerant players themselves into his plays. These individuals, masqueraders (*arbāb al-masākhir*), appear at the end of the first and second acts of *al-Salīt al-hasūd* to amuse the audience.

He coined a number of stage terms, many of which continued in use; he calls an act *fasl*, a scene *juz'*, the dramatis persona *shakhs*, and the curtain *sitār*. The first edition of his plays is full of useful advice to directors and actors. Al-Naqqāsh suggests that the person playing the compelling figure of Sam'ān "should most of the time display a talent for mockery, ridicule and unnatural imitation of, and contempt for, those with whom he is appearing on stage *(mal'ab)*, especially by exactly replicating the movements and gestures of his adversary." He provides a few details of the scene: Act II, Scene 1 of *Abū 'l-Hasan al-mughaffal* is set "in a royal chamber in the palace of the caliph, where one finds regal clothing, a crown and sceptre," *al-Salīt al-hasūd*, Act II, Scene 1, "in open country in the direction of Abū 'Īsā's house performed on a rainy night," and Scene 14 "good to see the flash of lightning and (hear) thunder." Many other stage instructions occur: "they drink and go off drunk", "angrily", "three times in their loudest voices and they leave" and "he sits a little, then returns and sleeps."

As in many works of contemporary literature Mārūn is careful to praise the Ottoman sultan and the local Ottoman authorities in his plays. In *al-Bakhīl*, Act II, Scene 5, Qarrād sings the praises of the sultan ʿAbd al-Majīd (Abdülmecit); this is repeated by the actors behind the curtain. In Act III, Scene 23, of *Abū 'l-Hasan al-mughaffal* the actors, singing the praises of the character Jaʿfar, are actually addressing Wāmīk Pacha, sitting in the first row of the spectators. *Al-Salīt al-hasūd* ends with a prayer to God to punish the enemies and bring victory to the Sultan, followed by the epilogue, a prayer for sultan ʿAbd al-Majīd and the Foreign Minister ʿĀlī Pasha, sung by the actors at the performance in the new theatre. Thanks are also addressed to Amīn Mukhlis Pasha, the governor of Sidon, who had encouraged Mārūn to set up the theatre and write the plays to open the "door of civilization" in the country.

For those unacquainted with theatre Mārūn introduced his first play with a long speech before the performance, explaining what drama is and what his objectives are. He exhorts spectators to follow his example by creating other works. He explores the causes of European progress and Arab backwardness. Historically, he says, the East had been more advanced: "we are the roots, they are the branches; we the spring and they the river." Yet Europeans have become more advanced than the Arab people, especially in the arts and sciences. Mārūn was determined to present to his audience a theatre that was morally based, European gold cast in an Arab mould. He confided to his brother Niqūlā that the

elegance of the play, its splendour and its unprecedented beauty are one third connected with excellent writing, one third with the skill of the actors and a final third with a suitable venue, costumes and appropriate props.

Theatres in Europe, Mārūn found, were divided into two categories: the first, called *prosa (brūzah)*, was divided into comedy *(kumidiyā)*, drama *(drāmmā)* and tragedy *(trājīdiyā)*. This form was presented without poetry, and not set to music. The second, called by them *opera (ūbirah)*, incorporates like the other, drama, tragedy and comedy, but within the framework of music. Though the first was simpler and more useful, Mārūn preferred the second, be-

cause it appeared to him more delightful, desirable and brilliant. He chose a dramatic form that emulated musical theatre, because he was convinced that, bearing in mind the Arab fondness for singing, opera would prove more popular with audiences. Mārūn admitted there would be difficulties, because adequate venues, suitable scenery and costumes were lacking. In theatre he had discovered a means to refine human nature. Though the form of the stories told was ostensibly figurative and comic, the core was both truthful and virtuous. Through repetition the audience would come to see benefits that were hard to describe, since drama was filled with good counsel, moral messages, wise sayings, and sheer wonderment. The failings of mankind were revealed; any sensible person could learn a lesson and take heed. Apart from acquiring a good education and sipping a draught of good advice, civilisation, and culture, spectators would at the same time learn classical vocabulary and avail themselves of good ideas; by its very nature theatre is composed of well ordered words and well-contrived meter. Audiences would enjoy seeing physical exercise, listen to musical instruments, learn musical tunes and the art of singing amongst boon companions; they would be able to enjoy wondrous spectacles and entertainments, comic acts and delightful occasions. They would come to understand both global affairs and domestic events. They would be trained in correct deportment and how to behave before kings. For Mārūn therefore theatre was an earthly paradise full of splendour.

In *al-Bakhīl*, Act II, Scene 6, Ghālī talks of the didactic effects of theatre:

It is an assembly of tales, all of it literature. In it shameful deeds are exposed entertainingly to the ignorant, then advice is expounded as a warning to the intelligent. It is an art characterized by benefits, an art that stimulates both body and spirit. (In it) they give an account of seriousness through a kind of humour.

Mārūn's plays continued this tradition of incorporating a number of moral precepts and wise sayings for the edification of the audience but with no direct relevance to the play's major topic. In *al-Salīṭ al-ḥasūd*, Act III, Scene 4, for example, Samʿān comments at length on theatre and Mārūn's plays:

First of all I admire this play al-Bakhīl *because it is the first to have been written in the Arabic language; to a degree this comedy has managed to gain for itself a good reputation. It is said … that this art carries advice, because it contains the essence of jest and humour, reveals defects and shameful deeds, educates intelligent people and provides moral counsel for the ignorant.*

Samʿān acknowledges that the author of *al-Bakhīl* has recognised his shortcomings. Mārūn admits that he has adopted his ideas from European plays and is not concerned about the purity of Arabic words used in his plays (which are full of grammatical errors and weaknesses of style). He has decided to go along with public taste. By using words not found in the dictionary, Niqūlā admits, "the author has not been meticulous with regard to the correctness of the Arabic used in the play; he has only paid attention to the meaning."

Mārūn's *Abū 'l-Ḥasan al-mughaffal*, more commonly known as *Hārūn al-Rashīd*, remained in the repertoire of the Syrian troupes of Aḥmad Abū Khalīl al-Qabbānī, Yūsuf al-Khayyāṭ, Sulaymān al-Qardāḥī, Iskandar Farah, and others active in Egypt till the 1890s. In 1860 Niqūlā revived *al-Salīṭ al-ḥasūd* on the anniversary of Mārūn's birthday. It was performed on his old stage, before an audience of local dignitaries, including the Governor ʿAzīz Pasha. In 1867 *Abū 'l-Ḥasan al-mughaffal* was performed by the St. Vincent de Paul Society in Niqūlā's house before Kāmil Pasha. Mārūn's pupils produced *al-Salīṭ al-ḥasūd* for charitable purposes at the opening of the new Arab Theatre (al-Marsaḥ al-ʿArabī) in Beirut c. 1868 before Nāṣr Allāh Frānqū Pasha, provincial governor of Mount Lebanon. In about 1869 *Abū 'l-Ḥasan al-mughaffal* was also performed before Frānqū. In 1874 Niqūlā presented *al-Salīṭ al-ḥasūd* at his uncle's house.

Salīm al-Naqqāsh (1850-1884) was to continue in the footsteps of his uncle, Mārūn, forming a troupe in Beirut, including actresses, and performing *al-Bakhīl*, *Abū 'l-Ḥasan al-mughaffal* and *al-Salīṭ al-ḥasūd* before the Beirut public in 1875 and 1876. In the latter year he took his troupe to Egypt and thus participated in the developing tradition of Egyptian Arabic theatre, a trend that was to be followed by other Lebanese and Syrians who were attracted by the Egyptian ruling family's support for the theatre and the much more vital theatrical scene. Amongst the plays performed by the troupe in Alexandria were *Abū 'l-Ḥasan al-mughaffal* and *al-Salīṭ al-ḥasūd*.

After these few years of activity in the 1840s and 1850s the theatre and the dramas performed there disappeared along with their creator and were almost entirely forgotten. Mārūn's absence may have been critical. Given the difficulties that the theatre had faced from the outset, Mārūn thought the survival of the art in the Lebanon was unlikely. He was certainly aware that such a process would not be easily achieved. Even so he continued throughout his relatively short life to encourage others to write something for the stage. He was hopeful for the future, and yet he died without ever tasting the fruits of what he had planted. Mārūn was convinced that his successors would surpass him, providing they worked seriously and strenuously. Niqūlā was to confirm this prediction, when he said that Mārūn's students, whom he had taught with the sweat of his brow, had not only continued to learn what he had taught them, but had progressed beyond all expectation. By 1869 the public's enthusiasm for this art was notable; people had begun to flock to performances, in comparison to the early days when Mārūn had been forced to resort to all kinds of blandishment and flattery in order to persuade them to attend his plays; even then only a few had responded. By the 1860s outstanding figures were competing with each other to write fine plays. Not a year went by without a number of notable offerings. What Mārūn had hoped for had indeed happened. But Niqūlā felt that there was still more to be done in the world of theatre, in that what had been achieved thus far was a mere shadow of what could be done.

REFERENCES

M. M. Badawi, *Early Arabic Drama* (Cambridge: Cambridge University Press, 1988), 43-53;

—— (ed.), *Modern Arabic Literature*, The Cambridge History of Arabic Literature series (Cambridge: Cambridge University Press, 1992), 331-334;

Hédi Ben Halima, "Abū 'l-Hasan al-Muġaffal de Mārūn al-Naqqāš (1817-1855), première composition originale dans le théâtre arabe", *Arabica* 11 (January 1964): 73-79;

Regina Karachouli, "Mārūn an-Naqqāsh (1817-1855) – Pionier des arabischen Theaters", *Asien, Afrika, Lateinamerika* 9 (1981): 305-311;

Joseph Khoueiri, *Théâtre arabe* (Louvain-la-Neuve: Cahiers théâtre Louvain, 1984), 41-81;

M. A. al-Khozai, *The Development of Early Arabic Drama (1847-1900)* (London: Long-man, 1984), 31-79;

Matti Moosa, "Naqqāsh and the Rise of the Native Arab Theatre in Syria", *Journal of Arabic Literature* 3 (1972): 106-117;

David Urquhart, *The Lebanon (Mount Souria): A History and a Diary*, vol. 2 (London: Thomas Cautley Newby, 1860), 178-180;

ʿAbd al-Rahmān Yāghī, *Fī 'l-juhūd al-masrahiyyah: al-ighrīqiyyah, al-ūrubiyyah, al-ʿarabiyyah (min al-Naqqāsh ilā 'l-Hakīm)* (Beirut: al-Muʾassasah al-ʿArabiyyah li'l-Dirāsāt wa'l-Nashr, 1980), 93-113;

——, "Mārūn al-Naqqāsh wa-tajribatuhu al-rāʾidah", in: *al-Masrah al-ʿarabī bayn al-naql wa'l-taʾsīl*, ed. ʿAlī al-Rāʿī et al. (Kuwait: Majallat al-ʿArabī, 1988), 56-68;

Hishām Zayn al-Dīn, "Mārūn al-Naqqāsh: al-rāʾid al-awwal li'l-masrah al-lubnānī wa'l-ʿarabī", *al-Masrah fī Lubnān* 2 (Beirut: 1996), 11-23

Mīkhā'īl Nuʿaymah
(Mikhail Naimy)
(1889 – 1988)

GREGORY J. BELL
Princeton

WORKS

al-Ābā' wa'l-banūn ("Fathers and Sons", New York: Shirkat al-Funūn, 1917);

al-Ghirbāl ("The Sieve", Cairo: al-Matbaʿah al-ʿAsriyyah, 1923);

al-Marāhil: siyāhāt fī zawāhir al-hayāh wa-bawātinihā ("Stages: Travels among Life's Outward and Inner Signs", Beirut: Matbaʿat Sādir, 1933);

Jubrān Khalīl Jubrān: hayātuh, mawtuh, adabuh, fannuh ("Jubrān Khalīl Jubrān: His Life, Death, Literature, and Art", Beirut: Matbaʿat Lisān al-Hāl, 1934);

Zād al-maʿād ("Provisions for the Hereafter", Cairo: Matbaʿat al-Muqtataf, 1936);

Kāna mā kān ("Once Upon a Time", Beirut: al-Makshūf, 1937);

Hams al-jufūn ("The Whispering of Eyelids", Beirut: Maktabat Sādir, 1943);

al-Bayādir ("Threshing Floors", Cairo: Dār al-Maʿārif, 1945);

al-Awthān ("The Idols", Beirut: Maktabat Sādir, 1946);

Karm ʿalā darb ("Vineyard by a Path", Cairo: Dār al-Maʿārif, 1946);

Liqāʾ ("A Reunion", Beirut: Maktabat Sādir, 1946);

The Book of Mirdad: A Lighthouse and a Haven (Beirut: Sader, 1948);

Sawt al-ʿālam ("Voice of the World", Cairo: Dār

al-Ma'ārif, 1948);

Mudhakkirāt al-Arqash ("The Memoirs of Scarface", Beirut: Maktabat Sādir, 1949);

al-Nūr wa'l-dayjūr ("Light and Darkness", Beirut: Maktabat Sādir, 1950);

Kitāb Mirdād: Manārah wa-mīnā' ("The Book of Mirdād: Lighthouse and Port", Beirut: Maktabat Sādir, 1952);

Fī mahabb al-rīh ("Storm-swept", Beirut: Maktabat Sādir, 1953);

Durūb ("Paths", Beirut: Dār al-'Ilm li'l-Malāyīn, 1954);

Akābir ("VIPs", Beirut: Dār Sādir, 1956);

Ab'ad min Mūskū wa-min Wāshintun ("Beyond Moscow and Washington", Beirut: Dār Bayrūt/Dār Sādir, 1957);

Abū Battah ("The Big-Calfed Man", Beirut: Dār Bayrūt/Dār Sādir, 1958);

Sab'ūn... Hikāyat 'umr ("Seventy... The Story of a Life", 3 vols., Beirut: Dār Sādir, 1959-60);

al-Yawm al-akhīr ("The Last Day", Beirut: Dār Sādir, 1963);

Hawāmish ("Marginalia", Beirut: Dār Sādir, 1965);

Ayyūb: masrahiyyah fī arba'at fusūl ("Job: A Play in Four Acts", Beirut: Dār Sādir, 1967);

Yā ibn Ādam: hiwār bayna rajulayn ("O Mankind: A Dialogue between Two Men", Beirut: Dār Sādir, 1969);

Fī 'l-ghirbāl al-jadīd ("In the New Sieve", Beirut: Mu'assasat Nawfal, 1971);

Ahādīth ma'a 'l-sihāfah ("Conversations with the Press", Beirut: Mu'assasat Badrān, 1973);

Najwā 'l-ghurūb ("Sunset Soliloquy", Beirut: Mu'assasat Nawfal, 1973);

Min wahy al-Masīh ("Inspired by the Messiah", Beirut: Mu'assasat Nawfal, 1974);

Wamadāt: shudhūr wa-amthāl ("Sparks: Fragments and Proverbs", Beirut: Mu'assasat Nawfal, 1977);

Periodical Publications

"Fajr al-amal ba'da layl al-ya's", *al-Funūn* 1.4 (1913): 50-70;

"Li-majd al-maslūb", *al-Funūn* 1.7 (1913): 44-52;

"Mahrajān al-mawt", *al-Funūn* 2.2 (1916): 391-408;

Review of al-Majallah al-'Arabiyyah, *al-Funūn* 2.6 (1916): 540-542;

"al-Hintah wa'l-ziwān: Nazrah fī 'l-*Ayyūbiyyāt*", *al-Funūn* 2.8 (1917): 732-735;

"Min ajl al-mardā wa'l-musābīn wa'l-masbīyīn", *al-Funūn* 3.3 (October 1917): 169-170;

Introduction to *Majmū'at al-Rābitah al-Qalamiyyah li-sanat 1921* (New York: al-Matba-'ah al-Tijāriyyah al-Sūriyyah al-Amrīkiyyah, 1921);

"Man anta? Mā anta?", *al-Sā'ih* 24 (August 1922); reprinted in *Sab'ūn... Hikāyat 'umr 1889-1959* (see above), 2, 218-220;

"The Endless Race", *The New York Times* vol. 77, no. 25.617 (Wednesday, March 14th, 1928), 24;

"A Strange Little Book", *Aramco World* 15.6 (November/December 1964): 10-15;

"The Long Strides", *Aramco World* 16.6 (November/December 1965): 26-27;

"A Strange Little Book", *Aramco World* 34.2 (March/April 1983): 8-9; while a work of the same title, this is a separate piece from the entry listed above.

(Many of Naimy's English poems are included in Hussein Dabbagh's *Mikhail Naimy: Some Aspects of his Thought as Revealed in his Writings*, see References).

Collected Works

al-Majmū'ah al-kāmilah, 8 vols. ("Collected Works", Beirut: Dār al-'Ilm li'l-Malāyīn, 1970-74).

Translations by the Author

Kahlil Gibran: A Biography (New York: Philosophical Library, 1950); translation of Naimy's own Jubrān biography (1934);

al-Nabī (Beirut: Mu'assasat Nawfal, 1956); Arabic translation of Jubrān Khalīl Jubrān's *The Prophet*;

Memoirs of a Vagrant Soul: or, The Pitted Face (New York: Philosophical Library, 1952); translation of Naimy's own *Mudhakkirāt al-Arqash* (1949);

"The Oasis of Peace," *The Aryan Path* 24.1 (January 1953): 3-7; translation of *Wāhat al-salām*", *al-Bayādir* (1945): 179-186;

Till We Meet ... and Twelve Other Stories (Banglore: Indian Institute of World Culture,

1957); translation of *Liqā'* and other stories.

Works in Translation

A New Year: Stories, Autobiography and Poems, selected and translated by J.R. Perry (Leiden: Brill, 1974); Journal of Arabic Literature Arabic Translation Series, vol. 3; includes several brief excerpts from Naimy's autobiography, eight poems and nine short stories;

Gregory J. Bell, *Theosophy, Romanticism and Love in the Poetry of Mikhail Naimy*, Ph.D. Dissertation, University of Pennsylvania, 2001 (UMI no. 3031639); contains translations of all of Naimy's original Arabic poetry;

(Translations of some of Naimy's poems are available in a number of anthologies, including the following:)

Gregory Orfalea and Sharif Elmusa (eds.), *Grape Leaves: A Century of Arab-American Poetry* (New York: Interlink Books, 2000);

Salma Khadra Jayyusi (ed.), *Modern Arabic Poetry: An Anthology* (New York: Columbia University Press, 1987);

Mounah A. Khouri and Hamid Algar (eds. and transl.), *An Anthology of Modern Arabic Poetry* (Berkeley: University of California Press, 1974).

Mīkhā'īl Nu'aymah's (Mikhail Naimy's) literary career spanned more than six decades and his impact on modern Arabic literature as a critic, poet and writer can still be seen today. Naimy's earliest works were critical articles calling for a rejuvenation of Arabic literature. Equally important were the poetry and prose he wrote while living in the United States between 1911 and 1932, where he was a central figure in the Arab émigré literary association, The Pen League. Naimy's early writing helped usher into Arabic letters a period of Romanticism in poetry and maturity in the short story.

After returning to Lebanon in 1932, Naimy embarked upon a simple life of contemplation and writing. He largely abandoned poetry for prose and his output focused increasingly on spiritual concerns influenced by his marked religious eclecticism and his familiarity with modern Theosophical thought. Naimy's œuvre encompasses nearly every modern genre, including poetry, drama, the short story, the novel, the essay, biography, autobiography and spiritual reflections. The range, volume and influence of Naimy's writing make him one of the most significant figures in modern Arabic literature.

Mikhail Naimy was born in the autumn of 1889 in the village of Baskinta, at the foot of Mount Sannin in Lebanon. The day of his birth was not recorded, but based on a dream, Naimy claimed that he was born on October 17th. Baskinta was an agricultural community of about 2,000 Maronite and Orthodox Christians and Naimy's family farmed a small piece of land near the village called al-Shakhrūb. Poverty in the region led thousands of Lebanese to emigrate in search of work during the latter part of the 19th century and, when Naimy was only ten months old, his father joined this exodus. As a result, Naimy's mother played a prominent role in his early life. She saw that Naimy was educated in the local two-room primary school and later in a new Russian Orthodox school built in Baskinta. Naimy excelled in his studies and in 1902 was chosen to be sent to the Russian Teachers' College in Nazareth to train for a post in one of the Russian Imperial Orthodox Society's regional schools. The Teacher's College exposed Naimy to a broad curriculum, including courses in both Arabic and Russian literature, which fed his growing interest in poetry and prose. Naimy finished at the top of his class and was awarded a full stipend to continue his education at a Russian Orthodox seminary in Poltava, Ukraine.

Naimy arrived in Poltava in the fall of 1906 and tackled the seminary curriculum with the same energy and success he had displayed in Nazareth. Apart from his studies, which included courses in theology, Russian and Arabic, life outside the classroom had a great influence on Naimy. Russian art, music and literature stirred his creative impulses and the political and social activism of his classmates, coupled with the inequities Naimy saw in Russian society, made him aware of the problems of modern Western civilization. Naimy made new friendships in Poltava, one of which led to a relationship with an unhappily married woman named

Varya, the sister of one of his classmates. Their fraught relationship continued for two years until Naimy left the Ukraine and Varya was forced to return to her husband.

Naimy's spiritual life also developed in Poltava. He grew more introspective and his faith more personalized and, ironically for a seminarian, he began to draw away from Church doctrine. Naimy was encouraged in his spiritual independence by his reading of Gorky and Tolstoy, whom he saw criticizing the Church for obscuring rather than professing the truth of Christianity. Naimy maintained his belief in the divinity of Christ and the importance of the Gospels, while at the same time beginning to develop a more mystical approach to God that would continue throughout his life.

Naimy read widely in Russian literature in Poltava and was impressed by writers such as Lermontov, Gogol, Pushkin, Turgenev and Chekhov, though none affected him as deeply as Tolstoy, whom he adopted as a teacher and spiritual guide. It was at this time that Naimy began to envision a literary life for himself and to develop specific ideas about writing. He made his first literary efforts in Russian with poems admired by his classmates and teachers. One of these poems, "The Frozen River," would later become Naimy's first published poem when he translated it into Arabic in 1917. While immersing himself in Russian, Naimy was also able to follow contemporary Arabic letters through journals such as the Egyptian periodical *al-Hilāl*, available to him in Poltava. Inevitably, Naimy compared Arabic and Russian literature and judged the literature of his homeland to be lagging far behind. This disparity did not lead him to despair, but spurred his ambition to bring about a renewal of Arab literature.

During Naimy's fourth year at the Poltava seminary, the students staged a strike over infringements on their freedoms and Naimy reluctantly served as the students' spokesman. As a punishment, he was not readmitted to classes and instead had to spend the year studying on his own in preparation for his fourth-year examinations. Naimy passed the examinations, was awarded a degree, and returned to Baskinta in May of 1911.

Once back in Lebanon, Naimy was able to arrange a stipend through the Church that allowed him to continue his education. At the same time, Naimy's older brother Adīb, who had been living in Walla Walla, Washington, returned to Lebanon for a visit and convinced Naimy to return with him to the United States and apply to the University of Washington in Seattle. Naimy thus set out with Adīb for the New World in the fall of 1911.

He began learning English in Washington and was soon admitted to a combined bachelor of law and arts program at the University of Washington. Although not entirely enthusiastic about university life in the United States, he did well in his studies and continued to expand his literary horizons, now adding English literature to his repertoire.

During the spring of Naimy's second year of college, he received the inaugural issue of *al-Funūn*, an Arabic literary journal published in New York City and co-edited by one of his friends, Nasīb 'Arīdah. Its aims were revolutionary and in complete harmony with Naimy's own. It published new Arabic writing, translations of Western literature and articles which introduced Arab readers to the riches of Western literature. Signaling its radical departure from the monorhymed, monometric neoclassical poetry of the time, the opening piece of the first issue was a prose poem by Jubrān Khalīl **Jubrān**.

Naimy was so excited by *al-Funūn* that he wasted no time in joining its literary revolution, immediately composing what was to be the first in a long line of articles of literary criticism. That article, "Fajr al-amal ba'da layl al-ya's" (The Dawn of Hope after the Night of Despair), appeared in the fourth issue of *al-Funūn* and lamented the weakness of Arab cultural and literary life. In it, Naimy criticized contemporary Arab writers for resting on the laurels of their glorious literary past while producing derivative works. The piece concluded with a detailed review of Jubrān's *al-Ajnihah al-mutakassirah* (Broken Wings) and other works which Naimy saw as the first rays of a dawning literary sun.

Throughout the next two years, Naimy devoted whatever free time his university studies and a part-time job left him to writing and thinking about the literary revolution. He published three more articles of criticism in *al-Funūn* in 1913, and his reputation among Arab readers in both the United States and the Arab world began to grow. He also contributed poetry and fiction to *al-Funūn* and to another New York Arab publication, *al-Sā'ih*.

Naimy's early short stories are noteworthy for their realistic style and their straightforward yet highly literate Arabic. The stories focused on social issues and were part of a nascent trend among Arab writers of the period who took up the Western short story format to address social and political issues. Representative of this thematic focus was one of Naimy's best early works, "Sanatuhā al-jadīdah" (Her New Year, 1914), which addresses the pressure on families to produce sons and the crime of infanticide. In the story a father of seven daughters is presented with his eighth child, another girl. He grabs the newborn from the midwife's arms and is seen digging behind the village church as a storm rages around him. Some of Naimy's other early short stories focus on social issues not generally tackled by Arab writers of the time. "Al-'Āqir" (The Barren Woman, 1915) is the heartbreaking account of a couple's loving marriage which disintegrates when they fail to produce children; although the wife is blamed and eventually driven to suicide, it is the husband who is sterile. This story was followed by a another fictional piece of social commentary, "Mahrajān al-mawt" (Festival of Death, 1916), which centers on a woman who is forced into an unwanted marriage in order to feed her starving family amidst the plague that struck the Levant during World War I. The story concludes with a satirical swipe at the ineffectual pronouncements of a committee of émigrés in New York. These and other stories place Naimy among the pioneers of the short story in modern Arabic literature. What sets him apart is the economy of his storytelling and the unembellished language he employs. Where other Arab writers of this period sometimes obscured their plots with divergent story lines or excessive authorial intrusions, Naimy does not lose sight of his themes or unnecessarily complicate his narratives.

At the same time that he was launching his literary career, Naimy's interest in spiritual matters continued to develop. During his third year at the University of Washington, Naimy shared a room with a Scottish student who was a member of the Theosophical Society and, through him, Naimy gradually became intrigued by theosophical beliefs. Theosophy draws upon world philosophies, religions and esoteric traditions, ancient and modern, and espouses beliefs in reincarnation, the karmic balance of punishment and reward, a One-God from which all creation emanates, and a bifurcation of the soul into passionate and spiritual aspects. Naimy was particularly taken with the idea of reincarnation and states that the

doctrine of repeating [life's] *experimentation by repeating lives with the aim of complete knowledge and ideal freedom became the great pillar upon which the philosophy of my life was established.*   (*Sab'ūn*, II [1983], 49).

After graduation from college in June of 1916, Naimy undertook his first large literary project, a full-length play entitled *al-Ābā' wa'l-banūn* (*Fathers and Sons*), which was serialized in *al-Funūn* and later published as a book. *Al-Ābā' wa'l-banūn* explored generational change in early twentieth-century Lebanon by focusing on the tradition of arranged marriage, obedience to one's parents, and the role of love in marriage. In the play, a young girl is promised to an influential but morally questionable older man. The girl's older brother opposes the marriage and, after the girl nearly dies, their mother is forced to see that the match is a bad idea. In the end, the daughter marries a poor, religiously free-thinking young man, while her brother marries a young woman from a differing Christian denomination. Although Badawi (1992, 356) finds *al-Ābā' wa'l-banūn* melodramatic and unconvincing, Naimy's heavy reliance on dialogue and the play's lack of dramatic action suggest an attempt at the sort of "intellectual drama" *(al-masrah al-dhihnī)* later authored by Naimy's contemporary, Tawfīq al-**Hakīm**, in Egypt.

al-Ābā' wa'l-banūn is also notable for Naimy's use of colloquial Arabic. Naimy was fully aware of the arguments for and against the use of colloquial rather than standard literary Arabic in dialogue and recognized the particular importance of this issue to drama. His solution was to base the register of Arabic each character spoke upon their level of education: thus, the educated son in the play speaks standard Arabic, while his illiterate mother speaks in Lebanese colloquial. He abandoned this practice in his later fiction and drama.

In the fall of 1916, Naimy joined Nasīb ʿArīdah in New York City, although a job with the Bethlehem Steel Company soon entailed a move to Allentown, Pennsylvania. Before this move, Naimy translated his early poem "The Frozen River" from Russian into Arabic and submitted it to al-Funūn, which published it in the February 1917 issue. The poem shows the clear influence of Western Romanticism and is a departure from traditional Arabic poetry (see the discussion of Naimy's poetry below).

About this time, Naimy composed several other poems of social and political commentary. The most famous of these was "Akhī" (My Brother), which was published in al-Funūn and reprinted in journals in the Arab world. The poem vividly describes the terrible suffering in Naimy's homeland and draws a stark contrast between his countrymen's fate and that of Western warriors who will exalt when the Great War finally ends. Rather than exalt, Naimy asks his countrymen to "kneel in silence as I do with a humble, bloodied heart / so that we may weep over the fate of our dead." The poem closes with self-condemnation:

The world smells rotten because of us, just as it stinks from our dead. / So, bring the spade and follow me so we may dig another ditch / in which to bury our living...

(*Hams al-Jufūn*, 1988, 14-15)

Naimy began writing his first novel, *Mudhakkirāt al-arqash* (The Memoirs of Scarface), while living in Allentown in 1917. World War I postponed the novel's completion until 1949, but the first few chapters were serialized in *al-Funūn*. The novel provides an early example of the sort of spiritual concerns that Naimy would focus on throughout the rest of his life. The story's anti-hero, al-Arqash, is a taciturn loner with a pock-marked face who has disappeared

from his job as a waiter in a small New York coffee shop. The novel's narrator procures al-Arqash's diary which is full of his spiritual and philosophical musings and hints at a terrible secret in his past, which is finally revealed to be his brutal murder of his bride on their wedding night. Naimy uses the character of al-Arqash to give voice to a number of spiritual beliefs, including reincarnation (al-Arqash describes death as "shed[ding] this garment and put[ting] on another", *Arqash*, 1998, 17), the importance of fate or karmic allotment, and the tension between the soul's higher and lower aspects.

While Naimy was working on *Mudhakkirāt al-Arqash*, the United States entered World War I and, although opposed to war and not a United States citizen, Naimy followed his "law-abiding nature" and registered for the draft. He was called up on May 25, 1918 and sent to North Carolina for a month of basic training before sailing for France; by mid-October 1918, he was performing reconnaissance near the front lines. Fortunately, the armistice was only two weeks away and Naimy survived his short war experience without physical injury. While awaiting return to the United States, Naimy enrolled in university classes in Rennes, France, where he studied French history, literature, art and law.

Naimy returned from France to Walla Walla, but within several months moved back to New York City where he rented a room and found employment in a trading company. The room Naimy rented was in the Manhattan home of an unhappily married American man and wife and, in striking similarity to his relationship with Varya in Poltava, Naimy soon became romantically involved with his landlady. Their relationship lasted five years and Naimy claims that it was the inspiration for a number of his poems which explore the struggle between the intellect and the heart.

Once back in New York, Naimy rejoined the literary circle of Syrian and Lebanese Christian Arabs that had formed around *al-Funūn*. On April 20, 1920, this group formally established one of the most famous literary associations in modern Arabic letters, the Pen League (al-Rābitah al-Qalamiyyah), although, as Nadeem Naimy (1967, 121) notes, a previous attempt to form the Pen League had been made in 1916, as is evident from the appearance of the association's name in early issues of *al-Funūn*; however, the name had quickly disappeared until its revival in 1920. The League committed itself to forging a new Arabic literature freed of neoclassical norms and built upon Western literary models. In addition to Naimy, the association's founding members included the poets and writers Nasīb 'Arīdah, Jubrān Khalīl **Jubrān**, Īliyyā **Abū Mādī**, 'Abd al-Masīh Haddād, Rashīd Ayyūb, Nadrah Haddād, and three Arab businessmen Wilyim Kātsflīs, Wadī' Bāhūt, and Ilyās 'Atā Allāh.

The group chose Jubrān as its leader and Naimy as its secretary. Naimy was assigned the task of drafting the association's constitution, the preamble of which he used to describe the Pen League's vision of a modern Arabic literature. Naimy states that true literature must draw its inspiration from the world in which it lives and that a good writer must be able to express the impact of that world upon his or her soul. He calls the effort to confine Arabic literature to classical traditions "a worm eating away at the body of our literature and language." The Pen League, he asserts, sought to propel Arabic literature from tradition and stagnation to innovation and renewed life.

In the summer of 1923, one of the most important events in Naimy's literary career took place when many of his early critical articles were published in Cairo in a volume entitled *al-Ghirbāl* (The Sieve). Significantly the introduction was written by 'Abbās Mahmūd al-'Aqqād, who, along with 'Abd al-Rahmān **Shukrī** and Ibrāhīm al-**Māzinī** (together known as the *Dīwān* Group), was engaged in a parallel but independent attack on Arabic literary traditionalism in Egypt. *Al-Ghirbāl* presents arguably the most articulate and consistent of the Arab voices calling for literary change in the early part of the 20th century. In the book, Naimy argues that Arab writers of his age were simply mocking a classical tradition that, however glorious, no longer spoke to the contemporary age. In particular, Naimy criticizes the dominant neoclassical poetry of the era written by such towering figures as Ahmad **Shawqī** and Hāfiz

Ibrāhīm, which employed traditional Arabic literary models to address contemporary topics. Naimy derides this sort of imitation and writers who allow themselves to be bound by traditional language, themes, forms and rules rather than shaping these to serve their literary purposes.

The view of literature expressed in *al-Ghirbāl* is a Romantic one centered on the individual. Naimy argues that man is the "pivot" around which all art and philosophy must rotate and that an individual's search for the self should be the motivation behind all art. For Naimy, a true writer is one who is awake to the emotions and ideas within all humans, and who then awakens others to these emotions. He famously defines the poet as "a prophet, philosopher, molder, musician and soothsayer." Not surprisingly, the models which Naimy recommends to Arab writers are primarily Western ones. In a piece entitled "Fal-nutarjim!" (Let's Translate!), Naimy compares the Arab world to a thirsty man who must turn to his richer neighbor (the West) for water, here representing translated Western literature.

Unlike many Arab poets of his day, Naimy was able to successfully apply the vision he set forth in *al-Ghirbāl* to his own verse. Naimy's most productive years as a poet coincided with his 1920-1932 membership in the Pen League, although his poems were not collected in book form until the publication of *Hams al-Jufūn* (The Whispering of Eyelids) in 1943. The collection omits a few of Naimy's early poems, but it does contain Naimy's own Arabic translations of fourteen poems he wrote in English. Several of these poems were published in American newspapers, including the *New York Times*. In addition, the collection is noteworthy for including a number of illustrations by Naimy and one by Jubrān. The poetry in *Hams al-jufūn* reflects Naimy's Romantic understanding. The poems are lyrics that explore the poet's innermost thoughts and the imagery draws heavily upon nature. The form of his poetry follows the Western models he so admired: rather than traditional monoryhme, Naimy generally relies on metered lines of varying lengths set in stanzas employing a variety of rhyme schemes. The language of his poetry is delightfully uncluttered; nowhere does one find the recherché vocabulary or linguistic games of some of the poetry that preceded him, nor does Naimy draw upon classical language, imagery or themes that bear no relation to his age. His use of imagery can be delightful, as when the poet addresses a frozen, seemingly dead river:

Here around you are the willows, leafless and no
longer beautiful,
Sadly genuflecting each time the north wind
passes through them;
The white poplar mourning over you, spreading
its branches
With no goldfinch to flit about in them and ring
out with its song.

Despite this desolation, the poet is able to envision a springtime thaw when,

The full moon will spread over you a silver veil
from its night-sky,
And the sun will cover your naked shoulders
with flowers.

As in his later prose, Naimy used his verse to explore spiritual issues. In his poems, he grapples with existential issues and, in particular, with the tension between human passions and loftier aims. As noted, Naimy states that a number of his poems were inspired by the relationship he had with his landlady in New York and the conflict this aroused is evident in poems such as "Afāq al-qalb" (The Heart Awakened) and "Yā rafīqī" (O Companion), where the poet expresses his surprise at being stirred from his spiritual contemplation by earthly love. In one of his latest poems, "Ilā M. D. B." (To M. D. B.), Naimy moves beyond the torment of his passions and argues that a companion for his heart is necessary. He ends that poem with a bold statement to his beloved and the world:

So give me your hand, and take mine
in comfort and hardship,
and say to those who are ignorant,
"Together we were from eternity,
together we shall remain forever!"

After struggling with his passions and with questions about God, existence, and the soul's ultimate aim, Naimy's later poems display a quiet spiritual contentment. "Al-Tuma'nīnah" ("Tranquility"), for example, plays on the New Testament parable of the man who builds his house on rock to proclaim this contentment:

The roof of my house is iron, its foundation
stone.
So rage O winds, and wail O trees
and float O clouds, and pour with rain
and roar O thunders, I do not fear any danger.
...
I am not afraid of torment, I am not afraid of
injury.
Fate is my ally and Destiny is my companion!

By the late 1920s, Naimy longed to leave the hectic life of New York for his beloved Lebanese village. He felt that the literary revolution to which he had dedicated so many years in America had by now largely succeeded and its struggle had been transplanted to the Arab world where it would continue. Thus, on April 19, 1932, Naimy boarded a steamship bound for Lebanon. Unlike many immigrants, Naimy was not disappointed to return home without riches from the New World; he had already decided that his life in Lebanon would be one of simplicity and contemplation of life's great mysteries. He arrived in Beirut on May 9, 1932 and was soon reunited with his family in Baskinta.

The homecoming of such an eminent literary figure was celebrated at gatherings in Baskinta and throughout the Levant, where Naimy was invited to speak. Many of these speeches were later published in a volume entitled *Zād al-ma'ād* (Provisions for the Hereafter, 1936). Most of the pieces in *Zād al-ma'ād* are sermon-like addresses which touch on topics that would appear again and again in Naimy's subsequent writing, such as the spiritual poverty of materialism compared to the virtues of honest labor, the beauty of nature, the unity of all creation, the importance of overcoming the soul's worldly passions, the goal of achieving knowledge of one's soul and the divinity within it through repeated lifetimes, and the unerring role of karmic justice.

In keeping with the philosophy outlined in these essays, Naimy worked on his family's farm and, when not working, would retreat to a small hut to think and write. The many visitors who came to see him were often surprised to find the famous writer tending cattle or working in the fields. One journalist who visited Naimy in 1932 dubbed him the "Hermit of al-Shakhrūb," a nickname that became so widespread Naimy was asked to write an article explaining his withdrawal from society. In the article (included in *Sawt al-'ālam*, see below), Naimy says that, far from rejecting his fellow man, his home and heart remained open to visitors. However he felt he needed to quiet his mind when he returned from the United States and where better to do so than in the beauty and solitude of his Lebanese home? As for his indifference to politics, money and everyday concerns, Naimy simply had different goals for his life than most people.

However ascetic and independent Naimy's life had become (he had by this time decided not to marry), he and his family did need money. Occasional legal work and translating earned him little and, although for several years he managed the Baskinta primary school, he did so without pay. To support himself and his family, the author turned to his pen, gathering several articles that had not been included in *al-Ghirbāl* and publishing them in a slim volume entitled *al-Marāhil: siyāhāt fī zawāhir al-hayāt wa-bawātinihā* (Stages: Travels among Life's Outward and Inner Signs, 1933), a book he was forced to publish and market himself, but which eventually earned a profit. Perhaps the most interesting article in *al-Marāhil* is "Thalāthat wujūh" (Three Faces), which is a discussion of the Buddha, Lao-tse and Jesus, whom Naimy describes as

Three lighthouses on the shore of existence. Their light deriving from one source. And illuminating one path to a single harbor... Let your shining faces be my refuge from the faces of men, and my escape from the caves of delusion, and my guide to the face of truth.

(*al-Marāhil*, 1982, 54)

Working in a grotto near his family farm (a spot commemorated today by a statue of the author), Naimy next wrote his controversial biography, *Jubrān Khalīl Jubrān: hayātuh, maw-*

tuh, adabuh, fannuh (Khalil Gibran: His Life, Death, Literature and Art, 1934). While some praised the book, others criticized Naimy for revealing too much personal information about Jubrān, particularly concerning his relationships with women. Some also questioned the accuracy of parts of the book. In response, Naimy explained that the book was never intended to be a research work or historical biography, but an artistic portrait of a friend who shared Naimy's love of literature and many of his spiritual beliefs. Naimy wrote the book in part to counter the mythical figure Jubrān was already becoming only a few years after his death. Thus, Naimy does not hesitate to describe some of the less attractive sides of Jubrān's character, just as he praises his better qualities, and includes candid and often critical evaluations of a number of Jubrān's works.

1937 saw the publication of perhaps Naimy's best known collection of short stories, *Kāna mā kān* (Once Upon a Time). All of the stories in this volume had been written while Naimy lived in the United States, including "Sanatuhā al-jadīdah" and "al-'Āqir," mentioned above. Another of the stories, "Shūrtī" (Shorty), drew upon Naimy's war experiences to tell the tale of a soldier who is hospitalized with a venereal disease and who dictates a farewell letter to his beloved before forcing his own sentries to shoot him down. The lead story in *Kāna mā kān*, "Sā'at al-kūkū" ("The Cuckoo Clock"), elaborates one of Naimy's favorite themes, that of a materialistic and spiritually dead West versus a more spiritual East. In the story, a young Lebanese man's fiancée runs off with a man who had recently returned from America and who had brought back, among other wonders, a cuckoo clock, which enchants the young woman. The jilted young man blames his tragedy on his ignorance and backwardness and soon himself emigrates to America where he succeeds in business, but fails to find spiritual contentment. Recognizing the contrast between the peaceful, natural life he had been leading in Lebanon and the "civilized" one that had fallen apart around him, the hero returns to Lebanon where he teaches those he meets to value their honest lives and to shun the artificial lures of modern civilization.

World War II brought both hardships and new opportunities for Naimy. During the war, the French established a radio station in Beirut and Naimy was paid to deliver monthly radio addresses. These talks continued after the war ended and were supplemented by public appearances in Lebanon and other Arab countries. The 1940s also saw the rise of a publishing industry in Lebanon and the Arab world, which provided new outlets for Naimy's writing.

Many of the radio addresses and talks Naimy had given during the war were published in 1945 under the title *al-Bayādir 1940-1944* (Threshing Floors 1940-1944). These essays developed many of the major themes of Naimy's thought, such as the veneration of nature, the unity of all creation and the importance of striving to overcome the limitations of one's senses and the lure of one's passions. Several of the talks focus on Naimy's antipathy toward greed and materialism and contrast Western "sight" with Eastern "insight," i.e., the West's material wealth with the spiritual wealth of the East. Other familiar themes also occur, including Naimy's belief in reincarnation and karmic justice; his recognition of many possible paths to God; his disappointment with organized religion's failure to encourage spiritual growth; his belief in God as the source of all, and the divine essence within every human soul. Given the fact that these addresses were delivered during the war, it is not surprising that Naimy derides warfare, nationalism and military industrialization; however, his concern is not with war *per se*, but rather with the greater spiritual war he encourages his listeners and readers to undertake.

In the years immediately following the war, Naimy published three more non-fiction collections: *Karm 'alā darb* (Vineyard by a Path), *al-Awthān* (The Idols) and *Sawt al-'ālam* (Voice of the World). *Karm 'alā darb* is a collection of thoughts, aphorisms and a few vignettes offering observations on topics such as life and death ("Do you fear death? Then how can you put your trust in life?"), human nature ("The innocent's heart is in his eyes"), spiritual growth ("The doors to knowledge are innumerable; as for the key, there is but one") and nature ("The earth's poetry is its trees"). *Al-Awthān* was yet another critique of modern materialism. The idols Naimy identifies in the book are money, power, political authority, public opinion, nationalism, the printed word and science. He argues that the worship of these idols, particularly money, goes on side by side with the worship of God and that human beings cannot serve two masters. Unfortunately, the idols have become ends for most people rather than means which they should be using to achieve more important spiritual goals. The essays in *Sawt al-'ālam* likewise focus primarily upon spiritual matters and what Naimy sees as the crisis of modern life. Naimy again argues that modern, particularly Western, civilization, despite its technological and material progress, has failed to bring its goals in line with those of the universe because it ignores the imagination and spiritual understanding so important to Eastern cultures.

Naimy returned to fiction in 1946 with the publication of the short novel *Liqā'* (A Reunion). *Liqā'* tells the story of a musician whose masterful violin playing enchants a young woman, sending her into a trance-like swoon from which she cannot be awakened. During the course of the novel, the musician reveals that he is the reincarnation of a shepherd whose reed long ago enchanted another young girl and that his beloved is the reincarnation of that girl. Thus, the two are destined to be lovers in this life because of their relationship in a previous one. The story ends as the musician revives the girl with his playing; however, just as she recovers, both collapse and join one another in death as the last notes of his violin fade.

Naimy next embarked on the book that he has described as the pinnacle of his thought and a summary of his view of life, *The Book of Mirdad: A Lighthouse and a Haven* (1948), a work that was followed by translations into English by Naimy of several of his earlier works, including the biography of Jubrān (1950), *Mudhakkirāt al-Arqash* (1952), and *Liqā'* and a dozen of his short stories (1952). Naimy also translated Jubrān's famous English novel *The Prophet* into Arabic in 1956. Naimy decided to write *The Book of Mirdad* in English in order to reach as wide an audience as possible. His aim in *Mirdad* is startlingly ambitious: as one reviewer noted, the work presents nothing less than "a new scripture for humanity." *Mirdad* opens with a narrator who has been captivated by the legend surrounding a ruined monastery, which sits atop a local mountain. The monastery was allegedly built by one of Noah's sons and, over many generations, grew wealthy and its abbot greedy. A stranger named Mirdad joined the monastery, won the monks' allegiance away from their abbot and convinced them to disburse their wealth and abandon the monastery. Mirdad struck the greedy senior monk dumb and cursed him to wander the grounds of the monastery.

The narrator makes an arduous and harrowing climb up the flint-covered mountain leading to the monastery, where he eventually meets the cursed senior abbot, whose tongue is freed upon his arrival. The abbot enjoins the narrator to publish to the world the *Book of Mirdad*, which is the story of the years following Mirdad's arrival at the monastery. The second and much longer part of Naimy's novel, then, is this *Book of Mirdad*, which is composed of thirty-seven short chapters that impart Mirdad's lessons. Not surprisingly, these lessons reflect Naimy's worldview. Thus, Mirdad preaches the unity of creation, endorses the concept of reincarnation, subscribes to a dualistic view of the human soul, with a "transient" and "abiding" self, and decries the allure of worldly desires and humans' attachment to their "coarse and inadequate senses." The book ends with Mirdad's call to humankind:

> Let those who would break their moorings from
>   the Earth; and those who would be unified;
>   and those who yearn to overcome them-
>   selves—let them come aboard.
> The Ark is ready.
> The wind is favouring.
> The sea is calm.
> So taught I Noah.
> So I teach you.   (*Mirdad*, 2002, 184-185)

Clearly a book like Mirdad is not to every reader's taste. Indeed, the book was originally turned down by a British publisher before Naimy found a publisher in Beirut. Once in print, however, *Mirdad* was well received in many parts of the world and was translated into

many languages. It continues to find an audience and has been reprinted in English several times, most recently in 2002. It was also adapted for the stage in Bombay in 1973.

The decade of the 1950s saw the rise of literary "commitment" among Arab writers who viewed literature as a tool of social and political change. Naimy's own commitment, however, remained to more transcendent concerns, sometimes making him seem "a strange voice coming from another world" (see Jayyusi 1977, 116-117). He published three collections of articles in the first half of the decade, viz., *al-Nūr wa'l-dayjūr* (*Light and Darkness*, 1950), *Fī mahabb al-rīh* (Storm-swept, 1953), and 1954's *Durūb* (Paths). Most of the pieces in these collections are short essays and addresses, some of which, "Difā' 'an al-zulmah" (In Defense of Darkness) in *Durūb* for example, are reminiscent of traditional Arabic epistolary art *(risālah)*. Although Naimy touches on a wide variety of themes in these articles, almost all return to the central theme of the necessity for human beings to come to understand themselves, overcome the animal passions within them, and grasp the divine that lies in every soul. Thus, while Naimy discusses contemporary issues such as the war, colonialism, education or literature, he generally uses these as platforms for larger spiritual messages. Naimy offers some loving descriptions of nature and his Lebanese home, but does not hesitate to criticize Arab society, arguing for greater intellectual freedom and the need for Arab self-reform. Despite the many problems Naimy discusses in these essays, a quiet optimism runs through them, based on his deep belief that human life has a purpose and divine end and that human development will continue to that end, however long it may take.

Naimy returned to fiction with another collection of short stories in 1956, entitled *Akābir* (VIPs). These stories again demonstrated his ability to craft interesting plots and capture a telling moment in an economical, clear and direct style of Arabic. Several of the stories in *Akābir* focus on Lebanese village life and on the poor. The title story, for instance, is the tale of a poor family which must contend with the visit of their rich landlord. Although the story is a bit melodramatic—the peasants are forced to give their son's favorite animals to the landlord—it does offer insight into the difficulty of peasant life. Naimy does not portray all villagers as innocent victims: another story in the collection, "Masraʿ Sattūt" (The Death of Sattut), for example, focuses on a malicious village gossip.

In August of 1956, Naimy was invited to the USSR by a Soviet writers' union. His journey was the impetus for a fascinating travelogue, *Abʿad min Mūskū wa-min Wāshintun* (Beyond Moscow and Washington), which recounts Naimy's first return to now-communist Russia since his days in Poltava. Naimy is less concerned in the book with the particulars of Soviet communism than he is with the more universal elements of the worldwide contention between communism and capitalism. He champions neither system, arguing that a proper world order would be one that helps lead all the world's peoples to true freedom through self- and spiritual knowledge. Naimy's trip to the USSR was followed by many other trips abroad, including lecture tours in Egypt, Kuwait, Tunisia and Iraq in the 1950s and 60s. He also returned to Moscow in 1962 to attend an international peace conference and traveled to India in 1965.

Naimy followed *Akābir* with another collection of short stories in 1958, titled *Abū Battah* (*The Big-Calfed Man*). Its stories are peopled with a variety of everyday characters caught in unusual circumstances, such as a musician whose dream seems to explain a mysterious accident or a young man whose patience is tested by a craftsman who trims his nails rather than complete a job. Perhaps the most engaging story in *Abū Battah* is "al-Bankārūliyā" (The Baccalaureate), which tells the tale of a man whose wife forces him to sell his herd of goats to pay for their son's college education. Despite earning his degree and emigrating, the son never finds work and ultimately writes to his father asking for money to return home; the father sends back everything that the "bankārūliyā" has left him, some strands of goat's hair and bits of dung.

Naimy celebrated his seventieth birthday in October of 1959 and began work on what may well be the most fascinating story he ever authored, that of his own life. His autobiography, *Sabʿūn... Hikāyat 'umr* (Seventy... the Story of a Life) was published in three volumes between 1959 and 1960 and is an absorbing account of Naimy's remarkable life. Alongside autobiographies by writers such as Tāhā **Husayn** and Salāma Mūsā, *Sabʿūn* was an influential contribution to the development of the modern Arab autobiography. It is moreover an invaluable document of modern Arabic literary history. The nearly 900-page work provides a wealth of information about Naimy's life in Lebanon, the Ukraine, the United States and even as a soldier in France. In addition to his many discussions of literature and culture, Naimy devotes a great many pages to his philosophy of life and spiritual questions. *Sabʿūn* is surprisingly frank and can be very serious, but there are also passages of humor and self-deprecation. As in his fiction, Naimy's eye for important detail is quite keen, which makes those aspects of his life he chooses to share with his reader all the more engaging.

In 1963, Naimy published one of his most compelling attempts to explain his philosophy of life in novel form, *al-Yawm al-akhīr* (The Last Day). *Al-Yawm al-akhīr* plays on the uncanny and fantastic throughout, beginning when the hero, Mūsā al-ʿAskarī, is awakened at midnight by a mysterious voice commanding him to "Arise and bid farewell to your last day!" The novel is composed of twenty-four chapters, each covering one hour of Mūsā's final day. Naimy fills these hours with a remarkable series of events that provide opportunities for Mūsā to muse upon the meaning of life and many of the spiritual issues familiar to readers of Naimy's writings. The story's strange events lend *al-Yawm al-akhīr* an interest and forward momentum that balance the hero's philosophical musings. The novel ends with Mūsā al-ʿAskarī awakening to bid farewell to the "old Mūsā al-ʿAskarī" and welcome the first day of life for a new Mūsā al-ʿAskarī.

Naimy next published *Hawāmish* (Marginalia, 1965), a work primarily composed of short vignettes in which ordinary characters are captured in telling moments. A school teacher's pride, for example, is dented when he is not accorded the title he feels he deserves, a variety of characters pray and find their prayers answered in unexpected ways, or a woman is mortified when she discovers she has worn mismatched stockings to her first high-society party. In these pieces, Naimy has honed his storytelling to bare essentials and yet is able to say a great deal: as Nadeem Naimy (1985, 101) observes, in *Hawāmish* "things normally deemed marginal in life are discovered, when seen in their cosmic setting, to be universally symbolic."

Naimy returned to drama in the late 1960s with two new intellectual plays. 1967's *Ayyūb* (Job) adapts the Old Testament story of Job and focuses on the conflict between Job and God. The play is short on dramatic peaks, but is engagingly written in Naimy's usual fluid style. Naimy uses his characters to explore some of his favorite themes: Job's patience, for example, becomes a model for acceptance of the good and bad fate doled out by an impartial universe; Naimy likewise has Job engage in several Socratic-like dialogues with a weaver, whose drawing together strands of wool on his loom symbolizes the unity and interconnectedness of the universe.

Another dramatic piece, *Yā Ibn Ādam: hiwār bayna rajulayn* (O Mankind: A Dialogue between Two Men) followed in 1969. The events of the play take place in a hut in the woods where the inventor of a powerful weapon has been hiding, leading a hermit-like existence. A reporter chances upon the hut and engages the inventor in a long conversation, during which the inventor relates a mystical experience through which he came to an understanding of life and the crime against life he had perpetrated with his invention. The inventor also elaborates on the shortcomings of science, with its limitation to the material world, and on the spiritual basis of life, which some day even scientists will recognize. By the play's end, the reporter is ready to follow his interlocutor's ascetic example, but a search party arrives under orders to take both men into custody.

Naimy read literature from around the world and wrote reviews and critical articles throughout his life. Many of these pieces were collected in *Fī 'l-ghirbāl al-jadīd* (In the New Sieve,

1971), a book whose title recalls his earlier critical collection, *al-Ghirbāl. Fī 'l-ghirbāl al-jadīd* contains short literary biographies, reviews, criticism, introductions Naimy wrote for other works, and correspondence with a variety of Arab writers. Not surprisingly, the first piece in the book is about Naimy's spiritual and literary guide, Tolstoy, written on the fiftieth anniversary of the Russian's death. Other non-Arab writers Naimy treats include Nietzsche, Rabinath Tagore, Walt Whitman, Pushkin, Gorky and Emerson; Arab literary subjects include Ilyās Abū Shabakah, Khalīl **Mutrān**, Īliyyā **Abū Māḍī**, and many others.

As Naimy neared the end of his life, his writings concentrated ever more on considerations of the Divine. At the age of 83 he composed a series of poetic meditations addressed to God on the wonders of creation in a book titled *Najwā 'l-ghurūb* (Sunset Soliloquy, 1974). Here, Naimy celebrates the greatness of God and expresses awe for the world around him and for the most miraculous element of that world, humankind. The meditations are expressed in beautiful language and build upon one another as the book proceeds. Once again arguing that full knowledge of the wonder of creation cannot be achieved in a single lifetime, Naimy asserts that people should welcome death as but a transition from one life to another on a long journey back to union with God.

Naimy next published a book of reflections on the life and meaning of Jesus, entitled *Min wahy al-masīḥ* (Inspired by the Messiah, 1974). The book contains accounts of Christ's mission that reflect Naimy's sometimes unorthodox interpretations. Naimy questions, for example, the doctrine of the virgin birth and he finds in the Gospel story of Jesus and the man who had been blind since birth an allusion to reincarnation, an argument he had earlier addressed in his novel *al-Yawm al-akhīr*.

Naimy's last published work was 1977's *Wamaḍāt: shudhūr wa-amthāl* (Sparks: Fragments and Proverbs). Like *Karm 'alā darb*, *Wamaḍāt* is a collection of aphorisms ranging from the simple to the profound and exemplifying many of the tenets of Naimy's thought. One finds among these sayings those extolling humility, the importance of perceiving with the heart and spirit, the dignity of honest poverty, and an antipathy to greed, materialism and superficial religious faith. Also evident in many of these sayings are notions of karma, the importance of freeing oneself from the material entrapments of the world if one is to come to know God, the unity of all being and reincarnation.

Naimy's immense contributions to Arabic and world literature were recognized many times late in his life. He was awarded the Lebanese Presidential Prize for literature in 1961 and in 1969 received an honorary doctorate from the University of Washington. In April of 1978, an international festival was held in Beirut celebrating Naimy's 90th birthday, for which a documentary film was produced, commemorative postage stamps issued, special music composed, a play staged and a commemorative book published. Naimy was also awarded the Insignia of the Knights of Cilicia in 1980 and in 1984 received UNESCO's Baghdad Prize for literature. He is also reported to have been nominated for the Nobel Prize in literature.

Mikhail Naimy died in Beirut on Sunday, February 28, 1988 after developing pneumonia. He was 98 years old. During his long life, Naimy had become a truly international literary figure. He is regarded today as one of the pioneers of modern Arabic letters and his influence lives on through his many writings, which remain in print, and through new generations of readers in Lebanon and throughout the Arab world.

REFERENCES

Ihsān 'Abbās and Muhammad Yūsuf Najm, *al-Shi'r al-'arabī fī 'l-mahjar*, 2nd ed. (Beirut: Dār Sādir, 1967);

Muhammad 'Abdul-Hai, *Tradition and English and American Influence in Arabic Romantic Poetry: A Study in Comparative Literature*, St. Anthony's Middle East Monographs, no. 12 (Oxford: St. Anthony's College for The Middle East Centre, 1982);

Jareer Abu-Haidar, "Romanticism and Modern Arabic Literature", in: *Tradition and Mod-ernity in Arabic Language and Literature*, ed. J. R. Smart (Richmond: Curzon Press, 1996), 3-17;

Khalīl Dhiyāb Abū Jahjah, *al-Ru'yah al-kaw-niyyah fī adab Mīkhā'īl Nu'aymah* (Beirut: Ittihād al-Kuttāb, 2004);

Na''ūm Abū Jawdah, *al-Mujtama' al-mithālī fī fikr Jubrān wa-Nu'aymah* (Beirut: Dār al-Fikr al-Lubnānī, 1981);

Roger Allen, "Poetry and Poetic Criticism at the Turn of the Century", in: *Studies in Modern Arabic Literature*, ed. R. C. Ostle (England: Aris and Phillips, 1975), 1-13;

——, *The Arabic Novel: An Historical and Critical Introduction* (Syracuse: Syracuse University Press, 1982);

M. M. Badawi, *A Critical Introduction to Modern Arabic Poetry* (Cambridge: Cambridge University Press, 1975);

——, *Modern Arabic Literature and the West* (London: Ithaca Press, 1985);

——, "Arabic Drama: Early Developments", in: *Modern Arabic Literature*, ed. M. M. Badawi, Cambridge History of Arabic Literature series (Cambridge: Cambridge University Press, 1992), 329-357;

Gregory J. Bell, *Theosophy, Romanticism and Love in the Poetry of Mikhail Naimy* (Ph.D. dissertation, University of Pennsylvania, 2001, UMI no. 3031639);

Issa J. Boullata, "Mikhail Naimy: Poet of Meditative Vision", *Journal of Arabic Literature* 24.2 (July 1993): 173-184;

Mitrī Salīm Būlus, *al-Khawāriq fī riwāyāt Mīkhā'īl Nu'aymah wa-aqāsīsih*, juz' 1-2 (Lubnān: Matba'at Fu'ād Baybān, 1985, 1993);

Pierre Cachia, "Freedom from Clerical Control: The Portrayal of Men of Religion in Modern Arabic Literature", *Journal of Arabic Literature* 26.1-2 (special issue *The Quest for Freedom in Modern Arabic Literature: Essays in Honour of Mustafa Badawi*, March-June 1995): 175-185;

Raja Choueiri, *Baskinta et Neaimeh, ou La novella montagne inspirée* (Beirut: F. Beryte, 2000);

Hussein Dabbagh, *Mikhail Naimy: Some Aspects of his Thought as Revealed in his Writings*, Occasional Papers series, no. 19 (Durham:

Centre for Middle Eastern and Islamic Studies, University of Durham, 1983);

'Afīf Dimashqiyyah, *al-Infi'āliyyah wa'l-ablaghiyyah fī ba'd aqāsīs Mīkhā'īl Nu'aymah* (Beirut: Dār al-Fārābī, n.d.);

Afifa Ghaith Ghaith, *La Pensée religieuse chez Ğubrân Ḫalīl Ğubrân et Miḫā'īl Nu'aymah*, Orientalia Lovaniensia Analecta series, no. 35 (Leuven: Peeters Press, 1990);

Sabry Hafez, "The Modern Arabic Short Story", in: *Modern Arabic Literature*, ed. M. M. Badawi, Cambridge History of Arabic Literature series (Cambridge: Cambridge University Press, 1992), 270-328;

Muhammad Ibrāhīm al-Hasārī, *al-Tajribah al-wujūdiyyah fī "al-Yawm al-akhīr" li-Mīkhā'īl Nu'aymah* (Sūsa/Tunis: Dār al-Ma'ārif, 1990);

Salma Kh. Jayyusi, *Trends and Movements in Modern Arabic Poetry*, 2 vols. (Leiden: E. J. Brill. 1977);

Mounah Khouri, "Nu'ayma as Critic", chapter in her *Studies in Contemporary Arabic Poetry and Criticism* (Piedmont, California: Jahan Books, 1987), 42-52;

Nabil I. Matar, "Adam and the Serpent: Notes on the Theology of Mikhail Naimy", *Journal of Arabic Literature* 11 (1980): 56-61;

Shmuel Moreh, *Modern Arabic Poetry, 1800–1970*, Studies in Arabic Literature series of the *Journal of Arabic Literature* (Leiden: E. J. Brill, 1976);

Nadeem N. Naimy, *Mikhail Naimy: an Introduction*, Oriental series, no. 47 (Beirut: American University of Beirut, 1967);

——, *The Lebanese Prophets of New York* (Beirut: American University of Beirut, 1985);

Cornelis Nijland, *Mīkhā'īl Nu'aymah: Promotor* [sic] *of the Arabic Literary Revival* (Istanbul: Nederlands Historisch-Archaeologisch Instituut, 1975);

——, "Nu'aymah, Mikha'il (1889-1989)", in: *Encyclopedia of Arabic Literature*, ed. J. Meisami and P. Starkey, 2 vols. (London: Routledge, 1998), II, 588-589;

Bishārah al-Sab'alī, *Mīkhā'īl Nu'aymah yuhaddithunī* (Beirut: n.p., 1998);

Jūrj Saydah, *Adabunā wa-udabā'unā fī 'l-mahājir al-amīrikiyyah* (Beirut: Dār al-'Ilm li'l-Malāyīn, 1964); revised and enlarged ed.;

Muhammad Shafīq Shayyā, *Falsafat Mīkhā'īl Nu'aymah: tahlīl wa-naqd* (Beirut: Manshūrāt Bahsūn al-Thaqāfiyyah, 1979);

Tunsī Zakkā, *Bayna Nu'aymah wa-Jubrān* (Beirut: Maktabat al-Ma'ārif, 1971);

Farhat J. Ziadeh, "Mikhail Nu'ayma (Naimy)", *al-'Arabiyya* 15.1-2 (spring and autumn 1982): 5-6.

Ahmad Abū Khalīl al-Qabbānī

(1833 – 1902)

PHILIP SADGROVE
University of Manchester

WORKS

Abū Ja'far al-Mansūr ("Abū Ja'far al-Mansūr", n.p., n.d.);

al-Amīr Yahyā ("Prince Yahyā", n.p., n.d.);

Riwāyat lubāb al-gharām, aw al-Malik Mitrīdāt ("The Quintessence of Love, or King Mithridate", Cairo, 1895 and 1900-1);

al-Amīr Mahmūd, najl shāh al-'ajam ("Prince Mahmūd, Son of the Shāh of the Persians", Cairo: al-Matba'ah al-'Umūmiyyah, 1900-1);

Riwāyat 'Antar b. Shaddād ("'Antar b. Shaddād", Cairo: al-Matba'ah al-'Umūmiyyah, 1900);

Riwāyat Hārūn al-Rashīd ma'a 'l-amīr Ghānim, aw al-Sidq bi'l-najāh ("Hārūn al-Rashīd and Prince Ghānim, or Truth though Success", Cairo: al-Matba'ah al-'Umūmiyyah, 1900);

Riwāyat nākir al-jamīl ("The Ingrate", Cairo: Mansūr 'Abd al-Muta'āl al-Kutubī, 1906?);
'Afīfah wa'l-amīr 'Alī ("'Afīfa and Prince 'Alī", Cairo: Matba'at al-Najāh, 1907);
Riwāyat Hārūn al-Rashīd ma'a Uns al-Jalīs ("Hārūn al-Rashīd and Uns al-Jalīs", Cairo: n.p., 1910?);
Riwāyat nākir al-jamīl ("The Ingrate", Cairo: Matba'at al-Nīl, 194?).

Collected Works

Muhammad Yūsuf Najm (ed.), *al-Masrah al-'arabī: dirāsāt wa-nusūs, 2. al-Shaykh Ahmad Abū Khalīl al-Qabbānī* ("Arab Theatre: Studies and Texts, 2. Shaykh Ahmad Abū Khalīl al-Qabbānī", Beirut: Dār al-Thaqāfah, 1963); includes the following plays: *Riwāyat Hārūn al-Rashīd ma'a 'l-amīr Ghānim b. Ayyūb wa-Qūt al-Qulūb*; *Riwāyat Hārūn al-Rashīd ma'a Uns al-Jalīs*; *Riwāyat al-amīr Mahmūd, najl shāh al-'ajam*; *Riwāyat 'Afīfah*; *Riwāyat 'Antar bin Shaddād*; *Riwāyat lubāb al-gharām, aw al-Malik Mitrīdāt*; *Riwāyat hiyal al-nisā' al-shahīrah bi-Lūsiyā*, and *Riwāyat nākir al-jamīl*;

Nāsir al-Ansārī (ed.), *Silsilat al-mi'awiyyāt: min masrah al-shaykh Ahmad Abū Khalīl al-Qabbānī* ("The Centennial Series: From the Theatre of Shaykh Ahmad Abū Khalīl al-Qabbānī", n.p. [Cairo?], 2005); includes the same plays;

'Alī Haytham Misrī (ed.), *Muwashshahāt Ahmad Abī Khalīl al-Qabbānī* (Damascus: Dār Talās li'l-Dirāsāt wa'l-Tarjamah wa'l-Nashr, 1991).

First Stagings

Nākir al-jamīl ("The Ingrate"), Damascus, c. 1865;
al-Malik Waddāh wa-Misbāh wa-Qūt al-Arwāh ("King Waddāh, Misbāh and Qūt al-Arwāh"), Damascus, c. 1871;
Darwīsh Misbāh wa-Qūt al-Arwāh ("The Dervish Misbāh and Qūt al-Arwāh"), Damascus, 1875;
'Itr Shām wa-ward al-jinān ("The Perfume of Damascus and the Rose of Paradise"), Damascus, 1875;
Wallādah bint al-Mustakfī, aw 'Iffat al-muhibbīn

("Wallādah, Daughter of al-Mustakfī, or The Virtue of the Lovers"), Damascus, 1876;
al-Amīr Mahmūd, najl shāh al-'ajam ("Prince Mahmūd, Son of the Shāh of the Persians"), in the Damascus Theatre, 1879;
'Ā'idah ("Aida"), in the summer theatre in al-Afandī Garden, Damascus, 18??;
Nafh al-rubā ("The Breeze of the Hills"), Danube Café, Alexandria, 1884;
Hārūn al-Rashīd ma'a Uns al-Jalīs ("Hārūn al-Rashīd and Uns al-Jalīs"), Danube Café, Alexandria, 1884;
'Antar b. Shaddād, Danube Café, Alexandria, 1884;
Lubāb al-gharām, aw al-Malik Mitrīdāt ("The Quintessence of Love, or King Mithridate"), Politeama, Cairo, 1884;
Hamzah al-muhtāl ("The Cunning Hamza"), Politeama, Cairo, 1884;
'Afīfah, aw 'Āqibat al-siyānah wa-ghā'ilat al-khiyānah ("'Afīfa, or Chastity Rewarded and Perfidy Punished"), Politeama, Alexandria, 1885;
Majnūn Laylā ("Layla's Madman"), Danube Café, Alexandria, 1885;
'Abd al-Salām al-ma'rūf bi-Dīk al-Jinn ma'a zawjatihi Ward ("'Abd al-Salām Known as Cock of the Demons and His Wife Ward"), Ezbekieh Theatre, Cairo, 1885;
Jamīl wa-Jamīlah ("Jamīl and Jamīlah"), Tanta, 1886;
Hārūn al-Rashīd ma'a al-amīr Ghānim, Cairo, 1890;
Asad al-Sharā, aw Kisrā Anūshirwān ("The Lion of Sharā or Khosrow Anoushirwan"), al-Qardāhī Theatre, Alexandria, 1896;
al-Sultān Hasan ("Sultān Hasan"), al-Qardāhī Theatre, Alexandria, 1896;
Hiyal al-nisā' al-shahīrah bi-Lūsiyā ("The Trickeries of Women, Known as Lucia"), Cairo or Helwan, 1898.

Ahmad Abū Khalīl ibn Muhammad Āghā ibn Husayn Āghā Āqbīq al-Qabbānī al-Dimashqī, the Syrian playwright, director, musician, actor, singer, composer, writer, and poet, is the most important Syrian theatrical figure of the nineteenth century. His efforts led to the foundation of the modern Damascus theatre and his subsequent long sojourn in Egypt did much to firmly establish the theatrical arts in that country, nurturing the talents of many major actors, singers, writers and composers.

The Qabbānī family was of Turkish origin and came from Konya; their original family name was *Ak Bıyık*, meaning "white moustache" in Turkish. Al-Qabbānī was born and died in Damascus. The family owned a weighbridge at the al-Jābiyah Gate. He studied first at a Quranic school, then in the mosques, and then with leading scholars and writers. He learned Turkish and Persian, but knew no European language. He studied music and a popular local dance form of Andalusian origin, called *samāh*, under the guidance of his teacher and friend, Shaykh Ahmad 'Uqayl al-Halabī. He was also influenced by al-Sayyid 'Alī Habīb, who presented *samāh* dancing and *karākūz* (shadow theatre, from Turkish *Karagöz*) in Damascus cafés.

By way of precedents to his career, the first Arabic drama in the history of modern Damascus theatre was Habīb Ablā Mālatī's *al-Ahmaq al-basīt* (The Idiot Simpleton), composed some time before 1855; Mālatī states that no one in Arabic literature had preceded him. In 1860 al-Sayyid Sulaymān Sāfī is said to have performed plays in the town of Homs. The Lebanese playwright Ibrāhīm al-Ahdab took a troupe to Damascus c. 1868, to perform *Iskandar al-Makdūnī* (adapted from Racine's *Alexandre le Grand*) for the circumcision ceremony of the sons of the Governor, Rāshid Pasha.

The history of al-Qabbānī's theatre in Damascus is obscure and riddled with contradictory statements. During the term of office of the Governor, Subhī Pasha (1872-1873), al-Qabbānī is said to have received his first taste of theatre, watching a performance of Molière's classic, *L'Avare*, performed by a French theatrical troupe at the Lazarist school at Tūmā Gate. It is asserted that the first play written by him was *Nākir al-jamīl* (The Ingrate), staged c. 1865 (or more likely some years later) at his grandfather's house in front of friends and relatives. The play tells the story of a good-natured young man, Halīm, who cures a sick youth, Ghādir, and makes him his close friend. In attempting to murder his patron, Ghādir kills the Crown Prince

by mistake and then frames Halīm for the murder. The latter is sentenced to death. However, the identity of the real murderer, Ghādir, is revealed through dreams and visions. Halīm is pardoned by the King and marries the latter's daughter.

The authorship of this play is open to debate. There are two versions: one by al-Qabbānī, the other by the Beiruti Antūn Shihaybar (written in 1879). Both are closely related in both structure and wording. Professor Najm reconstructed the dialogue of his version of al-Qabbānī's play from a novel based on the play.

Shaykh 'Abd al-Hādī al-Wafā'ī from the city of Homs, having got to know al-Qabbānī in Damascus, on returning home, wrote a number of plays and gave theatrical performances there beginning in 1870. Subhī Pasha heard of al-Qabbānī's activities, and asked him to form a troupe. Al-Qabbānī put on *al-Malik Waddāh wa-Misbāh wa-Qūt al-Arwāh* (King Waddāh, Misbāh and Qūt al-Arwāh) in a friend's house, and then before the public at the Italian Casino in al-Jābiyah Gate. He distributed the parts amongst his friends, using beardless youths in the roles of women. Another version of his play *Darwīsh Misbāh wa-Qūt al-Arwāh* (The Dervish Misbāh and Qūt al-Arwāh) was put on in June 1875; at this time it was common for plays to appear with slightly amended titles. In November 1875, al-Qabbānī's play *'Itr Shām wa-Ward al-Jinān* (The Perfume of Damascus and the Rose of Paradise) was performed, and in May 1876 yet another play, *Ibn Zaydūn wa-Wallādah* (Ibn Zaydūn and Wallādah), was put on at the home of Muhyī al-Dīn Bayhum as part of the celebrations at a circumcision ceremony; this is perhaps al-Qabbānī's play known under the title *Wallādah bint al-Mustakfī, aw 'Iffat al-Muhibbīn* (Wallādah, Daughter of al-Mustakfī, or The Virtue of the Lovers), about Ibn Zaydūn (d. 1070), a famous Andalusian poet who became a vizier and his stormy relationship with the poetess, Wallādah, daughter of the Umayyad caliph, al-Mustakfī, who eventually left him for his rival, Ibn 'Abdūs.

Midhat Pasha, the enlightened governor of Syria from 1878 until 1880, criticized Damascenes for their interest in shadow theatre, a spectacle notorious for its sexual innuendo that was to be seen in many cafés. He offered financial support to anyone in Damascus who would set up a theatre to perform edifying plays. On 22 January 1879 the Damascus Theatre (al-Marsah al-Dimashqī) was opened; Midhat attended the first performance, at which al-Qabbānī presented his operetta, *al-Amīr Mahmūd, najl shāh al-'ajam* (Prince Mahmūd, Son of the Shāh of the Persians), taken from the *Thousand and One Nights*. Prince Mahmūd, having fallen in love with a woman in a portrait, finds out in India that she is Zahr al-Riyād, daughter of the Chinese Emperor. Rewarded for preventing a Persian invasion, the King of India flies Mahmūd to China on a magic carpet. There he rescues Zahr al-Riyād from a jinn, who has forced the Emperor to make her his wife; instead she is married to Mahmūd.

Midhat Pasha is said to have asked Iskandar Farah, an assistant in the custom's department, to help al-Qabbānī form a troupe. They rented space in al-Afandī garden in the Tūmā Gate quarter and also put on performances at the Customs' Caravanserai between the Silk Souq and al-Barīd Gate. Among their performances was *'Ā'idah* (Aida), an adaptation by al-Qabbānī from a French translation by Camille de Laclos of the libretto of Verdi's opera (1871), that had been commissioned by the Khedive of Egypt; it tells the tragic tale from ancient Egypt of the love affair between Radames and the slave girl Aida.

Various reasons are given for the closure of al-Qabbānī's theatre. Apparently it proved so inviting that women complained to the ulema that their husbands were never at home. Employers also claimed that work was being neglected. According to one version of the story, the ulema demanded that one of the following governors, Midhat Pasha, Fādil Pasha or Ahmad Hamdī Pasha, close the theatre. Another version suggests that certain shaykhs objected to the appearance of the caliph Hārūn in a comedy, Mārūn al-Naqqāsh's *Abū 'l-Hasan al-mughaffal, aw Hārūn al-Rashīd* (The Fool Abū 'l-Hasan or Hārūn al-Rashīd), thus denigrating both the Caliph's office and person. Shaykh Sa'īd al-Ghabrā complained to sultan 'Abd al-Hamīd

that, as a result of the theatre's increasing popularity, adultery and sin were spreading in Syria, and women were mixing with men. It is alleged that an order was issued banning acting in Damascus in 1884, and al-Qabbānī's theatre was burnt to the ground, perhaps as the result of an arson attack.

Al-Qabbānī now wrote to his friend, the rich Syrian merchant Sa'd Allāh Hallābū, in Alexandria. The latter advised him to try his luck in Egypt, where there had been a tradition of modern Arabic theatre since 1870 and long established French and Italian theatres. In 1884 al-Qabbānī took his troupe to Egypt, including actors, writers, poets, composers, singers, musicians, and a group of *samāh* dancers who performed to the rhythms of the Andalusian verse form, the *muwashshahāt*. Al-Qabbānī sang, and the role of the protagonist was frequently entrusted to Iskandar Farah. Each play often included dancing and was followed by a pantomime, a one-act farce, or a farce with a dance with sword and shield, presented by Muhyī al-Dīn al-Dimashqī or the comic actor and carpenter, Abū 'l-Khayr al-Najjār.

Between 1884 and 1900, c. 150 performances were given. The first performances in Alexandria were in the Sulaymān Bey Rahmī Café known as the Danube Café (June-July 1884), then at the Zizinia Theatre (July-August). Certain plays became part of the repertoire of al-Qabbānī and other leading Syrian troupes that dominated the Egyptian scene: *Uns al-Jalīs, Wallādah aw 'Iffat al-muhibbīn, Nafh al-rubā* (The Breeze on the Hills), *Nākir al-jamīl, al-Amīr Mahmūd najl shāh al-'ajam, Lubāb al-gharām aw al-Malik Mitrīdāt, 'Antarah al-'Absī, 'Ā'idah, 'Āqibat al-siyānah wa-ghā'ilat al-khiyānah, al-Shaykh Waddāh wa-Misbāh wa-Qūt al-Arwāh,* all by al-Qabbānī himself, the musical *al-Khill al-Wafiyy* (The Loyal Friend), *'Alā 'l-bāghī tadūr al-dawā'ir* (Calamities Overtake the Unjust) by Shim'ūn Mūyāl, and *al-Saydaliyyah* (The Pharmacy). The troupe also performed at the Danube Bath's Theatre in Alexandria (September-October). In Cairo he rented the Politeama, near the Ezbekieh Gardens (October-November), and added his comedy *Hamzah al-muhtāl* (Cunning Hamza) to the repertoire. The troupe proved very popular with the Egyptian public and was widely praised for its excellent acting and musicals.

The plays are culled from a wide variety of sources. *Al-Khill al-wafiyy wa 'l-ghadr al-khafiyy* (The Loyal Friend and the Hidden Treason, translated by either Habīb Misk or Muhammad al-Maghribī), for example, is taken from Alfred de Musset's *Lorenzaccio* (1834). *Hārūn al-Rashīd ma'a Uns al-Jalīs* (Hārūn al-Rashīd and Uns al-Jalīs) is al-Qabbānī's dramatisation of a tale of the *Thousand and One Nights*. Al-Fadl Ibn Khāqān, vizier of the Governor of Basra, Muhammad b. Sulaymān, is ordered to buy him a slave girl to take the place left by the death of his favourite singer. Uns al-Jalīs, the girl he finds, enchants his son, 'Alī Nūr al-Dīn. Al-Fadl gives her to him, hoping to find another girl. 'Alī and Uns al-Jalīs flee, when another vizier, al-Mu'īn ibn Sāwī, arrives, saying that Ibn Sulaymān is waiting for the girl. They reveal their story to the caliph Hārūn and his minister, Ja'far. Al-Mu'īn tries to have al-Fadl, 'Alī and Uns al-Jalīs executed. The wicked al-Mu'īn and Ibn Sulaymān are ordered to appear before Hārūn and are imprisoned; al-Fadl is rehabilitated and made governor.

Lubāb al-gharām, aw al-Malik Mitrīdāt (The Quintessence of Love or King Mithridate, translated for al-Qabbānī by Iskandar Farah) is inspired by Jean Racine's tragedy *Mithridate* (1673). In it Mūnim appeals to Mitrīdāt, King of the Greeks, to avenge the death of her father by waging war against Rome. In Mitrīdāt's absence his two sons, Aksīfār and Farnās, rush to win the hand of Mūnim, who is already betrothed to their father. Mitrīdāt manages to get Mūnim and Aksīfār to confess to their love. Aksīfār is thrown into prison where he joins his brother and Mūnim. When Aksīfār and Mūnim remain steadfast in their love, Mitrīdāt orders their execution. Mitrīdāt now learns that Farnās has led an army to join the Romans; Farnās wages war against his father, but is captured and killed by him. Before Mūnim puts a poisoned cup, sent by Mitrīdāt, to her lips, the victory of Aksīfār over the Romans is announced. The King, critically wounded in the fight, abdicates in Aksīfār's favour and cedes Mūnim to him.

'Antar b. Shaddād or *'Antarah al-'Absī* is based on the story of the semi-mythical hero, the black slave 'Antarah. A rival tribal chief, Mas'ūd, insults him by proposing to his wife, 'Ablah, who, Mas'ūd asserts, has been married to 'Antarah against her wishes. Mas'ūd infiltrates some of his men into 'Antarah's tribe, but 'Antarah defeats them and rejects help offered by Mas'ūd. Mas'ūd is killed, and the Arab tribes unite. The plot of al-Qabbānī's play *'Afīfah wa 'l-Amīr 'Alī* ('Afīfa and Prince 'Alī), also known as *'Āqibat al-siyānah wa-ghā'ilat al-khiyānah* (Chastity Rewarded and Perfidy Punished), is inspired by *Geneviève de Brabant* by Madame de Staël (1766-1817). Prince 'Alī leaves with his army, confiding the principality and his wife, 'Afīfah, to Salīm. Salīm lies to 'Alī, claiming that his wife has committed adultery and is expecting a child. He gets the order to kill her and the child. However, the men charged with the task take pity and abandon her and the child. When 'Alī returns, he learns the truth; once he has found his wife, he kills Salīm. This particular play was revised after al-Qabbānī's death and published with additional music by his friend and associate, Kāmil al-Khula'ī.

Tawfīq, the Khedive (ruler) of Egypt, is said to have been much impressed by the troupe's performance of the musical *al-Hākim bi-Amr Allāh,* a play about the famous Fatimid caliph (985-1021), that was presented at the Opera House in Cairo in December 1884. The troupe next performed at the theatre in Ezbekieh Gardens (January 1885), then at the Politeama, Cairo (February and March), then at the Politeama in Alexandria (March-April), adding *al-Intiqām* (Revenge). They then performed at the Danube Café, adding al-Qabbānī's *Majnūn Laylā* (Layla's Madman), the tale of the lovelorn poet Qays b. al-Mulawwah, and at the Ezbekieh Theatre in Cairo (November-December), where they added al-Qabbānī's *'Abd al-Salām al-Ma'rūf bi-Dīk al-Jinn ma'a Zawjatihi Ward* ('Abd al-Salām Known as Cock of the Demons and His Wife Ward), the story of the Syrian poet Abū Muhammad 'Abd al-Salām bin Raghbān, who, after killing his wife in a fit of jealousy, dedicated a famous elegy to her.

In December 1885 an article in the Egyptian

press complained that the performances put on by al-Qabbānī's company at the Ezbekieh theatre were corrupting public morals. Male actors who had shaved off their moustaches and beards were assuming women's roles. Had they confined themselves to women's clothes or to the gestures of cultured women, the article suggested, it might have been acceptable. Instead however, they were being utterly shameless, flirting immoderately with the audience and showing no concern for moral values. These actors had already been expelled from Syria, when the Governor, fearing the consequences, banned them and issued a strong reproach to the actors for appearing on stage as women. Even prostitutes, it was asserted, would disapprove of such behaviour. The paper was confident that the necessary measures would be taken to prevent these male actors from performing in this fashion in Egypt. In 1884 some school-children in Syria had decided to imitate them, and the Syrian government had had to punish the director of the school. The paper asked whether it was right that a group which had been expelled from its own country and was bringing shame on religion should be allowed to perform in Egypt. However, the storm caused by this article seems to have subsided, since the same newspaper was later supportive of the troupe.

Al-Qabbānī's troupe then performed in towns in the Nile Delta, in Tanta (March-April 1886) during the annual celebrations of the local saint, Ahmad al-Badawī, adding *Jamīl wa-Jamīlah* (Jamīl and Jamīlah) by al-Qabbānī to the repertoire, then in al-Mansūrah in May. Audiences continued to appreciate the quality of the acting. At the end of performances or between acts 'Abduh al-Hamūlī, the most popular singer of the era, used to sing.

When al-Qabbānī returned to Syria, Iskandar Farah served as the troupe's director. Thus it was that in the middle of 1888 Farah left the troupe and established his own along with some of the other actors. With the great Egyptian actor/singer Salāmah Hijāzī (who had previously been active in other Syrian troupes) as one of its pillars, the new troupe enjoyed spectacular popularity from 1891 to 1904. Meanwhile, al-Qabbānī's troupe had been losing audiences, and

so, when he returned to Egypt, he added some new elements in order to attract a larger public. This time they were more successful, due in no small part to the presence of the singer Laylā in the troupe. In February 1889 they performed once again at the Opera House and were in residence at the Danube until May 1889, then in Tanta till the end of 1889, and then back to Cairo where they performed at a theatre on 'Abd al-'Azīz Street (September 1889-January 1890). They now added two other plays to the repertoire: *Mayy wa-Hūrās* (May and Horace), Salīm al-Naqqāsh's adaptation of Corneille's *Les trois Horaces et les trois Curiaces,* a love story set in the time of the war between Alba and Rome, and al-Qabbānī's *Qūt al-Qulūb* or *Hārūn al-Rashīd ma'a al-Amīr Ghānim*. The troupe was joined by two Syrian actresses, the beautiful Miryam Sammāt and her sister Labībah, and went on tour to Upper Egypt where they performed in Minya, Asyut, and Fayyum (April-June 1890). *Hārūn al-Rashīd ma'a 'l-Amīr Ghānim* (Hārūn al-Rashīd and Prince Ghānim) is derived from a tale taken from the 52nd night of the *Thousand and One Nights.* Hārūn's wife Zubaydah, jealous of his favourite concubine, Qūt al-Qulūb, orders her to be killed. Ghānim, a young merchant, finding her abandoned, falls in love. Hārūn discovers his wife's plot, and learning of the lovers orders that they be put to death. Ghānim escapes. The Caliph, on discovering that Qūt al-Qulūb has not been unfaithful to him, generously marries her to Ghānim, while he himself marries Ghānim's sister.

In 1893 the troupe was invited to perform at the Chicago World's Fair, the performances being intended for Syro-Lebanese immigrants to America. In the same year al-Qabbānī returned to Syria, renounced the theatre, and opened a starch factory in Homs. However, unable to free himself of his attraction to the theatre, he returned to Egypt, reformed the troupe, and gave performances in Tanta (November 1894 – January 1895), the Egyptian Theatre (al-Tiyātrū al-Misrī) in Cairo (January–February), then at al-Qardāhī Theatre in Alexandria (November–December 1896). A number of works were now added to the repertoire: the opera *al-Kawkāyīn*; al-Qabbānī's *Asad al-Sharā, aw Kisrā Anūshirwān* (The Lion of

Sharā, or Khosrow Anoushirwan) concerning the Sassanid Khosrow Anoushirwan (531-579, Greek Chosroes), perhaps another tale from the *Thousand and One Nights*, *al-Sultān Hasan* (Sultān Hasan), and Hannā Naqqāsh's one-act comedy, *al-Faylasūf al-ghayūr* (The Jealous Philosopher). Al-Qabbānī himself returned to Cairo to put on performances in the New Theatre (al-Masrah al-Jadīd), a building near the Opera House that had been specially built for him by 'Abd al-Razzāq Bey 'Ināyat, an inspector in the Ministry of Education. His troupe now included leading actors such as Ahmad Abū 'l-'Adl, the Syrian director Sulaymān al-Qardāhī, Sulaymān al-Bustānī, the brilliant Syrian singer Labībah Mālilī, and the sisters Miryam, Hīlānah and Hanīnah Sammāt, with 'Abduh al-Hamūlī singing between acts. His continuing success was also due to the presence of the famous Aleppan singer, the young Malikah Surūr, who used to end each performance with her songs. The Syrian actor, Sulaymān al-Haddād, who had his own troupe for a number of years, also worked for a while with al-Qabbānī.

Between January and May 1897 the troupe put on performances at both the New Theatre in Cairo and the theatre in Helwan to the south of the city. During that period they added Tawfīq Kan'ān's play *'Izzat al-mulūk* (The Power of Kings) to their repertoire, and when a new season began (August-September 1897), it included *al-Malik Iskandar al-Kabīr al-mulaqqab Dhī al-Qarnayn* (Alexander the Great, Called the Two-Horned) by Khalīl Haslab; *Shīrīn bint al-malik Kisrā* (Shirin, Daughter of Khosrow), the story of the famous Christian mistress of Khosrow, and *al-Mu'tamid b. 'Abbād* by Ibrāhīm Ahdab, about the unfortunate Spanish sultan and poet who died in a Moroccan prison in 1095. A few months later they added *al-Wālidayn wa'l-waladayn* (The Two Parents and the Two Children); *al-Liqā' al-ma'nūs fī harb al-Basūs* (The Familiar Encounter in the War of al-Basūs), a tale of pre-Islamic tribal conflict, by Jirjis Murqus al-Rashīdī; *al-Bakhīl* (The Miser), adapted from Molière by Najīb al-Haddād, *Makāyid al-gharām* (The Schemes of Love), *Lūsiyā, Hārūn al-Rashīd wa-Khalīfah al-sayyād* (Hārūn al-Rashīd and Khalīfah, the Fisherman), another tale from the *Thousand and One Nights*, by Mahmūd

Wāsif, and *Rūbirt wa-Albirt* (Robert and Albert).

The plot of al-Qabbānī's play *Hiyal al-nisā' al-shahīrah bi-Lūsiyā* (The Trickeries of Women, Known as Lucia) concerns the departure to war of Comte Frīdrīk (Frederic), the governor of Messina in Sicily and uncle of Jān (Jean), whom he is thinking of marrying to his daughter Ūjīn (Eugène). Lūsiyā (Lucia), his second wife and step-mother of Ūjīn, seizes the occasion to try to seduce Jān. He rejects her advances since he loves only Ūjīn. The intendant of the palace, Imīl (Émile), persuades Lūsiyā to help him marry Ūjīn. On his return the Comte rejects this mismarriage and unites Jān and Ūjīn. Leaving on a yet another mission, Frīdrīk takes his nephew with him on the insistence of Lūsiyā, who wishes to separate the young couple. Imīl, governor in the interim, follows Lūsiyā's advice and attempts to win Ūjīn's favours. Some months later, Lūsiyā treacherously informs Imīl that Jān has drowned and that he can now marry the widow. Ūjīn takes flight and finds her husband. The couple return to Messina, where the Comte inflicts just punishment on Imīl and Lūsiyā.

With al-Qabbānī's return to Cairo at the end of 1899, a new troupe was formed that included Labībah Mālilī, her sister Miryam, and other young actresses. Al-Qabbānī toured Upper Egypt once again, performing in Minya (January 1900) where he added *Hamdān*, an adaptation of Victor Hugo's (1802-85) *Hernani*, the story of a noble outlaw at war with society, in a translation by Najīb al-Haddād; at the New Theatre in Cairo (February), adding *Matāmi' al-nisā', aw Kātirīn Hawār* (The Schemes of Women, or Catherine Howard), adapted by Tawfīq Kan'ān from *Catherine Howard ou La Cupidité des femmes* by Alexandre Dumas père (1802-70), the story of the reputedly adulterous wife of Henry VIII; in Fayyum (February-March), adding two adaptations by Najīb al-Haddād, *Salāh al-Dīn al-Ayyūbī* (Saladin, the Ayyubid), inspired by Scott's *Talisman*, and *al-Sīd, aw Gharām wa-'ntiqām* (The Cid, or Love and Revenge), from Pierre Corneille's tale of the famous Castilian knight, *Le Cid* (1637). In April 1900 they presented Muhammad al-'Ibādī's play *Muqātil Misr Ahmad 'Urābī Bāshā* (Egypt's Warrior Ahmad 'Urābī Pasha), which is critical of the leader of the

Egyptian revolution of 1882; its performance apparently led to violent protests from the audience. In the town of Bani Suwayf to the south of Cairo (April), the troupe added *al-Ifrīqiyyah/ L'Africaine* by the French dramatist Eugène Scribe (1791-1861), translated by Dā'ūd Barakāt and Yūsuf Hibīsh, concerning the adventures and love affair of the African queen/slave, Selika, and Vasco da Gama, and *Hifz al-widād* (The Preservation of Love) by Salīm al-Naqqāsh.

It has been claimed that in May, while al-Qabbānī was on tour, his enemies once again encouraged the mob to set fire to his theatre. With no theatre in which to perform, the troupe split up and al-Qabbānī returned to Damascus. In 1900 he was invited to appear before sultan 'Abd al-Hamīd (Abdülhamid) in Istanbul and sang a collection of *muwashshah*s that he himself had set to music. Soon after his return to Damascus, he died of cholera.

It has been estimated that, of the 150 performances put on by al-Qabbānī's troupe, 45 were plays of foreign origin, 28 of them 19th century works, and 17 tragedies. Only eight of his own plays have been published, some of them adaptations or free translations of European works, others original works. Others are either lost or remain in manuscript. Among other plays included in his repertoire were *Abū Ja'far al-Mansūr,* the story of the 'Abbasid caliph and founder of Baghdad; *al-Amīr Yahyā* (Prince Yahyā), both by al-Qabbani himself; *Asmā wa-Salīm* (Asmā and Salīm); *Jamīl Buthaynah* (Buthaynah's Jamīl), the story of the lovelorn Umayyad poet, Jamīl, by Ibrāhīm al-Ahdab; *Kliyūbātrā* (Cleopatra) by Iskandar Farah; *Multaqā al-khalīfatayn* (The Meeting of the Two Caliphs); *Multaqā al-habībayn* (The Meeting of the Lovers), *Yazīd bin 'Abd al-Malik ma'a jāriyatayhi Habbābah wa-Sallāmah* (Yazīd b. 'Abd al-Malik and his Two Slave-Girls, Habbābah and Sallāmah), the story of the dissolute Umayyad caliph, also by Ibrāhīm al-Ahdab, and *Yūsuf b. Tāshifīn,* the story of the Almoravid sultan, who defeated the kings of Spain.

Al-Qabbānī composed his plays in a highly rhetorical classical Arabic, almost entirely in rhymed prose and verse, but the verse drama is not of the calibre to be found in the plays of Ahmad **Shawqī** performed in the 1920s. Al-Qabbānī had a talent for composing simple verse into which he incorporated lines from celebrated classical poems of the pre-Islamic, Umayyad and Abbasid periods, together with *hadīth*s and verses from the Qur'an. Responding to public taste, the plays provide an opportunity for a string of songs and musical interludes, and choral singing of the strophic Andalusian *muwashshahāt*, with melodies composed by him. The leading roles are written to be performed by singers; when performed by the leading singers of the day such as Salāmah Hijāzī, they were very popular with his audiences.

Al-Qabbānī himself describes his plays, most of which have four or five acts, as being musical *(talhīniyyah),* literary, dramatic, historical, romantic, moral, and warlike *(harbiyyah).* They seek to uphold justice and morality, using the dramatic genre as a means of preaching moral lessons. Characters address the audience in a series of long soliloquies, full of stern moralising, maxims, and sayings. Good is made to be victorious over evil, with divine vengeance sooner or later punishing evildoers. There is hardly a single principal character who does not believe in the power of fate. Though the theme of love dominates, the plays are also filled with tales of deception and treason, the perfidy of friends, wives or servants, intrigues, jail scenes, murder, and attempted murder. His simple, one-dimensional characters are stereotypes, incarnating every possible trait, whether good or evil; the very Arabic names used for the characters will often suggest a particular trait. Laughter is provoked by introducing stock characters from classical literature, oafs, beggars and parasites, and by making use of facetious remarks and parodies. He situates his plays against a backdrop of miraculous and improbable events, unlikely reunions, and supernatural phenomena (such as jinns appearing on stage); *coups de théâtre* produce characters, who are supposedly dead but have miraculously escaped disaster. As in folk literature, plays usually end happily, with wicked characters being implausibly forgiven. They are all very episodic, and the dialogue is monotonous and flat. As is the case with occasional poetry *(shi'r al-munāsabāt)* from the same period, al-Qabbānī often begins and ends his performances with a chorus singing hymns of glory in praise of Khedive 'Abbās of Egypt, or with praise or prayers for the Ottoman caliph and sultan, 'Abd al-Hamīd. When he praises Hārūn al-Rashīd's justice in the epilogue of one play, he compares it to that of 'Abd al-Hamīd.

A man of many talents, al-Qabbānī designed costumes, sang, danced, set the words of plays to music, and wrote poetry in Arabic and Persian. He was a major figure in the establishment of an Arab national theatre inspired by Arab history, literature and legend. By using a variety of themes culled from tales of storytellers *(hakawātī)* in the cafés of Damascus, for example, those of 'Antar and the *Thousand and One Nights,* and from the picaresque tales of the *maqāmah* genre with their treatment of love, passion, separation and reunion, marriage and divorce, war, comedy and tragedy, he was aiming to reach a broader audience. The stories of his own plays are drawn from legends, folk tales and popular literature of the Arabic and Islamic heritage, Arabic literature, and Arab and Islamic history; some are products of his own imagination. In addition he also turned to classical European drama, mostly French, as a source for translation, Arabisation or adaption. Audiences in both Egypt and Syria were already accustomed to being offered such adaptations and were fond of French classical drama.

Al-Qabbānī was one of the major figures in laying the foundations of a theatre tradition in Egypt and Syria. Described as the father of melodrama, he helped popularize musical drama or operetta. Himself a master of the musical theatre, he also trained a number of renowned Arab musicians. Amongst his disciples were the Egyptian musician and composer, Muhammad Kāmil al-Khula'ī (1879-1938), and Dā'ūd Qustantīn Khūrī (1860-1939), the actor, composer, poet, and writer. Al-Qabbānī was a leading member of the group of Lebanese/Syrian dramatists and actor-managers, whose activities from the 1870s to the early 1900s served as the basis for the firm establishment, prosperity and popularity of the theatre in Egypt.

REFERENCES

Atia Abul Naga, *Les Sources françaises du théâtre égyptien (1870-1939)* (Algiers: SNED, 1972), 16, 20, 129-159;

'Ādil Abū Shanab, *Rā'id al-masrah al-ghinā'ī al-'arabī: Ahmad Abū Khalīl al-Qabbānī* (Damascus: Dār al-Shumūs li'l-dirāsāt wa'l-nashr wa'l-tawzī', 2005) ;

M. M. Badawi, *Early Arabic Drama* (Cambridge: Cambridge University Press, 1988), 56-64;

'Abd al-Qādir Hisnī and Husayn Jum'ah, *Abū Khalīl al-Qabbānī: rā'id al-masrah al-'arabī* (Damascus: Ittihād al-kuttāb al-'Arab, 2007);

'Adnān Ibn Dhurayl, *al-Masrah al-sūrī mundhu Abī Khalīl al-Qabbānī ilā 'l-yawm* (Damascus, 1971), 19-34;

Sayyid 'Alī Ismā'īl, *Tārīkh al-masrah fī Misr fī 'l-qarn al-tāsi' 'ashar* (Cairo: Maktabat Zahrā' al-Sharq, 1997), 157-69, 237, 314;

Ilyās Tu'ma Jirjis, *Abū Khalīl al-Qabbānī: rā'id al-masrah al-sūrī* (Diploma, Beirut: Lebanese University, c. 1972);

Husnī Kan'ān, "Abū Khalīl al-Qabbānī: bā'ith nahdatinā al-fanniyyah", *al-Risālah* (Cairo) 16.804 (29 November 1948): 1120-1, 1351-3, 1461-2, and 17.811 (1949): 1397-9;

Regina Karachouli, "Abū Halīl al-Qabbānī (1833-1902), Damaszener Theatergründer und Prinzipal", *Die Welt des Islams* 32 (1992): 83-98;

Haytham Yahyā al-Khawājah, *Harakat al-masrah fī Hims min al-bidāyāt li-ghāyat 'ām 1979: dirāsah wa-tārīkh* (Homs: Matābi' al-Rawdah al-Namūdhajiyyah, 1984), 7-10;

M. A. al-Khozai, *The Development of Early Arabic Drama (1847-1900)* (London: Longman, 1984), 80-122;

Ibrāhīm al-Kīlānī, "Ahmad Abū Khalīl al-Qabbānī", *Majallat al-Mu'allim al-'Arabī* 1.1 (January 1948): 46-50;

Shākir Mustafā, *Muhādarāt 'an al-qissah fī Sūriyyah hattā al-harb al-'ālamiyyah al-thāniyah* (Cairo: Matba'at al-Jabalāwī, 1957), 188-202 and 207-9;

Muhammad Yūsuf Najm, *al-Masrahiyyah fī 'l-adab al-'arabī al-hadīth, 1847–1914* (Beirut: Dār al-Thaqāfah, 1980), 61-70, 115-126, 210-15 and 371-9.

Ma'rūf al-Rusāfī

(1875 – 1945)

TERRI DeYOUNG

University of Washington, Seattle

WORKS

Collected Poetry

Dīwān al-Rusāfī, ed. Muhyī al-Dīn Ahmad Khayyāt and Mustafā al-Ghalāyinī (Beirut: al-Maktabah al-Ahliyyah, 1910);

Dīwān al-Rusāfī, bi-hā qasā'id lam tunshar min qabl, ed. 'Abd al-Qādir al-Maghribī (Beirut: Matba'at al-Mu'arrid, 1932);

Dīwān al-Rusāfī, ed. 'Abd al-Sāhib Shukr al-Bādirā'ī (Cairo: al-Maktabah al-Tijāriyyah al-Kubrā, 1957; revised and enlarged ed., 1963);

Dīwān al-Rusāfī, ed. Mustafā 'Alī, 4 vols. (Baghdad: Manshūrat Wizārat al-I'lām, 1972-76; revised and enlarged ed., 1986).

Other Works

Daf' al-hujnah fī 'rtidākh al-lujnah ("Defense Against Defects in Speaking Arabic With a Foreign Accent", Istanbul: Idārat Majallat Lisān al-'Arab, 1912-1913);

Nafh al-tīb fī 'l-khitābah wa'l-khatīb ("The Sweet Breeze for Oratory and Orators", Istanbul: Matba'at al-Waqf al-Islāmī, 1917);

Muhādarāt al-adab al-'arabī ("Lectures on Arabic Literature", Baghdad: al-Matba'ah al-'Irāqiyyah, 1921);

al-Anāshīd al-madrasiyyah ("School Anthems", Jerusalem: n.p., 1920); revised and enlarged as *al-Anāshīd al-madrasiyyah wa'l-al'āb* (Baghdad: al-Matba'ah al-'Asriyyah, 1926);

Tamā'im al-tarbiyah wa'l-ta'līm ("The Amulets of Upbringing and Education", Beirut: n.p. 1924);

Rasā'il al-ta'līqāt ("Commentary Essays", Baghdad: al-Matba'ah al-'Irāqiyyah, 1944);

al-Adab al-'arabī wa-mumayyizāt al-lughah al-'arabiyyah fī adwārihā al-mukhtalifah al-adabiyyah ("Arabic Literature and the Distinctive Characteristics of the Arabic Language in Its Different Literary Phases", Baghdad: Matba'at al-Ma'ārif, 1952);

al-Adab al-rafī' fī mīzān al-shi'r wa-qawāfīh ("Refined Literature in the Balance of Poetry and Its Rhymes", Baghdad: Matba'at al-Ma'ārif, 1956); ed. with an introduction by Ibrāhīm Kamāl and Mustafā Jawād;

Khawātir wa-nawādir ("Thoughts and Observations"), revised as *Silsilat al-a'māl al-majhūlah, li-Ma'rūf al-Rusāfī*, ed. Najdah Fathī Safwat (London: Riad el-Rayyes Books, 1988);

Kitāb al-ālah wa'l-adāh wa-mā yatba'uhumā min al-malābis wa'l-marāfiq wa'l-hanāt ("Book of Instruments and Mechanisms and What is Connected With That Among Clothes, Conveniences, and Comforts"), ed. 'Abd al-Rahmān al-Rashūdī (Port Sa'īd: Matba'at al-Thaqāfah al-Dīniyyah, 2001);

'Alā bāb sijn Abī 'l-'Alā' ("At the Prison Door of Abū 'l-'Alā' [al-Ma'arrī]", Baghdad: Dār al-Hikmah li'l-Nashr wa'l-Tawzī', 1946; special ed., 2002);

Kitāb al-Shakhsiyyah al-muhammadiyyah, aw: Hall al-lughz al-muqaddas ("The Muhammadan Personality, or Solving the Holy Puzzle", Köln: Manshūrat al-Jamāl, 2002).

Translations by the Author

Nāmik Kamāl, *Ru'yā* (Baghdad: Matba'at al-Shābindar, 1909).

Translated Works

A. J. Arberry, *Arabic Poetry: A Primer for Students* (Cambridge: Cambridge University Press, 1965), 164-169;

Salma Khadra al-Jayyusi, *Modern Arabic Poetry* (New York: Columbia University Press, 1987), 95-96;

Hussein N. Kadhim, *The Poetics of Anti-Colonialism in the Arabic Qasīdah* (Leiden:

E. J. Brill, 2004), 91-93;
Safā' A. Khulusi, "Ma'rūf ar-Rusāfī, 1875-1945", *Bulletin of the School of Oriental and African Studies* 13 (1950): 616-626;
Muhammad Saghir Hasan al-Masūmī, "Rusāfī—A Modern Poet of Iraq", *Islamic Culture*, Jan. 1950: 50-59.

Al-Rusāfī was one of three major poets who dominated the Iraqi literary scene in the last decade of the nineteenth century and the first half of the twentieth century. The other two were Jamīl Sidqī al-Zahāwī (b. 1863) and Muhammad Mahdī al-**Jawāhirī** (d. 1997). All three represented the trend in Arabic literature known as neo-Classicism, which involved taking inspiration from the poets who wrote in the earliest periods of Arabic literature, beginning in the sixth century C.E. or even earlier. They sought to bring Arabic poetry into the modern world, while maintaining its ties to an indigenous cultural legacy that still commanded great respect throughout the Arabic-speaking world.

Each of the three poets nevertheless approached the political and social currents of their times very differently. Al-Zahāwī without hesitation cooperated with whatever group was exercising power, whether it be the Ottomans, the British or Arab Nationalist politicians. He felt that poetry should serve the causes of social reform and intellectual modernization, independent of whoever dominated the political order at any given moment. Al-Jawāhirī, in contrast, as a committed Communist, believed that politics and social reform were inextricably linked and that the latter could only be achieved under a favorable regime.

Al-Rusāfī's forays into the political arena were based more on reactions to specific circumstances. Sometimes he took positions on principle that cost him dearly. Thus, at the end of his life, in 1941, he found himself cast into the political wilderness because of his support of the unsuccessful Rashīd 'Alī coup against the British re-occupation of Iraq during the Second World War and, for a time, had to make ends meet selling cigarettes on the streets of Baghdad. At other times, he seems to have worked unquestioningly for the goals of a particular political party, even when they might be seen as conflicting with his personal beliefs. Such was the story when he allied himself with the Committee for Union and Progress (CUP), the political party controlling Ottoman politics between 1908 and 1918.

Though there has never been a shortage of accolades for al-Rusāfī's work, no one has ever made the argument that he stood in the vanguard of innovation for the Arabic literature of his time. His work is consistently regarded by most critics as solid and effective, consolidating the tendencies of the neo-Classical school to which he belonged, rather than breaking new ground. Yet there are also elements of his work that can be seen unexpectedly distinctive, even from the earliest period of his career. At one extreme, these included an interest in presenting finely honed description that owes more to a discerning eye than poetic tradition. At the other, we find a lifelong commitment to championing the dispossessed and downtrodden, as is shown in his many early poems dealing with widows and orphans, divorced women, prostitutes and convicts, long before such figures became acceptable subjects for poetic treatment.

Al-Rusāfī has thus been most favorably remembered as a poet of passionate social protest who brooked no compromise at a time when many poets expressed a traditionalist, elitist point of view. His protest and patriotic poems have best survived the test of time, being frequently included in the curricula of the schools throughout the Arab world up until the present, having secured an unassailable position in the canon of modern Arabic poetry.

Al-Rusāfī was born on an unknown date in 1875 in a poor district of Baghdad. His father was Kurdish, a veteran of the Russo-Turkish war of 1878, who became a provincial policeman and was thus frequently absent from home. His mother belonged to a Sunni clan of the Shammar tribe, long settled in the southern part of Iraq. Her parents had moved northward seeking a better life. It seems unlikely that she found that better life with her husband. The young Ma'rūf remembered his father as a taciturn, pious man with a short temper who frequently lashed out at his son and his wife. It is not surprising, then, that al-Rusāfī seems to have spent much of the time during his formative years living in his maternal grandfather's house in Baghdad.

The trajectory of al-Rusāfī's education at first followed a path common for a child of an ambitious lower middle class family of the times. When barely three years old he was sent to a *kuttāb* (Qur'an school). After passing through several levels of these traditional educational establishments, he entered the Baghdad Rushdiyya academy, an elite school that specialized in preparing students for military and civil service positions at the highest levels in Istanbul. Al-Rusāfī's hopes of a comfortable future were crushed, however, when he failed one of the third-year exams (in arithmetic) and was dismissed from the school.

In the early 1890s, then, he dramatically re-oriented his educational focus by enrolling for advanced studies in the traditional educational system. The two sets of school curricula—secular and traditional—differed most notably at this time in their linguistic emphasis. The government schools emphasized Turkish, the administrative language of the Ottoman dynasty, key to government employment, while the traditional system relied on Arabic for instruction—the native language of most Iraqis—and focused on religious and philological studies.

Al-Rusāfī excelled in the study of Arabic. He tells us that he had a naturally retentive memory and he became known as "Mr. Citation" among his peers and teachers for his ability to recall extemporaneously the examples of word usage, usually drawn from classical poetry, quoted in the grammar textbooks. This facility led him naturally to an interest in the study of Arabic literature.

He has left us a charming personal description of his first efforts in the poetic arena. He was inspired one night while studying to compose a eulogy honoring his most revered professor, Shaykh Mahmūd al-Alūsī, who occupied in Iraq much the same position as leader of the reformers held by Muhammad 'Abduh in Egypt. He duly recited his effort in front of al-Alūsī, but when pressed to reveal the name of the object of his praise—which should traditionally be included somewhere in the poem—he became

tongue-tied and fled the scene in embarrassment. Thus ended his first foray into poetry. Shortly thereafter, he returned to writing, this time because he had fallen head over heels in love. He tells us he spent hours scribbling in his notebook pouring out his suffering in poem after poem of unrequited longing. Later, he would burn the notebooks containing those poems, as well as some short satirical pieces they contained, so we know very little about their content beyond their author's laconic descriptions.

These experiences, however, led al-Rusāfī to re-evaluate his attitude toward writing verse. From that point on, he tells us, he sought to approach poetry from a different angle, more as a craft than an outlet for his feelings. He chose to hone his skills by composing descriptive works depicting the events of everyday life around him. This decision is reflected in the earliest dated poems he chose to include in his *dīwān*: "al-Ghurūb" (The Setting Sun) from 1894, and "Laylah fī malhā" (A Night of Entertainment) and "al-Qitār" (The Train), both from 1898. These juvenilia bristle with an exactitude in describing the subject matter that frequently turns inward upon itself, often to the detriment of the forward momentum of the poem. This tendency is juxtaposed, often rather incongruously, with ardent exhortations about the need to reform society. Nowhere is this more noticeable than in "Laylah fī malhā," where he depicts the atmosphere of a famous Istanbul nightclub that he visited with a group of young friends. He lavishes great care on the most minute description of a female dancer's performance, as she weaves among the audience, only to turn abruptly in line 40 of the poem to address his home city of Baghdad, lamenting its backwardness in comparison to the refinements of Istanbul, and expressing the hope that social reform and education will transform it into a beacon of light to others still oppressed by the darkness of ignorance.

It is interesting that both "Laylah fī malhā" and "al-Qitār" are set in Turkey proper. Their siting in Istanbul and on the rail line to Salonika (an industrial center at the head of the Aegean Sea that would later become the headquarters of the CUP) certainly indicates that al-Rusāfī was already traveling outside of Iraq even in the 1890s. Nor should one forget that his most revered teacher, Mahmūd al-Ālūsī, was temporarily exiled for "subversive activities" in 1902. These factors, along with the early protests against social conditions in Baghdad that we see in his poetry, suggest that he may have already been involved in secret political activities well before he publicly announced his support for the CUP in 1908. Such a supposition would be further confirmed by a statement he made in a letter to King Faysal of Iraq written in 1923, where he says that he had struggled for Iraq's freedom "for twenty-five years," suggesting he had become politically active in 1898, the same year that both "Laylah fī malhā" and "al-Qitār" were composed.

Whatever the case may be, in 1908 al-Rusāfī made his political allegiance public in a very dramatic way. Even before this, he had begun to carve out for himself a promising career in Baghdad, as a teacher in the prestigious government I'dādī (Preparatory) school, which trained students for the Rushdiyyah Academy and, at the same time, as a professional panegyric poet (along with al-Zahāwī), employed by the governor and his staff to welcome dignitaries and recite on public occasions. The poems "al-Sadd fī Baghdad" (The Dam in Baghdad) and "Sū' al-munqalab" (Evil of the Flood), both included in the *dīwān*, are typical examples of this kind of poem. He had begun to send more fiery poems, like "Īqāz al-ruqūd" (Waking the Sleepers) and "al-Sijn fī Baghdād" (The Jail in Baghdad), to publications abroad like Kurd 'Alī's *al-Muqtabas*, as well as other journals, especially in Egypt, which had less strict censorship laws than the territories directly under Ottoman control. His work thus soon obtained an international reputation outside of Baghdad proper.

The announcement lifting the suspension of the Ottoman Constitution in July 1908 meant, however, that political debate could flourish at home in anticipation of the elections scheduled for the autumn of that year. Newspaper publishing in Iraq also received a boost, because the strict censorship 'Abd al-Hamīd had imposed was lifted and licenses to publish private newspapers could more easily be obtained. Al-Rusāfī was approached in August to edit the Arabic section of the new CUP newspaper *Baghdād*. It was sponsored by the head of the local branch of the CUP, Murād Beğ Sulaymān, the brother of General Mahmūd Shawkat Pāshā, head of the Ottoman Third Army, out of which the leaders of the CUP had emerged. Murād Beğ's younger half brother, Hikmat Sulaymān (who would himself be Prime Minister of an independent Iraq several times), was al-Rusāfī's pupil and would remain a lifelong friend and supporter of the poet.

Al-Rusāfī's work for the newspaper threw him into the thick of CUP politics. When, in mid-October, a delegation of CUP leaders was sent from Istanbul to drum up support for the Party in advance of the elections, he led the welcoming committee, who rallied their supporters at the Wazīr Mosque. It was a Saturday and the crowd contained an unusually large number of the local Jewish supporters of the CUP. It also happened to be the middle of the Muslim fasting month of Ramadān. The group flowed into the mosque as sunset prayers were ending. Al-Rusāfī mounted the *minbar*, the rostrum where the prayer leader would normally give the Friday sermon, and began to harangue and encourage the assembly. The Muslims present were outraged at the behavior of al-Rusāfī and his fellows, and the resulting furor forced the Governor to confine them for a few days in the local prison to protect them from reprisals. One local religious leader even issued a *fatwā*, or legal opinion, sentencing the group to death.

Not long after this incident, al-Rusāfī received an invitation from Ahmad Jawdat, owner of the newspaper *al-Iqdām* in Istanbul, to come to the capital and edit a new Arabic edition of the paper he was planning to start. By mid-December, then, as the newly elected Parliament was assembling in Istanbul, al-Rusāfī had left Baghdad and was on his way to Turkey. Jawdat's newpaper project stalled, however, and al-Rusāfī found himself with nothing to do and few prospects.

It may have been during this period that he had the leisure to explore the new literary trends and sample the marketplace of new philosophical and aesthetic ideas, mainly coming from Europe and especially France, that had been spreading since the 1860s among Turkish intellectuals. Certainly, al-Rusāfī's understanding of various trends in Western literature consistently bears the marks of filtration through the medium of Turkish.

Much later in his career, for example, he attempts to reconstruct his initial response to the then fashionable Western doctrine of "art for art's sake," which he encountered for the first time in those heady pre-War days. He tells us that he heard of it in conversations with "reforming *(mujaddid)* Turkish authors in Istanbul," who told him that they believed "literature—and the arts in general—have no purpose. When someone composes a poem, or produces any work of art, his purpose is that poem," and nothing else. Puzzled by the implications of an aesthetic theory that seemed so antithetical to his own traditional Islamic education, which stated that "nothing in the world could exist without a purpose," al-Rusāfī was moved to explore the background of the idea further. Lacking direct knowledge of a European language, he consulted instead "a book on psychology *('ilm al-nafs)* translated from French into Turkish by a teacher of psychology at the Dār al-'Ulūm (House of Sciences), the Ottoman institution of learning set up to infuse new ideas from the outside into the traditional curriculum. From this book, al-Rusāfī learned that "art for art's sake" expounded the theory that the poet's purpose in his poetry should be "to illuminate and stir the emotions, and leave an influence on the souls [of others]," not to compose solely in response to the external stimuli of events and occasions. In addition, he learned, "the words that he uses in his poetry should not be external to that purpose. They are instead the purpose itself, because when he speaks these words and recites them to his listeners, he has achieved his desired purpose." This explanation—however much it may or may not distort the subtleties of "art for art's sake" as originally conceived by nineteenth-century French authors—is one with which al-Rusāfī can comfortably reinforce his own dedication to the cause of using poetry to move people to reform

their lives and reorder society's priorities, so he declares it with satisfaction "a sound theory *(ma'nā)* that cannot be faulted."

However much the intellectual delights of his new milieu may have imprinted themselves on al-Rusāfī's poetic practice at the time, the political spectacle, as the Ottoman government attempted to cope with democratic aspirations that had been pent up for more than thirty years, must have been equally mesmerizing for the bright young man from the distant, backward province of Iraq. The rapid pace of change in those months following the return of Constitutional rule gave him plenty of opportunities to be a witness to history in the making. He was there, for example, in March to see the Conservatives' counter-revolution against the CUP, and its bloody suppression by Mahmūd Shawkat at the head of the Third Army, marching from Salonika to rescue his erstwhile political allies. By the end of spring, the new order seemed once again to be firmly in place as martial law was imposed, 'Abd al-Hamīd was deposed, and replaced by the young and more cooperative heir apparent, Muhammad Rashād.

General Mahmūd Shawkat now became a key figure in Imperial politics. But al-Rusāfī decided he could no longer wait at loose ends in Istanbul; he made plans to return to Baghdad at the end of the summer 1909. He travelled via Beirut, where he made the acquaintance of several important intellectuals, including Amīn al-Rīhānī (d. 1940), newly returned to Lebanon from the United States. The two became fast friends and several poems in al-Rusāfī's *dīwān* are addressed to the modernizing Arab American intellectual.

He also sold the publishing rights to all the poems he had written up to that point to Muhammad Jamāl al-Dīn, owner of the publishing house al-Maktabah al-Ahliyyah, in return for funds sufficient to continue his journey. Jamāl al-Dīn hired two well-respected local scholars, Muhyī al-Dīn al-Khayyāt and Mustafā al-Ghalāyīnī to edit and annotate the poems. They took some care in their work, but in many places the text showed the marks of hasty publication. Over the years, many more editions were produced, and al-Rusāfī's letters indicate that he took a careful interest in their presentation and editing, but the circumstances surrounding this first edition gave rise to the impression that he cared little about the fate of his poems after they were composed. But the fact that the first edition of his *dīwān* came out so early in his career gives us good data for establishing the chronology of his poems.

Once in Baghdad, al-Rusāfī barely had time to wipe the dust from shoes before he received a telegram from his friends in Istanbul, telling him that there was a position available teaching Arabic language and literature at the Shāhāniyyah Mulkiyyah School, which he could combine with editorial work at the newspaper *Sabīl al-Rashād*, owned by 'Ubaydallāh, the Parliamentary Deputy from the Anatolian city of Aydīn, who would soon make a name for himself in 1910 and 1911 as a defender of Turkish superiority and opponent of the Arab deputies who were beginning to call for complete independence and severance of the Arab territories from the Empire. During these years, al-Rusāfī lived with 'Ubaydallāh, even marrying his sister Bilqīs in 1914. But in the early days of their companionship, al-Rusāfī struck up an even more immediately rewarding acquaintance with one of 'Ubaydallāh's neighbors, Tal'at Pāshā, a powerful figure in the CUP hierarchy. In those days, Tal'at already held the Cabinet position of Minister of Internal Affairs, but soon he would become part of the CUP's inner circle of governance, the famous "triumvirate" that also included Enver Pāshā and Cemal Pāshā. Tal'at would gain a reputation as the most pro-Arab of the CUP leaders, and he engaged al-Rusāfī in those early days of his rise to power as his teacher of Arabic. In 1912, this relationship would lead to al-Rusāfī's appointment to the Chamber of Deputies, the Ottoman Parliament, as member for the Iraqi district of al-Muntafiq. Thus, al-Rusāfī found himself very securely placed after his return to Istanbul, with two powerful patrons to whom he could turn in need: his new neighbor, Tal'at Pāshā, and the brother of his old sponsors in the Sulaymān family from Iraq, General Mahmūd Shawkat Pāshā, who by 1913 had become Prime Minister, with the support of the CUP. Shawkat's influence was soon lost, as he was assassinated in June 1913,

but Tal'at Pāshā would remain active at the highest levels of government, even becoming Prime Minister himself in the last year of the war, only resigning and fleeing to Germany in October 1917, just prior to the cease-fire of Mudros that put an end to hostilities between the Empire and the Allies.

It is not surprising, then, to find that al-Rusāfī composed many of his poems during this period as vehicles for support of CUP policies. In one notable case, he became involved in the controversy over the Arab Congress held in Paris, June 18-24, 1913, held to discuss the position of the Arabs in the Ottoman Empire and their demands for greater autonomy, a policy that had been discussed for some time under the rubric of "decentralization." Especially since the Balkan Wars of 1912 and 1913 had deprived the Ottomans of many of their European territories, the Empire was increasingly becoming an association of Arabic speakers and Turkish speakers, and this cast into higher relief the role of the Arab territories in the fabric of the state. This new awareness of their importance made the Arabs ever more conscious of the strictures imposed by the CUP's advocacy of "Turkification" in the territories they ruled, that is, the deliberate adoption of rules specifying Turkish as the only language to be employed in all official activities, from the schools to the law courts, and (as some Arabs believed) a preference for the appointment of ethnic Turks in upper level government positions. To counter this, influential Arabic speakers, including members of the Chamber of Deputies—as well as even some CUP officials like Tal'at Pāshā—advocated decentralization, or greater local autonomy, in the Ottoman dominions, while still maintaining the integrity of the Empire as a bulwark against European colonization.

In later years, al-Rusāfī would maintain that decentralization was the position he supported, and at first he welcomed—in the poem "Fī mu'rid al-sayf" (The Flat of the Sword)—the proposals of the sponsors of the Arab Congress, within the framework of adherence to the Empire. But shortly thereafter, responding to the increasing CUP hostility to the Congress, he composed a biting satire of the whole affair,

calling the delegates' motives and Arab patriotism into question, suggesting that they were
agents for European colonial designs on the
Ottoman provinces.

This critique of the holders of positions contrary to his own in the struggle for the development of an Arab identity would re-surface in
1916 with even more intensity. In June of that
year, Sharīf Husayn of Mecca, with British
support, would revolt against Ottoman suzerainty and declare himself the leader of all the
Arabs in their struggle for independence from
Turkish rule. One of the many ripostes to this
among Arab loyalists to the Ottoman Empire
was al-Rusāfī's poem "Thālith al-thalāthah" (The
Third of Three), which linked Sharīf Husayn to
two other Husayns seen as traitors to the Ottoman cause: Husayn al-Kāmil, who accepted the
position of Khedive of Egypt when the British
declared that country a Protectorate at the beginning of World War I, completely severing it
from any ties to the Ottoman Empire (which by
then had entered the War on the German side),
and Husayn al-Rushdī Pāshā, the Egyptian Prime
Minister who had loyally followed his master
into the British camp. This satire was so scathing
in its denunciation of Sharīf Husayn of Mecca
that it was only published in truncated form in
al-Rusāfī's *Dīwān*, with many of the most offensive verses omitted.

This poem would later come back to haunt
him, when Sharīf Husayn's son, Faysal, became
King of Iraq in 1921. But during the war years,
al-Rusāfī's life was one of increasing success.
Even when his term of office as a Parliamentary
Deputy came to an end in 1916, he had steady
employment teaching Arabic language and literature in the Shāhāniyyah Mulkiyyah School
and the Divinity School run by the Ministry of
Religious Endowments. His poetry was widely
known and admired, and he had many friends
and a comfortable marriage. As a crowning
achievement, he could take pride in the fact that
he was finally able to send money to support his
family in Baghdad, where his aged mother still
lived.

But British forces were slowly moving
northward along the Tigris and Euphrates Rivers, conquering Iraqi territory. As early Novem-

ber 1914, they had taken Basra. In March 1917,
Baghdad finally fell. Al-Rusāfī's mother died in
the disorder following the British occupation, a
loss that he felt keenly. But al-Rusāfī was unable
to return to his homeland in the wake of the
Ottoman defeat and the establishment of British
authority in Iraq, because the English army was
still involved in hostilities with Turkish units
over the exact demarcation of the boundary
between the two countries north of Mosul.

All Iraqis coming south from Istanbul were
being arrested as "Turkish sympathizers," which
al-Rusāfī certainly was. So he headed first to
Damascus, where Sharīf Faysal, accompanied by
many former Ottoman Army officers of Arab
heritage, was attempting to set up an independent Arab state. These efforts would soon come to
naught, as Syria had been awarded to France as
a sphere of influence by the secret Sykes-Picot
Agreement of May 1916, which had apportioned
the Arab territories of the former Ottoman Empire between Britain and France. France was to
administer Lebanon and Syria, in addition to its
colonies already in the Maghrib—Algeria, Tunisia and Morocco—while Britain was to control
Iraq and Palestine, in addition to its protectorate
Egypt.

But this was all in the future. As al-Rusāfī, in
the confused days following the cessation of
hostilities when everything seemed fluid and
possible, tried to get an audience with Faysal, he
was informed by Nūrī al-Sa'īd, an ex-Ottoman
officer who was rapidly becoming Faysal's
right-hand man, that the Sharīf remembered only
too well al-Rusāfī's insulting poem about his
father in 1916, and there would be no place for
him in the new regime.

While al-Rusāfī was considering his options
in the face of this rejection, a telegram arrived
from 'Ādil Jabr, Director of Education for Palestine, offering him a position teaching Arabic
language and literature at the Dār al-Mu'allimīn
(Teachers' Training College) in Jerusalem. On
March 3, 1920 he arrived at his new home, to be
welcomed by his old friend, Khalīl al-Sakākīnī
(whose successor he was to be at the Teachers'
Training College) and Muhammad Is'āf al-
Nashāshībī, a rising young author and journalist
from a famous and influential Palestinian family.

According to the letters he wrote to his friend and former host in Damascus, 'Abd al-Qādir al-Maghribī, these were some of the happiest days in his life. His only frustration seems to have been his inability to bring his Turkish wife, Bilqīs, from Istanbul. It is unclear whether this was by her choice or because of the restrictions on travel, but after this point, the two irrevocably drifted apart and eventually divorced.

With the end of the 1920-1921 school year, however, the interlude in Jerusalem came to an end. He received a telegram from the head of a leading family in Basra, al-Naqīb Tālib Pāshā, asking him to return to Iraq to serve as editor of a newspaper Tālib Pāshā was planning to finance. In July of 1920, Sharīf Faysal had been forced to relinquish his position in Syria, and now the British wanted him to occupy the throne of Iraq. Although the conclusion was foregone, they wished to hold an "election" so that it would seem Faysal was being chosen by the Iraqi people and not forced upon them. Tālib Pāshā had a strong traditional power base in Iraq, and he (along with several others) had decided to challenge Faysal, in an attempt to turn the contest into a real election. He needed a newspaper to serve as a public forum for his ideas in the campaign.

Al-Rusāfī arrived in Baghdad on April 9, staying with his old student, Mahmūd Shawkat's brother, Hikmat Sulaymān, who was already beginning his rise in postwar Iraqi politics. But in May Tālib Pāshā was exiled by the British to Ceylon and the planned newspaper never materialized. Faysal arrived in the country on June 12, was duly elected king in late July, and allegiance was sworn to him in a ceremony held on August 23, 1921.

Now al-Rusāfī found himself in essentially the same situation he had experienced in Syria two years earlier. By his own admission, he made matters worse by refusing to let bygones be bygones and questioning Faysal's motives and integrity to his face in their only meeting a few months later. Although he sought a high position in the Iraqi state, commensurate with his former rank as a deputy in the Ottoman parliament, the only position he was offered was as Vice-Chairman of the Translation Committee in the Ministry of Education. The miserliness of the offer rankled even more, since chairmanship of the Committee was vacant, and remained so.

For the next few years, al-Rusāfī would refuse to accept his lot, trying various strategies to find a way around the obstacle of King Faysal's ill will. His first instinct was to leave his homeland entirely, and in late 1922, he left for Beirut, not intending to return. The famous, but atypical, poem "Ba'd al-nuzūh" (After Exile), composed after he had made his decision, gives frank expression to the building despair and bitterness that had led him to prefer self-imposed exile. This poem is perhaps most notable for its deployment of the traditional ordering of the *qasīdah (nasīb, rahīl* and *madīh)* as a structural device for contrasting the idyllic past with the ruined present where dishonor and humiliation are his constant companions.

But news that elections were finally scheduled to be held at the end of 1923 prompted al-Rusāfī to come back the next year. The optimism he seems to have nurtured on their account was not widely shared, however. Many segments of society had been angered by the provisions included in the Anglo-Iraq Treaty, an agreement designed to formalize the provisions of the Mandate over Iraq granted by the League of Nations to Great Britain. Drafting the language of this Treaty had occupied much of the government's attention in 1922, and now the people of Iraq unexpectedly found themselves obligated to spend a quarter of the country's revenues on building up a military infrastructure mainly intended (as some saw it) to safeguard British oil investments in neighboring Iran and the Mosul area. Equally, another large segment of government funds were to be devoted to paying reparations imposed on all former Ottoman territories by the Allies, to repay the victors' war debt (a similar obligation had already been laid upon the Germans and the former Austro-Hungarian territories). As a final insult, the term of the Treaty was to last for twenty years, which meant that even nominal independence for Iraq was expected to be delayed at least that long. It is not surprising, then, that many Iraqi citizens were disposed to boycott elections for a Constituent Assembly whose first act would have to be the ratification of the widely hated treaty.

Al-Rusāfī responded to the situation rather differently. Following his return to Iraq, his first move was to declare his candidacy for a seat in the Assembly. In his campaign literature, he urged his fellow citizens to "follow their patriotic duty" and participate in the elections. Only in this way could they elect deputies who would make it their business to debate the Treaty and push for "complete independence," which, he explained, must entail economic as well as political self-determination. Such sentiments were more than likely to attract unfavorable attention from the authorities. So al-Rusāfī seems to have decided to deflect this by simultaneously with his campaign publishing a newspaper, *al-Amal*, that he used to express the most sycophantic approval and support for the British position on every issue that emerged on the local political scene. This attempt at a smokescreen seems, however, to have been to no avail; he lost badly in the election. But by the end of the year, long before the new Assembly would be summoned for its first session in March of 1924, he would be back working at the Education Ministry, in the even more prestigious position of Inspector of Arabic for the schools. So his long-term career prospects do not seen to have been materially harmed by his foray into politics. The various conciliatory gestures he attempted during his campaign seem to have been more helpful than his political opposition to authority seems to have harmed him. Even before announcing his candidacy, he had written an apologetic letter to the King begging his forgiveness for past offenses. No doubt even more helpful was his cultivation of a friendship with Abū Khaldūn Sāti' al-Husrī, an ardent Arab nationalist who had served in the Ottoman Education Ministry and was now the Head of the Iraqi Department of Education. Al-Husrī appreciated al-Rusāfī's talents, and now the more rewarding appointments in the field came his way. In 1927, for example, he followed up his selection as Inspector of Arabic with an appointment as Lecturer in Arabic Language and Literature at the Teachers' College, the closest thing Iraq had to a university in those days. He was also en-

gaged to give special lectures on these subjects elsewhere, and transcripts were published in various Department publications.

He also seems to have built upon his already extensive contacts in the Iraqi political establishment. Along with Hikmat Sulaymān, he renewed his friendship and became a political protégé of 'Abd al-Muhsin al-Sa'dūn, who had been Prime Minister in 1922, resigning over the crisis of Shi'a unwillingness to participate in the elections and ongoing discord between him and Faysal (an antipathy he shared with al-Rusāfī). But, when he became Prime Minister again in 1928, he saw to it that al-Rusāfī was chosen as the Deputy for Amara in the May elections that brought a huge majority for his party into the Chamber.

From that point on—with the exception of two brief periods: August-November 1930 and 1934—he was a Deputy in Parliament, and this was a job he took seriously, regularly attending the sessions and speaking out on issues that mattered to him and his party. Probably his most memorable moment was his speech in November of 1931, urging delay on the ratification of the Anglo-Iraqi Pact of 1930. This pact was designed to give Iraq nominal independence, but al-Rusāfī believed (quite rightly as it turned out) that it would in fact leave Iraq even more firmly under the dominance of British economic policy.

Al-Rusāfī's poetry during this period parallels the concerns foregrounded by his political career. Almost all of his poetry in the 1930s can be classified as "poetry of occasion," that is, poetry composed for immediate public consumption (either on the rostrum or in the newspaper), responding to the events of the day. It also undergoes a profound simplification and streamlining of its diction and literary allusions. Clarity is cultivated, to complement the poems' overriding concern with the gap between the words used in political discourse and the reality of the impact political policies had on people's lives. The schizophrenic tension generated by these contradictions is nicely reflected in al-Rusāfī's poem "Freedom in the Policy of the Colonialists," which relies on an insistent use of irony and antithesis to drive home its point that the rhetorical lexicon of British liberal democracy (words like "freedom," "equality," "representation," and "rights") means something quite different when politicians apply it to an Iraqi context. As al-Rusāfī aged and became more enmeshed in political controversies of the 1930s and 1940s in Iraq, his poems gradually became fewer and farther between.

This was also a period, when al-Rusāfī became increasingly involved in controversies with his fellow intellectuals and poets. His disenchantment with his ability to effect reform through his parliamentary position and involvement in political discourse seems to have been at least partially deflected into an increasing irascibility in his literary writings. His first target was his fellow poet, Jamīl Sidqī al-Zahāwī. The two had started their careers as cordial colleagues who spoke favorably of each other's work, if not fast friends. But in the 1920s a series of minor incidents between them seemed to indicate a cooling of relations, and in 1925 al-Rusāfī wrote a very cutting review of al-Zahāwī's translation of 'Umar al-Khayyām's Rubā'iyyāt, which sparked an equally hostile reaction from al-Zahāwī, who from then on engaged in a covert campaign against al-Rusāfī. This antagonism persisted until al-Zahāwī's death in 1936. Afterwards al-Rusāfī seems to have regretted his stance, and wrote an elegy praising al-Zahāwī, which he recited at a ceremony honoring him. But, by then, he had become involved in an equally distracting controversy with another old colleague—and this time a much closer friend—the Lebanese American poet and author, Amīn al-Rīhānī. In 1935, al-Rīhānī published a book called Qalb al-'Irāq (Heart of Iraq), in which he reported several remarks by al-Rusāfī critical of Iraq government policy. Al-Rusāfī seems to have felt that this made him look bad—as a member of the Chamber of Deputies and a public figure—so he wrote a letter to a local paper categorically denying what al-Rīhānī said in his book, and henceforth cut off relations with him.

In 1933, in the middle of his active parliamentary career, al-Rusāfī moved to Fallujah, a medium-sized town located not too far west of Baghdad on the Euphrates River. Although some have characterized this period of al-Rusāfī's life as an exile, he in fact remained involved in the normal range of social and political activities throughout most of the period. The initial motivating factor for his move seems to have been an offer of free housing from a prominent local family, which gave him greater financial security.

This was also the time when he was able to turn his increasing willingness to engage literary controversy to good account, in the sense that it motivated him to launch or revisit several writing projects In his last years, after he finally left the Chamber of Deputies in 1939, he finished a book on the famous medieval poet Abū 'l-'Alā' al-Ma'arrī, and wrote critical evaluations of several works by other authors, most notably the Egyptian critics Zākī Mubārak and Tāhā Husayn, as well as the Italian Orientalist Leone Caetani, whose Annali dell'Islam had recently been translated into Arabic. When these writings were finally published in 1944, he was officially accused of atheism and heresy by several conservative religious scholars. The Director of Religious Endowments, Ra'ūf al-Kubaysī, was compelled to open an official inquiry into the charges. These were summarily refuted by al-Rusāfī's old friend, Fahmī al-Mudarris, by then a respected academic administrator, who pointed out that al-Rusāfī was, for the most part, merely quoting the controversial opinions of others, that he "emphatically believed in God and His Prophet, and the words of the Qur'ān" and that charges against him had no basis. This defense ended the immediate threat to al-Rusāfī, but it probably also contributed to that fact that his last work, al-Shakhsiyyah al-muhammadiyyah (The Muhammadan Personality)—an analysis, using modern academic techniques, of the character of Muhammad and the impact it had on the formation of Islam—remained in manuscript for nearly fifty years, only being published in 2002.

In 1941, in the wake of the defeat of the forces who had rallied around Rashīd 'Alī, and the British re-occupation of Iraq to secure its oil supplies during World War II, al-Rusāfī had returned to Baghdad. There he lived in extreme poverty, largely forgotten except for a few faithful friends. At the end of 1944 the poet's health started to decline precipitously, and he was in and out of the hospital. One of his last visitors in these final days of his life was Muhammad Mahdī al-Jawāhirī, who had begun a literary correspondence with al-Rusāfī in the early 1940s, in which he emphasized his great admiration for the older poet's work and the great influence it had had on his own style. In March of 1945, al-Rusāfī's chronic lung disease turned into acute pneumonia, and on the fifteenth of that month, he died.

LETTERS

al-Rasā'il al-mutabādalah bayna al-Rusāfī wa-mu'āsirīh, edited and introduced by 'Abd al-Hamīd al-Rashūdī (Beirut: al-Mu'assasah al-'Arabiyyah li'l-dirāsāt wa'l-nashr, 1994).

REFERENCES

M. M. Badawi, *A Critical Introduction to Modern Arabic Poetry* (Cambridge: Cambridge University Press, 1975), 55-62;

Hanna Batatu, *The Old Social Classes and the Revolutionary Movements of Iraq* (Princeton: Princeton University Press, 1978);

Rafā'īl Buttī, "Ma'rūf al-Rusāfī," in: *al-Adab al-'asrī fī 'l-'Iraq al-'arabī* (Baghdad: al-Maktabah al-'Arabiyyah, 1923), 67-96;

Terri DeYoung, "This Other Eden", in: *Placing the Poet: Badr Shakir al-Sayyab and Postcolonial Iraq* (New York: State University of New York Press, 1998), 23-63;

Jalāl al-Hanafī, *al-Rusāfī fī awjihi wa-hadīdih: naqd bayānī li-qasā'id al-dīwān* (Baghdad: Matba'at al-ānī, 1962);

Salma Khadra Jayyusi, *Trends and Movements in Modern Arabic Poetry*, 2 vols. (Leiden: E. J. Brill, 1977), I, 188-193;

Hussein N. Kadhim, "Ma'rūf al-Rusāfī and the Poetics of Anti-Colonialism", in: Kadhim, *The Poetics of Anti-Colonialism in the Arabic Qasīdah* (Leiden: E. J. Brill, 2004), 85-130;

Qāsim al-Khattāt, Mustafā 'Abd al-Latīf al-Saharatī and Muhammad 'Abd al-Mun'im al-Khafājī, *Ma'rūf al-Rusāfī: shā'ir al-'arab al-kabīr* (Cairo: al-Hay'ah al-Misriyyah al-'Āmmah li'l-Ta'līf wa'l-Nashr, 1971);

Safa A. Khulusi, "Ma'rūf ar-Rusāfī, 1875-1945", *Bulletin of the School of Oriental and African Studies* 13 (1950): 616-626;

Bernard Lewis, *The Emergence of Modern Turkey* (Oxford: Oxford University Press, 1961);

Stephen Hemsley Longrigg, *Iraq, 1900 to 1950* (Oxford: Oxford University Press, 1953);

Muhammad Saghīr Hasan al-Masūmī, "Rusāfī—A Modern Poet of Iraq", *Islamic Culture* no. 24 (Jan. 1950): 50-59;

'Abd al-Hamīd al-Rashūdī, *al-Rusāfī: hayātuh, āthāruh, shi'ruh* (Baghdad: Dār al-Shu'ūn al-Thaqāfiyyah al-'Āmmah, 1988).

Ya'qūb Sannū'

(1839 – 1912)

DINA AMIN
Villanova University

WORKS

Plays and Dramatic Dialogues

[NOTE: Sannū' claims to have composed some 30 plays, but critical opinion tends to believe that the majority of them were both short and ephemeral. Whatever the case, none of them were published in his own lifetime, and only some 8 of them survive in printed form. They are now listed in alphabetical order.]

al-'Alīl ("The Invalid");

al-Amīrah al-iskandarāniyyah ("The Alexandrian Princess");

Ānisah 'alā 'l-mūdah ("A Fashionable Young
Lady");

Būrsat Misr ("The Egyptian Stock Exchange");

al-Durratayn or *al-Hashshāsh* ("The Rival Wives"
or "The Hashish Smoker"); the original play
was known by both titles;

Ghandūr Misr ("The Egyptian Dandy");

Mūlyīr Misr wa-mā yuqāsīh ("Egypt's Molière
and His Sufferings".

Collected Works

al-Lu'bāt al-tiyātriyyah ("The Theatrical Plays",
Cairo, 1987);

Muhammad Yūsuf Najm, *al-Masrah al-'arabī:
dirāsāt wa-nusūs: Ya'qūb Sannū'* (Beirut:
Dār al-Thaqāfah, 1961); works by and studies
on Sannū'.

Newspaper Articles and Other Works

Abū Naddārah (published intermittently between 1877 and 1910; repr. Beirut: Dār Sādir,
1974); periodical;

*Abū Naddārah zarqā': jarīdat musalliyāt wa-
mudhikāt* (Cairo: 1877); periodical;

Abū Naddārah, mes soixante neuf ans (Beirut,
Dār Sadir, 1974);

Suhuf Abū Nazzārah (Paris, 1878-1910); periodical;

*Abou Naddara et son voyage en Espagne, Por-
tugal, Maroc, Algerie, Tunisie* (Paris, 1890);
travelogue;

al-Badā'i' al-ma'radiyyah bi-Bārīs al-bahiyyah
("The Splendors of Exhibitions in Paris the
Radiant", Paris, 1899);

Ma vie en vers et mon théâtre en prose (Montge-
ron, 1912); memoirs of the author's experiences in theatre;

Mulhaq li-Abī Nazzārah (Paris, 1909);

Husn al-ishārah fī musāmarāt Abī Nazzārah
(Cairo, 1910).

Born to an Italian father and an Egyptian mother,
Ya'qūb Sannū' (1839-1912, also transliterated
as Sanua) was given the honorary title "Father of
Egyptian Theatre" by many scholars in recent
years. In his lifetime, the Khedive Ismā'īl of
Egypt bestowed upon him another title, "The
Molière of Egypt," a title which Sannū' cher-
ished deeply. Although he was a well known

journalist running his own satirical newspaper
entitled *Abū Nazzārah* (commonly spelled *Abou
Naddara*), which was read widely in Egypt, he is
mostly known today as the playwright, director
and theatre producer who introduced Euro-style
theatrical performances to Egypt in the mid-
nineteenth century.

Sannū''s personality, achievements and religious identity are today a subject of various debates. While maintaining that his contributions to
Egyptian theatre and the nationalist movement
were of great importance, his biographers and
scholars who have studied his theatrical productions point out that there was a good deal of exaggeration, largely driven by Sannū' himself, concerning the nature and level of his role in fostering both theatre and nationalist movement in
Egypt. A number of researchers have challenged
the extent of his participation in the resistance
movement against the British occupation. Furthermore, doubts have developed in recent times
concerning the passages in his autobiography
where Sannū' claims that his mother had made an
oath to raise him Muslim if he did not die in
infancy as did his three older siblings. A number
of studies have called that story into question, no
doubt for varying agendas, and concluded that
that pledge was never taken seriously by the
mother or Sannū' himself since not only did he
marry in a Jewish temple but was also buried in a
Jewish cemetery in France. Other scholars have
disputed Ya'qūb Sannū''s impact on Egyptian
theatre and argued that it was not any greater than
that of some of his contemporaries such as Muhammad 'Uthmān Jalāl (1829-1898). Other controversies revolve around the number of plays
Sannū' claimed to have written. Since very few of
his dramatic pieces are extant today, it is difficult
to form any definitive judgments. But, in spite of
all these disagreements concerning aspects of
Sannū''s life, art and politics, today he is constantly referred to by Egyptian and non-Egyptian
scholars and theatre practitioners alike as the
"Father of Egyptian Theatre." Furthermore
Sannū' self-identifies in his autobiography as an
Egyptian nationalist.

While Ya'qūb Sannū''s theatre established an
enduring theatrical tradition in Egypt, it did not
lay the foundation for a dramatic literary heri-

tage. Hence, theatre in Egypt remained within the realm of entertainment until Tawfīq al-**Hakīm** and others of his contemporaries, such as Ibrāhīm Ramzī and Khalīl **Mutrān**, started to make serious contributions by writing a body of well constructed dramatic works as well as producing top quality translations of international classics. With the establishment of the national theatre in Egypt in 1935, plays in the colloquial were banned from production on that stage which confirmed that Sannū''s original plays written in the Egyptian vernacular were neither going to be in repertoire nor admitted within the canon of literature. Thus, while Sannū''s contribution continues to be regarded as important from the point of view of the emergence and development of modern Arab theatre, his plays are not seen as major examples of the developmental stage of dramaturgy since they do not for the most part constitute independent and original compositions; instead they are creative adaptations of both European plays (and particularly those of Molière) and Arab folk tales.

Ya'qūb Sannū''s father, Raphael, was a court staff member in Prince Ahmad Yakan's retinue. Ahmad Yakan who was governor of Hijāz and leader of the Egyptian military campaign in Yemen, was also Muhammad 'Alī Pasha's nephew. Some sources support the idea that Raphael Sannū' was one of Yakan's close consultants. At a very early age Ya'qūb learned Arabic to read the Qur'ān, Hebrew to read the Old Testament, and English to read the Bible. According to his own recollections of his early childhood recorded in his various memoirs and autobiographies, he seems to have had an exceptional penchant for learning languages. Exceedingly impressed by the talents of the thirteen year-old Ya'qūb, who had accompanied his father on a court visit, the Prince considered the boy his protégé and granted him a scholarship to study in Italy.

In Livorno, Italy, Ya'qūb Sannū' studied art and literature for three years, and it is reported that he wrote three plays in Italian during this period. We also learn that this particular stage in his life was to shape his character as a revolutionary with a thirst for freedom in all spheres, whether intellectually, socially or nationally. Living in the regions of Tuscany from 1852 to 1855, he was there during an important historical moment, during the rise of resistance against the Austrian occupation and in the hub of the Italian nationalist movement which was demanding a united Italy. The teenage Ya'qūb became exceedingly influenced by the verve with which Italian nationalists called for their independence and freedom. Returning to his homeland, Egypt, he had already embraced the ideals which would shape his art and politics in the years to come. The European industrial revolution and that region's intellectual vitality gave him a critical perspective vis-à-vis outmoded social traditions and archaic institutions in his own country.

Upon his return to Egypt, Ya'qūb Sannū' soon found himself in the unhappy situation of having to be financially responsible for himself and his family at the age of sixteen. Six months after his homecoming, his patron, Prince Yakan, died and not long afterwards his own father passed away too. Instead of continuing his education, as his father had planned, he had to seek employment. At first, he worked as a court tutor for the children of nobility for almost three years. From 1863 he taught languages at the *Muhandiskhānah* (Polytechnic) for six years. This turned out to be an important period in his life since he established close friendships with his students in the military sciences, law, business and engineering departments, something that strengthened his affiliations with and influence on that rising educated class. Through that close association with students, he managed to spark in them a keenness for freedom and patriotism as well as a sense of responsibility for civic society and human rights. Many people have claimed that this very same group of students was indoctrinated into the concepts of nationalism by Sannū'; after their graduation they were to become activists who participated in the first modern Egyptian revolution calling for independence (1882), led by the nationalist leader, Ahmad 'Urābī. Some studies have even argued that, since 'Urābī himself attended *al-Muhandiskhānah* as a student, it is most likely that he met and befriended Sannū' there and was possibly attracted by the ideas he was expressing.

While Ya'qūb Sannū', like many educated young Egyptians in the mid-nineteenth century, was an avid nationalist, he is today known mainly for his theatrical contributions. At an early age he had attended theatre and opera presented by visiting European companies, and had at times participated as an actor in French and Italian productions. In his autobiography, Sannūʿ attests that his interest in theatre was aroused when he went to watch performances of plays by Molière, Sheridan and Goldoni. A few western travelers to Egypt have recorded that western-style performances of plays were being produced as early as 1840. However, they were staged in European languages, and thus only Europeanized Egyptians, mostly the upper class, were able to attend and understand. Moreover, the Egyptian opera was built in 1869 under the sponsorship of the Khedive Ismāʿīl, and during his reign other playhouses were also established to accommodate dramatic performances by foreign troupes such as the Comedy Theatre in al-Azbakiyyah, Cairo, as well as the Zizinyah and Alfieri playhouses in Alexandria. Meanwhile, Sannūʿ's enthusiasm for theatre soon turned into a realization that all Egyptians, not only the elite, needed to be introduced to the newly imported Euro-style drama. According to him theatre was essential to the modernization of Egypt since it provided an effective means for the promotion of ideals of progress and support for the cultivation of enlightened thinking.

Until the second half of the nineteenth century, Egyptians were accustomed to watching less formal dramatic performances of local street players, whose acts were based on improvisation, stock characters and familiar plots. Those troupes were comprised of male actors who played female roles (cf. entry on Abū Khalīl al-**Qabbānī**); they used to tour villages and market places presenting their skits wherever and whenever there was an audience ready to watch. With the introduction of ʿrealisticʾ performances through adaptations of European plays, the concept of drama as ʿimitatingʾ life was embraced by the creators of theatre and slowly accepted by the audience. Other new elements were also introduced, for instance the presentation of text-based drama and attendance at performances scheduled at a certain time of day. Most importantly, buildings to house plays

became imperative, a necessity that constituted a considerable change for a local population that up to that point had considered dramatic shows as mobile and was thus unaccustomed to the idea of a dramatic tradition set in a specific ʿtheatrical spaceʾ for performance.

In 1870, under the auspices of the Khedive Ismāʿīl, Sannūʿ formed a company of actors from a group of his pupils and opened his theatre, which would become the first Egyptian playhouse. While the script of the first play performed on that stage is not available today, the plotline as described by the author himself was a mix of elements. It contained an imitation of Molière's signature dramatic elements—trickery and role-playing, set in an *A Thousand and One Nights* atmosphere complete with song and dance.

Realizing that one of the primary dictates of the new dramatic form, namely realism, required that women play female roles, Sannūʿ went against the tradition of men playing women's parts in street performances by bringing female actresses to the Egyptian stage. He found two talented but illiterate Jewish girls whom he claimed to have taught to read and write as well as trained to become performers and introduced them to his audience as the first two Egyptian actresses. They were immediately embraced by the audience. From that point onwards women have continued to play a central role in Egyptian theatre, whether as actresses, directors, producers or playwrights.

In his autobiography, Sannūʿ asserts that the hardest achievement for him was to erect a fourth wall between the audience and actors on stage. He declares that both Egyptian audience and actors, who until that point were used to interactive street dramatic acts, continued to acknowledge each others' presence even as a performance was in progress, thus disrupting a basic principle of realism which assumes that a silent audience ʿpretendsʾ to be peeping into someone's private home and performers are ʿpretendingʾ not to be watched.

Yaʿqūb Sannūʿ is alleged to have written and produced thirty-two plays within the short period of the existence of his theatre (1870-1872); another version puts the number at seventy two, although only the thirty-two were produced on stage. He also declared that the plays received over one hundred performances. However only eight full-length plays are available in full text today, while the plots of a few others are known through descriptions included in his autobiography and his many journalistic writings.

Wishing to perform at court, Sannū' sent a copy of his first play to be reviewed by the Khedive who gave it his seal of approval and allowed the play to be performed at the Qasr al-Nīl palace. With an audience of Egyptian and European dignitaries headed by the ruler himself, Sannū' reported in his autobiography that the performance was a huge success. He presented a bill of three plays that he had written, directed and produced. At the end of the show Khedive Ismā'īl conferred on Sannū' the title "The Egyptian Molière," wishing also, with that bestowed honor, to be himself compared with Molière's illustrious patron, Louis XIV. Sannū' was also awarded the sum of £E 100 by the Khedive for the quality of his dramatic entertainment.

The three plays presented that evening were: *Ānisah 'alā 'l-mūdah* (A Fashionable Young Lady), *Ghandūr Misr* (The Egyptian Dandy), and *al-Durratayn / al-Hashshāsh* (The Two Rival Wives / The Hashish Smoker). The text of the first and second plays are not available, but Sannū' describes them thoroughly in his prose writings. The first play is about a young woman who, taking advantage of her beauty, courts a number of young men simultaneously. When her deceptions are discovered, she is ultimately abandoned by all of them and left to regret her shameless conduct. When the play was first performed in public, the audience did not like such an unhappy ending. After the first show, Sannū' found himself forced to address his audience. They objected to the way the play had ended and defended the female protagonist as a "good sort of girl"; since she hadn't flirted with anyone outside the play (i.e. the audience), she deserved a husband. Bent on keeping his audience entertained and satisfied, Sannū' gave the play a happy ending by adding a scene in which the girl repents of her misconduct and finds a suitable young man to marry.

The second play, as described briefly by Sannū', revolves around a young woman's choice of marriage between a mindless fop and an intelligent gentleman. She chooses the former for his charm. The third play, *al-Durratayn*, is an important dramatic piece as it constitutes Sannū''s first stark criticism of local social institutions; it was in fact this ever escalating satirical attitude that ultimately caused a rift between him and the palace. Set in an ordinary household, the play portrays a middle-aged man, depicted as a-good-for-nothing hashish smoker, who decides to take a sixteen year-old young woman as a second wife. To introduce the idea to the first wife, he pretends to be marrying another woman in order to relieve her of housework. The two women, each one set on expelling the other from the house, do everything in their power to make each other's life miserable. As a result the husband divorces both of them and harangues the audience about the negative aspects of polygamy. He stresses the immense disruption that occurs within the family as a result of the discord and resentment between rival wives. To please his audience, Sannū' ends the play with a reconciliation between the husband and his first wife. While the play contains witty dialogue, that being a characteristic feature of Sannū''s writing, the dramatic construction and characterization is weak. What is more, it is reported to have offended the Khedive since both he and his retinue maintained large harems.

For two years after his theatre opened, Sannū' produced numerous plays. Among the full-length works preserved till today are the following titles, mentioned in the chronological order in which they are believed to have been written and produced: *Ānisah 'alā 'l-mūdah* (A Fashionable Young Lady); *Ghandūr Misr* (The Egyptian Dandy); *al-Durratayn / al-Hashshāsh* (The Two Rival Wives / The Hashish Smoker); *al-Amīrah al-iskandarāniyyah* (The Alexandrian Princess); *al-'Alīl* (The Invalid); and *Būrsat Misr* (The Cairo Stock Exchange); also his autobiography, written in dialogue form, *Masrahiyyāt Mulyīr Misr wa-mā yuqāsīh* (Quandaries of the Egyptian Molière; a dialogue). These plays were all collected and anthologized in an edition by Muhammad Yūsuf Najm entitled *al-Masrah al-'arabī: dirāsāt wa-nusūs: Ya'qūb Sannū'*

(Arab Theatre: Texts and Critical Studies, 1961).

Al-Amīrah al-iskandarāniyyah marks a shift in Sannū''s dramatic writing and his control over structure. It is a blatant attack on social pretentiousness and blind imitation of the west. The play tells the story of an affluent westernized family where the mother, Maryam, desires to have her daughter marry a Frenchman even though the young woman loves an Egyptian. By way of role-playing, the Egyptian young man pretends to be the Frenchman and asks the mother for her daughter's hand in marriage. Immediately consenting to the proposal, the mother marries her daughter off to the Frenchman. After the wedding she discovers the truth and faints, but, realizing that she has no power to change the situation, she reluctantly accepts. The humor in the play arises from a number of sources. There is, for example, the mother's ridiculous westernized posturing evident in the way she inserts French words into her dialogue; this particular device constitutes a counter-motif in Sannū''s comedy where he regularly derives humor from the portrayal of Europeans butchering the Arabic language with mispronunciations and consistently using broken Arabic words in wrong contexts. Other humorous encounters in the play occur when Maryam tries to teach her servant, Hasanayn, to imitate European butlers, and he consistently fails to metamorphose.

In the next play, *al-'Alīl*, Sannū' pokes fun at both 'unconventional' medical practices, such as magic, and the custom of arranged marriages in Egypt. Written as a comedy, the playwright uses misunderstanding as a comic *modus operandi*. The play tells the story of Hannem who is in love with a young man, Mitrī, and her ailing father who seeks treatment through magic from a Moroccan medicine man called Hajj. Under the influence of the latter, the father, Habīb, vows to marry his daughter off to whoever is able to cure him. Thus, when he is moved to the Hulwān sanatorium for treatment, Mitrī makes a pact with the European doctor in charge: if the latter succeeds in treating the father, he will help the lovers marry. In the meantime Ilyās, Mitrī's friend, who has a funny speech impediment, joins them at the sanatorium. In a Feydeau-like scene, the father laughs so hard at Ilyās's stam-

mer that he believes himself cured, which means that he has to give his daughter in marriage to the latter. In spite of Hannem's loud refusal the father insists. The final scene is a funny cacophony of protests in which virtually every character on stage objects to what the others want. This climactic moment is however resolved with the arrival of Dr. Kabrīt, the foreign doctor. Similar to the Greek dramatic technique, the *deus ex machina*, he settles all disputes by declaring that actually what cured the father was the good air and healthy sulfuric water of Hulwān, which he had prescribed. This means that he was the person who has treated the father and maintains his position in regards to the pact he had made with Mitrī, upon which he steps down to allow the lovers to unite in marriage.

While the play is not a political satire, it does contain strong social criticism regarding the tradition of not asking the daughter's consent before giving her away in marriage. It is thus a call for fathers/patriarchy to listen to the wishes of the females in their care. Another important element in this play lies in the fact that it tells the story of a Christian family. Though religion is not a factor of importance in the play, the work is reflective of the diversity within the Egyptian population. The representation of minorities on stage (and later on screen and television) has slowly disappeared throughout the twentieth century; it is only recently that it has started to re-emerge as an effective means of changing the socially unhealthy attitude whereby only the Muslim majority is represented on stage.

One of Ya'qūb Sannū''s most important plays is *Būrsat Misr*. The renowned Egyptian critic, Lūwīs 'Awad (d. 1990) speculates that it was written in 1873, thus implying that Sannū' continued to produce and write plays even after his playhouse was closed. This play is a direct attack on the Khedive's failed economic policies; it refers to specific loans that the Egyptian ruler had received from European banks such as the Oppenheim Bank in 1873. The contemporary audience of such events was probably much better able to understand the subliminal meanings and humor of the play than today's readers. The play is believed to have been the beginning of the serious falling-out between Sannū' and the Khedive, one that ultimately led to the former's exile.

Set against the tension-inducing swings of the stock-market pendulum, the play presents a parallel between the brokerage of stocks and marriages, putting them both on a more-or-less equal footing and thus providing the basic thrust of the humor and Sannūʿ's message. The two major characters around whom the play revolves are the two bankers, Salīm and Halīm. They are given the title of *khawājāt* (a title given to non-natives or non-Muslims); throughout the play it remains ambiguous as to whether they are Levantine or Jewish. Two subordinate characters, Yūsuf and Antoine, try to sell the bankers stocks for commission; they also try to be matchmakers. Antoine tries to convince Salīm to marry his daughter, Labībah, to Halīm, while Yūsuf tries to persuade him to marry her off to Yaʿqūb, the suiter whom Labībah herself prefers. Salīm agrees to marrying Labībah to Halīm as he believes the latter to be rich, whereas, while Yaʿqūb is an honorable young man, he is only an employee and has limited financial resources. However, Labībah declares to her father that it is Yaʿqūb whom she loves. Unhappy with such information the father convinces his daughter to accept Halīm as a fiancé for six months as a kind of test period. Halīm requests the sum of £E 6,000 as dowry, and, even though Salīm realizes it is a very large sum, he agrees. Yūsuf intervenes to help the lovers unite and uses trickery to demonstrate Halīm's greed to Salīm. Once the latter realizes that money is the only thing driving Halīm's interest in the marriage, he cancels the engagement and agrees to the union between Labībah and Yaʿqūb.

The play is in two acts, each one containing a large number of short scenes and ending with a song. The structure reveals some weakness in Sannūʿ's dramatic writing, but the use of the colloquial provides the play with a great deal of vitality and authenticity in character portrayal. The playwright's biting satire is evident in his comparison of marriage with stock-brokerage, allowing him to pass negative comment on human relationships governed by materialism and on a rigid class system in the society of his time that marginalized the poor, a view that illustrates both his socialist tendencies and sense of resentment at any form of exploitation.

While Sannūʿ was a dedicated artist devoted to the establishment of a theatre movement and dramatic appreciation amongst his audience, he was also an avid nationalist. Once he started using theatre as a platform for the promotion of his political agenda and present biting socio-political satire, the ruler of Egypt withdrew his support and closed down his theatre. Although the Khedive was able to disrupt Sannūʿ's theatrical career, he could not stop him projecting his nationalist sentiments by other means, joining secret cultural and political organizations such as the Masonic Society, for example, something over which the Khedive had no authority. However, such societies were exclusive and did not allow Sannūʿ to spread his revolutionary ideas widely. Thus between 1872 and 1875 (after the closure of his theatre) he formed two cultural clubs, *Mahfal al-taqaddum* (Progress Society) and *Jamʿiyyat muhibbī al-ʿilm* (Society of the Devotees of Knowledge), through which he was able to denounce foreign occupation, give lectures on the values of political freedom, and forward his advocacy of social egalitarianism. When both platforms were shut down by Khedival order in 1874, he turned to journalism as a forum of last resort. He was to continue writing journalistically until his death.

The reason for the closing of Yaʿqūb Sannūʿ's theatre has always been a subject of debate. In one of his autobiographies, *Ma vie en vers et mon théâtre en prose*, Sannūʿ accuses certain influential figures of having artfully swayed the Khedive's opinion so that he decided to close the theatre down. Among those forces were ʿAlī Mubārak (d. 1893), the Minister of Education, and Draneht Beğ, the Superintendent of the Khedival Theatres. The first had a clearly conservative outlook and considered dramatic performances to be a challenge to the tradition of gender segregation, a social custom that he endorsed. Draneht Beğ, who was opposed to the existence of an Arab theatre in the first place, construed the Khedive's attention to Sannūʿ as a threat to both the funding of the state-owned Comedy and Opera theatres that he supervised and his own status within the cultural scene in

Egypt. He too was thus eager to kill off any competition by inciting the closure of Sannū''s theatre. Furthermore, according to Sannū', after he had staged a play entitled *al-Watan wa'l-hurriyyah* (The Nation and Liberty)—a critique of existing social structures and a call for a better treatment of the peasants and downtrodden elements in society—, the watchdogs of the British occupation came to regard his playhouse as being dangerous since it was spreading a nationalist agenda potentially threatening to their occupational rule. They proceeded to point out to the Khedive the satirical and politically subversive nature of Sannū''s plays; their advice to the Khedive involved the immediate silencing of Sannū''s theatrical voice, one that was constantly undermining the Khedive's rule and their own authority in Egypt. Thus, while the various studies that take Sannū''s art and/or politics as their focus have been unable to point to the single overwhelming factor that brought about the closure of his theatre, their conclusions invariably include a mixture of all the above possibilities.

For four years after the demise of his theatre, Ya'qūb Sannū' taught at the elite missionary school in Cairo, the Frères de la doctrine chrétienne. He also gave private lessons to European travelers and children of local dignitaries. As a result of the same court censorship that he had encountered in his theatre, the Egyptian press did not welcome his journalistic contributions. In order to find a forum for his political commentaries, he first established a number of short-lived newspapers in Italian and French, and then in March 1877 founded his most enduring publication, a satirical newspaper entitled *Abū Naddārah Zarqā'* (Man with Blue Spectacles), a title that has continued to serve as his *nom de plume*. It was the first Arabic newspaper to be written in the colloquial dialect and to present satire through cartoons, the illustrations for which were sketched by Sannū' himself. The paper took as its main subject matter criticism of the Egyptian ruling family and British authority over the country. He often expressed his views by way of dialogues, assigning symbolic names to authority figures. The Khedive's epithet, for example, was *shaykh al-ḥārah* (the quarter headman), a figure who consistently appears in the

cartoons or satirical dialogues as greedy, despotic and corrupt. Others figures—merchants, court minions, peasants and British personalities—were referred to by particular labels that could identify them for readers. In May 1878, this paper too was suppressed by authorities, and in June 1878 he was exiled by vice-regal order.

Ya'qūb Sannū' spent the rest of his life in Paris, but he never stopped writing about his nostalgia for Egypt nor did he stop his satirical newspaper writing. *Abū Naddārah Zarqā'* appeared intermittently and clandestinely in Egypt and other Arab countries. Ironically, while he himself was in exile, his paper was widely read in Egypt by people from virtually all walks of life, from officers in the military to denizens of the countryside, aristocrats and middle class readers alike. To escape censorship, Sannū' published his weekly under different pseudonyms: *al-Naddārah al-Misriyyah* (1879-1880), *Abū Zummārah* (1880), *Abū Suffārah* (1881), *Muqaddimat al-Hawī* (1881) and *al-Watanī al-Misrī* (1883).

During his years in Paris, Sannū' was invited to return to Egypt a few times, but he consistently refused to do so as long as the British still occupied the country. In *Abū Naddārah* of August 1882, following the defeat of Ahmad 'Urābī Pasha by the British, he expressed his endless support for the nationalist movement, terming 'Urābī the most heroic of all heroes. To his old patriotic comrades he wrote that he considered himself to be the representative of all Egyptians in Europe, "where I can defend my nation in European newspapers," he wrote. "While I may be far away, my heart and spirit are with you." When 'Urābī was exiled to Ceylon, Sannū' kept up a regular correspondence with him for at least ten years. From his Parisian exile, Sannū' continued to lobby for the support of France and Turkey in order to free his country from British occupation. It is not a little ironic that his call for French help coincides with a period in history when the French themselves also had enormous imperial ambitions in the Arab world.

In 1910, with old age impinging and his eyesight waning, Ya'qūb Sannū' gave up writing altogether. He died in 1912 and was buried in Paris, survived by his daughter who preserved his writings and aided 20th century scholars in the publication of much of his unpublished work.

REFERENCES

Roger Allen, "Drama and Audience: The Case of Arabic Theatre", *Theater Three* 6 (1989): 25-54;

——, "Egyptian Drama after the Revolution," *Edebiyat* 4.1 (1979): 97-134;

——, *The Arabic Literary Heritage: The Development of its Genres and Criticism* (Cambridge, U.K.; New York: Cambridge University Press, 1998);

Lūwīs 'Awad, *Tārīkh al-fikr al-misrī al-hadīth: min 'asr Ismā'īl ilā thawrat 1919* (Cairo: Maktabat Madbūlī, 1986);

M. M. Badawi, *Early Arabic Drama* (Cambridge: Cambridge University Press, 1987);

——, "The Father of the Modern Egyptian Theatre: Ya'qūb Sannū'", *Journal of Arabic Literature* 16 (1985): 132-145;

——, *Modern Arabic Drama in Egypt* (Cambridge: Cambridge University Press, 1987);

Rosella Dorigo Ceccato, "Autobiographical Features in the Works of Ya'qūb Sannū'", in: *Writing the Self: Autobigraphical Writing in Modern Arabic Literature*, ed. Robin Ostle, Ed de Moor, & Stefan Wild (London: Saqi Books, 1998), 51-61;

Irene L. Gendzier, *The Practical Visions of Ya'qūb Sanū'* (Cambridge: Harvard University Press, 1966);

'Abd al-Hamīd Ghunaym, *Sannū': rā'id al-masrah al-misrī* (Cairo, 1966);

Salma Khadra Jayyusi and Roger Allen (eds.), *Modern Arabic Drama: An Anthology* (Bloomington: Indiana University Press, 1995);

Jacob M. Landau, *Studies in the Arab Theater and Cinema* (Philadelphia: University of Pennsylvania Press, 1958);

Moosa Matti, "Ya'qûb Sanû' and the Rise of the Arab Drama in Egypt", *International Journal of Middle East Studies* 5 (1974): 401-33;

Shmuel Moreh, "New Light on Ya'qub Sanua's Life and Editorial Work through his Paris archive", in: *Writer, Culture, Text*, ed. Ami Elad (Fredericton, New Brunswick: York Press, 1993), 101-115;

—— and Philip Sadgrove (eds.), *Jewish Contributions to Nineteenth-Century Arabic Theatre: Plays from Algeria and Syria: A Study and Texts* (London: Oxford University Press, 1996);

'Anūs Najwā, *Masrah Ya'qūb Sannū'* (Cairo: al-Hay'ah al-'Ammah li'l-Kitāb, 1984);

'Alī al-Rā'ī, *Masrah al-sha'b: al-kumīdya al-murtajalah, funūn al-kumīdya, masrah al-dam wa'l-dumū'* (Cairo: Dār al-Sharqiyyāt, 1993).

Abū 'l-Qāsim al-Shābbī

(1909 – 1934)

MOHAMED-SALAH OMRI

Washington University, St. Louis

WORKS

al-Khayāl al-shi'rī 'ind al-'Arab ("Poetic Imagination among the Arabs", Tunis: Matba'at al-'Arab, 1929);

al-Shābbī: hayātuhu wa-shi'ruhu ("al-Shābbī: His Life and Poetry"), ed. Abū 'l-Qāsim Muhammad Karrū (Beirut, 1952);

Aghānī al-hayāt ("The Songs of Life"), ed. Muhammad al-Amīn al-Shābbī (Cairo: Dār al-Kutub al-Sharqiyyah, 1955; 2nd ed. Tunis: al-Dār al-Tūnisiyyah li'l-Nashr, 1966; 3rd ed. 1970);

Rasā'il al-Shābbī ("al-Shābbī's Letters"), ed. Muhammad al-Hilīwī (Tunis: Dār al-Maghrib al-'Arabī, 1966);

Mudhakkirāt ("Diaries", Tunis: al-Dār al-Tūnisiyyah li'l-Nashr, 1966).

Complete Works

al-A'māl al-kāmilah ("The Complete Works", 6
vols., Tunis: Dār al-Maghrib al-'Arabī, 1994).

Translated Works

Songs of Life (Tunis: Bayt al-Hikmah, 1987);
translation of *Aghānī al-hayāt*, tr. by Lena
Jayyusi and Naomi Shihab Nye;

"Life's Will" and excerpts from "Songs of Ecstasy", in: *Modern Arabic Poetry: An Anthology*, ed. Salma Khadra Jayyusi (New
York: Columbia University Press), 97-103;
translation of "Irādat al-hayāt" etc.

"I Weep for Love", translated by A. J. Arberry,
in: *Modern Arabic Poetry* (London: Taylor's
Foreign Press, 1950), 52-53; translation of
"Abkīkī...li'l-hubb";

"In the Valley of the Shadow of Death", translated by Mounah Khouri and H. Algar, in:
Modern Arabic Poetry: An Anthology
(Berkeley: University of California Press,
1974), 136-7; translation of "Fī zill wādī al-
mawt";

"A Storm in the Dark", translated by M. M.
Badawi, *Journal of Arabic Literature* 6
(1975): 32; translation of "Zawba'ah fī 'l-
zalām";

"The Song of Sorrow", translated by S. Masli-
yah, *Maghreb Review* 6 (1981): 98-99; translation of "Nashīd al-asā";

"Fate Must Respond", translated by Jamal
Ahmad, in: *Modern Islamic Literature* (New
York: Rinehart, 1970), 161-2; translation of
"Irādat al-hayāt".

Abū 'l-Qāsim al-Shābbī was one of those rare
figures who managed to capture the spirit of
their time in memorable metaphors and encapsulate it in their lives and personalities. He was
able to give expression to a period marked by
the rise of the liberationist spirit in his native
Tunisia and the yearning for emancipation from
colonialism and underdevelopment which swept
across much of the Arab world in the first half of
the 20th century. And nowhere was this truer

than in a poem which was on the tip of millions
of tongues, taught in schools from Morocco to
Yemen, sung by some of the most influential
Arab stars, written on protest banners, shouted
by students in the face of French and English
occupiers, and more recently against their own
governments. The couplet even entered the
folklore of global protest music and poetry and
was adopted by the International Solidarity
Movement. The opening lines of the poem now
form the closing part of Tunisia's national anthem and adorn an archway in the poet's native
city, Tozeur.

If one day people should embrace life,
Fate is certain to respond.
The night will surely dissipate
And chains will be broken.

Yet despite their global appeal, the humanistic
spirit they embody, and their seeming timelessness, these words were the product of a specific
historical context and a personal temperament
fashioned by colonialism and the movement of a
poetry which was undergoing transformations of
profound proportions. In poetry as in criticism,
al-Shābbī needs to be understood within schools
of thought and poetic composition known as *al-
Dīwān*, *al-Mahjar* and *Apollo* (see the articles on
Jubrān, **Nu'aymah**, and **Abū Shādī** in this
volume). Al-Shābbī sought to rebel against
Arabic tradition in the way that European Romantics had rejected classicism. He was a poet's
poet, rather like the French Arthur Rimbaud,
keenly conscious of his mission as poet and as
visionary. At a time when contact between the
Arab East and North Africa was minimal, he
served as a bridge, gaining fame and a canonical
status across the Arab world in the 20th century.
With such reputation and impact, it may appear
that he had a prolific input and a long life. The
reality is quite different. The poet produced just
over one hundred poems and lived for only 25
years. In fact al-Shābbī's impact was such that
there is more poetry about him than by him. (By
1994, no less than 140 poems celebrating the
poet have been recorded.) He also kept a diary
and published several pieces of literary and
cultural criticism.

Abū 'l-Qāsim ibn Muhammad ibn Abū 'l-

Qāsim ibn Ibrāhīm al-Shābbī was born on 24 February 1909 in the district of al-Shābbiyyah in Tozeur, an oasis town in the South West of Tunisia. His family is said to have settled in the area 300 years earlier after they were expelled from power as rulers of the renowned city of al-Qairawān. Among famous members of the family were Ahmad ibn Makhlūf al-Shābbī, founder of the al-Shābbiyyah *tarīqah* (Sufi path) and a famous scholar. The poet's father was a traditional judge (*qādī*) who had received a religious education in Tunisia and degrees from the al-Azhar mosque-university in Cairo where he met the famous reformist, Muham-mad 'Abduh (d. 1905). Following the father's appointments, the family moved around Tuni-sia quite frequently, giving the poet exposure to life across the country. He lived in Silyānah and Tālah in the centre; Gafsa and Gābis in the south; and Majāz al-Bāb, Zaghouane and Rā's al-Jabal in the north. As a result, he did not really live in his native town until the last five years of his life. Al-Shābbī studied at Quranic schools before moving to the Islamic university in Tunis, al-Zaytūnah, in 1920 from where he graduated in 1928. In accordance with his father's wishes he then joined the School of Law and started training in Tunis in 1930. In the capital, he stayed in student accommod-ation, frequenting the Khaldūniyyah and al-Sādiqiyyah libraries and spending vacations with his family wherever they happened to be. Al-Shābbī's education was exclusively in Arabic. Although he was always keen to read foreign literature in translation, he suffered from his lack of knowledge of a foreign lan-guage at a time when most of his friends were bi-lingual. "I know that I can only fly in the world of literature on a single wing," he wrote in a letter dated 22 February 1933. He hated his legal studies in Tunis, and focused instead on literary activities and attempts to reform educa-tion at al-Zaytūnah.

When his father died in December 1929, the poet became the head of the household. He married soon afterwards and had a child by 1931. But despite the need, he refused to take up a job saying:

I am a poet and the poet must be free like a bird

in the forest. Legal jobs in particular stifle the spirit and destroy the songs of the heart and personal serenity.

In Tozeur, he often spent time near a water-spring on the outskirts of town (now a shrine to him and an obligatory stop for tourists), reading or socializing with friends, walking in the oasis, or attending Sufi ceremonies, all of which he reports in letters to his friend at the time. He also helped found the Association of Tozeur Students and tried to start a fund to help writers publish their work.

Some of al-Shābbī's ideas about poetry are scattered in articles, letters and private diaries. In his introduction to the Egyptian poet **Abū Shā-dī**'s collection *al-Yanbū'* (The Water Spring), published in 1932 and solicited by the latter, al-Shābbī gives a useful overview of contemporary Arabic poetry and advocates innovation. He does however express his firm belief that respect for the rules of the Arabic language and its roots should be maintained. In 1931 he considered Jubrān's rebellion against the rules of Arabic "a mistake which will be outweighed by the intel-lectual revolution he left behind." In a veiled criticism of Abū Shādī, he mentions that the latter is prolific without saying much about the quality of his work. But in a letter dated 19 December 1933, he explains that the Egyptian poet appears hurried, opting for quantity over depth. In 1929 al-Shābbī caused a memorable stir across the cultural landscape in Tunisia with his lectures on "al-Khayāl al-shi'rī 'ind al-'arab" (Poetic Imagination among the Arabs). Reports say that hundreds of people from all orientations attended the talk and were soon divided into supporters and detractors of the poet. The lec-tures were the third in a series of daring talks which brought out into the open a conflict be-tween two sides, known as the conservatives *(al-taqlīdiyyūn)* and the modernizers *(al-mujaddi-dūn)*, that marked the cultural scene in Tunisia at the time. In the literary field, al-Shābbī spear-headed the second group, whereas his friend, al-Tāhir al-Haddād, led a parallel debate about the rights of women and the working class. A year later, al-Shābbī published his lectures in book form through the subscription system prevalent at the time. By then, he had become part of the poetry scene, but a poet with no collection to his name. This was in fact his first book.

al-Khayāl has been seen within a number of contexts. One is the controversy which arose from skepticism regarding the origins of pre-Islamic poetry, introduced by the Egyptian Tāhā **Husayn** in his famous work on the subject (1926) and the hostile responses that it had aroused across the Arab world, including Tunisia. Scholars have suggested that al-Shābbī's real target was a book entitled *al-Khayāl fī 'l-shi'r al-'arabī* (Imagination in Arabic Poetry) that had been published in 1922 by Muhammad al-Khadr Husayn (1873-1958), who was *muftī* of al-Azhar in Egypt but Tunisian in origin. He too had previously attempted to refute Tāhā Husayn's ideas in a work entitlted *Naqd kitāb "Fī 'l-shi'r al-jāhilī"* (A Critique of the book "On Pre-Islamic Poetry", 1927). A further context was the rising influence of Western ideas, particularly Romanticism.

Al-Shābbī, clearly aware of the polemical nature of his ideas, presents them as personal beliefs rather than research findings, although he does so in a methodical, clear, learned and stylistically polished piece. He divides imagination into two types. One he calls "technical" because it involves verbal skills which can be learned, such as metaphors, imagery, and other forms of verbal mastery. Imagination here plays an ornamental role. The second type of imagination and the main thrust of the lectures is called 'poetic' and is used by human beings to understand themselves and the world around them. Philosophy, religion, and myth all come under this category. Al-Shābbī focuses on myth, nature, woman and narrative poetry as subjects of his analysis and draws comparisons between Arabic and Western literatures.

According to al-Shābbī, the earliest form of imagination was myth, since it constituted the first formulation whereby human consciousness created meaning in life and the world. "Myth may be considered the childhood of poetry during the childhood of the human kind." After establishing this premise, he moves on to ask whether Arab culture has had its own myths. He declares that myths are rare in the early history of Arab civilization and wonders whether it is a

question of record. In other words, could it be that narrators have neglected to transmit any myths to us? The answer provided is no, since there was in fact very little for them to preserve. It seems, al-Shābbī suggests, that, unlike the Greeks and Romans, the Arabs neither cared about their myths nor included them in their poetry. For him, even the few Arab myths and deities that existed—and he gives several concrete examples— show a lack of imagination. For instance, the deities of the ancient Arabs were "simple statues," revered ancestors or deities borrowed from neighboring cultures. They did not invest these gods with life or integrate them into their concerns and aspirations. The goddess Ashtar, borrowed from the Assyrians by both Arabs and Greeks, is an example of the varying uses of myth. Al-Shābbī suggests that while the Arabs turned Ashtar into a statue the Greeks called her Aphrodite and created around her stories and genealogies that were unknown even to the Assyrians. The Greeks, he concludes, seem to have associated their deities with ideas, feelings or forces of nature, and constructed stories and poems around them, whereas the Arabs failed to do so. Al-Shābbī's ideas fall within the way his contemporary Arab intellectuals tried to analyze their own history and culture in comparison to Western civilization. By giving this prime importance to myth, al-Shābbī, like others in his generation and even the one after it, such as the Egyptian Tawfīq al-**Hakīm** and the poets Adonis (i.e., 'Alī Ahmad Sa'īd, b. 1928) and Badr Shākir al-Sayyāb (d. 1964) tried to understand and explain why Western literature and philosophy have developed at a pace unmatched by their Arabic counterparts. But the poet, unlike al-Hakīm for instance, was not interested in applications such as the representation of myths in theatre or dramatic poetry. His interest was in the foundations themselves.

Al-Shābbī goes on to point out the close link between poetic imagination and nature. In other words, nature in a nation's poetry is related to the environment that shapes that nation. Arab poets, he argues, have excelled in their nature poetry, particularly with regard to the environments they know best, the desert in early poetry, and mountains and meadows in the poetry of Spain (al-Andalus), to cite just two examples. However, the Arabs did not establish a poetic relationship with nature; rather they talked about it like "story tellers." al-Shābbī gives ample citations from Arabic poetry on the subject and compares them with 18th and 19th century European Romantics, particularly Lamartine and Goethe. His conclusion is that Arabic poetry was naïve while its western counterpart was marked by depth. Al-Shābbī 's own poetry, as we will see shortly, attempts to redress this perceived problem.

The third issue is the relationship between poetic imagination and women, not from the point of view of how women dealt with imagination—in fact women poets are completely absent from al-Shābbī's otherwise impressive anthology in this book—; rather, he focuses on how poetry portrayed woman. The Arabs, he suggests, have given woman a very high position, to the point that no poem has really been free from reference to this theme. The initial part in the structure of the canonical *qasīdah* (Arabic ode) is often about a woman. However, he thinks that this presence was limited to the woman as body and one of life's pleasures, not as a soul or an inspiration. There are, he argues, social and historical reasons for this position. One such is the fact that the culture links women to guile (*kayd*); the other is that women never had "real freedom" at any point in Arab history. Al-Shābbī contends that the Arabic literary heritage includes a good deal of poetry devoted to erotic love (*ghazal*) but not about love itself, except perhaps in the case of Ibn al-Rūmī (d. 896) and, more recently, Jubrān. With regard to narrative, he notes the presence of this genre in the poetry of Mankhal al-Yashkarī and Imru' al-Qays (d. circa 540), but suggests that these narratives were part of the overall structure, not an independent genre as one would find in Greek and Roman poetry. 'Umar ibn Abī Rabī'ah (d. 712) was an exception, but his example was emulated by his successors. In prose, narrative either focused on moral exemplars and wisdom or else on literary humor and linguistic entertainment (such as the *maqāmah* genre).

After this general analytical overview, the poet concludes that Arabic poetry has been 'materialistic,' unwilling to look into the essence of things or explore the unknown. This, he insists, should not be seen as meaning that this literature did not express the aspirations and worldview of the Arab people across the ages, but rather that this literature "is no longer appropriate to our present-day spirit, our mood, hopes and wishes." The pre-modern tradition should not be emulated because such an act would pull the culture back into the past at a time when it should be looking to the future. But before it can move onwards, the culture needs to become conscious of the fact that the past does not fill "our hunger nor does it cover our naked bodies." al-Shābbī therefore sees his own task as one of disseminating this consciousness.

The key point, made again and again, is that Arab writers should not look to the past for answers to present-day problems. Instead, inspiration should be sought in Western culture. The basic reason for this inadequacy and the "shallowness" of Arabic poetic imagination, he argues, is related to the Arab spirit, which he describes as "rhetorical" and "materialistic." The Arabs made no distinction between poet and orator; both were expected to express the spirit of the tribe and defend its honor. Likewise, poetry remained largely unchanged for centuries. Sections of the culture maintained a religious understanding of literature, overvaluing pre-Islamic convention as a dogma not to be changed while others understood literature solely as a form of entertainment. Both tendencies focused on form and expression. In addition, the Arabs did not translate the literatures of other nations and thus failed to benefit from them. They avoided Greek and Roman literatures, not only because they perceived them as idolatrous but also because they had an arrogant sense of the value of their own literary culture. Modern-day life demanded a drastic departure from this tradition.

We need a new fresh literature which expresses the hope, life and feelings inside us; when we read this literature, we should find in it a representation of our very heartbeats, the movement of our souls and the yearnings of our hopes and

dreams. Ancient Arabic literature cannot pro-
vide such things; it was not composed for us, the
people of the present era, but for hearts now
silenced by death.

Critical reactions to *al-Khayāl* vary a great
deal. It has been called a pamphlet against tradition; a manifesto for new poetry written in the
rhetoric of missionaries; an immature study of
Arabic poetry; a prelude to a modernism which
cuts ties with tradition; a study of the absence of
poetic imagination among the Arabs. Others
considered it an extreme case of infatuation with
the West, particularly the European classical age
and Romanticism, and even a form of self-hate
and masochism. But some critics have argued
that it would be wrong to look for al-Shābbī the
critic in this book because his intention was to
mount a vigorous rebellion against a stagnant
culture rather than to provide an objective analysis of its history. For them, *al-Khayāl* marks a
moment of intellectual struggle against repression of opinion and forces that, according to the
poet, were impeding creativity and progress. The
book is not so much about Arabic poetry as it is
about the position that Arabs have adopted
towards their poetic tradition and how they have
understood the function and mission of poetry in
the past. Some of the ideas expressed in *al-
Khayāl* can also be found in al-Shābbī's poetry,
making the book both a summary of the poet's
work until 1929 and a manifesto for what he
would write thereafter.

Some of al-Shābbī's biographers have suggested that from 1928 he went into a deep depression as the result of the death of a woman he
loved; but information about this is vague and
widely contested. In letters to friends and in his
diaries, the poet often mentions his nightmares,
extreme sensitivity, and frequent bouts of weeping. He talks of a loss of hope and feelings of
worthlessness and despair. "In this life," he
wrote to his life-long friend Muhammad al-
Hilīwī on the 22nd of February 1933,

nothing makes me sadder than the thought that I
am going to die before fulfilling the mission for
which I feel I was born.

In moments of despair, al-Shābbī thought that

Tunisia was too small for him, and that people
in general were beneath the mission he had for
them. He called himself an unknown prophet, a
visionary who saw the right path and felt the
need to lead the people to it through poetry and
willful action. In periods of greater hope, he
expressed his belief in the will of the people to
change their destiny and regained his sense of
belief in the validity of his own mission. It is in
this sense, one critic has observed, that Romanticism for al-Shābbī was a life experience as
much as it was a mode of poetic expression.

In 1933, despite depression and illness, he
started editing his poetry for publication as a
collection, a project that involved both copying
and amendments and one that was to remain
unfinished until 20 years after his death. It seems
that that his connection with the group of poets
who worked around the Egyptian journal *Apollo*
and the poet Ahmad Zakī **Abū Shādī** gave him
both a natural home and renewed impetus. In
fact, al-Shābbī had started writing poetry at the
age of 15, but, fearing his father's disapproval,
had not published his work until three years later.
Appearing first in Tunisian newspapers and
magazines, it was then published in the Cairo-
based journal, *Apollo*, where from 1933 eighteen
of his best-known poems appeared and were the
subject of two critical articles in 1934. It is
through *Apollo* that he would become known
across the Arab World. In 1933, encouraged by
Abū Shādī, he selected 83 poems to form a
collection (*dīwān*). As he reports in his letters,
he started gathering subscriptions ahead of publication. But when the book was finally published in 1955, it contained 91 poems. The 1984
edition increased the number to as many as 132
pieces, but *The Collected Works* published in
1994 included only 105 poems dated between 1
August 1924 and 20 August 1934. These discrepancies reveal serious disagreement as to how
much of al-Shābbī's poetry should have been
allowed to circulate. The poet himself discarded
or amended several poems. For example, his
most famous poem, "Irādat al-hayāt" (The Will
of Life), appeared in three different versions: 60
lines in the version published in 1935; 58 in the
book by Karrū published in 1952; and 63 in the
1955 collection. In addition, there are 29 in-

stances of internal differences in wording between the earlier and later versions. This controversy over poems and versions is indicative not only of the disputed poetic quality of particular poems, lines or expressions, but also of a contested image of the poet himself. Some editors have been motivated by the desire to increase the volume of what al-Shābbī published so as to boost the size of his anthology, while others have preferred to remove poems that might reflect negatively on his reputation. A third group has aimed to abide by the poet's own selection, since he seemed determined to weed out a large number of poems that he had published earlier because he considered them naïve and worthless (as he himself notes in a letter dated 19 December 1933).

Some critics have noted that al-Shābbī never really speaks of a specific location or time. Likewise, no specific woman is mentioned in his love poetry, making woman in his work an archetype or an ideal rather than a specific lover. The latter is debated, and an early love story was alleged. (A 2005 television drama about the poet's life plays up this story, giving more def-inition to the woman by dressing her in a specific regional costume). This enabled his poetry somehow to transcend its geographical and temporal origins, namely Tunisia in the late 1920's and early 1930's, and it may help to explain why his poetry was more widely read 20 years after his death (and even up till now) than was the case during his own lifetime. Beyond the canonical nature of his poetry, the appeal remains largely untouched, no more so than in his most famous poems. Five of these, each representing an aspect of the poet's art and thought, will be treated in some detail below. School curricula in Tunisia and elsewhere, as well as singers, have made other poems famous. Among them, we find "Yā ibna ummī" (My Mother's Son, 20th Feb. 1929), "Shakwā al-yatīm" (The Orphan's Plaint, 31st Aug. 1926), "al-Nabī al-majhūl" (The Unknown Prophet, 21st Jan. 1930); "al-Jannah al-ḍā'i'ah" (The Lost Paradise, 9th Jan. 1933); "Falsafat al-thu'bān al-muqaddas" (The Philosophy of the Sacred Snake, 20th Aug. 1934) and "Ilā tughāt al-'ālam" (To the Tyrants of the World, 8th Apl. 1934).

Critics divide al-Shābbī's work into two distinct phases, perhaps taking their cue from the poet himself; in a letter he states that his attitude changed from a view of a life of despair and pain to one involving sarcastic smiles and strong belief, especially at the time when he wrote "al-Sabāh al-Jadīd" (The New Morning). According to some critics, the poem even shows a move away from tones of confession and mourning, often mixed with loud and direct rhetoric, in order to focus on sound, rhythm and allusion. At the level of form, al-Shābbī makes full use of the Arabic meters in all their variety, using 9 out of the 16, something that is rare among modern poets. About one third of the poems are multirhymed. The five poems discussed below are: "al-Sabāh al-jadīd" (The New Morning); "Irādat al-hayāt" (The Will of Life); "Nashīd al-jabbār aw hākadhā ghannā Brūmīthyūs" (The Song of the Mighty One, Or Thus Sung Prometheus); "Salawāt fī haykal al-hubb" (Prayers in the Temple of Love) and "Fī zill wādī al-mawt" (In the Shadow of the Valley of Death).

Many critics have termed "Prayers in the Temple of Love," written 13 October 1931, "a poetic event" in modern Arabic literary history; it remains a favorite in anthologies of love poetry. The origin of the poem and the motivations behind it remain unclear. The poem starts with the description of the beloved in a series of similes, none of which is concrete, unlike the traditional tendency in Arabic poetry where woman's body and high birth are celebrated in the opening section of the ode.

You are gentle as childhood,
*   As a dream, a melody, a morning light.*
Gentle as the laughing sky,
*   As a moon-rich night.*
Sweet like roses,
*   Or a newborn smile.*

Further on in the poem, there is a description of the body in terms of music and rhythm rather than shape and feel:

You sway in the world,
*   Like melody of divine perfection.*
Your steps are drunk with song,

Your voice echoes the distant sound of a flute.

The beloved is described as someone who can save the poet from the disintegration of his soul and descent into despair. The woman here is akin to the poetic muse; she even assumes attributes of the divine, a life-giver who is called upon to save the poet from an alienating existence among people who do not appreciate beauty and the purity of love. The poem concludes with a supplication that, by regenerating the poet's voice and art, she not extinguish the hope created by her beauty. The prayers in her temple are bound to be answered:

For a great God does not stone a slave
   When he is kneeling down in ardent worship.

"The New Morning," written 9 April 1933, is often cited as a key example of al-Shābbī's attempts at innovation in Arabic poetry, involving both form and rhythm. The poem has varied rhyme, in itself a reflection of a departure from the mono-rhymed classical Arabic poem. It is also made up of a set of three lines, called *qaflah* or *qarār* (refrain), repeated after two sets of 4 quatrains, creating a lyricism and musicality through repetition with variation. On the page, the poem looks unusual as it comes close to, but does not emulate, the sonnet in Western poetry, being three sets of 11 lines each, rather than 14. The poem is further admired because of the profound meanings that it conveys. Here the poet sees light not as representing life on earth but rather as a deliverance from it through death or a form of permanent existence beyond suffering. The refrain goes like this:

Let wounds heal!
         Let sorrows recede!
For the age of weeping is gone,
      The time of madness too.
And from beyond the ages,
      Morning has broken.

Wounds and sorrows are transcended by turning life's pain into a song (al-Shābbī titled his collection *Songs of Life*):

In death's gullies,
         I buried my pain.
To the vanishing winds,

I scattered my tears.
Out of life,
   I made a melodious organ.
And played on it
   Across the expanse of time.

At the end, the poet sails in the "great ocean", answering the call of the new morning and bidding farewell to life's troubles and "weary spaces."

Yet, despite the appeal of meditative pieces and love poems, al-Shābbī remains best known for his 'political' poetry. This should not be understood to mean a specific political line or affiliation with a given agenda or party. In fact, the poet did not really belong to any political institution or group. His poems gave expression to the general desire for freedom from colonialism; they were hymns to liberation and rebukes against tyrants rather than calls for specific action. His most-quoted poem, "Irādat al-hayāt" (The Will of Life), written a year before his death (16. 9. 1933), was said to have resulted from an encounter with the nationalist, al-Tāhir Sfar, in 1933 in the mountainous region of ʿAyn Drāhim where al-Shābbī was convalescing and where both men discussed the rising tensions with the French. But to his readers the poem did not come as a surprise, since it had been preceded by a number of other poems on the same theme, dating back to the poet's earliest published work. For example, "To a Tyrant" written on 17 February 1927, displays an equally revolutionary spirit but does not contain the element of a dialogue with nature, which is the structuring principle of the later poem. The poems show belief in the power of the people, reveal the transient nature and fragility of domination and repression, and, above all, express an unwavering hope in freedom as the ultimate outcome no matter what the suffering and setbacks involved. "To the Tyrants of the World" ("Ilā tughāt al-ʿālam," dated 8 April 1934—just a few months before the death of the poet) is further imbued with references to nature. The poem contains one of his most quoted lines:

Beware! For under dying ashes, lives fire.
   Whoever sows thorns is certain to harvest wounds.

Yet, despite the general nature of the appeal early on in his career, the poet left no doubt that occupied Tunisia was his preoccupation. In the poem "Beautiful Tunisia," written when he was 18, he says:

This is the age of darkness,
But I have glimpsed the morning beyond it.
 Beautiful Tunisia! I have ridden the waves
  of your love.
 Deep love is my covenant with you,
And I have tasted its bitter sweetness.
 […]
 Time has dissipated the glory of my peo-
 ple
 But life is certain to adorn them with glory
 once again.

It is in fact this certitude that guides the poet's seemingly unstoppable belief in the power of the people in "The Will of Life." Here, the poet takes his anguished questions and doubts to nature, and she responds with resounding certainty:

If one day people should embrace life,
 Fate is certain to respond.
The night will surely dissipate
 And chains will be broken.

After a statement of the overall message (This is what life said to me/This is how her hidden spirit spoke), there follows a dialogue with various elements of nature. Storms, forests and the seasons are interrogated, and the secret of life and its progress from the darkness of Winter to the brightness of Spring is revealed. The message is unequivocal:

Across the universe it was proclaimed:
 Ambition is the flame of life,
  And the spirit of victory.
 If souls reach for life,
 Fate is certain to respond.

Read within the context of a society where fate is a matter for God alone, the poem challenges a deep-seated belief in pre-ordained destiny. The statement was nevertheless embraced by a revolutionary Arab world, particularly during the colonial period and at the height of pan-Arab nationalism in the 1950s and 1960s. In 1987,

when the Prime Minister of Tunisia removed President Bourguiba from office, one of the first steps he took in order to transform state discourse was to amend the national anthem by adding to it al-Shābbī's opening lines.

In a poem entitled "Falsafat al-thuʿbān al-muqaddas" (The Philosophy of the Sacred Snake, dated 20 August 1934), al-Shābbī explains the colonial strategy of assimilation which was the dominant strategy of the French in education, religious conversion, language policy and cultural measures. In a clear reference to the biblical story of the tempting snake, he introduces the poem with a short statement where he calls assimilation "the philosophy of educated power." He then goes on to explain that in the dialogue between the snake and the bird in the poem, the former uses mystical philosophy to convince the bird that its death is a necessary sacrifice in order to achieve permanence. The poem describes a bird chirping away on a spring day when it is attacked by a snake. The bird realizes that he has been attacked because he remains weak as long as power resides in the hands of the mighty. The snake then tries to convince the bird to sacrifice itself in order to contribute to a more noble cause, gaining everlasting existence by becoming part of a bigger whole and a more powerful being. The bird resigns itself to death, but not before showing that it fully understands the ploy:

Let nature, for whom I have sung
 The dreams of youth and wonder, bear wit-
 ness!
Peace is a forged truth,
 Justice is the language of the dying fire.
 There can be no equality unless the forces
  are equal,
 And terror is met with terror.

The poem is a direct reflection on, and a rejection of, the argument advanced by the French that small colonies can achieve power and progress only by becoming part of a the victorious French empire.

This intellectual political poem exemplifies al-Shābbī's tendency to write contemplative and philosophical poetry. He did so perhaps under the influence of Jubrān and readings in classical

Arabic literature, particularly the poet Abū 'l-'Alā' al-Ma'arrī (d. 1057). With the poem "Fī zill wādī al-mawt" (In the Shadow of the Valley of Death; written on 5 April 1932), al-Shābbī presents a more sustained view of life. Here the poet questions the purpose and logic of life. He complains of emptiness and strives to experience death in the hope of discovering the meaning of existence, not unlike the poem "The New Morning" discussed above.

Yet, despite his engagement with contemporary issues, innovative style and poetic skill, al-Shābbī's key distinction was his belief in poetry, in the role of the poet, and in his own mission in life. He wrote numerous pieces about poetry itself, the bard and art in general. In fact, rarely in his collection do we find a poem that does not refer in some way to poetry, song or the poet as such. This tendency links al-Shābbī with a new consciousness in the Arabic literary scene: by emphasizing lyricism and the self, it gives additional focus to the art of poetry itself. Putting into practice the ideas he had earlier discussed in *al-Khayāl*, al-Shābbī compared himself to an unknown prophet, a visionary who is meant to show the way. He also saw himself as someone who would remain alone and misunderstood because of his particular nature. All of which led him to adopt a variety of stances towards other people. He saw himself as a constructive force but also as destroyer; as a man destined to lead but also as a solitary figure who must shun society. The poem "al-Nabī al-majhūl" (The Unknown Prophet; dated 21 January 1930), illustrates this movement between the two impulses. It starts with a desire to destroy and uproot:

Oh, people! I wish I were a wood cutter,
  So that I may strike roots with my axe.

People are incapable of understanding the sheer depths of what it is the poet is urging them to embrace:

You do not grasp reality,
  Except through touching and feeling.

The poet presents beauty and hope to the people as flowers and music but they respond by stamping on his heart and roses. He then decides to leave them:

I am going to the forest
  To spend life alone, in despair.

But when the poet turns away from people, they accuse him of being possessed and shun him like a devil:

Expel the non-believer form the temple,
  He is the source of all evil.

Between the poet and his people stand inherited ignorance and deep mistrust. The poet is fated to live torn between two realities, "a prophet according to life itself" but a "madman" in the view of his folk. The only solution is communion with nature, for she alone understands the poet. It is this element above all else that makes al-Shābbī one of the key figures of Romanticism in the Arabic tradition.

But reaction to people's neglect can also take the form of hardened will and a stronger belief in the poet's mission. In this aspect, al-Shābbī can be linked to a long Western tradition of the poet as a Prometheus, particularly in its modern articulation where the Greek hero is freed from his chains. "Prometheus Unbound" by Shelley comes to mind. In "Nashīd al-jabbār aw hākadhā ghannā Brūmīthyūs" (The Song of the Mighty One, or Thus Sung Prometheus; written on 15 December 1933, the use of Greek mythology links al-Shābbī with a tradition that was to develop soon after his death whereby poets would recall local mythology in their art, and even in politics, particularly in Iraq, Syria, Lebanon and Egypt. The movement involved such figures as al-Sayyāb (d. 1964), Sa'īd 'Aql (b.1912), and Adūnīs/Adonis (i.e., 'Alī Ahmad Sa'īd, b. 1930). In the poem, al-Shābbī recalls the images from the original myth, such as the eagle, Prometheus' defiance of the Gods, and his commitment to arts and beauty. The poet proclaims that he will transform pain—by this time al-Shābbī was actually very ill—and rejection into poetry and music.

Despite illness and enemies,
I will live upon soaring summits,
Like a proud eagle.

The poet thrives in the face of adversity and is

strengthened by hardship and solitude, laughing off people's chatter and worldly interests. The direct occasion for this poem was a particularly bad setback: the poet lost his luggage and assumed he had lost his collection of poetry (as he records in a letter dated 19 December 1933). A graphic illustration of these famous lines, which have become a slogan of defiance and resistance in the face of adversity, now adorns the sandy hilltop just outside the poet's oasis town; the monument features the statue of a giant eagle spreading its wings on top of a mound, with the line of poetry written underneath.

Despite problems, not least of which was the difficulty the editors of the journal *Apollo* encountered in reading his North African handwriting, al-Shābbī became widely read in the Arab East. "He was almost an Egyptian poet," commented the critic Muhammad Mandūr. Others even considered him the strongest of the *Apollo* group in "poetic power, intensity of feeling and rebellion of spirit." For his part, al-Shābbī preferred *Apollo* to other Egyptian journals. He wrote to al-Hilīwī on 22 February 1933 that the newspaper *al-Siyāsah al-usbū'iyyah* represented the arrogance and Pharaonic tendencies in Egypt whereas *Apollo* represented a more inclusive group of young people who had yet to be touched by fame, and who genuinely supported modern poetry.

At home in Tunisia, al-Shābbī had powerful opponents, but also enjoyed the unwavering support of friends and fellow reformers. Al-Hilīwī had an unquestioned belief in al-Shābbī's genius and so had all his friends, as is revealed in their letters and accounts. They also appear to draw inspiration from his courage and the sincerity of his critical opinions and poetry. In a letter dated 26 March 1930, al-Hilīwī says,

You are the unknown prophet among your people; but history, yes history, will ensure that your name will be eternal and that future generation will crown your head with glory long after you and I have passed away.

In a letter dated 10 December 1933, al-Hilīwī joked that in the current context, al-Shābbī would be Lamartine, and al-Hilīwī himself would be his friend and critic, Saint Beuve. He went on:

The voice of reason then returns me to reality, although I believe that you are the Lamartine of Arabic poetry.

By then the poet was quite well-known. But ironically, until the age of 20 al-Shābbī had made his impact on the local cultural scene not so much through poetry as through criticism. Aged only 22, al-Shābbī had already been diagnosed with an enlarged heart; he was advised to avoid stress and to travel to mountainous regions for cleaner air, something that he did throughout the year 1932-33. However he was often very ill; he was hospitalized in 1933 and confined to bed for four months in 1934. In October of the same year, he fell ill again and died in hospital on 9 October at the age of 25.

For some unknown reason, al-Shābbī kept a diary in 1930. He wrote summaries of his activities and reflections on ideas and feelings in an elegant style. The diary confirms contemporary sources, letters and testimonies about the poet and his time. It reveals a thriving literary scene in the city of Tunis and offers insights into the poet's daily life, his routine, and the esteem that he enjoyed among his contemporaries. He was at the heart of this activity, a founding member of the The Literary Club, in close touch with key figures like Zayn al-'Ābidīn al-Sunūsī (1901-1965) and 'Uthmān al-Ka'āk (1903-1976), along with theatre groups and other cultural figures. He and his peers received ideas from Egypt and the Arab East with a blend of eagerness and a desire to compete. Tāhā Husayn's book on pre-Islamic poetry (1926) led to further studies written within the same spirit in Tunisia. Egyptian journals were always read with great interest. Al-Shābbī was clearly well read; he was courted by the literati of his day and consulted by colleagues. He found his company among liberal young people, some of whom were explicitly atheist, as he notes in the entry for 20 January 1930. He avoided traditional figures and, whenever the occasion arose, poured scorn on their literature and ideas. We also learn that he was accused of blasphemy because of his ideas, particularly those expressed in *al-Khayāl*.

The diaries—and one never really knows if they were destined for publication since their style is so polished— provide glimpses into the poet's temperament, which oscillated between spontaneous anger, melancholy, sensitivity, and an overwhelming intensity of feeling and expression. Al-Shābbī emerges as someone engrossed in the poetic life, a course to which he believed himself destined. He used to take daily walks in the lush fields and gardens around the city, always accompanied by a book and pen and paper. When he was made aware of the burdens of life and responsibility, something from which he had been sheltered by his father—added to which was the prospect of social prestige and a career that awaited the son of a respected and well-connected judge—he totally rejected such a prospect. It also emerges from the diaries that he cared deeply about the fate of Arabic and scorned writers in the Arab East for mixing standard Arabic with colloquial in their stories, creating what he called a "bastard" language. Just like his compatriot Mahmūd al-**Masʿadī**, he wanted popular ideas and expressions to be incorporated into standard Arabic and made to fit its grammar and syntax.

Seventy five years on, al-Shābbī's position remains unrivalled in Tunisia's poetic scene, even becoming a major complex that confronts aspiring poets. If anything, his status has now been so integrated in the fabric of the culture and even its institutions that interest in him can only increase. The yearly commemoration of his death at his home-town in the month of October keeps this interest alive and ensures that it proliferates. Al-Shābbī has become even an integral part of the economy of the town, the show-piece of a local economy based on tourism. He is also anthologized and studied in all the major books on the subject of Arabic poetry. In fact, it was this wide reputation that created a tolerance for his more daring poetry. His credentials as both a nationalist poet and an integral part of the re-vival of Arab culture made accusations of blasphemy leveled against him seem cheap. His opponents who are unable to ignore his poetry have even resorted to amending what they consider objectionable elements in it. His ideas about poetry are now decidedly dated and largely academic, but his status as an Arab poet and a Tunisian icon remain unquestioned. There are over 40 books about him in Arabic, hundreds of shorter studies in a variety of languages, more than 30 songs, a musical, a television drama, statues, streets and schools bearing his name, poetry prizes as well as other forms of commemoration.

REFERENCES

M. M. Badawi, *A Critical Introduction to Modern Arabic Poetry* (Cambridge: Cambridge University Press, 1975), 157-168;

Mongi Chemli, "Un poète romantique tunisien: Aboul-Qasim Chabbi", *Confluent* 37 (January 1964): 53-60;

Ronak Husni, "al-Shābbī and his Nature Poetry: romantic or revolutionary?", *British Journal of Middle Eastern Studies* 22.1-2 (1995): 81-92;

Abū 'l-Qāsim Muhammad Karrū, *al-Shābbī: Hayātuhu wa-shiʿruh* (Beirut, 1952; reprinted 7 times);

Mounah Khoury, "al-Shābbī as a Romantic", *Mundus Arabicus* 2 (1983): 3-17;

Hammādī Sammūd, *Dirāsat fī 'l-shiʿriyyah: al-Shābbī namūdhajan* (Tunis: Bayt al-Hikmah, 1988);

Muhammad al-Saqānijī (ed.), *al-Shābbī bayna shuʿarāʾ ʿasrihi* (Tunis: al-Dār al-Tūnisiyyah li'l-Nashr, 1986);

R. Marston Speight, "A Modern Tunisian Poet: Abū 'l-Qāsim al-Shābbī (1909-1934)", *International Journal of Middle East Studies* 4.2 (April 1973): 176-189.

Ahmad Shawqī

(1868 – 1932)

IRFAN SHAHID

Georgetown University

WORKS

The Poems: *Mawsū'ah* [see below], vols. ii-v;

'Alī Beǧ al-Kabīr ("Ali Beg the Great", composed in 1893, publ. 1932): *Mawsū'ah*, VII, 209-310;

'Adhrā' al-Hind ("The Maid of India", published in 1897, 2005);

Lādiyās ("Ladiyas" [proper name], 1898): *Mawsū'ah*, VIII, 11-101;

Dall wa-Taymān ("Dall and Tayman" [proper names], 1899-1900): *Mawsū'ah*, VIII, 293-455; an adaptation of the novel *Eine Ägyptische Königstochter* (1864) by Georg Ebers;

Shaytān Bintā'ur ("The Satan of Bintā'ur", publ. 1901-1902): *Mawsū'ah*, VII, 73-200;

Waraqat al-ās ("The Myrtle Leaf", 1904): *Mawsū'ah*, VI, 451-530;

al-Hikāyāt ("The Fables"): *Mawsū'ah*, IX, 139-263; interspersed in these *Hikāyāt* are poems in the *rajaz* meter, not related to the "Fables";

al-Azjāl ("Zajal Poetry"): *Mawsū'ah*, IX, 267-290; short pieces written in dialectal, Egyptian Arabic, which were set to music and sung;

al-Bakhīlah ("The Miser", composed in 1907 but not published): *Mawsū'ah*, VI, 381-445;

Amīrat al-Andalus ("The Princess of Andalusia", composed during his exile in Spain, but published later, 1932): *Mawsū'ah*, VI, 271-374;

Duwal al-'arab wa-'uzamā' al-islām ("Empires of the Arabs and Great Men of Islam", composed in Spain, but published later, 1933): *Mawsū'ah*, IX, 5-136;

Masra' Kilūbatra ("The Death of Cleopatra", 1927): *Mawsū'ah*, VIII, 207-287;

Majnūn Laylā ("The Madman of Layla", 1931; most recently: Cairo, 2002, with commentary): *Mawsū'ah*, VIII, 107-199;

Qambīz ("Kambyses", 1931): *Mawsū'ah*, VII, 429-527;

'Antarah ("'Antarah b. Shaddād", 1932): *Mawsū'ah*, VII, 317-407;

al-Sitt Hudā ("Madame Hudā", 1969): *Mawsū'ah*, VII, 8-65;

Aswāq al-dhahab ("The Gold Markets", 1932): *Mawsū'ah*, VI, 9-144;

Miscellany of prose compositions: *Mawsū'ah*, VI, 147-238.

Collected Works

al-Mawsū'ah al-Shawqiyyah, ed. Ibrāhīm al-Abyārī, 10 vols. (Dār al-Kitāb al-'Arabī, Beirut, 1995, 1998); henceforth *Mawsū'ah*; this is now the standard edition of Shawqī's complete works and has superseded all previous editions with the exception of:

al-Shawqiyyāt ([Collected Poems], publ. by Shawqī himself in 1898); with an Introduction;

al-Shawqiyyāt al-majhūlah, ed. Muhammad Sabrī (Dār al-Kutub al-Misriyyah, 1961/1962); Sabrī collected an impressive number of poems and prose pieces by Shawqī unknown before;

Masrahiyyāt ("Plays", Cairo: al-Hay'ah al-Misriyyah al-'Āmmah li'l-Kitāb, 1982).

Works in Translation

The best translations of Shawqī are in French and English and may be found in the following works:

L'Espagne vue par les voyageurs musulmans de 1610 à 1930, tr. Henri Pérès (Paris, 1935); translation of Shawqī's Spanish period;

Des Shawqiyyāt en Arabe dialectical, tr. Antoine Boudot-Lamotte, *Arabica* 20 (1973): 225-245;

Ahmad Shawqi: L'Homme et l'œuvre, tr. Antoine Boudot-Lamotte (Damas, 1977); translations of Shawqī's poetry in all its varieties;

Majnūn Laila: A Poetical Drama in Five Acts,

tr. Arthur J. Arberry (Cairo, 1933);
Arabic Poetry, tr. Arthur J. Arberry (Cambridge, 1965), 154-161;
Poetry and the Making of Modern Egypt, 1882–1922, tr. Mounah Khouri (Leiden: E. J. Brill, 1971).

Ahmad Shawqī was the foremost neo-Classical poet of Modern Arabic literature. In the course of the last forty years of his relatively short life (d. 1932), he emerged as the poet of Revivalism, the return to the Golden Period of Arabic poetry (the Abbasid, 8th–11th centuries) for inspiration. In so doing, he continued and perfected the work of his precursor, the distinguished Revivalist poet, al-**Bārūdī** (d. 1904). But he also succeeded in adding to Arabic poetry what it had sadly lacked—the dramatic genre, in which he had no real successors. This has made him not another Shakespeare but the Shakespeare of Arabic poetry.

Shawqī was born in Cairo in 1868 to a good middle class family in whose veins ran Turkish, Kurdish, Circassian, Greek, and Arab blood. But he was a natural aristocrat and moved in aristocratic circles, palatial and other, all his later life. He received his education in the secular school system of Egypt. After his elementary education, he entered in 1885 the School of Law where he spent four years studying, first law then the art of translation, graduating in 1889. These four years were crucial for his formation and for his future career in three important respects. Firstly, it was at this school that he acquired his impressive command of Classical Standard Arabic and his intimate knowledge of Abbasid poetry expressed through it, on the cunning manipulation of which, some, even much of his poetry depended for its appeal. He owed this to a talented teacher, Husayn al-Marsafī, who also wrote that volume titled *al-Wasīlah al-adabiyyah*, in which he tastefully included the best of Abbasid poetry not forgetting that of the heroic figure of the Revivalist precursor, al-Bārūdī, whom he admired, and who, in Marsafī's estimation, sometimes excelled his Abbasid predecessors. It was to this that Shawqī most probably owed his desire to appear not only as the foremost poet of his age but of all Arabic poetry. The other volume which he studied at the Law School was *al-Kashkūl* of Bahā' al-Dīn al-'Āmilī (d. 1621) to which Shawqī owed his initial knowledge of *tasawwuf*, Islamic mysticism, which was to appear fitfully in his work. A third book, *al-Kalim al-thamān* (The Eight Words), was a composition of al-Marsafī, possibly inspired by Rifā'ah al-**Tahtāwī**, the enlightened Egyptian reformer of the earlier part of the century. Such were the inspiring volumes and such was the tutor, who inspired the future poet and fired his imagination in these impressionable years.

Secondly, the School of Law provided Shawqī with an opportunity for acquiring a sound knowledge of the French language, an attainment that was to distinguish him to his advantage from his Revivalist predecessor, al-Bārūdī, who moved in the strictly Islamic orbit of Arabic, Turkish and Persian. French opened for Shawqī spacious opportunities for the flowering of his native genius in areas inaccessible to the less fortunate of his contemporaries, who remained innocent of the *lingua franca* of the world in the nineteenth century. Thirdly it was at this School that Shawqī met two figures, close to the Khedive Tawfīq, namely, Muhammad al-Basyūnī and 'Alī al-Laythī, who used to compose panegyrics on the Khedive and sometimes would consult with Shawqī for refining their poems. It was through them that Shawqī became attached to the Khedival court, where he spent two years in the service of Tawfīq, 1889-1891. He acquitted himself remarkably well and his education at the School of Law stood him in good stead. His performance earned him the friendship and appreciation of the Khedive, who as a result, decided to send him to France as a Government scholar for further advanced study, a decision which changed the course of his poetic career and affected its orientation.

His triennium in France from January 1891 till November 1893 was the first of two turning points in his poetic *floruit*. These three years witnessed his total immersion in French literature, especially the poetry of the Romantic trio, Victor Hugo, Alfred de Musset, and Lamartine, to whom may be added La Fontaine. His future poetry clearly reflected the influence of these four French literary figures. But even before his return to Egypt, he started composing in the new Romantic style, expressed in a love lyric, which began *khada'ūhā* "They deceived her", which was later set to music and sung by the leading Egyptian singer and ward of Shawqī, Muhammad 'Abd al-Wahhāb (d. 1991).

The French influence was not limited to these poets. Paris itself, the city of light and of the arts, especially the Parisian stage, impacted profoundly the future apostle of dramatic Arabic poetry and the patron of the arts in Egypt. And his reaction was immediate; it was in Paris and before he returned that he composed his first verse drama on the Mamlūk period in Egyptian history.

On his return to Egypt he was attached to the Khedival court as he had been before, and so he spent two decades of his life until 1914 attached to the new Khedive 'Abbās Hilmī. As the poet laureate of a Muslim ruler who even aspired to be caliph, Shawqī could not compose under the French influence which had impacted him in Paris and which the Khedive Tawfīq had frowned upon, when the latter did not welcome his first verse drama *'Alī Beğ al-Kabīr* with open arms. So, he postponed composing under that influence until the end of his life when he wrote the series of verse drama with which his name is indelibly linked.

As the poet laureate of a Khedive in Egypt, who was related to the Ottoman sultan in Istanbul, Shawqī composed on 'Abbās Hilmī as his spokesman and panegyrist, on his country Egypt and its history, and on the incumbent of the Islamic caliphate in Istanbul. Yet he found time to compose sometimes outside these three contexts. The landmarks of these years relevant to his poetic career may be outlined as follows:

In 1894 he attended the Congress of Orientalists at Geneva, as a representative of the Egyptian Government and of his patron 'Abbās Hilmī. He delivered a paper in French in which he reminded the audience of the Egyptian renaissance under Muhammad 'Alī and the 'Alawī Dynasty to which belonged 'Abbās Hilmī, his patron. He also reminded his audience of the Arab literary Revival, no longer medieval but modern, giving as examples his own verse drama, *'Alī Beğ al-Kabīr*; his long monumental ode on Egypt, the

hamziyyah; and the collection of poems put in the mouths of animals symbolically, in the style of La Fontaine.

In 1898 he published his collected poems, his *dīwān*, under the title *al-Shawqiyyāt*, which established his reputation in the Arab world as the leading poet of his generation. As important as the poems was the valuable Introduction, in which he outlined his views on poetry, of which the following may be noticed: he regretted and deprecated the abundant composition of panegyrics in medieval Arabic poetry as unworthy of poets, a bold statement coming from a post-laureate; he maintained that it is possible for a poet to be a prose writer also. Most important was his view of poetry, namely that it is the child of two parents, Nature and History, a view which his life's work fully illustrates. His nature poetry, attractive as it is, remained photographic as that of Classical and medieval nature poetry in Arabic had been, not reflective of a true Romanticism in its lack of the spiritualization and idealization of nature. He also wrote on the rejuvenation of Arabic poetry. Shawqī who had endured the animadversions of Khedive Tawfīq for his involvement in verse drama is now cautious and recommending rejuvenation, not as a revolutionary but as a gradualist, who believed in evolution, not revolution. Yet, and despite this, Shawqī was not spared the violent criticism of conservatives who did not accept his modernist views of Arabic poetry; such were Muhammad al-**Muwaylihī** (d. 1930) and Ibrāhīm al-**Yāzijī** (d. 1906), both of whom criticized him and what he said in that Introduction.

In the course of these twenty years or so while he was a court poet, he composed poems of exceptional length, a remarkable performance for a poet who was writing in conformity with the metrical forms of classical Arabic poetry, monorhymed and monometered, a reflection of his powerful command of Arabic and its metrical system. These long odes reflected the two main themes he addressed in this period—Egypt, its history and problems; and the Islamic caliphate in its Ottoman version:

– The year 1894 witnessed the long ode on Egyptian history delivered to the Orientalist Congress in Geneva, a poem of 290 verses, monorhymed and monometered, which goes through Egyptian history from Pharaonic times till the 'Alawī dynasty, reaching the reign of his patron, 'Abbās Hilmī;

– the Islamic Ottoman caliphate was also addressed in this period in odes reflecting Shawqī's Islamism and his pro-Ottoman sentiments, as well as those of his patron 'Abbās Hilmī, who looked at the Ottoman sultan as the natural ally of Egypt in its struggle for independence against the British who had occupied it in 1882. In 1897 appeared his very long ode of 260 verses, also monorhymed and monometered, on the Turkish/Greek war of the same year, in which he saluted sultan 'Abd al-Hamīd and the Turkish victories in the war, not forgetting the heroism of Turkish women. In 1913, he wrote on the fall of Edirne to the Bulgars a long ode of 105 verses, almost an elegy on it, which opened "O Sister of Andalus!" alluding to the loss of al-Andalus in 1492. To this period belongs also his famous panegyric on the Prophet Muhammad, *Nahj al-Burdah*, a long poem of 190 verses which he composed in 1909 as *mu'āradah*, a "contrafaction" written in imitation of a famous earlier poem by al-Būsīrī, the Egyptian mystic of the 13th century. It was later set to music and sung by the foremost Arab songstress, Umm Kulthūm (d. 1975).

In spite of opposition to Shawqī's efforts to renovate and rejuvenate Arabic poetry, both Khedival from Tawfīq and 'Abbās, and conservative from al-Muwaylihī and al-Yāzijī, Shawqī was able to compose a verse comedy, *al-Bakhīlah* (The Miser), in 1907. The scene was set not in the court surrounding of Qasr al-Qubbah or 'Ābidīn, but in a modest neighborhood in Cairo, and the plot turned around a rich widow, surrounded by a grandson and suitors who were less interested in her than in her wealth. In writing *al-Bakhīlah*, the French influence asserted itself since it is practically certain that Molière's *L'Avare* was his inspiration. But he did not publish it until much later in his life.

Shawqī ignored also what the conservatives had said in their criticism of *al-Shawqiyyāt* and its Introduction and published a series of prose romances, also French inspired, most probably by Victor Hugo. In the course of five years, he published four of these prose romances: *'Adhrā' al-Hind* (The Maid/Virgin of India) in 1897; *Lādiyās* in 1898; *Dall wa-Taymān* in 1899; and *Shaytān Bintā'ūr* (The Satan/Demon of Bintā'ūr) in 1901-1902. The first three were narratives while the fourth was cast in the form of dialogue. They all are set in Pharaonic Egypt and convey a political message against the British occupation of Egypt, a theme which Shawqī continued to remember in his poetry until 1915 and which caused his exile from Egypt in that year.

In this period appeared also the prose romance *Waraqat al-ās* (The Myrtle Leaf) on the publication of which there is some uncertainty, since sometimes it is presented as published in 1904 and sometimes in 1911. It was different in almost every way from the four Pharaonic prose romances. Northern Mesopotamia, not Pharaonic Egypt, was where the plot unfolded, and the protagonist was al-Nadīrah, the Arab princess of al-Hadr (Hatra), which she had surrendered to the Persian king, Shapūr. The romance ends with the tragic death of al-Nadīrah at the hands of her paramour, the Persian Shāh.

The second phase of his poetic *floruit* opened during the First World War. His patron Khedive 'Abbās Hilmī was deposed while he was in Istanbul in 1914 and Shawqī, who was known for his pro-Ottoman sympathies and his anti-British stance, was exiled to Spain, which was his own choice. His exile reflected the importance of poetry in the political life of Egypt and how it became a force to be reckoned with by Britain, the occupying power. Shawqī was exiled not for any political activity he had indulged in, as al-Bārūdī had been, but for being a poet of Egyptian nationalism and of Khedival opposition to the British presence. But his exile to Spain turned out to be a blessing in disguise, as it emancipated him from the court and it constituted the second turning point in his career.

This quinquennium in Spain 1915-1919 was a period of reflection and total immersion in Spanish Arab history and civilization. Spain had been alive in his consciousness even while he was a court poet, as reflected in his ode on the fall of Edirne, "Andalusia's sister", to the Bulgars in 1913. Now emancipated from court duties, he concentrated on his calling as a poet. Just before his return from Spain to Egypt in 1919, he left Barcelona, where he had resided, and visited Andalusia, in Southern Spain, to treat himself to the visual dimension of the Arab presence: its art and architecture in Granada and Cordoba in his *sīniyyah*, his poem rhyming in *-s-*; his strophic ode on 'Abd al-Rahmān al-Dākhil, the founder of the Umayyad dynasty in Spain; and his *nūniyyah*, rhyme in *-n-*, in which he expressed his nostalgia for Egypt. And he composed these odes in the same meter and rhyme of some of his distinguished predecessors, al-Buhturī (d. 897) on Īwān-Kisrā, and Ibn Zaydūn (d. 1070) on Wallādah, the daughter of the caliph al-Mustakfī of the 11th century; and Lisān al-Dīn Ibn al-Khatīb (d. 1375) on his patron. The most Andalusian of these odes was the one on 'Abd al-Rahmān al-Dākhil, since Shawqī not only composed memorably on the distinguished Umayyad figure, but also in his ode succumbed to the *muwashshah*, the strophic metrical form invented and perfected by the Arab poets of Andalus, which Shawqī did not attempt before or after.

In addition to these few but splendid odes, Shawqī tried two new literary forms: the prose drama and the long *urjūzah*. In the first, he wrote *Amīrat al-Andalus* (The Princess of al-Andalus), in which the protagonist is Buthaynah, the daughter of the Arab ruler of Seville, al-Mu'tamid ibn'Abbād (d. 1095). The second, the *urjūzah*, the long poem written in the *rajaz* meter, was a panorama of Arab and Islamic history, from the birth of Islam to the end of the Fatimid Dynasty in Egypt. Although written in the meter usually reserved for didactic verse, Shawqī restored to this meter its effectiveness in the most spacious canvas he painted of Arab Islamic history in 1526 (!) verses, within which obtained many a purple patch of true poetry and not only rhymed and metered verse.

Shawqī returned to Egypt in 1919, which year opened the third and last phase of his poetic career. It lasted thirteen years till his death in 1932. During his stay of five years in Spain, Egypt, the Arab and the Islamic worlds had experienced fundamental changes as a result of the cataclysm of the First World War, all of which affected Shawqī's poetic career and output, especially in the first part of this period, the eight years which extended until 1927. In Egypt the nationalists were clamoring for independence and the termination of the British Protectorate and occupation. The period witnessed the famous uprising of 1919, the Milner Report of 1921, the Declaration of February 1922, the Constitution of 1923, and the first elected Parliament of 1924. The nationalist figure who dominated the scene was now Sa'd Zaghlūl, who died in 1927, after securing for Egypt its independence. The tensions and excitements of these years naturally touched the political sensibilities of Shawqī, the Egyptian patriot and nationalist, who as such had thundered in his poetry before his exile, as spokesman of Khedive 'Abbās Hilmī. Now he entered the political arena and composed, not as a court poet associated with 'Ābidīn or Qubbah palace, but as the spokesman of the Egyptian people, living in his own home, Karmāt Ibn Hāni'. He saluted Egypt's struggle for independence from Britain in poems in which his intimate knowledge of political life and his training in law helped him compose odes that presented the case for Egypt with the skill of a lawyer, but also with the passion of a poet. Egypt received also some of his odes in this period in an area other than the struggle for independence. It was in this period that Lord Carnarvon and his associate Howard Carter made their truly sensational discovery, the Tomb of the Pharaonic king Tut, which elicited from Shawqī odes, one of which he himself considered his best poem. Two or three years before, in 1921, he had returned to the history of Egypt in a long poem of 153 verses, titled "The Nile", in which Pharaonic Egypt received the lion's share of 94 verses, the famous *qāfiyyah* (poem rhyming in *-q-*), which he dedicated to D. Samuel Margoliouth, the Laudian Professor of Arabic at Oxford, whom he had met a few years before in 1912 at the Orientalist Congress in Athens.

Egypt's artistic life also became Shawqī's concern in this period. He became a patron of its arts, especially of music and song, shepherding the talents of the young Muhammad 'Abd al-Wahhāb, who, thus, became the foremost Arab singer of the century. He set to music and sang many of Shawqī's lyrics and, in so doing, he imparted to them the auditory dimension, both instrumental and vocal, which has kept them alive in the consciousness of the very wide circle of listeners and not only the preserve of the few passionate connoisseurs and silent readers of Arabic poetry.

The new Arab World, born after the First World War, separated from the Ottoman Empire but now under British and French mandates, attracted Shawqī; during this period he accorded it much attention. His total immersion for five long years in the strictly Arab history and culture of Spanish Islam had already put him in a singularly receptive mood to respond to this facet in the new orientation of his poetic career after his return from exile. And he responded *con brio*. Some of his best poems were composed on the struggle of the Syrian Arabs against France, witness his *Dimashqiyyāt*, "the Damascene Odes", the *qāfiyyah*, the *nūniyyah*, and the *lāmiyyah*, which are still in the front rank of all his poems. As a result, Shawqī emerged as the poet of that nationalist wave which swept over the new Arab world from Iraq to Morocco, thus becoming almost the apostle of Arab unity, translated later into the Arab League after the Second World War.

Shawqī's new interest, the new Arab world and Arab nationalism, was enhanced by the defeat of the Muslim Ottoman caliphate in the First World War, the rise of Turkish nationalism, and the final abolition of both the sultanate and the caliphate by Mustafa Kemal. The victory of the latter at the battle of Sakarya had elicited from Shawqī a splendid epinician ode, saluting the victory, which Shawqī then thought was a victory for Islam. It was an ode which he composed in the meter and rhyme of the Abbasid poet Abū Tammām's (d. 845) celebrated ode, saluting al-Mu'tasim, the Abbasid caliph, for his conquest of Amorium in A.D. 838. Little did he know that Mustafa Kemal was going to turn his back to the sultanate and the caliphate, both of which he abolished in 1922 and 1924 respectively, and that the Turkish parliament was later (1934) to endow him with the title "Atatürk" (Father of the Turks). Shawqī, however, addressed to him a poem in which he chided the

victor of Sakarya for what he had done, and composed two odes on the demise of the Muslim caliphate.

Of an entirely different order was a problem, a personal one, which faced Shawqī on his return to Egypt in 1919. As has been said before, Shawqī's efforts to rejuvenate Arabic poetry on his return from France in 1893 had been greeted with opposition from the Khedive Tawfīq, and from conservative circles, represented by Muhammad al-Muwaylihī and Ibrāhīm al-Yāzijī. Now a more serious criticism, indeed a violent storm awaited him on his return from Spain in 1919. While Shawqī was away, a new generation of critics and poets appeared in Egypt, influenced by English poetry and criticism—the Romantic School of the so-called *Dīwān*, at the head of whom was none other than the intellectual and literary critic 'Abbās Mahmūd al-'Aqqād whose powerful and influential voice was heard in Egyptian and Arab circles and who remained Shawqī's nemesis for almost half a century until his death in the sixties. His contemporary Tāhā **Husayn**, the Dean of Arabic Letters, was also critical but moderately so. The Egyptian School of Romantics, the *Dīwān* group, was joined in its opposition to Shawqī by the Romantics of the Arab-American School. Their critic was Mikhā'īl **Nu'aymah** (Naimy) who wrote deleteriously of Shawqī's poetry and published his criticism in a volume titled *al-Ghirbāl* (The Sieve), to which al-'Aqqād wrote the introduction. A third broadside was fired against Shawqī by Ahmad **Abū Shādī**, another Romantic, who was to found *Jamā'at Abullū*, the "*Apollo* Group", in the early thirties. So, while al-Muwaylihī and al-Yāzijī had accused Shawqī of going too far in his efforts to rejuvenate, the new group of critics accused him of not going far enough! Shawqī remained imperturbable and continued to compose in his favorite style odes, which only went to enhance the general recognition of him as the leading poet of his generation. His paramountcy among the large and not so silent majority in the Arab world was reflected in 1927 when delegates from the Arab countries converged on Cairo and saluted him. Thus the Poet of Princes became the Prince of Poets, *amīr al-shu'arā'*, the sobriquet that was coined in his honor on that memorable occasion.

More important, much more important, than the odes he composed in these past eight years were the series of verse dramas with which he gifted Arabic poetry. In the course of the last five years of this period and of his life, his prolific talent found its greatest expression when no less than eight or seven plays flowed from his pen, some of which were performed during his lifetime and some after his death. Some of them he had worked on before, such as *al-Bakhīlah*, which he had attempted in 1907, and *Amīrat al-Andalus*, which he had begun in Spain. The others were new and may be briefly described as follows:

Masra' Kilūbatra (The Fall and Death of Cleopatra): the plot turns around the struggle between Rome under Octavian, and Egypt, Hellenistic Egypt under Cleopatra, the Macedonian queen and her paramour, the Roman commander Marc Antony; the defeat of the latter at the Battle of Actium in 31 B.C., and the suicide of Cleopatra, who chose to die rather than to be led captive in the triumph of Octavian in Rome.

Shawqī evinced much originality in the composition of this play, especially in his departure from the well-known Shakespearean play *Antony and Cleopatra*, reflected mainly in the delineation of the character of Cleopatra. Shakespeare had taken the side of the Roman conqueror and presented Cleopatra as a "the viper of the Nile" while Shawqī painted an entirely different picture of the Macedonian Queen as a loving mother and highly cultured woman, ruling a prosperous country, blessed with a civilization, the Hellenistic, which was superior to that of the Roman adversary Octavian, and above all as a patriot, defending Egypt against the aggressive imperialism of Rome. In so doing, Shawqī intelligently set his verse drama against the background of an Egypt struggling against the British occupation, in which Cleopatra patriotically defends her country, thus endearing the play to its Egyptian spectators. He was also mindful of the fact that the Khedives of Egypt, the 'Alawī dynasty, had hailed from Kavala in Macedonia whence the Ptolemies, to whom Cleopatra belonged, had also hailed. In addition to the plot, the play is remarkable for the poetry, the many purple patches with which Shawqī endowed it. Unlike the plot, which has lost some of its appeal after Egypt attained full sovereignty, the poetry in the play has not lost any of its appeal and constitutes the main attraction of the play for lovers of Arabic poetry.

Majnūn Laylā (The Possessed/Mad Lover of Laylā): the second of Shawqī's verse dramas, which he composed in the short period of five months after the success of *Masra' Kilūbatra*. The plot turns round the well-known, star-crossed romance of Qays and Laylā in early Islamic times. After Laylā's father denied Qays the hand of his daughter and married her off to someone else, the latter became distraught and roamed the deserts of Najd, mad with love; hence his sobriquet *al-Majnūn*, "the one possessed by a demon". The play owes much to Shawqī's innovations, such as the scene of *Qaryat al-jinn*, "the village or preserve of the *jinn*, genii, demons". The insertion of this scene in the play chimed well with the Arab tradition, which conceived of poetry as inspired by Jinn, almost the platonic concept of poetry as "divine madness". The concept of love develops in the play. It begins with Laylā as a lady whose love is *'udhrī*, chaste and pure, and progresses to become *sūfī*, the Islamic term for "mystic", and both loves give the play a strong Arab and Islamic complexion and relate it to the classical Arab heritage.

Majnūn Laylā was very close to Shawqī's heart since the male protagonist, Qays, was a poet as Shawqī was, and what is more, a love poet who wrote *'udhrī* poetry, hence the play is replete with love lyrics, which haunted and has continued to haunt Arab readers; and some of it has been set to music and sung, such as the one in which a mountain, Mt. Tawbād, is apostrophized.

The play is significant in the comparatist context, both Islamic and non-Islamic. Within the Arabic Islamic, Shawqī's achievement consisted in his gathering together the accounts of this love affair, sporadically scattered in the sources, and presenting them within a play, the plot and characters of which are well defined. In so doing he also did justice to Arabic literature and poetry, since that poetry had lacked a literary work, which told the story of this celebrated love affair as Islamic Persian literature had done. Shawqī filled this vacuum in Arabic poetry, which previous Arab poets had forgotten or neglected to do. In the non-Islamic comparatist context, the play which was the Romeo and Juliet of Arabic poetry naturally involved his relation to the Bard. His Romeo and Juliet had been translated into Arabic and surely Shawqī was aware of it, and this may have been an additional incentive, which has impelled him to compose *Majnūn Laylā*.

Qambīz (Cambyses): It had been the prose romance *Dall wa-Taymān* which Shawqī had written when he was a court poet, and now he wrote it as a verse-drama. Its plot turns round the occupation of Egypt by the Persian king Cambyses (Qambīz), who, thus, terminates the long period of Egyptian Pharaonic independence. Confusion and violence reign in Egypt and Qambīz appears as a tyrant who destroys the temples and kills the calf Ābīs (Apis), while the Egyptians were celebrating it. Just as *Masra' Kilūbatra* was allegorical, indirectly attacking the British occupation of Egypt, so was *Qambīz*, but in a much more open manner. Women play an important role in the play and this was perhaps a reflection of the importance of the women's movement in Egypt in this period. Unlike the two previous plays, *Qambīz* is not graced with fine lyrics, and the concentration is on the plot, perhaps due to the fact that critics had accused Shawqī of being in his plays more of a lyric poet than an accomplished dramatist.

'Alī Beğ al-Kabīr (Ali Beg the Great) was the play that Shawqī had originally written in France and on which the Khedive Tawfīq had frowned. Now, towards the end of his life in this quinquennium, Shawqī returned to it, re-wrote it, and published it. The plot treats the Mamlūks of Egypt and their leader, 'Alī Beğ, who tries to win independence for Egypt and himself from the Ottoman sultans, one of whom, Salīm, had annexed Egypt in 1517. The protagonist is 'Alī Beğ, a Circassian, whose ally was the chivalrous Zāhir al-'Umar, who also had carved for himself an independent existence in northern Palestine and whom Shawqī calls, because of his chivalry, Samaw'al al-Wafā', "The Samaw'al of Fidelity"

(Samaw'al ibn 'Ādiyā' being a pre-Islamic poet proverbial for his loyalty). The play ends with the violent death of 'Alī Beğ. In its revised second version of 1932, some forty years after the first, the play is even closer to the Egyptian spectator than *Masra' Kilūbatra* and *Qambīz*, both of which belonged to the distant past of Egypt and not the Arab or Muslim worlds. But it shares with *Qambīz* its concentration on the plot and on characterization and is almost free of lyricism. Again, this was probably in response to the criticisms leveled against Shawqī à propos *Kilūbatra* and *Majnūn*, namely, that he appeared in these two plays more of a lyricist than a dramatist.

'Antarah was one of the last of the plays that Shawqī wrote, and it was published posthumously. It was the second Arab play after *Majnūn Laylā* and one in which a poet, 'Antarah, was the protagonist. 'Antarah, however, was a half-Arab, whose mother was an Abyssinian slave and whose love for 'Ablah, the daughter of the chief of his tribe, became celebrated in pre-Islamic times. At that time 'Antarah was regarded as the picture of courage and chivalry and he appears in the plays as such, and as the leader of the Arabs against the Persians, inaccurate historically as that was. It was his courage that won him manumission as a slave and also the hand of 'Ablah after it had been denied him. The lyrics naturally return to the play since the protagonist was a poet and lover at that. The new dimension to 'Antarah's personality, the nationalist, was imparted to it by Shawqī, consonantly with the new wave that swept over Egypt and the Arab world, in which Shawqī became involved after the abolition of the sultanate and the Muslim caliphate.

Al-Sitt Hudā (Lady/Madame Hudā): As Shawqī re-worked *'Alī Beğ al-Kabīr* forty years after he wrote its first version, so did he re-work *al-Bakhīlah* "The Miser", written in 1907. *Al-Sitt Hudā* is a verse comedy singularly free of the lyrics with which Shawqī endowed three of his other plays, and which Shawqī apparently avoided in response to the criticism that his plays were more lyrical than dramatic. It is the story of a rich lady who had ten husbands, all of whom are not interested in her and her personality, but in her wealth. The dialogue is clever, the plot well-constructed and so is characterization. The play is at its most amusing when al-Sitt Hudā herself reveals the character of each and everyone of her former husbands, some of whom had died while others had been divorced. The scene is set in Hayy al-Hanafī in Cairo, the very same neighborhood that Shawqī lived in before he moved to the more courtly surroundings and before his life became associated with the Khedival palaces; hence the appeal of the comedy to the Egyptian public and their rapport with it.

Shortly after his death and the end of this quinquennium appeared in print a prose work of his, *Aswāq al-dhahab* (The Markets of Gold), which he had apparently composed during his exile in Spain in 1915-1919. It was a collection of meditations and essays in rhyming prose, which contained his attractive apostrophe to the Mediterranean.

The last five years of Shawqī's life thus witnessed the peak of his output and innovative spirit. In the course of the three decades or so before, he had rejuvenated Arabic poetry as a Revivalist when he composed, inspired by the Classical Arab heritage, but in a creative manner and not as a *muqallid* "slavish imitator", as his critics had unfairly dubbed him. Now in the course of these five years, he confounded his critics when he innovated entirely outside the Arab tradition and it was a massive innovation—not less than endowing Arabic poetry with a genre it had lacked—drama. His achievement as a Revivalist had been rewarded with the amirate (the princeship) of poetry in 1927; now his achievement as the distinguished innovator and rejuvenator of Arabic poetry was recognized, when at the end of these five years he became the president of the literary circle called *Jamā'at Apollo* (The Apollo Group), the avant-gardiste Romantic movement in Egypt, whose founder and moving spirit was Ahmad Abū Shādī, the very same critic who had joined the chorus of hostility towards Shawqī in the twenties. So, Shawqī passed away in 1932, full of honors, if not of years.

Although Shawqī died in 1932, he has remained alive in the literary consciousness of the Arab reader despite new storms which blew against him and his poetry posthumously. During his lifetime, a large group of poets who might be appropriately called the "School of Shawqī" grew and remained faithful to him long after his death. Its members in various parts of the Arab world continued to compose in the classical mould of the Arabic metrical system, which he had perfected, and these looked up to him as their leader. Such was Bishārah al-Khūrī, his friend and admirer, and his most successful creative imitator, who composed on him a truly moving elegy.

The storms which broke out after his death took a variety of forms. Firstly, his old nemesis, 'Abbās M. al-'Aqqād, who had attacked him ferociously in the twenties, did not abate his hostility towards Shawqī posthumously; he even intensified it in a monograph and in articles which appeared in the fifties of the twentieth century before his death in 1964. The other influential critic, Tāhā Husayn, who had animadverted on Shawqī's poetry, although more fairly than al-'Aqqād, also lived long, decades after the death of Shawqī, dying in 1973. But both were outlived by the poet who dominated neo-Classical poetry in the second half of the twentieth century, the Iraqi Muhammad Mahdī al-**Jawāhirī** (d. 1997), who remained steadfastly composing in the neo-Classical idiom of Shawqī, the living monument to the vitality of Shawqī's school throughout the century.

Secondly, the Egyptian Revolution of July 1952 led by Jamāl 'Abd al-Nāsir did not help his cause. Since it brought about the downfall of King Fārūq, the last ruler of the 'Alawī family, everything associated with that dynasty was now out of grace, especially as Fārūq proved unworthy of the heritage passed on by previous rulers of Egypt, such as the founder, Muhammad 'Alī, his son, Ibrāhīm, and grandson, Ismā'īl. Those associated with the dynasty and the Khedival court were frowned upon, and thus Shawqī, who had been the poet laureate of 'Abbās Hilmī, naturally suffered from the hostility of the new Egypt and its ideology, not well disposed to the 'Alawī court.

Third and most significant was the rise and development of an entirely new type of poetry, a sharp departure in the history of Arabic poetry from the classical traditional style, namely that of Free Verse *(al-shi'r al-hurr)*, under the influence of its practitioners in England and the United States, especially Edith Sitwell and T. S. Eliot. It was a true revolution, and its Arab converts did not stint Shawqī and his School their sharp criticisms. The monorhyme and monometer which distinguished Arabic poetry from all other metrical systems were discarded. A new metrical form was now developed, the basic unit of which was no longer the single verse with its two hemistiches but the one foot, the *taf'īlah*, which was repeated as many times as was thought appropriate by the poet, with hardly any employment of rhyme. A new concept of poetry was also born, which did not chime well with the old Classical one. The movement swept over the Arab world from Morocco to Iraq and almost all poets at one time were writing in the new metrical idiom, often with hostility towards the Classical and neo-Classical school of Shawqī.

Shawqī, however, has managed to weather all these storms. In 1982 the Egyptian government decided to celebrate the semi-centennial anniversary of his death. Poets and critics from the Arab and non-Arab world descended on Cairo for the occasion, which officially celebrated the memory of the great poet. Of late, some of the devotees of Free Verse began to return to the old Classical idiom of Shawqī. Most importantly, the *œuvre* of Shawqī which had been published indifferently, sporadically, and in a manner unworthy of the great poet, has now been published in a de luxe edition which has given a new lease of life to the Prince of Poets. In ten massive volumes, all his works, the poetry and the prose, have been collected, edited and commented upon by Ibrāhīm al-Abyārī, in his *al-Mawsū'ah al-Shawqiyyah*. This work, which has appeared in its complete form in 1995, has included also the material in the two volumes of Muhammad Sabrī, which had appeared in 1961-1962, called *al-Shawqiyyāt al-majhūlah* (The Unknown Shawqiyyāt), in which he collected a vast number of poems and prose works by Shawqī, previously unknown. The appearance of this splendid edition has now laid the ground for

a return to the poet and his work in order to explore new dimensions in it and to re-examine old dimensions that had been explored, for a more refined evaluation of the poet and his astounding *œuvre*.

In an entry written in English for the benefit of an Anglophone readership, and in a century that has witness globalization, it is *à propos* to re-evaluate Shawqī and explore the various dimensions of his significance within this remoter background of world and comparatist literature. And if Arabic can present a poet within this new and complex contextualization, it is surely this one, Ahmad Shawqī, who broke through the Arab Islamic template and, profoundly influenced by French poetry, the window through which he looked at new horizons, was able to rejuvenate Arabic poetry and endow it with more than Arab Islamic scope, appeal, and resonance.

In later pre-modern times (indeed up till the early 20th century) the former Arab Empire and the Islamic caliphate, now represented by the Ottoman sultans and caliphs in Istanbul / Constantinople, found no poet to interpret them in verse other than Shawqī. These, unlike some other polities such as those of the Far East, were closely linked to Europe and the West, not only geographically and historically, but also within the history of religion and culture, since Islam is an Abrahamic religion, the third monotheistic religion after Judaism and Christianity. Hence what Shawqī had to say about them is of much relevance to the Western reader. In his long poem of (1526) verses he sang the epic rise and development of the Islamic Movement from its birth in seventh century Arabia till the period of the Fātimids of eleventh century Egypt. This long poem is not didactic; it is interspersed with flashes of true poetic feeling. The Islamic caliphate, that venerable institution which lasted for some thirteen centuries, was the counterpart of the Holy Roman Empire in the West and the Christian Roman Empire in the East (Byzantium). Its wars and relations with these two polities which Shawqī remembered in his poetry are of much relevance. Previous Arab poets had remembered this or that caliph, but Shawqī, in addition to remembering one particular sultan/caliph, the Ottoman ʿAbd al-Hamīd, who was well known to Europe, viewed the caliphate as an institution and composed on it and on its abolition by Mustafā Kamāl (M. Kemal "Atatürk") some five elegies, even as the Habsburg Empire and that of the Russian Romanovs, with whom the caliphate collided, also crumbled after the First World War. So the poetry of Shawqī treated stirring events that convulsed the world in the East and in the West. Memorable in this context are his poems on such historical events as the Turkish/Greek war of 1897, the Fall of Edirne in 1913 to the Bulgars, and the victory of Mustafa Kemal at the battle of Sakarya over the Greek invading army in 1923. For him these wars echoed the epic of the Arab-Byzantine conflict in Medieval times. Nor did he forget the prime mover of the Revolution in world history brought about by the Prophet Muhammad, on whom Shawqī composed long odes.

In addition to the poetry on the Islamic caliphate, Shawqī may be considered the foremost Arab poet of the Mediterranean and its world. The sea which witnessed the birth of civilization, religions, and empires has been visited by poets of various nationalities, such as the Spanish-American George Santayana, the Italian Eugenio Montale, and the Latin American Rubén Darío, let alone Homer in both his epics, *The Iliad* and *The Odyssey*, the scene of which was the Mediterranean in its Eastern and Western halves. But no one remembered the Mediterranean with such detail and feeling for history as Shawqī, who remembered it both as a Muslim lake and as a Christian *mare nostrum*, Bahr al-Rūm. The image of the Mediterranean in Shawqī's poetry may be summarized as follows: He knew this sea personally, criss-crossing it many times: to France, to Spain, to the Balkans, and to Switzerland. He addressed apostrophes to it in prose and verse; he analyzed the civilization that arose and fell on its shores; Pharaonic, Greek, Roman, Byzantine, Islamic, Arab, and Ottoman. He remembered it in details: composed on its islands, the waterways such as the Bosporus and the Suez Canal, on its great rivers, especially the Nile, on which he wrote a poem of epic dimensions. And he did not stint its great cities: he remembered Cairo and Alexandria, the Hellenis-

tic city, Damascus in his two celebrated odes, Istanbul and Ankara in Turkey, Rome and Napoli in Italy, Athens in Greece, and Geneva in Switzerland. Paris, where he spent some time as a student, naturally received from him apostrophes, as did Napoleon, one of his heroes, whom he remembered in some of his best poetry. Especially remarkable is his long elegy of eighty-four verses after a visit to his tomb at Les Invalides in Paris. The elegy recalls that of Manzoni's *Il Cinque Maggio* and Hugo's *Le Retour de l'Empereur* on Napoleon, and is, at least, as impressive as either.

Of special interest in this connection are his Andalusian poems, which he composed during his exile there. Andalusia has inspired many a literary artist, but Shawqī's relation to it was unique as he spent in it the five years of his exile. His long ode after he visited Andalusia in 1919, just before his return to Egypt, an ode of some 110 verses, is the Arab Islamic elegy on Spain and the Fall of Granada to Ferdinand and Isabella in 1492. The two purple patches in it are on the great Mosque of Cordova and on Alhambra, the palace-fortress of Granada. These are splendid examples of *Ekphrasis* in Arabic, when the poetic art describes another work of art, in this case masterpieces of Islamic architecture. In composing, Shawqī reprised what the last Arab poets of Andalusia had done in the fourteenth and fifteenth centuries, when the Arab presence in the Peninsula was drawing to a close at the onslaught of the Spanish Conquistadors. But, Shawqī gave the theme of the fall of Andalusia a fuller and more expressive context and was the last Arab poet to visit Spain and compose memorably on it before the demise of the Islamic caliphate. Thirteen years later the poet-philosopher, the Indian Muslim Muhammad Iqbāl, made the pilgrimage to Andalusia and composed his famous hymn on the Mosque of Cordova.

Lastly we come to the topic of Pharaonic Egypt. As important as his poetry on the Mediterranean and its world is, his poetry on one region in it, namely Pharaonic Egypt, is of considerable interest to Western readers. Napoleon's invasion of Egypt and the French *mission civilatrice* enhanced European interest in Pharaonic Egypt with the discovery of the Rosetta stone and the deciphering of the hieroglyphics by Champollion. A certain Egyptomania swept over Europe in the nineteenth century and poets such as Shelley, Hunt, and Pierre Loti in literature did not fail to remember Pharaonic Egypt. The climax of this interest took place when the tomb of King Tut was discovered. The mummified pharaoh has never lost his universal appeal; witness his exhibition which is displayed periodically in various museums around the world. While other Arab poets referred to it *en passant* (as did Europeans such as Shelley in his Ozymandias), Shawqī's interest in Pharaonic Egypt was a romance that riveted his attention most of his life. His interest in it was especially aroused when he was a student in France, the country most related to the resuscitation of the glories of Pharaonic Egypt. On his return to Egypt, he started doing justice to the civilization that was born and grew in his own country, Egypt, particularly as the reign of 'Abbās Hilmī, his patron, witnessed much interest in collecting its Pharaonic artifacts for the Museum of Egyptian Antiquities, which had such distinguished directors as Auguste Mariette and after him Gaston Maspero. Shawqī used to visit the Pyramids every week until he moved, after his return from Spain, to his new mansion, from the balcony of which he could easily see the Pyramids.

The Pharaonic presence in his consciousness was first expressed in the long *hamziyyah* (poem rhyming in *hamzah*, the glottal stop), delivered before the Orientalist Congress in Geneva in 1894. After his poetic trajectory was diverted by Khedive Tawfīq away from drama, he published four prose works on it: three historical romances and one dialogue conducted with its poet (or so Shawqī thought), Pentā'ūr, and he used to refer to it sporadically in his poems and in the introductions to his poems. One such poem with a prelude in prose was addressed to the American president Theodore Roosevelt, when he visited Egypt in 1910. A long poem, almost epic, on the Nile, addressed (as noted above) to D. Samuel Margoliouth, the Professor of Arabic at Oxford, included much on Pharaonic Egypt. And there were poems exclusively devoted to it, such as his poem on the Sphinx.

It was, however, after his return to Egypt from his Spanish exile in 1919 that he returned again to Pharaonic Egypt in a series of poems, after his imagination had been fired by the discovery of the Tomb of King Tut. This elicited from him poems on the King and later an elegy on the death of Lord Carnarvon. When asked about what he considered his best poem he answered without any hesitation that it was his poem on King Tut, which opened *darajat 'alā 'l-kanzi 'l-qurūnu*... "Generations have passed over the treasure...".

These Pharaonic odes represent important contributions to world literature, and they are unique examples of *ekphrasis*. The Oriental poet-philosopher 'Umar Khayyām (d. c. 1123) was fortunate enough to have such a talented dragoman as Edward FitzGerald to advertise his genius to the English reader, and the odes of Shawqī deserve such a dragoman in order to introduce them into the caravan of world literature.

In his thoughtful essay "What is a Classic?", addressed to the Virgil Society in 1944, T. S. Eliot has argued that Virgil is the classic poet of European Literature. Arab literary critics and admirers of Shawqī have raised the same question in the twentieth century and concluded that Shawqī is the classic of Arabic poetry. But the criteria were rather simplistic and have failed to carry conviction to the serious literary critic. It was left to the American poet/critic to supply the true sophisticated criterion for answering the question, posed by the Arab admirers of Shawqī. *Maturity* was the concept, which he argued is the correct criterion; maturity in all its dimensions: maturity of mind, manners, language, and style. He also added comprehensiveness of the poet's *œuvre* and his being born at the right moment in the development of the particular language and history that he represents. If a poet in the Arabic Islamic tradition can be said to have passed the test of this criterion with all its dimensions, it was Ahmad Shawqī, just as Zuhayr or al-Nābighah, may be said to have passed the test for pre-Islamic Arabic poetry. Shawqī spent a lifetime, almost from the cradle to the grave, in the service of the Muse of poetry, without any distraction, mastered the Arabic language as no other poet of his generation did, and lived in the ambience of a mature sophisticated society during the reign of the Viennese educated 'Abbās Hilmī.

Furthermore, circumstances or fate had prepared him to be born in the last days of the caliphate in its Ottoman version, which he saluted when it was prospering and which he elegized when it was abolished. Before its demise he could and did view the whole panorama of the history of the Islamic caliphate from its birth in the seventh century to its fall in the twentieth in the Easter Mediterranean, as well as the sunset glow of the Arab supremacies of Andalusia in the fifteenth century in the Western Mediterranean. His moving compositions on both are the epic of Islam. Ahmad Shawqī, thus, is truly and demonstrably the classic of Arab and Islamic poetry. As Egypt, in the words of Herodotus, was "the gift of the Nile," so was Shawqī the gift of Egypt to the world of Arabic and Islamic poetry.

Few poets have been honored as Shawqī has been in his lifetime and after his death. He was buried in the family mausoleum in al-Sitt Nafīsah, Cairo, and on his marble tomb is inscribed the epitaph he himself had chosen. It is expressed in calligraphic Arabic and it reflects his deep religious faith so à propos, coming as it does, from the poet who was truly the poet of Islam and dār al-islām. The epitaph is touching in its humility and in the hope and confidence that Shawqī reposes in the "mighty fortress" of God's forgiveness. It is one of the verses in the panegyric he had composed on the Prophet Muhammad in 1909, the famous Nahj al-Burdah.

REFERENCES

For more extensive bibliographies, see the two following works:

Salih J. Altoma, Fī 'l-'alāqāt al-adabiyyah bayn al-'arab wa 'l-gharb (Jiddah, 2003), 132-144;

Azīz Abāzah, "Chawki", Mélanges de l'institut dominicain d'etudes orientales du Caire 7 (1962-63): 199-206.

Other references:

Ahmad Abū Shādī, "Shawqi, Hāfiz and Mutrān:

The Three Leading Neoclassical Poets of Contemporary Egypt", Middle Eastern Affairs 3 (1952): 239-244;

Fu'ād H. 'Ali, "Shawqi, der Fürst der Dichter", Orientalistische Studien, Enno Littmann überreicht (Leiden: E. J. Brill, 1935), 139-148;

Roger Allen, "Poetry and Poetic Criticism at the Turn of the Century", in: Studies in Modern Arabic Literature, ed. R. C. Ostle (Exeter: Aris and Phillips, 1975), 1-17;

Arthur J. Arberry, "Hafiz Ibrahim and Shawqi," Journal of the Royal Asiatic Society 35 (1937): 41-58;

'Abbās Mahmūd al-'Aqqād, Shu'arā' Misr wabī'ātuhum fī 'l-jīl al-mādī (Cairo: al-Nahdah al-Misriyyah, 1965);

Shakīb Arslān, Shawqī aw sadāqat arba'īna sanatan (Cairo: 'Īsā al-Bābī al-Halabī, 1936);

M. M. Badawi, "Convention and Revolt in Modern Arabic Poetry", in: Arabic Poetry: Theory and Development, ed. G. E. von Grünebaum (Wiesbaden: Harrassowitz, 1973), 181-208, esp. 185-189;

——, A Critical Introduction to Modern Arabic Poetry (Cambridge, 1975), esp. 28-42;

Antoine Boudot-Lamotte, Ahmed Šawqi: l'homme et l'œuvre (Damascus, 1977);

Shawqī Dayf, Shawqī: shā'ir al-'asr al-hadīth (Dār al-Ma'ārif, Cairo, 1953);

Franceso Gabrieli, "Commemorazione di Ahmad Shawqi", Oriente Moderno 39 (1959): 486-497;

'Abd al-Hakīm Hassān, Antūniyū wa-Kilūbatra bayna Shakespeare wa-Shawqī (Cairo: Maktabat al-Shabāb, 1972);

Īliyyā Hāwī: Ahmad Shawqī (Beirut: Dār al-Kitāb al-Lubnānī, 1980);

Tāhā Husayn, Hāfiz wa-Shawqī (Cairo: Matba'at al-I'timād, 1933);

Salma Khadra Jayyūsi, Trends and Movements in Modern Arabic Poetry, 2 vols. (Leiden: E. J. Brill, 1977), esp. 46-51;

Waddāh al-Khatīb, "Rewriting History, Unwriting Literature: Shawqī's Mirror-Image Response to Shakespeare", Journal of Arabic Literature 32 (2001): 256-283;

Mounah A. Khouri, Poetry and the Making of Modern Egypt (1822-1922) (Leiden: E. J. Brill, 1971);

Jacob M. Landau, *Studies in the Arab Theater and Cinema* (Philadelphia: University of Pennsylvania Press, 1958), esp. 125-138;

Muhammad Mandūr, *Masrahiyyāt Shawqī* (Cairo: Ma'had al-Dirasāt al-'Arabiyyah, 1965);

Shmuel Moreh, *Modern Arabic Poetry, 1800– 1970: The Development of its Forms and Themes under the Influence of Western Literature* (Leiden: E. J. Brill, 1976), esp. 70-71, 171-172;

Mikhā'īl Nu'aymah, *al-Ghirbāl* (Cairo, 1923);

Mattityahu Peled, "al-Muwailihī's Criticism of Shawqi's Introduction", *Middle East Studies* 16 (1980); reprinted in *Modern Egypt: Studies in Politics and Society*, ed. Elie Kedouri and Sylvia Haim (London: F. Cass, 1980), 115-124;

Hasan K. al-Sayrafi, *Hāfiz wa-Shawqī* (Cairo,

1948);

Irfān Shahīd, "Arabic Literature", in: *Cambridge History of Islam*, vol. 2, ed. P. M. Holt et al. (Cambridge: Cambridge University Press, 1970), 668-671;

——, *al-'Awdah ilā Shawqī aw ba'da khamsīna 'āman* (Beirut: al-Ahliyyah, 1986);

——, "Greece in the Arabic Poetic Mirror", *Graeco-Arabica* (Athens, 1991), 33-42;

——, "The Arabic Mirror", in: *Napoleon: One Image, Ten Mirrors* (Georgetown University, 2002), 61-86;

Husayn Shawqī, *Abī Shawqī* (Cairo: al-Nahdah al-Misriyyah, 1947);

Muhammad al-Tarābulsī, *Khasā'is al-uslūb fī 'l-Shawqiyyāt* (Tunis, 1981);

Tāhā Wādī, *Shi'r Shawqī al-ghinā'ī wa'l-masrahī* (Cairo: Dār al-Ma'ārif, 1981).

Ahmad Fāris al-Shidyāq

(1804 – 1887)

WALID HAMARNEH
Swarthmore College

WORKS

Khabariyyāt As'ad al-Shidyāq ("The Story of As'ad al-Shidyaq", no publisher, 1833);

al-Bākūrah al-shahiyyah fī nahw al-lughah al-Inkilīziyyah ("The Appetizing Introduction to English Grammar", Malta, 1836);

al-Lafīf fī kull ma'nā zarīf ("Encyclopedia of Witty Constructs", Malta, 1839);

al-Muhāwarah al-unsiyyah fī 'l-lughatayn al-Inkilīziyyah wa'l-'Arabiyyah ("Pleasant Dialogue on the Arabic and English Languages)", Malta 1840);

al-Ajwibah al-ghaliyyah fī 'l-usūl al-nahwiyyah ("Precious Answers, Concerning the Rules of Grammar", Malta, 1841);

Panegyric of Ahmad Pasha Beğ of Tunisia, tr. with commentary by Gustave Doreau (Dugha), in: Imprimiére de Bineteay, Paris 1851;

al-Sanad al-rāwī fī 'l-sarf al-faransāwī ("The

Quenching Support Concerning French Grammar", Paris: Imprimérie Impériale, 1854);

al-Sāq 'alā 'l-sāq fī-mā huwa al-Fāriyāq ("One Leg Over Another/The Pigeon on the Tree-Branch, Concerning al-Fāriyāq", Paris: Benjamin Dupart, 1855);

al-Wāsitah fī ahwāl Māltah ("Mediation Concerning Malta", Tunis, 1863);

Kashf al-mukhabbā 'an funūn Ūrubbā ("Disclosing the Hidden of the Crafts of Europe", Tunis, 1863);

Sirr al-layāl fī 'l-qalb wa'l-ibdāl ("The Secrets of Morphology and Metathesis", Istanbul, 1884);

Ghunyat al-tālib wa-munyat al-rāghib fī 'l-sarf wa'l-nahw wa'l-ma'ānī ("The Satisfying Answer to Morphology and Semantics", Istanbul: Matba'at al-Jawā'ib, 1288 H./1871);

Kanz al-raghā'ib fī muntakhabāt al-Jawā'ib ("The Heart's Desire, [consisting of] Selections from [the periodical] *al-Jawā'ib*"), ed. Salīm al-Shidyāq, 7 vols. (Istanbul: Matba'at al-Jawā'ib, 1288-1299 H./1871-1881);

Salwān al-shājī fī 'l-radd 'alā Ibrāhīm al-Yāzijī ("The Curative Comfort: In Response to Ibrāhīm al-Yāzijī", Matba'at al-Jawā'ib, Istanbul, 1289 H./1872);

Kanz al-lughāt: Fārisī wa-Turkī wa-'Arabī ("The Treasure of Languages: French, Turkish and Arabic", Beirut, 1876);

al-Jāsūs 'alā 'l-qāmūs ("Spying on the Dictionary", Istanbul: Matba'at al-Jawā'ib, 1299 H./1882);

Muqaddimah wa-hawāmish tawdīhiyyah li-Lisān al-'Arab li-Ibn Manzūr ("Introduction and Clarifying/Explanatory Glosses on Ibn Manzūr's [dictionary] *The Language of the Arabs*"), 20 vols. (Cairo: Matba'at Būlāq, 1883-1889);

Muqaddimat dīwān Ahmad Fāris Afandī ("Introduction to the Collected Poems of A. F. Effendi", Istanbul: Matba'at al-Jawā'ib, n.d.);

al-Maqāmah al-bakhshīshiyyah, aw: al-Sultān Bakhshīsh ("The Bakhshish Maqāmah, or: Sultan Bakhshīsh", Algiers, 1893); publ. together with a French translation by R. Arnaud;

Falsafat al-tarbiyah wa'l-adab ("Educational Philosophy"), ed. 'Alī Muhammad al-Khattāb (Cairo, n.d.);

Mukhtārāt min Fāris al-Shidyāq ("Selections from F. al-Sh.", Beirut: Maktabat Sādir, 1963);

Munāzarāt al-Shidyāq wa-Ibrāhīm al-Yāzijī ("Debates Between al-Shidyāq and Ibrāhīm al-Yāzijī", Beirut, n.d.).

Probably Lost Works

al-Ujrūmiyyah; probably an interpretation of the *Ājurrūmiyyah* of Muhammad b. Muhammad b. Ājurrūm al-Sinhājī (672-723/1273-1323);

Dīwān al-Shidyāq; this anthology, according to al-Ziriklī, includes 22 000 verses but is about one fourth of Shidyāq's poetic production;

Fusūl wa-rasā'il shattā; selection of articles from *al-Makshūf* and *Majallat al-Salām*;

Lā ta'wīl fī 'l-injīl ("No Interpretation in the Gospels");

Malhūzāt 'alā 'l-shi'r al-'arabī ("Notes on Arabic Poetry"); probably the introduction to his collected poetry;

al-Mir'āt fī 'aks al-tawrāt ("The Mirror in Refuting the Torah"); a manuscript of about 700 pages in the refutation of the Holy Bible which he did not want published prior to his death;

Muntahā al-'ajab fī khasā'is lughat al-'Arab ("The Exquisite Wonders of the Language of the Arabs"); this manuscript concerned with the lexicography and phonology of Arabic on which al-Shidyāq worked for a number of decades was lost in a fire during his lifetime;

al-Nafā'is fī inshā' Ahmad Fāris ("Precious Items Concerning Ahmad Fāris's Compositions");

Nubdhah shā'iqah fī 'l-radd 'alā Mutrān Mālta ("An Exciting Brief In Refuting the Bishop of Malta");

al-Taqnī' fī 'ilm al-badī' ("The Satisfaction Concerning Figurative Language");

al-Rawd al-nādir fī abyāt wa-nawādir ("The Recherché Garden on Poetry and Anecdotes");

Tarājim mashāhīr al-'asr ("Biographies of Famous Contemporaries");

al-Masā'il al-mufakhkhamah fī 'l-'aqā'id al-mubhamah ("The Grand Issues of Ambiguous Creeds");

I'tirādāt Injīl Sharīf ("[Objections to the Holy Bible]"); this title was mentioned in the list of books of an Ahmad Tawfīq Pasha whose private library was sold following his death in 1893; it is described as a fine manuscript in 150 pages which was copied in Beirut in the year 1281 of the Islamic calendar;

al-Maghnā li-kull ma'nā ("A Treatise on Meaning").

Unpublished Works

Irtibāt al-tamaddun bi'l-dīn al-islāmī ("[The Connection of Civilization to Islamic Religion]"); an apologetic text that defends Islam against those who maintain it is a religion of backwardness;

Lamm al-qurūd fī dhamm al-yahūd ("[An invective of the Jews]", probably written 1248 H./1832-33); a long poem that mocks and critiques the Old Testament;

Mumāhakāt al-ta'wīl fī munāqadāt al-injīl ("The
  Contentions of Interpretation in the Contradictions of the Bible"); there exist two manuscripts of this text dating from Feb 20th, 1851,
  and Nov. 20th, 1856; the essay points out to
  many contradictions in the Bible and relates
  their impact on biblical hermeneutics;
Nutq al-sitt bi'l-durar wa'l-yāqūt ("The
  Woman's Enunciation of Jewels and Rubies"); a *maqāmah* dealing with issues of
  language and poetry.

Translations by al-Shidyāq into Arabic

al-Kanz al-mukhtār fī kashf al-arādī wa'l-bihār
  ("The Treasure Digest of Lands and Seas",
  Malta, 1836);
Tārīkh al-kanīsah 'alā wajh al-ikhtisār ("Church
  History Digest", Malta, 1839);
*Kitāb al-salawāt al-'āmmah ma'a mazāmīr Dā-
  wūd* ("The Book of Common Prayer with the
  Psalms of David", Malta, 1840); there are
  many editions of this prayer-book with the
  psalms added; some editions and reprints appeared in London as well as Beirut and other
  places;
Sharh tabā'i' al-hayawān ("Natural History Explained", Malta, 1841); a rather free translation of the first volume of W. F. Maier's
  Natural History for the Use of Schools;
al-'Ahd al-jadīd ("The New Testament", London: Christian Knowledge Society, 1851); a
  translation of the New Testament made in
  collaboration with Samuel Lee and others;
*Tarjamat al-Kitāb al-Muqaddas (aw tarjamat al-
  Tawrāh)* ("Translation of the Bible (or translation of the Torah)", London: The Society
  for Promoting Christian Knowledge, 1857); a
  translation of the Holy Bible made in collaboration with Samuel Lee and others;
Majallat al-ahkām al-'adliyyah ("The Magazine
  of Laws", Istanbul, 1869-1876, reprinted 1897).

Works in Translation

Faris Chidyaq, *La jambe sur la jambe*, roman
  traduit de l'arabe par René R. Khawam (Paris: Phébus, 1991).

It needs to be stressed at the outset that any
discussion of the works and ideas of al-Shidyāq

is, at the present level of research, preliminary.
This is mainly due to the fact that many of his
works are still unpublished or have been lost.
But what adds to the difficulties is the liberal
editorial work done to his published works. Here
we encounter editors giving themselves the right
to delete passages and even complete pages
whenever they think these pages are offensive to
the reader or even not suitable from a writer and
intellectual the caliber of al-Shidyāq. The research and critical works of Abier Bushnaq in
German and Fawwāz Tarābulusī and 'Azīz al-
'Azmah in Arabic have contributed to a better
understanding of the present state of al-Shidyāq
scholarship.

Al-Shidyāq is arguably the most controversial and problematic thinker and writer in Arabic
during the nineteenth century. One of the main
problems associated with the discussion of his
ideas, especially those outside the sphere of
language, is the difficulty of classifying his
works. They seem to defy both the classical
generic classifications as well as the modern
ones. A case in point is his most important work,
al-Sāq 'alā 'l-sāq. Most Arab and many Western
commentators have considered it an autobiographical work and have used it as an historical
source for his biography as well as a source for
his ideas. But *al-Sāq* is a literary work that has
clear connections to classical Arab narrative
genres as well as fictive elements. Added to all
this is the underlying sarcastic and playful sub-
stratum that forms the basis of the work and its
structure. This, however, does not mean that *al-
Sāq* does not include and should not be used as a
source for al-Shidyāq's biography or his ideas. It
merely means that the text cannot be seen only
as a social text, it is a multi-layered one.

Ahmad Fāris al-Shidyāq was born in 1804 in
'Ashqūt, a small town in Kisrawān in today's
Lebanon. In those times, Mount Lebanon was
nominally a part of the Ottoman Empire but was
in reality ruled by the emir Bashīr al-Shihābī
(1789-1840). Of great authority was the Maronite patriarch Yūsuf Hubaysh (1823-1845)
who was to play an important role in the negative attitude of Shidyāq to the Maronite Church.
The Shidyāq family was one of the renowned
and rich Maronite families of Mount Lebanon,

but some of them were rebellious or made unwise decisions concerning their alliances with the many contenders of power, which led, in some cases like that of al-Shidyāq's grandfather Butrus, to tragic ending. However, the incident that had the greatest impact on the young Fāris was the conversion of his brother As'ad to Protestantism. Patriarch Hubaysh summoned As'ad in March 1826 and detained him in the monastery of 'Almā. But As'ad was able to flee to Beirut and reported his story in a letter to the American missionary, Isaac Beard. As'ad's family, however, handed him back to the Patriarch who imprisoned him in the Qannubīn monastery, where he died in 1830. As'ad was supposed to be a lesson to all those who thought of converting from the Maronite Church to Protestantism. The causes of As'ad's death are not known. Some maintain that the prison conditions and possibly torture were the causes of his death. While others maintain that it was due to having had dropsy (as maintained by Shidyāq's cousin, Būlus Mis'ad, who later became the Maronite Patriarch himself). Fāris grew disgusted with the Maronite Church, became a Presbyterian in 1825, and left for Egypt.

He lived in Egypt until 1834. During his stay there he studied Islamic sciences with renowned Azhar scholars and taught Arabic to American missionaries. During the latter part of stay in Egypt he succeeded al-**Tahtāwī** as the editor of the official government newspaper, *al-Waqā'i' al-Misriyyah*. He also married the daughter of a Syrian Christian émigré family (al-Sūlī) who bore him two sons, Fāris (1826-1906) and Fāyiz (1828-1856).

In 1834 the American missionaries invited al-Shidyāq to become the director of their printing press in Malta. He spent the next fourteen years there, mostly working on his studies and readings. He only left Malta twice: once was an almost secret visit to Lebanon, Syria and Palestine in 1840; the other was to London in 1846 when he was invited by the Society for the Propagation of the Gospel to help Dr. Samuel Lee in translating the Bible and the Book of Common Prayer into Arabic. While in Malta in 1836 al-Shidyāq wrote a grammar book of the English language, *al-Bākūrah al-shahiyyah fī*

nahw al-lughah al-inkilīziyyah; he later republished it in Istanbul in 1881. Four years later, in 1840, he published another book in Malta with essays on the Arabic and English languages entitled *al-Muhāwarah al-unsiyyah fī 'l-lughatayn al-inkilīziyyah wa'l-'arabiyyah* (a second printing appeared in Istanbul in 1881). In 1841, while still in Malta, he published a book on Arabic language and grammar *(al-Ajwibah al-ghaliyyah fī 'l-usūl al-nahwiyyah)* in which he summarized the work done in the field by Archbishop Jirmānūs Farhāt of Aleppo (1670-1732) who was one of the most outstanding scholars in the area of Arabic studies during his times. In 1854 he published in Paris a textbook of French grammar, *al-Sanad al-rāwī fī 'l-sarf al-faransāwī*. What is important about these grammar and language books is that they were probably the earliest textbooks composed to teach Arab learners the grammars of English and French.

In September of 1848, al-Shidyāq decided to move to England to do the work for Dr. Lee. He first lived in London, then relocated to a small village (Purley) close to Cambridge where Dr. Lee was teaching Arabic. The translations were completed and published in 1857 (after the death of Dr. Lee). And although Shidyāq had many issues and differences with Dr. Lee relating to the translation, especially as pertains to using terms closer to Qur'anic and classical Arabic, which Dr. Lee rejected and preferred terms associated with Syriac and Hebrew, many commentators think that this was the best Arabic translation of the Bible and that it surpassed the one that was made by Smith and van Dyke with the help of Butrus al-Bustānī and Nāsīf al-**Yāzijī** which is the one used by most protestant Churches in the Arab World. It seems that al-Shidyāq's critical attitude toward the church establishment and his later conversion to Islam has contributed to the animosity toward his better translation by the Eastern Churches.

After completing his work on the translation, he tried to get a job at Cambridge, then at Oxford, but to no avail. So he left for Paris where he spent a total of 30 months in two occasions that were the most productive and most enjoyable for him. During his Paris stay he contacted many orientalists, poets, writers, as well as Arab merchants. He also wrote some of his most important books: *al-Sāq 'alā 'l-sāq*, *Sirr al-layāl fī 'l-qalb wa'l-ibdāl*, *al-Jāsūs 'alā 'l-qāmūs*, and *Muntahā al-'ajab fī khasā'is lughat al-'arab*.

As noted above, *al-Sāq 'alā 'l-sāq* is widely acknowledged as being his most important work. The full title of the book is *al-Sāq 'alā 'l-sāq fī mā huwa al-Fāriyāq: aw ayyām wa-shuhūr wa-a'wām fī 'ujm al-'arab wa'l-a'jām* (literally, One Leg over Another / The Pigeon on the Tree-branch, Concerning the Person Called al-Fāri-yāq, or: Days, Months, and Years Among Foreign Arabs [those who are incapable of speaking Arabic well] and Foreigners; another reading would be *'ajm* instead of *'ujm*, the former meaning, literally, "to bite on a coin in order to know whether it is genuine or not"; this reading turns the subtitle into "Days, Months, and Years [Spent] With Testing [or Critically Observing] Arabs and non-Arabs," a reading which would correspond to the French subtitle of the original edition, which has *Observations critiques sur les arabes et sur les autres peoples* "Critical observations on Arabs and non-Arabs"). This is important to highlight from the outset as the title and its form can provide us with a pretty good idea of the text. Some recent commentators and editors of the text have felt uncomfortable with the title because they had a preconceived idea of what the text is, namely an autobiographical piece. The editor of the text, 'Imād al-Sulh, who also wrote a book about al-Shidyāq, even went as far as changing the title into: *I'tirāfāt al-Shidyāq fī kitābih al-Sāq 'alā 'l-sāq* (The Confessions of al-Shidyāq in His Book *al-Sāq 'alā 'l-sāq*). It goes without saying that this turns the book not only into a piece of autobiography but also confessions, very intimate and subjective and associated not with memories of the external world and what impact it had on the person, but rather with the development of the inner self and psyche and thus very subjective. According to al-Sulh it is thus similar to confessions in the religious mode and should be read as such. Such an interpretation of the text would, for sure, necessitate a change in the title; indeed it required the excision of certain passages that al-

Sulh thought inappropriate, although this may be seen as contradictory to his interpretation of the text as a confession.

The title of the text gives us some clues as to what it is, at least in the mind of its author. First of all we have the rhyme in the title which connects this with classical traditional Arabic writings. But it also includes the word Fāriyāq which is a concoction of the first part of Shidyāq's first name and the last part of his last name. The interpretation of *al-sāq 'alā 'l-sāq* as "leg over leg" can be more problematic (not to mention the fact that the phrase can also mean "the pigeon on the tree-branch"). It may be seen as referring to the posture taken by people who are westernized in sitting. But it can also refer to the touching of the legs as a sexual reference as Tarābulusī and al-'Azmah maintain. There may be some strength to this interpretation as issues of sexuality are central to the text. However, a closer and open-minded examination of the text clearly shows that it is difficult, if not impossible, to force it within any strict categorization or classification as concerns genre. The text utilizes and combines many different genres and styles, both classical and modern, and its subject matter is also mixed. In what follows, I will try to describe some of the main characteristics of *al-Sāq* and try to show where it can be situated within the institutions of Arabic literature and intellectual life in the nineteenth century.

The narrator of the text is al-Hāris ibn Hithām which is clearly a reference to the two narrators in the two most well-known collections of *maqāmāt* in classical Arabic literature, namely 'Īsā ibn Hishām (the narrator of al-Hamadhānī [d. 1008]) and al-Hārith ibn Humām (the narrator of al-Harīrī [d. 1122]). The narrator in these *maqāmāt* tells a story in which he gets entangled in a plot or situation with the protagonist, who is generally a bright and somewhat cunning but funny character. The protagonist of al-Hama-dhānī is Abū 'l-Fath al-Iskandarī and that of al-Harīrī is Abū Zayd al-Sarūjī. The protagonist of al-Shidyāq is Abū Zulāmah al-Fāriyāq. The plots of the different chapters of the book are similar to those of the *maqāmah*, in which the protagonist appears unexpectedly and gets involved with the narrator who is already in a curious situation, only to be resolved through the words of the protagonist.

Maqāmāt were written in rhyming prose *(saj')*, and so was *al-Sāq*. But the rhyming prose would sometimes be interspersed with lines of poetry. In *al-Sāq*, poetry is resorted to more often, especially in the pieces of advice that is given by al-Fāriyāq to al-Hāris. Although the classical *maqāmah* had comic elements, yet it derived its ludic character from the situation and characters. *Al-Sāq* is undoubtedly funny, but its ludic character is more satirical of itself. It mocks its own style and conventions. It uses rhyming prose so efficiently as to verge on the super-artificial and almost forces the reader to laugh at its almost perfect utilization. The smile or giggle is extricated through reflection on the method and not only through subject matter or situation or linguistic play. The literary and linguistic conventions resorted to so efficiently become the object of reflection and, thereby, the source of the pleasure of the text. It is exactly this aspect of the text that irritated an outstanding historian of Arabic literature like Shawqī Dayf with his traditionalist bent and made him judge *al-Sāq* negatively both as a bad imitation of al-Harīrī and al-Hamadhānī and also as opposed to *Majma' al-bahrayn* by Nāsīf al-**Yāzijī** who was a contemporary of al-Shidyāq and wrote in the more serious and venerable mode of the classical *maqāmah*.

Al-Sāq is actually glued together in many ways. One is the anecdotal but ironic depiction of the life of al-Fāriyāq. But this is further complicated by the introduction of his wife, al-Fāriyāqah, who is full of life and curiosity and has about her character a warmth of portrayal that was new for Arabic literature. Yet she functions somehow as the other with whom al-Fāriyāq is contrasted. Through such juxtaposition of the two a kind of dramatic irony is achieved, and al-Fāriyāqah becomes the moral corrective for al-Fāriyāq. So despite the lack of a novelistic plot in the modern sense, a certain unity is achieved through an ironic interplay between parallelisms and anti-theses and between similarities and contrasts. In that sense it is closer to the work of Fielding in ironically turning the protagonist into an anti-hero as in

Tom Jones and *Shamela*. Another aspect that contributes to the ironic effect is the continuous posturing of the implicit author and his intervention and commentaries on the text, the characters, the themes, as well as the narrator himself. The implicit author, in line with a venerable tradition in Arabic story telling generally associated with the second person narration, directs his discourse directly to the reader bypassing the narrator, and thus provides a possibility for the reader to reflect.

As to themes, al-Shidyāq tells us in his introduction to *al-Sāq* that he has in mind two main ones: women and language. Language is not only a theme, but also the medium of writing. The play with language becomes the object upon which we read many reflections but is also elaborated through the very same language that the author is using. This form of linguistic reflexivity runs in tandem with the ironic aspects mentioned earlier and reinforces them. It also adds to the ludic effect of the text.

The theme of women is central to the book; indeed the presence of al-Fāriyāqah makes the discussion of women very different from those discussions of the issue during his times and even well into the twentieth century. Not only does al-Shidyāq use his characters to discuss intimate relations between the sexes, something regarded as obscene by many commentators and critics who have studied al-Shidyāq, but also and probably for the first time in the Arabic language, the perspective of women is foregrounded. This has resulted in much uneasiness amongst critics and lots of apologetics as well as editorial censorship (the same applies to his criticism of religion and religious institutions, but especially the religious bureaucracy). One cannot but agree with Tarābulusī and al-'Azmah, namely that al-Shidyāq was a feminist many decades before feminism and many more before Arab feminism.

To summarize, here are the main themes and topics treated in *al-Sāq*:

1. A harsh critique of religion in general, but especially religion in the Arab East. A special object of criticism are priests and monks who have assumed a lot of worldly power that they misuse and who preach ethics, morality, and

purity but are themselves slaves of their sexual urges both hetero- and homosexual. He pokes fun at Catholic priests whom he calls *sūqiyyūn* ("marketers," from *sūq* meaning market) because they turn religion into a business, as well as Protestant priests who merely change the form of things but are essentially the same as Catholics. He even calls the Pope the *shaykh* of immorality *(fisq)*. He goes on to narrate the story of his brother (a passage that was censored by the translator into French, Part I, chapter 19). Al-Shidyāq also emphasizes the necessity of the division between religion and politics. He stresses that religion belongs in the sphere of the individual; it is a matter of personal belief. Thus, unlike language or culture, religion cannot serve as the basis for a modern community.

2. Women and men, sexuality and the body, marriage and celibacy are discussed in different places (examples: education of women: I, 10; advantages and disadvantages of celibacy: IV, 13; rights and obligations of the husband: II, 18; marriage and divorce: II, 13-14; the good aspects of women: III, 19; fights in marriage: III, 13; jealousy: IV, 2; kissing in public: II, 6; women of London: IV, 6; no differences between a married woman and a virgin amongst Europeans: IV, 17; comparison between English and French women: IV, 17; fashion and women: III, 6; erotics: III, 5; love and marriage: III, 2; the right of a woman to have a relationship outside of marriage: III, 18; prostitution: I, 8 and IV, 4. It should also be noted that, in many of these chapters, al-Shidyāq resorts to his great knowledge of the Arabic language and its rich traditions of vocabulary concerning the description of body parts as well as shapes and forms of women which some editors, especially 'Imād al-Sulh, have expurgated from the text (see especially II, 14; III, 5; IV, 16).

3. As in most other writings by al-Shidyāq, language is an important theme here. Many issues are broached and discussed, such as mistranslations of the Bible (II, 11; III, 9; III, 18) and style and grammar (I, 11), as well as one of his obsessions, namely, the descriptions of bad smell and ways of getting rid of it (III, 2; II, 11; IV, 8).

4. We find many comparisons between Westerners and Easterners. It is noteworthy that al-Shidyāq is much more insightful in discerning the positive habits of Westerners: hard work, respect for women and wives, habits of reading, little talk and more work, and keeping promises. But he also sees many of the social and economic problems facing the poor in both country and city. He criticizes Orientalists and merchants, and makes comparisons between different European cities, observing the better situation of housing in London when compared to Paris, especially concerning the danger of fire. But it needs to be emphasized that these themes and topics are always treated from within stories that are fictive, though not necessarily fictitious.

Peled maintains that *al-Sāq* can be classified as Menippean satire. His analysis of the text is, unlike most other critics, literary. He compares *al-Sāq* with some other contemporary texts like al-Shirbīnī's (late 17th cent.) *Hazz al-quhūf fī sharh qasīdat Abī Shadūf*, the works of Ibn Sūdūn (d. c. 1464) and Ibn 'Ishrīn, as well as other works within this tradition of humor (as Shawqī Dayf terms it). The fact that these works share with *al-Sāq* a number of characteristics—parody, satirical posture, the play on parallelisms and contrasts, and an emphasis on humor—should not make us forget or minimize the differences between them. The tradition of al-Shirbīnī is a part and parcel of a clear culture of humor in the Bakhtinian sense of opposition. It is embedded within the culture of the lower classes, one that pokes fun in a direct manner at the culture of the upper classes through reversals and oppositions but also through parody of high literary genres.

The earlier Arabic tradition of parody of genres and themes in a humorous manner was resorted to by al-Wahrānī (d. 1179), who used both the *maqāmah* as the genre of parody and the epistolary tradition *(rasā'il)* and made fun of poets, philosophers, kings. In his *Hazz al-quhūf fī sharh qasīdat Abī Shādūf*, Yūsuf al-Shirbīnī developed this tradition still further, especially in the second part of the work, where he parodies the tradition of *shurūh* (explications and commentaries) by providing a *sharh* of the poem on the theme of food. *Shurūh* were usually commentaries on either religious or poetical texts that were considered important, but here the *sharh* is of a poem on food most probably written by al-Shirbīnī himself. He adds other "food parodies," this time resorting to short and long Friday sermons in mosques. Al-Shirbīnī explicitly mentions his indebtedness to Ibn Sūdūn, as Dayf notes (Dayf 1985, 112). However, in contradistinction to this work of al-Shirbīnī which is a clear parody, *al-Sāq* is more complicated, not so much because it parodies many different genres, but rather because its mode of parody is different. It does not involve opposition from without, but rather from within. The *maqāmah* in and of itself is not sufficiently important to become the object of satire or of parody. Parody is merely a means, and the main objective is clearly to break down generic classifications and conventions in a manner analogous to the need to break out of the classicist and conservative attitude to language. It is not so much parody and Menippean satire that is at play here, but more Occam's razor, leading inexorably *ad absurdum*. If the parodic attack on genres has the limited aim of engendering laughter—no small feat in itself, then al-Shidyāq's aims were much more radical, amounting to a challenge of the entirely of literary and linguistic institutions in his own times.

It is through this prism that his whole work can be seen as a project, and an important and subversive one at that, something for which he made use of every means available to him. He had to work hard in his attempt to become a public intellectual in his time, something was extremely difficult since intellectuals in the Arab World were by definition servants of either the state or religious institutions. In this sense al-Shidyāq differs from many other leading intellectuals of the Arab renaissance in the nineteenth century in that, for most of his life, he distrusted the dominant institutions. He did not believe in an etatist reform project, although he did support and work for reformist leaders. Yet, despite his cooperation with those reformist leaders, he never believed that the enlightenment project could be entrusted to them. In this matter too he differed greatly from contemporaries like al-Tahtāwī for whom reform and modernization could only be the work of an enlightened ruler

and even a despot. Al-Shidyāq seems to have known better. This may help us understand why he is generally neglected within the intellectual institutions of the Arab World which continue to be implicated with institutions of power and religion.

Following the death of his first wife al-Shidyāq married an English woman in 1857. Also in 1857 he composed a panegyric of the reformist ruler of Tunis, Ahmad Pasha, who in turn invited him to come to Tunis where he was well treated and became the editor of the newspaper, *al-Rā'id*, as well as the director of the Education department. While in Tunis, al-Shidyāq published two travel books in one volume (either 1863 or 1865): *al-Wāsitah fī ahwāl Māltah* and *Kashf al-mukhabbā 'an funūn Ūrubbā* (a second augmented edition was published in Istanbul in 1867). The first work describes Malta and its inhabitants, both Maltese and English, and is based upon his long experience of the island in which he lived for 14 years. It discusses the geography of the island, its demography, climate, ethnic and social structure, its politics, language, and its arts, especially archeology and music. The second work is mostly based on his experiences in England and France. But the two books are different in many ways from similar books written by Arabs who visited or spent longer periods in European countries and wrote about these countries and their experiences in them. A paradigmatic example and one that has been much more influential than al-Shidyāq is al-**Tahtāwī** whose *Takhlīs al-ibrīz* is a description of Paris during the earlier decades of the nineteenth century. Both al-Tahtāwī and al-Shidyāq are very keen observers. But al-Tahtāwī is more interested in the society from the perspective of organization and politics. He describes how the political and social as well as legal system works. He is interested in the constitution and parties. Whenever he approached social life, it is through the perspective of a Muslim and an Egyptian. And although al-Tahtāwī was an open-minded person, his observations and comments on the social life of the Parisians were mostly framed from within the perspective and the frame of reference of a Muslim scholar. The case of al-Shidyāq is different. Though interested in political and social organization, he is more of an anthropologist looking at society in its totality. He is interested not only in political and social organization and laws, but also the economic life of the different segments and classes of society. He discusses material culture, daily life, as well as habits and customs. He is as much interested in cooking, eating and drinking, in death and birth rituals and gossip, as in government and governing. His keen sense of the daily and mundane and his sharp eye that misses nothing make him an accurate observer of life. His comments and observations related to women in England, France, and the East are a very good example of this. Another important aspect that characterizes his observations, especially the comparative ones stems from his open-minded view of different cultures. He seems to be almost post-modern in his attitude and understanding of cultures. He emphasizes the differences without passing absolute judgments. There are things that he likes or dislikes about England, France and the East. But such value judgments are tempered by his conviction, which he never tires of stating, that different cultures operate and can be better understood from within rather than from without; that cultures function internally rather well, and what seems strange, odd, or exotic from the perspective of one culture is only natural from the perspective of another. It would take anthropologists decades to come to such an understanding, not to mention the centuries of modernity's conviction in its own superiority or for that matter Islam.

It was also during this period spent in Tunis that in 1860 al-Shidyāq converted to Islam and changed his name to Ahmad Fāris. This conversion has been a highly controversial topic. Father Cheikho, an outstanding scholar of Arabic language and literature, maintains that Shidyāq's conversion was based on advice from some dignitaries in Tunis who thought that this was the way to get promoted by the Sultan in Constantinople. This may be true and may have contributed, in a small or large amount, to Shidyāq's conversion. But it does not fully explain it. Some sort of change was sure to come. Shidyāq became as disillusioned with Protestantism as he

was with the Maronite Church. He poked fun at both in his writings, especially in *al-Sāq 'alā 'l-sāq*, and his criticism of Christianity and the church was extremely harsh. One could also discern a general antipathy to all kinds of metaphysics and all sorts of religious beliefs in his writings. This became more pronounced during his stay in France where he became more acquainted with socialist ideas and materialist philosophies. A man of al-Shidyāq's education and knowledge, with outstanding competence in English, French, and Turkish as well as a fine competence in other tongues, once exposed to writings by different figures in Europe who were highly critical of Christianity and the church, was clearly much influenced by these various factors. But "why Islam?" remains the big question. Tarābulusī and al-'Azmah interpret the choice of Islam as being both a combination of self-interest as well as a cultural choice associated with his emphasis on Arabic and the culture of Arabic which is intricately associated with Islam as a religion and culture. What makes such an interpretation plausible is that it seems to fit with al-Shidyāq's ideas and pronouncements and to explain his vision of Islam as expressed in some of his later writings.

Another panegyric, but this time of the Ottoman sultan 'Abd al-Majīd, brought about an invitation to settle in Istanbul in one of the Sultan's palaces. There he translated the legal journal *Majallat al-ahkām al-'adliyyah* into Arabic between the years 1869-1876. But his more important project was to launch an Arabic newspaper, *al-Jawā'ib*, which is considered the first true non-governmental newspaper in the Arabic language with a very wide circulation both within and outside the Ottoman Empire. It typically included news, both official and non-official, with special emphasis on news items from the Arab parts of the Empire as well as Lebanon. Each issue also contained literary articles, poems, discussions related to language, and it also published a history of the Ottoman Empire in serialized form. However, from issue 36 the journal began to face financial problems to the extent that it announced its imminent closure. However, the financial intervention of the Ottoman Prime Minister, Fu'ād Pasha, saved it, and it rapidly became the most popular Arabic newspaper in the sultanate and an almost official mouthpiece of the government. It was now read in Baghdad, Damascus, Beirut, Cairo as well as the Maghreb. But al-Shidyāq was well aware that, even though he supported and received support from the sultan, he had to preserve some kind of financial independence if he was to preserve his political autonomy. He diversified his sources of financial support to include the governor of Tunis and the Khedive of Egypt both of whom were reformers. As long as the reformists had the upper hand in Istanbul, al-Shidyāq supported them. But as soon as the reformist movement became increasingly associated with a nationalist Turkish ideology, he felt estranged from it and started to face difficulties with the authorities to the extent that in 1879 al-Jawā'ib was temporarily closed by the authorities and virtually ceased publication in 1884.

During his stay in Istanbul the radical, almost revolutionary Shidyāq mellowed. He became less radical and a supporter of reforms. We can nevertheless still discern in his writings the sarcastic and critical attitude of the rebel and the renegade. During the latter parts of his life, political and ideological movements seemed to lose their attractiveness for him and the Arabic language moved to the centre of his convictions. Arabic language was always important for al-Shidyāq both intellectually and as an object of study. But during the latter years of his life, it became the determinant of the Arab race, something in which he preserved his conviction, despite his extremely critical attitude of the Arabs of his day, their social habits and beliefs. Among the more important contributions that al-Shidyāq made to language studies are his contributions to Arabic grammar and philology. In 1871 (1288 H.) he published an Arabic grammar textbook in Istanbul, *Ghunyat al-tālib wa-munyat al-rāghib fī 'l-sarf wa'l-nahw wa'l-ma'ānī*, which has been reprinted many times, most recently in Beirut (1994). In 1876 he published in Beirut a trilingual Persian-Turkish-Arabic dictionary. His work on Arabic philology and dictionaries was initiated by the book *Sirr al-layāl fī 'l-qalb wa'l-ibdāl*, a huge work of 609

pages published in 1876 in Istanbul, in which al-Shidyāq discusses commonly used verbs and nouns and traces the ways in which they changed, especially with regard to phonological shifts and transformations throughout history. He explains their synonyms and shows differences in their semantic fields both diachronically and synchronically. He also discusses critically Fīrūzābādī's (d. 1414) *al-Qāmūs al-muhīt*, one of the most comprehensive dictionaries of the Arabic language from the late medieval period, and mentions many words that have escaped him. He continued his critical examination of Arabic dictionaries with his *al-Jāsūs 'alā 'l-qāmūs*, published in Istanbul in 1882. This is probably the most learned and critical review of classical Arabic philology as it has been transmitted through dictionaries like *Lisān al-'arab*, *al-Qāmūs al-muhīt*, and *Tāj al-'arūs* by Murtadā al-Zabīdī (d. 1790). Al-Shidyāq is extremely critical of al-Zabīdī who was more of a linguistic purist and rejected the appropriation of foreign words as well as those from the different Arabic dialects. In that sense al-Shidyāq differed from many of his contemporaries like al-Tahtāwī in Egypt as well as the Bustānīs and Yāzijīs in Lebanon who held al-Zabīdī in great esteem. A further step was taken by al-Shidyāq when he published in Cairo between 1883 and 1889 an edition of *Lisān al-'arab* by Ibn Manzūr in 20 volumes, a work that is considered one of the greatest classical dictionaries of the language. He wrote an extensive and critical introduction as well as added thousands of footnotes and additions to the huge dictionary. This was such a great feat that some commentators wrote that any one wishing to write about Arabic philology after al-Shidyāq should be ashamed as no one will be able to equal, not to mention surpass, him.

During his lifetime al-Shidyāq engaged in many controversies concerning Arabic grammar and philology with the greatest luminaries of the era, especially on the pages of journals like his own *al-Jawā'ib* but also others like *al-Jinān*. Some of these discussions were later collected in book form, like *Salwān al-shājī fī 'l-radd 'alā Ibrāhīm al-Yāzijī*, published in 1872 in Istanbul, and *Munāzarāt al-Shidyāq wa-Ibrāhīm al-Yāzijī*, published in Beirut.

Yet another area within the broader field of Arabic language to which al-Shidyāq made major contributions was that of translation. As mentioned earlier, his translation of the Bible and the Book of Common Prayer is considered one of the best. But as a translator and writer he introduced many new words into Arabic. Many of his contemporaries, especially those who traveled to Europe and wrote about western civilization, attempted to find or develop or invent Arabic words for European products or ideas. As is usual in these early attempts, success is rare. The Egyptian al-Tahtāwī is a case in point. Many of the terms he adopted to describe French products and ideas have not survived the times. In the case of al-Shidyāq we can confidently say that he was the most successful among early Arab renaissance intellectuals. We owe him many words that have survived for over a century and a half. He was the first to use *jarīdah* for "newspaper" (and not Ibrāhīm al-Yāzijī, as some maintain). We also owe him the word *ishtirākiyyah* for "socialism", as well as words like *tābi'* "stamp", *intikhāb* "election", *majlis al-nuwwāb* "parliament", *al-madrasah al-jāmi'ah* "university", *mathaf* "museum", *jawāz* "passport", *mustashfā* "hospital", *mulākamah* "boxing", *i'lān* "advertisement", and *saydalī* "pharmacist". He also developed the word *hāfilah* for "bus" which was not used a lot but is now more popular in standard Arabic.

In 1886 al-Shidyāq visited Egypt where he met the politicians, intellectuals, and dignitaries of Egypt including the Khedive Tawfīq. As Jurjī Zaydān reported at the time, the old man was still sharp and intelligent but also very playful despite his age. Following his return to Istanbul he died a few months later on September 20th, 1887; his body was sent to Lebanon to be buried there on October 5th of the same year. There is a well-known story concerning the fight between Muslims and Christians in Lebanon as to where and how al-Shidyāq was to be buried, a conflict that was resolved by the decision that both Muslim and Christian clerics would lead his funeral. He was buried, according to his will, in al-Hazmiyyeh suburb of Beirut with a crescent on his grave in a cemetery of the Christian Pashas of Lebanon.

REFERENCES

Mārūn 'Abbūd, *Saqr Lubnān* (Beirut: Dār Mārūn 'Abbūd, 1977);

——, *al-Shidyāq wa'l-Jāhiz wa'l-Mutanabbī* (Beirut: Dār Mārūn 'Abbūd, 1977);

A. J. Arberry, "Fresh Light on Ahmad Faris al-Shidyaq," *Islamic Culture* 26 (1952): 155-168;

'Azīz al-'Azmah and Fawwāz Tarābulusī, "Ahmad Fāris al-Shidyāq: Su'lūk al-Nahdah," *al-Nāqid* 79 (January 1995): 18-36;

M. M. Badawi (ed.), *Modern Arabic Literature*, The Cambridge History of Arabic Literature series (Cambridge: Cambridge University Press, 1992);

Trevor Le Gassick, *Major Themes in Modern Arabic Thought: An Anthology* (Rexdale: The University of Michigan Press, 1979), 11-15;

Muhammad 'Abd al-Ghanī Hasan, *Ahmad Fāris al-Shidyāq*, A'lām al-'Arab, no. 50 (Cairo: al-Dār al-Misriyyah li'l-Ta'līf wa'l-Tarjamah, n.d.);

John A. Haywood, *Modern Arabic Literature. 1800-1970: An Introduction with Extracts in Translation* (London: Percy Lund, Humphries & Co. Ltd., 1971), 53-59;

Albert Hourani, *Arabic Thought in the Liberal Age, 1798–1939* (Cambridge: Cambridge University Press, 1983), 77-79;

Shafīq Jabrī, *Ahmad Fāris al-Shidyāq* (Beirut: Mu'assasat al-Risālah, 1987);

Sulaymān Jubrān, *al-Mabnā wa'l-uslūb wa'l-sukhriyyah fī kitāb al-Sāq 'alā 'l-Sāq li-Ahmad Fāris al-Shidyāq* (Cairo: Qadāyā Fikriyyah li'l-Nashr wa'l-Tawzī', 1993);

A. G. Karam, "Fāris al-Shidyāq", in *Encyclopaedia of Islam*, 2nd ed. (Leiden: E. J. Brill, 1954-2004);

'Isām Mahfūz, *Hiwār ma'a ruwwād al-nahdah al-'arabiyyah*, (London: Riyād al-Rayyis, 1988), 13-27;

Muhammad al-Hādī Matwī, *Ahmad Fāris al-Shidyāq, 1801–1887: hayātuhu wa-atharuhu wa-ārā'uhu fī 'l-nahdah al-'arabiyyah al-hadīthah*, 2 vols., Série Universitaire, Faculté des lettres Sciences humaines de Kairaouan, Tunisie (Beirut: Dār al-Gharb al-Islāmī, 1989);

Muhammad Yūsuf Najm, *al-Qissah fī 'l-adab*

al-'arabī al-hadīth, 1870-1914 (Beirut: Dār al-Thaqāfah, 1966), 245-250;

Mattityahu Peled, "al-Sāq 'alā al-sāq: A Generic Definition," in: Aspects of Modern Arabic Literature, ed. M. Peled (Paris: Peeters Louvain, 1988), 69-84;

Henri Pérès, "Les premières manifestations de la renaissance littéraire arabe en Orient au XIX siècle. Nasif al-Yazigi et Faris ash-Shidyaq", Annales de l'Institut des études orientales, Alger, 1 (1934-5): 240ff.;

Muhammad 'Alī Shawābikah, al-Shidyāq wa'l-naqd: muqaddimat dīwān Ahmad Fāris al-Shidyāq (Amman: Dār al-Bashīr, 1991);

'Imād al-Sulh, Ahmad Fāris al-Shidyāq: atharuhu wa-'asruhu (Beirut: Sharikat al-Matbū'āt li'l-Tawzī' wa'l-Nashr, 1987);

Rotraud Wielandt, Das Bild der Europäer in der modernen arabischen Erzähl- und Theaterliteratur (Beirut: Franz Steiner Verlag, 1980), 77-98;

Jurjī Zaydān, Bunāt al-nahdah al-'arabiyyah (Cairo: Dār al-Kātib al-'Arabī, 1982), 189-200.

'Abd al-Rahmān Shukrī

(1886 – 1958)

TERRI DeYOUNG

University of Washington, Seattle

WORKS

Adwā' al-fajr ("Lights of Dawn", Alexandria: Matba'at Madrasat Wālidat 'Abbās al-Awwal, 1909);

La'ālī 'l-afkār ("Pearls of Thought", Alexandria: Matba'at Jurjī Ghazūrī, 1913);

Anāshīd al-sibā ("Hymns of Youth", Alexandria: Matba'at Jurjī Ghazūrī, 1916);

Zahr al-rabī' ("Flowers of Spring", Alexandria: Matba'at Jurjī Ghazūrī, 1916);

al-Khatarāt ("Musings", Alexandria: Matba'at Jurjī Ghazūrī, 1916);

al-I'tirāf wa-huwa qissat al-hayāh ("Confession: [auto-] biography", Alexandria: Matba'at Jurjī Ghazūrī, 1916-1917);

al-Thamarāt ("Fruits", Alexandria: Matba'at Jurjī Ghazūrī, 1916-1917);

Hadīth Iblīs ("Conversation with the Devil", Alexandria: Matba'at Jurjī Ghazūrī, 1916-1917);

al-Afnān ("Branches", Alexandria: Matba'at Jurjī Ghazūrī, 1918);

al-Sahā'if ("Pages", Alexandria: Matba'at Jurjī Ghazūrī, 1918);

Azhār al-kharīf ("Flowers of Autumn", Alexandria: al-Matba'ah al-Misriyyah, 1919).

Collected Works

Dīwān 'Abd al-Rahmān Shukrī, ed. Niqūlā Yūsuf and Muhammad Rajab al-Bayyūmī (Alexandria: Munsha'at al-Ma'ārif, 1960); revised with an introduction by Fārūq Shūshah (Cairo: al-Majlis al-A'lā li'l-Thaqāfah, 2000);

al-Mu'allafāt al-nathriyyah al-kāmilah ("Complete Prose"), edited with an introduction by Ahmad Ibrāhīm al-Harāwī (Cairo: al-Hay'ah al-'Āmmah li-Shu'ūn al-Matābi' al-Amīriyyah, 1998).

Works in Translation

Mounah Khouri, *Poetry and the Making of Modern Egypt* (Leiden: E. J. Brill, 1971), 173-198, *passim*;

— and Hamid Algar, *An Anthology of Modern Arabic Poetry* (Berkeley: University of California Press, 1974), 132-33.

'Abd al-Rahmān Shukrī was an Egyptian poet who was active mainly during World War I and the years immediately following. He is considered the most gifted representative of the literary movement known as the *Dīwān* School—for the name given to the manifesto published by two of the group's members in 1921—who revolted against what they perceived as the traditionalism of the preceding generation. They introduced many concepts of European Romanticism, especially the work of English poets, into Arabic literature. Shukrī was the oldest member of the *Dīwān* group (whose other mainstays were ʿAbbās Maḥmūd al-ʿAqqād and Ibrāhīm al-**Māzinī**), and his deep understanding of both the Arabic literary tradition and Western literary movements had an important impact on the thought of his colleagues. He and al-Māzinī quarreled during the latter years of World War I, mainly over mutual accusations of plagiarism, causing Shukrī to abandon writing almost entirely from 1919 until the mid-1930s. Therefore, he is seen as having little role in the momentous developments occurring in Arabic poetry following the end of World War I.

Shukrī's introductions to his *dīwān*s were the first sustained critical statements by a practicing Arab poet in modern times. Further, the articles he published in numerous important literary journals, like *al-Risālah* (The Message) and *al-Muqtaṭaf* (Selections), in the 1930s, give an unprecedented insight into the intellectual developments and literary concerns of Arab authors in the early years of the twentieth century. For the totality of his work, then, more than for any outstanding individual effort in poetry or prose, he is remembered and consulted by historians and scholars of modern Arabic literature.

Shukrī was born late in 1886 in Port Said, the Egyptian commercial town that guards the Mediterranean entrance to the Suez Canal, where his father worked in the government administrative offices. Muhammad Shukrī had succeeded in obtaining a coveted civil service position in the late 1870s and was initially posted to Alexandria. There he became involved in the ʿUrābī Revolution, perhaps through his friend ʿAbd Allāh al-Nadīm (d. 1896), who was one of the leaders of the movement. In the wake of the failure of the Revolution, Shukrī's father was dismissed from his position and sentenced to prison. Four years later, he was released and reinstated. He was then posted to Port Saʿīd, where the poet was born.

Shukrī began his schooling at the age of eight in a traditional *kuttāb* school where the rudiments of reading and writing, along with memorization of the Qurʾān, were taught. After a year he left and transferred to the primary school attached to the Tawfīqī Mosque in Port Saʿīd. He records that during this period of his schooling, he was taught by traditional methods that seemed calculated to snuff out all interest the pupils might have had in the poems. But in his grandfather's library, he discovered *al-Wasīlah al-adabiyyah* (The Literary Method), a textbook of Arabic rhetoric and literature composed by Shaykh Ḥusayn al-Marṣafī (d. 1890). Al-Marṣafī had been a good friend and mentor for the Egyptian nationalist poet Maḥmūd Sāmī al-**Bārūdī** and had used many of the latter's verses as illustrations for the topics treated in his rhetoric textbook. Shukrī tells us that at this time his family did not read any of the many newspapers or literary journals in circulation among educated Egyptians, so al-Bārūdī's work constituted his first exposure to the work of a contemporary poet. Since the poet's involvement in public occasions and momentous national events—so characteristic of al-Bārūdī's work—was a practice decisively rejected by Shukrī and the rest of the *Dīwān* school, this would not seem an adequate explanation for his attraction. He tells us, instead, that he was impressed by how al-Bārūdī was able to allude to major medieval Arabic poems in his writings, and shape them to his own, more contemporary, concerns (following a technique known as *muʿāraḍah*, "contrafaction"). Allusion, adaptation and imitation—even when they crossed the line into plagiarism—became central preoccupations of Shukrī both as author and critic throughout his career, so it would seem especially important to recognize al-Bārūdī's influence on the formation of his taste in this regard.

In 1900, Shukrī graduated from the primary school in Port Saʿīd and transferred to the Raʾs al-Tīn school in Alexandria for his secondary education, since there were no secondary schools operating in Port Saʿīd at the time. In Alexandria, he continued to study Arabic, but he began to study English more seriously, including English literature. His teachers, Mr. Stephens and Mr. Steed, encouraged their pupils to read outside the classroom, helping them purchase the inexpensive editions of classic English texts becoming increasingly available in Egypt under British occupation. Shukrī read these avidly, and his interest in more contemporary authors, besides the plays of Shakespeare and passages from Milton's *Paradise Lost* set in the school curriculum, grew. Undoubtedly it was here, under the tutelage of his young English mentors, that his later interest in the themes of beauty, love, truth, the suffering of the artist, and moral perfection (or its lack) began.

In 1904, with his secondary school certificate in hand, Shukrī left Alexandria for Cairo and one of the most prestigious educational institutions then operating in Egypt, the Khedival School of Laws. When Shukrī entered, the program was best known for two things: its demanding French-based curriculum, and the political activism of its students. Shukrī became embroiled in the latter when the students, encouraged by the nationalist leader, Mustafā Kāmil and his supporters, called a strike and in February 1906 closed the school in protest over what they saw as the Director's unfair policies. Additionally, he may have found the curriculum alien and difficult for someone trained, as he was, in an English-speaking secondary school. At any rate, he was expelled from the school at the end of the 1906 academic year, and was fortunate enough to obtain a place the following year at the Advanced Teachers' College, which, according to Shukrī himself, was facing a shortage of students and welcomed all qualified enrollees.

The Teachers' College (Dār al-Muʿallimīn) was also a premier educational institution in Egypt at the turn of the century, known for its wide-ranging curriculum and its emphasis on preparation in English. The basic text for the literature courses was the most influential educational anthology produced in nineteenth-century England, Francis Palgrave's *Golden Treasury*. Palgrave was the Professor of Poetry at Oxford University from 1885 to 1895, and his anthology, first published in 1861, by the turn of the century governed the curriculum of all English schools, both at home and abroad in England's many colonies. The *Golden Treasury*, of course,

was dominated by short lyric works, and came to a close with a heavy dose of the English Romantic poets, but included no later writers. It was through this lens, then, that Shukrī was introduced to a systematic treatment of European literature, and it had a discernible impact on his perception of what was of greatest interest and importance in the English canon. From his classroom readings in the lyrics of Shelley, Byron, Coleridge and Wordsworth, he progressed to more systematic readings of their critical prose, and eventually developed a relatively sophisticated understanding of their theories of imagination and art. He would seek to incorporate these into his Arabic writings, in order to communicate them to his fellow countrymen who were not able to read them in the original and to familiarize them with these new ideas from Europe.

His first major pupil in this regard was his fellow student, Ibrāhīm al-**Māzinī**, who would go on to become an important author in his own right. Unlike Shukrī, al-Māzinī dabbled in poetry, but pursued prose fiction and literary criticism with greater vigor. Shukrī and al-Māzinī would eventually collaborate with another rising Egyptian intellectual from outside the circle of the Teachers' College, ʿAbbās Mahmūd al-ʿAqqād, to form the *Dīwān* Group after Shukrī's return from England in 1913. Although Shukrī and al-Māzinī would quarrel at the end of World War I, becoming bitter enemies for many years, in 1934 al-Māzinī sought to reconcile himself with his former friend and acknowledged that he would have been nothing without the latter's guidance, that Shukrī even at their first meeting was already a mature thinker while he was a mere neophyte. He was still reading late medieval Arabic authors like Ibn al-Fārid (d. 1235) and Bahā' al-Dīn Zuhayr (d. 1258) or popular European authors like Sir Arthur Conan Doyle and Maria Corelli, and Shukrī opened his eyes to "Shakespeare, Byron, Wordsworth, Shelley, Milton, Hazlitt, Carlyle, Rousseau and many others," as well as Arab authors of the great classical canon like "Abū Tammām [d. 845], al-Buhturī [d. 897], al-Sharīf al-Radī [d. 1015], al-Maʿarrī [d. 1058] and Ibn al-Muʿtazz [d. 908]."

Shukrī's years (1906-1909) in the Teachers'

College were characterized by an increasing amount of political activity, including the publication, in newspapers like Lutfī al-Sayyid's *al-Jarīdah*, of a not inconsiderable number of "poems of occasion." The first of these was an elegy for Mahmūd Sāmī al-Bārūdī, commissioned by Khalīl **Mutrān**. Then he composed "al-Thabāt" (Steadfastness) to protest the Dinshaway show trial held in June 1906. These were followed by an elegy for Qāsim Amīn, author of a manifesto calling for the liberation of Egyptian women, and another for the nationalist leader Mustafā Kāmil (1908), both of whom had been idolized by the youthful Shukrī. With the exception of the Bārūdī poem, these were collected and published in his first collection, *Adwā' al-fajr* (Lights of Dawn), which appeared in 1909, just before he left for England.

Shukrī had graduated at the top of his class from the Teachers' College, and he was selected for a government fellowship to go on an educational mission to pursue university studies at the University of Sheffield, located in a large industrial town in the English Midlands. During his time in Sheffield, Shukrī pursued a rigorous curriculum, including not only English language and literature, but also English and European history, Political Economy, Philosophy and Sociology. In his scarce leisure time, he frequented the local Botanical Garden and traveled around the English countryside close to the University, but he did not find his surroundings appealing and became deeply homesick. He wrote numerous poems about his restless sadness and depression—including a verse letter to al-Māzinī—but most of them were not published until the 1930s.

Having successfully obtained his baccalaureate degree, Shukrī gladly returned to Egypt in 1912. He was immediately put to work as a teacher of English, history and translation at the same secondary school in Alexandria, Ra's al-Tīn, where he had graduated less than ten years before. He re-established his relationship with al-Māzinī, now working for the newspaper *al-'Ukāz*, but mostly he wrote feverishly, and the next year he published a second *dīwān*, *La'ālī' al-afkār* (Pearls of Thought), with an introduction by al-Māzinī's new friend, 'Abbās Mahmūd al-'Aqqād.

In 1915, he would publish a third *dīwān*, this time with a relatively brief introduction of his own composition. In this prefatory discussion, he focuses on identifying the nature of poetic inspiration and defining the criteria for the composition of good poetry. He locates the central touchstone for literary excellence in what he calls the "poetry of emotion." By this, he tells us, he does not mean just "pain and flowing tears," but the use by the poet of his imagination, "to study the emotions, learn their secrets and analyze them." In this, he appears to be echoing William Wordsworth's famous definition of poetry in the preface to his *Lyrical Ballads*, "poetry is the overflow of powerful feelings, recollected in tranquility." In the rest of the introduction, however, Shukrī directs most of his attention to exploring more deeply the connection between poetry and emotion, returning to his declaration in the first sentence of the introduction, "the spirit of the poet is like a musical instrument," and making an extended comparison between poetic composition and musical performance. In this, Shukrī is certainly extending, but not radically altering, the definition of poetry as it was conceived by the preceding generation. Al-Bārūdī, after all, the pioneer of the neo-Classical movement in Arabic, had characterized poetry as a "lightning spark of the imagination" in the introduction to his *dīwān*, using a similar metaphor framed in the discourse of Nature to emphasize the transformative power of the poet's mind and its effect on his material. Although Khalīl **Mutrān**, Shukrī's other potential model, does not give us so succinct a definition of poetry as al-Bārūdī does, his poems attest that his vision of the poet's role in the writing process was similar. Rather than attempt to split hairs by highlighting the differences in detail of these remarkably similar approaches to defining poetry, what should be kept in mind is how much all of them differ from the traditional definition of the art given by Arabic grammarians and rhetoricians through the centuries: Poetry is "words with meter and rhyme" *(kalām mawzūn muqaffā)*.

Interestingly, at the very end of this introduction, Shukrī locates the most authentic spirit of poetic genius in pre-Islamic poetry, rather than in later periods of Arabic literature, because "their souls were great and their emotions strong, not having been damaged by [the] weakness and luxury" to which later generations fell prey. This is one of the few places in Shukrī's criticism where he distances himself from his early idol, al-Bārūdī, who explicitly venerated the later Abbasid writers and paid substantially less attention to the earlier poets. Here he does appear to be more directly affiliating himself with Muṭrān, who is known to have similarly expressed a preference for pre-Islamic poetry.

In contrast to the reticence of his critical introductions to these two collections—representing the fruit of his experience at Sheffield University—the poems they contain are some of his most innovative and well-crafted compositions. "al-Shāʿir wa-sūrat al-kamāl" (The Poet and the Picture of Perfection), "ʿUsfūr al-jannah" (The Bird of Paradise), and "Nubūʾat shāʿir" (A Poet's Prophecy) provide particularly apt examples of the more sophisticated Romantic spirit (emphasizing the qualities of emotion and imagination) now suffusing his work.

Taken as a whole, 1916 was a particularly productive year for Shukrī. He published, along with two new *dīwān*s of poetry, two collections of articles culled from his journalistic activities, and a thinly disguised autobiography, *al-Iʿtirāf* (Confession) clearly modeled on the famous work by Jean Jacques Rousseau. Although the new *dīwān*s represent important extensions of the ideas expressed in his previous *dīwān*, *al-Iʿtirāf* has been recognized as a seminal work in the autobiographical genre of modern Arabic literature and an important counterpoint to the even more famous *al-Ayyām* (The Days) published by Ṭāhā **Ḥusayn** in the late 1920s. Much more than the somewhat distanced and ironic *al-Ayyām*, *al-Iʿtirāf* concentrates on depicting the interior, psychological development of its nameless protagonist and dares to present many uncomfortable revelations (including his thoughts of suicide) in the name of a full exploration of its subject's mind and personality.

Beside the highly intimate revelations of *al-Iʿtirāf*, the other two prose works, *al-Thamarāt* (Fruits) and *Ḥadīth Iblīs* (Conversations with the Devil), mine a much lighter vein in the genre of the informal, or personal, essay. *Al-Thamarāt* is a miscellany discussing such topics as memory vs. expectation, weeping vs. laughter, the power of the imagination to create reality, overcoming despair, nature as seen through the poet's eyes, the formation of sound taste in literature, and the pursuit of the ideal. It ends with a celebration of the sea, and its ability to inspire the poet. *Ḥadīth Iblīs* comprises an imaginary dialogue, ironic in tone, between the author and Iblīs (the fallen angel, tempter of mankind in the Qurʾān) on the follies of humanity and the nature of good and evil.

The introductions to Shukrī's *dīwān*s from this period project an increasing analytic seriousness, culminating in the lengthy preface on literary technique in the fifth volume, *al-Khaṭarāt* (Musings). He begins in the fourth volume, *Zahr al-rabīʿ* (Flowers of Spring) by reiterating his condemnation of poets who specialize in "occasional verse." He complains that their output is limited to celebrations of ribbon-cutting ceremonies for government offices, the opening of schools and hospitals, or the commemoration of a battle or a king's visit. Though this may have been appropriate in the past, now poets must take on a more socially active role, as "prophets" whose task is to "polish souls and move them, increasing their light and fire." He then moves on to define poetry again as emotion *(wijdān)* and states that the most fitting theme for poetry is love, because the love of a beautiful woman is only the reflection of a general love for life. Love for life subsumes all categories of emotion. Similarly, desire for another person can serve to instill a more general desire for excellence on the lover's part, and a thirst to achieve great things in order to attract the beloved's attention. This can be an important factor, then, in creating a healthy striving among the citizens of a single nation and between nations that will end up promoting the common good.

Shukrī is careful to disassociate his concept of love from lust or eroticism. He conceives of the desire he celebrates as desire for the beautiful, which he equates with the good, and in this he endorses a re-introduction of the sort of spiritualized love imagery associated in Arabic literature with Islamic mysticism, or Sufism, which the neo-Classical poets had rigorously excluded from their poetry.

In the introduction to *al-Khaṭarāt*, Shukrī, instead of again pleading a case for poetry's importance, simply asserts that it "is not something that rounds out life, but is the basis for it." But he also reveals an innate elitism by declaring that poetry is not something that simply comes naturally to the individual but is a talent that must be constantly refined. The poet must not write to please the common people or simply respond to the emotion of the moment, for he writes "for human reason and the soul of humanity, wherever they may be." To this end, he must range broadly and constantly seek out new inspiration in unfamiliar sources, especially through the "study of the literature of other nations who have peopled the world, built civilizations, and produced great works of art and science." But the danger of this approach is that people who themselves have dedicated their lives to imitating *(ihtidhā')* their forefathers will accuse those adventurers who have left the well-trodden paths of imitating and plagiarizing their new models. Shukrī then goes on to describe the effect of these accusations with such detail and in such emotional terms, that it is easy to assume that he himself had been the target of these accusations, especially since he was known for his interest in English and European literature. Uncertainty and anxiety had clearly been imported with the introduction of new material of foreign origin into a system where a poet's engagement with his predecessors had been governed and contained by practices such as *mu'āradah* (see above, p. 329) that gave the writer accepted avenues whereby he might work out his preoccupations without being labeled a plagiarist. But, if *mu-'āradah* is signaled by using the same meter and rhyme as the precursor poem, how can a similar mechanism be worked out for poems written in foreign languages? This is an issue that would engage Arabic poets increasingly in the decades to come.

Shukrī, however, does not choose to pursue the issue in this fashion in the remainder of his introduction. Instead, he takes quite a different tack. He brings up several examples from al-Māzinī's poetry that have, in his opinion, clearly

been plagiarized from the works of European writers like Shakespeare, Shelley and Heine. Then he excuses al-Māzinī by saying he is sure that this was not done intentionally, but he also insists that his friend will be "criticized for what he has done in the past until he remedies his error and attributes everything to its source." On this note of challenge, virtually demanding that al-Māzinī acknowledge his borrowings publicly, Shukrī ends his essay.

Many years later, al-Māzinī would write an article in which he would give an account of the events that led up to his quarrel with Shukrī. There, he says that Shukrī had, on a visit al-Māzinī made to Alexandria, brought up the examples of plagiarism that were included in the preface. But, when al-Māzinī offered to publish something explaining how he might have inadvertently used imagery and themes from the European writers because of the vast amount he was reading and his faulty memory, Shukrī had prevaricated and discouraged him from doing so, because "people would not appreciate such frankness." That being the case, al-Māzinī was shocked to find the very same verses mentioned in the introduction to *al-Khaṭarāt*. He now adamantly refused to publish an acknowledgement of plagiarism.

Despite the efforts of mediation by the two poets' friends, neither would compromise and the quarrel became the talk of literary circles all over Egypt and abroad. It began to interfere with Shukrī's ability to write, and the output of his poetry and criticism dwindled rapidly, to the point where he would declare many years later that, by 1917, he had ceased to write. This was not entirely true, as works continued to come out containing previously composed material, but new items did not appear. The final nail was hammered into the coffin of Shukrī's literary career in 1921, when al-Māzinī and al-'Aqqād came out with their groundbreaking literary manifesto entitled *al-Dīwān*. There, al-Māzinī contributed a chapter accusing Shukrī of arbitrariness and ambiguity in his poetry, which he attributes to "the vagueness of the idea in his head", suggesting, none too subtly, that his confusion came from mental imbalance and even incipient madness, citing passages from *al-*

I'tirāf as evidence for his contentions.

Shukrī was deeply wounded by this *ad hominem* attack on the part of his former friend, and completely abandoned literature. He turned, instead, to his career in the Egyptian public schools and slowly climbed the ladder of responsibility, serving as principal in a number of schools in the Egyptian Delta region and eventually being appointed as an Inspector in the Literature division of the Ministry in Cairo in 1935.

In that same year, he again began to publish poems, but promptly fell afoul of his superiors with one, "al-Nushū' wa'l-irtiqā'" (Development and Rise), which endorsed the theory of evolution, and shortly thereafter another criticizing the patriotism of Egyptian people. His promotion was also rescinded temporarily because the government lost power. So, in 1938, he was asked to retire from government service and take his pension. Having done so, he moved to Port Saʿīd and began to eke out his income by writing literary criticism and essays regularly for *al-Risālah* and *al-Muqtataf*, as well as a few new poems. He continued this way for many years, eventually going to live with family in Alexandria after he suffered a paralytic attack in 1952. He died on December 15, 1958, having outlived al-Māzinī by nearly ten years, but never having entirely succeeded in resuscitating his poetic reputation from the blows it had suffered that fateful day in 1921.

REFERENCES

ʿAbd al-Badīʿ ʿAbd Allāh, *Ibrāhīm ʿAbd al-Qādir al-Māzinī* (Cairo: al-Hayʾah al-Misriyyah al-ʿĀmmah li'l-Kitāb, 1994);

Muhammad Mustafa Badawi, *A Critical Introduction to Modern Arabic Poetry* (Cambridge: Cambridge University Press, 1975), 92-105;

Jan Brugman, *An Introduction to the History of Modern Arabic Literature in Egypt* (Leiden: E. J. Brill, 1984), 112-121;

Ahmad ʿAbd al-Hamīd Ghurāb, *ʾAbd al-Rahmān Shukrī* (Cairo: al-Hayʾah al-Misriyyah al-ʿĀmmah li'l-Kitāb, 1977);

Salma Khadra Jayyusi, *Trends and Movements in Modern Arabic Poetry*, 2 vols. (Leiden: E. J. Brill, 1977), I, 156-162;

Mounah Khouri, *Poetry and the Making of Modern Egypt* (Leiden: E. J. Brill, 1971), 173-178;

Hamdī al-Sakkūt and Marsden Jones, *ʾAbd al-Rahmān Shukrī* (Cairo: Dār al-Kitāb al-Misrī, 1980).

ʿAlī Maḥmūd Ṭāhā
(1901? – 1949)

TERRI DeYOUNG
University of Washington, Seattle

WORKS

al-Mallāh al-tāʾih ("The Wayward Sailor", Cairo: Matbaʿat al-Iʿtimād, 1934);

Layālī al-mallāh al-tāʾih ("Nights of the Wayward Sailor", Cairo: Sharikat Fann al-Tibāʿah, 1940);

Arwāh shāridah ("Spirits Astray", Cairo: Sharikat Fann al-Tibāʿah, 1941);

Arwāh wa-ashbāh ("Spirits and Ghosts", Cairo: Sharikat Fann al-Tibāʿah, 1942);

Ughniyyat al-riyāh al-arbaʿ ("Song of the Four Winds", Cairo: Sharikat Fann al-Tibāʿah, 1943);

Zahr wa-khamr ("Flowers and Wine", Cairo: Sharikat Fann al-Tibāʿah, 1944);

al-Shawq al-ʿāʾid ("Desire Returning", Cairo: Sharikat Fann al-Tibāʿah, 1945);

Sharq wa-gharb ("East and West", Cairo: Sharikat Fann al-Tibāʿah, 1947).

Collected Works

Dīwān, edited and introduced by Suhayl Ayyūb
  (Damascus: Dār al-Yaqzah al-'Arabiyyah
  li'l-Ta'līf wa'l-Tarjamah wa'l-Nashr, 1962;
  revised ed., Beirut: Dār al-'Awdah, 1982);

Sharh dīwān 'Alī Mahmūd Tāhā, edited with an
  introduction by Nabīl Tarīfī (Beirut: Dār al-
  Fikr al-'Arabī, 2001).

Translated Works

Modern Arabic Poetry: An Anthology (New
  York: Columbia University Press, 1987),
  104-105;

Mounah Khouri and Hamid Algar, *An Anthology
  of Modern Arabic Poetry* (Berkeley: University of California Press, 1974), 134-35.

'Alī Mahmūd Tāhā's career is an object lesson
in the uncertainties of literary fame. In the 1930s
and 1940s his popularity in Egypt, his homeland,
and across the Arab world was unrivalled. Today, few know his name, except possibly as the
author of the lyrics to "Ughniyat Jundūl" (A
Gondola Song) and "Layālī Kilyūbatrah" (Cleopatra's Nights), classic popular songs recorded in
the 1940s by Egypt's best-known modern male
singer, Muhammad 'Abd al-Wahhāb.

Tāhā's fall from notoriety was precipitous
beginning with the 1970s, but the signs were
visible even as early as the later 1960s. His complete *dīwān* appeared in 1962, and three major
studies of his poems appeared in 1964 and 1965,
but by 1969, when the Egyptian poet Salāh 'Abd
al-Sabūr went looking for Tāhā's works in Cairo
bookshops, he found they were no longer available, even though they had been reprinted five or
six times during the poet's lifetime. Yet, his
poetry was, almost without exception, enormously influential on the Free Verse poets who
revolutionized both the form and content of
Arabic verse following World War II. As Nāzik
al-Malā'ikah, one of the leaders of this revolutionary group, noted in her landmark study of
Tāhā, he was lionized by her generation because
"he innovated in the content of the Arabic poem
and moved it to the center of modern life."
Besides al-Malā'ikah, poets who have acknowledged their debt to Tāhā include Badr Shākir al-
Sayyāb and Muhammad Mahdī al-**Jawāhirī** in

Iraq, Nizār Qabbānī in Syria and Salāh 'Abd al-
Sabūr in Egypt. For this influence, if nothing
else, Tāhā's work merits preservation and examination.

'Alī Mahmūd Tāhā was born in either 1901
or 1902 (more likely the former) in the north-
eastern Nile Delta town of al-Mansūrah. His
family, originally from the Arabian peninsula
and claiming descent from al-Husayn, grandson
of the Prophet Muhammad, had long been established as textile merchants in the town. Their
relative wealth meant that they became frequent
hosts for the religious gatherings of the local
Sūfīs, and they actively cultivated local intellectual and political connections. 'Alī's relatives
sheltered leaders of the 'Urābī Revolution, like
'Abd Allāh al-Nadīm, and they would be steadfast supporters of Mustafā Kāmil's National
Party and then the Wafd Party during the poet's
youth. Sa'd Zaghlūl, leader of the Wafd Party,
was a family friend.

Historically al-Mansūrah had been famous as
the spot where King Louis IX of France was
captured and incarcerated during his ill-fated
Crusade of 1248. By the early twentieth century
it had become a town known for its beautiful
lakes and beautiful women, both motifs that
dominated 'Alī Mahmūd Tāhā's poetry in later
years, though the references were mostly set in
exotic foreign locales. But certainly they may
also be seen as allusions to the poet's idyllic
youth spent in his home town, where nothing
seems to have interfered with his march through
the progression of schools and personal milestones typical for a well-to-do young man of the
period. The only thing at all unusual was his
decision to attend a technical school, rather than
the more customary secondary institution that
would have led to university-level training in
Cairo.

In 1924, Tāhā graduated from al-Mansūrah's
School of Arts and Crafts, with a diploma in
architecture. He was employed shortly thereafter
by the al-Mansūrah municipal authorities in the
Building Department. Even before his graduation, he had begun to forge lasting literary collaboration that would be instrumental in helping
him develop his poetry and further his career.

While still a teenager, Tāhā had been introduced to Ahmad Hasan al-Zayyāt, also from al-Mansūrah, who would soon become, as the publisher of one of the most influential literary journals of the 1930s and 1940s, al-Risālah (The Message), a supporter whose patronage would be of incalculable value. It was al-Zayyāt who helped him place his first poem, a short piece entitled "Ālām al-shāʿir" (The Sufferings of the Poet), in the avant-garde journal al-Sufūr (Unveiling) in 1918. He even wrote a short preface introducing it. Later, of course, Tāhā's work would frequently grace the pages of al-Risālah, once the journal began appearing in 1934.

Even more important to Tāhā than the mentoring of Ahmad Hasan al-Zayyāt, however, was his friendship with three other young poets of al-Mansūrah who all went on to distinguished literary careers in Cairo. Sometime during 1927 Tāhā became the inseparable companion of a young physician and aspiring poet, three years his senior, by the name of Ibrāhīm Nājī, who had moved to al-Mansūrah from Cairo for health reasons. The two of them then made the acquaintance of a pair of students at the secondary school, Muhammad ʿAbd al-Mutiʿ al-Hamsharī and Sālih Jawdat, with similar interests. Together—since they had all learned English in school—the four began to read and discuss the poetry of the English Romantic poets Byron, Shelley, Keats and Wordsworth, to which they appended the verse of Rupert Brooke. In short order, they also turned to the French Romantic poets (although Tāhā would still be struggling with learning the language in the mid-1930s). During this period, both Nājī and Tāhā composed translations of Alphonse de Lamartine's "Le Lac" (The Lake) that would have an immense impact among their contemporaries and on the formation of poetic taste in the succeeding generation. During this time, Tāhā also made a return to the Cairo publishing scene, when ʿAlā 'l-sakhrah al-baydāʾ" (On the White Stone) and "Qithāratī" (My Lute)—typical elegiac Romantic poems of the period—were published in the newspaper, al-Siyāsah al-Usbūʿiyyah, in 1927 and 1929 respectively.

In 1931, the entire group of friends moved to Cairo. Nājī had been transferred to the Egyptian Public Railway Hospital, Tāhā had found a job at the Ministry of Works, and al-Hamsharī and Jawdat entered the university. Here, in the heart of Egyptian literary life and the cultural scene, as well as under the renewed attention of al-Zayyāt, Tāhā's poetry blossomed. The feverish pace of maturation in his work was helped by the involvement of all four friends with the Society of Apollo (Abullū), and its journal of the same name, founded in 1932 by Ahmad Zākī **Abū Shādī**. The poets of Apollo celebrated European Romantic ideals in their compositions and, like their European counterparts, drew inspiration from classical Hellenism, which additionally represented for the Arab poets a reminder of the common heritage from antiquity they shared with the West.

Although Tāhā briefly served on the Executive Committee of Apollo, he in fact published little in the journal. Nājī and al-Hamsharī contributed far more. Nevertheless, the program of the Society left an impression, as can be seen in Tāhā's choice much later (in 1942) to place his innovative dialogue poem Arwāh wa-ashbāh (Spirits and Ghosts) in a Greek setting, using Greek names for the characters.

More immediately, love, as both inspiration and torment to the lover, became a central theme of Tāhā's work after his move to Cairo. Poems composed during this period, like "al-Mallāh al-tāʾih" (The Wayward Sailor) and "Ghurfat al-shāʿir" (The Poet's Room) betray the fashionable fascination with the poet's suffering in love as an avenue to creative expression. They are also tinged with imagery borrowed from the Sūfī mystical tradition in Arabic poetry, that lends them an aura of allegorical idealism suggesting the poet is speaking about issues of greater depth than the incidental personal pangs of erotic desire. But the implications are largely left undeveloped, potential rather than fully explored.

1934 was a watershed year in Tāhā's career, both professionally and literarily. He gathered his poetry to date into a dīwān that was reviewed by one of the leading critics and cultural arbiters of the time, Tāhā **Husayn**. Husayn's review was essentially favorable, though not devoid of a certain disparagement of ʿAlī's depth of cultural background and his lack of grammatical finesse.

Nevertheless, the attention from one of the leading voices in contemporary literary studies propelled the *dīwān*—its title drawn from the poem "al-Mallāḥ al-tāʾih"—into the national spotlight and made Tāhā's reputation as a young poet to be reckoned with.

Similarly, Tāhā received an important promotion at the Ministry of Trade (where he had moved as Director of Special Exhibitions in 1932). He was appointed private secretary to the Minister. This would shortly be followed by a new position at the Secretariat of the Wafd Party in Parliament, where he would reap even greater financial rewards that would ensure him a comfortable living, as well as the opportunity to associate with politicians and men of influence.

As early as 1932, with the death of the important neo-Classical poets Ahmad **Shawqī** and Hāfiz **Ibrāhīm**—who had both been supporters of *Apollo*—Tāhā had been called upon to compose occasional poems to accompany the official ceremonies of remembrance for these towering spokesmen for the Egyptian nation. In 1933, this trend was further reinforced with his elegies mourning the death of King Faysal of Iraq and the moderate Egyptian politician, ʿAdlī Yakan Pāshā.

Now, with his employment in the halls of political power, Tāhā would be called upon ever more frequently to produce topical verse articulating the public consciousness and, most especially, the Wafd viewpoint on issues of the day. For example, in this period he composed verses-to-order on the dedication of Saʿd Zaghlūl's tomb ("al-Nahr al-zāmiʾ", The Thirsty River), the death of a Wafd General Secretary ("ʿĀlam al-dhikrā", World of Remembrance), and the publication of Muhammad Husayn Haykal's modern biography of the Prophet Muhammad ("Sadā al-wahy", Echo of Inspiration). Also, after World War II, he broadened his reach to compose a number of poems on world events, condemning the Axis powers, mourning the destruction in Europe, and supporting the aspirations of the Palestinian people and their leaders who opposed the partition of the British Mandate in 1948. For the most part, however, Tāhā completely compartmentalized these poems from his lyrical works (which he also continued

to produce intermittently), developing for the occasional poems a distinctive declamatory style remarkably reminiscent of Shawqī in his prime.

If Tāhā was distracted to a degree from developing his lyric poems in the mid-1930s, the latter part of the decade would give him a new opportunity to pursue the development of his literary talents. At the end of 1937, plagued by a series of setbacks and scandals, the Wafd government fell. Parliament was dissolved in February, and a new government, with a non-Wafd majority, was installed in May 1938. Tāhā seems to have found himself temporarily without employment, and he resolved to spend the summer in Europe, the first time he has traveled outside of Egypt.

He spent most of his time in Italy but traveled widely, and the journey was a revelation. In particular, his poems celebrating the fantasy worlds of the carnival in Venice and the tourist attractions at Lake Como—"Ughniyat jundūl" and "Buhayrat Kūmū"—expressed a fascination with the aesthetics of sensual enjoyment that had long been absent in modern Arabic poetry, where the reigning Romantic consensus had enforced an idealization of the emotions of desire and longing. The veiled eroticism of these poems—though probably too hesitant and timid for modern taste—impressed the younger generation because they do not ignore the temptations and negative consequences of surrendering oneself to the senses and do not shy away from exploring the outcome of the lovers' obsessions, both positive and negative. Later, voices would be raised claiming that Tāhā's poems from this trip, and a similar one in 1939 to Germany and Switzerland as well as Italy, did not go far enough in pressing the boundaries of conventionalism, while others would point out that they ignored the darkening clouds of war and conflict lurking beneath the glittering surface of the pre-war capitals. But in the early 1940s, they seemed a breath of fresh air. As Salāh ʿAbd al-Sabūr has also pointed out in his introduction to Tāhā's *Selected Poems* (published in 1969), Tāhā's wartime lyrics are consistent with a pattern of writings from this era that represent incidents of Arab men romancing and bonding with European women as a sort of allegory for peaceful conquest of the West by the Arab world, or at least for the formation of a closer rapprochement between them. This vision was also enormously attractive to a younger generation much more sophisticated in the ways of the West than their fathers, and still optimistically confident of the similarities between the cultures.

Tāhā had always been something of an innovator in poetic form, known for his willingness to experiment with unusual meters, verse forms, and generic amalgamations. The European lyrics, for example, were mostly composed in *ramal* meter, a somewhat unusual rhythm that, in the regularity of its beat, anticipates the first experiments of the Free Verse poets in the postwar years. But at the height of the war years, in 1942 and 1943, he published two long works that were even more clearly framed as attempts at formal innovation and were received favorably as such, again particularly inspiring younger readers. These were *Arwāh wa-ashbāh* (Spirits and Ghosts), generally characterized as "a dialogue poem" rather than a truly dramatic work, and *Ughniyat al-riyāh al-arba'* (Song of the Four Winds), a more conventional closet drama.

The more unusual poem is *Arwāh wa-ashbāh*, which tells the story of how three nymphs—Sappho, Thais, and Belitis—dispute with a poet over the sinful nature of women and the forms of Platonic love, as the Greek god Mercury prepares to bring him to earth to take human form. The elevated philosophical nature of this dialogue over love, and its daring metrical experiments, so inspired the young Iraqi poet Badr Shākir al-Sayyāb when he read it in 1944 that he promptly went out and composed his own imitation of it, entitled *Bayna al-rūh wa'l-jasad* (Between Body and Soul). He sent the manuscript to Tāhā, but it was lost among the older poet's papers when he passed away unexpectedly a few years later.

After the boldness of *Arwāh wa-ashbāh*, Tāhā seems to have retreated into greater formal conventionality with *Ughniyyat al-riyāh al-arba'*, though it is equally unusual in its own way. It is an adaptation of a French version of an ancient Egyptian dramatic work, composed in 2000 B.C.E. Though it attempts to do with ancient Egyptian literature what had already

been rather successfully carried out by Tāhā and his contemporaries with ancient Greek literary works, it did not resonate with the modern Arabic literary public in the same way and had little impact at the time, despite the interest Tāhā's works usually generated with his contemporary audiences, and is regarded today as mainly a curiosity.

After World War II, Tāhā went back to the pattern of his pre-War writing. He continued to write occasional verse, along with his trademark Romantic lyrics. A trip to Europe in 1946 yielded more poems in the same vein as those published in his 1940 collection *Layālī al-mallāh al-tā'ih*. Tāhā also continued to hold various short-term jobs in the Wafd Party establishment, until in 1949 he finally obtained a post much to his liking as Deputy Director at the National Library (Dār al-Kutub). But unfortunately he was not to enjoy the position for long. In November he died, after briefly being hospitalized at the Italian hospital in Cairo, from a "sudden illness".

REFERENCES

M. M. Badawi, *A Critical Introduction to Modern Arabic Poetry* (Cambridge: Cambridge University Press, 1975), 137-145;

Jan Brugman, *An Introduction to the History of Modern Arabic Literature in Egypt* (Leiden: E. J. Brill, 1984), 173-181;

Salma Khadra Jayyusi, *Trends and Movements in Modern Arabic Poetry*, 2 vols. (Leiden: E. J. Brill, 1977), II, 397-410;

Anwar al-Ma'addāwī, *'Alī Mahmūd Tāhā: al-shā'ir wa'l-insān* (Baghdad: Wizārat al-Thaqāfah wa'l-Irshād, Mudīriyyat al-Thaqāfah al-'Āmmah li'l-Kitāb, 1965; revised ed., Cairo: al-Hay'ah al-Misriyyah al-'Āmmah li'l-Kitāb, 1986);

Nāzik al-Malā'ikah, *Muhādarāt fī shi'r 'Alī Mahmūd Tāhā: dirāsah wa-naqd* (Cairo: Jāmi'at al-Duwal al-'Arabiyyah, Ma'had al-Dirāsāt al-'Arabiyyah al-'Āliyah, 1964);

al-Sayyid Taqī al-Dīn al-Sayyid, *'Alī Mahmūd Tāhā: hayātuh wa-shi'ruh* (Cairo: al-Majlis al-A'lā li-Ri'āyat al-Funūn wa'l-Ādāb wa'l-'Ulūm al-Ijtimā'iyyah, 1964).

Rifāʿah Badawī Rāfiʿ al-Tahtāwī
(1801 – 1873)

WALID HAMARNEH
Swarthmore College

WORKS

Prose

Takhlīs al-ibrīz fī talkhīs Bārīz aw Dīwān al-nafīs bi-īwān Bārīs ("The Purification of Gold Concerning the Summarization of Paris, or The Precious Diwan on the Portico of Paris", Cairo: Matbaʿat Būlāq, 1834; other editions include: Mustafā al-Bābī al-Halabī, 1958; al-Hayʾah al-Misriyyah al-ʿĀmmah li'l-Kitāb, 1993); the edition used here is Cairo: Wizārat al-Thaqāfah, 1958;

Jumal al-Ājurrūmiyyah ("The Sentences in the Ājurrūmiyyah [a canonical medieval didactic poem on Arabic grammar]", Cairo: n.p., 1863/4);

Anwār Tawfiq al-jalīl fī akhbār Misr wa-tawthīq Banī Ismāʿīl ("The Lights of the Noble Tawfiq, concerning Events in Egypt and the Documentation of the Sons of Ismāʿīl", Cairo: Matbaʿat Būlāq, 1285 [1868/9]);

al-Tuhfah al-maktabiyyah li-taqrīb al-lughah al-ʿarabiyyah ("The Library Gift to Make the Arabic Language Accessible", Cairo: Matbaʿat al-Madāris, 1868/9?);

Manāhij al-albāb al-misriyyah fī mabāhij al-ādāb al-ʿasriyyah ("The Paths of the Egyptian Hearts in the Joys of the Contemporary Arts", Cairo: Matbaʿat Sharikat al-Raghāʾib, 1912);

al-Qawl al-sadīd fī 'l-ijtihād wa'l-tajdīd ("The Clear Word Concerning Individual Judgment and Modernization", Cairo: Matbaʿat Wādī al-Nīl, 1287 [1870/1]);

Kitāb al-murshid al-amīn li'l-banāt wa'l-banīn ("Guiding Truths for Girls and Youths", Cairo: Matbaʿat al-Madāris al-Malakiyyah, 1289 [1872/3]); edition used here is the one by ʿImād Badr al-Dīn Abū Ghāzī (Cairo: al-Majlis al-Aʿlā li'l-Thaqāfah, 2002);

Nihāyat al-ījāz fī sīrat sākin al-Hijāz ("A Compendium Concerning the Resident of the Hijaz Region"), ed. ʿAbd al-Rahmān Hasan Mahmūd and Fārūq Hāmid Badr (Cairo: Maktabat al-Adab, 1982);

al-Dawlah al-islāmiyyah, nizāmuhā wa-ʿamalatuhā: wa-huwa al-mutammim li-kitāb Nihāyat al-ījāz fī sīrat sākin al-Hijāz ("The Islamic Empire, Its Organization and Conduct, It Being a Completion of the Earlier Work *Nihāyat al-ījāz* ..."), ed. ʿAbd al-Rahmān Hasan Mahmūd and Farūq Hāmid Badr (al-Qāhirah: Maktabat al-Adab, 1990).

Poetry

Manzūmah misriyyah wataniyyah (Cairo: Dār al-Tibāʿah, 1855/6);

Muqaddimah wataniyyah misriyyah (Cairo: n.p., 1867/8);

al-Kawākib al-nayyirah fī layālī afrāh al-ʿAzīz al-muqmirah ("Gleaming Stars on the Moonlit Nights of Celebration for al-ʿAzīz", Cairo: al-Matbaʿah al-Amīriyyah, 1872/3);

Takhmīs qasīdat al-Shihāb Mahmūd ("al-Shihāb Mahmūd's Ode as a Quintain", Cairo: n.p., 1891/2);

Tahniʾah ʿīdiyyah wataniyyah ("National Congratulations on the ʿĪd Festival", Cairo: n.p., n.d.);

Tahniʾah wataniyyah li'l-wizārah al-saniyyah ("National Congratulations on the Cabinet", Cairo: al-Matbaʿah al-Misriyyah, n.d.).

Collected Works

al-Aʿmāl al-kāmilah li-Rifāʿah Rāfiʿ al-Tahtāwī, ed. Muhammad ʿImārah (Beirut: al-Muʾassasah al-ʿArabiyyah li'l-Dirāsāt wa'l-Nashr, 1973);

Yūsuf Zaydān, *Fihris makhtūtāt Maktabat Rifāʿah Rāfiʿ al-Tahtāwī* (Cairo: al-Munazzamah al-ʿArabiyyah li'l-Tarbiyah wa'l-Thaqāfah wa'l-ʿUlūm, Maʿhad al-Makhtūtāt al-ʿArabiyyah, 1996); a catalogue of the manuscripts of al-Tahtāwī in three vols.;

Dīwān Rifā'ah al-Tahtāwī, ed. Tāhā Wādī (Cairo: al-Hay'ah al-Misriyyah al-'Āmmah li'l-Kitāb, 1979); collected poetry.

Translations by the Author

al-Ta'rībāt al-shāfiyyah li-murīd al-jughrāfiy-yah ("The Satisfying Arabization for the Student of Geography", Cairo: Matba'at Būlāq?, 1834/5);

al-Ma'ādin al-nafīsah li-tadbīr ma'ā'ish al-khalā'iq ("Precious Metals in the Economy of Human Life", Cairo: Matba'at Būlāq, 1832/3);

Qalā'id al-mafākhir fī gharīb 'awā'id al-awā'il wa'l-awākhir ("The Honourable Necklaces Concerning the Curious Customs of the Ancients and Moderns", Cairo: al-Matba'ah al-Amīriyyah, 1833/4);

Qudamā' al-falāsifah ("Ancient Philosophers", Cairo: n.p., 1836/7);

al-Jughrāfiyyah al-'umūmiyyah ("General Geography", 4 vols., Cairo: n.p., n.d.);

al-Mantiq ("Logic", Cairo: n.p., 1838/9);

Mabādi' al-handasah ("The Principles of Engineering", Cairo: al-Matba'ah al-Amīriyyah, 1842/3);

Ta'rīb al-qānūn al-faransāwī al-madanī ("French Civil Law in Arabic", 2 vols., Cairo: al-Matba'ah al-Amīriyyah, 1866/7);

Ta'rīb qānūn al-tijārah ("Commercial Law in Arabic", Cairo: al-Matba'ah al-Amīriyyah, 1868/9);

Mawāqi' al-aflāk fī waqā'i' Tilimāk (Cairo: n.p., 1867-8; Cairo: Matba'at Dār al-Kutub wa'l-Wathā'iq al-Qawmiyyah, n.d.); translation of *Les aventures de Télémaque* by Fénelon.

Works in Translation

An Imam in Paris: Account of a Stay in France by an Egyptian Cleric (1826-1831) (London: Saqi Books, 2004); translation of *Takhlīs al-ibrīz fī talkhīs Bārīz*, tr. by Daniel L. Newman;

L'or de Paris: relation de voyage 1826-1831, traduit de l'arabe, présenté et annoté par Anouar Louca (Paris: Sindbad, 1988); translation of *Takhlīs al-ibrīz fī talkhīs Bārīz*;

Ein Muslim entdeckt Europa: Bericht über seinen Aufenthalt in Paris 1826-1831 (Munich: C. H. Beck, 1989); translation of *Takhlīs al-ibrīz fī talkhīs Bārīz*, tr. by Karl Stowasser;

L'Emancipation de la femme musulmane: le guide honnête pour l'éducation des filles et des garçons, traduit de l'arabe, présenté et annoté par Yahya Cheikh (Beyrouth, Liban: al-Bouraq, 2000); translation of *Kitāb al-Murshid al-amīn li'l-banāt wa'l-banīn*.

Rifā'ah Badawī Rāfi' al-Tahtāwī (1801-1873), Egyptian author and educationist, was a leading intellectual figure of his generation, one of the first and most prominent initiators of the Egyptian *nahdah* (awakening) of the 19th century. Al-Tahtāwī was born into a family of prominent *'ulamā'* in the Upper Egyptian town of Tahtā on October 15, 1801. He spent his childhood there and went to a traditional school *(kuttāb)* in his home town. Following the death of his father in 1817, he went to Cairo and enrolled in al-Azhar. One of his teachers there was Hasan al-'Attār (d. 1834) who had the greatest and most lasting influence on him. Al-'Attār had come into contact with the French during their occupation of Egypt (1798-1804) and became interested in European thought and sciences. He became the Grand Shaykh of al-Azhar during Muhammad 'Alī Pasha's rule (1805-48). Al-Tahtāwī held a teaching position at al-Azhar between 1822 and 1824, and then became the imam of a regiment in the new Egyptian army of Muhammad 'Alī. Hasan al-'Attār intervened again in 1826 to have al-Tahtāwī appointed as one of the four imams accompanying the first mission of 44 army students sent to France by Muhammad 'Alī to complete their higher military and scientific education.

In Paris, Rifā'ah, on his own initiative, studied French in order to be able to read works in that language. During his stay he made friends with leading French orientalists, such as A. I. Silvestre de Sacy (d. 1838) and E.-F. Jomard (d. 1862). His readings included books of the new discoveries of Egyptology and of western values and culture in general. He read books on ancient history, logic, arithmetic, geography, philosophy, and mythology. He read some French

poetry including Racine, as well as lives of great
leaders like Napoleon. But the most important
and lasting readings were those of the French
Enlightenment of the eighteenth century especially Condillac, Voltaire, Montesquieu, and
Rousseau's *Social Contract*. But his other aim
was not only to read books in French but to
master the art of translation from French into
Arabic, and so it was that he passed his translation exams under the supervision of some of the
greatest French orientalists of the time with
distinction. On the recommendation of Jomard,
Muhammad 'Alī appointed him as the general
supervisor of Egyptian students in Paris. After
his return to Egypt and at Muhammad 'Alī's
request, he published his observations and impressions of Paris in a work which he had already written there with the title: *Takhlīs al-ibrīz
fī talkhīs Bārīz* in 1834 (henceforth *Takhlīs*), a
colorful title typical of earlier times and meaning
something akin to "The Purification of Gold
Concerning the Summarization of Paris." This
description became very well known and until
the 1850s it remained the sole work in which
Arabic-speaking readers were offered a description of a European country.

Of the many books that al-Tahtāwī wrote,
translated, or edited, *Takhlīs al-ibrīz fī talkhīs
Bārīz* is not only the most influential but also
arguably the most important literary and social
document of the first half of the nineteenth
century in Egypt. It was probably the first book
in Egypt that adopted an evolutionary and modern conception of society that did not completely
conform to the dominant Islamic interpretations
of civilization and history during that period of
time. The book, however, is characterized by the
tension between a rather open-minded, yet traditionalist mentality and a great admiration for,
and acknowledgement of, the scientific, technological, and socio-political advancement of
France. This tension is manifest at all levels,
linguistic, rhetorical, ideational, as well as political. And the attempts of al-Tahtāwī to resolve
this tension are never successful. This document
can, therefore, be considered both foundational
and emblematic of all later attempts by Muslim
reformers who wanted to achieve economic,
scientific, political, and cultural modernization

while insisting that modernization is neither contradictory to traditional Islam nor to the social
and moral norms and conventions of traditional
Muslim societies.

One of the first obstacles that al-Tahtāwī attempts to overcome is the then dominant conception amongst Muslims of the division of the
world into the Land of Islam *(dār al-islām)* and
the Land of War *(dār al-harb)* which is a spatial
division, but also the backward-looking attitude
that considers early Islam (the period of the
Prophet and the Rāshidī caliphs) as the point of
reference for any truly Islamic society. Al-Tahtāwī adopts what may be termed a universalist
conception of world history that allows him to
introduce time as a developmental concept in
tandem with the dominant theories of Western
Enlightenment. He introduces advancement in
what he calls "human arts and civic sciences"
(art understood here in the classical Greek sense
of all human activities of production and sciences as all sorts of knowledge) as a criterion for
dividing societies based upon progress in those
fields and the temporal distance from the primitive or natural state. Based upon such criteria he
develops a hierarchy of ranks: The first and
lowest rank: that of the savages; the second
rank: that of the crude barbarians; and the third
and highest rank: that of the civilized, cultured,
literate, and urban (6). He also insists that what
he is interested in and wants Egypt and the lands
of Islam to introduce is related to technologies,
arts, and "foreign sciences" (*al-'ulūm al-barrā-
niyyah*, a concept used in Muslim scholarship to
differentiate between the indigenous or Islamic
sciences and the foreign ones like philosophy
and other branches of knowledge not derived
from Islamic sources) and justifies this by references to the sayings of the Prophet (9) as well as
the advice of his own teacher and mentor,
shaykh Hasan al-'Attār.

Takhlīs has the structure of a travel book. The
trip to Paris and the return to Egypt are its formal framework. There is a preface *(khutbah)*
followed by an introduction *(muqaddimah)* which
is divided into four chapters *(bāb)* and provides
the context, causes, and justification of the trip.
This is followed by six parts (essays or *maqālāt*)
of different lengths which make up the bulk of

the book and which are divided in turn into subsections *(fasl)*. The first two essays of the main part are the shortest and describe the journey to Paris while the third essay is a description of Paris itself. The fourth essay is a report of the mission sent by Muhammad Alī to which al-Tahtāwī was attached. The last two essays are additions and further explications, and the last part of the book is a conclusion *(khātimah)* that describes the trip back to Egypt. So from a formal perspective the book's structure, subtitles, and divisions conform to traditional Arabic methods of authoring. On the other hand, from the perspective of organization and description of topics and subject matter, it is much closer to the then popular genre of books called manners and customs. This genre developed in contrast to travel books that were also popular, but filled with imaginary stories and exaggerations. Manners and customs books were interested in the strange and exotic but attempted to be as descriptive and anthropological as possible. They followed rules and conventions that became known as voyage instructions, emphasizing aspects described such as the environment, geography, climate, land, habitat, homes, and food. Then there was the necessity to describe the human beings, their customs and habits, their economic activities, and their political systems. While in Paris, al-Tahtāwī translated one of these books by G. B. Depping into Arabic; it was a part of the documentation he presented in his translation examination mentioned earlier.

Al-Tahtāwī had to surmount some difficulties associated with his potential readers who were the traditional class of religious *'ulamā'* as well as the newly educated elite in the schools that Muhammad ʻAlī had founded in Egypt. He emphasized simplicity and conciseness of style (5) but confronted the huge problem of the lack of terms, concepts and equivalents for the products and ideas he was trying to explain, a situation that forced him to resort to analogical terms in traditional Muslim scholarship, to use an Arabicized form of the French word, or in other cases to invent a term as an equivalent. But he also wanted to make sure that his readers understood what he was discussing as well as to authenticate his credibility by emphasizing that

everything he mentioned, no matter how strange or incredible it might sound to his readers, was the truth that he had seen or witnessed. Whenever possible, he provides comparisons with Egypt in order to bring things closer to the minds of his readers. For example, he compares the Seine with the Nile (47) and the water distribution systems of Paris and Cairo (50).

Al-Tahtāwī tries to treat matters that are controversial for his times in a rather distanced manner, as, for example, when he discusses the shape and form of the globe and whether it is flat or round (without committing himself to any of the opposing views). And yet he begins his description of Paris by noting without any further elaboration or discussion that scientists have shown by proof that the earth is round (4). He also tries to explain some scientific principles whenever this is related to his topic, discussing the climate in Paris, for example, and the way that temperature is measured by degrees, which he explains as derived from a scale between the points of freezing of water to that of its boiling (43).

What al-Tahtāwī emphasizes in *Takhlīs* are three constellations of issues. The first is related to science and civilization, the second to political systems, and the third to translation as a vehicle of cross-cultural communication and learning. His discussion of the sciences and the manifestations of civilized life fill almost all his description of Paris. He gives us a list of the different branches of knowledge and sciences (10-11, 188), a list of the names of colleges, educational institutions, scientific, literary and cultural societies (138, 143), lists of libraries, museums, and public parks (134, 145), means of communication and transportation (125), and even nightclubs and places of entertainment (96-7).

Conforming to his model of positivistic description, he tries to fill his account with statistics, data, names, and concepts. But he explains his insights through examples. He is also keen on pointing out how knowledge and sciences have spread amongst the French when compared to the Egyptians (12, 132). But his insights go much deeper than merely comparing appearances, as, for example, when he discusses banks and financial institutions and points out how profit is an important incentive for people's work and activities (123). In conjunction with the spread of literacy and knowledge (52-3), al-Tahṭāwī stresses the important role played by journalism (144) and introduces the word "journal" into Arabic (with a regular feminine plural, as is the case with most loan words in Arabic). He also emphasizes the importance of literacy for all classes of people (52), the non-traditional and non-imitative character of the French, and their emphasis on invention and the creation of the new (52). He also points out that, in contra-distinction to Egypt, scientists (implying people of knowledge) are not the priests, whom he describes as "scientists in religion only" (133), but that scientists are in different fields and specializations and that knowledge is not restricted or judged by knowledge of religious and theological matters only (133).

Another aspect of culture that seemed important to al-Tahṭāwī was the theatre. He goes into details explaining what it is and the kind of entertainment and education it offers while differentiating the two different types of plays, comedies and tragedies (95-7). Although he is somewhat critical of the theatre, he still sees in it great educational and moral potential (97). He also points out that actors are educated and well-respected individuals. Dance and dancing is also an art form that he tries to elevate in the eyes of his readers. He invokes a comparison between dance and wrestling and stresses that dance is performed by men as well as women with an emphasis on artistic and physical finesse and abilities in contradistinction to dance in Egypt (belly dancing) which is performed by women only and used to arouse sexual urges (98). It is interesting to note that al-Tahṭāwī discusses women in French society in a positive manner. He highlights women's participation in life, economics, culture and literature. "Women," he notes, "have written great works; some are translators of books from one language to another" (68).

As there was no immediate danger or threat of Europe invading or occupying Egypt during the time he was writing *Takhlīs*, al-Tahṭāwī does not see Europe as an enemy or a political or colonial threat. Despite his enthusiasm for certain aspects of French society and political culture, he remains critical of the dominant mentality that he sees as regulating human affairs, one that is derived from reason and not from divine law. So despite his acknowledgement that the French constitution embodies the principle of justice, it is still based not on the ethical principles of religion (i.e. Christianity) but on the belief in human reason.

The French are of those who believe that it is human reason which ascribes goodness or badness to things. They deny that miracles can occur and believe it is not possible for the laws of nature to be broken. They believe too that religions have come only to encourage men to do good and avoid that which is opposed to it, that general welfare and human progress can take the place of religion, and that ... the intelligence of their learned men is greater than that of the prophets. (81)

Based on such an interpretation, it can be seen that al-Tahṭāwī shared the opinion that has been very popular in the Arab and Islamic world for over two centuries, namely that, despite the superiority of the West in matters of science, economics, military power, technology, and social organization, it fails in the religious, moral, and ethical domains where Islamic societies remain superior.

Despite many reservations related especially to the moral and social aspects of life in France, al-Tahṭāwī is extremely enthusiastic about the political order there. His enthusiasm is clear in his exposition of the political system and his translation of the French constitution. But within his exposition we can discern an implicit criticism of the political life and system in Egypt. Yet this implicit criticism is never fully formulated, mostly because al-Tahṭāwī, despite his enthusiasm for a constitutional monarchy, was still encumbered by his traditional attitude toward politics. This was to be left to the political elite *(ūlī al-amr)* and to the ruler *(walī al-niʿam)*. This is also in tandem with al-Tahṭāwī's belief that reform and change do not, and probably should not, come from the people, but are the jurisdiction of the ruler and in this case the

benevolent despot. So despite his great enthusiasm for the democratic system of government,
he ends his discussion of it with two lines of
poetry to the effect that any one who maintains
that there is a need for things that do not conform to Islamic jurisprudence *(sharʿ)* should not
be considered a friend as his advice will only
bring detrimental effects (85).

In his discussion of the French political system he is interested in the division of powers and
the rule of law. These two points make sense to
a person who is an Islamic legal scholar, someone well aware of the fact that the independence
of legal institutions which had clearly existed
throughout much of Islamic history but was no
longer the case during the Ottoman period nor
during the reign of Muhammad ʿAlī, is something desirable. This accounts for al-Tahtāwī's
detailed exposition of the parliamentary and
legislative system and that of constitutional
monarchy. He then translates the constitution of
Louis XVIII, adding that he is doing this despite
the fact that "most of what is to be found in it, is
neither in God's book nor in the sayings of his
prophet" (73). But al-Tahtāwī is interested in
providing connections between the constitutional system of government and the basic freedoms and the concept of liberty.

Upon his return to Egypt in 1831, Rifāʿah
had been employed as a translator at the School
of Medicine and later became the head of the
translation staff. He was appointed supervisor of
the Māristān school where students studied
mathematics, astronomy, natural history, logic
and ancient and modern history to prepare them
for the medical school. Then, in 1833, he was
appointed at the Artillery School mostly because
he preferred translating materials related to
engineering and the art of war. During the cholera epidemic in Cairo of the year 1834 he went
back to his hometown Tahtā. While there he
translated the first volume of the huge geography
textbook by Conrad Malte-Brun to which he
returned later in his life and translated other
parts. Upon returning to Cairo, he presented his
translation of Malte-Brun's book to Muhammad
ʿAlī who promoted him to the rank of major in
the army. In 1836 he was appointed to a teaching position at the School of Administration

founded by Muhammad ʿAlī to teach present
and future government officials. The real breakthrough, however, came in 1836 in connection
with the reorganization of the Administration of
Schools when he was chosen as one of the permanent members and the only Egyptian on the
Council. In 1837 he was appointed head of the
newly-created School of Translation (later renamed the School of Languages), where 50
young excellent students of ages between 14 and
18 were chosen by al-Tahtāwī to be taught languages and translation. The number was raised
to 60 in the year 1841. Al-Tahtāwī introduced a
system at the school that adapted the traditional
system of education of al-Azhar to that of
Europe. The languages taught at the school were
Arabic, French, Turkish, Persian, English, and
Italian but the emphasis was on Arabic and
French. The School of Translation was continu-
ously expanded to include a section for studies
in government administration in 1844. Two years
later a section of agricultural sciences was added
followed by a section for Hanafi law (one of the
four main Sunni schools of Islamic law and the
official school of the Ottomans). The translation
section was the dearest to al-Tahtāwī and was
divided into four subsections; one for mathematics, another for medical and natural sciences, a
third for social sciences, and a fourth for Turkish. In 1842 al-Tahtāwī was entrusted with the
editorship of the official newspaper *al-Waqāʾiʿ
al-Misriyyah* for a time. But without question,
his most important work was as a translator and
supervisor of translators. He was rewarded in
1846 with the honorific title Beğ.

Al-Tahtāwī saw translation as both a linguistic and cultural activity. Development and reform, learning and advancement can only be
achieved through awareness and knowledge of
the materially and scientifically more advanced
other (France). However, as a prerequisite there
needs to be a proper understanding, the foundations of which can only be found in cultural and
scientific translation. For al-Tahtāwī translation
was not merely an individual activity but rather
a social and educational project, one to which he
dedicated most of his energies and for which he
gathered and taught his best students. As al-
Tahtāwī saw it, translation was a foundational

segment of Egypt's development, but if it was to function in such a manner it had to mould the language to which books are translated (in this case, Arabic) in such a way as to capture the spirit of the original as well as make sense to its readers who might not be acquainted with the objects and ideas being discussed. So, in addition to the terminological issues of translation, al-Tahṭāwī was aware of the other cultural and ideational factors related to the different mindsets. Thus, in his own translations and those that he supervised and edited he tried to create an equilibrium between faithfulness to the original on the one hand and the prerogatives of communicability on the other. He was especially aware of the problems associated with the rendering of scientific terminology into Arabic and the necessity of preparing specialized bi-lingual dictionaries for such sciences. His contribution to such a project was to attach to the books and monographs he translated a glossary of the terms used in the book with their Arabic equivalent. For his *Qalā'id al-mafākhir fī gharīb 'awā'id al-awā'il wa'l-awākhir* (1834) he appended (as Mohammad Sawaie notes) "a core scientific Arabic glossary in which he provided annotations for neologisms that he had adopted in the translation of this work" (400). It is important to point out that, according to Sawaie, the text of the translation of this book amounts to 112 pages while the glossary consists of 105 pages, an apt illustration of the importance that al-Tahṭāwī attached to dictionaries and scientific vocabulary.

As stated earlier, al-Tahṭāwī resorted to different methods in translating new French words and concepts into Arabic. One way was through Arabization, implying transliterating a foreign word as is or with minimal changes into Arabic script. Examples of these words abound in his works; some have since then been accepted and became loan words that are generally used in modern standard Arabic, such as: *ūbirah* (for opera), *banūrāmā* (panorama), *al-biyānū* (the piano), *jūrnāl* (journal), *kāzītah* (gazette), *amnībūsah* (omnibus), *insṭīṭūt* (institute), and *akdamah/akdimah* or *akadimyah* (academy). These words were even treated according to Arabic grammatical and word-formation rules, such as using the regular feminine plural or deriving a

verbal form from the noun. He sometimes even borrowed a foreign word and attached it to an Arabic word as a compound term as in *ayyām al-karnawāl* (carnival days). Another method of translating concepts was to resort to classical Arabic words and applying them to a new meaning that is somewhat related to the original one. He also attempted to recover some of these scientific concepts from classical Arabic scientific writings, but this proved difficult since most Arabic scientific writings from the Classical period were unavailable during his time. He also had the courage to resort to using words and concepts from the colloquial, especially Egyptian urban dialects that had, in addition to Arabic words, many words derived from Turkish or Persian, especially terms associated with vocations and administration.

Muhammad ʿAlī was succeeded upon his death by his grandson ʿAbbās (1848-54), who did not share his grandfather's views. In November 1849 the School of Languages was closed, and in the following year al-Tahṭāwī was sent to the Sudan to become the principal of a newly created primary school there. Some historians interpreted this as a virtual exile by ʿAbbās because he did not like the opinions of al-Tahṭāwī concerning just rule as these were expressed in *Takhlīs*. Other historians maintain that ʿAlī Mubārak, another Egyptian intellectual and educator of the times who was close to ʿAbbās, became jealous of al-Tahṭāwī and caused this exile, while still other historians see his exile as resulting from the animosity of the conservative Azhar sheikhs who were opposed to al-Tahṭāwī's teaching, especially his liberal and innovative interpretation of Islamic law.

While in the Sudan, al-Tahṭāwī worked on a translation of Fénelon's *Les aventures de Télémaque*. He published his translation in 1867 in Beirut, Lebanon, and not in Egypt. When Saʿīd (1854-63) succeeded ʿAbbās following the latter's assassination in 1854, al-Tahṭāwī returned to Cairo where he was appointed translator in the Cairo Directorate, then vice-principal at a military school, then assistant director of the school of the chiefs of staff in 1856. Following the retirement of its director, al-Tahṭāwī took over the directorship and developed the school in a manner similar to that of the School of Languages. The syllabus he developed gave the students the choice of one Eastern (Persian or Turkish) and one Western Language (French, English, or German). He also founded a department of translation and one for accounting. He was also appointed director of the Royal School of Engineering and Architecture thus becoming a dominant power in the field of education in Egypt. But this did not last long, for in 1861 the school was closed and al-Tahtāwī remained unemployed for two years until Ismāʿīl (1863-79) became the Khedive and re-established the Education Ministry (Dīwān) to which al-Tahtāwī was appointed as a member of its board that looked into planning the opening of new schools. He assumed membership of many committees at the Ministry, including curriculum development as well as heading the commission responsible for the translation of the French legal code. From 1870 until his death he was the editor of *Rawdat al-Madāris*, a periodical for the Ministry of Education. Despite such a heavy load, al-Tahtāwī found time to translate and encouraged the editing and publication of many classics of Arabic thought such as the works of Ibn Khaldūn. He also wrote a number of books such as *Kitāb al-murshid al-amīn li'l-banāt wa'l-banīn* (Albert Hourani renders the title which rhymes in Arabic as: Guiding Truths for Girls and Youths) and *Manāhij al-albāb al-misriyyah fī mabāhij al-ādāb al-ʿasriyyah* (Albert Hourani again: The Paths of the Egyptian Hearts in the Joys of the Contemporary Arts) as well as an incomplete history of Egypt, *Anwār Tawfīq al-Jalīl fī akhbār Misr wa-tawthīq Banī Ismāʿīl* (literally, The Lights of the Noble Tawfiq concerning Events in Egypt and the Documentation of the Sons of Ismāʿīl), and a history of Islam of which the first volume is a biography of Muhammad, *Nihāyat al-ījāz fī sīrat sākin al-Hijāz* (again literally, A Compendium Concerning the Resident of the Hijaz Region).

If *Takhlīs* had been written earlier with the objective of providing Egyptians with an understanding of France and its social and political structure in a generally sympathetic manner, then these later books by al-Tahtāwī were more concerned with his views on the reform of Egyptian society, especially in the field of education. They can in fact be considered a continuation of the project he initiated in *Takhlīs*. In *Manāhij al-albāb al-misriyyah fī mabāhij al-ādāb al-ʿasriyyah* (henceforth *Manāhij*), he discusses how a society can become civilized or developed, repeatedly emphasizing the concept of love for one's homeland *(watan)*, a rather new concept for Egyptians who still considered themselves as part of the Ottoman Empire and owing allegiance to an Islamic state. He then proceeds to discuss progress along the lines of his discussion in *Takhlīs*. For a society to reach the highest levels of civilization and development, two factors need to be present: one is the ethical and moral education of character achieved through religion and human virtues; the second is what he calls public benefits *(manāfiʿ ʿumūmiyyah)* that produce wealth for society and advancement to the community (7-8). In other words he points to two origins of civilization that need to come together, namely the spiritual and the material. But he is also aware that each nation *(millah)* possesses a different religion and may therefore be different from other nations in its spiritual aspects (9). He is also aware of the differences in the impact of the various arts and industries on progress. By way of example, he points out the superiority of seafaring and associated trades to that of agriculture (133). He later defines what he means by public benefits, resorting to the Arabization of the French word *industrie* and explaining it as progress in those skills and crafts that allow human being to change the raw materials created by God but unusable in their natural form, thus converting them into new and useful forms. He gives the examples of turning cotton and wool into textiles, crafts that his compatriots know very well. Al-Tahtāwī then proceeds to give a more general definition, noting that *industriyah* is the art of work and accompanying activities that lead to an increase in resources in the three important areas of agriculture, industry, and commerce and thus help bring about human happiness (129).

However, in addition to these two prerequisites, al-Tahtāwī also comments on the political and social aspects of civilization and progress. Invoking Montesquieu's idea of the distinction between the three branches of power (legislative, administrative, and legal or juridical), he draws a link to the classical Islamic idea of the supremacy of Sharī'ah law over the ruler, even though he also acknowledges the idea of the ruler's complete authority. The limits of the ruler to exercise his authority are those provided by Islamic law. But the real guardians of Islamic law are the scholars of religion who make up one of the four orders or estates of society according to traditional Islamic scholarship, namely the ruler, the religious scholars ('ulamā'), soldiers, and those engaged in economic production. Religious scholars are important for al-Tahtāwī, not only because they have been sanctioned by Islamic law to be the guardians who are to make sure that the law is not broken, but also because this was the group that fielded most of its members from ordinary Egyptians (unlike the other orders which were made up mostly from non-Egyptian Turks, Albanians, Circassians… etc.). This gives al-Tahtāwī's thinking a certain nationalist overtone, as Albert Hourani notes. But for the 'ulamā' properly to perform their duties as advisers to the ruler and as protectors of the law, they need to come to terms with the new learning and sciences and accept those who master the new sciences as members within their order of "people of knowledge". Yet ultimately al-Tahtāwī's fundamental conception of Islamic law is traditionalist and conforms to the dominant understanding of legal scholars during the late Middle Ages, namely that law is to be understood as a restraining factor that sets limits of action for everyone in society, including the ruler. However, it neither prescribes nor sets the principles in accordance with which the ruler should act.

In the latter parts of Manāhij, al-Tahtāwī writes about the changes that were the consequences of Muhammad 'Alī's economic policies, especially advances in agriculture which resulted from the special attention paid to the irrigation system, that being a policy that had characterized the greatest rulers of Egypt throughout its long history. He also discusses the economic potential and possibilities of development in Egypt resorting to different sources and documents as well as one European author. But

again there is the important point that al-Tahtāwī stresses in this as well as in his other works, that social virtues based upon religious and ethical beliefs are a prerequisite for economic and social progress. These social virtues can be instilled in people through proper education.

As a teacher and one of the planners and directors of the educational policies in Egypt during his times, al-Tahtāwī wrote another important work concerning education, namely al-Murshid al-amīn li'l-banāt wa'l-banīn (henceforth al-Murshid). This book was written as a commission from the "Ministry of Education to write something which would be equally suitable for teaching boys and girls", as Hourani points out. Therefore, according to him, the book reflects the official policies and aims of the Khedive Ismā'īl Pasha. In this book, al-Tahtāwī emphasizes the connection between education and society as well as loving one's homeland (which can be translated into the modern political jargon of good citizenry). Primary education should be universal and available to all. Secondary education should be of superior quality as it will produce the best minds in society. But he also stresses the importance and necessity of the education of girls. His reasoning has little to do with integrating women in the economic and social production of society as he still held the traditional view that women should stay home and take care of their families. That in fact is one of the reasons he gives for the need to educate them, the purpose being to make them lead a harmonious family life and better nurture their children. But education will also minimize the emptiness of a life of gossip in their restricted households. When the need arises, it will also give them the opportunity to work, but only within the limits of their capacity as women.

Such an attitude towards women was, needless to say, much more progressive than the general opinion amongst the 'ulamā' and elite in his time, but is hardly revolutionary in that it does not contradict the basic tenets of the traditionalist view of women. He also held to the Qur'anic view that men could marry more than one woman (up to four at the same time) but only on condition that they are capable of being just to them all.

Al-Tahtāwī's works on the history of Egypt and Islam are in many ways traditionalist and lack originality. We notice, however, a few interesting aspects in these historical books. In the first part of his history of Egypt, *Anwār Tawfīq al-Jalīl fī akhbār Misr wa-tawthīq Banī Ismā'īl* (1868), which was continued in the incomplete history of Islam, posthumously published as *Nihāyat al-ījāz fī sīrat sākin al-Hijāz* (1874) and *al-Dawlah al-islāmiyyah, nizāmuhā wa-'amalatuhā* (collected from his manuscripts, edited and published in 1990), al-Tahtāwī divides history into two epochs, ancient and modern. However, he gives this fundamentally Western division an Islamic twist by using the rise of Islam as the dividing line between the two, while differing from traditional Muslim historians in that he does not consider the pre-Islamic period unworthy of study. He is also aware of Egyptian history and civilization before the coming of Islam in the 7th century CE, and conceives the history of Egypt as a continuum between its ancient civilization and that of Islam. *Anwār* covers the whole era from the times of the ancient Egyptians through Alexander the Great, the Romans and the early Byzantine period to the times of the Arab conquest of Egypt. The two other volumes cover periods of Egyptian history following the Arab conquest.

Although al-Tahtāwī subscribes to the traditional view that Egypt is a part of the Islamic nation, it is also his view that its own history makes it a special nation within the larger Islamic community (the word for "nation" being the same as for "Islamic community", *ummah*). This idea, coupled to the notion of the continuity of Egyptian history since ancient times, constitutes the embryonic form of Egyptian nationalism that was to develop later in the nineteenth century, especially following the British occupation in 1882. This feature also marks his other works discussed above, and can also be seen in some patriotic poems *(wataniyyāt)* he wrote that bear witness to the beginnings of a new sense of Egyptian identity.

Al-Tahtāwī's thinking revolved around issues that were already manifest in his early work *Takhlīs* and crystallized during his stay in Paris. All his other activities can be seen as further elaborations and developments of the insights in this early work. These ideas can be summarized as follows: the welfare of society and its members lies in civilization which in turn is based upon the spiritual and material development of society. As the worldly object of government is human welfare of the citizens, it is the function of government to promote the spiritual and material well-being of the populace. The people, in return, have to submit to the authority of their rulers. Religious scholars will advise the ruler so that he does not commit actions prohibited by law. Science and knowledge as well as material progress have been best developed in the West, and Egypt and other Muslims need to learn from the West, especially France, in order to achieve a higher level of civilization. Since Muslims were in the forefront of scientific knowledge and civilization during earlier periods, it is all but natural that they learn to redevelop, since the reasons for their decline are related to the dominance of the Mamluks (slave soldiers) in earlier centuries, a set of rulers who were not interested in knowledge and science. To achieve this goal, the lands of Islam and Egypt in particular need to adopt Western science and its fruits.

Because France provided a principal model for al-Tahtāwī, he initiated a tradition of cultural francophilia in Egypt that became even more pronounced following the British occupation of the country in 1882, all as a means of expressing anti-colonial sentiments amongst the educated. The trend survived well into the second half of the twentieth century.

Al-Tahtāwī was neither a modern liberal nor a radical thinker. Instead he was a reformer, someone who did not shy away from acknowledging the weaknesses of Egyptian society and the strengths of Western societies. Even if we acknowledge the revolutionary effects of al-Tahtāwī's ideas on Egyptian thought, especially during the nineteenth century—statements by the late Lūwīs 'Awad, for instance, that al-Tahtāwī was the "first to introduce into Egyptian thought the concept of libertas in the civic, as opposed to the legal, sense" or "his unreserved acceptance of the emancipation of women" (31), such claims seem somewhat exaggerated. He can be seen as an enlightened traditionalist in the sense that his starting point was tradition which he interpreted in a non-dogmatic and non-literalist manner. For him economic and social progress did not contradict Islamic beliefs and norms and could be achieved through the guidance and leadership of an enlightened state, even in fact an enlightened despot who would have a group of similarly minded advisers surrounding him. In his opinion a constitutional democracy was not alien to Islamic teachings. Modernization could be launched from within tradition, but only if it were aided and forwarded by modern knowledge and gainful pursuits. In more than one way, al-Tahtāwī was one of the earliest and most influential proponents of modernization and progress in Egypt and by extension other Arab and Muslim societies. And yet, at the same time he laid the foundation for the problematic and sometimes contradictory tension between tradition and modernity that has plagued Arab and Muslim societies for the past two centuries. One of his ideas which became an important component of enlightened Arab and Muslim thought from the middle of the nineteenth to the middle of the twentieth centuries and which was the basis for the different social projects of liberal modernizing thought was the central importance of education for all classes of society.

REFERENCES

A. Abdel-Malek, *Idéologie et renaissance nationale: L'Egypte moderne* (Paris: 1969);

Ibrahim Abu-Lughod, *The Arab Rediscovery of Europe* (Princeton, N.J.: Princeton University Press, 1963), 50-53;

Louis Awad, *The Literature of Ideas in Egypt: Part I* (Atlanta, Georgia: Scholars Press, 1986), 25-47;

Ahmad Ahmad Badawī, *Rifā'ah Rāfi' al-Tahtāwī* (Cairo, 1959);

Jan Brugman, *An Introduction to the History of Modern Arabic Literature in Egypt* (Leiden: E. J. Brill, 1984), 18-25;

Y. M. Choueiri, *Arab History and the Nation-state: A Study in Modern Arabic Historiography 1820-1980* (London-New York: Routledge, 1989); new ed. with the title *Modern Arab Historiography: Historical Discourse and the Nation-State* (London: Routledge-Curzon, 2003);

J. A. Crabbs Jr., *The Writing of History in Nineteenth-Century Egypt: A Study in National Transformation* (Detroit: Wayne State University Press, 1984);

Gilbert Delanoue, *Moralistes et politiques musulmans dans l'Egypte du XIXe siècle (1798-1882)* (Cairo: Institut français d'archéologie orientale du Caire, 1982);

Peter Gran, *Islamic Roots of Capitalism: Egypt, 1760-1840* (Austin: University of Texas Press, 1979);

R. A. Hamed, *The Japanese and Egyptian Enlightenment* (Tokyo, 1990);

J. Heyworth-Dunne, "Rifā'ah Badawī Rāfi' al-Tahtāwī: the Egyptian revivalist", *Bulletin of the School of Oriental Studies* 9 (1937-9): 961-967, and 10 (1940): 399-415;

Albert Hourani, *Arabic Thought in the Liberal Age, 1798-1939* (Cambridge: Cambridge University Press, 1983), 69-84;

Khaldun Sati' Husari, *Three Reformers: A Study in Modern Arab Political Thought* (Beirut: Khayats, 1966);

Muhammad 'Imārah, *Rifā'ah al-Tahtāwī: rā'id al-tanwīr fī 'l-'asr al-hadīth* (Cairo: Dār al-Mustaqbal al-'Arabī, 1984);

Sulaymān al-Khatīb, *al-Dīn wa'l-hadārah fī fikr al-Tahtāwī: qirā'ah islāmiyyah* (Cairo: al-Markaz al-Islāmī li-Dirāsat al-Hadārah, 1992);

Bernard Lewis, *The Muslim Discovery of Europe* (London: Weidenfeld and Nicolson, 1982);

A. Louca, *Voyageurs et écrivains égyptiens en France au XIXe siècle* (Paris, 1970), 55-74;

Husayn Fawzī al-Najjār, *Rifā'ah al-Tahtāwī* (Cairo: al-Dār al-Misriyyah li'l-Ta'līf wa'l-Tarjamah, 1969);

Rifā'ah al-Tahtāwī, 1801-1873: al-kitāb al-tidhkārī fī 'l-dhikrā al-mi'ah wa'l-'ishrīn (Cairo: Wizārat al-Thaqāfah, al-Hay'ah al-'Āmmah li-Qusūr al-Thaqāfah, 1993);

Mohammad Sawaie, "Rifā'ah Badawī Rāfi' al-Tahtāwī and his Contribution to the Lexical Development of Modern Literary Arabic", *International Journal of Middle Eastern Studies* 32 (2000): 395-410;

Jamāl al-Dīn Shayyāl, *Rifā'ah Rāfi' al-Tahtāwī, 1801-1873* (Cairo: Dār al-Ma'ārif, 1980); al-Badrāwī Zahrān, *Rifā'ah al-Tahtāwī wa-waq-* *fah ma'a 'l-dirāsāt al-lughawiyyah al-hadīthah: ma'a tahqīq nass kitābihi al-Tuhfah al-maktabiyyah* (Cairo: Dār al-Ma'ārif, 1983).

Mahmūd Taymūr

(1894 – 1973)

STEPHAN GUTH

Dept. of Culture Studies and Oriental Languages (IKOS), University of Oslo

WORKS

al-Shaykh Jum'ah, wa-qisas ukhrā ("Shaykh Jum'ah, and other stories", Cairo: al-Matba-'ah al-Salafiyyah, 1925);

'Amm Mitwallī [Mutawallī], wa-qisas ukhrā ("'Amm Mitwallī, and other stories", Cairo: al-Matba'ah al-Salafiyyah, 1925);

Fann al-qasas ("The Art of Storytelling", Cairo: Matba'at al-Raghā'ib, 1925);

al-Shaykh Sayyid al-'abīt, wa-aqāsīs ukhrā ("Shaykh Sayyid the Fool, and other stories", Cairo: al-Matba'ah al-Salafiyyah, 1926); contains as an introduction a study that was published in 1936 in an enlarged version as *Nushū' al-qissah wa-tatawwuruhā* (see below);

Rajab Afandī: qissah misriyyah ("Rajab Efendi: an Egyptian Story", Cairo: al-Matba'ah al-Salafiyyah, 1928);

al-Hājj Shalabī, wa-aqāsīs ukhrā ("Hājj Shalabī, and other stories", Cairo: Matba'at al-I'timād, 1930); includes *al-Infijār* ("The Explosion"), a one-act play intended for reading;

"al-Nizā' bayn al-fushā wa'l-'āmmiyyah fī 'l-adab al-misrī al-hadīth" ("The Clash of Standard and Colloquial Arabic in Modern Egyptian Literature"), *al-Hilāl* 41 (1931): 185-8;

Abū 'Alī 'āmil artiste, wa-qisas ukhrā ("Abū 'Alī Trying as an Artist, and other stories", Cairo: al-Matba'ah al-Salafiyyah, 1934); revised as *Abū 'Alī al-fannān* (1954, see below);

al-Atlāl: riwāyah qasasiyyah misriyyah, wa-qisas ukhrā ("The Ruis: an Egyptian Fic-tional Story, and other stories", Cairo: al-Matba'ah al-Salafiyyah, 1934); revised as *Shabāb wa-ghāniyāt*, in: *Shabāb wa-ghāniyāt, wa-aqāsīs ukhrā* (1951, see below);

Nushū' al-qissah wa-tatawwuruhā ("Growth and Development of the Story", Cairo: al-Matba-'ah al-Salafiyyah, 1936);

al-Shaykh 'Afā Allāh, wa-qisas ukhrā ("Shaykh 'Afā Allāh, and other stories", Cairo: al-Matba'ah al-Salafiyyah, 1936); reprinted as *Zāmir al-hayy* (1953, see below);

Thalāth masrahiyyāt min fasl wāhid ("Three One-Act Plays", Cairo: Matba'at 'Atāyā, n.d. [1942?; Nazīh al-Hakīm gives "Cairo: Muhammad Hamdī, 1936"]); contains *Abū Shū-shah*, *al-Mawkib*, and *al-Su'lūk*, all in Egyptian vernacular (later republished in *fushā*);

Hājatunā ilā 'l-fann ("Our Need for Art", Cairo: Dār al-Nashr al-Hadīth, 1937);

al-Wathbah al-ūlā ("The First Step", Cairo: Dār al-Nashr al-Hadīth, 1937); revised versions of stories from the first three collections;

Qalb ghāniyah, wa-qisas ukhrā (Cairo: Dār al-Nashr al-Hadīth, 1937);

Fir'awn al-saghīr, wa-qisas ukhrā ("Little Pharaoh", Cairo: Matba'at al-Ma'ārif, 1939); includes as its preface *al-Masādir allatī alha-mat-nī al-kitābah*;

Nidā' al-majhūl ("The Call of the Unknown", Beirut: Dār al-Makshūf, 1939);

Maktūb 'alā 'l-jabīn, wa-qisas ukhrā ("Written on the Forehead, and other stories", Cairo: Matba'at al-Ma'ārif, 1941);

Hūriyyat al-bahr ("The Sea-Houri", Beirut: Dār

al-Makshūf, 1941);

'Arūs al-Nīl: masrahiyyah ghinā'iyyah bi'l-'āmmiyyah ("Nile Bride: a Musical Play in the Vernacular", Cairo: Dār Majallat al-Hawādith [?], 1941); revised as *Fidā'* (1951);

al-Makhba' raqm 13 [talattāshar] ("Shelter No. 13", Cairo: Dār Majallat al-Hawādith [?], 1941 [?]); annotated phonemic transcription by Stig T. Rasmussen (København: Akad. Forl., 1979);

Abū Shūshah wa'l-Mawkib: masrahiyyatān bi'l-'arabiyyah al-fushā ("Abū Shūshah and The Procession: Two Plays in *fushā*", Cairo: Matba'at al-Taraqqī, 1942; Damascus: Maktabat al-Taqaddum, 1943);

'Awālī: masrahiyyah bi'l-'arabiyyah al-fushā fī thalāthat fusūl ("'Awālī: a Three-Act Play in *fushā*", Cairo: al-Maktabah al-Tijāriyyah al-Kubrā / M. al-Istiqāmah, 1942);

al-Munqidhah, wa-Haflat shāy ("The Savior, and The Tea-Party", Cairo: Dār al-Kutub al-Ahliyyah, 1942);

Qāl al-rāwī ("The Narrator Said", Cairo: al-Maktabah al-Tijāriyyah al-Kubrā, 1942);

Suhād, aw al-Lahn al-tā'ih: masrahiyyah 'arabiyyah bi'l-fushā fī thalāthat fusūl ("Suhād, or The Lost Melody: an Arabic Three-Act Play in *fushā*", Cairo: 'Īsā al-Bābī al-Halabī, 1942);

Qanābil ("Bombs", Cairo: Lajnat al-Nashr li'l-Jāmi'iyyīn, 1943);

Bint al-shaytān, wa-qisas ukhrā ("Satan's Daughter, and other stories", Cairo: Dār al-Ma'ārif, 1944);

'Itr wa-dukhān: khawātir wa-maqālāt fī 'l-adab wa'l-fann wa'l-masrah ("Perfume and Smoke: Ideas on Literature, Art, and Theatre", Cairo: Lajnat al-Nashr li'l-Jāmi'iyyīn, Maktabat Misr, 1944/45);

Fann al-qasas, ma'a taqdīm fī qadiyyat al-lughah al-'arabiyyah wa-nusakh min ahdath aqāsīs al-mu'allif ("The Art of Story-Telling, with an Introduction Concerning the Arabic Language Issue, and the Latest Specimens of the Author's Stories", Cairo: Majallat al-Sharq al-Jadīd / Dār al-Hilāl, 1945);

Hawwā' al-khālidah ("Eternal Eve", Cairo: Dār al-Istiqāmah, 1945);

Kilyūbātrah [Cleopatra] fī Khān al-Khalīlī ("Cleopatra in Khan al-Khalili", Cairo: Matba'at al-Istiqāmah, 1946);

Shifāh ghalīzah, wa-qisas ukhrā ("Thick Lips, and other Stories", Cairo: Matba'at al-Istiqāmah, 1946);

Abū 'l-hawl yatīr ("The Sphinx Takes Off", Cairo: Matba'at al-Istiqāmah, 1947);

Salwā fī mahabb al-rīh: Qissah misriyyah ("Salwa Blowing the Wind", Cairo: Maktabat al-Ādāb, 1947);

Khalf al-lithām ("Behind the Veil", Cairo: Matba'at al-Kātib al-Misrī, 1948); partially reprinted as *Dunyā jadīdah* (1957, see below);

Ihsān li-'llāh, wa-qisas ukhrā ("Charity for God, and other stories", Cairo: Dār al-Ma'ārif, 1949);

al-Yawm khamr ("Today's It's Wine", Cairo: Dār al-Ma'ārif, 1949 [?; "1945" according to others]);

Khutuwāt 'alā 'l-shallāl ("Steps in the Rapids", Cairo: Matba'at al-Kaylānī al-Saghīr, 1950);

Kull 'ām wa-antum bi-khayr, wa-qisas ukhrā ("Happy New Year!, and other stories", Cairo: Dār al-Ma'ārif, 1950);

Malāmih wa-ghudūn: suwar khātifah li-shakhsiyyāt lāmi'ah ("Features and Issues: Impressions about Prominent People", Cairo: Maktabat al-Ādāb, 1950); repr. as *al-Shakhsiyyāt al-'ishrūn* ("Twenty Personalities", 1969);

Dabt al-kitābah al-'arabiyyah ("Writing Arabic", Cairo: Matba'at al-Istiqāmah, 1951);

Fidā' ("Sacrifice", Cairo: Dār Ihyā' al-Kutub al-'Arabiyyah, 1951); revised version of *'Arūs al-Nīl* (1941);

Ibn Jalā ("[a name]", Cairo: Dār al-Ma'ārif, 1951);

al-Nabī al-insān, wa-maqālāt ukhrā ("The Prophet [as] a Human Being, and other articles", Cairo: Maktabat al-Ādāb, [194?; 1951, 1956, or 1959, according to others]);

Shabāb wa-ghāniyāt, wa-aqāsīs ukhrā ("Young Folk and Pretty Girls", Cairo: 'Īsā al-Bābī al-Halabī, 1951); previously published as *al-Atlāl* (1934, see above);

Shifā' al-rūh ("Soul's Cure", Cairo: Dār al-Kātib al-'Arabī, 1951);

Abū 'l-Shawārib, wa-qisas ukhrā ("[a name, meaning:] The One with the Moustache, and other stories]", Cairo: Dār al-Ma'ārif, 1953);

Ashtar min Iblīs ("Cleverer than the Devil", Cairo: Dār al-Ma'ārif, 1953);

al-Muzayyafūn: masrahiyyah misriyyah fī sittat fusūl ("The Forgers: an Egyptian Six-Act Play", Cairo: Maktabat al-Ādāb, 1953);

Kidhb fī kidhb: masrahiyyah misriyyah fī arba'at fusūl ("Lie Upon Lie: an Egyptian Four-Act Play", Cairo: Matba'at Misr, 1953); *fushā* version of *Kidb fī kidb* (staged 1952, but never published in the vernacular);

Zāmir al-hayy ("Quarter Flautist", Cairo: Dār al-Ma'ārif, 1953); previously published as *al-Shaykh 'Afā Allāh* (1936, see above);

Abū 'Alī al-fannān ("Abū 'Alī the Artist", Cairo: Dār al-Ma'ārif, 1954); revised version of *Abū 'Alī 'āmil artist* (1934, see above);

Thā'irūn ("Revolutionaries", Cairo: Dār al-Hilāl, 1955); the title story is a long narrative classified as a novel by some;

Kalimāt al-hayāh al-'āmmah ("A Word on Life in General", Cairo: Matba'at al-Istiqāmah, [1956]);

Mushkilāt al-lughah al-'arabiyyah ("Problems in the Arabic Language", Cairo: Maktabat al-Ādāb, 1956);

Saqr Quraysh: masrahiyyah 'arabiyyah ("The Falcon of Quraysh: an Arabic Play", Cairo: Maktabat al-Ādāb, 1956);

Tāriq al-Andalus ("Tāriq of Andalusia", Cairo: Maktabat al-Ādāb, 1956);

Dirāsāt fī 'l-qissah wa'l-masrah ("Studies on Fiction and Drama", Cairo: Maktabat al-Ādāb, 1957 [?; Funk gives "1950"]);

Dunyā jadīdah ("A New World", Cairo: Maktabat al-Ādāb, 1957); partial reprint of *Khalf al-lithām* (1940, see above);

Muhādarāt fī 'l-qasas fī adab al-'arab: mādīhi wa-hādiruh ("Lectures on Arabic Literature, Past and Present", Cairo: al-Jāmi'ah al-'Arabiyyah, 1958);

Shumrūkh: riwāyah qasasiyyah ("Shumrūkh [personal name]", Cairo: Dār al-Hilāl, 1958); revised as *al-Dhahab al-aswad* ("The Black Gold", Cairo: Wizārat al-Tarbiyah, 1965);

Nabbūt al-khafīr ("The Guard's Cudgel", Cairo: Maktabat al-Ādāb, 1958);

Shams wa-layl ("Sun and Night", Cairo: Maktabat al-Ādāb, 1958);

Tamr hinnā 'ajab (Cairo: Maktabat al-Ādāb, 1958);

al-Adab al-hādif ("Committed Literature", Cairo: Maktabat al-Ādāb, 1959);

Ilā 'l-liqā' ayyuhā 'l-hubb ("Farewell, O Love", Cairo: al-Sharikah al-'Arabiyyah li'l-Tibā'ah wa'l-Nashr, 1959);

al-Masābīh al-zurq ("Blue Lamps", Cairo: al-Nāshir al-Hadīth, 1960);

Anā 'l-qātil, wa-qisas ukhrā ("I'm the Murderer, and other stories", Cairo: Dār Nahdat Misr / Dār al-Qalam, 1961);

Mu'jam al-hadārah ("Lexicon of Civilization", Cairo: Maktabat al-Ādāb, 1961);

Munājayāt li'l-kutub wa'l-kuttāb ("Intimations on Books and Writers", Cairo: Dār al-Jīl, 1962);

Intisār al-hayāh, wa-qisas ukhrā ("Life's Victory, and other stories", Cairo: Dār al-Ma'ārif, 1963);

Jazīrat al-jayb: siyāhah fī Ītāliyā, wa-mashāhid ukhrā ("The Pocket Isle: a Tour in Italy, and views of other places", Cairo: Maktabat al-Ādāb, 1963);

Khamsah wa-khmēsah (khumaysah) (Cairo: al-Dār al-Qawmiyyah, 1963); includes as its first item *Hakamat al-mahkamah*, translated by Medhat Shaheen as *The Court Rules*, in: *Arabic Writing Today: Drama*, ed. Mahmoud Manzalaoui (Cairo: American Research Center in Egypt, 1977), 53-63;

Talā'i' al-masrah al-'arabī ("Early Phases of Arabic Theater", Cairo: Maktabat al-Ādāb, 1963);

Zilāl mudī'ah: falsafat al-fann wa-mushkilat al-mujtama' wa'l-hayāh ("Shadows in the Light: Philosophy of Art and the Issue of Society and Life", Cairo: Maktabat al-Nahdah al-Misriyyah, 1963);

al-Adīb bayn al-fann wa'l-hayāh ("The Littérateur between Art and Life", Cairo: Maktabat al-'Ālam al-'Arabī, 1965 [?]);

al-Bārūnah Umm Ahmad, wa-qisas ukhrā ("Baroness Umm Ahmad, and other stories", Cairo: Dār al-Ma'ārif, 1967);

Adab wa-udabā' ("Literature and Littérateurs", Cairo: Dār al-Kātib al-'Arabī, 1968); reviews, criticism, literary-autobiographical essays;

al-Ayyām al-mi'ah, wa-mashāhid ukhrā ("A Hundred Days, and other impressions",

Cairo: Dār Nahdat Misr, 1968); includes *al-Ayyām al-mi'ah*, *Khutuwāt 'alā 'l-shallāl* (republished), *Ilā madīnat al-nasr*, and *Abū 'l-Hawl yatakallam*, *Hikāyat Abū 'Awf, wa-qisas ukhrā* (Cairo: Dār Nahdat Misr, 1969);

Qunfudhah wa-Amūrah wa-mā jarā lahumā fī 'l-junaynah al-mashūrah: haddūtah ("Qunfudhah [Little Hedgehog] and Amūrah and What Happened to Them in the Enchanted Garden: a Tale", Cairo: Dār Nahdat Misr, 1968 [?]);

Bayn al-mitraqah wa'l-sindān ("Between Hammer and Anvil", Cairo: Dār al-Kātib al-'Arabī, 1969);

Ma'būd min tīn ("Clay Idol", Cairo: Maktabat al-Ādāb, 1969;

Ittijāhāt al-adab al-'arabī fī 'l-sinīn al-mi'ah al-akhīrah ("Literary Tendencies in the Last Hundred Years", Cairo: Maktabat al-Ādāb, 1970);

al-Shakhsiyyāt al-'ishrūn: suwar li-shakhsiyyāt min al-mādī al-qarīb ("Twenty Personalities: Portraits of Persons from the Recent Past", Cairo: Dār al-Ma'ārif, 1970); reprint of *Malāmih wa-ghudūn* (1950);

Zawj fī 'l-mazād ("Marriage for Auction", Alexandria: Dār al-Kutub al-Jāmi'iyyah, 1970?);

Bint al-yawm ("Today's Girl", Cairo: Mu'assasat Akhbār al-Yawm, 1971);

al-Qissah fī 'l-adab al-'arabī, wa-buhūth ukhrā ("The Story in Arabic Literature, and other studies", Cairo: Maktabat al-Ādāb, 1971).

Works in Translation
Collections and Novels

Mahmoud Teymour, *Tales from Egyptian Life*, translated by Denys Johnson-Davies (Cairo: The Renaissance Bookshop, 1949);

Bonne Fête (Paris: Nouvelles Editions Latines, 1954); French translation of *Kull 'ām wa-antum bi-khayr* (1950) and nine other stories.

Mahmoud Teymour, *The Call of the Unknown*, translated by Hume Horan (Beirut: Khayats, 1964); translation of *Nidā' al-majhūl*;

Mahmoud Teymour, *Sensuous Lips, and other stories*, translated by Nayla Naguib (Cairo: General Egyptian Book Organization, 1993).

Single Stories

"Summer Journey", translated by Denys Johnson-Davies, in his *Modern Arabic Short Stories* (London: Heinemann, 1976 [originally Oxford University Press, 1967]), 167-72;

"The Enemy," translated by Anthony McDermott, in: *Arabic Writing Today: The Short Story*, ed. Mahmoud Manzalaoui (Cairo: The American Research Center in Egypt, 1968), 47-53.

Plays

Shelter No. 13 (København: Akad. Forl., 1979); annotated phonemic transcription of *al-Makhba' raqm 13* [*talattāshar*] (1941?), by Stig T. Rasmussen;

"The Court Rules", translated by Medhat Shaheen, in: *Arabic Writing Today: Drama*, ed. Mahmoud Manzalaoui (Cairo: American Research Center in Egypt, 1977), 53-63; translation of *Hakamat al-mahkamah* (first item in *Khamsah wa-khmêsah*, 1963).

Articles

"Le Conflit des langues arabes dans la littérature égyptienne moderne", in *Actes du 18e Congrès International des Orientalistes*, Leiden 1932; translation of "al-Nizā' bayn al-fushā wa'l-'āmmiyyah fī 'l-adab al-misrī al-hadīth" (1931).

Other

Muhammad Taymūr, *Mu'allafāt* ("Works"), ed. Mahmūd Taymūr, 3 vols.: 1. *Wamīd al-rūh* ("Sparks from the Spirit"; includes as "Book 4" the first edition of *Mā tarāhu 'l-'uyūn*, "What the Eyes See"), 2. *Hayātunā al-tamthīliyyah* ("Our Theater Life"), 3. *al-Masrah al-misrī* ("Egyptian Theater") (Cairo: Matba-'at al-I'timād, 1922);

Muhammad Taymūr, *Mā tarāhu 'l-'uyūn* ("What the Eyes See"), 2nd edition, ed. Mahmūd Taymūr (Cairo: al-Matba'ah al-Salafiyyah, 1927);

Majallat al-Qissah, general editor Mahmūd Taymūr (Cairo: Wizārat al-Thaqāfah wa'l-Irshād al-Qawmī, Jan. 1964-Aug. 1965); monthly, suspended with no. 20.

Mahmūd Taymūr is a key figure for modern Egyptian, and Arabic, literature. As a most prolific writer who with hundreds of short stories and a number of programmatic studies contributed substantially to the breakthrough, and lasting establishment, of a new prose genre as a recognized form of literary expression, he is usually referred to as the "father," or "shaykh" (grand old man, chief, master), of the modern Arabic short story. The remaining part of his œuvre, hardly less voluminous than his output in the field of the short story, and in many cases of an acknowledged high quality, has received comparatively little attention: almost ten novels, some twenty plays, a number of studies on Arabic language and literature (some of them pioneering), a handful of travel accounts as well as numerous essays, collections of "reflections, ideas, inspirations" *(khawātir)* and memoir-like reminiscences.

Mahmūd Taymūr was born in Cairo in the Darb Saʿādah quarter where his great-grandfather had built a large domicile in 1816 after having settled in Egypt. The Taymūrs were of mixed Arab-Kurdish origin and had lived in the region of Mosul before Mahmūd's ancestor came to the Nile as an officer in the army of the Ottoman provincial governor and "opened" the country for the family (this is why he was called "the Pioneer"). In time he even rose to the position of the Governor's right hand, a position that allowed him to acquire the wealth, real estate, 'aristocracy', and also educational facilities which later generations could profit from. The palais in Darb Saʿādah was to house three generations of major officials and highly cultivated men of letters. "The Pioneer's" son, Mahmūd's grandfather Ismāʿīl (1815-72), served as educator of the princes at the court of the 'vice-king' (khedive) of Egypt. Mahmūd's aunt ʿĀʾishah (1840-1902), Ismāʿīl's daughter, was instructed in religious matters, grammar and literature by renowned teachers, mastered not only Arabic, but also Persian and Ottoman, started to write poems and prose fiction after her husband's early death, and thus became ʿĀʾishah al-**Taymūriyyah**, the famous pioneer of women's writing in modern Arabic literature. Her (half-) brother, Ismāʿīl's son from another woman, that

is, Mahmūd's father Ahmad (1871-1930), received his education, among many others, from his sister ʿĀʾishah and became one of the finest Arabic philologists of his time who penned numerous studies on Arabic language and Arab life and culture (folklore) and enjoyed an international reputation. If ʿĀʾishah, thirty years his senior, can still be seen as a representative of the Ottoman era and its 'pure' esthetics, Ahmad Taymūr's interests and efforts focussed on Arabic and Arab culture not without a certain utilitarianism—like many of his contemporaries he hoped to be able to revive the spirit of the Arabs' 'golden ages' and in this way initiate an Arab *nahdah*, a "renaissance", at a time when the Middle East had already begun to become dominated by European powers politically and economically (England had occupied Egypt in 1882 and established a colonial regime and economic system); the intellectuals had to find answers to the challenges of technical modernization and the Middle Easterners' seemingly evident civilizational backwardness, from which also began to result a feeling of inferiority. Classicism seemed to be an answer and was widespread throughout the Arab world. Yet another age, that of the quest for national independence and then the consciousness of being free—and at the same time responsible—, is what the next generation of Taymūrs stands for, especially Mahmūd and his elder brother Muhammad.

These two, and their still elder brother Ismāʿīl, were the children of Ahmad Taymūr, the classicist encyclopedian and philologist, and his wife Khadījah, the daughter of Ahmad Pasha Rashīd, then Minister of the Interior, from a Greek wife. Ahmad Taymūr and Khadījah married in 1890, Ismāʿīl was born in 1891, Muhammad in 1892, and Mahmūd in 1894.

Darb Saʿādah, situated between al-Mūskī and Bāb al-Khalq in Old Cairo but bordering on the 'modern' city to the West, was still a rather mixed quarter at that time. There were the little palaces of pashas and houses of begs, but also a lot of workshops, stores and shops; in an autobiographical essay published in 1960 in al-*Ādāb*, Taymūr remembers it even as an "authentically popular" quarter in which many "different groups and classes" were living side by side. Although upper class families usually were eager to keep their children away from those of the lower classes, the Taymūr boys were allowed to mix freely with the craftsmen's, shopkeepers' and domestics' children, playing soccer, having races and enjoying all other kinds of children's amusements, observing also the adults at their work, listening to old men's stories, the alley's gossip and the women's songs. The father's tolerant attitude thus enabled Mahmūd and his brothers to get to know, in spite of their 'aristo-cratic' background, those aspects of the life of the Egyptian 'common man' that would later become the focus of attention in Muhammad's and Mahmūd's early writings.

The first tragic blow that seems to have left a lasting imprint on Mahmūd's personality was his mother's untimely early death. She died—from measles!—in 1899 when Mahmūd was only five years old, and since the father did not remarry he grew up motherless. There are no autobiographi-cal statements as to the effect of this loss, but judging from the many short stories, both by Muhammad and Mahmūd, which made orphans their protagonists, it can be assumed that the children suffered severely from it. The love and affection with which aunt 'Ā'ishah (the poetess, then approaching her sixties already) tried to replace the mother seem to have helped them to overcome the stroke of fate, but obviously this was not enough to compensate wholly for the loss.

The place left by their mother was filled, at least partially, by their father, whose influence on Mahmūd would perhaps not otherwise have been as deep as it came to be. Together with the old family tradition, the children's increased fixation on their father may have given the world of books and learning in which he lived an additional appeal. This was even more so when, only three years after the mother's death, their aunt 'Ā'ishah also passed away (1902). At the time Mahmūd was still attending the Nāsiriyyah Primary School where he received a standard education of the modernized, mostly secular type from a crème of teachers who had to pre-pare intelligent students from the high society for the secondary level of the *lycée khédivial*. In

his free time, Mahmūd continued to play with the children of the quarter and appears to have been a happy and sociable boy.

Though Ahmad Taymūr was still in his early thirties when his wife died, he seems to have suffered from a kind of rheumatism which his doctor attributed, among other things, to the unfavorable climatic conditions in the old family residence. The large house that "the Pioneer" had built more than eighty years ago was now quite rotten, and its cold and damp interior was certainly not the environment in which Ahmad's health could improve. He therefore decided, in 1903 or 1904, to give up the Darb Sa'ādah domicile—which in Mahmūd's recollection of his early childhood resembled a "ruined for-tress"—and move to 'Ayn Shams, then still at the north-eastern outskirts of Cairo, where the family possessed a fine spacious cottage in a rural, and much drier, area, not too far from the city. The idea of a change of location may well have helped him get over the loss of his beloved wife and his elder sister.

In 'Ayn Shams several things became impor-tant for the young Mahmūd and impressed him so deeply that they left their marks/traces in his writings. The first was the experience of life in the country. While he had come to know the milieu of the urban common people in Darb Sa'ādah, here in 'Ayn Shams he could gain a first-hand knowledge of the life of the fellaheen (Egyptian peasants). Although the enormous social distance separating these Egyptians from urban 'aristocrats' was never forgotten, Muham-mad and Mahmūd were allowed to mix freely with the people of the neighborhood, playing soccer with the other boys, joining the fellaheen at work on the fields, and joining their custom-ary evening gatherings, when they sat together talking, gossiping, disputing, telling stories, and singing songs. According to the memoirs of Ignatiĭ Yu. Krachkovskiĭ (1883-1951), the fa-mous Russian Arabist, the Taymūr boys were looked at by the local population as "real fella-heen". The local color which, a few years later, was to become a characteristic feature of the early short stories of both Muhammad and Mah-mūd was thus chiefly nourished in its imagery, selection of characters, and 'Egyptianness' from impressions that the two boys obtained from encounters outside their aristocratic homes in Darb Saʿādah and ʿAyn Shams.

At home meanwhile, the atmosphere of traditional Taymūrian erudition and learning began to exert more and more influence on Mahmūd as he went to school and started learning to read and write. Ahmad Taymūr possessed an immense private library, and, according to Mahmūd's recollection, he gave it "all his attention" and "spared neither time nor money" on it. Having lost his wife, he never remarried; instead, as some biographers have it, he "married" his own library. Mahmūd recalls that the library grew up with him; from which stemmed his own love for books. In time it was to become one of the finest in the Middle East (with more than 7,000 titles in 1914 and more than 18,000 at the end of Ahmad Taymūr's life). Because it included a large number of precious manuscripts the collection also attracted numerous visitors, among them sheikhs from al-Azhar, intellectuals, writers and scholars, not only from Egypt but also from abroad (among them the above-mentioned Krachkovskiĭ). These people of course also sat down with Ahmad, sought his opinion and advice, held discussions with him (and often in small circles as well) about matters of shared interest or common concern; this intellectual atmosphere inside the home was to be as important for the two boy's development during their formative years as the milieus outside where they were consorting with the poorer people in both city and country.

Even before they were able to grasp the meaning of classical Arabic poems, their father made them learn some of the finest pieces by heart. However this introduction to the world of the classical heritage became much more appealing to Mahmūd when his father introduced him to the stories from "A Thousand and One Nights," perhaps because their folkloristic simplicity made them seem closer to the kind of popular stories that Mahmūd had heard in Darb Saʿādah and ʿAyn Shams or else they were simply more attractive for a child of his age.

It must have been still during their time in ʿAyn Shams that Mahmūd's brother, Muhammad, began to compose poetry himself. He showed such extraordinary talent that he soon became known as "the poet of the Ecole Khédivale". In 1905, at the age of fourteen, he is also said to have published his first articles in one of the most important papers of the time. Mahmūd admired his brother for that very much. From early age, he used to regard him not only as a playmate and intimate friend but also as an example to follow.

So it was also Muhammad who introduced him to modern, contemporary Arabic literature after their father had started to familiarize them with the classical heritage. While Ahmad Taymūr continued in his efforts when the boys joined the Ilhāmiyyah Secondary School in order to complete their standard education on the next level, Muhammad had begun to read the works of the *mahjar* (diaspora) authors, that is, of the Arab, mostly Syro-Lebanese, writers who had left their home countries and settled in the New World, among them, in the first place, Jubrān Khalīl **Jubrān** (1883-1931), Amīn al-Rīhānī (1876-1940), and Mīkhā'īl **Nuʿaymah** (Naimy, 1889-1988), and of course tried to make his younger brother-friend share his ideas and feelings. Mahmūd may still have been too young to fully understand what these writings were really about but, judging from the first poetry he composed some years later (and eventually published in 1915), it must already have fallen on a fertile ground: it was in that same free-verse form for which Jubrān had become famous, and its sentimental tone very much reflected the spirit of the diaspora authors.

The impact of his reading of *mahjar* writers is evident also from the first piece of fiction at which Mahmūd tried his hand in 1908, at the age of fourteen. Reportedly, the experiment bore the title *al-Sharaf al-rafīʿ* (Noble Sense of Honor) and told the story of an Indian girl whom an English officer had assaulted and who was rightly revenged after that by her people. This plot, which of course epitomizes the colonial situation and advocates retaliation for injust treatment at the hands of the colonial power and self-defense of the local population against foreign aggression, clearly shows that romantic nationalism was appealing very much to Mahmūd, as it was to Arabs in general at the time, especially so in Egypt where a number of events had heightened anti-British emotions and produced a nationalist movement that accused the colonial regime of 'despotism' and began to call for independence. The British had themselves added fuel to the mass feelings directed against them through unjustified executions of local peasants in the Delta village of Dinshawāy in 1906. The year 1908 in which Mahmūd penned *al-Sharaf al-rafīʿ* saw the foundation of the Egyptian National Party as well as, for example, the opening of the Egyptian (now Cairo) University, a private initiative aimed at raising the level of local higher education to international standards. An Egyptian author who was also very much *en vogue* then, especially among young men in their late teens, was Mustafā Lutfī al-**Manfalūtī** (1876-1924). Mahmūd, though still a bit younger, was no exception, and the sadness and exaggerated melodramatic mood of *al-Sharaf al-rafīʿ* reveals the influence of his readings of al-Manfalūtī. (The father, however, whom Mahmūd had approached to help him publish the story, did not grant the boy this favor because he found it still not mature enough.)

One or two years earlier, the family had moved back to Cairo (ʿAyn Shams seems to have been a bit too far from the center of intellectual life) and found a new domicile there in the Hilmiyyah al-Jadīdah quarter which had been built only recently and was now a favored place to live for many government officers. While the children continued to go to school, received additional instruction from their father and read al-Manfalūtī and the *mahjar* authors, they also used to 'stage' some plays before an audience of family members, friends and guests (Muhammad was to become a dramatist and an actor later in his life!), and also trained their pens further by editing a family newspaper.

In 1911 Muhammad finished his secondary education and, like many sons of upper class families, was sent to Europe for further studies. While Muhammad stayed in Europe (1912-1914, most of the time in Paris), Mahmūd completed his school diploma *(baccalauréat)* (1912), registered at the Higher School for Agriculture (perhaps because he had liked the rural atmosphere of ʿAyn Shams and at the same time sympathized with the poor fellaheen), and studied there for two years.

However, the year 1914 was to be a kind of turning-point in his life. Firstly, he suffered a heavy attack of typhoid which not only forced him to abandon his studies but also changed his life completely; from then on, he was constantly under medical control, had to follow a diet and a certain daily rhythm, and was restricted in his movements. Thus, from the age of twenty till the end of his life he felt like living "in a cage" (interview, in Campbell). In retrospect, Taymūr even interprets his illness as possibly the main factor in his writing, in that, as a means of distracting himself from his suffering he decided to train himself to write fiction.

The second turning-point was Muhammad's return to Egypt due to the outbreak of World War I. During the two years he had spent in France Muhammad had not so much attended university but rather read European literature and frequented theaters. He came back full of new ideas, and it was he who recommended to Mahmūd the writers of modern European short fiction, and particularly Guy de Maupassant (1850-93). This latter was to become "the greatest short-story writer" in Taymūr's eyes, a model whose artistic level he constantly tried to attain by working on his style. With his own literature, he desired to achieve what de Maupassant had achieved for the French; his early short stories he even signed as *Mūbāsān al-misrī* (the Egyptian Maupassant). Another European author whom Muhammad recommended enthusiastically was Anton Chekhov 1860-1904). Chekhov appealed to him as a sharp analyst of the depths of the human psyche. He too was to become one of the main models for Taymūr, but only when he made his 'psychological turn' in the late 1920s. Among local Egyptian writers, Muhammad considered only two texts worth reading: *Hadīth ʿĪsā b. Hishām* (ʿĪsā b. Hishām's Tale, first published as a series of articles starting from 1898) by Muhammad al-**Muwaylihī** (1858-1930) and Muhammad Husayn **Haykal**'s (1888-1956) *Zaynab* (heroine's name, 1913). European short story writers as well as the chief representatives of local socio-political satire and 'romantic nationalism' in literature thus widened

Mahmūd Taymūr's horizon in his early twenties, a few years before he published his own first short stories.

Having recovered sufficiently from the attack of typhoid, Taymūr started to work, still in 1914, in the Ministry of Justice. After a year, he transferred to the Ministry of Foreign Affairs for another six months, after which he decided that he should give up this kind of occupation altogether because it did not suit his character and talents. Since the Taymūrs were rich, there was no need to earn a living by working; thus, from 1917 onwards, he lived the life of a wealthy man of letters, dedicating himself to reading, writing and (later in his career) delivering lectures. His decision may have been enhanced also by the successful publication, in 1915, of some pieces of prose poetry *(shi'r manthūr)*, still in the style of Jubrān, in the reformist, national-oriented avant-garde review, *al-Sufūr*, and in 1916 the publication of *al-Hubb bayn al-ya's wa-qublat al-amal* (Love between Desperation and the Kiss of Hope), a story which, like his early poetry, showed the influence of his readings of neither European literature nor of al-Muwaylihī or Haykal, but was simply still highly sentimental.

The decision to quit his bourgeois job may also have been influenced by Muhammad's example: after his return from Paris, the elder brother was living the life of an artist (actor and dramatist). Not only did he bring out some poetry, but also published his first seven short stories (1917, in *al-Sufūr* as well). Furthermore, judging from Muhammad's first play which bore the title *al-'Usfūr fī 'l-qafas* (The Bird in the Cage, 1918), the fact that the two younger brothers abandoned the careers that they were expected to pursue may also be interpreted as a kind of rebellion against the restrictions of the 'gilded cage' of their education (without ever blaming their father explicitly for that, of course).

The second half of the 1910s was of utmost importance for modern Egyptian literature because it is then that a group of writers who demanded for Egypt a modern and at the same time authentically *Egyptian* literature, constituted itself. At first it centred around *al-Sufūr*, but later they formed themselves into *al-Mad-*

rasah al-hadīthah, the Modern School. The main literary vehicle for the achievement of their goals was the short story, a genre previously unknown to Arabic literature, and it was largely due to their efforts that it eventually came to be established as one of the major genres of modern Arabic fiction. Muhammad Taymūr was an active member of the group, and through him also Mahmūd was introduced into this circle of kindred revolutionary-minded reformist spirits, just one year before the national uprising of 1919 under the charismatic leader Sa'd Zaghlūl which finally lead to Egypt's (at least formal) independence in 1923.

Just one year after the 'Revolution', in 1920, Mahmūd Taymūr married Zaynab Dhū 'l-Fiqār, the daughter of the King's chamberlain. He was then twenty-six and was not allowed to see his wife before the wedding; but, unlike the hero in Muhammad's *Bird in the Cage*, Mahmūd did not rebel against the traditional custom of arranged marriage. There was also no need—he fell in love with the bride, and Zaynab even seems to have become his life's great love. They had a boy and two daughters. However, this happy marriage at the end of 1920 was followed by a terrible stroke of fate a few weeks later. In February 1921 Muhammad died very suddenly. His death hit Mahmūd very hard, and he obviously reckoned the best way to cope with the loss of his beloved brother, intimate friend and admired example was to carry on and accomplish what death had prevented Muhammad from accomplishing. First, he edited his Collected Works (*Mu'allafāt Muhammad Taymūr*, 3 vols., 1922) and later cared for a book edition of the stories that had appeared earlier under the heading *Mā tarāhu 'l-'uyūn* (What the Eyes behold, 1927), thereby honoring the brother's memory, making his art available to a greater public (and preserving it better for posterity). Secondly, he tried 'to take over' and continue Muhammad's work. Mahmūd's *al-Shaykh Jum'ah*, the title story of the collection that came out three years later, was first published in 1922 in *al-Sufūr* where Muhammad had played such an important role. Unlike the earlier sentimental attempts, this story was written in the spirit of Maupassant'ian realism—as his lifelong reverence for this author may perhaps also be explained, partly at least, as Brugman (255) suggests, from loyalty towards his brother, who "cultivated and refined" Mahmūd's love for literature and to whom he therefore often referred as *ustādhī* (my master).

In the three years following Muhammad's death, Mahmūd devoted himself not only to editing the latter's œuvre but also to propagating 'modern' forms of writing, first by selecting, translating, and publishing a number of exemplary stories from world literature, then more and more by composing himself "authentically Egyptian" stories in the spirit of the Modern School and their call for an *adab qawmī*, a "national literature". After the stories had appeared in newspapers and journals, he brought out many of them again in his early collections: *al-Shaykh Jum'ah* (Sheikh Jum'ah [also: Gom'ah], 1925), *'Amm Mitwallī* ('Uncle' Mitwalli, 1925), and *al-Shaykh Sayyid al-'abīt* (Sheikh Sayyid the Fool, 1926). Since classical literature was regarded as being out-dated and the writings of the *mahjar* authors and al-Manfalūtī (as well as the foreign, or foreign-inspired, yet extremely popular boulevard novels) were considered too melodramatic and unrealistic to be able to play a positive role in the construction of new independent Egypt, Mahmūd Taymūr and the writers of the Modern School sought to create a literature that would both mirror reality and not remain silent about the evils and 'diseases' that stood in the way of progress. In his early stories he and his 'brothers-in-arms' saw themselves as their society's doctors and believed that literature could serve as a remedy and thus help to pave the way for a better future. The diseases which he and the other Modernists identified were, for example, alcoholism and gambling, the corruption and hypocrisy of religious leaders, arranged marriages, despotic husbands, the lack of education, and widespread superstition. But it was not only the themes that had to be 'typically Egyptian', but also the characters and the settings. This is why many of the stories were given the heroes' names as their titles, give detailed descriptions of the surroundings, of the protagonists' and other persons' outward appearances and habits, ways of living and thinking. In the early collections, Taymūr lets them

even talk in the Egyptian vernacular (a *faut pas* according to traditional esthetics).

Most stories in these collections are set in the countryside and deal with characters who reportedly were modelled after persons whom Mahmūd had met in his childhood in 'Ayn Shams. From the way he portrays these rural (and also urban) Egyptians in his first collections it becomes clear that as a writer he has not yet been able fully to overcome his aristocratic background. Quite often, he seems to be amused at their "exoticness" (Jad 1983, 37). Two of these early collections are also preceded by programmatic introductions. In the forword to *al-Shaykh Jum'ah* Taymūr discusses the nature of the short story genre, its usefulness and prospects, as well as the desired 'realism', including the question of 'literarizing' the vernacular. *Al-Shaykh Sayyid al-'Abīt* opens with a lengthy study on "The Beginnings and Development of the Arabic Story," an important document in which the author scans the classical Arabic—elite as well as popular—literary tradition in search of what could serve as autochthonous predecessors to which the new 'European' genres, short story and novel, could be linked in order to root them in the Arab culture (he is however well aware that, in general, "the Arabs did not care much about prose fiction"). These forewords can be considered landmarks in modern Arabic literary theory and literary history.

From the mid-1920s, Taymūr published a new collection of stories almost every one or two years. In many of them he also re-published texts that had appeared already in earlier collections but which he thought could still be improved. In many cases, the revised texts differ considerably from their predecessors and show his striving for perfection as well as the development of his art.

The constant flow of texts did not stop even when in 1925 he left Egypt for a two-years stay in Europe (mainly in Switzerland). With the principal aim of stabilizing his health, he spent most of his time there reading European fiction, obviously reckoning his previous readings in this field to be still insufficient. The reading absorbed him almost totally and, together with the direct exposure to European civilization, impressed him deeply. In an autobiographical document, *al-Masādir allatī alhamatnī al-kitābah* (The Sources Which Inspired My Writing; published as preface to *Fir'awn al-saghīr*, 1939), he recalls that what he read and saw often "shocked" him and used to "linger in my heart of hearts." It is no wonder then that he felt the stay in Switzerland had made him more mature, nor is it surprising that the new insights and experiences stood at the beginning of what would soon lead to a new stage in his writing. In his recollection it was here that he realized that local color was not everything, that literature should deal, though perhaps still in a local garment, with matters of a more general significance and that he should therefore focus more on *al-nafs al-bashariyyah*, "the human soul".

It took some time however to translate these insights into a new type of narrative. Literary historians differ as to whether Taymūr's 'analytical psychological turn' took place already in the late 1920s or not before the mid-1930s. Wielandt notes that already in *Rajab Afandī* (Rajab Efendi, 1928) the author's sophisticated analysis of the protagonist's character goes far beyond the patterns and categories of characterization he had applied, rather mechanically, in earlier texts. Brugman, on the other hand, is convinced that the first example in which the author got past his former exotist, "tourist-like" attitude towards his heroes—preferably "folksy people" and "strange characters" with "distorted appearances" in "dilapidated surroundings," as Jad describes them (Jad 1983, 37) —, is the novella *al-Atlāl* (The Ruins, 1934). Be that as it may, both *Rajab Afandī* and *al-Atlāl* give evidence of the fact that the writer was entering a new phase in which the 'inner worlds' of his characters received increased attention, but not without relating them to the conditions of upbringing and *milieu* as well as connecting them organically with the behavior of the environment with which they interacted. That is, whereas the earlier stories were either rather static studies of a character or a milieu (tableaux of manners), or effectively focussed on a curious event, or aimed at discussing a certain social problem (Wielandt's four "types of narrative"), the texts now became more and more complex and accord-

ingly also longer. *Rajab Afandī,* though still a linear one-string narrative no different in principle from earlier stories, consists of more than a hundred pages in the book edition, *al-Atlāl* ninety. With *al-Atlāl* Taymūr also performed, consciously, a 'novelist turn': he subtitled the text a *riwāyah qasasiyyah misriyyah*, "an Egyptian novel".

Mahmūd Taymūr's increased interest in psychology parallels the same tendency in the Modern School during the second half of the 1920s. Yahyā **Haqqī**, himself a member of the group and also its chronicler, recalls in his *Fajr al-qissah al-misriyyah* (The Dawn of Egyptian Fiction, c. 1959/60) that the change in their understanding of what 'realism' in literature could mean was brought about essentially by their reading of Russian literature; whereas the French authors had appealed to their intellect, they found the Russians much closer to their hearts. Though Taymūr was staying in Europe when the Modern School started to run their review, *al-Fajr* (The Dawn), in 1925, he does not seem to have been cut off from the discussions going on in his home country; it is also known that he read Tolstoy in 1926. As is indicated not only by the founding of their new literary review (only two years after the granting to Egypt of a limited degree of independence) but also in the subtitle of *al-Fajr, sahīfat al-hadm wa'l-binā'* (The Paper of Demolition and Reconstruction), this group of writers believed that it was now definitely time to lay new and sound foundations for Egypt's future national culture. In addition to authenticity (through local color) and technical maturation, the turn to human universals qua psycholocial analysis was believed to guarantee a breakthrough to global standards of modernity.

However, in the year that Taymūr returned from Switzerland, *al-Fajr* was discontinued, and the group soon separated. The revolutionary vigor had soon cooled down and began to give way to a sometimes rather desperate mood. As *Rajab Afandī* as well as *al-Mahkūm 'alayhi bi'l-i'dām* (Death Sentence), the story included in the same collection (1928), show, Taymūr reacted to this situation with stories "dedicated totally to the dark sides of human existence"

(Brockelmann 221). At the same time, *Rajab Afandī* is the first in which he gives up the use of the vernacular for the dialogues—his tribute to the hope of winning recognition beyond a local reading public as well as the result of a consideration striving for aesthetic perfection: he now regarded two languages in one work as a contradiction that reduced the value of a piece of art (preface to *Rajab Efendī*). In matters of language, Taymūr began to become the purist for which he was later to become well known.

From this time on, the author's private life developed rather "smoothly" (Brugman), but with two major exceptions: the deaths of his father (1930) and son (1940). As an author, he gained more and more confidence in himself, evidenced by not only his turn to the more complex novel genre but also the fact that, in 1937, he brought out a collection of stories that contained exclusively revised versions of texts from his first three books, under the title *al-Wathbah al-ūlā* (The First Step), implying that in the meantime he had transcended this early stage and reached maturity. This was paralleled by the edition of collected articles and lectures on "The Beginnings and Development of Fiction" (*Nushū' al-qissah wa-tatawwuruhā*, 1936) and "Our Need for Art" (*Hājatunā ilā 'l-fann*, 1937), which suggest that the maturation process was accompanied by theoretical reflection. By the end of the 1930s Taymūr also seems to have gained the recognition which literary circles had denied him as a member of the Modern School, and must have felt he had become something of a celebrity; otherwise he would hardly have opened his 1939 collection, *Fir'awn al-saghīr* (Little Pharaoh), with an autobiographical essay entitled "The Sources Which Inspired My Writing" *(al-Masādir allatī alhamatnī al-kitābah)*. On the other hand, the achievement of a maturity in crafting the short story genre also meant, according to critics and literary historians, that in spite of uninterrupted production, rewriting (to improve style or plot), rearrangement and republishing, Taymūr from now on was not adding anything substantially new to the field. By and large, this may be true with regard to narrative technique and his fondness for certain modes such as the grotesque, the tragicomical,

the satirical, or the simple sketch, as well as perhaps with regard to the stories' personnel and setting, although a shift in preference from rural to urban may be observed in his later œuvre. Thus, whereas peasants or village sheikhs and imams had been the favorite subjects of the early collections, now urban characters such as government officials and employees, writers and actors or, from the lower social strata, craftsmen, artisans, shopkeepers, workers, caretakers, woman matchmakers, and also the marginalized—orphans, beggars, tramps, prostitutes—became more present from the 1930s onwards. Together with the psychological turn there is also a shift away from the exotist predilection for the queer and extreme (e.g., religious obsessions, insanity, strange cases of superstition) to more common, everyday problems and situations. There is, for example, the hard social reality seen through the eyes of a child whom his brutal foster-father forces to sell sweets in the streets (title story of *Nabbūt al-khafīr*, The Guardian's Stick, 1958); the mocking exposure of sensational journalism (*Najāh mi'ah bi'l-mi'ah*, A Hundred Percent Successful, in the same collection); the moving description of a woman beggar who has to decide whether she should sacrifice her honor or pass up an opportunity to provide for her child's living (*Umm Shahlūl*, Shahlūl's Mother, in *Thā'irūn*, The Rebels, 1955); or a biting satire on the hypocrisy and cringing of some lower officials (*Jā' al-shitā'*, Winter has come, *ibid.*).

Strangely enough, in his first full-length novel, *Nidā' al-majhūl* (1939; translated as *The Call of the Unknown*, 1964), Taymūr departs from the realism and Egyptianness of his previous fiction. The events take place in the Lebanese mountains and consist of a rather fantastic adventure, a "Gothic romance" which at the same time can be read as a "novel of spiritual quest" (de Moor, *Encyclopedia of Arabic Literature*), of "man's search for something more meaningful than the surface truths of social existence" (Jad 1983). The text was announced as the story of a girl who "loved truly and faithfully, but suffered disappointment from her Beloved, therefore left her country and made her imagination the place of her adventures, searching for an unknown (…) whom she could make her guide". This can serve as a metaphorical description of a widespread feeling among intellectuals on the eve of World War II, almost two decades after the uprising of 1919. Nationalist intellectuals had seen their former ideals being shattered by political, economical and social reality and were now suffering from desillusionment. Many of them turned to radical ideologies (socialism, communism, fascism, islamism—the longing for a guide, a leader, a 'Führer'!), while others, among them the Taymūr of *Nidā' al-majhūl*, tried to cope with the situation by resorting to the unfathomable, the mysterious, the mystical.

Obviously not satisfied with this kind of solution, he too fell prey later to 'stronger' ideas (though only for a moment). His pensiveness gave way to a sort of Darwinism that sought to retrieve at least *something* positive from the pre-war and war situation. In the essay "al-Tabī'ah al-qāhirah" (The Cruelty of Nature, in *'Itr wa-dukhān*, Perfume and Smoke, c. 1945), for instance, he holds that life is essentially a fight for survival and that this "law of nature" is always for the benefit of humanity "because it exterminates the weak who are of no use to the world"; accordingly, also wars are seen as "an appropriate means to remove unsuccessful civilizations, to absorb weak states".

Fortunately, Taymūr the writer soon outgrew Taymūr the 'philosopher', and his essentially humanist attitude vis-à-vis the struggling of his characters as well as his sense of realism and detail reclaimed the upper hand over implicit contempt of the weak and ideological platitude. An indication for this 'recovery' is his entering into what Nazīh al-Hakīm lists as a next stage after the sentimental, the analytical, the local color, and the novelistic approaches—drama. With the exception of *al-Infijār* (The Explosion), subtitled "A Theatrical Piece Intended for Reading" and published within a collection of short stories (*al-Hājj Shalabī*, 1930), Taymūr had not tried his hand at drama before the mid-1930s, and three pieces which he probably wrote in the second half of the decade. During the war years, however, he suddenly came out with no less than ten plays. Many of them were issued in two versions, one in the Egyptian colloquial (intended for the stage), and one in *fushā* (standard written Arabic, for reading). They are either comedies or social drama set in contemporary Egypt, or historical plays dealing mostly with more 'eternal' questions. While the early one-acters for the most part satirize "the weakness and pretensions of the upper classes" (Badawi 1987, 90)—*Hakamat al-mahkamah* (The Court Rules; early 1940s but published only in 1963) being an exception in that it deals with a case of baby murder in the countryside, two other plays of the first half of the 1940s clearly let the reader/spectator feel the pulse of the Second World War: *al-Makhba' raqm talattāshar* (Shelter No. 13, 1941) describes the emotions and reactions of some Egyptians of different social standing who become trapped in an air-raid shelter, while in *Qanābil* (Bombs, 1943)—"perhaps Taymur's greatest comedy," according to Badawi (98)—the author "delights both in revealing the hollowness of most people's pretexts, as well as in pointing out the gulf that exists in Egyptian society between town and country" (Landau 151), taking as his starting point a situation where the city lives in fear of bombardments during the war. Another play, quite similar in intent and pointing to a realist 'recovery,' is *Haflat shāy* (A Tea-Party, 1942, together with *al-Munqidhah*), "perhaps the best Arabic farce" (again Badawi), "a hilarious though scathing satire on the blind imitation of Western manners (Badawi, "Introduction", 6) and "the emptiness of French-inspired snobbery" (Landau 254). Unlike the characters in these plays who are all very lifelike and "seem copied *in toto* from everyday society in Egypt" (Landau 152), those of the other war-time productions—*'Arūs al-Nīl* (The Bride of the Nile), *Suhād* [heroine's name], *'Awālī* [heroine's name], *al-Munqidhah* (The Woman Saviour), and *Hawwā' al-khālidah* (Eternal Eve), all published 1942-45 and all set somewhere in the Arab or pharaonic past—appear quite artificial, and the themes seem either fairly romantic or rather studied (again 'philosopher-like'). They all center round female protagonists. The picture of woman as emerging from these texts is however a very traditional one; the author ascribes to the 'fair sex' certain unchanging, essentially 'feminine' features (as the title "Eternal Eve" already suggests), and it is another "law of nature" that woman can never be man's equal.

The dualism, just observed, of down-to-earth realism and pseudo-philosophical idealism and abstraction in search of 'universal truths' (where Taymūr is certainly not at his best) continues right into the author's post-war writings—and can be observed in the field of short story, novel and drama alike. Thus, on the one hand, the writer goes on to depict the various everyday problems, hopes and yearnings of his fellow-countrymen, studies both peasant and urban personalities as well as their social situations. As a result of the war-time experience, one can detect in many of these works a sharper edge or even a shift to socially committed literature (as de Moor (*Encyclopedia of Arabic Literature*) and Brugman (259) have it). In the novel *Kilyū-bātrah fī Khān al-Khalīlī* (Cleopatra in Khān al-Khalīlī, 1946), for instance, Taymūr sits in judgment on politicians and the world of international congresses, using satire in order to describe the seemingly inescapable temptation of power and the mechanisms of moral decay. *Salwā fī mahabb al-rīh* (Salwā in the Whirlwind, 1947), subtitled "an Egyptian story" and probably the author's best-known novel, is dedicated to the difficult circumstances now faced by the New Woman in the wake of the war. By now she had gained a high degree of self-consciousness and freedom, but that had only exacerbated her sense of privation as social conditions succeeded in preventing her from living the way she would like; as a result, she was blown to and fro by the "whirlwinds" of fate, personalized partly through the men on whom she had to set her hopes.

On the other hand, there is still a tendency to abstraction, intellectualization, and studied intervention, a feature that may perhaps originate in his early romantic idealism and/or be based on his notion of the writer as a thinker and authority of learning, but which sometimes interferes with or superimposes itself on his quest for realism. As Funk (94) has observed, Taymūr's short stories at this period usually lack specific temporal or spatial coordinates. Two

plays of the earlier post-war years are again set in the Arab past and thus show his inclination towards 'literary' subjects: *al-Yawm khamr* (Wine Today, 1949) retells the life of the pre-Islamic poet Imru' al-Qays and *Ibn Jalā* (Ibn Jalā, 1951) that of the famous Umayyad governor, al-Hajjāj b. Yūsuf (d. 714); both are meant to deal with universal human problems, for which the author thought a 'dignified' classical Arabic to be the most appropriate level of language.

The 'aristocratic' style which Taymūr also utilized, one that is "usually lucid, precise and economical," yet quite "*deliberately* made to sound suggestive of the Arabic of the classical age"; one that is therefore not entirely free of mannerisms and that Jad describes very aptly as that of a "philologist and classical Arabic revivalist" (Jad 1983, 124), this style, together with his services to Arabic literature as a pioneer of the short story, eventually earned Taymūr the First Story Prize of the Academy of the Arabic Language in 1947, followed two years later by membership of the same institution. In 1950 he was awarded the King Fu'ād Prize for Literature. Until then, the author had affirmed his aesthetic conservatism not only through his fiction and drama, but also in an account of his journey to the United States (*Abū 'l-Hawl yatīr*, The Flight of the Sphinx, 1947) as well as in a number of essays, collected in *Fann al-qasas* (The Art of Story-Telling, with an Introduction to the Case of the Arabic Language, 1945) and the above-mentioned *'Itr wa-dukhān* (Perfume and Smoke, c. 1945), subtitled *Khawātir wa-maqālāt fī 'l-adab wa'l-fann wa'l-masrah* (Reflections and articles on literature, art, and theater).

Despite Taymūr's 'aristocratic' origins, the Revolution of 1952, which sought to abolish the *ancien régime*, did no damage to his reputation. Although some hostile voices maintained that, "as an aristocrat, he knew nothing about the life of the common people or their feelings" (Paxton 1974, 177), he was awarded the first-class decoration for Distinguished Services in 1962 and in the following year the State Prize for Literature, clearly showing that, despite his earlier monarchist affiliations, he was acceptable to the new regime. Judging from his play *al-Muzayyafūn*

(The False Ones, 1953), written before 1952, he had already sensed the need for, and indeed been in favor of, political change. The novella/novel *Thā'irūn* (Rebellious Ones, 1955) may even be taken as evidence for the idea that, at least at that particular moment, the author had not managed to avoid the spell of revolutionary pathos and identified Nasser as that strong leader whose advent one of the protagonists had so longed for in the closing scene of *al-Muzayyafūn*. The novel retells the events of the last seven months before the Egyptian Revolution of July 23, 1952 through the lives of three young Egyptians who rebel against the prevailing pre-revolutionary conditions.

Yet it goes without saying that Taymūr never became a 'revolutionary.' It is true that in his later fiction he can slip into the role of under-privileged protagonists so convincingly that he manages to make even criminal acts of rebellion plausible. Furthermore, he obviously also felt no difficulty in harmonizing his own ideas concerning the role of literature in society with the concept of *littérature engagée* that became a postulate of the new times: in 1959 he published a collection of essays under the title *al-Adab al-hādif* (Committed Literature) in which he stressed that "the writer is a helper of mankind in the widest sense" and that "the products of his pen will soon lead society to new horizons and give them the confidence they need in order to fight the struggle for life successfully." Even so the writer who penned these words is clearly more a humanist nobleman than a proletarian socialist.

Taymūr continued to write until briefly before his death, but, as a work such as *Shumrūkh* (A Stalk of Dates, 1958; revised as *al-Dhahab al-aswad*, Black Gold, 1965) makes clear (it being a novel about the political and social implications of the discovery of oil in an imaginary "Oil-Land" *(Zaytistān)*), he always remained the observer, the analyst, the visionary warner, without ever becoming a rebellious activist. Since he was already in his sixties during the early years of the Egyptian Revolution, he may well have been too old for such a role in any case. Schoonover, who met him around 1957, describes him as "mild in speech,

courteous in manner, careful in attire, … in every way the gentleman and scholar the Taymūr family represents" (Schoonover 1986, 36). He clearly regarded himself more as a member of the Language Academy than a child of the Revolution. Of his twenty-odd books on Arabic language and literature, three-quaarters were written after he had been elevated to the Academy's olympus. Among these, *Mu'jam al-hadārah* (The Dictionary of [Modern] Civilization, 1961) deserves special attention. Taymūr here picks up the thread of his earlier work, *Mushki-lāt al-lughah al-'arabiyyah* (Problems of the Arabic Language, 1956), where he had already advocated the Arabization of loanwords from European languages. In the later work he tries to provide Arabic equivalents for a large number of terms. As a linguistic purist and authority, he also composed a children's story intended for class reading, *Qunfudhah wa-Amūrah wa-mā jarā lahumā fī 'l-junaynah al-mashūrah* (Qunfudhah and Amūrah and What Happened to Them in the Enchanted Garden, 1968?).

Mahmūd Taymūr died in 1973 in Lausanne/Switzerland where he had gone for medical treatment. His life and work have become the subject of numerous studies, some of them not a little hagiographic. Histories of modern Arabic literature remember him foremost as a pioneer of the modern Arabic short story, and the remainder of his vast output has not really been able to add to his fame. Other authors, Najīb Mahfūz in the field of the novel, Tawfīq al-Hakīm in that of drama, are considered the great pioneers. Among his plays, the non-historical, non-abstract, realist ones, especially the comedies and farces, are usually regarded as his best. The novels have had a rather ambiguous reception: some critics (e.g. Vial) hold that, as a master of the short story, he should not have turned to another genre at all, while others (e.g. Jad 1983,) mainly criticize his stylistic classicism as being inappropriate mannerisms in certain places. Still others (e.g. Husayn) point out that he often failed to write up to his own standards; in his own essays on literary theory, for example, he maintained that an author should not impose himself on his own characters, a feature that, according to Husayn, is not translated with sufficient consistency into his own narratives.

Throughout his life, Taymūr contributed to the literary life of his country, writing articles in various newspapers, reviews and journals, and touring Egypt and the Arab world giving public lectures on Arabic language and literature. He was highly sought-after as a participant in interviews and discussions, and also renowned also as a great patron and promoter of younger talents. Today, his short stories continue to be read as classics of modern Arabic literature, while the novels and plays are viewed more as documents of a distant past.

REFERENCES

M. M. Badawi, *Modern Arabic Drama in Egypt* (Cambridge: Cambridge University Press, 1987);

Carl Brockelmann, *Geschichte der arabischen Litteratur*, Dritter Supplementband (Leiden: Brill, 1942);

Jan Brugman, *An Introduction to the History of Modern Arabic Literature in Egypt* (Leiden: E. J. Brill, 1984);

Robert Campbell (ed.), *A'lām al-adab al-'arabī al-mu'āsir: siyar, wa-siyar dhātiyyah* (Beirut: Orient-Institut & Wiesbaden: Steiner, 1996);

Ed. C. M. de Moor, "Mahmūd Taymūr," in: *Encyclopedia of Arabic Literature*, ed. Julie S. Meisami and Paul Starkey, 2 vols. (London: Routledge, 1998), II, 761-762;

——, *Un Oiseau en cage: Le discours littéraire de Muhammad Taymūr (1892–1921)* (Amsterdam & Atlanta/GA: Rodopi, 1991);

Ladislav Drozdík, "La conception linguistique de Mahmūd Taimūr," in: *Studia semitica philologica necnon philosophica Ioanni Bakoš dicata*, ed. Stanislaus Segert (Bratislava: Vydavatel'stvo Slovenskej Akadémie Vied, 1965), 111-8;

Harald Funk, "Zu einigen neueren Erzählungssammlungen Mahmūd Taymūrs," *Mitteilungen des Instituts für Orientforschung* 15 (1969): 86-98;

Eugenia Gálvez Vázquez, *El Cairo de Mahmūd Taymūr: personajes literarios* (Sevilla: Univ., 1974);

Sabry Hafez, *The Genesis of Arabic Narrative Discourse: A study in the Sociology of Modern Arabic Literature* (London: Saqi Books, 1993);

Nazīh al-Hakīm, *Mahmūd Taymūr, rā'id al-qissah al-'arabiyyah: Dirāsah tahlīliyyah* (Cairo: Matba'at al-Nīl, 1944);

Yahyā Haqqī, *Fajr al-qissah al-misriyyah* (Cairo: Dār al-Qalam, c. 1960);

Hamdī Husayn, *al-Shakhsiyyah al-riwā'iyyah 'inda Mahmūd Taymūr: bayn al-nazariyyah wa'l-tatbīq* (Cairo: Dār al-Thaqāfah, 1988);

Fathī al-Ibyārī, *'Ālam Taymūr al-qasasī: dirāsah fī fann al-qissah wa'l-riwāyah 'inda shaykh al-qissah al-'arabiyyah Mahmūd Taymūr* (Cairo: al-Hay'ah al-Misriyyah al-'Āmmah li'l-Kitāb, 1976);

Ali B. Jad, *Form and Technique in the Egyptian Novel, 1912–1971* (London: Ithaca, 1983);

Biyār Khabbāz, *Mahmūd Taymūr wa-'ālam al-riwāyah fī Misr: dirāsah nafsiyyah tahlīliyyah* (Beirut: Dār al-Mashriq, 1994. [PhD thesis al-Jāmi'ah al-Lubnāniyyah, 1992]);

Hilary Kilpatrick, "The Egyptian Novel from *Zaynab* to 1980", in: *Modern Arabic Literature*, ed. M. M. Badawi (Cambridge: Cambridge University Press, 1992), 223-69;

Ignatiĭ Ĭulyanovich Krachkovskiĭ, *Nad arabskimi rukopisĭami* (Moscow, 1948); translated as *Among Arabic Manuscripts: Memories of Libraries and Men* by Tatiana Minorsky (Leiden: E. J. Brill, 1953);

Jacob Landau, *Studies in Arab Theater and Cinema* (Philadelphia: University of Pennsylvania Press, 1958);

Arpag Mekhitarian, "Tawfīq al-Hakīm et Mahmoud Taymour face aux problèmes de l'arabe parlé," *Acta Orientalia Belgica* (31.5.1963/1.-2.6.1964) = *Correspondance d'Orient* 10 (1966): 137-54;

Evelyn Paxton, "Taha Husain and Mahmud Taimur: An Appreciation," *Asian Affairs* 61 (1974): 176-8;

Mattityahu Peled, "Reading Two Versions of a Story by Mahmūd Taymūr: A Study in the Rhetoric of Fiction," *Israel Oriental Studies* 7 (1977): 309-30;

Issa Peters, *Mahmūd Taymūr and the Modern Egyptian Short Story* (Unpublished Ph.D. thesis, Columbia University, 1974);

Kermit Schoonover, "Contemporary Egyptian Authors, III: Mahmūd Taymūr and the Arabic Short Story," *Muslim World* 47 (1957): 36-45;

Charles Vial, "Mahmūd Taymūr," in: *The Encyclopedia of Islam*, new ed., vol. VI (Leiden: E. J. Brill, 1986);

Rotraud Wielandt, *Das erzählerische Frühwerk Mahmūd Taymūrs: ein Beitrag zu einem Archiv der modernen arabischen Literatur* (Beirut: [s.n.]; Wiesbaden: Komm. Franz Steiner, 1983);

Lūsī Ya'qūb, *al-Usrah al-Taymūriyyah wa 'l-adab al-'arabī* (Cairo: Maktabat al-Ādāb, 1993).

'Ā'ishah al-Taymūriyyah

('Ā'ishah 'Ismat bint Ismā'īl Taymūr)

(1840 – 1902)

MARILYN BOOTH

University of Edinburgh

WORKS

[*Hilyat al-tirāz*] ("Embroidery Decoration", Cairo: al-Matba'ah al-'Āmirah al-Sharafiyah, 1303 [1885/86]); 1327 [1909/10]; full title: *al-Dīwān al-muhyī rifāt al-adab, albāligh min funūn al-balāghah ghāyat al-arab, al-muhtawī min husn al-barā'ah 'alā mā bihi imtāz, al-musammā tibqan li-ma'nāhu bi-Hilyat al-tirāz*;

Natā'ij al-ahwāl fī 'l-aqwāl wa 'l-af'āl ("Results of Circumstances in Statements and Deeds"), Cairo: Matba'at Muhammad Efendī Mustafā, 1305 [1887/88]);

"Lā tuslah al-'ā'ilāt illā bi-tarbiyat al-banāt" (Family reform comes only through the education of girls), originally published as "'Asr al-ma'ārif", *al-Adāb* 9 (Jumādā II 1306 [10 Feb. 1889]), repr. in: Zaynab Fawwāz al-'Āmilī, *al-Durr al-manthūr fī tabaqāt rabbāt al-khudūr* ("Scattered Pearls Concerning the Classes of Cloistered Women", Cairo/Būlāq: al-Matba'ah al-Kubrā al-Amīriyyah, 1312 [1894]), 306-8;

Mir'āt al-ta'ammul fī 'l-umūr ("Mirror of Contemplation on Matters", Cairo: Matba'at al-Nīl, 1310 [1892/93]; Alexandria: Matba'at al-Mahrūsah, 1310 [1892/93]);

Üşküfe or *Şüküfe* (Istanbul, n.p., n.d.); Turkish *dīwān*; contemporary sources say that it was "in publication" in the 1890s.

Later Editions

Hilyat al-tirāz: Dīwān 'Ā'ishah al-Taymūriyyah, ma'a al-qasā'id allatī lam yusbaq nashruhā ("Embroidery Decoration"), ed. Lajnat Nashr al-Mu'allafāt al-Taymūriyyah (Cairo: Matba'at Dār al-Kātib al-'Arabī, 1952);

Mir'āt al-ta'ammul fī 'l-umūr ("Mirror of Contemplation into Matters"), ed. Mirvāt Hātim (Cairo: Multaqā al-Mar'ah wa'l-Dhākirah, 2002).

Works in Translation

"Family reform comes only through the education of girls," translated by Marilyn Booth, in: *Opening the Gates: A Century of Arab Feminist Writing*, ed. Margot Badran and Miriam Cooke (London: Virago, 1990; Bloomington and Indianapolis: Indiana University Press, 1990), 129-33;

"Introduction to *The Results of Circumstances in Words and Deeds*," translated by Marilyn Booth, in: *Opening the Gates: A Century of Arab Feminist Writing*, ed. Margot Badran and Miriam Cooke (London: Virago, 1990; Bloomington and Indianapolis: Indiana University Press, 1990), 126-28.

ʿĀ'ishah Taymūr is one of the earliest Arab women of the modern era to have been published in her lifetime as well as recognized before her death as a notable poet and prose writer. Composing poetry in Persian and Turkish as well as Arabic—and strophic colloquial Arabic poetry as well as the monorhyme *qasīdah* of Arabic poetic tradition—she also wrote and published allegorical fiction and nonfictional essays addressing gender politics at the inception of discourse on gender and nation in Arab and Muslim-majority societies. Celebrated in her lifetime as a paragon of the educated woman, she has been claimed since her death for varying agendas, first an Arab feminist perspective and now a scholarly-political agenda that privileges Islamic identity in early modern women's discourse, though in the case of Taymūr this means emphasizing certain works and contacts over others. Her name is justly in the forefront as scholars recognize women's precedence in the emergence of Arabic gender-conscious discourse in the nineteenth century before the more famous contributions of Qāsim Amīn (1865-1908) and other turn-of-the-century male intellectuals.

Because she used the descriptive term *(nisbah)* al-Taymūriyyah ("the female Taymūr") to refer to herself—for example, characters in her allegorical tale consistently make reference to "al-Taymūriyyah's proverb-verse" on a given theme—I use it here.

ʿĀ'ishah Taymūr is noteworthy and unusual for having left a rich commentary on her own life, in passages throughout her prose and poetry. Yet, students of her legacy have tended to take al-Taymūriyyah's self-writing as simply transparent autobiographical commentary, although these passages are perhaps better seen as literary elements within her overall artistry, weaving constructions of female experience into the tapestry. Such passages offer an ambiguous, complex commentary on markers of identity—female, Muslim, Egyptian, elite—within the tumultuous political and nationalist-discursive context of late-nineteenth-century Egyptian and Ottoman public life.

Born into an illustrious intellectual family with close ties to Egypt's ruling family and high positions in the Turco-Egyptian bureaucracy, al-Taymūriyyah was elder sister of the renowned bibliophile and writer-compiler on linguistic subjects, Ahmad Taymūr (1871-1930). At his birth (just over one year before their father's death), and a few years later when he took his first steps in reading, she composed occasional poems, and she took her fatherless brother's earliest education in hand, for she was 31 years the elder. Two of Ahmad's three sons were renowned writers, Muhammad (1892-1921) and Mahmūd (1894-1973) **Taymūr**; in an essay written for the fiftieth commemoration of al-Taymūriyyah's death, her nephew Mahmūd remembered his aunt's poems as part of his earliest literary education.

The Taymūr family had Kurdish roots; Muhammad Taymūr Kāshif (d. 1264 [1847/48]) had left the Ottoman province of Mosul after quarreling with his brother, joined the Ottoman army, and came to Egypt with Muhammad ʿAlī (reg. 1805-48). In 1230 (1814/15), he built the family home in which al-Taymūriyyah was born, on Darb Saʿādah in Cairo's Darb al-Ahmar district. Favored by Muhammad ʿAlī and involved in his schemes, Taymūr was granted substantial land holdings in the area of al-Kushūfiyyah, source of the appellation "Kāshif". Late in life, he apparently had a warm relationship with Muhammad ʿAlī's son Ibrāhīm (reg. 1848), and this close link continued through the next two generations. Taymūr Kāshif was married to ʿĀ'ishah al-Siddīqiyyah, daughter of ʿAbd al-Rahmān Efendī al-Islāmbūlī, a senior bureaucrat in the court of Ottoman sultan Selim III (reg. 1789-1807). Al-Taymūriyyah would be married into this Turkish family from the Ottoman capital, who had moved to Egypt in 1224 (1809/10) as a result of the sultan's death and accession of his rival, Mahmūd II (reg. 1808-39).

ʿĀ'ishah's father, Ismāʿīl Taymūr Pasha (1230/1815-1289/1872), a career bureaucrat, was drawn to intellectual pursuits, is said to have known six languages, and for a time headed the "foreign section" of the Khedivial Dīwān. His son recalled him as a reluctant government servant, "gentle and modest but fierce when necessary," who preferred the solitude of his farm and his books.

Taymūr's mother, like so many women throughout world history, is not survived by her name or by birth or death dates. Known to us only as "the Circassian," she is presumed to have been Ismāʿīl's *jāriyah* (slave/concubine) initially, but as was often the practice, was freed (*maʿtūqah,* as al-Taymūriyyah's contemporary and acquaintance Zaynab **Fawwāz** [c. 1850-1914] refers to her). Through al-Taymūriyyah's writing, she appears as an assertive and accomplished mistress of the household. Her daughter wrote an elegy for her, but her more famous appearance comes in the preface to the allegorical tale *Natāʾij al-ahwāl fī 'l-aqwāl wa'l-afʿāl* (Results of Circumstances in Statements and Deeds), which opens with recollections of the author's childhood. The passage has been quoted or paraphrased in virtually every evocation of this figure's life ever since. The plot of this evoked childhood is the parental negotiation over defining young 'Ā'ishah's upbringing; the mother tries to yoke her training to the conventional elite female pursuits of needlework while *she* attempts to "escape" into her father's gatherings of other intellectual men, to listen in on their discussions. Her father, famously, instructs her mother to train their other daughter in the womanly arts, while he takes responsibility for 'Ā'ishah's bookishness, hiring tutors to coach her in memorizing the Qurʾān, learning calligraphy, studying the basics of Islamic jurisprudence, Arabic grammar, Turkish, and Persian. (They had another sister, Munīrah, who—unlike 'Affat, subject of one of al-Taymūriyyah's elegies—survived her.)

Another autobiographical evocation goes into more detail; this one is available to readers of Arabic due to Mayy Ziyādah's careful culling (and acknowledgement) of sources in her study of al-Taymūriyyah (see below, p. 375). Translated into Arabic for Ziyādah by Muhibb al-Dīn al-Khatīb, this longer recollection appeared in al-Taymūriyyah's Turkish *dīwān,* in publication approximately five years after *Natāʾij* appeared.

I habitually went out to our reception hall to linger near whichever writers were there and listen to the melodious tones of their voices. But this act of mine wounded my mother—God settle her in the gardens of Paradise. She would con-

front me with severity, intimidation, warnings, and threats, diverging sometimes to pleasant promises and awakening my desires for pretty ornaments and clothes. My father, God's mercy upon him, said: "Beware of breaking this little girl's heart and sullying its purity with harshness. As long as our daughter has a natural inclination for inkwells and paper, do not stand in the way of her preferences and desires. Come, let us divide our daughters: take 'Affat and give me 'Ismat. And if 'Ismat emerges a writer and poet, that will bring mercy upon me after my death."

The writer mentions the tutors her father engaged, for this was before the founding of schools for girls in Egypt, and in any case, in an elite family such as this, home tutoring—if any—was the norm for girls (and still for many boys). She recalls his own teaching—and parenting:

my father did not give me permission to go into the sessions of men. He himself undertook to teach me the books of Persian eloquence, such as Firdawsī's Shāhnāmeh *and the Noble* Mathnavī; *he set aside two hours every evening when I would read to him.*

She began to read and compose poetry "in the easy meters" during this period, and she relates the affecting story of reciting her first couplet—in Persian—to her father, noting that she felt

very shy and cautious, because whenever my father saw a book of poetry in my hands he would say to me, "If you read a lot of ghazal [love] *poetry, that will cause all your lessons to go out of your head."*

Yet, with her evident interest in poetry, he promised her lessons in the poetic meters from a female teacher. "But," comments the memoirist, "after a long wait, no sooner did the coming year begin than I was bound by the tie of marriage."

If the Arabic text closely translates the Turkish, it is worth noting al-Taymūriyyah's characterization of marriage. Drawing on a conventional trope of marriage as a "tie" while emphasizing the binding, restricting connotation of that metaphor, this brief reference stands out as the sole first-person reference to her marriage in the entire corpus, a silence all the more telling as she is so relatively forthcoming about other events in her life. (In the Arabic *dīwān*, at least, there is no elegy for her husband; while elegies do appear for both parents, one sister, and her daughter, as well as an intricately metaphoric, moving remembrance of one Shaykh Ibrāhīm al-Saqqā.) Her father betrothed her to Muhammad Tawfīq Beǧ Zādāh, son of Mahmūd Bek al-Islāmbūlī b. 'Abdallāh (d. 1292/1875). Her betrothed followed the family occupational pattern, as a senior bureaucrat; according to al-Taymūriyyah's grandson, Ahmad Kamāl Zādāh, he was a senior figure in the state treasury. They were married in 1271 (1854/55); 'Ā'ishah was fifteen. And at that, says her contemporary and first biographer Zaynab **Fawwāz**,

she stopped reading and composing poetry, and turned to managing the household ... especially when God rewarded her with sons and daughters.

Her brother and her grandson also refer to "boys and girls" and "her children," but these are stock phrases, perhaps not to be taken literally; she may have had only two children who survived beyond early childhood (though Fawwāz refers to "children" in the plural as among those who tried to convince Taymūr later to emerge from her mourning after the death of her eldest child).

The first child, Tawhīdah, was probably born no later than 1276 (1859/60) and likely earlier. Taymūr's elegy for Tawhīdah is dated 1294 (1877); she is said by most sources to have died aged eighteen, although Taymūr's grandson gives "twelve." Dating back from the elegy and presuming eighteen Hijrī (lunar) years, 1276 would be the latest birth date possible. But it is possible that Taymūr did not compose this elegy immediately, as she was in deep mourning. The preface to the Turkish *dīwān* suggests Tawhīdah was born only a year or two after the marriage, as it also evokes her as an emblem of harmonious balance between the "feminine" pursuits that little 'Ā'ishah had rejected—and that she had at first been compelled to practice—and the intellectual pursuits she loved. Her daughter, presumably, was forced into neither area, and thus enjoyed both.

After ten years [of marriage, presumably] *the first of my heart's fruits, Tawhīdah ... reached age nine, and I enjoyed seeing her spend ... from morning to noon among inkwells and pens, and work ... until evening with her needle, crafting wondrous things. I prayed that God would grant her success, sensing my own sorrow about what had slipped from my grasp at her age, my aversion to the likes of this work. When my daughter reached the age of twelve, she was determined to serve her mother and father, and moreover assumed management of the household and servants .... I was able to withdraw to the niches of repose.*

With Tawhīdah running the household, and—by 1875—with her father and husband dead, Taymūr—who now, as Fawwāz put it bluntly, "had charge of herself"—decided to return to poetry. She engaged two female tutors to teach her advanced Arabic grammar and the science of poetic meter, Fātimah al-Azhariyyah and the entrancingly named Sittītah al-Tablāwiyyah. To judge from the Turkish preface she may have begun to lead a more contemplative and intellectual life before her husband's death, but only as a widow did she engage tutors and resume sustained study. Thus, her writing life saw a 21-year hiatus (from 1854 to 1875), or so it appears. There is much that we do not know about her life: biographers' focus on al-Taymūriyyah's childhood, and their silence on her adulthood, is most likely a product of her own silence.

It was after this second period of study, said Fawwāz, that al-Taymūriyyah began to compose "long odes." It is not clear whether some of her most moving poems—such as her elegy for her father—were written after this date or closer to events that inspired them, thus before she resumed formal training in the *ars poetica*.

But the interruptions were not at an end. Taymūr's attempt to pick up her intellectual pursuits was tragically suspended by Tawhīdah's death. Like many a poet before her, Taymūr articulated this tragedy in a poem memorializing her daughter. Among her most moving poems, and generally regarded as one of or perhaps the finest of her odes, this elegy is characteristic for its poetic genre in evoking the autobiographical while constructing of it a universal *cri de cœur*. The poem transcends conventional tropes, and voices a final "conversation" between mother and daughter that echoes long after the death of both. The witness of contemporaries and of Taymūr herself tells us that she was plunged into seven years of mourning. In fact, al-Taymūriyyah wept so long and so hard for her daughter that the *ramad*, the eye disease she was afflicted by, is said to have been caused by her crying. Yet this hardship, too, produced some of her most arresting poetry. The "*ramad* odes" are signaled in her *dīwān* by explanatory glosses that they were composed "during" or "after" or "in a relapse of" the disease.

The presence of Taymūr's son, Maḥmūd Bek Tawfīq (d. 1332/1914), later a judge, was a motive for her to emerge from her long and intense mourning. Maḥmūd apparently was instrumental in collecting and publishing her poetry and other works; in the Turkish *dīwān* preface, she recalls telling him that although she had burned much of her earlier poetry after his sister's death—in penance, she suggests, for her turn to the pen—he could have what remained: "if you find it worthy to be printed, publish it."

It was her Arabic poetry that came out first, in what is probably the earliest book by a female author to be published in Egypt (and it is also worth noting that there was more than one printing, before World War I, of her poetry and her allegorical tale). Sparse dates of composition in the *dīwān* span 1288-1296 (1871 or 1872 to 1881), suggesting that she started again to compose poetry before her husband's death. Many of the undated poems may well have been composed 1881-1885 (at the end of the *dīwān*, it is said printing was completed in early Rabīʿ II, corresponding to January 1886).

The 1952 *dīwān* produced by the Committee to Publish Taymūr [Family] Writings—on the occasion of the fiftieth year following al-Taymūriyyah's death—includes previously unpublished poems found among Aḥmad Taymūr's papers; most, said chairman Khalīl Thābit, were in her handwriting. Those dated were composed 1305-1308 AH (1887/88-1890/91), and it seems likely that almost all are poems composed after *Ḥilyat al-ṭirāz* (Embroidery Decoration) had appeared. A fuller redaction—if these manu-

scripts are extant—awaits future scholars. So does assessment of principles that might have guided the original *dīwān*'s organization—for the 1952 *dīwān* also reorganizes Taymūr's poetic corpus.

It is unfortunate that this edition moves one of her most famous poems, "Bi-yad al-ʿifāf," from its position as first poem in the original *dīwān* to number 207, buried in a section of *akhlāqī* (moral commentary) verse. This poem builds on the poet's self-introduction in her preface, as modest and (conventionally) seeking readers' indulgence, but simultaneously as carrying on a long legacy of Arab women's poetic declamations. Taymūr deploys notations of invisibility and modesty standard among the (few published) female poets and prose writers of her time; it can be argued, though, that these gestures serve to *highlight* limitations placed on women and the "ruses" women employ to subvert them, thus subverting also the timeworn linkage of "female" and *kayd* (trickery) by showing *kayd* to be a literary survival skill and social necessity. And modesty is invoked with great pride and ringing force; the narrator is subject rather than object of discourse or target of social "protection"—for it is *she* who "guards," who maintains her feminine status through seclusion or covering (*ḥijāb*) rather than being "the well-protected," epithet of the respectable woman at the time (*al-masūnah*). She uses another term of epithetic resonance, *ʿismah*, which not only echoes one of her given names but refers to a constellation of values: chastity, virtuousness, self-guarding, moral impeccability.

With virtuous purity's hand I guard the glory of
 my hijāb
And by my faultless self-guarding I rise above
 my peers
With radiant thought and piercing talent
Have I perfected my literary skills

The trope of modesty yields less-than-modest aims and signals anything but invisibility! Taymūr appears to answer—at the start of her *dīwān*, her earliest published work—potential critics, perhaps especially women, to whom she refers dismissively in another poem as concerned with the form over the content of *tahdhīb* (education as refinement). She beautifully addresses this shortsighted attitude by referring to her "perfecting" or "completing" of *ādāb*—literary skills but equally translatable as "refinement," education in the broadest sense, literary, moral, and social; that this rhymes with *atrābī,* "my peers," makes the implicit attack, the distancing of her own trajectory from that of most of her acquaintance, all the more pointed and forceful. Having dealt with those of her era, she then turns for sustenance to her female forbears, her chosen lineage, as she did in her preface:

I composed poetry of the character of an assemblage
Before me, women of secluded rooms and high regard

Yoking seclusion and "high regard" suggests that one does not preclude the other, in her life or, as attested by their fame, in the poetic careers of earlier women. Yet, Taymūr denies the linkage between poetry and life—or does she?

I uttered it only as the jesting of a speaker
Passionate for the eloquence of logic and books

She plays coyly with the notion of "passion" here, gesturing to the thematic genre of *ghazal* with the verb *hawā*—to love passionately—and yet her "love" is directed at rhetoric, eloquence, logic, the mind. And in this she has impeccable antecedents; she echoes her preface in alluding to the poets 'Aliyyah bint al-Mahdī (160/776-210/825) and Laylā al-Akhyaliyyah (d. 85/704):

al-Mahdī's daughter and Laylā are my models
And with my innate intelligence I rendered my concluding words.

Fasl al-khitāb ("concluding words"; also the end of a formal greeting in a letter) connotes both finality and judgment; *khitāb* also suggests public communication: it is "oratory" as well as a letter or message. With a reference to God-given poetic talent, the poet then takes up the feminine poetic conceit, found widely in writings of that time, of writing as adornment, but more importantly as self-reflection; it is writing rather than external adornment that captures her time and attention:

The brow of my notebooks I made my mirror

And of the etching of ink I made my dyestuff

The poet goes on to draw on the tropes of protective amulets, of female solitude and the veil *(khimār)*, not as deterrents to writing but as productive of it. And the poem itself enacts a different register of visibility.

Although it has been often supposed that *Natā'ij al-ahwāl* appeared first in 1888, the earlier publication of the *dīwān* explains why unpublished poems dated 1305 (1887/88) and later were found among her brother's papers, and it also explains why Fawwāz suggests that the publication of the Arabic *dīwān* convinced Taymūr that "she was able to write." It had, says Fawwāz, "great impact on sensibilities and was received especially well by the literati." Thus, al-Taymūriyyah embarked on her first prose work. As noted, *Results of Circumstances* is most famous for its widely quoted preface; the rest of the book is hardly mentioned. With a rhetorical yawn, Ziyādah summarizes it for the reader, noting that she is "fatigued" by the effort. Yet the tale, with her preface, interests: if it is a "traditionally" set story, about kings and princes and quests, it is also set within its late-nineteenth-century publication context in that it is a narrative about the uses and benefits of education. Through his own trials and embedded tales to which he listens, the young prince Mamdūh is guided to right practice, a sense of responsibility toward himself, his family, and his future subjects. In its subject focus, the tale does not diverge markedly from al-Taymūriyyah's poetry in praise of the royal family: but it does put in the foreground the importance of education and responsibility. It highlights the author's own presence, steadily offering lines of her poetry to encapsulate messages the embedded stories also convey.

As and before she wrote and published, Taymūr had a social presence beyond her household. She maintained her family's close relationship to the Muhammad 'Alī dynasty. Qadriyyah Husayn, daughter of sultan Husayn Kāmil (reg. 1914-17), recalled that

often this fine poet came to 'Ābidīn Palace to visit my grandmother ... who had all respect and admiration for "Sayyidah 'Ā'ishah".

The reference in fact may be to Qadriyyah's great-grandmother, for in *Results of Circumstances* we learn in an authorial digression that Taymūr occasionally served as Persian interpreter for her. Late in the tale, the Persian shah's daughter is returned to her father's household in somewhat incredible circumstances and onlookers utter a long exclamation. "The Persians say this when struck with sudden fright," explains the text:

Her Excellency, Treasure of Pearls, mother of His Highness, Ismā'īl Pasha the former Khedive—God grant her His mercy and His vastest paradise—would call me to the exalted palace to translate upon the arrival of the relatives of the kings of the Persians, and I would hear this expression from the women's mouths… I would remain with them as long as they stayed, conversing with them and asking about their customs and moral beliefs.

It is not known how often al-Taymūriyyah performed this service. And, rather than any move into a putative "public sphere," such a role was in line with the circumspect, private, and interconnected lives of Cairo's female elite.

Al-Taymūriyyah wrote numerous poems in praise and flattery of Egypt's rulers and consorts, and commemorated royal births. In this, she was a product of her time and her class; like many others who published such paeons in the press—at least one of al-Taymūriyyah's appeared in the nationalist and pro-Khedive daily *al-Mu'ayyad*—these poems invoke Misr, but hardly in terms of a sense of national belonging, as al-Taymūriyyah's poems have recently been suggested to do; and "Misr" hovers between the larger geographical entity "Egypt" and the localized scene in Cairo. Her poem commemorating Tawfīq II's return to Egypt after the 'Urābī revolt (1881-82)—the only text that can be considered overt political commentary—is aligned fully in sympathy with the ruling family. In this poem as in others, al-Taymūriyyah articulates a traditional concept of the relationship between the ruler and the ruled, as one based on paternalistic concern without space for the voices of the ruled. No nationalistic celebration, this.

Beyond the palace, Taymūr corresponded with, perhaps met, and knew something of the writings of, other female intellectuals. She participated in a conventional circulation of works and compliments among the era's small elite, but like these other writing women, she highlighted women's intellectual and artistic output. Thus, she wrote poems celebrating the publication of other women's books and magazines. Within her texts, she linked her own writing to that of others. But rather than a specifically "Islamic" sense of identity, as has been argued, if this suggests a sense of community at all it seems to be one of shared endeavor and linguistic medium as well as gender and place. As she mentions earlier Arab Muslim poets, in her preface to the *dīwān*, she follows them with the name of an Arab Christian contemporary, Wardah al-Yāzijī (1838-1924). The encomia she wrote to other women's achievements celebrated those of a (Shi'i Lebanese) Muslim—Zaynab Fawwāz—and the poetry and women's journal, respectively, of two women of Syrian and Christian origin, Wardah al-Yāzijī and Hind Nawfal. It is clear from their exchange of letters and poems that Taymūr knew al-Yāzijī's *dīwān Hadīqat al-ward* (Rose Garden, 1867, 1886). Likewise, al-Taymūriyyah's books were announced and praised in journals run by Egyptians and Syrians, Muslims and Christians. Networks of intellectuals, the agendas and issues their work addressed, and their venues of publication, accommodated more complexity than does recent scholarly dichotomizing.

Yet, there is no doubt that Taymūr spoke from her own experience as a Muslim woman (who according to her brother was very devout and dedicated to daily rituals of Muslim practice). She did so forthrightly and richly, with a productive ambiguity or tension, suggesting the conventions of upper-class Muslim practice to be simultaneously protective, supportive and comforting, and yet confining; and suggesting a continuum of relationship between daily practice and religious requirement. At the same time, analysis of the imagery of female seclusion or separation in her poetry must recognize that her fund of images drew on a shared rhetoric of "adornment," "modesty," and gender segregation. Recent attempts to dichotomize "Islamic"

versus "secular" approaches to female experience and aesthetic presence alike are obliged to
ignore the ambiguities and richness of actual
texts; for example, one cannot merely highlight
prefatory allusions to the divine nature of
writerly talent as signaling an Islamic outlook.
Conventional rhetoric, this was equally posed by
writers of Christian origin.

Similarly, in her essayistic prose, al-Taymūriyyah draws on the notion of "Eastern societies" as did Christian Arab writers of the era.
This is the context in which her 1889 essay
"'Asr al-ma'ārif' (The Age of Knowledge)
makes its appeal, in the newspaper 'Alī Yūsuf
published before he founded his better-known
daily al-Mu'ayyad. This and the longer Mir'āt
al-ta'ammul fī 'l-umūr (Mirror of Contemplation
on Matters), published as a 16-page booklet,
must be regarded as among the earliest texts in
the gender debates that suffused the Arab/ic
public sphere of the late nineteenth century. The
latter probably came out in early 1893 rather
than 1892, as has been supposed; it is announced
in the newspaper al-Nīl (whose printing press
published it) and in al-Mu'ayyad in March 1893,
and in 'Abdallāh Nadīm's al-Ustādh in April.

In both "The Age of Knowledge" and Mir'āt
al-ta'ammul fī 'l-umūr, as in her poetry, al-Taymūriyyah draws on the imagery of seclusion as
she makes the conventional plea that readers will
excuse limitations of her writing. Like Zaynab
Fawwāz in her preface to her biographical dictionary, Taymur gestures to the specifically
gendered nature of (class-specific) experience
that underlies women's rhetorical presence in
the public sphere at this early moment for modern Arab women's public, written expression.
She emphasizes social pressures hampering
women's ability to acquire and then to exhibit
and use formal learning; the content of her essays, thus, echoes the autobiographical testimony found in the prefaces to Results of Circumstances and the dīwān. The autobiographical
passages become significant not only as self-
writing but as public testimony of the political
nature of domestic behavior, the ways that parental expectations and the "bonds" of marriage
act to suppress girls' and women's powers of
self-articulation and intellectual participation.

Both texts proceed from the grounds of Divine
omnipotence to make an argument for gender
equivalence. "The Age of Knowledge" argues
that the existence of two genders is evidence of
God's plan for humanity, wherein each needs
the other and thus has obligations toward the
other. Mirror of Contemplation grounds a discussion of the state of marriage in Egypt in
Qur'ān exegesis; exercising her right as a well-
informed believer to practice ijtihād, or independent inquiry into the meanings of the sacred
sources of Islamic law, the author explicates the
principle of men's authority over women as
based on a system of reciprocal rights and duties; when men cede their duty to support the
family, instead pursuing marriages based on
material interest, they also cede their rights to
authority over the family. Interweaving text
interpretation and social commentary, this powerful text sets a discussion of family law within
the context of changing social relations and the
vectors of class; as in her poetry of mujāmalah
(encomia), al-Taymūriyyah's own class posi-
tioning is evident here as she bemoans the vulnerability of the elite household to servants who
lure their dissatisfied mistresses from the home,
now that the end of slavery (abolished in 1877)
has meant the disappearance of jawārī (slave-
girls) from household service. Slaves' depend-
ence on the household, argues al-Taymūriyyah,
made them fearful of disobedience or spilling
family secrets. At the heart of her critique,
though, lie new values of consumption and
notions of entertainment among both men and
women, which have upset the putatively ideal
balances of (elite) family life to which al-Taymūriyyah nostalgically looks back.

Like many writers of her time—of Muslim
and of Christian origins, and of complex origins
within those two rather unsatisfactory identity
rubrics—al-Taymūriyyah criticizes zakhrafah
(excessive adornment) and the rise of consumer-
ist attitudes linked to infatuation with European
products and ways. The very titles of her works,
as well as the narrative progression of each (both
essays and allegorical tale), signal her central
preoccupation with notions of social responsibility: the young are not taught to think about "the
results of circumstances and the outcomes of

matters." Rather, they bask in presentist arrogance, living for the day and for its transitory adornments. In both essays, she puts preponderant blame on the educated men of her society, and she speaks from a collective female position. It is possible to gloss this as a "Muslim" identity, for al-Taymūriyyah defines that collective as "we, society of the secluded." Yet, if *Mirror of Contemplation* does find its logic in a specifically Qurʾān-centered investigation, the concerns voiced in "The Age of Knowledge" are not specific to Islamic practice but rather focus on women's practical knowledge of child raising, while the larger, social collective that she invokes at the start is "the East." She has recourse to a comparison with "the western state" in the matter of acknowledging the presence and benefit of knowledge among women; like other writers of her time, she puts this in the context of marriage relations:

It may be that the man finds a certain matter intricate or tangled, and it bewilders him; his wife draws him close gently with her delicate fingers and extinguishes a searing ember, soothes anguish with her painstaking ministrations. Even so, he works mightily to conceal her merit among society's individuals and is on his guard against announcing her worth, fearing lest it be said that she is a woman of knowledge.

Yet families are "infatuated" with their daughters' external adornments, rather than with "the rubies of knowledge." Taymūr dismisses the argument—found throughout the Arabic periodical press of the time—that teaching girls to read will lead to "passionate flirtation… and exchanges with others" as "a pretext flimsier than a spider's web"; and she warns "men of our lands, you who control our affairs" that they are only reaping what they have sown:

As you have been miserly in extending to these females humanity's true adornment, and have been content to pull them away and isolate them from its brilliant jewel, when they were under your authority, more pliable than a reed pen… why do you now raise your hands in confusion, like one who has lost hold of the meaning of things in the hour of need?

For the last several years of her life—her grandson says four—Taymūr was ill. She died on the 2nd of May, 1902. Like other Arab female writers, Taymūr had achieved visibility not only through book publication but in the press—the daily newspapers, a new feature of public discourse at the time, as well as the novel presence, from 1892 on, of magazines dedicated to women's articulations of gender politics. Like a few other notable intellectual women, obituaries in major publications commemorated her passing—*al-Manār*, *al-Hilāl*, *al-Muqtataf*. Already, she was seen as a beacon—although the obituary in *al-Manār* mostly praised her brother Ahmad for not succumbing to the much-censured but popular elaborately emotional public funeral practices of the time, in either his sister's funeral or that of his mother, who died a few days later.

Fawwāz suggests that Taymūr became widely known following publication of her poetry. If this has the hagiographic flavor of the era's biography, it is true that in the early 1890s al-Taymūriyyah's writings were announced and praised in the press, as was the practice of the time; at least one of her poems in praise of the Khedive appeared in *al-Muʾayyad*. Moreover, it appears she was known beyond Egypt. An essay published in *al-Muqtataf* two months after her death offers a lovely personal testimony to this, by a woman living in Ottoman Syria who, when she traveled to Cairo, sought the poet out and met with her several times. (Penned by "one of the female readers of *al-Muqtataf*," it also illustrates women's understandable reluctance to name themselves in print.)

Taymūr was the subject of biography during her life: Zaynab Fawwāz's monumental 1894 biographical dictionary of women featured her among a few other living Arab subjects. Fawwāz's biography remains a key source for Taymūr's life; it is possible, although not documented, that Fawwāz obtained her information from Taymūr herself. Fawwāz highlights female networks: this became a leitmotif in later constructions of al-Taymūriyyah.

Indeed, in her lifetime, al-Taymūriyyah's writing itself had become *hujjah*, "proof": the act of writing and the visibility of its writer, her signature on the work, are arguments in favor of—and in demonstration of—women's intellectual participation in public life. Both Taymūr and her books become artifacts in a discourse on gender. This began even before Fawwāz's biography; it is evident in the *taqrīz* (text in praise of a text and author) for her *dīwān* (1303/1886) sent to her by Salīm Bek Rahmī:

After this [publication of the *dīwān*], *is it admissible to have it said that women are less excellent than men? O sons of the East, why is it that we have been so insolent about what was due to them, a futile pursuit, and have ruined their homes* [or: *brought low their standing*] *when they are the preservers of homes, and neglected their upbringing when they are the raisers of our children? ... This* dīwān *is to be counted among this era's refined* [*works*]. *Let those who love the progress of homelands take good signs from it, and not limit themselves to educating merely the boys....*

Al-Taymūriyyah was part of an early discourse on writing women by writing women. Fawwāz's biography of the poet was reprinted (in December 1906) as one of the earliest of the women's journal *Fatāt al-Sharq*'s long-running "Famous Women" series, and al-Taymūriyyah was featured in other women's journals. Most famous was the series of essays on her life and work by the Lebanese writer, orator and salon hostess Mayy Ziyādah (1886-1941), published in *al-Muqtataf* in 1922 and then in book form. Ziyādah's study, couched in a critical feminist stance and her immersion in the literature of romanticism, is a highly sympathetic one, emerging from her remark that the critic's most important trait is *'atf*, not as a simple sympathy but as a critical stance based on the careful evaluation and respect of a subject and her environment. While reductively accepting the emerging liberal—and imperial—critique of veiling and seclusion as curtailing females' opportunities for self-expression and active social participation—and using this study, like her other biographically shaped studies of Arab women, to mount a critique of gender practices in Arab and Muslim-majority societies (often through long digressions)—Ziyādah also recognizes and lauds possibilities for women's activism within an

Islamically defined context. She heralds al-Taymūriyyah as a "beacon" of Arab women's articulations of self and social being, calling her "the harbinger of feminist awareness in these lands." She highlights al-Taymūriyyah's ascription of responsibility for prevailing understandings of gender's prescriptive role to men, even as she underscores women's own articulations of present and ideal gender regimes. She thus pointed out—long before contemporary scholars did—that al-Taymūriyyah's as well as other women's commentary preceded Qāsim Amīn's famous and explosive tracts on gender politics (1899, 1900), arguing—probably incorrectly—that al-Taymūriyyah likely influenced Amīn. For Ziyādah's liberalist outlook, al-Taymūriyyah is exemplary as an instance of how formal education for girls leads to a quality of judgment that creates individual responsibility within social practice.

Ziyādah contextualizes Taymūr's poetry within the poetic production of the era, which she characterizes as conventional, inexpressive of emotion, and often imitative. Yet, she does not dismiss Taymūr's poetry. To the contrary, spending almost a third of her study on it, she emphasizes the strong emotional content and sincerity of this poetry despite its being situating within the highly stylized world of nineteenth-century Arabic poetry; indeed, noting "faults" of the era allows Ziyādah to suggest that Taymūr's poetry was stunningly able to transcend these limitations even as it partook of them. Ziyādah illustrates this through a rather daring simile.

What charms me in her poetry is that her persona appears through the preserved material [of conventional poetic diction], *as the body appears portrayed in a painting, from within diaphanous weaves.*

As a romantic, it is crucial to Ziyādah that the female Taymūr is "in the forefront of sincere poets"; thus, to characterize her poetic voice as *sādhijah* (naïve) is a compliment rather than a criticism.

REFERENCES
Marilyn Booth, "Biography and Feminist Rhetoric in Early Twentieth-Century Egypt: Mayy

Ziyadah's Studies of Three Women's Lives", *Journal of Women's History* 3.1 (Spring 1991): 38-64;

Zaynab Fawwāz al-'Āmilī, *al-Durr al-manthūr fī tabaqāt rabbāt al-khudūr* (Cairo/Būlāq: al-Matba'ah al-Kubrā al-Amīriyyah, 1312 [1894];

Mervat Hatem, "'A'isha Taymur's Tears and the Critique of the Modernist and the Feminist Discourses on Nineteenth-Century Egypt", in: *Remaking Women: Feminism and Modernity in the Middle East*, ed. Lila Abu-Lughod (Princeton: Princeton University Press, 1998),

73-87;

'Umar Ridā Kahhālah, *A'lām al-nisā'* (Beirut: Mu'assasat al-Risālah, 1982), III, 162-79;

Hudā al-Saddah (ed.), *'Ā'ishah al-Taymūr: Tahaddiyāt al-thābit wa'l-mutaghayyir fī 'l-qarn al-tāsi' 'asharah* (Cairo: Mu'assasat al-Mar'ah wa'l-Dhākirah, 2004);

Ahmad Taymūr Pasha, *Tārīkh al-usrah al-Taymūriyyah* (Cairo: Lajnat Nashr al-Mu'allafāt al-Taymūriyyah, n.d.);

Mayy Ziyādah, *'Ā'ishah Taymūr: Shā'irat al-talī'ah* (Cairo: Dār al-Muqtataf, 1926).

Nāsīf al-Yāzijī

(1800 – 1871)

PAUL STARKEY
University of Durham

WORKS

Majma' al-bahrayn ("The Meeting Place of the Two Seas", Beirut, 1856, 1872, several later reprints and editions);

Fākihat al-nudamā' fī murāsalāt al-udabā' ("Fruit for the Companions, Concerning the Correspondence of Littérateurs", n.p., 1866?, 1904);

Nafhat al-rayhān ("The Scent of Basil", n.p., 1864, 1898);

al-'Arf al-tayyib fī Dīwān Abī 'l-Tayyib ("Fragrant Perfume, Concerning the Poetry of Abū 'l-Tayyib [al-Mutanabbī]", Beirut: al-Maktabah al-Adabiyyah, 1887);

Thālith al-qamarayn ("The Third of Two Moons", Beirut: n.p., 1883, 1903).

Collected Works

Dīwān al-'ālim al-'allāmah al-shā'ir al-shaykh Nāsīf al-Yāzijī (Beirut: al-Maktabah al-Adabiyyah, 1898).

Works in Translation

Extract from one of the *maqāmāt* from *Majma'*

al-bahrayn, in J. A. Haywood, *Modern Arabic Literature, 1800-1970* (London: Lund Humphries, 1971), 51-52.

Nāsīf al-Yāzijī (1800-71) has been generally regarded as one of the most important figures of the Arabic *nahdah* (literary and cultural revival, sometimes translated as "renaissance") in nineteenth-century Lebanon. He was considered by many to be the greatest Arabic scholar of his age, and as such, together with contemporaries such as Butrus al-Bustānī and Fāris al-**Shidyāq**, has been given the credit for helping to re-establish the Arabic language, which had fallen into decline under the Ottomans, as an effective medium of self-expression both in Lebanon and in the wider Arab world. Like many of his colleagues active in Lebanon at the time, he was Christian rather than Muslim by religion, but he nonetheless had a profound knowledge of the classical Arabic literary tradition, including the Qur'ān itself. Although by temperament a conservative rather than an innovator, he has thus been seen as a key figure in the transition from the medieval tradition of Arabic literary expression to the more modern forms of Arabic literature, as well as helping to pave the way for the later Arab nationalist movement.

Nāsīf al-Yāzijī was born in 1801 in Kafr Shīmā, a village on the Lebanese coast near Beirut, into a prominent family that had originally come from the Homs region of Syria and converted to the Maronite version of Catholicism towards the end of the eighteenth century. The family name, al-Yāzijī—which means "writer" in Turkish (yazıcı in modern spelling)—indicates that at least one member of the family had worked as a clerk in the Ottoman Turkish administration. Nāsīf's father was a doctor with literary tastes, which he passed on to his son, whose love for Arabic language and literature soon became evident. Almost entirely self-taught, apart from some lessons from a monk named Matthew, Nāsīf set about, in traditional Middle Eastern fashion, memorising a large quantity of classical literature in Arabic, including not only the whole of the poetry of al-Mutanabbī but also the Qur'ān—an indication of the esteem in which the sacred book of Islam was held by at least some of the leading Christian Arab intellectuals of the day as the prime authority for the Arabic language. He also composed popular poetry in zajal form, not all of which has yet been published.

From 1816 to 1818 Nāsīf worked as a clerk for the Greek Catholic Patriarch at Dayr Qarqafah, before being appointed, on the recommendation of the court poets Niqūlā al-Turk (1763-1828) and Butrus Ibrāhīm Karāmah (1774-1861), to the court of Bashīr II al-Shihābī at Beiteddin. From 1827 to 1840 he served as Bashīr's confidential secretary, before moving to Beirut, where he taught successively in the "National School" founded by the scholar and writer Butrus al-Bustānī, in the "Patriarchal School" administered by the Greek Catholics, and in the Syrian English College (later to become the American University of Beirut). In the course of his teaching career, he produced at least fifteen schoolbooks on various topics, including grammar, rhetoric, poetics, logic and medicine; among the best known of these was a book entitled Jawf al-fanā', a verse work of approximately 1000 lines on Arabic syntax probably modeled on the medieval grammarian Ibn Mālik's Alfiyyah.

Like many other leading figures of the nineteenth-century Syro-Lebanese nahdah, Nāsīf also became involved with Western missionary movements. He was a leading member of the literary and cultural society called al-Jam'iyyah al-sūriyyah (The Syrian Society), established by the missionaries in Beirut in 1847, and from 1849, despite knowing no European languages himself, worked as a proof-reader for the American missionaries on a new Arabic translation of the Bible—a project in which Butrus al-Bustānī and Yūsuf al-Asīr were also involved. He also versified the translation of several hymns, and produced a number of original religious poems, in some of which he sought to prove the divinity of Christ.

The intellectual environment in which al-Yāzijī and his Lebanese contemporaries functioned, though highly productive, appears to have been an intense and at times probably an unpleasant one. Despite the friendships of many of those involved, personal rivalries and animosities were also much in evidence, and their concern with the minutiae of the Arabic language at times reached extraordinary lengths. "Fault finding" exercises (takhti'ah) were commonplace, and al-Yāzijī's later career was marked by a series of furious quarrels with his fellow countryman al-Shidyāq over matters as seemingly trivial as whether al-Yāzijī had really written fithal rather than fitahl in his best-known work Majma' al-bahrayn. Al-Shidyāq, indeed, was even said to have paid another colleague, Yūsuf al-Asīr (1815-89) to attack his rivals al-Yāzijī and Salīm al-Shartūnī on his behalf.

Be that as it may, it is to this later period that most of Nāsīf al-Yāzijī's published works belong. They all confirm his status as an essentially conservative scholar, with few, if any, of the popularising or progressive tendencies of contemporaries such as Fāris al-Shidyāq or the Egyptian Rifā'ah Rāfi' al-**Tahtāwī** (1801-73). His output includes works in both prose and poetry, but his best known work, and the one on which his enduring reputation is based, is undoubtedly the collection of maqāmāt (a traditional Arabic literary form, for which see below) entitled *Majma' al-bahrayn* (The Meeting Place of the Two Seas), published in 1856. His interest in this literary form appears to have been originally prompted when the French consul in Beirut suggested to him that he should study the medieval Arabic *maqāmāt* of al-Harīrī in the recently published edition by the French orientalist Baron Silvestre de Sacy. Al-Yāzijī's suggested corrections to de Sacy's edition were set out in a letter to the French scholar, and he subsequently embarked on the composition of a series of *maqāmāt* of his own, which were consciously modelled on those of al-Harīrī; these aroused a good deal of interest, not only in the Arab-speaking world but also in Europe, where a number of translations soon appeared.

Al-Yāzijī's poems, which conform entirely to the norms of medieval Arabic verse in terms of their metre and rhyme schemes, were collected in three volumes, entitled respectively *Nafhat al-rayhān* (The Scent of Basil, 1864), *Fākihat al-nudamā' fī murāsalāt al-udabā'* (Fruit for the Companions Concerning the Correspondence of Littérateurs, 1866?), and *Thālith al-qamarayn* (The Third of Two Moons, 1883); they were later reedited and reissued by his son Ibrāhīm. Nāsīf's early interest in al-Mutanabbī, which had originated in his youth, also found fruition after his death when the materials that he had prepared for a commentary on al-Mutanabbī's work were published by Ibrāhīm as *al-'Arf al-tayyib fī dīwān Abī 'l-Tayyib* (Fragrant Perfume Concerning the Poetry of Abū 'l-Tayyib [al-Mutanabbī]) in 1882.

By his later years, al-Yāzijī had acquired a considerable reputation as a scholar, both among Western orientalists, with some of whom he continued to correspond, and in the Arab world itself. His contribution to the development of Arabic literature and scholarship was recognised when he was elected a member of the Syrian Academy, founded in 1848. Despite this extensive reputation, however, Nāsīf's own geographical and intellectual horizons remained extremely limited by comparison with those of many of his contemporaries; in addition to his lack of knowledge of foreign languages, he seems to have been uninterested in travel and indeed, is never

known to have left Lebanon.

In 1869 Nāsīf al-Yāzijī suffered a stroke, which left him paralysed on his right side. He is said to have borne the consequences with considerable fortitude, but died from a second stroke in 1871, not long after the death of his eldest son, Habīb, in 1870. Habīb's death was commemorated by his father in one of his most expressive poems.

In addition to Nāsīf himself, several other members of the family also played prominent roles in the literary life of their country. Among these were Nāsīf's younger brother Rājī (1803-57), who wrote poetry; and a number of Nāsīf's children. These included his sons Habīb (1833-70), already mentioned, who predeceased his father; Ibrāhīm (1847-1906), who later emigrated to Egypt and wrote a famous poem praising the Arabs to the detriment of their Ottoman rulers; Khalīl (1858-89), a writer and poet; and a daughter, Wardah (1838-1924), who produced a considerable volume of poetry, in addition to essays for publication in periodicals.

Nāsīf al-Yāzijī's best-known work, *Majma' al-bahrayn* [The Meeting Place of the Two Seas], was first published in Beirut in 1856. The title refers to the mingling of poetry and prose, and the work consists of a collection of sixty short pieces in the traditional medieval Arabic *maqāmah* (pl. *maqāmāt*) form. This form, which had almost certainly originated with the writer Badī' al-Zamān al-Hamadhānī (d 1008), had been brought to its highest level of perfection about a century later by al-Harīrī (d. 1122). Sometimes described as the nearest medieval Arabic equivalents of the modern short story, *maqāmāt* were usually composed as collections of short independent narratives, each involving a hero and a narrator, with a 'plot' that often, though not invariably, involved some trickery, and subsequent exposure, on the hero's part. The narrative itself was conventionally composed in *saj'* [rhymed prose], with verse insertions of a greater or lesser extent depending on the author's inclinations and abilities. Although the form had continued in constant use after the high point of al-Harīrī, the creative and imaginative qualities that had marked the early medieval collections had more recently been overtaken by

a tendency to use the form as a vehicle for demonstrations of verbal dexterity, and there is
general agreement among critics that by the end
of the eighteenth century the form was no longer
fulfilling a creative literary role.

It is important to note that, although al-
Yāzijī's attempt to breathe new life into the form
has been regarded as in some way occupying a
pivotal position in the development of nineteenth-century Arabic literature, his approach is
essentially imitative. As such, it stands in stark
contrast to the iconoclastic approach of Fāris al-
Shidyāq, whose incorporation of four *maqāmāt*
into his pioneering part fictional, part autobiographical *al-Sāq 'alā 'l-sāq* (an untranslatable
title, in that it exploits the ambiguities of the
Arabic lexicon, but roughly equivalent to: One
Leg Over Another, or The Pigeon on the Tree-
Branch; see p. 321 ff. of entry on al-Shidyāq),
may be regarded as an attempt to subvert the
traditional *maqāmah* format in the interests of a
somewhat eccentric modernism. The imitative
and traditionalist approach of al-Yāzijī's *maqāmāt*
also stands in contrast to that of the later Egyptian writer Muhammad al-**Muwaylihī** (1858?-
1930), whose *Hadīth 'Īsā ibn Hishām* (originally
published 1898-1902, republished in book form
1907), attempted to marry the formal and stylistic aspects of the traditional *maqāmah* with a
degree of contemporary social criticism clearly
directed at the Egypt of the day. It is worth
noting that although al-Muwaylihī's work has
been commonly regarded as the last great work
of Arabic literature to be written using the
maqāmah form, the form has continued to be
used intermittently through the twentieth century, at times to stunningly good effcct, by authors anxious to exploit the indigenous Arabic
literary tradition; the outstanding examples of
this phenomenon are probably the satirical *maqāmāt* of the Tunisian/Egyptian Mahmūd Bayram al-Tūnisī (1893-1961), whose *maqāmāt* explore the subtleties of Egyptian everyday life in
a language often far removed from the classical
subtleties of al-Harīrī and his successors.

For his part, al-Yāzijī made no secret of the
fact that his aim was to produce, in *Majma' al-
bahrayn*, a work that would emulate that of al-
Harīrī both in form and in content. Indeed, his

decision to include in his collection sixty
maqāmāt rather than al-Harīrī's fifty possibly
suggests a desire to surpass him. Al-Yāzijī's
lack of concern with "originality", however—
even by comparison with many of his contemporaries—, marks his approach as traditionalist
rather than modernist, and arguably little to
modern taste. Be that as it may, his attempt to
emulate the achievements of al-Harīrī was
judged so successful that some commentators
even began to speak of the "three great collections of *maqāmāt*" in reference to al-Hamadhānī,
al-Harīrī and al-Yāzijī himself.

In his own short introduction to the work, al-
Yāzijī describes himself simply as a "Christian
from Mount Lebanon" who has "poached on"
the preserves of Arab littérateurs by composing
stories that resemble *maqāmāt* in name only. He
explains that the names of his hero, Maymūn ibn
Khuzām, and of his narrator, Suhayl ibn 'Abbād,
are imaginary and belong to no specific country,
and begs the reader's forgiveness (forgiveness
being one of the marks of nobility) for his pre-
sumption in putting forward such a composition.
Most of this may, of course, be dismissed as a
simple literary conceit. Unlike the later Muhammad al-Muwaylihī—the name of whose protagonist, 'Īsā ibn Hishām, deliberately echoes
that of the hero of al-Hamadhānī's *maqāmāt*—
al-Yāzijī employs new names for his characters;
but any illusion that the reader of the introduction might have had that this indicates a new
approach is quickly dispelled, for in their mixture of *saj'* and verse, in their narrative structure,
and in their preoccupation with the intricacies of
the Arabic language, al-Yāzijī's *maqāmāt* are in
no sense original.

The collection begins with a "Desert *maqāmah*", which relates the first meeting between al-
Yāzijī's hero, Maymūn, and his narrator, Suhayl.
The narrative, which follows almost slavishly
the pattern established by al-Hamadhānī and al-
Harīrī, describes how Maymūn succeeds in
retaining for himself the spoils from an encounter with some brigands in the desert, leaving the
narrator with nothing but his camel and a witty
note of thanks in verse. This pattern forms what
might almost be described as a "template" for
many of the subsequent *maqāmāt* in the collec-

tion. As in the medieval collections of al-Harīrī and al-Hamadhānī, al-Yāzijī's individual *maqāmāt* are titled individually, and as in the earlier collections, many are given place-names as titles (Yemen, Baghdad, Aleppo and Iraq, for example); but the locations in which the individual tales are set are in many instances (hardly surprisingly, in view of the fact that al-Yāzijī himself had almost certainly never left Lebanon) in practice almost entirely random. By contrast, the setting of the final *maqāmah*, the "Jerusalem *maqāmah*", is obviously highly symbolic: here, Maymūn, who has now apparently given up his trickster habits, takes leave of the narrator in the al-Aqsā mosque, telling him that they will meet again in Paradise—a neat conclusion to the series of episodes that preceded it.

The arcane nature of the language employed by al-Yāzijī is evidenced by the large number of explanatory footnotes to be found in most editions of *Majma' al-bahrayn*, which at least equal those to be found in a modern edition of al-Harīrī's *maqāmāt*; on some pages, the footnotes occupy more space than the actual text. Literary allusions also abound, including references to, and occasionally direct quotations from, the Qur'ān itself. In this connexion, the traditional phrase "*al-lughah al-'arabiyyah lā tatanassar*" (the Arabic language cannot be Christianised) has been quoted by more than one commentator with reference to al-Yāzijī's work, though the precise significance, both of the phrase itself, and of the commentators' interpretation of it, has not always been totally clear.

The linguistic gymnastics in which al-Yāzijī and his colleagues indulged is nowhere better evidenced, perhaps, than in the twentieth *maqāmah* ("The *maqāmah* of Basra"), which includes a fourteen-line poem in which the first and second halves of every line form a palindrome (if not always a totally precise one), as in the following example (which omits short vowels):

qmr yfrt 'mda ms̲h̲rq : rs̲h̲ ma' dm' trf yrmq

Although the linguistic and phonological structure of Arabic make this a slightly easier feat than it would be in English (not least because short vowels on Arabic do not form an integral part of the script), the modern reader is likely to come away from a reading of this particular *maqāmah* with the feeling that the author was better equipped to be a crossword or sudoku champion than an author of imaginative literature. A similar concern with arcane linguistic skills is evidenced in al-Yāzijī's partiality for chronograms, as will be seen below in the brief discussion of his poetry.

Al-Yāzijī's poetry, which was published in three *dīwān*s (collections), entitled respectively *Nafḥat al-rayḥān* (1864), *Fākihat al-nudamā' fī murāsalāt al-udabā'* (1866?), and *Thālith al-qamarayn* (posthumous, 1884) is, like his collection of *maqāmāt*, essentially imitative, reflecting an interest in medieval Arabic poetry that was primarily scholastic and philological. In turning to al-Mutanabbī and the other great Abbasid poets for a model, al-Yāzijī's poetry reflects the values of the early pioneers of the neo-classical verse movement, soon to find perhaps its first distinguished exponent in the Egyptian Maḥmūd Sāmī al-**Barūdī** (1839-1904); unlike al-Bārūdī and the later neo-classicists, however, al-Yāzijī appears to have lacked the ability, or inclination, to find a way of redirecting the classical themes and motifs towards the concerns of the modern world. These limitations were arguably reinforced by his personal experience, for his attachment to the court of Bashīr II for a period of some dozen years (itself reminiscent of the status of the medieval Arabic court poet) had involved the frequent composition of poems in traditional genres, most obviously those of the elegy *(rithā', marthiyah)*, and poems of praise *(madīh)* or, less commonly, self-praise *(fakhr)*. Although many of the poems included in his collections are addressed to Bashīr or to other local dignitaries with whom he had some contact, others are not: one, for example, was written on the accession of Queen Victoria to the throne of England.

There is no doubt that, compared with most of those who had gone recently before him, al-Yāzijī's poems demonstrate a remarkable linguistic talent. Critics have spoken of some at least of his poems as reminiscent of those of great Arabic medieval poets such as al-Mutanabbī (d. 965) and al-Sharīf al-Radī (d. 1015), and the last poem that he wrote, lamenting the death of his son Habīb, has been especially praised for its sincerity and simplicity. It is notable, however, how many of his poems, although clearly "written to order" for specific occasions, are only tenuously connected with the particular people involved, suggesting yet again that the author's interest in poetry was primarily a linguistic and technical one.

The essentially imitative nature of al-Yāzijī's poetry reveals itself not only in the traditional genres that he favoured. Despite his early experiments in the popular poetic *zajal* forms, based on stanzaic structures more flexible than the strict metrical patterns and monorhyme of "classical" Arabic poetry, he shows little if any inclination to formal experimentation in his later verse. Rather, his poems are full of the complex wordplay and rhetorical figures characteristic of later medieval Arabic poetry, of which the most popular and productive was undoubtedly *jinās* ("paranomasia"), the use in close proximity to each other of two words based on the same, or similar, roots. This figure, which assumed a wide variety of forms, had proved particularly productive in medieval Arabic because of the structure of the language itself, based largely on tri-consonantal roots (*k-t-b*, *n-z-l*, etc), each capable of generating a large number of vocabulary items (*kataba*, *kātib*, *maktab*, *maktaba*, *kitāb*, *kutub*, *kātaba*, *kutayyib*, etc.). In addition, the traditional structure of the Arabic poem, based on single lines divided into hemistiches (half-lines) with matching metrical patterns, encouraged the use of various sorts of parallelism in verse, of which al-Yāzijī, like his predecessors, was not slow to take advantage. Allusions to his poetic predecessors, another common feature of many medieval writers, also abound in his verse: at least two of his poems, for example, begin with the word "*qif*" or "*qifā*" (stop!), an allusion to the opening line of the pre-Islamic *mu'allaqah* ("ode") of Imru' al-Qays (d. ca. 550) a line which can almost certainly claim to be the best known and most frequently imitated line of classical Arabic poetry.

Al-Yāzijī's pedantic, archaising tendencies are nowhere better evidenced than in his fondness for chronograms, a form of expression that depends on the fact that each letter in the Arabic alphabet is also associated with a numerical value. (A parallel, albeit an imprecise one, is provided by the use of letters for numbers in "Roman" numbers such as LXVII.) This implies that any expression in Arabic, short or long, can be assigned a numerical value by summing the total value of the individual letters—a procedure that in certain contexts has acquired magical or mystical overtones. Of more immediate relevance to the discussion of al-Yāzijī is the fashion that had sprung up during the Ottoman period for poets to compose short poems, the sum of whose letters formed a relevant date; if this was a person's date of death, the poem might then be inscribed on his tombstone. Al-Yāzijī's *Thālith al-qamarayn* includes over forty pages of such compositions at the end of the collection, and in one poem, addressed to the Ottoman sultan, the author develops the technique still further—the initial letters of the lines of an extended poem being used to form a shorter two-line poem containing four chronograms.

Despite the enduring reputation of al-Yazijī as a pillar of the Arabic nineteenth-century literary and cultural revival, he may well strike the reader of this brief discussion of his life and works as a slightly problematic figure. Certainly, al-Yāzijī shared few if any of the attitudes and experiences of his more progressive contemporaries with whose names he is often linked. Unlike al-Shidyāq, for example, he had not travelled to Europe; he showed no apparent interest in the formal or structural development of the traditional Arabic forms of literary expression; he knew no European languages; and he could thus make only an indirect and probably marginal contribution to the "translation movement" that was soon to play such a crucial role in the development of Arabic literature. Although his role as a teacher is beyond dispute, and his unparalleled knowledge of the Arabic language certainly gave him an almost "iconic" status among his contemporaries, it may therefore be suggested that some further research is necessary to clarify more precisely the extent of his contribution to the *nahdah* as a whole.

REFERENCES

Mārūn ʿAbbūd, *Ruwwād al-nahdah al-hadīthah* (Beirut: Dār al-Thaqāfah, 1977);

Thomas Bauer, "Die *badīʿiyya* des Nāṣīf al-Yāziǧī und das Problem der spätosmanischen arabischen Literatur", in: *Reflections on Reflections: Near Eastern Writers Reading Literature*, ed. A. Neuwirth & A. C. Islebe (Wiesbaden: Reichert, 2006), 49-118;

Louis Cheikho, *al-Ādāb al-ʿarabiyyah fī ʾl-qarn al-tāsiʿ ʿashar*, 2 parts (Beirut: al-Matbaʿah al-Kāthūlīkiyyah, 1924-26);

A. J. Gully, "Arabic linguistic issues and controversies of the late nineteenth and early twentieth centuries", *Journal of Semitic Studies* xlii (1997): 75-120;

——, "al-Yāzidjī", *Encyclopaedia of Islam*, 2nd ed. (Leiden: E. J. Brill, 1954-2005), XI, 317-8;

John A. Haywood, *Modern Arabic Literature 1800–1970: an introduction with extracts in translation* (London: Lund Humphries, 1971);

S. Kh. Jayyusi, *Trends and Movements in Modern Arabic Poetry*, 2 vols. (Leiden: E. J. Brill, 1977), I, 18-20;

I. Kratschkowsky, "al-Yāzidjī", *Encyclopaedia of Islam*, 1st ed. (Leiden: E. J. Brill, 1913-36), VIII, 1170-1;

Henri Pérès, "Les premières manifestations de la Renaissance littéraire arabe en Orient au XIXe siècle", *Annales de l'Institut d'études orientales d'Alger* 1 (1936): 233-56;

P. C. Sadgrove, "al-Yāzijī, Nāsīf", *Encyclopedia of Arabic Literature*, ed. J. S. Meisami and P. Starkey, 2 vols. (London: Routledge, 1998), II, 813.

Jurjī Zaydān

(1861 – 1914)

WALID HAMARNEH
Swarthmore College

WORKS

Al-Falsafah al-lughawiyyah waʾl-alfāz al-ʿarabiyyah ("Linguistic Philosophy and Arabic Expressions", Beirut, 1886);

Tārīkh Misr al-hadīthah ("History of Modern Egypt", 1889);

Al-Tārīkh al-ʿāmm mundhu al-khalīqah ilā ʾl-ān ("General History from Creation Till the Present", Beirut, 1890);

Al-Mamlūk al-shārid ("The Mamluk Who Escaped", 1891);

Mukhtasar jughrāfiyyat Misr ("Compendium of Egyptian Geography", Cairo: Matbaʿat al-Taʾlīf, 1891);

Jihād al-muhibbīn ("Lovers' Struggle", 1892);

Istibdād al-Mamālīk ("Mamluk Despotism", 1892);

Asīr al-Mutamahhidī ("The Captive of the Mahdi Pretender", 1892);

Fatāt Ghassān ("The Young Girl of Ghassan", 1898);

Armanūsah al-misriyyah ("The Egyptian Armanusa", 1899);

Tārīkh al-māsūniyyah al-ʿāmm ("General History of Masonry", 1899);

ʾAdhrāʾ Quraysh ("The Virgin of Quraysh", 1899);

Al-Sābiʿ ʿashar min Ramadān ("The 17th of Ramadan", 1899);

Tārīkh Injiltirā ilā ʾl-dawlah al-yūrkiyyah ("History of England Till the House of York", Cairo: al-Hilāl, 1899);

Ghādat Karbalāʾ ("The Young Woman of Karbala", 1901);

Al-Hajjāj ibn Yūsuf al-thaqafī ("Hajjāj ibn Yūsuf from [the tribe of] Thaqīf", 1902);

Tarājim mashāhīr al-sharq fī ʾl-qarn al-tāsiʿ ʿashar ("Biographies of Famous Nineteenth

Century Celebrities", 1902);

Tārīkh al-tamaddun al-islāmī ("History of Islamic Civilization", 1902-06);

Fath al-Andalus ("The Conquest of al-Andalus", 1904);

Shārl wa-'Abd al-Rahmān ("Charles and Abd al-Rahman", 1904);

Tārīkh al-lughah al-'arabiyyah ("History of the Arabic Language", Beirut, 1904);

Abū Muslim al-Khurāsānī ("Abū Muslim from Khorasan", 1905);

Al-'Abbāsah ukht al-Rashīd ("Abbasah, the Sister of al-Rashid", 1906);

Al-Amīn wa'l-Ma'mūn ("Al-Amin and al-Ma'-mun", 1907);

Muhammad 'Alī ("Mohammed Ali", 1907);

'Arūs Farghānah ("The Bride from Farghana", 1908);

Al-'Arab qabla al-islām ("The Arabs Before Islam", Cairo, 1908);

Ahmad ibn Tūlūn ("Ahmad ibn Tūlūn", 1909);

'Abd al-Rahmān al-Nāsir ("'Abd al-Rahmān al-Nāsir", 1909);

Al-Inqilāb al-'Uthmānī ("The Ottoman Coup", 1911);

Tārīkh ādāb al-lughah al-'arabiyyah ("History of Arabic Literature", 1911);

Fatāt al-Qayrawān ("The Young Girl of Qayrawan", 1912);

'Ajā'ib al-khalq ("The Wonders of Creation", 1912);

Salāh al-Dīn wa-makā'id al-hashshāshīn ("Saladin and the Conspiracies of the Assassins", 1913);

Shajarat al-Durr ("Shajarat al-Durr", 1914);

Ansāb al-'Arab al-qudamā' ("Genealogies of Ancient Arabs", Cairo: al-Hilāl, 1921); published posthumously;

Tabaqāt al-umam ("Classes of Nations", Cairo, no date);

Tārīkh al-Yūnān wa'l-Rūmān ("History of Greece and Rome", Cairo, no date).

Other Writings

'Ilm al-firāsah al-hadīth ("Modern Physiognomy", 1901);

Mukhtārāt Jurjī Zaydān ("Selections from Jurjī Zaydān", 1920).

Jurjī Zaydān was born in 1861 (most probably December 14) in Beirut where his father's family had migrated due to the early death of his grandfather. Zaydān's father owned a small restaurant in the popular quarter of the city. He spent most of his time at work and rarely saw his children who were brought up by their mother. Zaydān attended schools, but at the age of eleven he was taken out to help his father at the restaurant, ostensibly for a few weeks but in fact a period that lasted seven years. Later he became an apprentice in a shoemaker's shop, only to return to his father's restaurant after a brief period. While working with his father in the various restaurants (which moved from one place to another many times but remained in the same general area close to the city center), he met students from the Protestant College (later renamed the American University of Beirut) as well as intellectuals and teachers who made a strong impression on him and gave him the idea of pursuing his own studies. He also seems to have made an equally positive impression on many of them, and they gave him encouragement to complete his studies.

In 1881, at the age of twenty and with virtually no regular academic background, Zaydān decided to apply to the Medical School of the Protestant College. He had to take the entrance exams, including arithmetic, algebra, geometry, physics, chemistry, biology, Arabic and English. Passing them all, he was admitted to the School of Medicine, only to be forced to leave the College a year later when he supported one of his professors (named Louis) who delivered a lecture defending Darwin. The administration of the College had insisted on dismissing Louis, and the students responded by forming a union in his support headed by Zaydān. Attempts were made to resolve the issue, but the conservatives at the college had the upper hand. Some of the students, including Zaydān, were dismissed but were allowed to return only if they withdrew their signatures from a letter in which they had supported Louis. Following this incident Zaydān decided in 1883 to go to Egypt in order to continue his studies there. Borrowing some money from a neighbor to cover the cost of his trip, he was able to repay him within a year since he started working rather than enrolling at a university in Egypt.

The job that Zaydān found was with a small newspaper called *al-Zamān*, owned by another Syrian who was living in Egypt. In 1884 Zaydān worked as a war correspondent and interpreter with the British army that was sent to the Sudan to rescue General Gordon. It was at this time that his interest in history developed, and he began to immerse himself in reading, studying languages, and writing. In 1885 he decided to return to Beirut. He spent ten months studying Hebrew and Syriac and in 1886 published his book on linguistic philosophy, upon the basis of which he was made a member of the Royal Asiatic Academy in Italy.

Al-Falsafah al-lughawiyyah wa'l-alfāz al-'arabiyyah (Linguistic Philosophy and Arabic Words) appeared in Beirut and was soon translated into Turkish (and published in Istanbul in 1893). The main hypothesis in the book is that language as an acquired activity is consonant with the laws of evolution, especially regarding some points on which he provides examples and analysis, mostly from Arabic. Among these general hypotheses are:

1. Utterances that are similar or close in both meaning and phonology are variants of one word;

2. particles, prepositions, conjunctions and similar words that denote meaning in other words that are necessarily contiguous are residues of formerly meaningful utterances;

3. most utterances or words that are meaningful in themselves can be deductively reduced to monosyllables (mostly a combination of a consonant and a vowel) that have a mimetic relationship to sounds from nature;

4. words like pronouns and demonstratives can be deductively reduced to one or a small number of utterances;

5. utterances involving mental or non-material significances originally denoted meanings associated with the material senses that shifted throughout time through metaphors and similes due to resemblances or analogies in mental images.

Based upon these points, Zaydān arrives at the conclusion that the Arabic language was originally composed of a few monosyllabic utterances, most of which were imitations of sounds in nature and which are instinctively and spontaneously enunciated by humans. Arabic developed out of these basic units, their transformations and combinations, to become what it has become in order to satisfy the needs of its speakers and according to the laws of evolution. In the two concluding chapters Zaydān discusses the invention of writing and its history (hieroglyphic, cuneiform, Hittite, and Chinese), which he associates with nature, then the process of computation and the invention of numbers.

Following the success of his early work on linguistic philosophy, Zaydān decided to pursue further studies in Europe. In 1888 he traveled to London where he spent most of his time studying books and manuscripts related to the history of Islam and Arabic. By the end of that year he was back in Egypt working as the editor of the well-known journal, *al-Muqtataf*, but left the post after two years in order to join the staff of the Greek Orthodox School in Cairo where he taught from 1889 to 1891. It was in 1891 that he started making plans for a journal of his own. Named *al-Hilāl*, it was founded in 1892 and was to become the center of Zaydān's life and intellectual energy (and it remains today one of the most important journals in the Arab world). He used it to publish most of his writings, including the novels for which he is chiefly remembered, published (like their European forebears) in serialized form. He was to remain its most prolific contributor until his death in 1914.

In the same year (1891) Zaydān published his first historical novel, *al-Mamlūk al-shārid* (The Mamluk Who Escaped). Over the next several years he was to compose no less than 23 novels, only one of which, *Jihād al-muhibbīn* (Lovers' Struggle, 1892), is not a historical novel; they cover the history of Islam from the period of the conquests to the early twentieth century. A complete list now follows, along with the original dates of publication in book form:

Al-Mamlūk al-shārid (The Mamluk Who Escaped, 1891);

Jihād al-muhibbīn (Lovers' Struggle, 1892);

Istibdād al-Mamālīk (Mamluk Despotism, 1892);

Asīr al-Mutamahhidī (The Captive of the Mahdi Pretender, 1892);

Fatāt Ghassān (The Young Girl of Ghassan, 1898);

Armanūsah al-misriyyah (The Egyptian Armanusa, 1899);

'Adhrā' Quraysh (The Virgin of Quraysh, 1899);

Al-Sābi' 'ashar min Ramadān (The 17th of Ramadan, 1899);

Ghādat Karbalā' (The Young Woman of Karbala, 1901);

Al-Hajjāj ibn Yūsuf al-thaqafī (Hajjāj ibn Yūsuf from [the tribe of] Thaqīf, 1902);

Fath al-Andalus (The Conquest of al-Andalus, 1904);

Shārl wa-'Abd al-Rahmān (Charles and Abd al-Rahman, 1904);

Abū Muslim al-Khurāsānī (Abū Muslim from Khorasan, 1905);

Al-'Abbāsah ukht al-Rashīd (Abbasah, the Sister of al-Rashid, 1906);

Al-Amīn wa'l-Ma'mūn (Al-Amin and al-Ma'mun, 1907);

Muhammad 'Alī (Mohammed Ali, 1907);

'Arūs Farghānah (The Bride from Farghana, 1908);

Ahmad ibn Tūlūn (Ahmad ibn Tūlūn, 1909);

'Abd al-Rahmān al-Nāsir ('Abd al-Rahmān al-Nāsir, 1909);

Al-Inqilāb al-'uthmānī (The Ottoman Coup, 1911);

Fatāt al-Qayrawān (The Young Girl of Qayrawan, 1912).

For each of these novels a significant period in history would be selected, and the story placed within it. However, the novels were not written as a series that reflects the chronological order of their accumulated subject matter; rather each work was authored independently. Since their initial publication, these novels (which are collectively referred to as *Riwāyāt tārīkh al-islām*, Novels on the History of Islam) have retained their popularity and have had an enormous impact on readers in the Arab World. At the same time literary critics have varied widely in their estimates of the novels' literary merits. Many critics have simply ignored them, while others have studied them merely as educational works with little "artistic" value.

In his introduction to the first edition of *Tārīkh al-tamaddun al-islāmī* (History of Islamic Civilization, to be discussed below), Zaydān notes that his purpose in writing historical novels is to make the uninitiated reader better acquainted with the history of Islam. Since the majority of readers in the Arabic-speaking world during his own time will find reading works of history a heavy burden, he says, he has needed to resort to tricks (*ihtiyāl*) in order to provide such educational material; for him, the novel has offered the most effective way of attracting such readers. In the introduction to the novel *al-Hajjāj ibn Yūsuf al-thaqafī* (1902), he further explains that his purpose in writing historical novels differs from that of the European historical novel (he probably has such writers as Sir Walter Scott in mind). His aim, he says, is to write history in the novel or story form. For that reason he has no desire to deviate from history, nor is he interested in using it as a vehicle for narrative; rather his aim is to use narrative as a vehicle for history.

Many critics have observed that his novels are composed of two basic elements. The first element consists of the historical background, which can be subdivided into two types—historical time, usually composed of long passages (sometimes with footnotes and references to historical works) that provide the reader with an elaborate temporal context; and a second type associated with space, where Zaydān provides elaborate and detailed descriptions of cities or areas in which the action takes place. The second element in Zaydān's novels is the love-story. This typically involves a man and woman who fall in love, then are separated by circumstances, only to meet again and in most case come together in a happy ending. The plot structure can thus be considered closed and dominated by historical facts.

From among the many examples provided by these novels we will illustrate these features with summaries of three. *Al-Amīn wa'l-Ma'mūn* (1907) portrays a critical period in the history of the Abbasid rule following the death of the caliph,

Hārūn al-Rashīd (d. 809). Civil war erupts between his two sons, al-Amīn and al-Ma'mūn, each of whom is eager to inherit the throne, a struggle that was not merely a personal one involving two brothers but also a confrontation of traditional elites (mostly ethnic Arabs) with the newer elites composed of both ethnic Persians and Arabs. The struggle ended with the killing of al-Amīn and with al-Ma'mūn assuming the throne. Zaydān develops his plot around a love-affair involving Maymūnah, the daughter of Ja'far al-Barmakī (the minister of Hārūn al-Rashīd who was very close to him and married Hārūn's sister al-'Abbāsah but was later executed), and Bahzād, the grandson of Abū Muslim al-Khurāsānī (who led the Abbasid armies from Khurāsān that defeated the Umayyads and allowed the Abbasid family to assume the caliphate). Within this skeletal plot-structure, Zaydān creates an interesting picture of contemporary society. He uses characters to show the wealth of the period and the emerging levels of scientific learning, most especially through the character of al-Ma'mūn himself who patronized the sciences and built a renowned library in Baghdad to house books from different languages translated into Arabic. Zaydān also portrays the new modes of education through the characters of Zaynab, al-Ma'mūn's daughter, and her slave-governess or nursemaid, Danānīr. Zaynab is highly educated and has as strong a will and independence of mind as her father, while Danānīr, though a slave, is particularly well versed in astronomy and astrology, subjects she has acquired during her early career in the palace of Yahyā al-Barmakī, one of the patrons of science who had commissioned the translation of Ptolemy's *al-Magest*.

A second novel, *Armanūsah al-misriyyah* (1899), is set during the Muslim conquest of Egypt. Under the leadership of 'Amr ibn al-'Ās the Muslim armies have been ordered by the caliph 'Umar to invade Egypt. The events of the conquest in 640 are presented through the story of a love-affair between Armanūsah, the daughter of al-Muqawqis, the Byzantine ruler of Egypt who had quickly surrendered to the Muslims, and Arcadius, the son of the Byzantine army commander. However Armanūsah is a beautiful young woman, and the Byzantine Emperor Heraclius has ordered her father to send her to his imperial palace in Constantinople so that he can marry her. Unwilling to go to Constantinople, Armanūsah joins the invading Arab armies, and their commander, 'Amr, offers her his protection and friendship. She travels with the army until they reach Alexandria, Egypt's capital at the time. The city soon surrenders, and while Armanūsah is in the city, she meets Arcadius; they are joined in marriage. Zaydān uses the plot of this novel to explain the rapid collapse of the Byzantine forces in Egypt, pointing to not only the fervor of the conquering Muslim armies and the chivalric values that led them to treat their enemies with respect, but also to the degeneration of those same values within the Byzantine Empire.

However not all Zaydān's novels have a happy ending. *'Adhrā' Quraysh* (The Virgin of Quraysh, 1899) takes place during one of early Islam's most controversial periods, the aftermath of the murder of the third caliph, 'Uthmān ibn 'Affān, and the civil wars that resulted. As soon as 'Alī, the Prophet Muhammad's cousin and son-in-law, declared himself caliph and successor to 'Uthmān, the supporters of the latter, led by Mu'āwiyah in Syria, 'Amr ibn al-'Ās in Egypt, and other enemies such as Talhah and al-Zubayr, duly supported by 'Ā'ishah (the young widow of the Prophet and daughter of the first caliph, Abū Bakr), all declared war on him. The novel, however, covers only the earlier years of this schism that was to divide Islam between Sunnis and Shiites (i.e. the supporters of 'Alī), and especially the battles of al-Jamal (the Camel) and Siffīn.

Zaydān uses a love-story involving Asmā' and Muhammad ibn Abī Bakr (the son of the first caliph and 'Ā'ishah's brother) in order to lead us into this maze. Mariam, Asmā''s mother, is married to Yazīd, a member of the Umayyad clan, who is not Asmā''s father. Mariam dies before divulging this secret to Asmā'; all we learn is that her father was an important member of the Quraysh, the Prophet Muhammad's own clan. It is Asmā''s efforts to unravel this secret that make her a witness to the historical incidents related in the novel. While searching for

'Alī, Asmā' meets Muhammad ibn Abī Bakr, and the two are quickly attracted to each other. However, Marwān ibn al-Hakam, a prominent and cunning member of the Umayyad family whose sons and grandsons are later to become Umayyad caliphs and who is related to Asmā''s step-father, falls in love with her, but the feeling is not reciprocated. Asmā' spends time in the caliph 'Uthmān's household and is on friendly terms with his wife, Nā'ilah, who tries unsuccessfully to arrange a match between Asmā' and Marwān. After 'Uthmān's murder, Asmā' also gets to meet Muhammad's ibn Abī Bakr's sister and the Prophet's wife, 'Ā'ishah. As a result, she witnesses the fighting between 'Alī's camp and that of 'Āishah and her co-conspirators, Talhah and al-Zubayr. She tries to trace a priest in Syria, hoping to find out who her father is (a search that allows Zaydān to indulge in a description of that region, and especially the city of Antioch). However, she ends up witnessing the Umayyad conspiracy against 'Alī. Her beloved, Muhammad ibn Abī Bakr, has been appointed governor of Egypt by the new caliph, 'Alī, and she travels there to look for him. However, the Umayyad revolt in Egypt is successful; Muhammad is killed, then burned. Upon seeing his burning face, she herself plunges into the fire.

This novel has many subplots. The trips and tribulations of Asmā' may be somewhat exaggerated, and yet Zaydān manages to make many of her encounters with members of the ruling elite credible based upon her family connections. All in all, this novel is more successful than some of his other novels in linking reports of historical incidents with the love-theme. Zaydān is also clearly aware that he is venturing into dangerous terrain by portraying important and controversial characters from early Islamic history who are venerated by some but cursed by others. Most of the characters are portrayed from within their perspective, thus showing them in a somewhat sympathetic light without necessarily taking sides. The exceptions are the Umayyads and their two main representatives, Marwān and Asmā''s step-father, Yazīd, who are the novel's villains.

In these and other historical novels by Zaydān, characters are generally static and show very little development. The good ones are good, the bad ones bad, and they remain so mostly from beginning to end, with very little delving into characterization as generally understood in prose fiction and the novel. The psychology of his characters seems almost Pavlovian, with similar and even exaggerated reactions to similar stimuli. Such features noted however, we can point to certain other factors that may help explain the continuing popularity of these novels in the Arab world. They do not necessarily always reflect his own attitudes, and the path to an eventual outcome is more complex than is generally thought. Zaydān subordinates the story to the structure of the historical narrative. The closed basic theme to be found in his novels is tailored to his particular version of the historical narrative; Zaydān's understanding of history is not teleological but rather based on two governing principles: chronology (temporality) and causality. In the process of subordinating the narrative to this historical structure, results will vary. However the structures of history will occasionally crack open the closedness of the narrative, resulting in a novel crafted in such a way as to be closer to a *fabula* (in Russian Formalist terminology, the "story" in its chronological sequence), while in others it is closer to a *sjuzhet* (a plotted narrative), although never pure, but always "contaminated." In Zaydān we witness the first steps in the shift from story to plot, from mere chronology to causal structuration. This tendency can also be seen in another element in which story and history meet, namely chance. In Zaydān novels (and in many others) the love-story is full of chance meetings and separations, and yet chance is not a *deus ex machina* that emerges from nowhere. Rather it is derived from and a part of the historical narrative governed by causality. So what appears to be mere coincidence at the level of the story is in many cases causally determined at the level of history. Yet probably the most important and understudied aspect concerns the impact that these novels had on the literary taste of readers and the contribution they made to transformations in prose styles through the creation of an entirely new community of readers.

A number of scholars have noted that journalism and its language have had an immense effect on changing styles and expectations of readers. In the context of the Arabic language this factor is of considerable significance. For a number of reasons, and principally because of the sacred aspects associated with the language of the Qur'an, the different levels of Arabic (the written language being different from the language of daily communication), and the great respect for older "classical" texts as being the best models for emulation, Arabic literary styles in both poetry and prose had remained rather stagnant for many centuries. This began to change during the course of the nineteenth century with the beginning of the Arab renaissance. Although Zaydān was not the first to innovate in modes of prose writing, it was through his journalism and particularly his novelistic writings that he broke away from traditional styles and helped develop a new mode of expression, one constructed around linguistic choices based on the primacy of communication. This issue has proven to be of enormous importance in the development of modern Arabic literature and writing in general. Zaydān's contribution to it was central.

Zaydān was to make use of the pages of his journal, *al-Hilāl*, to publish two enormous historical projects: one on Islamic history, *Tārīkh al-tamaddun al-islāmī* (History of Islamic Civilization, 1902-06), and a second on Arabic literary history, *Tārīkh ādāb al-lughah al-'arabiyyah* (History of Arabic Literature, 1911). There is a certain amount of overlap between the two histories, and, while the first of the two was written about a decade earlier, it has proven to be of more lasting value.

In his history of civilization his approach mixes the diachronic and synchronic; in some parts narrative dominates, but in many others analysis, exposition, and comparison are more prevalent. The subdivisions within each section are based on what Zaydān regarded as being the most important aspects of social life: politics, administration and state organization, economics, social life, and the organization of knowledge. The work consists of five volumes, of which we will now provide a brief summary.

The first volume gives a short historical survey of the rise of the Islamic Empire, its prehistory in Arabia and the Middle East and its rise

and later divisions. This is an introduction to the analysis of the structures of state administration, including different positions—caliphs, emirs, *wālī*s (governors), and *wazīr*s (chancellors)— and to a review of the administrative divisions of the state in different periods. He also discusses military organization, means of communication within the Empire, the position of the *qādī* (judge) and his role within the administration, the organization of the police force, the court and its offices, and concludes with a discussion of the positions of *naqīb al-ashrāf* (marshal of the Prophet's descendants) and leaders of the different Sufi movements and brotherhoods.

The second volume discusses the economic organization of the state and society, showing clearly the large amount of research that Zaydān undertook in order to complete these volumes, using not only Arabic sources and history books but also more recent works by orientalists. He compares revenues and expenditures between the first Abbasid period and later periods, detailing the many reasons for the large revenues in the earlier period and the comparative decrease during the later. The second volume closes with a short but useful and informative discussion of some of the principal cities in the empire, especially those in the central regions such as Basrah, Kūfah, and Baghdād (all in today's Iraq) and Fustāt (old Cairo) in Egypt.

The third volume of the history is a survey of learning and the sciences, ranging from literature to history and medicine. The topic is subdivided into three sections: traditional modes of knowledge and culture inherited from pre-Islamic times and developed further during the Islamic eras, including literature, genealogy, veterinary medicine, and history; the Islamic sciences that developed as a result of the needs associated with the new religion and its expansion to large segments of the old world and different cultural and linguistic groups; and the "foreign" sciences that resulted from the interaction of the Arabs with other civilizations, especially Greek, Persian, Syriac, and Indian. Zaydān's discussion concentrates on the latter two which had a major impact on literature, language and philology, while being impacted upon in turn by the more traditional Islamic sciences. This volume also includes a discussion of schools and libraries in Islam. (Zaydān added an appendix to this volume to which we shall return later.)

In the fourth volume, Zaydān returns to political history. Here his exposition is mostly historical and narrative, tracing political changes from the times of the Prophet through the period of the "Righty-Guided *(rāshidūn) Caliphs*", then the Umayyad and Abbasid dynasties of caliphs, including those periods when actual political power lay with Persian, then Turkish, elements in the Empire. He discusses the Buyid, Seljuk, Fatimid, and Mughal eras, and includes the Umayyad state in Spain (al-Andalus).

The fifth and last volume in this monumental project deals with social history. As usual, Zaydān starts with a short survey of the social situation in the different parts of what will become the Islamic Empire prior to Islam, followed by a short discussion of the society during the era of the early caliphs and the Umayyad period, as well as social mores, habits, and customs during the various sub-periods. He then surveys architecture in the urban centers of the empire, especially in Syria, Iraq, al-Andalus, and Egypt, before moving to a discussion of literary and artistic salons in the courts. He concludes both the volume and the book with a survey of sports and leisure activities like hunting.

As is obvious from a summarization of this work, it presents a comprehensive history of Islamic civilization, one that resulted from meticulous preparation by Zaydān. It quickly became a classic, and that in spite of many attacks directed against it, particularly by traditionalists who were unhappy with Zaydān's rational and detached approach to his subject matter. It goes without saying that he made a few errors here and there and was limited by the state of knowledge during his own time, and yet the learning he displays is truly encyclopedic. Beyond that, his mastery of many languages allowed him to assemble materials of such variety that only he could have put together. Despite more recent and detailed research in economic and social history in particular, this work still retains its value.

A final note on this work concerns the chapter appended to the third volume in which he discusses a letter sent to him by the orientalist scholar David (D. S.) Margoliouth, the translator of the work's first volume into English. Margoliouth draws Zaydān's attention to the work of Robertson-Smith concerning totemism and matriarchy among ancient Arabs, noting that his conclusions differ significantly from Zaydān's. In response Zaydān first provides a summary of what "totem" means (it being unfamiliar to Arabic readers of his time). He then surveys the work done on matriarchy since Bachofen and proceeds to refute Robertson-Smith and his successors. What is significant about this chapter is that it clearly demonstrates Zaydān's overall method. He first writes over fifty pages of detailed exposition, then moves to refutation based upon information and fact. What is important here is not which scholar (Zaydān or Robertson-Smith) was closer to the historical facts, but rather that Zaydān chooses to invoke as many facts and indicators as possible rather than to resort to conjecture and guess-work.

In 1904 Zaydān published a second work on Arabic philology, *Tārīkh al-lughah al-ʿarabiyyah* (History of the Arabic Language). It starts where his earlier work, *al-Falsafah al-lughawiyyah* (1891, discussed above), ended, tracing developments in the Arabic language since the period of its maturation. Unlike the first book, it adopts an almost chronological and historical description. Divided into eight chapters it reflects the eight phases in the development of the Arabic language, which can be briefly summarized as follows:

1. The *pre-Islamic* period: In this period Arabic developed and changed mainly through internal developments and changes pertaining to its users, but also due to its contacts with other languages like Ethiopic, Persian, Sanskrit, Ancient Egyptian, and Greek. In his discussion Zaydān maintains that, prior to determining the origin of words and whether or not they are loan words and from what language, one should examine historical, geographical, economic, and other aspects related to possible contacts, direct or indirect, between peoples, cultures and languages.

2. The period of *early Islam:* In this period Arabic was enriched, in that the newly emerging Islamic sciences, including jurisprudence and

Islamic law, theology, Islamic hermeneutics, and philology, added many new words to the language.

3. The period of *the Muslim conquests* saw the addition of huge areas that were formerly parts of the Byzantine and Persian Empires, resulting in Arabic becoming the language of the ruling elites and soon thereafter the language of administration. This necessitated the adoption of many new words, especially those associated with government and administration. The shift from tribal society to urban culture also brought with it many usages and words associated with the new modes of life, many of them borrowed from the languages of the conquered areas, especially Persian and to a lesser extent, Latin.

4. The lengthy era of *the Abbasid dynasty* witnessed translation initiatives, first from Persian, but then the great translation movement from Greek and the ensuing rise of an Islamic scientific and philosophical Golden Age. Arabic borrowed but also developed many new words and concepts associated with the new sciences, especially mathematics and medicine as well as philosophy.

5. Many other changes resulted from internal developments within the language itself, a phenomenon common to all language traditions. In tracing such changes, Zaydān notes firstly changes in the meanings of words (either through specialization or changes in emphasis), and secondly the impact of the various spoken Arabic dialects.

6. With *the fall of Baghdad* in 1258 C.E. and the emergence of first the Mamluk, then the Ottoman dynasties, new ruling classes emerged that were not of Arab origin (mostly Turkish, Circassian, or Kurdish). Many words were borrowed from these languages, especially those related to administration and government.

7. *The nineteenth century* brought closer contact with the West, its culture, science, and economy. Arabic started importing many new words in all spheres of life or else developed neologisms from within the language to give expression to the new concepts, objects and aspects of life imported from the West. Most of the new words came from French, Italian, and then English.

The second of the two large-scale historical projects that were alluded to above is Zaydān's *Tārīkh ādāb al-lughah al-'arabiyyah* (History of Arabic Literature, 1911). Although a small number of Orientalists had compiled histories of Arabic language and literature in the nineteenth century, Zaydān was to be the first modern Arab scholar to compose such a work, the most comprehensive history of its kind during his own times and one that retains its usefulness to this day. It traces Arabic literature from its early known beginnings in the Arabian Peninsula during the pre-Islamic era to the late nineteenth century, but adopts a broader definition of "literature" than the one in common use today, incorporating within its purview, in addition to *belles-lettres*, works in the natural, mathematical, and metaphysical sciences. The periodization that he adopts for this work echoes that of his earlier studies, following mostly dynastic rather than literary or artistic criteria: Pre-Islamic; Early Islamic; Umayyad; Abbasid; Period of Decline; and *Nahdah* (Renaissance). The subsections can be summarized as follows:

In dealing with the Pre-Islamic period (to 622 A.D.), Zaydān begins by tracing the earliest manifestations of Arabic literature to what he calls the early Jāhiliyyah, before turning to the period immediately preceding Islam. He examines hundreds of terms and words in order to illustrate the modes of life, then examines the literature itself, highlighting the most important characteristics of first poetry, then oratory (which for him is the mode of prose expression closest to poetry). He also discusses other aspects of pre-Islamic culture: history and especially genealogies and tribal divisions which were of central importance for a tribal society like that of pre-Islamic Arabia, and closes his discussion by commenting on the scientific knowledge of the Arabs, especially as related to medicine, veterinary medicine, and climate.

The early Islamic period (622-660 A.D.) witnesses the rise of the new religion and its central text, the Holy Qur'an. According to Zaydān, the period was characterized by a relatively lesser regard for poetry and increased importance of rhetoric and witnessed the earliest stages of the influence that the Qur'an was to exert linguistically on modes of Arabic expression.

The Umayyad period (661-750 A.D.) sees the first encounter between Arabic culture and those of Byzantium and Persia in the newly conquered territories. During this period, two categories of "science" developed: the purely Islamic sciences themselves, including the Qur'an and *hadīth* (accounts of saying and actions of the prophet Muhammad), *tafsīr* (the science of interpreting these holy texts), and *fiqh* and *sharī'ah* (Islamic jurisprudence); and other fields of study that emerged as the result of both the developing Islamic sciences and new elements being introduced through contact with Byzantine and Persian cultures. Zaydān classifies the various subgenres of poetry and enumerates the different important poets, identifying the subgenres or purposes of their poetry and offering evaluations of each of them. This period brings the first volume of this literary history to a close.

The second volume opens with the five centuries of the Abbasid Caliphate (750-1258 A.D.), which Zaydān subdivides into four periods, the first three amounting to about a century each and the last extending to almost two. The discussion of each period is prefaced by a section devoted to the impact of the Qur'an and the Islamic sciences on Arabic language and literature. The first period witnessed important developments in all branches of science: the Arabic sciences associated with language and literature, Islamic sciences associated with religion, and "foreign" sciences derived from the Greeks, Persians, Byzantines and the other civilizations of the region. In discussing the poetry of the period, Zaydān identifies changes in the conception of literature and connects them to new works devoted to literary study written in this period. This particular period also witnessed the standardization of Arabic grammar and the development of different styles of writing. Zaydān discusses the major grammarians of the earliest schools of Arabic grammar in the twin (Iraqi) cities of Basrah and Kūfah and traces the development of other studies related to language, especially the prosodic system described by al-Khalīl ibn Ahmad al-Farāhīdī (d. 791). He goes on to examine the development of writing styles, including that of literary studies and professional

bureaucrats and scribes associated with courts, most notably Ibn al-Muqaffaʿ (d. 755?). Lastly he quickly reviews the development of Islamic jurisprudence and the formation of the four main Sunni schools of law, concluding with a discussion of the founding figures of historical writing in Islamic civilization, especially those who wrote histories of the Muslim conquests and genealogies.

In his discussion of the second Abbasid period (equivalent to the century from the middle of the ninth to the middle of the tenth centuries C.E.) he focuses on firstly major poets, then developments in composition, especially in prose. He highlights authors such as al-Jāhiz (d. 869) and continues with a survey of studies in philology and grammar, including pioneers who compiled the early dictionaries that were to be further developed during the third stage. The third period (from the mid-tenth to mid-eleventh centuries C.E.) is dubbed "the golden age of Arabic sciences." Competition between rival dynasties of rulers resulted in greater support for science and literature, most especially as a result of newly constructed libraries and schools and the modes of writing associated with such institutions (most especially encyclopedic works). However it was mostly in poetry that the features of the new era can be seen, with the development of a more sophisticated poetic language influenced by the sciences and new types of knowledge, particularly philosophy. Discussing prose writing of the period, Zaydān highlights the shift to a more elaborate and ornate style, involving an emphasis on prose rhyme (*saj'*), and rhetorical and linguistic tropes that was to become the dominant mode of prose writing for many centuries to come. He also mentions several of the lengthy story-collections and sagas that gained in popularity during this period: that of ʿAntarah, the pre-Islamic black poet, for example, others describing ancient wars between Arab tribes (Bakr and Taghlib), still others concerning courtly love-poets, not to mention those of Indo-Persian origin such as *Alf laylah wa-laylah* (A Thousand and One Nights).

Zaydān portrays the final period in the lengthy Abbasid period (from the middle of the eleventh century to the fall of Baghdad in 1258) as being one of stagnation in literature, with little or no innovation and no great poets or prose writers. This leads directly into the so-called "period of decline," which is seen as starting with the fall of Baghdad to the Mongols in 1258 C.E. and is said to last until the nineteenth century. While acknowledging that some of the most important products of Islamic civilization were written during this period—a prominent example being Ibn Khaldūn's (d. 1406) history along with its renowned "introduction" *(al-Muqaddimah)*—, Zaydān nevertheless characterizes the entire era as being one of stagnation and imitation, and especially in literature. In other branches of learning activities focused on the compilation of materials from earlier sources and the composition of encyclopedic works.

The *Nahdah* ("Renaissance") movement is shown to begin in eastern parts of the Arab world: in greater Syria via western missionary activities and then in Egypt with the Napoleonic invasion. Well aware of the tension in discussing this period between the values of traditional Arab civilization and those of the modern West, Zaydān sees the most significant manifestations of the "renaissance" as being education (modern schools), the printing press and journalism (to which he himself contributed a great deal), the spirit of personal freedom, literary and scientific societies and clubs, public libraries, museums, acting and the theatre, and, last but not least, the increasing interest of orientalist scholars in studying Arabic literature and culture.

For many decades following the publication of this pioneer work of literary history, historians of Arabic literature in both East and West have followed the pattern (if not necessarily the breadth of knowledge) laid out by Zaydān in this work. But as mentioned earlier, such a division into periods based mostly on political history has been criticized also for failing to trace the development of literary and artistic criteria that serve as a basis for literary history. It is clear that Zaydān's literary history exemplifies the kind of erudition and breadth of knowledge possessed by many historians of literature and culture during the nineteenth and early twentieth centuries. But this contribution to literary history also reveals the limitations of such works that sacrifice the autonomy of the literary field and reduce it to an appendage of the general history of culture, science and politics.

Zaydān published over forty books during a relatively short life, a remarkable achievement by any yardstick. Many of them have remained standard reference works for a number of decades since his death in 1914, the year when his final historical novel, *Shajarat al-Durr*, was published. Those novels, his most popular works, have retained their pedagogical function and their popularity until the present day.

REFERENCES

Hamdi Alkhayat, *Ǧurǧī Zaidān: Leben und Werk* (Köln: Orient Mercur-Verlag, 1976);

'Abd al-Muhsin Tāhā Badr, *Tatawwur al-riwāyah al-'arabiyyah al-hadīthah fī Misr, 1870-1938* (Cairo: Dār al-Ma'ārif, 1963);

Encyclopedia of Arabic Literature, ed. Julie S. Meisami and Paul Starkey, 2 vols. (London: Routledge, 1998);

Ignaz Kračkovskij, "Der historische Roman in der neueren arabischen Literatur", *Die Welt des Islams* 12 (1930): 51-87;

Matti Moosa, *The Origins of Arabic Fiction* (Washington DC: Three Continents Press, 1983);

Thomas Philipp, *Ǧurǧī Zaidān: His Life and Thought* (Wiesbaden: Steiner Verlag, 1979).

Entry Index

Find entry by Arabic spelling